AMERICAN REVOLUTIONARY SOLDIERS OF FRANKLIN COUNTY PENNNSYLVANIA

COMPILED BY
VIRGINIA SHANNON FENDRICK
FOR THE
FRANKLIN COUNTY CHAPTER
DAUGHTERS OF THE AMERICAN REVOLUTION
CHAMBERSBURG, PENNA.

Southern Historical Press, Inc.
Greenville, South Carolina

This volume was reproduced from
An 1944 edition located in the
Publisher's private Library
Greenville, South Carolina

All rights reserved. No part of this publication may be reproduced,
stored in a retrieval system, transmitted in any form, posted
on to the web in any form or by any means without
the prior written permission of the publisher.

Please direct all correspondence and orders to:

www.southernhistoricalpress.com
or
SOUTHERN HISTORICAL PRESS, Inc.
PO Box 1267
375 West Broad Street
Greenville, SC   29601
southernhistoricalpress@gmail.com

Originally published: Chambersburg, PA, 1944
Copyright 1944 by The Franklin County Chapter of the D.A.R.
ISBN #0-89308-752-1
All rights Reserved.
Printed in the United States of America

Affectionately dedicated to

Virginia Shannon Fendrick

of Mercersburg, Pa. A geneologist of note in Franklin County and recognized as such by the National Societies of Geneological Research. A Charter Member of our chapter through whose untiring efforts over a long period of years has made the publishing of these Records possible.

FOREWORD

The names of all the Revolutionary Soldiers who have been born, died, or have been buried in Franklin County are included in this book as accurately as possible.

Mrs. Virginia Shannon Fendrick of Mercersburg, Penna., our late Chapter Genealogist and Historian, spent many years searching for data in Court Records, Genealogical, Historical and Ramily Records, also in the files of old newspapers. The record of every soldier herein has been carefully proven.

Many thousands of pioneers and their families came through the port of Philadelphia into Lancaster County, Pennsylvania which, after the Revolution, was divided into five counties of which Franklin County is one. From Franklin County many settlers moved on into Western Pennsylvania, then into Ohio and Indiana and later to the far West. Many went over into Maryland and others settled in the Shenandoah Valley of Virginia, still others moved into North Carolina, Kentucky and Tennessee.

In publishing these Records we hope to preserve this valuable information for their descendants.

CONTENTS

American Revolutionary Soldiers of Franklin County .... 17 to 234
    Names arranged alphabetically

GRAVEYARDS

Browns Mill	237
Cedar Hill	241
Early Presbyterian and Lutheran	243
Fairview	244
Falling Spring Presbyterian	244
First Lutheran, Chambersburg	252
Hokes	253
Moss Spring	254
Old Johnston	255
Old McClellan	256
Old Reformed and Lutheran	256
Old Reformed Church	257
Old Shannon	258
Presbyterian	259
Quincy	260
Rocky Spring	260
The Royer	264
Slate Hill	265
Snively	267
The Robert Kennedy Memorial Presbyterian	268
The White Church	269
White Church	269
Waddell's	274
Old Union	278
Grindstone Hill	280
Zion Reformed, Chambersburg	282
Rangers On The Frontiers	285
Colonial Records	287
McConnellsburg	292

The Church Hill Graveyard, Mercersburg, Pa.

The large tomb in the foreground marks the grave of Rev. John King, D.D. Many valuables were concealed within this tomb during the Civil War. The four flat stones cover the grames of the Bards. The monument in the distance, surrounded by an iron fence, marks the grave of Archibald Irwin. Samuel Findlay, the Smiths, and other early settlers are buried here.

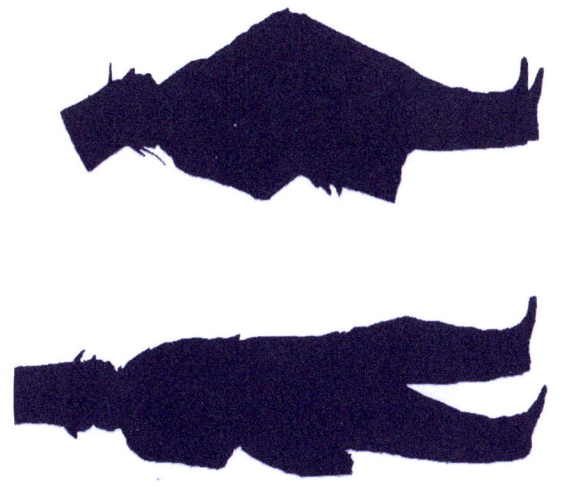

Silhouettes of 1826
1. Colonel John Findlay born in 1766
2. John Findlay Junior

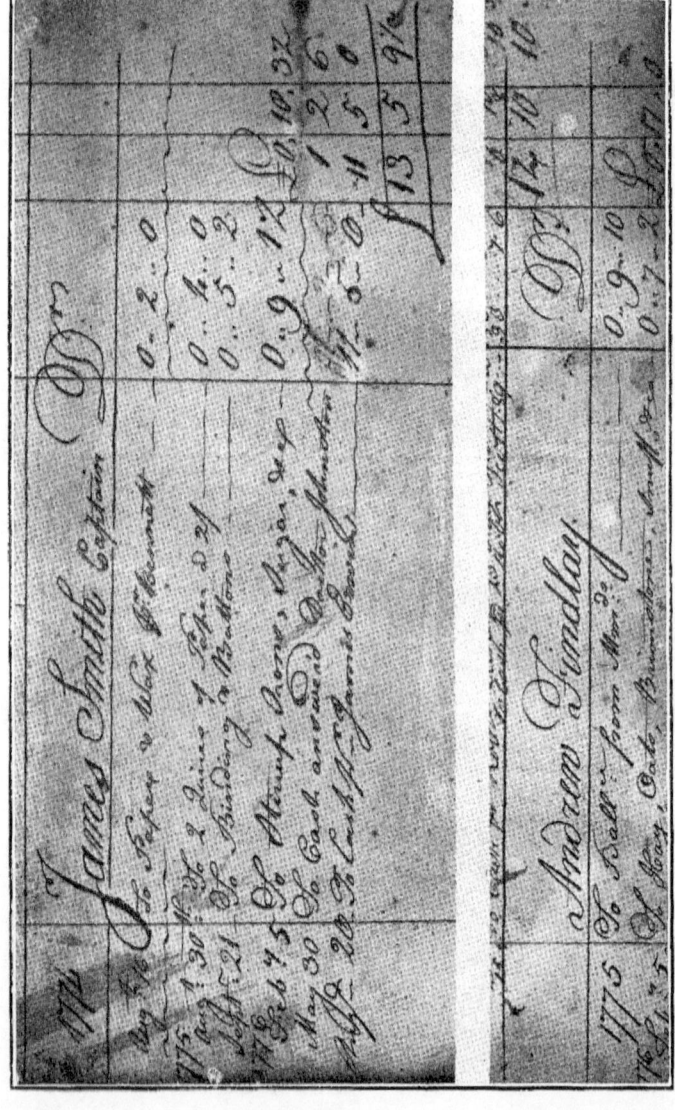

Page from an old ledger of Samuel Findlay

General Hugh Mercer

Bridge near McDowell's Mill
One of the many stone bridges which span Conococheague Creek

John McDowell LL. D.
First President of St. John's College, Annapolis, Md.
Later Provost of the University of Penna. Phila., Pa.

Colonel Benjamin Chambers

Site of Fort Davis

Site of Fort Wadell

Rock Spring Church — Built 1794

Interior of Rocky Spring Church

Remains of Fort Stover or Stauffer—near Wayncastle

First Schoolhouse in Waynesboro
built by John Bourns in 1770

On Sunday the cabin was used for Church Services by
Lutheran, Reformed and Presbyterian Congregations

AMERICAN
REVOLUTIONARY SOLDIERS OF FRANKLIN COUNTY

JOSEPH ALEXANDER

Appears in service 1778-80-81-82, with Capts. Adam Harmony, Wm. Strain and Conrad Snyder, probably the oldest son of Patrick Alexander, so named by his mother in the settlement of estate.

Penna. Arch. 5th Ser. Vol. 6, p. 87. 123, 391, 404, 538, 641.

PATRICK ALEXANDER

Was in service 1780-81-82, with Capts. James Young and Terrence Campbell. Under date of May 19, 1778, the estate of Patrick Alexander, Sr., came into Court showing the family to consist of a widow Martha and eleven children, the minors being, John; James; Margaret and Ann. Sons Patrick and Samuel chose Samuel Rennix as their guardian. It was the son Patrick who gave service 1780-81-82. The plantation in Guilford Twp., was bounded by George Hertzouch, James Crawford, John Cowden, Samuel Benedict and Robert English. Joseph was the oldest son of Patrick Alexander, Sr.

Penna. Arch. 5th Ser. Vol. 6, p. 82, 110, 125.

ROBERT ALEXANDER

Served as pvt. under Capt. Noah Abraham, 1780-82, also undated rolls. He mar. Margaret, dau. of George McConnell, of Cumb. Co., Penna. They had issue: George; Randall; Margaret; Polly; Wm.; He died 1815. Mary (Polly) Alexander, b. 1790, died Oct. 19, 1849, mar. John Flickinger, b. Oct. 31, 1787, d. Mar. 31, 1876, mar. 1815.

Penna. Arch. 5th Ser. Vol. 6, p. 85, 127, 140, 428.

JACOB ALBERT

(Mary) W9326 Pennsylvania. Washington Co., Md.,—April 1, 1818. Jacob Albert enlisted Reading, Penna., 1776 in 2nd Penn. Regt., commanded by Col. Harmer, Capt. Rower (?), Capt. Brown. Captured by Cornwallis at Stony Point, exchanged. Again enlisted 2nd Penna. Reg. Col. Harmer, Capt. Nice. Discharged at the conclusion of war at Philadelphia, Penna. by Gen'l. Mays (Mayn). Affidavit—John Barnhiser (age 87) that he knew Jacob and Mary Albert—was present at their marriage in Mar. 1781, Berks Co., Penna. served with Jacob in Rev. Jacob died May, 1830. Franklin Co., Penna., Mar. 15, 1839. Affidavit—Mary Albert, resident Washington Co., Md., age 74, Widow of Jacob Albert—they were married March 6, 1781, near Reading, Penna. by Rev. Jacob Sitzel (Litsel). Jacob Albert died May 4, 1830. She served with him in Rev. Has no record of births of children. Jacob Albert was born in Penna. enlisted with Capt. Spohn's 5th Battalion, 1776, Berks Co., Penna. Married Mariah Bermen (Beunen) of Berks Co. in 1778. That Mariah had served with him two years in Rev. after their marriage. Affidavit of John Barnhiser (a Rev. Sol.) Nov. 27, 1830 Washington Co., Md. Feb. 15, 1840, Mary Albert (age 74) widow unable to attend Court.

Penna. Arch 5th Ser. Vol. 2, p. 178, 709.

PETER ALBRIGHT

Served under Capt. Wm. Berryhill, Antrim Twp., in 1780-81. He died intestate leaving a widow Christiana and five children,—Mary mar. George Gerhart; Catherine; John; Peter; Jacob. Orphans' Court shows that Catherine mar. Jacob Appenseller. Salem Church records, Waynesboro, give births of children of Peter and Christina Albright as: Anamaria b. Dec. 28, 1810; Esther b. Oct. 31, 1811; Catherine b. Oct. 28, 1812; Johanes b. Jan. 30, 1814.

Penna. Arch. 5th Ser. Vol. 6, p. 80, 101.

WILLIAM ALLISON

Was appointed Justice of the Peace for Cumb. Co., Penna., Mar. 10, 1749, and again in 1750. In the will of William Allison of Antrim Twp., dated Sept. 22, 1777, he names wife Catherine (said to be Craig); sons Wm.; Patrick; Dau. Agnes, wife of Robert McCrea; Son Robert; Dau. Catherine, wife of James Hendricks; grandsons, Wm. McCrea and Wm. Allison; Nephew John Allison "for his great care and tenderness toward my brother Robert." Exrs: Wife, sons John, Robert, and William.

Penna. Arch. 2nd Ser. Vol. 9, p. 807.

DAVID ARROL (ARREL)

Served under Capt. Wm. Strain as a pvt. The will of Eleanor Ers (Erl) of Greene Twp., prob. in 1816, gives signature as Arrel. She names brothers George and William Erl. She mentions her interest in a tract of 202 acres in Poland Twp., of Youngstown, Trumbull Co., and Territory N. W. of the River Ohio, "subject to the monies I have paid," to my brother John Erl and brother-in-law Samuel Caldwell; 3 sisters: Ann Stewart; Ratchel Smith; and Margaret Caldwell. 9 nieces: Margaret and Martha Erl; Margaret and Martha Stewart; Betty; Margaret; Elinor and Kesiah Smith and Mary Caldwell; to be paid as they arrive at age. Betty Smith my saddle and Elinor Smith $200. and one set of silver teaspoons. Dated and Prob. in 1816. Deeds show that David Errell of Southampton Twp., was possessed of a negro girl at the passing of the act of the gradual abolition of Slavery in the year 1780, aged now 28 yrs; said negro girl Mariah "I am desirous of securing the freedom of said negro. She shall be free henceforth from me and my heirs," &c. Aug. 26, 1797. David Arrel was a pewholder in the Rocky Spring Church. In the Covenanter Graveyard, Scotland, is a stone to William Arrel, who d. 1860, in his 78th year.

Penna. Arch. 5th Ser. Vol. 6, p. 390, 430.

ANDREW ALSWORTH

Was Sergt., under Capt. Chas. Maclay, and pvt., under Capt. Js. Miller and Capt. Thos. Askey, 1780-81-82. He was a son of Benj. Alsworth of Lurgan Twp., whose will was prob. 1784.

Penna. Arch. 5th Ser. Vol. 6, p. 148, 151, 390, 436, 450, 631.

BENJAMIN ALSWORTH

Was a pvt., under Capt. J. Miller in 1782. He was a son of Benj. Alsworth of Lurgan Twp. His name appeared later in Westmoreland Co., Penna.

Penna. Arch. 5th Ser. Vol. 6, p. 435, 450.

JAMES ALSWORTH

Was a pvt., in 1781-82, under Capt. J. Miller, and under Lieut. Robert Quigley at Little's Fort Aug. 21, 1781. He was a son of Benj. Alsworth of Lurgan Twp. In the will of John Strain of Lurgan Twp., he names his dau. Margaret wife of James Alsworth.

Penna. Arch. 5th Ser. Vol. 6, p. 416, 425, 434, 449, 636.

DANIEL ALTICK

Is shown in service 1777-80-81, undated roll, under Capt. Alexdr. Peebles. Elizabeth Alteck, consort of Daniel Alteck, died May 25, 1829, aged 74 yrs. Elizabeth Alteck was buried in the Graveyard of Reformed Church, Shippensburg, Penna. Bodies removed to Spring Hill Cemetery. It is quite probable that Daniel Alteck was buried beside his wife. The Census of 1790, Franklin Co., Penna., shows the family of Daniel Oltick as, 1 man, 2 boys, 6 females.

Penna. Arch. 5th Ser. Vol. 6, p. 136, 389, 396, 421, 590.

MICHAEL ALTICK

From Franklin Co., residing in Maryland in 1825. Court records at Hagerstown, Md., show the Admr. of estate of Michael Alteigh, Aug. 8, 1826. No further data.

Penna. Arch. 2nd Ser. Vol. 13, p. 5.

DAVID ARMSTRONG

Served as pvt., 1779-81-82 under Capt. Noah Abraham. He was born 1748, d. 1811, buried at Plaingrove, Laurence Co., Penna. He was mar. in Path Valley, Penna., 1779, to Sarah, dau. of Rowland Harris. She d. in 1816. They had issue: George Armstrong b. 1780, mar. Elizabeth McCune; Rebecca Armstrong b. 1782, mar. Jas. McCune; Archibald Armstrong b. 1785, mar. Elizabeth Wallace; Thos. Armstrong b. 1787, mar. Frances Drake; Roland Armstrong b. 1790, mar. Jane Donnel; Mary Armstrong b. 1795, mar. Alexdr. McBride; David Armstrong b. 1798, mar. Jane Jack; Anna Armstrong b. 1800, mar. Samuel Jack; Samuel Armstrong b. 1803, mar. Jane Erwin; Elizabeth Armstrong b. 1807, mar. Wm. McNees.

Penna. Arch. 5th Ser. Vol. 6, p. 121, 128, 141, 384.

JAMES ARMSTRONG

4th son of Capt. Joseph Armstrong, pioneer, was a Colonel of the 8th Regt., North Carolina Line, from Nov. 1776 to June 1778. He later commanded a regiment of Rangers, and was reported among the killed and wounded at Stone Ferry, June 29, 1779.

Geo. O. Seilhamer, Esq.

JOHN ARMSTRONG

Son of Capt. Joseph Armstrong of Hamilton Twp., was a member of his father's Company in the Kittanning Expedition Sept. 1756. He removed to North Carolina, dying there in 1806, leaving issue: Margaret mar. James Wilson; Joseph mar. Frances Tinney; Thomas; James; Jennet; Mary; Elizabeth; Katrinah. He was an officer in the Cont. Line, rising to the ranks of Major and Lieut. Col., in the 4th Regt. of the line.

Penna. Arch. 5th Ser. Vol. 1, p. 37. Notes by H. H. Emmons.

COLONEL JOSEPH ARMSTRONG

Was an early esttler in Hamilton Twp. In 1755 he organized a company of rangers for the protection of the frontier against the incursions of the Indians. He was a Member of the Colonial

Assembly in 1750-51-53-54-55. He commanded a company of Militia under General Broadhead at destruction of the Indiantown Kittaning in Sept. 1756. He was paymaster of the Colony in the building of the great road from Fort Loudon to Pittsburgh, and he left an unusually fine will,—Sept. 3, 1760 it is dated and he bequeaths to Jennet, "my dear and well beloved wife, one equal third of all my movables or personal estate with other dowrie" &c; beloved and eldest son John my plantation in Orange County, N. C. &c; beloved son Thomas Armstrong, the tract of land lying between Robert Elliott's and Wm. Rankins in Hamilton Twp.; My beloved son Joseph Armstrong the plantation whereon I dwell; Beloved son James Armstrong; Beloved son Wm. Armstrong; to my beloved dau. Katherine Armstrong, otherwise Courey, 20 lbs., over and above what she has received; Beloved dau. Margaret, who is unmarried; Wit: Robert Elliott, John Stuart, Nath. Wilson. Prob. Jan. 30, 1761. The marriage of James Currie and Catherine Armstrong is recorded at Lancaster, under the St. James Episcopal Church records, on May 31, 1758, when the settlement had fled owing to the incursions of the Indians.

Penna. Arch. 5th Ser. Vol. 1, p. 37, 62, 70, 336.

JOSEPH ARMSTRONG

Appears as a pvt., in the Company of Capt. Saml. Patton, 1778-80- 81-82. Mr. Emmons places Joseph as the eldest son of Thomas Armstrong and further states that Joseph and wife removed to near Wooster, Wayne Co., Ohio, dying without issue.

Penna. Arch. 5th Ser. Vol. 6, p. 278, 287, 311, 380.

THOMAS ARMSTRONG

And his brother John, are shown in 1755, in service under their father, Capt., Joseph Armstrong, in a Company of rangers for the protection of the frontier against the incursions of the Indians. An old Map, shows the Disposition of the Penna. Troops, in the Western District, for the Winter Season, 1764, at "Arm strongs an Officer and 15"———— Thomas Armstrong, born 1734, died Sept. 26, 1776, the funeral services conducted by the Rev. John Craighead. He lived in Hamilton Twp., on land he inherited from his father, Joseph Armstrong, Sr. He left a widow Mary and issue: Jane; Sarah; Joseph; Wm.; Thomas. The widow Mary mar. 2nd Wm. Eckles, and in 1796, her name was Mary Satimore (Latimore) (?) Of the children Jean mar. John Blackburn and Sarah mar. Hugh McClelland. Thomas and wife Margaret were of Ross Co., Ohio. In 1804, John and Jean Blackburn removed to Columbiana Co., Ohio. Hugh McClelland and wife Sarah went to Stark Co., Ohio, they having issue six children. Service in the Rev. War has been claimed for the above Thomas Armstrong, but it is, as yet, unproven.

Penna. Arch. 5th Ser. Vol. 1, p. 37. McCauley's Hist. Franklin Co. p. 67.

THOMAS ARMSTRONG

2nd son of Capt. Joseph Armstrong, pioneer, removed to Orange County, N. C., before the Revolution. He entered the Cont. Service Apr. 16, 1776, as First Lieut. in the 5th Regt. North Carolina Line, made Captain Oct., 1777; served to the close of the war. Wounded and taken prisoner at Fort Fayette, June, 1779, exchanged Dec., 1779; captured the 2nd time at Charlestown, May, 1780, and exchanged July, 1781.

Geo. O. Seilhamer, Esq.

WILLIAM ARMSTRONG

5th son of Capt. Joseph Armstrong, pioneer, removed to Orange County, N. C. before the Revolution. He entered the Continental Service, Jan. 1776, as an Ensign in the 1st North Carolina Regt., promoted, and as Captain Aug., 1777. He retired Jan. 1, 1783, having been wounded at Ramsour's Mill June, 1780.

Geo. O. Seilhamer, Esq.

WILLIAM ARCHIBALD

Served as a pvt., under Capt. Patrick Jack in 1781. He mar. Margaret Thompson. Wm. Gillielmus Archibald and wife Margaret are buried in the family graveyard on the Archibald farm near St. Thomas. Some of the Thompsons were buried there prior to 1782. Issue of above: Martha, b. 1778; David b. 1780; Thomas b. 1782; Isabella b. 1783; Mary b. 1786; Wm. b. 1788; Margaret b. 1791; Daniel b. 1794; James b. 1797; Ruhannah b. 1799.

Penna. Arch 5th Ser. Vol. 6, p. 292, 296.

CAPTAIN THOMAS ASKEY

Is shown on July the 28th, and the First Call, July 31, 1777, with David Anderson as 1st Lieut., Richard Coulter as 2nd Lieut., William Elder, Ensign, all under Col. James Dunlap. Col. Askey's Service was from 1777 to 1782, being shown on guard at Frankstown, Apr., 1781. He was from Fannet Twp., and signed various petitions from there. Capt. Askey mar. Elizabeth, dau. of Col. Robert Baker, June 12, 1764, the marriage by the Rev. J. C. Bucher. He was born 1727, died 1807, his wife dying in 1830. They are buried in an old Presby., church yard in Centre Co., Penna. 6 miles east of Bellefonte, at Jacksonville. They had issue: John mar. Betty Evans; Wm. mar. Mary Baker; David mar. Jane Harrison; Robert mar. Mary Polly Evans; James mar. Jane Swanzey; Samuel mar. Lettie McKibben; Ann mar. Baptist Lucas; Rebecca mar. Joseph Lucas; Peggy mar. David Tipton; Polly, unmar.

GEORGE ANDERSON

Served as a pvt., under Capt. Conrad Snider in 1781. He was a weaver in Washington Twp., his will prob. Mar. 15, 1787. All personal estate to John Horner, Jr.

Penna. Arch. 5th Ser. Vol. 6, p. 108, 118.

HENRY ANDERSON

"March, 1756, Capt. Joseph Brandon, Lieut. George Huston, Ensign, all of Peters Twp." The will of Henry Anderson, of Peters Twp., 1778, names wife Ann; Allen; Rebeckah; John; Elizabeth as children of his brother John. Brother Thomas in Ireland; Sister Mary a widow. To the Asso. Presbyterian Congregation on the West side of Conococheague to Rev. John Rodgers, accepting the call xx. To nephew Henry Marshall son to my brother-in-law Wm. Marshall; To Henry Wray, son of John Wray; To Wm. Anderson, eldest son of Oliver Anderson and to his 2nd son Henry and dau. Jane; Exrs: David Humphrey; John Work; Oliver Anderson. Henry Anderson and wife Ann, are probably buried in "Slate Hill" Graveyard.

From old paper in State Library, Harrisburg, Penna., given by Miss Jessica Ferguson.

ISAAC ANDERSON

In November of 1788 Isaac Anderson mar. in Westmoreland Co., Penna., Euphremia Moorehead, eldest dau. of Fergus Moorehead, who had also been a Soldier of the Revoltion. Fergus Moorehead was the father of Joseph Moorehead who received an Ensign's Commission and marched to the west with the army under Gen'l. St. Clair. He was at the disastrous battle of Nov. 4, 1791, at Fort Recovery, where Gen'l. St. Clair and his army were defeated by the Indians. Mrs. Euphemia Moorehead Anderson died Aug. 26, 1851, aged 80 yrs. 11 mos.

McBride's Pioneer Biography, Vol. 1, p. 288.

ROBERT ANDERSON

Pvt., served until the end of the war, residing in Franklin Co., 1812. His will states "Late of Chambersburg." Names children: Thomas; Mary; Robert; Ann; David; Margaret. Robert Anderson received $96. per year as a Penna. pensioner, a private in Penna. Line. Was aged 80 yrs., in 1819. The Franklin Repository under date of Sept. 20, 1823, "Died Wednesday night last in this borough at an advanced age, Robert Anderson."

Penna. Arch. 2nd Ser. Vol. 13, p. 6.

WILLIAM ANDERSON

Chambersburg, Pa. Survey Book 2, p. 114, shows a warrent to William Anderson, May 24, 1753, Green Twp., part of 416 acres, now sells 170 acres to John Rea. p. 133, 158 acres sold off same to John Farry. On Dec. 20, 1773, one William Anderson, was married to Catherine McElhatton, of Mercersburg, or vicinity, by Rev. John King.

DAVID ANDREW

Is shown as a Soldier in the Cont. Line, from Cumb. Co. Pa. He was a son of John and Hannah Andrew of Guilford Twp., and married late in life, as recorded by Dr. David Denny: "David Andrie to Sarah Ritchie, Nov. 3, 1818." Their two daughters Misses Margaret and Sarah Andrew were early school teachers in Mercersburg, both buried in Fairview Cemetery. David A. Andrew, born Oct. 9, 1763, died March 31, 1841. Sarah Andrew died Feb. 9, 1846, aged 56 years, 6 months, 8 days. Both lie in the Presbyterian Cemetery, McConnellsburg, Penna.

Penna. Arch. 5th Ser. Vol. 4, p. 619.

JOHN ANDREW

Appears in service with Capt., Conrad Snider and William Long. In 1777 as Captain; as Ensign, and as a Court Martial man; during 1778-79-80-81, he is shown in service. Under persons to take subscriptions for the Continental Loan in 1777, John Andrew was one of eight men from Cumberland Co., Penna. John Andrew, Esq., of Guilford Twp., left a will dated Dec., 1803, prob. Jan., 1804. Son David first named; wife Hannah the possession of my mill and plantation with my children now at home; David; Nancy and Margaret; son James; son Robert; dau. Hannah and her husband Joseph Lamb; Grandson John Andrew, son of my son John, and to his sister Mary; son David; dau. Nancy Lindsay and dau. Margaret this plantation whereon I now dwell. Several plantations, one in Green Twp., called "Big Meadows" to be sold. The Executors of John Andrew transfer to the son David the land known as "Big Meadow" a tract of 90 acres. David Andrew bought out the right of his brother Robert, in June, 1809, and in July, 1809, James Andrew, now of North Carolina, states that David Andrew hath fully paid him and he transfers to David "my full right." A descendant states that wife Hannah was a Dixon, and that son Robert mar. Martha Dougherty. John Andrew and wife Hannah Dixon, had a dau. Agnes (Nancy) who mar. John Lindsay, and their dau. Margaret (Andrew) Lindsay mar. 1st

John Ritchey; mar. 2nd Wm. Metcalfe. From the Franklin Repository, Nov. 30, 1830.—"Died at the home of her daughter, Mrs. Ritchey, in Montgomery Twp., Sunday morning the 21st inst., Mrs. Agnes Lindsay, aged 64 years." The Falling Spring Graveyard "Agnes Lindsay, died Nov. 21, 1830, aged 64 years." The will of Agnes Lindsay of Montgomery Twp., was dated Apr. 26, 1830; prob. Dec. 6, 1831; son-in-law Samuel Renfrew; dau. Margaret Ritchey and son Andrew Lindsay. Exr: Son-in-law Samuel Renfrew. From the Franklin Repository Jan. 4, 1804,—"Died on Friday, the 30th ult., at his dwelling on the Falling Spring, John Andrew, Esq., an old inhabitant of this country. The decd., merited and obtained during a long and active life, the character of a devout christian and an honest man. On Saturday his remains were deposited in the Presbyterian burying ground in the town, attended by a numerous and respectable concourse of citizens."

Penna. Arch. 5th Ser. Vol. 6, p. 5, 70, 87, 118, 537, 545.

JOHN ANDREW, JR.

Son of Captain John Andrew, served in 1778 under Capt. Adam Harmony. The estate of John Andrew, Jr., was administered July 25, 1797, by John Dickson. The widow Catherine renounced her right to administer and she signed,—Kitty Andrew. Wit: John Andrew. Capt. John Andrew, in his will referred to "grandson John Andrew, son of my son John and to his sister Mary." Robert Andrew, who went south, was born at Chambersburg, Aug. 3, 1766, died Oct. 29, 1840. His wife was Martha Dougherty, probably the dau. of Thomas Dougherty of Hamilton Twp., Franklin Co., Penna.

Penna. Arch. 5th Ser. Vol. 6, p. 538.

Francis Bailey, an English Scientist who visited the United States in 1796, left a Diary, from which the following is taken: "Leaving Greencastle we had to go eleven miles farther that night to Mr. Lindsay's, whom we had engaged at Baltimore to carry our goods to Pittsburg in his wagons. We were hospitably entertained by Mr. Lindsay and his father-in-law, Mr. Andrews, who have a very excellent farm and live very comfortably in truly American style. The place at which he resides is called the Falling Spring they rise from under an oak tree and the stream does not proceed three hundred yards before it turns a cider mill and a little further on it turns a grist mill. These mills belong to Mr. Andrews, as also does a large quantity of the land around Mr. and Mrs. Andrews are brisk and their families are all settled in the neighborhood." Oct. 11, 1796. "About eleven o'clock in the morning we set off from Mr. Andrews." They proceeded to Chambersburg, and from there to McDowell's Mill, about thirteen miles distant.

NICHOLAS ANSMINGER (ENSMINGER)

Was in Service 1781, with Capt., Wm. Berryhill, of Antrim Twp. The names Christian, Daniel, Henry, Jacob, John, Michael and Peter Ensminger all appear, giving service from Lancaster Co., Penna., during the Rev. War.

Penna. Arch. 5th Ser. Vol. 6, p. 102.

AARON BOGGS SERGEANT

Was in service 1780-81-82, with Capt. John McConnell, Command of Col. Samuel Culbertson. Seilhamer states that Aaron Boggs settled near Strasburg and that he married after 1766, Rebecca (Clark) Baldridge, widow of John Baldridge.

Penna. Arch. 5th Ser. Vol. 6. p. 267, 302, 309.

SAMUEL BOGGS

Was serving under Capts. James Young and Conrad Snider, 1779-80-81.

Penna. Arch. 5th Ser. Vol. 6, p. 87, 119, 548.

WILLIAM BOGGS

Served in 1781, under Capt. John Rea. He is shown as applying for a pension, and is buried in "Upper Strasburg" Graveyard. No stone. State pension records at Harrisburg show him from Jan. 1835 to Nov., 1841, date of death.

Penna. Arch. 5th Ser. Vol. 6, p. 105, 107.

JAMES BURNS

Is shown in service under Capt. Alexdr. Peebles, 1777-78-79-80-81-82. It is probable there was another man of the name. James Burnes and Jene Gebby were mar. Nov. 7, 1780, by Dr. Alexdr. Dobbin of Adams Co., Penna. John Gabby of Letterkenny Twp., Franklin Co., Penna., left a will dated 1806 and prob. Dec. 20, 1810 and signed Gebby. He stated he "was old and Stricken in years," and named his wife Jane Gabby. Sons: John; Wm.; Archibald; and Joseph.. 2 daughters: Janet, wife of James Burns; Jane wife of Samuel Cooper. Son James of Washington, Co., Penna. The widow Jean Gabby of Chambersburg, formerly of Letterkenny Twp., directed as follows: "My body to be decently interred in the burying ground at Mr. Lind's Church in Greencastle." She named dau. Jenny wife of James Burns; dau. Jean, wife of Samuel Cooper. Brother James Brownlee 100 pounds if in this country. Exrs: son-in-law Samuel Cooper and Wm. Jamison, both of Chambersburg. The will was dated Jan., 1812, prob. Aug., 1813.

Penna. Arch. 5th Ser. Vol. 6, p. 31, 58, 136, 389, 296, 421, 433, 590.

JOHN BOURNS

Served as a pvt., under Capt. Daniel Clapsaddle in 1780-81. John Bourns, Sicklesmith, of York County, in Carroll's Delight, bought land in Wash. Twp., in Apr. 7, 1774. He forged the first Cannon made in America. It was Captured by the British at the battle of the Brandywine. He mar. Esther, dau. of Jeremy Morrow. His will begins,—"In Subordination to the Sovereign pleasure of the almighty, I, John Bourns of Washington Twp." &c. He died Apr. 20, 1802, his wife Esther having died June 8, 1797. They are buried at Willow Glen Farm, near Waynesboro, Penna.

We are indebted to Mr. C. W. Cremer, Esq., Waynesboro, Penna., in a paper read before the Kittochtinny Historical Society for above facts on John Bourns. See Kittichainny Magazine 1908-1910. Penna. Arch. 5th Ser. Vol. 6, p. 72, 94.

ABRAHAM BOYD

Is shown in service with Capt. Patrick Jack. Penna. Arch. 5th Ser. Vol. 6, p. 28.

ANDREW BOYD

Was in service, 1777, with Capt. Alexdr. Peebles. Under Orphans' Court, Dec. 22, 1794, at Chambersburg, Penna., is the following: "Came into Court Frances Boyd, aged 14 yrs., and upwards, minor child of Alexander Boyd, late of Cecil Co., Md., decd.; and prayed that Andrew Walker, of Peters Twp., farmer, might be appointed his guardian."

Penna. Arch. 5th Ser. Vol. 6, p. 589.

JAMES BOYD

Was in service in 1777-80-81-82, with Capt. John McConell, command of Col. Saml. Culbertson. In 1794, one James Boyd occupied Pew 12 in the Rocky Spring Church; James Boyd and Geo. McElroy in Pew 21, in 1800. James Boyd of Letterkenny Twp., left a will in which he names a son James; dau. Agnes; dau. Mary Morrow.

Penna. Arch 5th Ser. Vol. 6, p. 267, 302, 309, 373.

JAMES BOYD

Is shown in service 1779-80-81-82, with Capt. Wm. Moorehead, Command of Col. Jas. Dunlop.

Penna. Arch. 5th Ser. Vol. 6, p. 65, 399, 413, 415, 439.

JOHN BOYD

In the will of John Boyd of Letterkenny Twp., dated 1769, prob. 1770, he names wife Mary; dau. Elizabeth Boyd; and six sons: James; Robert; Wm.; Samuel; John; Thomas; each to have 1/6 share of estate; wife Mary and son James were Executors. John Boyd and wife Mary who died 1778, have stones in the Rocky Spring Graveyard, having occupied Pew No. 32, in the church.

ROBERT BOYD

Was in service 1779-80-81-82, with Capt. James Young; as a Clerk with Capt. Terrence Campbell in Aug., 1782.

Penna. Arch 5th Ser. Vol. 6, p. 100, 111, 127, 183, 290, 548.

THOMAS BOYD (BOYDE)

Was in service 1781, some undated rolls, under Capts. Charles Maclay and Patrick Jack. One Thomas Boyd occupied Pew 24 in the Old Log Church at Rocky Spring; with him were Wm. Archibald; Elizabeth Thompson and Jas. Nicklas. Thomas Boyd of Letterkenny, left a will, dated Jan., 1795, prob. Feb., 1795. To son John, when he comes of age, ⅔ of my estate and dau. Margaret one third; she was to be educated and was also to have her mother's clothing. The Exrs. were friends John Boyd of Berkeley Co., Va., and John Brotherton of Letterkenny Twp. Isaac Parker and John Boyd as witnesses.

Penna. Arch. 5th Ser. Vol. 6, p. 149, 151, 281, 292, 296.

WILLIAM BOYD

Was in service 1780-81-82, with Capts. Thos. Johnston and John Woods.

Penna. Arch. 5th Ser. Vol. 6, p. 91, 103, 114, 130.

WILLIAM BOYD

Was in service, as First Lieut., with Capt. Patrick Jack, 1777-78, undated rolls. He was with Capt. Jack at Newtown in his Company of Militia, and in Jan. 1778, he appears under Capt. John Campbell and Quarter master Archbd. Irwin.

Penna. Arch. 5th Ser. Vol. 6, p. 13, 31, 44, 144, 146.

(It is probable that four or five of these were sons of John Boyd of Letterkenny Twp. VSF).

ENSIGN DAVID BLAIR

In 1764, a group of Woodsmen or riflemen from Fredk. Co., Md., (now Wash. Co., Md.) marched to Fort Pitt to serve without pay. Among this Company were, Capt. Wm. McClellan; Lieut. James Dougherty; Ensign David Blair; Ensign John Moran; Ensign Edmund Moran; Privates David Shelby; James Ross; John Dougherty; Felix Leer. In the will of Andrew Blair whose plantation was on the Penna.

& Md. line, and whose will was dated 1787, prob. 1796, he names the following: dau. Cath. Moran; dau. Ann McClellan; dau. Susanna Dougherty; dau. Mary Shelvy.

The Penna. German in the Settlement of Maryland, By D. W. Nead.

JAMES BLAIR

Of Blair's Valley, wife Martha Elliott. They are buried on the original Blair farm on what is called Valley Road, from Clearspring, Md. to Mercersburg, Penna., the farm later owned by W. W. Seibert. No stone, but a D. A. R. marker was placed on grave. The N. S. D. A. R. has accepted the above James Blair. The will of Andrew Blair named three sons, John; James; David. Hagerstown, Md., Court records, the Admr. of John Blair, 1799; the will of James Blair, 1828; the Admr. of Charity Blair, 1837.

HENRY BRIM

Served as pvt., Col. John Patton's Regt., C. L. May, 1777, Baker's Co.; transferred to Powell's Co.; resided in Franklin Co. in 1820. Ap. Sergeant in Capt. Joseph Powell's Co., in service 3 years,—discharged by Capt. Powell. In battles of Burlington, Brandywine, Germantown, Monmonth. Enlisted again in Company of Capt. Luis of Md., line, and marched under Command of Gen'l. Wayne against the Indians, was discharged by Gen'l. Wilkison at Greenvale. He was a pensioner, his estate being admr., Feb. 26, 1835, in Franklin County, Penna.

Penna. Arch. 2nd Ser. Vol. 10, p. 810. Penna. Arch. 5th Ser. Vol. 4, p. 530.

RICHARD BROWNSON

Served as Surgeon under Col. Samuel Culbertson, 6th Batt., Cumb., Co. Militia, 1777-78-81-82, Samuel Findlay as Quarter Master in the same. Richard Brownson, b. 1737, mar. Mary, dau. of John and Agnes (Craig) McDowell, of Fort McDowell. In 1769, their family consisted of 2 children, John and Agnes; they also had Nathan; Timothy; Asa; Elizabeth; Abigal. Mrs. Brownson, b. 1743, d. Apr. 22, 1833. Dr. Brownson died Mar. 25, 1790. Their son John mar. Sally Smith, Oct. 7, 1807. She was the "little daughter Sally" named by William Smith, who laid out the town of Mercersburg, in 1786—his wife being Peggy (or Margaret) Piper. The dau. Agnes, shown in 1769, mar. on Mar. 11, 1788, John Findlay of Chambersburg, Penna. From Brownson Hist. by Dr. E. R. Brownson: Richard Brownson was born May 3, 1737, at Woodbury, Litchfield Co., Conn. The son of Timothy Brownson, he the son of Cornelius Brownson, and he the son of Richard Brownson, an original Immigrant who with his father, came to Mass., in 1633, and later moved to Hartford, with Rev. Hooker, in 1636. Mary, widow of Dr. Richard Brownson, is shown in 1796 taxed with 100 ac., warranted land, 2 Horses, 2 Cows, 2 slaves. She left a will, dated Aug., 1823, prob. Aug. 1833. She names sons John and Nathan Brownson; a dau. Elizabeth, unmar., Grandau. Eleanor Findlay. The Rev. David Elliott, a witness, Abigail Brownson, dau. of Dr. Richard and Mary Brownson, left a will dated and probated May, 1816—naming Jane and Eleanor Findlay, my nieces; Brother John Brownson; Sister Betsy Brownson; Brother Nathan Brownson; Wit: Jesse Magaw and A. Elliott. Timothy Brownson died Aug., 1777; Asa Brownson died Sept. 1805. Dr. Richard Brownson is undoubtedly buried in White Church graveyard. In the "White Church" Graveyard, near Mercersburg there are stones to John Brownson, Esq., and his wife Sarah Smith, at least five children died young. Miss Ellen D. Creigh, dau. of Dr. Thos. Creigh of Mercersburg, when pressed by the writer for "early recollections" talked much of "Grandma Irwin and Miss Jane" who were neighbors, and who petted this little girl, to her great delight. When it became apparent that "Grandma Irwin" was no other than Peggy (Piper) Smith who mar. 2nd, James Irwin, the questions came rapidly. "What did they look like?" "Well, Grandma Irwin was short and fat, and very much wrinkled, but Miss Jane was tall and stately and wore a green brocade silk dress"—and little Miss Ellie aged but seven when they died in 1852; a later picture than Mr. Fithian gave of Peggy Piper in 1775, aged ten years, "She seems to me to be remarkably intelligent; reads very clear, attends well to the quantity of words. Indeed I have not been so lately pleased as with this rosy-cheeked Miss Peggy Piper."

Penna. Arch. 5th Ser. Vol. 6, p. 298, 304, 367, 375.

JOHN BENEDICT

Served as pvt. under Capt. Saml. Royer, 1780-81. In the will of Abraham Knepper, dated 1811, prob. 1824, he names wife Catherine; son Samuel; John Benedict mar. to my decd. daughter Catherine, also sons, David; Abraham; Joshua (or Josiah).

Penna. Arch. 5th Ser. Vol. 6, p. 89, 112.

PETER BENEDICT

Served as pvt. under Capt. Samuel Royer, 1779-80-81. His estate was admr., 1798, which shows sons, John; Abraham; Jacob; Daniel and Peter; daus. Catherine mar. Fred. Hess; Barbara mar. Daniel Stover; Elizabeth, mar. Abraham Nipper; Christina; Mary; Susanna. He left 455 acres land in Washington Twp. The Rev. Stoever's marriage records show "Peter Benedict to Maria Elizabeth Laukster, Lebanon, Oct. 14, 1760."

Penna. Arch. 5th Ser. Vol. 6, p. 89, 112, 542.

MOSES BLACKBURN

Appears as a pvt., 1777-81-82, under Capts. James Young and Terrence Campbell. Moses and John Blackburn are said to have been born in Dauphin Co., Penna., sons of William, and grandsons of Alexdr. Blackburn, an early settler. Moses enlisted under Franklin Co. men and is shown on Tax lists, Guilford Twp., 1782-86. He was married to Margaret McKnight, Jan. 6, 1780, at Canniwago. Moses Blackburn occupied, with others, Pew No. 3 in the old Log Church at Rocky Spring.

Penna. Arch. 5th Ser. Vol. 6, p. 111, 126, 157.

ADAM BRATTON

Appears as 1st Lieut., with Capt. Thos. Askey, July ye 28, 1777, and in July 1778, "By order of Council for ye first and second classes ye second Tour for Three hundred Men to ye Standing Stone." Dated at Phila., July 14, 1778.

Penna. Arch. 2nd Ser. Vol. 15, p. 563.

JOHN BRATTON

Served as pvt. 1781-82, under Capt. Patrick Jack. The will of John Bratton was dated Sept. and prob. Oct. of 1804. Son Robert the plantation where he now liveth; dau. Elizabeth 75 pounds; son James 300 pounds when he arrives to the age of 21 years; daus. Margaret and Jane each 200 pounds; residue of estate to other 2 sons, John and William; wife Alice to remain in the family. In the will of Guan Morrow, 1796, he names a dau. Margaret as the wife of John Bratton.

Penna. Arch 5th Ser. Vol. 6, p. 291, 295, 312.

JOHN BRATTON

Appears in Aug., 1776, as a pvt., with Capt. Samuel McCune. In 1781, with Capt. Walter McKinnie—shown in the Cont. Line, as Soldiers of the Revolution, are Edward; James; John and Samuel Bratton, from Cumb. Co., Penna.

Penna. Arch. 5th Ser. Vol. 6, p. 587, 300. Penna. Arch. 5th. Ser. Vol. 4, p. 280, 621.

ROBERT BRATTON

Is shown in Service 1778, under Capt. Isaac Miller and Lieut. Col. James Johnston.

Penna. Arch. 5th Ser. Vol. 6, p. 39, 41.

ROBERT BRATTON

Was in service, 1778, under Capt. Isaac Miller.

Penna. Arch. 5th Ser. Vol. 6, p. 39-41.

SAMUEL BRATTON

Was in service 1776-78 under Capts. Samuel McCune and John Campbell.

Penna. Arch. 5th Ser. Vol. 6, p. 33, 587.

The following marriages were by Dr. David Denny of Chambersburg, Penna.:
Robert Bratton, Molly Dixon, March 31, 1803.
Mr. Shannon, Miss Bratton, March 17, 1807.
Mr. Armstrong, Miss Bratton, March 17, 1807.
James Dixon, Jane Bratton, June 16, 1814.
Valentine Feil, Mary Bratton, Oct. 27, 1831.

SAMUEL BRATTON

Appears 1760 in Col. Armstrong's Co., with some men from Fort Loudon. Robert Braddon also is with the Company. Samuel Bratton next appears Aug. 13, 1776, with Capt. Saml. McCune, and he is later shown as a Soldier in the Cont. Line, from Cumb. C., Penna.

Penna. Arch. 5th Ser. Vol. 1, p. 306. Penna. Arch. 5th Ser. Vol. 4, p. 280, 261. Penna. Arch. 5th Ser. Vol. 6, p. 33, 587.

ROBERT BRICE

Served as pvt. under Capt. Thomas Askey, 1780-81-82. Robert Brice is shown as a freeman, in Fannett Twp., during the above years.

Penna. Arch. 5th Ser. Vol. 6, p. 393, 408, 417, 441, 481.

JAMES BEARD

Served as pvt. 1780-81-82 under Capt. John McConnell. His wife was Jane, dau. of James McKean.

Penna. Arch. 5th Ser. Vol. 6, p. 268, 303, 310.

THOMAS BURNEY

Appears as a pvt. under Capt. Wm. Heyser, in the German Regt., under Baron Arendt, Colonel, at Quibble Town, May 22, 1777. Thomas Burney, John Dixon and Richard Venable are shown with Col. Benj. Chambers in 1767 as signers to the agreement between the trustees and the builders of the church at Falling Spring. Under a meeting of the Governors, Apr. of 1767, is Thomas Burney agt. James Elliott and submitted by Consent of Partys to the Determination of Col. Benj. Chambers, Thomas Beard, Richard Venables, Bobert Urie and Wm. Lyons or any three of them. A certain pricked line proposed by Col. John Armstrong was used for a Division which was first disagreeable to both parties, yet now Thos. Burney is willing to abide by it.

Penna. Arch. 5th Ser. Vol. 3, p. 794. Penna. Arch. 3rd Ser. Vol. 1, p. 171, 299.

HUGH BOND

Served with Capt. Samuel Patton, 1780-81-82, also serving in the Cont. Line, Cumb. Co. Militia. Hugh Bond was married by Rev. Alexdr. Dobbin, to Ann, dau. of Thos. Anderson, of Hamilton Twp., Dec. 26, 1775.

Penna. Arch. 5th Ser. Vol. 6, p. 264, 278, 287, 311, 643. Penna. Arch. 5th Ser. Vol. 4, p. 279.

JOHN BARCLAY

Served as pvt. 1780-81-82, under Capt. Alexdr. Peebles. Deeds at Chambersburg show that John Barclay died early owning a tract of land in Lurgan Twp., a dau. Margaret as his only heir,—said dau. mar. James Rankin. They sold land in 1786 to Andrew Hamilton, who sold from Fayette County, Penna., to Fredk. Hess in 1787.

WILLIAM BLEAKNEY

Of Washington Twp., served with Cumb. Co. Militia, in the Cont. Line, and was entitled to Depreciation pay. He served as a Ranger on the Frontier. His wife Jean, dau. of John Moorhead of Antrim Twp. In his will, dated and prob. Feb., 1798, he names 4 sons: James; Wm.; Fergus; Samuel and their heirs, 2/3 of the estate equally among them. Grandson Wm. the son of James, 5 lbs.; beloved daughters, Ann; Catherine; Jenat; Sarah; and their heirs 1/3 part of my estate. In April, 1804, Ann Bleakney is shown as the wife of Saml. Cox; Edward Bleakney of Westmoreland Co., had mar. Catherine Bleakney; Sarah and Jennet were then in Washington Twp., Franklin Co., Penna. Under the records of Dr. Robert Kennedy of Greencastle and Welsh Run, are these marriages: Moses McLean, Sally Bleakney, Sept. 22, 1808; Wm. Bleakney, Margaret Wilson, March 20, 1809.

Penna. Arch. 5th Ser. Vol. 4, p. 279, 620.

HENRY BUZZARD

Served as pvt. under Capt. Samuel Patton, 1780-82. He was a brother of John Bossart of Hamilton Twp.

Penna. Arch. 5th Ser. Vol. 6, p. 278, 311.

JOHN BUZZARD (BOSSERT)

Served as pvt. under Capt. Samuel Patton, 1780-81 82. He was born 1741, Alsace Loraine, mar. 1760, at Lancaster, Penna., to Catherine LaRue, born 1740, died 1805 near Chambersburg, Penna. John Bossert was a miller of Hamilton Twp. He owned the following property: land 1092 acres; mountain land, 50 acres; one mill; one negro; two horses; three cows. He left a will dated March 26, 1803. Issue of the above: Henry Bossart unmar.; Jacob Bossert no date; John Bossart mar. Margaret Kinard; Catherine mar. Henry Trout; Margaret mar. John Bonnet; Elizabeth mar. Jacob Shearer; Magdalena mar. George Weirich; Rebecca mar. John Mathews Mary mar. Dewalt Keefer; Esther unmar.

Penna. Arch. 5th Ser. Vol. 6, p. 277, 286, 288, 311.

HUGH BARKLEY (BERKLEY)

Served as pvt. under Capts. John Jack and Wm. Long in 1779-1780. Under the Rev. Dobbin's records is found the mar. of Hugh Bockley to Sarah McCullough, June 19, 1777, of "Cannigagig." A deed proves her a dau. of Robert McCulloch (Miller) of Antrim Twp., to his son-in-law Hugh Barkley of Baltimore, Md. Among the Rangers of the Frontiers, Hugh Barclay, Adjt. is shown.

Penna. Arch. 5th Ser. Vol. 6, p. 540, 557.

JAMES BOGLE

Served under Capt. Robert Shannon, Cumb. Co., 1780-81-82; he also served in 1777-78-79, and later moved to Franklin County, Montgomery Twp., where he bought and sold Kyle land to Jacob Brewer—conveyed to Robert Kyle by his father Samuel and sold by Robert to James Bogle. This tract was known as "Clifton Hall." In Oct., 1800, James Bogle and wife Sarah of Montgomery Twp., sold 100 acres to Jacob Brewer, part of the grant to Samuel Kyle in 1771.

Penna. Arch. 5th Ser. Vol. 6, p. 16, 67, 243, 252, 259, 445, 447, 628.

JOSEPH BOGLE

Served in Cumb. Co., 1777-79, undated rolls. His wife was Rachel Maise (Mayse) of Lancaster Co., Penna. dau. of Andrew Maise and sister to the wives of Cairnes Sterrett and Johnston Elliott. Joseph Bogle and wife also conveyed their (Kyle) land to Jacob Brewer. Joseph Bogle left a will dated 1807, prob. 1811. In 1801 Joseph Bogle and wife Rachel sold 235 ac. to John McMordie. The Bogles were from Newton Twp., Cumb. Co., Penna. In the will of Joseph he names brother Samuel; nephew Joseph, son of brother Robert, decd.; brother James; 3 sisters: Susanna, Margaret, Martha each 10 pounds. Joseph Bogle appears as a member of the Asso. Ref. Ch. of "Upper Conococheague" near Mercersburg, Penna.

Penna. Arch. 5th Ser. Vol. 6, p. 68, 243, 260, 445, 447.

ALEXANDER BIGGER

Served as a pvt in 1778. From Carlisle the will of Alexander Bigger, Apr. 18, 1778, names: To Agnes, eldest dau. of Andrew Bigger, 50 pounds in gold or silver now in the hands of brother Andrew. To my father and mother, 50 pounds to be sent to them the 1st opportunity. To Martha Bigger my sister, to be sent 1st opportunity. Brothers John and Ezekiel—part of land joining Wm. McDowell. Will prob. Oct. 3, 1778.

Penna. Arch. 5th Ser. Vol. 6, p. 375.

ANDREW BIGGART (BIGGER)

Served as pvt. in 1777 under Capt. Geo. Crawford, and in 1780-81 under Capts. James Patton, Robert Dickey and Thos. McDowell. He died in St. Thomas Twp.; letters of Admr. June 1829, leaving a widow Mary and issue 4: Nancy, widow of James Clayton; Mary, wife of Alexander Work; Jane, wife of Henry Westbay; Martha, wife of Spencer Madan. Grandchildren: John, Joseph, Washington, James, Daniel, Wm., Charlotte, Mary and Andrew of whom the last 8 are minors (Mark Brindle guardian) of John Biggert, decd., who had received his share in life time, and James Will Biggert, minor child of James Biggert, decd., (James Dixon guardian), leaving land in St. Thomas Twp., showing a stone 2 story house, kitchen, Bank barn and Spring house. Petition for division of estate was in Orphans' Court, Jan. 12, 1829. 1790 Census for Penna., shows family of Andrew Bigger as 2 men, 2 boys, 4 females.

Penna. Arch. 5th Ser. Vol. 6, p. 271, 284, 289, 314, 371.

JAMES BIGGERT

Served as pvt. under Capt. Pat. Jack 1777, and and under Capt. Walter McKinne 1781-82. In 1769 he was living in Dist--'t 7 of the Presbyterian Church of Merersbu with a wife, not named, and children, Su 1; John; Mary; Rebecca. They appear a. .ne household with the family of Patrick Cannon. 1790 Census shows family of above as: 2 men, 1 boy, 3 females.

Penna. Arch. 5th Ser. Vol. 6, p. 297, 300, 305, 372.

JAMES BIGGER

Served as private under Capt. Walter McKinnie 1781-82. He and wife Rosanna sold land in Franklin County and removed to Westmoreland Co., Penna., Unity Twp., where his will was dated 1803, and prob. 1809. He named wife Rosanna, "Cash due me in Franklin Co., Penna." dau. Martha White; dau. Hannah White; dau. Ann White of Juniata; dau. Mary White now of Ky.; son John and wife Elizabeth, no issue; daus. Amanda &c. The marriages of the above to Whites were performed by Rev. John King, Mercersburg, Penna.

Penna. Arch. 5th Ser. Vol. 6, p. 297, 305.

JOHN BIGGER

Served as pvt. under Capt. Walter McKinnie 1781-82. John Bigger of Peters Twp., sold land in 1798 to Daniel Ridenour. 1790 Census shows John Bigger family as, 2 men, 2 females.

JOHN BIGGER, JR.

Served as pvt. under Capt. Walter McKinnie 1781-82. John Bigger's child died Oct. 20, 1776, and Mrs. John Bigger died June 9, 1790.

Penna. Arch. 5th Ser. Vol. 6, p. 298, 306.

Marriages, Dr. John King, Mercersburg, Penna.: Mr. Work, Polly Bigger, July, 1803.
Mr. Wisbay, Jean Bigger, Apr. 23, 1807.
John Bigger, Mary Bigger, Dec. 25, 1787.
James White, Martha Bigger, Aug. 7, 1781.
Stephen White, Mary Bigger, Feb. 7, 1786.
Stephen White, Hannah Bigger, May 8, 1786.
Mr. White, Anne Bigger, Jan. 19, 1791.
John Bigger, Rebecca Elliott, June 20, 1825.

DANIEL BONEBRAKE

Served as a soldier in the Rev. War, in and about Philadelphia, 1777-1781, under Col. Abraham Smith, Capt. Conrad Snider, Corp. Daniel Bonebrake. He was the son of Daniel and Anna Maria Beinbrech (buried at Grindstone Hill), date and place of birth not known, but it is probably he was born in Germany, date and place of death after 1813 Westmoreland Co., Penna., as shown in abstract of will of one Jacob Smith proved Jan. 5, 1813—wife Marey and father-in-law Daniel Bonbrit—with whom Jacob Smith had a written agreement. In 1802 Daniel Bonebrake deeded his property to Daniel Leap, in Guilford Twp., Franklin Co., Penna. He is listed in same Twp., 1779-1780-1781-1782. The census for Franklin Co., Penna., 1790, lists Daniel Bonebrake as the head of a family with one boy and six girls under sixteen. His wife's name not known, but there is record of these children: Conrad Bonebrake, born Feb. 24, 1768—died Nov. 11, 1844, buried on Bonebrake farm, Washington Twp., Franklin Co., Penna.; Martha Bonebrake—died Aug. 24, 1862, aged 83 yrs. 6 mos. 9 days, mar. John Clugston, (buried at Brown's Mill); Mary Bonebrake, mar. Jacob Smith, lived in Westmoreland Co., Penna.

Penna. Arch. 3rd Ser. Vol. 23, p. 660, 656.
Penna. Arch. 5th Ser. Vol. 6, p. 87, 119, 538, 545.

DEWALT BONEBRAKE

Served as pvt. under Capts. Samuel Royer and Conrad Snider, 1779-80-81. For further data see Biographical Annals of Franklin Co., Penna., by Seilhamer on Bonebreak, which are thought to be excellent.

Penna. Arch. 5th Ser. Vol. 6, p. 74, 89, 119, 542.

FREDERICK BONEBREAK

Served under Capt Wm. Long in 1779, and under Capt. Conrad Snider 1780-81. The will of Fredk. Bonebreak was prob. Nov. 30, 1820. His wife was Christina. He mentions the heirs of son Dewalt, decd.; the children of Adam; Catherine mar. to George Crossland; Eve Hamilton and Henry. The husband of Eve was Wm. Hamilton. By Nov. 30, 1820 the widow, Christina, had mar. Baltzer Overcash. The above Frederick was a son of pioneer Daniel Beinbreght, wife Anna Maria of Guilford Twp.

Penna. Arch. 5th Ser. Vol. 6, p. 87, 119, 538, 546.

HENRY BONEBRAKE

Served as pvt., 1779-80-81, under Capts. Samuel Royer and Conrad Snider.

Penna. Arch. 5th Ser. Vol. 6, p. 74, 89, 119, 542.

PETER BONEBREAK

Served under Capts. Adam Harmony and Wm. Long, 1777-78, and under Snider, 1780-81. Peter Bonebreak is shown as a soldier in the Penna. Line, from Cumb. Co., Penna.

Penna. Arch. 5th Ser. Vol. 6, p. 87, 118, 537, 545. Penna. Arch. 5th Ser. Vol. 4, p. 621.

ALEXANDER BROWN

Was a Lieut. in Capt. Jeremh. Talbot's Co., recruited in Franklin Co., Penna.; he was commissioned Jan. 9, 1776. Alex. Brown is shown serving under Capt. Walter McKinnie, 1781-82. One Alexdr. Brown was mar. by Rev. J. C. Bucher, Aug. ye 6th, 1767, to Deborah Clark, and was taxable, 1781, in Peters Twp., with 420 acres of land. He appears 1817 to 1820 on the Ledger of "Squire McKinstry of Mercersburg, Credit—"By Pention." Alex. Brown is given in 1796, a taxable with one cow; his family in 1790 Census, consisting of three men. Alexander Brown wounded at Stony Point; discharged Jan. 11, 1781. General Accounting office, Washington D. C., states that Alexdr. Brown d. on July 1, 1823, in Franklin Co., Penna., arrears of pension paid to Joseph Boyd at Phila., Nov. 20, 1823, as Atty. for James McDowell, Admr. of the estate.

Penna. Arch. 5th Ser. Vol. 2, p. 208, 211. Penna. Arch. 5th Ser. Vol. 3, p. 72. Penna. Arch. 2nd Ser. Vol. 10, p. 556. Penna. Arch. 5th Ser. Vol. 6, p. 298, 300, 306.

GEORGE BROWN

Served in 1747-48, of the Asso. Regiment of Lancaster Co.," over the river Susquehanna under Col. Benj. Chambers. With Capt. George Brown were Lieut. John Potter and Ensign John Reynolds. The will of George Brown of Antrim Twp., directs "my two sons George and Lazarus to give my wife Agnes sufficient maintenance and cut and hall her firewood, and keep her horse, cows and sheep for her during her widowhood. Also 200 pounds and 2 negro wenches Silvy and Doll; her choice of one horse and saddle, two best cows, four sheep, one bed and furniture and furnishings for a Chamber according to station &c. all the plate furniture in the house to be wholly and absolutely at her disposal and while she remains my widow the further privilege of any Room she chooses in the house and my two sons George and Lazarus is to give her a sufficient maintainance &c. To my dau. Susanna McKnight the tract of land I possess in the Little Cove, in Bedford Co., adjoining widow Herad and 100 pounds. To my dau. Sarah Chambers the tract I possess in Westmoreland Co., that I purchased of Wm. Perry and 200 pounds &c. To my son Thomas Brown 2 tracts in Redstone Settlement xx negroes Jack and Philip xx. To my son Wm. Brown a tract in West Conococheague settlement xx to be clothed, schooled and maintained xx. To my sons George and Lazarus xx my Mill and certain land. Will dated Oct., 1785, prob. June, 1791. Executors: Son Thomas and brother-in-law James Maxwell, Esq.

Penna. Arch. 5th Ser. Vol. 1, p. 25.

HENRY BROWN

Resided in Franklin Co., 1835, aged 81 yrs. He served in the 6th Penna. Regt. Cont. Line.

Penna. Arch. 2nd Ser. Vol. 10, p. 593. Penna. Arch. 5th Ser. Vol. 3, p. 173.

JOHN BROWN, S. K. (STOREKEEPER)

Served as a pvt under Capt. Terrence Campbell in 1782. His wife was Elizabeth, dau. of Joseph Cooke, and grandau. of Thomas Brown, pioneer. He was a Merchant in Chambersburg, his will prob. Mar. 27, 1818. He left sons John and Robert, who probably left no heirs, as the Franklin Repository stated that John Steele Brown died Dec. 28, 1820, last of the family of John Brown, Esq. John Brown Esq., d. Mar. 26, 1818, aged 63 yrs. His wife Elizabeth and 2 sons lie with him in Cedar Grove Cemetery. The Franklin Repository of Nov. 3, 1807, gave this: "Died at Clarkesville, Tenn., on the 25th of Sept. last, Mrs. Jane Reynolds, youthful consort of Mr. James Reynolds, Mcht., and dau. of John Brown, Esq., of this place." The bodies were removed from the Asso. Ref. Ch. graveyard in Chambersburg, to Cedar Grove Cemetery.

Penna. Arch. 5th Ser. Vol. 6, p. 125.

SIMS (SIMSY) BROWN

Served under Capt. Walter McKinnie, 1781.

He was a freeman in Montgomery Twp., 1781. Sims Brown is shown as a private., in the Cont. Line; he was also a Ranger on the Frontier.

Penna. Arch. 5th Ser. Vol. 6, p. 281, 299, 301. Penna. Arch. 5th Ser. Vol. 4, p. 280.

OLIVER BROWN

Served as pvt. under Capt. Patrick Jack, 1781-82. The will of Oliver Brown, Sr., is prob. Feb. 24, 1807. He names sons John; Oliver; Wm.; Grandchildren named Thompson: Wm.; Mary; Sarah; Elizabeth; Ann; Grandau., Elizabeth McKean Brown, dau. of my son John. They were of Hamilton Twp.

Penna. Arch. 5th Ser. Vol. 6, p. 292, 296, 313.

WILLIAMS BROOKENS

The Valley Spirit, Chambersburg, Penna., May 4, 1850: "Died on the 27th Ult., in Shippensburg, Mr. William Brookens, a hero of the Revolution, aged about 85 yrs."

HENRY BLACK

Was in service with Capt. Askey, 1779, of the First Batt., of Cumb. Co. Militia, with "Capt. Alex. Piples at Sunbury, Sept. 1, 1779." In 1781, he substituted for Peter Houghenberry, at Little's Fort, and later was serving as Corporal with Capt. Robert Quigley. He appeared, also as a pvt. in the Cont. Line, from Cumb. Co., Penna.

REV. JOHN BLACK

Was married Nov. 15, 1773, by Dr. John King, Mercersburg, Penna., to Elizabeth Newell. Penna. Magazine, Vol. 10, p. 454; John Black, born in York Co., Penna., about 1750, his father Robert Black, an early settler, but removed to N. C., when John was an infant. John entered Nassau Hall 1769, graduated 1771, licensed by Donegal Presby., 1773, ordained in Upper Marsh Creek Congregation 1775. Served nineteen years, resigning in 1795. Delegate to Penna., Convention to ratify the Federal Constitution in 1787. He accepted a call to Unity and Greensburg, Penna., dying there Aug. 16, 1802. In the will of John Black, Minister of the Gospel, he named son John; daus. Margaret and Mary Black; his two eldest children were Ann McAllister and Robert Black.

WILLIAM BLACK

Enlisted in 1775 and served one year in Capt. Jeremiah Talbot's Co., Col. Irvine's Penna. Regt. He then enlisted and served in Capts. J. Torrey's and Lloyd's Companies, Col. Hazen's "Congress" Regt., was in the battles of Three Rivers, Lake Champlain and Brandywine and served six years and six months. He was wounded on board a gunboat on Lake Champlain, in the left hand; was hospitalized at Ft. George. He was discharged by Gen'l. Washington's order. Private William Black resided in Franklin County in 1815; and was allowed pension on his application executed May 15, 1818, while a resident of Franklin County, Penna., aged about 73 yrs. In 1820 he stated his family consisted of one dau. and grandson; their names not given.

Penna. Arch. 5th Ser. Vol. 2, p. 209, 6th Penna. Cont. Line.

JACOB BARNCOURT

Served as a pvt. under Capt. Walter McKinnie in 1781-82.

Penna. Arch. 5th Ser. Vol. 6, p. 298, 301, 306.

PETER BARNCOURT

Served as pvt. under Capt. Walter McKinnie, 1781-82. His will was prob. Nov. 30, 1796. He names 2 sons, Jacob and Peter; daus, Barbara; Eve; and Susannah; Grandson, Jacob Peeman; Grandaus, Mary and Elizabeth Crinkle. The son Peter Barncord died in 1814, leaving a widow Elizabeth and issue: Jacob; Catherine mar. Jacob Wilt; John; all above minority; Mary mar. Jacob Tritle, Mary now decd., leaving a son Jacob under 14 yrs., also Elizabeth Barncord, under 14 yrs. They owned land in Peters Twp.

Penna. Arch. 5th Ser. Vol. 6, p. 297, 305.

JAMES BRYAN

Served as pvt. under Capt. Noah Abraham, 1780-81-82. He was of Metal Twp., his will having been probated Apr. 6, 1804, he named a dau. Ledea (Lydia) McCurdy; 2 sons, Charles and Golden, land on which they now reside. Golden Bryan mar. Sarah Brown, Apr. 21, 1802, by Dr. John King, Mercersburg, Penna.

NATHANIEL BRYAN

Served as pvt. under Capt. Noah Abraham, 1777-80-81-82. An interesting petition sent to the Executive Council from Fannett Twp., June 29, 1778, shows both Nathaniel and James Byran among the signers. "We have repeated alarms of the Indians heading toward us, xxxx We have an ardent desire to maintain our Ground, and think we could if we have had Guards sent to us to join our people, either to reap the Grain, Guard our forts or scout the woods beyond us." The will of Nathaniel Bryan of Fannett Twp., was dated and prob., Feb. 1818. He was living in the family of James and Elizabeth McCurdy—to whose children he left bequests, also to certain Bryans in the State of Delaware and to the children of Charles Bryan living in the Western Country; $75. towards finishing the Upper Meeting house or church in Path Valley, and any surplus for schooling and supporting Poor children in Metal and Fannett Twps.

Penna. Arch. 5th Ser. Vol. 6, p. 86, 120, 128, 384, 392, 515, 620.

JOHN BROOKY

Served in 1778 under Capt. Joseph Culbertson. John Brooky mar. Mary McElhatton, Dec. 23, 1778, her sister Catherine having mar. Wm. Anderson, Dec. 20, 1773, both marriages by Dr. John King. A tract of land in Hamilton Twp., was granted to Wm. Rankin in 1751, who sold to Jas. McFarland 1765, who sold to Thos. Anderson in 1778. Thos. Anderson and wife Anne, sold to Robert Anderson, who with wife Mary transferred 86 acres to Benj. Caruthers. Benj. and wife Susan to Wm. Anderson and John Brookie. Wm. Anderson and wife Catherine, John Brookie and wife Mary, of Hamilton Twp., sell in 1779 to Andrew Davison—(Catherine signs as Kitty). In 1780 it is the property of Alexander Hill.

Penna. Arch. 5th Ser. Vol. 6, p. 382.

ADAM BURKHOLDER, SR.

Of Greene Twp., served as pvt. under Capt. Joseph Culbertson, 1780-81. His will prob. Feb. 5, 1800, names wife Maria, and children: Jacob; Adam; Catherine; Christian; Barbara; Mariah; Michael; Elizabeth; Henry; Easter; Joseph; Grandchildren, Robert Attison and John Lindsay, children of his dau. Ann. His lands joined Rev. Chaighead, James Findlay and others.

Penna. Arch. 5th Ser. Vol. 6, p. 280, 290.

ADAM BURKHOLDER, JR.

Served as pvt. under Capt. Joseph Culbertson, 1780-81. Undoubtedly a son of Adam, Sr.

Penna. Arch. 5th Ser. Vol. 6, p. 280, 290.

CHRISTOPHER (CHRISLEY) BURKHOLDER

Served as pvt., 1780-81, under Capt. Joseph Culbertson, probably the son "Christian" shown in will.

Penna. Arch. 5th Ser. Vol. 6, p. 279, 289.

JOHN BURKHOLDER

Served as pvt. under Capt. Joseph Culbertson, 1780-81.

Penna. Arch. 5th Ser. Vol. 6, p. 280, 290.

PETER BRICKER

Enlisted in 1776 in the 6th Regt. under Colonel North, in the Company of Wm. Findlay. He received an honorable discharge. In 1813 he resided in Franklin Co., Penna., and in 1835 he was living in Franklin Twp., Huntingdon Co., Penna., aged 77 years. Under April 26, 1799, deeds at Chambersburg show that Peter Bricker and wife Catherine of Franklin County sell to Alexdr. McCutcheon. John Bricker of Hamilton Twp., died intestate, owning land in Hamilton Twp., 175 ac. He left a widow and eleven (11) children, one of whom is the said Peter Bricker, who is by law entitled to a part.

Penna. Arch. 5th Ser. Vol. 4, p. 530. Penna. Arch. 2nd Ser. Vol. 13, p. 23. Penna. Arch. 2nd Ser. Vol. 10, p. 594.

DANIEL BAKER

The census of 1790 shows a DANIEL BAKER family consisting of one man, six boys, four females. He owned large tracts of land. Daniel Baker of Washington Twp., Franklin Co., Penna., left a will dated January 10, 1785, prob. Dec. 27, 1790. He names his wife Faronica; the son Jacob was to provide for his mother. Jacob was to get the plantation "whereon I now live." Son John 5 pounds and the plantation where he now lives. There were no executors, but witnesses were William Stover, Jacob Hess, Samuel Royer. He is probably the Daniel Baker who was taxed in 1782 in Washington Twp., on 265 ac. of land, with horses and cattle.

GEORGE BAKER

Was in Service, 1781, under Capt. Daniel Clapsaddle.

Penna. Arch. 5th Ser. Vol. 6, p. 117.

JACOB BAKER

Served under Capt. Saml. Royer, 1780-82. The Census of 1790, shows the family of Jacob Baker to consist of 2 men and 4 females. Peter Baker, Sr., and Jr.; Jacob Baker; Henry Baker all shown in 1782, with land and stock.

In the will of John Potter, Jr., dated 1821, he names a dau. Catherine Baker.

Penna. Arch. 5th Ser. Vol 6, p. 89, 112, 124.

JAMES BAKER SERGT.

Appears, 1779, in service with Capt. Samuel Royer.

Penna. Arch. 5th Ser. Vol. 6, p. 541.

JOHN BAKER

Appears in service 1779-81 under Capt. Samuel Royer. Under 1799 Taxables, John Baker is shown with land; merchant mill; 2 log houses; Stable; Horses and Cows. In the will of David Stoner, 1810, he names a dau. Sarah, wife of John Baker. The Census of 1790, shows man named

John Baker, in Washington Twp.,—as John Baker, 1 man, 3 boys, 5 females.
Penna Arch. 5th Ser. Vol. 6, p. 543, 113, 98, 90.

SAMUEL BAKER

Appears in service, 1778-81-82, undated roll, under Capts. Thos. Askey and Isaac Miller. Frances Baker of Fannett Twp., left a will dated 1789, prob. 1791, naming oldest dau. Rebecca Wallace; oldest son, Wm.; dau. Elizabeth Askey; second son John; Nancy McCrea; Rosannah Baker and Samuel Baker, a lot of ground in Wilmington. My right in a legacy from my aunt Rebecah Baker, arrearages of rent from Felix Doyle; Exrs: Samuel Baker and Rosannah Baker. The above Frances was the widow of Col. Robert Baker, (Provincial service) who died in 1768. They had issue: I. Rebecca mar. John Wallace; II. William; III. Elizabeth mar. Thomas Askey (Erskine); IV. Rosannah mar. Robert Lytle; V. John mar. Jane Ross; VI. Samuel mar. Mary Beatty; VII. Anne mar. John McCray (McCrea); VIII. Mary, unmarried.
Penna. Arch. 5th Ser. Vol. 6, p. 37, 39, 52, 132, 414, 440.
Marriage records, St. John's Lutheran Church, Hagerstown, Md.:
Christian Backer, Nancy Stoul, Stout or Stall, Jan. 17, 1797.
Fredk. Clopper, Sarah Backer, April, 1798.
Abraham Becker, Marg. Partoon, April, 1802.
Peter Backer, Sus. Otmen, March, 1804.
Philip Baker, Maria Thomas, March, 1814.
Nicholas Baker, Margaret Webb, February, 1805.
Peter Backer, Cath. Thomas, May, 1806.
John Backer, Marg. Schoffner, August, 1807.
Alexdr. (?) Backer, Mary Webb, March, 1808.
Richard Baker, Ann Webb, July 2, 1811.
James Murra, Margt. Baker, June, 1810.

ADAM BRECHT

Of Letterkenny Twp., served in Lancaster Co., under Casper Stoever. His will prob. Nov. 1797, in Franklin County, names wife Magdalena, and five children: Adam; Elizabeth; John; Catherine; Magdalena.
Penna. Arch 5th Ser. Vol. 7, p. 151.

JOHN BLACKBURN

Appears serving in 1777-78-79, as pvt., and as Lieut., in 1779 with Capt. Jas. Floyd. John Blackburn mar. Jean, dau. of Thomas Armstrong, shown in the final account of the estate of Thos. Armstrong. John Blackburn and Jane Armstrong were mar. Dec. 6, 1784. Jean and her husband, John Blackburn, settled in Columbia Co., Ohio. The will of Col. Joseph Armstrong, son of the pioneer, gave to Joseph Armstrong Blackburn, son of John Blackburn, above, a legacy, as promised to those named for him. John Blackburn and wife were living in Hamilton Twp., Franklin Co., Penna., in 1802, when they sold their land to Henry Lawson, in 1806, removing to Columbiana Co., Ohio.
Penna. Arch. 5th Ser. Vol. 6, p. 160, 168, 604.

JOHN BRINDLE

Served as a private under Capt. John Lamb, 1780—4th Comp., 3rd Batt., Cumb. Co. Militia. He was born 1734, d. 1817. His wife Catherine b. 1743, died 1818. Malachi Brindle d. 1862, aged 96 yrs. Buried in the old Brindle graveyard, St. Thomas Twp. In 1793, John and Malachi Brindle, late of Cumb. Co. Penna., bought from Adam and Sarah Holliday 486 ac. land which pioneer John Holliday had willed to his son Adam. In Dec. of 1800, John Brindle transferred all his interest in 2 tracts of land, called "Wrangle" and "The Addition to Wrangle" to John and Saml. Holliday. The Witnesses were Elliott T. Lane and John Riddle. In 1789, David Casner and wife, Catherine sold to John Brindle, a tract in Peters Twp., called "Ipswich" joining James Campbell and others. Burials of the above family are in the "Old Brindle Graveyard," St. Thomas Twp., a cement wall enclosing the graves.
Penna. Arch. 5th Ser. Vol. 6, p. 219, 225.

LAWRENCE BRINDLE (BRENDLE)

Appears as a pvt., 1780-81-82, with Capt. Wm. Strain, Cumb. Co. Militia. He is shown as a taxable in Lurgan Twp., 1778 to 1782, with land, horses and cattle and in Southampton Twp., in 1786, with both state and county taxes. The tax list of 1796 is signed by Geo. Johnston, Daniel Nevins and Lawrence Brindle. He removed to Westmoreland Co., Penna. where he died in 1809, one dau. having mar. ———— Harshman.
Penna. Arch. 5th Ser. Vol. 6, p. 142, 397, 416, 429.

SAMUEL BRINDLE

Of Southampton Twp., served under Capt. Wm. Strain, 1780-82, undated rolls. His will, dated and prob. 1804, in which he requested his youngest son Wm. to be sent to school "if a school can be had." He names six children: Peter; George; Catherine Brindle; Uley Brindle; Wm.; John; son John's son Samuel and dau. Elizabeth.
Penna. Arch. 5th Ser. Vol. 6, p. 142, 152, 398, 430.

SAMUEL BRENDLE

Served in 1780-82, undated rolls, with Capts. Benj. Blythe and Wm. Strain, Cumb. Co.

Militia. Samuel Brendle is shown as a taxable 1778 to 1782 in Lurgan Twp., with land, horses and cattle.

Penna. Arch. 5th Ser. Vol. 6, p. 142, 152, 398, 430.

ANTHONY BEVER (BEAVER)

Served as pvt. under Capt. Samuel Royer and Adam Harmony, in 1778-80. He was a son of Nicholas Beaver and was born Jan. 25, 1761, died Sept. 7, 1839. Married 1st, May (Mary) Clopper, mar. 2nd Susan Clopper. Issue: Henry and Susan to first wife and to 2nd wife, Catherine; Elizabeth; Margaret; Ann; Esther; John; Samuel; Anthony; Hannah. They moved to Huntingdon Co. (now Blair) Aug. 16, 1793. They later moved and built Marklesburg, Huntingdon Co., Penna., and died there.

Penna. Arch. 5th Ser. Vol. 6, p. 74, 89, 539.

BENJAMIN BEAVER, PVT.

Lived in Franklin Co., 1835, aged 77 yrs. He was a pvt., in the Penna. Line and a pensioner. Deed Book Vol. 11, p. 598, Chambersburg, Penna., —Benj. Beaver of Antrim Twp., for $130., sells to David Bever, his right in the estate of his father Nicholas Bever, partly in Franklin and partly in Adams Co., Penna., June 24, 1815.

Penna. Arch. 5th Ser. Vol. 2, p. 989. Penna. Arch. 3rd Ser. Vol. 23, p. 507.

BENJAMIN BEAVER

Served in Jackson's Company under Col. Craig, 1781, transferred to Steele, 1782, First Penna. Benj. and Christ'r. Beaver C. L. entitled to dep. pay.

Penna. Arch. 2nd Ser. Vol. 10, p. 389, 396. Penna. Arch. 5th Ser. Vol. 2, p. 748. Penna. Arch. 5th Ser. Vol. 4, p. 214.

BENJAMIN N. BEAVER

Son of Nicholas, mar. Caroline Snyder; issue: 4: John; David; Caroline; Jacob. John moved to Westmoreland Co., Penna.; David enlisted in War of 1812; Caroline, mar. Samuel Fisher, moved to Springfield, Ill.; Jacob lived near Waynesboro, Penna.

GEORGE BEAVER

Gravestone of George Beaver, Keefer's Church Graveyard, Letterkenny Twp.,—"George Beaver, born in Chester Co., Penna., 1755, died in Franklin Co., 1836. He served his country in the Struggle for American Independence as a member of Capt. Church's Company,—4th Penna. Battalion Commanded by Capt. Anthony Wayne." He was a private in the Penna. Line, and a pensioner. Gen'l. Wayne to Pres. Reed—1780.

Camp, at Totowa, Oct. 25, '80.
Dear Sir:

I did myself the honor to address you the 17th Instant, and took the liberty to ask for a quantity of thread and needles, to be forwarded by Mr. Little; but as he came away without them, I must beg leave to reiterate my request, and desire that they may be sent on with all possible dispatch, as every day adds to our distress, and renders an immediate supply of these articles Indispensably necessary—I believe no army before this was ever put to such shifts, in order to have even the appearance of uniformity— when the charge of the Penna. Division devolved on me after the removal of Gen'l. St. Clair to the Command of the left wing, I thought of an expedient of reducing the heterogenius of new, old, cock'd and floped hats and pieces of hats, to Infantry Caps, in which we succeeded very well—by making three decent caps out of one tolerable and two very ordinary hats, to which we added, as an embellishment, a white plume, and a Comb of flowing red hair. We now shall try the experiment of making three short coats out of three old tattered long ones. I must acknowledge they would answer much better for the Spring than fall; but without something done in this way, we shall be naked in the course of two or three weeks; nor will even this expedient answer longer than Christmas —For God's sake, use every possible means to procure Cloathing for both officers and men, by that time, at furthest.

Signed   Ant'y Wayne.

Penna. Arch. 1st Ser. Vol. 8, p. 593.

NICHOLAS BEAVER

Served as pvt., 1779-80-81, under Capt. Samuel Royer,—name written Bever and Beavor. Nicholas Beaver, born March 8, ——, died March 29, 1812, Franklin County, Penna. He mar. Katherine Simmer, 1746-1809. He had sons: Anthony; Benjamin; Jacob; Philip; John.

Penna. Arch. 5th Ser. Vol. 6, p. 75, 90, 113, 542.

BENJAMIN BRIGGS, SR.

An early settler in Fannett Twp., appears in service 1777-79, with Capt. Noah Abraham. He signed a petition, June, 1778, in which "We greatfully acknowledge the Favour xxx already done us, in sending some arms and amunition on our former petition, by Capt. Abraham, we pray the honorable Council to send us more arms xxx and two Companies of men xxx through the Divine assistance, we may be able to preserve the settlement xxx."

Penna. Arch. 5th Ser. Vol. 6, p. 21, 52, 131.

BENJAMIN BRIGGS, JR.

Was in service 1778-79, undated roll, under Capts. Thos. Askey and Isaac Miller.
Penna. Arch 5th Ser. Vol. 6, p. 37, 62, 132.

SAMUEL BRIGGS

Was in service 1779, undated roll, under Capt. Thos. Askey.
Penna. Arch. 5th Ser. Vol. 6, p. 61, 132.

ALEXANDER BUCHANAN

Pensioner, private in the Penna. Line, in Pike C., Penna., was 62 years of age on Dec. 1, 1818, and died March 25, 1819. He appears to have been living in or near Mercersburg as he had baptized a son William, June 5, 1770, and a child on Oct., 1774.

JOHN BRACKENRIDGE

Served as pvt. under Capt. Wm. Strain 1782, also under Capt. Alex. Peebles in 1777. The will of John Brackenridge, was probated Nov. 21, 1810. He names: Sons John and Samuel; dau. Gennit, wife of Benj. Johnston; Children of dau. Sarah, who mar. Archbd. Mahan; dau. Elizabeth, wife of James Herron; dau. Polly wife of James Shoop; dau. Nancy wife of Robert Culbertson; son Culbertson; son Andrew.
Penna. Arch. 5th Ser. Vol. 6, p. 143, 430, 26.

JAMES BROTHERTON

Of Guilford Twp., Tanner, served under Capt. James Young, 1779-80. His will dated July, 1— was prob. Aug., 1788, naming wife Margaret; Nephew James Brotherton, tanner, son of Robert Brotherton my plantation whereon I now live with the tanyard xxx; Nephew James Brotherton, son to Wm. Brotherton; Jean Patterson and Margaret Boyd my nieces; Nephew Hugh Brotherton; Sister Mary Ann Rogers in Ireland; Sister Janet Reed; Niece Jean Brotherton; Brother Wm.; Nephew Robert Brotherton, the tanner; Niece Matthew Brotherton; Nephews Samuel and John Brotherton; Sister-in-law Rebecca Tomson; Brother Robert Brotherton; Nephew David Brotherton and Niece Mary Brotherton; Margaret Brotherton dau. to my nephew William Brotherton; Rev. James Long 10 pounds; five pounds for the use and benefit of the College at Carlisle; Exrs: James Brotherton, George Delong, John Ward.
Penna. Arch 5th Ser. Vol. 6, p. 548, 82.

JAMES BROTHERTON

Served as 1st Lieut. under Capts. Thos. Johnston, John Jack and Samuel Royer, 1777-78-79-80-81. Orphans' Court records show that James Brotherton died in 1809 on or about March 30th, last. Issue: seven,—Margaret; John; Mary; Wm.; James; Robert; Martha, the last three minors. John, eldest son took the real estate; interest to widow Jane during her life. Heirs, in 1812 were Margaret Brotherton; John Roberts and wife Mary; Wm. H. Brotherton; James and Martha with guardians; John Brotherton and wife Esther took 193 ac., half of a tract by Patent to Wm. Brotherton, whose will (at Carlisle) was dated May 24, 1776 and who devised the whole tract to sons James and George. The widow Jane is said to have been Jane Henry.
Penna. Arch. 5th Ser. Vol. 6, p. 83, 108, 114, 168, 511, 514, 516, 532, 535, 539, 580.

JAMES BROTHERTON

Served as pvt., 1779-80, under Capt. James Young, Guilford Twp.
Penna. Arch. 5th Ser. Vol. 6, p. 82, 548.

ROBERT BROTHERTON

Of Letterkenny Twp., served as pvt. under Capt. John McConnell, 1780-81-82. His will dated July, 1807, was prob. May, 1808. "Old and Stricken in years." To son John 330¼ ac. land in Cumb. County, he paying to my son Robert 600 pounds; Son Samuel ½ the plantation I now live on, value 1600 pounds, and all my personal property; Son David 800 pounds; Son James 400 pounds; Dau. Jane, wife of Jas. Patterson; Dau. Mary, wife of John Laughlin. The following is probably the son of above Robert Brotherton. The will of Samuel Brotherton of Letterkenny Twp., Farmer, advanced in life. Son Wm. now of Bedford Co., Penna., on Sideling Hill. Son Robert all my landed estate in Franklin Co., and personal property. To Margaret Robison, my grandau., and dau of my late dau. Nancy, who was intermarried with Robert Robison, Esq., $100., when she is twenty-one. Grandson Samuel Robison brother of Margaret $250. at twenty-one. Dated Nov. 6, 1828; prob. Sept. 7, 1839. Robert Brotherton occupied pew No. 36 in the old Log Church at Rocky Spring. Samuel Brotherton died Sept. 1, 1839, in his 75th year. From "Franklin Repository" Chambersburg, Penna., Aug., 1822: "Died near Strasburg, the 29th, Mrs. Margaret Brotherton in her 58th year, consort of Samuel Brotherton."
Penna. Arch. 5th Ser. Vol. 6, p. 267, 302, 309.

ROBERT BROTHERTON

Was a pvt. under Capt. James Young in 1780.
Penna. Arch. 5th Ser. Vol. 6, p. 82.

WILLIAM BROTHERTON

Served 1779 under Capt. James Young and 1780-81 with Capt. John McConnell.
Penna. Arch. 5th Ser. Vol. 6, p. 267, 302, 548.

JAMES BARR

Appears as a Soldier from Westmoreland Co., Penna., in the Cont. Line, also as a Lieut. of Rangers. The above man was a son of Thomas Barr, an early settler near Fort Loudon. Rupp gives a letter from Sheriff John Potter, concerning the burning of Matthew Patton's house, Nov., 1755, stating "another on fire, that of Mesach James," about one mile up the creek from Thos' Barr's. Barr's son was wounded, and the Indians burned Barr's house and in it consumed their dead. In 1769, James Barr and wife Mary appear as a family, in the vicinity of Fort Loudon. They had baptized, by Rev. John King, of Upper West Conococheague Presbyterian Church, Margaret, May 13, 1770; Sarah, Oct. 8, 1771; Janet, Oct. 3, 1772; Thomas, Nov. 9, 1774. Undoubtedly Thomas Barr had died and his family in 1769 is shown as: Janet Barr; Robert Barr; Alexander Barr; David Barr; Sara Hutchinson; James Hamilton. From the Survey, the Barr tract was granted May 5, 1744, to Thos. Barr, and in June, 1774, the heirs sell: Janet Barr; James Barr and wife Mary; Robert Barr and wife Mary; Cumb. Co., Peters Twp., Penna.; They sell to Robert and Samuel Walker of same, for 1200 pounds land in Peters Twp., by North Mountain, Thos. McDowell, James Dickey, Robert Campbell, West Conococheague Creek, Enoch James; Middle tract from the Proprietaries March 1, 1737, granted to David Huston and from him to Saml. Moorehead, and from Moorehead to Thos. Barr, decd.; 259 acres, survey, Oct. 26, 1767; several tracts. Wit: John Walker and Alexdr. McConnell. Frontier Forts of Western Penna., furnishing interesting details on the Barrs, as does Caldwell's Hist. of Indiana Co., Penna.

Penna. Arch. 5th Ser. Vol. 4, p. 735. Penna. Arch. 3rd Ser. Vol. 23, p. 283.

ROBERT BARR

Appears as a Soldier in the Cont. Line, from Westmoreland Co., Penna. He was a son of Thomas Barr from vicinity of Fort Loudon. He married Mary Williamson, Apr. 23, 1771, and they had issue: Thomas, baptized by Rev. John King, Feb. 10, 1773; 3 children baptized for Robert Barr's wife, Feb. 21, 1778; The death of Robert Barr's child Jan. 10, 1772. It is quite probable that the Barrs, like many other early settlers, left their family, over the winter months, in Franklin County. It is proven in a number of cases. The tract of land upon which Barr's Fort was built, was located Apr. 3, 1769— warranted and granted to Robert Barr, for whom it was surveyed in 1789. One of the adjoining parties was James Barr, Esq. Barr's Fort stood about a mile north of New Derry, Wallace's Fort about five miles distant, and on one occasion, the "signs" of Indians had been seen in the woods for some days. Major Wilson, with a few of his men, found the Indians too numerous for his little band and they were compelled to retreat. About a mile from Wallace's (Alexander?) Barr was killed. Robert Barr, also fell, fighting manfully with the butt of his gun. Major Wilson shot one of the Indians, who fell dead on Barr. The next instant a tomahawk was buried in Barr's skull. In 1796, Thomas Barr, eldest son of Robert Barr, decd. conveyed to Wm. Gilson, the land granted to Robert Barr, by location in 1769. This fort was originally the house of the pioneer Barr, but later a stockade fort, and in the graveyard on this place, is the grave of Major James Wilson, and many early settlers, probably the oldest burying ground in that section.

Penna. Arch. 5th Ser. Vol. 4, p. 429, 735.

WILLIAM BARR

Is shown in service 1780-81-82 with Capt. Alexdr. Peebles. He was a member of the Middle Spring Church, and in the District of Col. James Dunlap. It is possible he was a brother of Thomas Barr.

Penna. Arch. 5th Ser. Vol. 6, p. 136, 150, 396, 422, 434, 406, 627.

THOMAS BARR

Of Lurgan Twp., is shown in service with Capt. Isaac Miller, 1782, command of Col. Jas. Dunlap. Thos. Barr left a will dated and prob., 1799. To wife Mary a comfortable mantainance and subsistance out of my estate and a desent interment at her decease, with a full ⅓ of my personal estate; Son Thomas 10 pounds and my large bible; Son James and son John, each ½ of the tract on which I live; Son-in-law Samuel Walker legal guardian for son John; 3 daus: Mary Patterson; Elizabeth Walker; Sarah Elder, each 20 pounds; Son Joseph 50 pounds; Agnes Barr 20 pounds; young negro Warwick, at my wife's decease to be valued and disposed as the rest of my personal estate and old negro Dinah is to stay as long as my wife lives, then to be sold for $40.

Penna. Arch. 5th Ser. Vol. 6, p. 435.

BENJAMIN BLYTHE

Served as Sub-Lieutenant of Cumb. Co., Penna., 1777-78-80-81. Deeds show Benj. Blythe, Township of Hopewell, Co. of Cumb., Esq., and wife Abigail to John, Eldest son of Benj. Blythe, "All those four several tracts in Twp. of Lurgan, known as "Wm. Reynolds pine Meadow Tract," granted by the name "Selavonia" to the said Benj. Blythe, Dec. 8, 1774. "Col. Benjamin Blythe, who lived at the head of Middle Spring, noted Indian fighter, Rev. Soldier, Sub. Lieut. of Cumb. Co.," is shown paying to Capt. Matthias Scott 256 pounds, 10 shillings for recruiting part of the 13th Penna., Regt., July, 1778, the names of nine recruits are given. In 1805, Henry Leer, sells land from John Leer's estate to Benj. Blythe, Jr., of Southampton Twp.

Penna. Arch. 5th Ser. Vol 6, p. 3, 41, 152, 426. Penna. Arch. 5th Ser. Vol. 3, p. 710.

BENJAMIN BLYTHE

Appears as a pvt., 1781-82, in service with Capt. Alexander Peebles.

Penna. Arch. 5th Ser. Vol. 3, p. 124, 422, 434.

JACOB BLYTHE

Served as a pvt. under Capt. Alex. Peebles in 1777.

Penna. Arch. 5th Ser. Vol. 6, p. 589.

JAMES BLYTHE

Sub-Lieut. of County of Cumberland, undated rolls.

Penna. Arch. 5th Ser. Vol. 6, p. 28.

JOHN BLYTHE

Served as Sergt. under Capts. Pat. Jack, Wm. Strain and John Campbell, 1778-80-81-82. John Blythe, Esq., is shown in the Cont. Line from Cumb. County.

Penna. Arch. 5th Ser. Vol. 6, p. 30, 143, 390, 397, 404, 429, 621. Penna. Arch. 5th Ser. Vol. 4, p. 270, 620.

SAMUEL BLYTHE

Of Southampton Twp., is shown as a pvt. in the Flying Camp, and as a Captain of a Comp. of Rangers in 1780. He served 1780-81-82. In 1796 Tax lists show him with 1400 ac. land, 4 Horses, 10 Cows, 2 Mills and 1 Saw Mill. The will of James Brotherton, Atty., Chambersburg, prob 1807, states, "Andrew Dunlop and myself lately purchased at Sheriff's sale 900 ac., of land with a forge thereon erected, sold as the property of Charles Leeper and Samuel Blythe, between Roxbury and the north mountain." Sept., 1781, Benj. Blythe of Hopewell Twp., Cumb. Co., Penna. Esquire, and Abigail, his wife, to Samuel Blythe of Lurgan Twp., son of the said Benjamin, for natural love and affection, land in Lurgan Twp., bounding John Blythe, John Lear's, Philip's heirs, and Benj. Blythe,—126 ac. 103 pchs. Patented to Benj. Blythe Dec. 8, 1774. In 1814 Samuel Blythe and Jemima, his wife sell to Benj. Blythe land in Green Twp., on which are Merchant, Grist and saw mills. Under date of Oct. 30, 1817, a Bedford, Penna., paper gives the following: "Married Tuesday 21st, inst., by Rev. Robert Lee, Alexdr. Thompson, Esq., of this boro, to Miss Abby Blythe, dau. of Samuel Blythe of Franklin Co., Penna., From the Franklin Repository, under Jan. 4, 1831: "Died in Southampton Twp., the 24th, Samuel Blythe, a Soldier of the Revolution."

Penna. Arch. 5th Ser. Vol. 6, p. 395, 421, 431. Penna. Arch. 2nd Ser. Vol. 15, p. 764.

WILLIAM BLYTHE

Served as Lieut. under Capt. Wm. Armstrong, the Penna. Regt. of Foot in 1757-58-1764, and in 1765 he was in the Garrison at Fort Augusta, later as Overseer of the King's Pastures at Carlisle. Blunston Licenses: Apr. 12, 1737, William Blythe, 150 acres joining to the Southwest of Joseph Clark On the South Side of a hill and North Side of the Waggon Road. Rev. Soldiers—Mrs. W. C. Bartol: William Blythe died ante, 1793, living in White Deer Twp., 1777. An Indian trader at Shippensburg, Penna., 1748; Captain-Lieutenant, Com. Dec. 24, 1757, in Penna. Regt. of foot, in service to the close of the Boquet expedition to the Ohio xx. On Committee of Safety, White Deer Twp., Northumberland Co. Feb. 13, 1777. He had two (2) daughters: Margaret mar. (1) Capt. John Reed, died ante 1778, and mar. (2) Capt. Chas. Gillespie; Elizabeth mar. Dr. Joseph Eakers.

Penna. Arch. 5th Ser. Vol. 1, p. 63, 91, 99, 105, 107, 121, 128, 180, 266, 335, 339, 343, 348.

JOHN BLAIR

Was in service as pvt., June 13, 1777, at Shippensburg, under Capt. Alexdr. Peebles and again in 1779, also on undated roll. One John Blair is shown in Letterkenny Twp., under tax lists of 1786, as a taxable, with state and county taxes.

Penna. Arch. 5th Ser. Vol. 6, p. 57, 136, 372, 589. From Hist. of Westmoreland Co., Penna: Copy of an affidavit in the possession of William R. Blair, Esq., of Pittsburgh, Penna., descendant of John Blair, Esq. of Blair's Gap:

Huntingdon County, SS:

"Before me, the subscriber, one of the Justices of the Peace in and for the County aforesaid, personally appeared Captain Samuel Brady who being sworn according to law, did despose and say that he served in the Provincial Troops raised by order of the King of Great Britain for the defence of the Province of North America immediately after General Braddock's defeat; that he was well acquainted with John Blair and his sons, Thomas and Alexander Blair of Cumberland County (now Franklin); that the said John, Thomas and Alexander to the knowledge of this deponent were each of them (besides other appointments) commissaries and acted in that capacity under Col. John Armstrong, General Forbes Stanwix and Mongtain and Colonel Bouquet; that the aforesaid Alexander Blair lost his life in the service in the defence of Fort Venango as the deponent believes from the reports of that time and further this deponent saith not.

     (Signed) Samuel Brady"

Sworn and subscribed before me at Allegheny Township in the County aforesaid, the 12th day of June, 1809.

     (Signed) JOHN BLAIR

THOMAS BLAIR

A brother-in-law of James Galbreath and William McClelland, moved to Bedford Co., died Sept. 8, 1810, in Allegheny Twp., Huntingdon Co., Penna. On Dec. 10, 1777, Thomas Blair was Capt. of 3rd Co. 2nd Batt., Bedford Co. Associators under Col. Geo. Ashman. He and his wife Jane McClellan had issue: John; Alexander; Ruth; Catherine; William. Deeds at Chambersburg show that Thos. Blair and wife Jane of Franks Town, Co. of Huntingdon sold a tract of land in Fannett Twp., called "Clover Green," "in the path valley," 237¾ ac. for 1904 pounds, part of a larger tract on warrant to Thomas Blair in 1762.

WILLIAM BLAIR

Is shown in service 1781-82, under Capt. Walter McKinnie.

Penna. Arch. 5th Ser. Vol. 6, p. 299, 301, 306.

ENSIGN DAVID BLAIR

In 1764, a group of Woodsmen or riflemen from Fredk. Co., Md., (now Wash. Co., Md.) marched to Fort Pitt to serve without pay. Among this Company were, Capt. Wm. McClellan; Lieut. James Dougherty; Ensign David Blair; Ensign John Moran; Ensign Edmund Moran; Privates David Shelby; James Ross; John Dougherty; Felix Leer. In the will of Andrew Blair whose plantation was on the Penna. & Md. line, and and whose will was dated 1787, prob. 1796, he names the following: dau. Cath. Moran; dau. Ann McCellan; dau. Susanna Dougherty; dau. Elenor Dougherty; dau. Mary Shelvy.

The Penna German in the Settlement of Maryland, By D. W. Nead.

JAMES BLAIR

Of Blair's Valley, wife Martha Elliott, They are buried on the original Blair farm on what is called Valley Road, from Clearspring, Md. to Mercersburg, Pa., the farm later owned by W. W. Seibert. No stone, but a D.A.R. marker was placed on grave. The N.S.D.A.R. has accepted the above James Blair. The will of Andrew Blair named three sons, John; James; David. Hagerstown, Md., Court records, the Admr. of John Blair, 1799; the Will of James Blair, 1828; the Admr of Charity Blair, 1837.

GEORGE BENEFIELD, PRIVATE

Served under Capt. James Patton, and Capt. Robert Dickey in 1778-80-81. He is said to have died in Jefferson Co., Ind., Apr. 1, 1832, buried in Jefferson, and a D. A. R. marker is on his grave. His wife was Mary Buchanan, b. York Co., Penna., Dec. 25, 1759. Their dau. Esther mar. Robert McClelland, son of Alexander McClelland and Isabella Futhey. Isabella was b. about 1772, mar. in Lexington, Ky., about 1790.

Penna. Arch. 5th Ser. Vol. 6, p. 272, 285, 381.

JOHN BENEFIELD, PRIVATE

Served under Capt. James Patton and Capt. Robert Dickey in 1780-1781.

Penna. Arch. 5th Ser. Vol. 6, p. 272, 285, 315, 643.

CAPTAIN WILLIAM BERRYHILL

Of Antrim Twp., served in 1780-1781. He died intestate, his estate being settled in 1808. He left a wife Ruth and seven children: Alexander; Ruth who mar. John Noble (decd); William; Samuel; 3 minors: Mary; Isabelle; Elias; The widow, Ruth d. May 30, 1836, aged 84 yrs. A. S. Berryhill d. March 27, 1846, aged 71 yrs. They are buried in Cross Creek graveyard, Washington Co., Penna.

Penna. Arch. 5th Ser. Vol. 6, p. 69, 79, 81, 100, 102.

WALTER BEATTY

Son of Henry and Catherine Beatty, served as pvt. under Capt. Terrance Campbell, 1778-82. He mar. March 3, 1781, Agnes, dau. of Samuel and Mary Smith of Antrim Twp. He was a "joiner" and is said to have built the first Court House in Chambersburg, Penna. His outstanding work was the building of the Rocky Spring Church, in 1794. He died at Chambersburg Aug. 11, 1821, "an honest man," his widow Agnes (Nancy) dying at an advanced age Sept., 1822. Their children are buried in Falling Spring Graveyard,—Martha; Samuel S.; Ann S.; Ruth Twin of Samuel; Harriet; Walter and wife. It is probable that Walter Beatty, Sr. and wife are also buried in Falling Spring Church yard.

Penna. Arch. 5th Ser. Vol. 6, p. 124, 125, 328.

ANDREW BLACKHEART (BLECHART)

Served as pvt., 1777-80-81-82, under Capts. Alex. Peebles, Thos. Askey and Noah Abraham. On March 3, 1794, Letters of Admr., were granted to Andrew Blechart of Providence Twp.,

Bedford Co., Penna., on the estate of above man. The Census of 1790 shows the family of Andrew Blackart to consist of 1 man, 2 boys and 3 females.

Penna. Arch 5th Ser. Vol. 6, p. 22, 27, 131, 409, 423, 442, 620.

AUBURN (URBAN) BEATES

Served under Capt. Samuel Patton, 1780-81 and said to have been born 1747, Franklin Co., Penna., mar. Dorothy Baker or Barker, buried Washingtonville, Ohio. Tax lists of Hamilton Twp., Franklin Co., Penna., show Lodowick Beates with 250 ac. land; Frederick with 80 ac. and Conrad, as a freeman, as well as above Auburn, 1778-1782. The 1790 Census of Penna., Franklin Co., shows Urban Beates with 1 man, 5 boys and 6 females.

Penna. Arch. 5th Ser. Vol. 6, p. 279, 288. Official Roster Rev. Soldiers of Ohio.

FREDERICK BYER, JR.

Served as pvt. under Capt. John Jack in 1779, also under Capt. Thos. Johnston, 1780-81-82. His wife was Anna Margaret Moyer and their son, Capt. John Byer was in the War of 1812. Capt. John mar. 1st Catherine Study; mar. 2nd Elizabeth Lantz.

Penna. Arch. 5th Ser. Vol. 6, p. 75, 84, 115, 130, 540.

NICHOLAS BITTINGER

Naturalized 1760, served as Capt. in the "Flying Camp," Rev. War. He was captured by the British at Fort Washington, Nov., 1776. He had a dau. Elizabeth, wife of Dr. Andrew Baum of Chambersburg, assessed in 1788-89 with House and lot, Horse, Cows &c. In 1790 Thos. Hartley, Esq., and wife Catherine of York County, Penna., lease in trust for Elizabeth Baum, a lot No. 23 in Chambersburg, David and Sarah Baum appearing as children of Elizabeth Baum. The heirs of Nicholas Bittinger were: Christina Duncan and Elizabeth Baum, widows; William Hamilton and wife Magdalena; Tobias Kepner and wife Susanna; above of Adams Co., Penna.; Samuel Lane and wife Barbara of Franklin Co., Penna.; John Clark and wife Margaret of York Co., Penna. and George Rudy of Kentucky. On page 658, of the 1887 Hist. of Franklin County, under "Lane" is this: "Samuel Lane mar. Anna Barbara, a dau. of Nicholas Bittinger, a wealthy land owner, who was signalized in the Revolution as an ardent Whig, and who was captured by the British at Fort Washington in November 1776." On May 19, 1777, Miss Bittinger, was mar. to Major Clarke of York, by Dr. John King of Mercersburg, Penna.

Penna. Arch. 5th Ser. Vol. 4, p. 227.

MICHAEL BEAR

Served in Lancaster County, Penna. as a pvt. during 1778-79-80-81-82 under Capts., John Smuller and Andreas Rehm. Deeds at Chambersburg show Michael Bear of "Athel" Twp., Lancaster Co., Penna., buying land, May, 1800, from Noah Abraham and Rebecca, his wife of Fannettsburgh, Penna. The land was a warrant to James Montgomery, Aug. 20, 1765, who sold to Nathaniel Brian, who with his wife Hannah conveyed to Noah Abraham, joining David Campbell, 343½ acres. Michael Bear of Fannett Twp., left a will dated April and Prob. May, 1801; to wife Margaretha all personal estate—if she is willing to give the estate to her sons, then they shall build her a house of stone 30 ft. long, by 28 broad and two story high, and provide her a comportable living; farms bot. from Noah Abraham and Andrew Douglas. Sons John and David; if two unmarried daus. should marry, they must be furnished with such necessaries as I have done by the married ones; each dau. 250 pounds, except Elizabeth, she, 300 pounds; grandson Simon Miller 100 pounds when twenty-one years old.

Penna. Arch. 5th Ser. Vol. 7, p. 226, 280, 315, 318, 884, 888, 903.

DENNIS BALF

Served as pvt. under Capt. Patrick Jack, 1781-82. In Deed Book 4, p. 135-136, May 4, 1768, Dennis Balf is witness on a deed where James Arthur sells land to Patrick Jack. With many others he is found later in Westmoreland Co., Penna. Dennis Balf was mar. to Bridget Brady, May, 1766, by Rev. J. C. Bucher, and they had a dau. Fanny. The widow Balf is head of the family in 1800; the name appears in Butler County where William is Commissioner and Sheriff until 1814. Wm. mar. Elizabeth, dau. of Nathaniel Stevenson (Rev. Soldier) and pensioner. James Balf born 1784, died 1862, mar. Elizabeth King. Both Wm. and James were in the War of 1812. Catherine Balf mar. Robert Leech who died 1813, and his widow mar. John Elliott. Catherine, aged 76 in 1850, and Margaret Leech aged 39 yrs. Under Marriages of James Power, D. D. at Mt. Pleasant are recorded:

Catherine Balph, Robert Leech, Dec. 23, 1794.
Joseph McGrew, Fanny Balph, Nov. 21, 1797.

Penna. Arch. 5th Ser. Vol. 6, p. 295, 291, 313.

CONRAD BEAMER

Served as a Lieut., under Capt. Noah Abraham, in 1777 and with Capt. Wm. Berryhill, 1780-81. Deeds in 1783, John Allison and wife, Elizabeth sold to Conrad Beymer, lot No. 7, in the Town of Greencastle, east side of Carlisle St. In 1783 Conrad Beamer of Baltimore, Md., sold a lot in Greencastle to Robert McCulloh. In 1786, Conrad

Beamer of Cumb. Co., Penna., and Juliania, his wife, sold a lot in Greencastle to James Watson. Feb. 6, 1787, Conrad Behmer and Juliana, his wife, sign before Justice of the Peace, John Herron. Conrad Beamer signed the Oath Allegiance before John Creigh, at Carlisle, Penna.

Penna. Arch. 5th Ser. Vol. 6, p. 17, 69, 79, 100, 139.

DAVID BRANDT

Served as pvt., in Lancaster Co., 1779-81-82. He came from Dauphin County to Franklin County in 1824, buying land in St. Thomas Twp., from James, Thomas and Campbell Montgomery, and from Erasmus and Martha Cooper. In the will of David Brandt, prob. 1836, he names sons David and John, and dau. Catherine, wife of Henry Alleman. "Brandts" Graveyard, in St. Thomas Twp., shows the following inscriptions: David Brandt, d. June 19, 1836, aged 75 yrs. 29 days. Catherine Brandt, d. June 20, 1841, aged 79 yrs. 7 mos. 1 day. Son John b. 1803, d. 1873. Wife Mary. Son David b. 1799, d.—— 1870, Wife Elizabeth Stoner.

Penna. Arch. 5th Ser. Vol. 7, p. 559, 917, 943, 963.

ISAAC BRAND

Shown in service, in 1782, under Capt. Jas. Poe.

Penna. Arch. 5th Ser. Vol. 6, p. 572.

JOHN BRAND

Served 1778-79, with Capts. Samuel Patton and Thos. McDowell, and shown at Legonere in June, 1779, Col. Wm. Chambers' Battalion. He appears under Freemen, in Peters Twp., 1778-79-80-81-82 and the Findlay Ledger had an account with John Brand. Court records fail to show either his will or Admr., so it is quite possible that he is the man buried in the Brandt or "Old Dutch" Cemetery, between Ligionier and Stahlstown, in a field. Mrs. Ruth Norris Berger gives the following: John Brandt died July 11, 1802, aged 81 years. Anna Maria, wife of John Brandt died Dec. 25, 1804, aged 83 years.

Penna. Arch. 5th Ser. Vol. 6, p. 314, 380, 602.

JOHN BRAND

Was in service 1778-79, with Capt. Samuel Patton, on the Western frontiers as a Ranger; in 1781 under Capt. Robert Dickey, Cumb. Co. Militia.

Penna. Arch. 5th Ser. Vol. 6, p. 285, 602, 610.

ANDREW BARRINGER

Was a pvt. under Capts. Wm. Smith and Wm. Huston, 1780-81. He also served in the Cont. Line. Andrew Benninger (?) mar. Mary Snyder, Feb. 22, 1789, at Mercersburg, by Dr. John King. In the 1790 Census he appears in Bedford Co., Penna., family consisting of 1 man, 2 boys, 3 females.

Penna. Arch. 5th Ser. Vol. 6, p. 275, 282. Vol. 4, p. 260.

LAWRENCE BARRINGER

Served 1780, under Capt. Wm. Smith.
Penna. Arch. 5th Ser. Vol. 6, p. 275.

GEORGE BACKER

York County, Penna. Will Book B, p. 158. The will of George Backer, Berwick Twp., York Co., Penna. Sons: John; George; Daniel; daus: Elizabeth, wife of Henry Brissel; Susannah; Cathrina; sons to have real estate and each son to give each dau. 60 lbs. Prob. Apr. 20, 1768. Note: Daniel was 19 at this time, was mar. 1772, at age of 23. Bakers, Snells, Brissells, named in Hist. of the Brethren—Brumbaugh—were members of Conewago, 14 miles S. W. of York. George Backer and son George buried about 3 miles north of Abbottstown, Penna. Son George left a family. Daniel Baker b. 1749, d. 1804, mar. May 19, 1772, Elizabeth Schnellin, b. Jan. 21, 1754; d. May 22, 1829 (75-3-29), a dau. of Philip and Judith Snell. Catherine Baker, b. Feb. 23, 1773, moved to Stark Co., Ohio. George Baker b. Dec. 1, 1774, moved to Bedford Co., Penna. Elizabeth Baker b. Dec. 21, 1776, moved to Tusc. Co., Ohio. John Baker b. Jan. 13, 1779, moved to Tusc. Co., Ohio. Mary Baker b. Apr. 7, 1781, moved to Tusc. Co., Ohio. Philip Baker b. and d. Oct. 13, 1783. Daniel Baked b. Dec. 20, 1785 moved to Tusc. Co., Ohio. Jacob Baker b. Feb. 8, 1788, stayed in county. Peter Baker b. March 7, 1790, stayed in county. Andrew Baker b. Mar. 25, 1792, unmar. Abraham Baker b. Mar. 25, 1796, moved to Tusc. Co., Ohio. Susanna Baker b. Aug. 12, 1798, stayed in county mar. (?) Above from a Bible published by Christopher Sauer, Germantown, A.D. 1763, copied by Susan Baker, wife of Andrew C. Baker, Roaring Springs, Penna., Jan. 13, 1898. Elizabeth Baker b. Dec. 21, 1776, mar. 1st. Abraham Thomas; mar. 2nd George Harmon. Issue: Susan Thomas b. Feb. 19, 1794. Elizabeth Thomas b. July 31, 1798. John Thomas b. Feb. 9, 1800. Jacob Thomas b. Nov. 23, 1801. Catherine Thomas b. May 18, 1804. Mary Thomas b. Feb. 20 1806, mar. Adam Swinehart. Anna Thomas b. Jan. 25, 1808. Abrahm Thomas b. July 31, 1810. Daniel Thomas b. Nov. 18, 1812. David Thomas b. Mar. 30, 1814. Rebecca b. Jan. 14, 1818. Philip Snell left will at Hagerstown, Md., names dau. Elizabeth, wife of Daniel Baker.

From a Report: "The supposed home of Daniel Baker's father after coming to this country, was Conococheague, Franklin Co. Penna." "The early home of George and Daniel Baker was in Franklin County and that he knows the farm owned by their father." George Baker, b. 1749, mar. Elizabeth Strengen, Jan. 14, 1771, issue; John; George; Jacob; David; Solomon; Daniel; Magdalena.

(1). Alex Mack b. 1679, d. Feb. 19, 1735, buried Germantown, Penna., mar. Ann Margaretha Klingend, b. 1679, d. 1720. (2). Johannes, "went to Antietam" d. ———; bought land 1749-52. (3). Alexander, b. ——— d. 1811, children born in Franklin Co. He went to Bedford Co. Will. (4). John mar. Anna Longenecker. Elizabeth mar. John Garber. Alexander, b. 1771, d. Aug. 31, 1824 mar. Catherine Baker Jacob. Sarah, d. 1857, mar. Daniel Longenecker. Anna mar. Daniel Garber. Peter Longenecker, d. 1803, Franklin Co., Penna., mar. Anna Mock— issue: (1). Daniel mar. Sarah Mock, d. Columbiana Co., Ohio. Abraham; Jacob; David; Joseph; Anna mar. John Mock. Dau. mar. ——— Winters. Alexander Mack and cousin William Mack served from Franklin Co., Penna.

Daniel Baker, father of Elizabeth Baker Thomas, moved from York Co. to Franklin about 1786, and on to Bedford Co., 1797.

JOHN BECKETT

S 15 324. John Beckett was pensioned on Certificate No. 19 613, issued Aug. 8, 1833; rate $20 per annum; act of June 7, 1832; Ohio Pension Agency. He alleged that he volunteered in September 1776; served at various times in the Pennsylvania Troops, under Captains Thomas Paxton, James Shelby, Thomas Blair and Colonel George Woods; was in two skirmishes with the Indians; served as Ensign. His alleged service totaled 6 months. He volunteered at Bedford Cove, Bedford County, Pennsylvania, place of residence then not given. About 1811, he moved to Butler Co., Ohio. He was born Sept. 15, 1755, in County Antrim, Ireland. The names of his parents not shown. It was not stated whether or not John Beckett married. The date of his death was not given.

JAMES BRACKENRIDGE

Was a private in Militia, born 1742, died 1809. His wife Elizabeth Culbertson, born 1760, died 1835. Orphans' Court records show issue as Martha mar. to James Brown; Joseph; Molly; Elizabeth; James; John and Robert Brackenridge. They occupied Pew 37 in the old Log church at Rocky Spring, Franklin Co., Penna. Joseph and Martha Brackenridge attest that he, their father, died July 14, 1809. He was a Ranger on the Frontier.

Penna. Arch. 5th Ser. Vol. 4, p. 392, 701.

JOHN BREDY

Allegheny Co. Penna., Court records, Book 1, p. 6, Apr. 14, 1788. The will of John Bredy of Franklin Co., Penna., Layman. Being now on my Journey from the Mouth of the Yough River to Post Vinston on the Wabash River; Estate to John McKee, if I should die or be killed by Indians before I come back. Exr.: John McKee.

WILLIAM BURGESS

Pvt. Gordon's Company, P. M. Dec. 24, 1816. Wm. Burgess of the town of Loudon, left a will dated March, prob. Apr. 2, 1821, in which he gives to wife Nancy 1/3; Dau. Suffia Jane, silver spoons; Brother Samuel my watch; Sister Sally Easton my cupboard furniture; Exrs: George Warner, James Colhoun. Wit: John Dickey and Wm. Pott.

Note: Hezekiah Easton mar. Sally Burgess, Dec. 18, 1817.

Penna. Arch. 3rd Ser. Vol. 23, p. 479, 480.

WILIAM BURKE

Sergeant 6th Penna. Cont. Line, William Burke, from Corporal, July 11, 1776, Capt. Abraham Smith. Court records, Chambersburg, Penna., show Letters Admr., March 12, 1824. William Burke enlisted 1777, served 13 months, 6th Penna., C. L. He was a pensioner, and died Feb. 29, 1824.

Penna Arch. 5th Ser. Vol. 2, p. 230. 2nd Ser. Vol. 10, p. 594

JAMES BUTCHEY

Is shown serving as a pvt., under Capt. Wm. Smith in 1780. The name is not a familiar one in the County.

Penna. Arch. 5th Ser. Vol. 6, p. 276.

TUBAIL CAIN

Was a pvt., in the Cont. Line, and a Ranger on the Frontier.

Penna. Arch. 5th Ser. Vol. 4, p. 281, 621.

ALEXANDER CALDWELL
ALSO JOHN, MATTHEW AND WILLIAM

Are shown in the Cont. Line, serving from Westmoreland Co., Penna., Chambersburg, Penna. Deed Book 6, p. 46, shows the heirs of Robert Rush (Indian Captive) one being Hester, wife of Alexander Caldwell in the year 1768.

Penna. Arch. 5th Ser. Vol. 4, p. 431.

DAVID CALDWELL

Was in service as a pvt. 1777-80-81-82, under Capt. Samuel Patton, Command of Col. Samuel Culbertson. David Caldwell was a taxable in Hamilton Twp. until 1782.

Penna. Arch. 5th Ser. Vol. 6, p. 278, 287, 311, 372.

HUGH CALDWELL

Appears in 1778, under Capt. John Rea. He was in service in 1780-81-82, with Capt. John McConnell. In the will of Thomas Dougherty, 1789, of Hamilton Twp., he named four married daughters, one being Eleanor, wife of Hugh Caldwell.

Penna. Arch. 5th Ser. Vol. 6, p. 268, 281, 303, 310, 529, 537.

JAMES CALDWELL

Gave service as an Ensign, 1777-78, and as a Lieut. 1780-81-82, under Capt. John McConnell. Little is found on the early Caldwells of Franklin County, but a Deed gives the following: John Graham, who had a 1755 warrant in Lurgan Twp., died intestate, leaving sons Wm. and John; a dau. Jennet who mar. James Caldwell; a dau. Hannah mar. John Allison; and the widow, Elizabeth, of John Graham.

Penna. Arch. 5th Ser. Vol. 6, p. 260, 301, 309, 370, 379, 381.

JAMES CALDWELL

Apears July 31, 1777, under the First Call, First Marching Company with Capt Thos. Askey. He gave service until 1782, with Capt. Alexdr. Peebles. Under Taxables in Letterkenny Twp., 1778-82, Robert and Stephen Caldwell had land, Horses and Cattle, the amount increasing yearly, and throughout those years, James Caldwell was taxed as a freeman. John Strain of Lurgan Twp., left a will prob. 1810, naming a dau Mary and grandau. Isabella Caldwell, whose guardian was son James Strain.

Penna. Arch. 5th Ser. Vol. 6, p. 8, 28, 58, 150, 263, 288, 302, 309, 389, 396, 421, 433.

JOSEPH, JOHN, ROBERT CALDWELL

Under Dec. 8, 1776, part of Capt. James McConnell's Company, Command of Col. James Armstrong, continued service until 1782.

Penna. Arch. 5th Ser. Vol. 6, p. 317, 268, 303, 310, 318, 643.

LIEUT. SAMUEL CALDWELL
ENSIGN JOHN CALDWELL

Were in the Company of Capt. John McConnell, 1780-81-82, pvts. Robert Caldwell, Sr.; Robert Caldwell Jr.; Hugh Caldwell; Joseph Caldwell. Robert and Stephen Caldwell, with Wm., John and James Harper, occupied Pew 28 in the old Log Church at Rocky Spring. John Colwell in Pew 38. In the will of Joseph Stevenson, prob, 1791, he names a dau. Mary, wife of Stephen Caldwell. In 1792, Stephen Caldwell sold land to Nicholas Eshway.

Penna. Arch. 5th Ser. Vol. 6, p. 266, 268, 301, 302, 303, 308, 309, 310.

JAMES CALHOUN

Serving as a pvt. He undoubtedly was under Capt. Robert McCoy who was killed at Crooked Billet. In 1809, Martha, widow of Wm. Dean, late of Peters Twp., Franklin Co., Penna., applied to the Indiana, Penna., Orphans' Court for a pension, stating that her husband was killed on May 1, 1778 at the battle of Crooked Billet as a soldier under Capt. Robert McCoy. In her behalf James Calhoun of Armstrong Co., swears before Robert Beatty June 1, 1809, that he was present as a soldier at battle of Crooked Billet under Capt. Robert McCoy, and saw Wm. Dean killed. James Calhoun received from the Penna Legislature a pension of $40.00 annually on March 29, 1802, in Westmoreland Co. In 1769 James Calhoun and wife Eleanor were living in District 10 of the Presby. Church of Mercersburg. Samuel Templeton was the Presiding Elder over that District and he was of Peters Twp. Eleanor Calhoun was his dau., dying May 14, 1777. James and Eleanor Calhoun had 3 sons: Moses baptized Oct. 21, 1770, and Wm. baptized, June 13, 1773. There was also a son James. Prior to 1784 James Calhoun mar. 2nd Mary Walker (nee Adams), widow of Robert Walker who had a grant of 100 ac. in 1767 in Fannett Twp., Franklin Co., Penna. James Calhoun died in 1824. Robert Walker and wife had issue: Benjamin; Margaret; Alexander; Samuel; Mary mar. David White; James; Robert; Abraham; they all later were in Armstrong and Indiana Counties. James Calhoun and wife Mary Walker had issue 2, one born in 1784 and one in 1786. Dr. John Calhoun of Pittsburgh has listed about 250 descendants of James Calhoun and his two (2) wives. He was born 1747. Thought to be buried in an old graveyard near his Indiana County line, with the other Calhouns with an old stone cut by his son Wm. badly erased by time. William (or Billy) Calhoun mar. 1797 Betsy Lytle,—they lived and died at Stewartsville, Penna.

Penna. Arch. 5th Ser. Vol. 6, p. 375, 433.

JEREMIAH CALLAHAN

Served as pvt., 1780-81-82 under Capts. James Poe and John Woods. He was also in the Cont. Line Official Roster Rev. Soldiers of Ohio given burial place as Greenford, Ohio.

Penna. Arch. 5th Ser. Vol. 6, p. 92, 104, 138, 583, 76. Penna. Arch. 5th Ser. Vol. 4, p. 281.

ARCHIBALD CAMBRIDGE

Of Franklin County, Yeoman, served as pvt.

with Lieut. Wm. Strain, undated roll. He left a will dated July, 1801, prob. Aug. 18, 1809; son John all my estate, he paying the following heirs: 3 daus. Hannah, wife of Andrew Love; Elizabeth, wife of Benjamin Futhey; Christian, wife of John Gelvin, 10 pounds each; son Archibald 10 pounds; grandson Archibald Love 5 pounds. Exr: Son John. In 1810, Benj. Futhey was head of a family of seven in Lexington, Ky. One Isabella Futhey, born abt. 1772, mar. Alexdr. McClelland about 1790 in Ky. or Penna.

Penna. Arch. 5th Ser. Vol. 6, p. 143.

ANDREW CAMPBELL, SR.

Appears in Capt. Thos. Askey's Company 1779-81-82. He was of Fannett Twp., and his estate is shown in Orphans' Court in 1797. He left a widow Esther, and John who took the tract of 358 acres, also sons Joseph and Andrew. Catherine mar. James Armstrong; Jean mar. Joseph Ward; Elizabeth mar. Joseph McMackin; Margaret mar. Andrew Wakefield; Esther mar. Thomas Wilson, Nov. 13, 1794—by Dr. Denny. One Joseph Campbell was also mar. by Dr. Denny, to Flora Galbreath, Dec. 6, 1796. The will of above Andrew Campbell was dated 1788; prob. 1789, and sons Mark, David and Alexdr. (youngest) were named; the Exrs: Brother Wm. Campbell and Robert Anderson.

Penna. Arch. 5th Ser. Vol. 6, p. 61, 132, 417, 409, 424, 442.

ANDREW CAMPBELL, JR.

Son of Andrew Campbell of Fannett Twp., served in 1781-82, with Capt. Thos. Askey. He was a son of Andrew Campbell, Sr., of Fannett Twp. There were ten men named Campbell in Capt. Askey's Co., May, 1779: Edward; Andrew; John; John, Sr.. John, Jr.; Joseph; Wm. Sr.; Wm. Jr.; Thomas and another John.

Penna. Arch. 5th Ser. Vol. 6, p. 408, 423, 441.

CHARLES CAMPBELL

Was the son of Michael Campbell, b. 1720, d. 1767, and his wife Rebecca Brown, who had issue: Sarah; Charles; Thomas; George; William; Michael (of Tenn.); James. Charles Campbell is said to have removed from Franklin County to what was later known as Campbell's Mills, about 1772, said to have been a native of the Conococheague Valley. He was taken captive by the Indians with Randall Laughlin, Dickson, John Gibson and his brother, then marched off, first to Kittanning where they had to run the gauntlet and undergo drill. They were then taken to Detroit where they were delivered to the British and thence conveyed to Quebec where they passed a severe winter and were exchanged in the ensuing autumn. His diary is first dated Sept. 25, 1777, and is full of most interesting experiences (to the reader) until the 14th of Oct. 1778, when they arrived in Boston Harbor and from there he traveled by foot and sometimes by vehicle, reaching home in about six weeks. For many years he was an Elder in Bethel Presby. Church. His connection with the Militia of the County and district was both honorable and effective. Westmoreland Co., Penna. Charles Campbell, Esq., Sub. Lieut. The State of Massachusetts Bay. Received from the government thereof, on his way home from captivity for the purpose of relieving his distresses, three hundred dollars, Oct. 16, 1778. Balance due Col. Campbell equal to 109 pounds 17 specie. For his pay while a prisoner from Sept. 25, 1777, to Nov. 16, 1778—416 days—at 20s and 12 days returning, Cont. money, 428 pounds. Paid per order of Council to Col. Charles Campbell in full for his services as commissioner for laying out a road, from the navigable waters of Juniata to those of Conemaugh, with expenses for assistants, provisions &c, 34 pounds-3s 1d. Mar. 9, 1778 Col. Chas. Campbell to Wm. Findlay, Feb. 1793. The letter concerns Pay Rooles for the Spyes and the Militia, Doctor bills for wounded Soldiers of the Militia, A Praisement of a Gun, the Best Tracts of land &c. He then adds, "If you Can Get A Good Gown Patren for Mrs. Campbell, as there is Not Any In the Goods that Mr. Deniston Sent to me." Inscriptions from Bethel Cemetery, Indiana Co., Penna. Copied by Mrs. R. E. Warden, Johnstown, Penna.— Lieut. Charles Campbell, Penna. Militia Revolutionary War, 1746-1828. In Memory of Margaret, Consort of Charles Campbell, (remainder illegible). Elizabeth, wife of Charles Campbell, died June 1, 1828, aged 75 years. Capt. Campbell mar. 1st, Margaret Clark; 2nd Mrs. Elizabeth Ramsey,— Issue: Barbara mar. James McLene, son of James McLene of Antrim Twp.; Michael mar. Elizabeth Ramsey; Rebecca mar. Samuel Denniston; Sarah mar. Fullerton Woods; Mary mar. John Denniston; Jane mar. Dr. Jonathan French; James mar. Amy Howard; Margaret mar. Abram Speares; Fenwell mar. Robert Doty; Eliza mar. Alexdr. Spears; Charles mar. 1st Matilda Henderson; 2nd Mary Cummins; Thomas mar. Elizabeth Fair.

Caldwell's Hist. of Indiana Co., Penna. Survey Book 1, p. 518, Chambersburg, Penna. Penna.Arch. 3rd Ser. Vol. 7, p. 131, 132, 220. Penna. Arch. 2nd Ser. Vol. 4, p. 626, 627.

DAVID CAMPBELL

Is shown in service 1780-81-82, with Capts. John Orbison and Wm. Huston.

Penna. Arch. 5th Ser. Vol. 6, p. 264, 274, 294, 308, 642.

DUGAL CAMPBELL

Died at Camden, N. J., Jan., 1777. He mar. Martha, dau. of pioneer James Johnston and wife Elizabeth of Antrim Twp. Dugal was the son of Wm. and Frances Campbell, early settlers south of Mercersburg. The Ledger of Samuel Findlay over Rev. War period, shows two men named Dugal Campbell, one a Schoolmaster, the other a neighbor. Dugal Campbell had a warrant for land, which later was patented to his daus., called Sisterhood—later the farm of Mrs. Agnes Bradley. Elizabeth Campbell mar. John Beatty, and her sister Frances mar. David Rankin. In 1800 the tract was divided.

Presbyterian Church records, Mercersburg, Penna.

FRANCIS AND JOHN CAMPBELL

Both appear as pvts in 1782, with Capt. John Orbison.

Penna. Arch. 5th Ser. Vol. 6, p. 307.

FRANCIS CAMPBELL

Appears as a pvt. in the Company of Capt. James A. Wilson, the Sixth Penna. Batt., under Col. Wm. Irvine. Capt. Wilson and Lieut. John Grier were captured at Grand Isle, July 24, 1776. The battalion reached Carlisle on its return, March 15, 1777 and was re-enlisted as the Seventh Penna. of the Cont. Line. Francis Campbell also served, in 1780, in Capt. James Fisher's Company. Francis Campbell was appointed Justice of the Peace, for Cumb. Co., Oct. 17, 1764. He was a Store-keeper and Inn-holder, and tax lists, 1778-1785, show him with from 483 to 663 acres of land, 2 negroes, horses and cattle. In his will, dated Aug., 1790, prob. March, 1791, he names wife Elizabeth; Sons: Francis; Ebenezer; Parker; George; Dau. Elizabeth and Son-in-law Robert Tate. By his first wife he had the Rev. John Campbell, D. D. born 1752, died at Carlisle. A 2nd son, Robert Campbell killed 1779. Francis Campbell mar. 2nd Elizabeth, dau. of John and Margaret (McClure) Parker. Issue: Francis mar. Sarah Duncan d. at Shippensburg, 1808; Ebenezer mar. Eleanor McCune; Nancy mar. Robert Tate; James mar. Cassandra Miller; Parker, 1768-1824, mar. Elizabeth Calhoun, dau. of Dr. John Calhoun and wife Ruhamah Chambers. They had a dau. Elizabeth, who mar. Wm. Chambers; Elizabeth, unmar.; George, living in 1790. The Military service has been attributed to Francis Campbell, Sr., but if his first son was born 1752, Francis Campbell, Sr., was born before 1737, as has been stated. It seems probable that the Military service belongs to the son Francis Campbell.

Penna. Magazine of History, Jan., 1904. Clemons Hist., Campbell Family. Penna. Arch. 5th Ser. Vol. 6, p. 625. Penna. Arch. 5th Ser. Vol. 2, p. 217, 219.

JAMES CAMPBELL

Served in 1781, also with Capt. Orbison, and appears as a pewholder in the Church at Welsh Run.

Penna. Arch. 5th Ser. Vol. 6, p. 294.

JOHN CAMPBELL

Opression in Militia, d. Oct. 30, 1776. As Capt. Jeremiah Talbott recruited in Franklin County, this John Campbell is probably the one shown in Capt. Talbott's Company, Jan., 1776.

Presbyterian Church records, Mercersburg, Penna.

JOHN CAMPBELL

Of Franklin County; in Capt. Samuel Blythe's Company of rangers in 1780, giving residence at the time of application for State annuity. In 1785, John Campbell and wife Mary of Shippensburg, sell to Peter Dickey, certain land in Lurgan Twp.

Penna. Arch. 2nd Ser. Vol. 15, p. 765.

JOHN CAMPBELL

Resided in Franklin Co., Pa., in 1824; a private in the First Penna. Cont. Line. His estate was administered March 9, 1824.

Penna. Arch. 2nd Ser. Vol. 10, p. 355.

PATRICK CAMPBELL

Served as pvt. 1780-81 under Capt. Wm. Huston and Capt. Thos. McDowell. In 1769 he was living in District 2 of the "Upper West Conococheague" Presby. Church. His wife was Eleanor and he had, James; John and Patt. He died Aug. 23, 1794, Eleanor dying in Oct., 1795. In his will he names wife Eleanor; Son William; Dau. Jenny, wife of Caleb Stockton; Sons John and Samuel; Sons Patrick and Robert; Sons David and Samuel. Of the above children Patrick born Sept. 9, 1760, mar. Frances Stockton Jan. 31, 1792. Chambersburg, Penna. Will Book A. p. 337. Patrick Campbell of Peters Twp. dated June 15, 1795; prob. Sept. 14, 1795; wife Eleanor 100 pounds; Son Wm. 300 Pounds; Dau. Jenny Stockton (wife of Caleb Stockson) 100 pounds; son John 500 pounds; son Samuel 100 pounds; my upper plantation in Peters Twp. of 400 ac., to my 2 sons Patrick and Robert; my other plantation in Peters Twp., of 300 ac.; to sons David and Samuel; Exrs: wife Eleanor, Son Robert and esteemed friend John Scott. Esq., of Chambersburg. Wit: Robert McFarland; James Erwin; John Riddle.

Penna. Arch. 5th Ser. Vol. 6, p. 265, 270, 283, 615.

PATRICK CAMPBELL

Served under Capts. James Young and Terrence Campbell, 1779-80-81-82. Patrick and Terrence Campbell were early store keepers in Chambersburg and in 1796 tax list he is shown as a Merchant, with a house and Lot, 3 unimproved Lots, 1 horse and 3 cows. In the list of 1791, in addition to above items, he is the owner of 2 Tablespoons and 6 teaspoons. From the Bedford Gazette, Jan. 18, 1820, is the following: "Died in the borough, at the home of Dr. John Anderson,—on Friday last, Patrick Campbell, Esq., of Chambersburg, aged about seventy years." It was stated that he emigrated to America in 1772. Under date of Jan. 2, 1820, Patrick Campbell left a will at Bedford, Pa. He names a sister Mary McDonnel, widow of Edward McDonnel, house, lots &c, in the borough of Chambersburg, also a tract of about 150 ac., on the N. side of the turnpike road, from Chambersburg to Camellstown. At death of said Mary to her children: Maria; Terrence; Edward and Catherine McDonnel. To Catherine Campbell, dau. of my brother Terrence, $600.; To Mary Campbell, dau. of Terrence $300.; The rest and residue equally between the widow and two daughters of Patrick Campbell, my nephew, late of Knoxville, Tenn. Wherever I should die, my body to be buried in the Roman Catholic burying ground at Chambersburg, and my brother's remains, who is buried at Bedford, to be taken to the same place, and put in the same grave with my body. Such tombstones shall be erected, as shall be directed by Edward Crawford, and Thomas McCollock. The witnesses were: Thomas Heyden, Samuel Riddle, and the date of probate Jan. 19, 1820. Through the courtesy of Mrs. Howard Cessna, Bedford, Penna.

Penna. Arch. 5th Ser. Vol. 6, p. 81, 109, 110, 125, 547, 640.

ROBERT CAMPBELL, LIEUT.

March 1776, under Capt. Wm. Peebles. Robert Campbell promoted Capt., Dec. 21, 1776. Family records state that Robert Campbell was killed in 1779,—a son of Francis Campbell of Shippensburg. As there were several men of the name, identification is uncertain. Mrs. Mary Fullerton, late widow of Capt Robert Campbell, states that he died in actual service, Oct. 5, 1779.

Penna. Arch. 5th Ser. Vol. 2, p. 357, 359, 360, 362, 366, 369, 453, 463. Penna. Arch. 5th Ser. Vol. 4, p. 557.

THOMAS CAMPBELL

Appears in 1779 as Lieut. Light Horse; Capt. in Flying Camp; taken prisoner at Fort Washington; released Nov. 9, 1778; subsequently Capt. of Rangers until 1780. President Reed appoints Thomas Campbell to a Captaincy of a Company of Rangers—owing to his claims or standing in the Cont. Line—"I think you will serve yourself and your Country more effectually in this Corps" &c., &c., Apr. 7, 1779. Letters from Hannastown, Dec. 8, 1779 to Council, from Capt. Thos. Campbell of Cumb. Co., Penna., his Lieuts. being Isaac Thompson, George Calhoun, and Alexdr. Parker. Thomas was the son of Michael and Rebecca Brown Campbell, and in 1813, Thomas Campbell and wife Mary sell to George Beaver, Lot 37 in the town of St. Thomas. The warrant to Michael, father of said Thomas Campbell, was dated Feb. 14, 1749. Thomas Campbell, 1751-1816, of Peters Twp., left a will prob. Apr. 23, 1816, in which he authorized his brothers-in-law, James McDowell, John McLean and Lazarus Brown, as Executors to sell,—divide in 3 shares equally; one to wife Mary Campbell, one to Jean McKean, one to Rebecca B. Campbell. Codicil names Grandson Thomas Campbell McKean, his sword and a tract in Crawford County; and to Thos. Campbell McDowell, my nephew, land in Crawford County. He also names his father-in-law, James McDowell, Esq., decd., his wife having been Mary McDowell, who was born 1762, dying in 1821. Janet Campbell was married to Joseph McKean, at Mercersburg, by Dr. John King, Jan. 19, 1808. They had a son Thos Campbell baptized, Apr., 1809; a dau. Mary Ann Elizabeth, on May 14, 1812.

Penna. Arch. 5th Ser. Vol. 6, p. 314, 613. Penna. Arch. 1st Ser. Vol. 8, p. 36, 37, 68, 69, 70, 109. Penna. Arch. 1st Ser. Vol. 7, p. 301, 447. Penna. Arch. 2nd Ser. Vol. 15, p. 764.

TERRENCE CAMPBELL

Is shown as Quarter Master 1777-78, under Col. Abram Smith, with Thos. Johnston as Adjutant, 8th Batt., Cumb. Co. Militia. To Col. Terrence Campbell, Chambersburg, Penna. The bearer John McMullen has cleaned and trimmed all the Shot first recd., at this post from your furnace, and thereby rendered them all fit for use except forty three 3pd., shot, which on account of their irregular figure, cannot be made of any use. Patrick and Terrence Campbell, "Have Opened at their stores in Chambersburg and Bedford an extensive assortment of Merchandise Suitable for the present season among which are Calicoes, Chintzes, Calimancoes, Stuffs, Moreens, Jone's spinning wild boars &c., Camel's hair needle wrought shawls, Best London pewter, window glass 10 x 8 & 9 x 7½". The first Borough Book of Bedford shows that in 1802, Terrence Campbell, Esq., was duly elected as Chief Burgess. On Jan. 21, 1815, Patrick Campbell of Chambersburg, was the surviving partner and heir at law of Terrence Campbell, late of Bedford, Merchant, deceased.

Penna. Arch. 5th Ser. Vol. 6, p. 125, 127, 511, 528, 530, 548, 531. Egles Hist. Register, p. 128, 129. Franklin Repository, May 20, 1805.

WILLIAM CAMPBELL

Non Cupative Will No. 46, sworn Oct. 29, 1782. James Wilkins swore that on the day William Campbell went away on his Journey, and on the Expedition with Col. Archibald Lochry to the Indian Country, that his request to this deponent was that if he did not live to return home, to inform his friends that he did really order all his worldly estate to become the property of his brother Michael Campbell forever free from all other claims of any other heirs, only two colts, being colts of a mare called the Sheely Mare and the oldest colts of said Mare which he allowed to his Brother Charles Campbell. In case of his death the above Non Cupative Will was ordered by said Deceased to be made known. The above William Campbell was the son of Michael Campbell and his wife Rebecca Brown, early settlers in Peters Twp., Franklin Co., Penna. The widow Rebecca died March 25, 1778. They had issue: Charles; Sarah, who mar. Samuel Holliday; Thomas; George; William; Michael; James (George and James since decd.)

Westmoreland County Penna., Court Records.

ADAM CASNER

Served in 1780-82 under Capts. John Woods and Patrick Jack. Deeds show a certain David Casner who had a Patent for land in Peters Twp., May, 1789, with James Campbell, Wm. McDowell, as neighbors. David Casner and wife Catherine granted above land to John Brindle, who with his wife Catherine, in 1791, conveyed the same to Melchor Brindle.

Penna. Arch. 5th Ser. Vol. 6, p. 91, 313.

PATRICK CAVENAUGH

8th Penna. Regt. Cont. Line, Private, enlisted at Carlisle in Capt. Huffnagle's Company; he saved Gen. Lincoln from capture by the British, in New Jersey; afterwards express rider for Gen. Greene; died in Washington County, Apr. 5, 1823, aged 83 yrs. A John Cavenaugh and Barny Cavenaugh, same page and all three in 8th. Penna. Cont. Line. 1786 Tax List of Freemen, Peters Twp., Franklin Co., Penna., appears the name of Patrick Cavana.

PATRICK CAVET

Served in 1781-82, under Capts. John Woods, Berryhill and Poe, undated rolls. In 1780, Patrick Cavitt is shown with land, horses and cattle in Antrim Twp.

Penna. Arch. 5th Ser. Vol. 6, p. 101, 137, 576, 583.

WILLIAM CAVIN

Pvt., in Penna. Line; was 81 in 1821. He was a pensioner.

Penna. Arch. 3rd Ser. Vol. 13, p. 507.

BALSOR (BALTZER) CEASE

Served as pvt. 1779, under Capt. Samuel Royer, also in 1781. In Deed Book 1, Feb., 1787, Baltzer Cees, late of Washington Twp., now of Peters Twp., sells to Nathaniel Lightner of York Town, County of York, 333 acres of land in Washington Twp., vested in a certain Christopher Cees, who lately died intestate, leaving a widow Catherine and lawful issue. (See Orphans' Court, Carlisle, May 29, 1780). Baltzer Cees, 2nd. son pays the widow and children and sells as above. In Sept., 1785, John Jack and wife Margaret of York Co., Penna., sold to John McCullough of Washington Twp., Pa., 336 ac. land, the same tract which Balser Ceese sold Jan. 1781 to Henry Hartman, who by 2 deeds, sold to John Jack.

Penna. Arch. 5th Ser. Vol. 6, p. 112, 541.

GASPER CEASE

Served as pvt. under Capt. Samuel Royer, 1779-80-82.

Penna. Arch. 5th Ser. Vol. 6, p. 89, 123, 542, 585.

MELCHER (WELKER) CEASE

Served under Capts. Samuel Royer and Walter McKinnie, 1779-80-82.

Penna. Arch. 5th Ser. Vol. 6, p. 89, 306, 542.

MAJOR JOHN CESSNA

(1726-1802) served as Major in 1777, Volunteer Comp., served thru the War. Sheriff of Bedford Co., born in Franklin Co., Penna., died in Friend's Cove, Bedford Co., mar. 1st Sarah Rose (1740-88). Will proven Apr. 15, 1802, stricken in years, wife Elizabeth; sons: Charles; Evan; James; and Henry; dau. Sarah Rose Cessna; Exrs: Sons, John and Jonathan Cessna and Henry Williams. In Oct., 1795, Samuel Hall, in his will states that he is at present lying in the house of his son-in-law, John Cessna, in a very low state. He was of Colerain Twp., and left a son Robert under age. The "Public Opinion" gives the following: John Cessna, son of John, a Huguenot, settled in Lurgan Twp., removed to Friend's Cove, one of the first Justices of Bedford Co., in 1771; a member of the Penna. Convention of 1776, and Sheriff of Bedford Co., 1777-78. John Cessna who represented this district in Congress was a great grandson.

D. A. R. Lineage Book, No. 94, p. 25.

JAMES CISNA (CESSNA)

Served with Capts. Alexdr. Peebles and Wm. Strain, 1777-79-80-81-82, commanded by Col. James Dunlop. James Cessna is shown in the Cont. Line, from Cumb. Co., Penna.

Penna. Arch. 5th Ser. Vol. 6, p. 58, 96, 136, 396, 404, 422, 433 590. Penna. Arch. 5th Ser. Vol. 4, p. 281.

JOHN CESSNA

Sheriff, Oct. 30, 1777, again in 1778; Collector of Excise Jan. 1, 1778; Justice of the Peace, Oct. 21, 1782, and Sept. 9, 1790. A delegate to the Convention of 1776. From the Miller Collection, State Library, is the following: John Cessna took up land in Southampton Twp., about 1½ miles south of Shippensburg. He is probably buried in Old Council House Graveyard, but no marker to be found today. His son James is lying in this early burying ground. The will of John Cessna, dated Oct. 24, 1793, gives to his son James a house in Shippensburg, land on the Juniata in Southampton Twp., and Blunston land in York County.

Penna. Arch. 2nd Ser. Vol. 3, p. 596, 672, 673, 674.

STEPHEN CISNA

Served with Capt. Alexdr. Peebles 1777-78-79-80-81 and is shown at Sunberry with Capt. Peebles Sept. 1779. He is also given as a soldier in the Cont. Line from Cumb. Co., Penna. Under the records of Rev. John Linn, Center Church Perry Co., Penna., is the marriage of Stephen Cisney of Bedford County to Mary Gardner of this congregation, on April 12, 1790.

Penna. Arch. 5th Ser. Vol. 6, p. 51, 57, 62, 136, 395, 421, 589. Penna. Arch. 5th Ser. Vol. 4, p. 282, 622.

THEOPHILUS CESNEY (CESSNA)

Served as Ensign, 1780-82, with Capt. William Strain, and also as a Captain in the Cont. Line, from Cumb. Co., Penna. One Theopilis Cisna was married to Nancy Richardson, Sept. 25, 1800, by Dr. David Denny of Chambersburg, Pa.

Penna. Arch. 5th Ser. Vol. 6, p. 143, 397, 429. Penna. Arch. 5th Ser. Vol. 4, p. 281, 622.

THOMAS CISSNA

Is shown serving in 1781, as Ensign, with Capt. Thos. Askey. He also was in the Cont. Line, as Ensign from Cumberland Co., Penna.

Penna. Arch. 5th Ser. Vol. 6, p. 630. Penna. Arch. 5th Ser. Vol. 4' p. 282, 622.

WILLIAM CESSNA

Served as a Lieut. with Capt. Joseph Culbertson, 1777-78-81 and he was also in the Cont. Line from Cumb. Co., Pa. Under Indian Massacres we have this note of July 18, 1757,—"Six men killed or taken near Shippensburg. These were reaping in Mr. John Cisney's field,—missing, John Cisney and three little boys, two of them his grandsons."

Penna. Arch. 5th Ser. Vol. 6, p. 290, 369, 377, 642. Penna. Arch. 5th Ser. Vol. 4, p. 281.

BENJAMIN CHAMBERS

Was the son of James. The date and place of his birth and the name of his mother are not shown. Benjamin Chambers was commissioned early in the year 1778, ensign in the 1st Penna. Regt. commanded by his father, Col. James Chambers; was promoted Lieut., and left the service after the conclusion of the campaign of 1780. He was in the battles of Springfield, Connecticut Farms and Bull's Ferry. He was allowed pension on his application executed Nov. 22, 1821, at which time he resided in Cooper County, Missouri, and was aged 57 years. In 1829, he was residing near Walnut Farm, Saline County, Missouri. He was at one time Deputy Surveyor of the public lands of the United States. Benjamin Chambers mar. first Ruth McPherrin, Dec. 27, 1796. She was a dau. of Rev. Thomas McPherrin, pastor of the Presby. Church at Welsh Run. They were mar. by Dr. John King of Mercersburg, Penna., They had issue: a child who died young, and a son, Thomas. The will of Rev. Thomas McPherrin, 1801, states: "$100. to grandson, Thomas Chambers, which his father, Benj. Chambers justly owes to my estate." Benjamin Chambers died Aug. 26 or 27 (both dates appear), 1850, in Cambridge Township, Saline Co., Missouri. At that time he was referred to as Col. Benjamin Chambers; no explanation for the title was made. In 1822, Benjamin Chambers referred to the following children: Oldest son (probably Thomas) aged 23 yrs. Sarah Bella, in her 15th year. George Washington in his 11 years. Catharine Judith in her 8th year, born 1815, mar. John C. Pulliam. Susan M. in her 6th year. Ludlaw in his 3rd year. John aged 14 months. Mother's name is not given. On Nov. 20, 1837, Benjamin Chambers mar. Jane Wooldridge, a widow. Both were then of Saline Co., Missouri. Soldier's widow, Jane, was allowed pension on her application executed Dec. 12, 1858, at which time she was aged 58 yrs, and resided in Saline Co., Missouri. In 1862, she stated that she had then lived in Missouri for 25 years, and previous to that time in Virginia. She died March 31, 1867. It was stated that when Mrs. Jane Wooldridge married Benjamin Chambers she had a large family of her own; her three sons are referred to, only name given is that of William Daniel Wooldridge, who, in 1879, lived in Cambridge, Missouri.

Veterans Administration—W. 10302.

EZEKIEL CHAMBERS

Served as a pvt. in 1778-79-80-81, under Capts. Adam Harmony, James Young, Conrad Snider. This Chambers family moved to Erie Co., Penna. In the will of James Stewart, Mill Creek Twp., he names wife Elizabeth; dau. Rebecca, wife of the late Ezekiel Chambers; a dau. Grace, decd., wife of Benjamin Chambers, and others. The Will prob. Aug. 18, 1825. Notice from "Franklin Repository," Dec. 27, 1803,—All those who are indebted to Ezekiel Chambers, Or his sons Ezekiel and Benjamin, are hereby informed that their notes and accounts are left in the hands of the subscriber to recover the money.—James McLene

Penna. Arch. 5th Ser. Vol. 6, p. 538, 546, 87, 119.

JAMES CHAMBERS

One of a patrol of four killed by the Indians, May, 1780, near French Jacob Groshong's Mill; buried Lewis Cemetery (unmarked) Northumberland County Militia. Son of Robert Chambers, Sr., who came from vicinity of Chambersburg, Penna., about 1775.

Mrs. Bartol's list Rev. Soldiers, Shikelimo, D. A. R.

ROBERT CHAMBERS

Died in 1825, lived in Buffalo Twp., 1778-87. Private and Ensign Northumberland Co., Militia. He mar. Catherine (Klinesmith) Campbell, widow of Daniel Campbell, also a Rev. Soldier. Son of Robert Chambers, Sr.

Mrs. Bartol's list Rev. Soldiers Shikelimo Chapter, D. A. R.

SAMUEL CHASE

Was a private in the Penna. Line. He was 81 years of age in 1822, and a pensioner.

Penna. Arch. 3rd Ser. Vol. 13, p. 507.

JOHN CHESSNO

Served with Capt. Wm. Smith in 1780, as a private. The name may be Chesney.

Penna. Arch. 5th Ser. Vol. 6, p. 276.

BENJAMIN CHESTNUT

Served as a pvt. under Capt James Young and Col. Jas. Johnson, 1780-81. He mar. Anne McKinnie of Mercersburg, Feb. 23, 1789. He bought from William Smith, Sr., in Mercersburg, 2 lots or pieces of ground, on the run, including a Tan yard and a sufficient quantity of water to supply said yard. On March 10, 1797, Benj. Chestnut and wife Ann sold the above to Enoch Skinner. Benjamin removed to Washington Co., Penna., where he is shown as a pensioner, May 11, 1833, then aged 77 years. Deed Books 4 and 12 contain full records on this family. Article of Agreement between Benj. Chestnut and Enoch Skinner: Article of agreement made and concluded this 11th day of January 1797, between Benjamin Chestnut of Mercersburg, Franklin Co., Pa., on the one part and Enoch Skinner of Bedford Co. and state aforesaid on the other part,—witnesseth, that the said Chestnut doth hereby grant, bargain and sell unto the said Skinner the Lot or plot of ground he now lives on including a Tanyard being all the property the said Chestnut now owns where he lives a conveyance to be made on the 1st day of April next, for the sum of 750 pounds to be paid as follows: Said Chestnut is to give up the possession on the 1st day of May next. Said Skinner is to have liberty to work in the tanyard anytime he may want. Said Chestnut is to give a six plate stove and what shingles is now made and lying in the yard. Said Chestnut is to give said Skinner the first offer of what hides he may have on hand between this and the 1st of May next. In testimony whereof both parties—

Wits: Robert McFarland   Benj. Chestnut
       James Irwin   Enoch Skinner

Rec'd Jan. 7, 1797 from Enoch Skinner the sum of Five Dollars in part of the within.

Benj. Chestnut

Presby Church records at Mercersburg, Penna., show baptisms for 3 children of Benj. Chestnut,—A child on Feb. 11, 1790; a child on Feb. 25, 1791; and Esther on Aug. 28, 1792.

Penna. Arch. 5th Ser. Vol. 6, p. 83, 100.

THOMAS CHESTNUT

Served as pvt. under Capt Samuel Patton 1780-81-82. Thomas Chestnut was left land by his father, 360 acres, on Back Creek in Franklin Co., Penna. He appears to have died 1814, the heirs being sisters and brothers,—viz: Margaret Chestnut, late of Hamilton Twp., now (1816) of Washington Co., Penna.; Matthew Ferguson and Wife Anne (Chestnut) of Pickaway Co., Ohio; Wm. Swan and wife Eleanor (Chestnut) of Huntingdon Co., Penna.; Benjamin Chestnut and wife Anne (McKinnie) of Washington Co., Penna.; and John Chestnut and wife Peggy of Northumberland Co., Penna. Between 1816-18 all heirs join in selling the land to John Wilson of Franklin Co., Penna. Survey Book 3, p. 494 shows the Thomas Chestnut land to have been in right of John Erwin, 365 acres, 139 pchs., in 1766, the Irwins having been early settlers. John Chestnut, pew No. 41 in old Log Church at Rocky Spring, also in the Brick Church in 1794; in 1800 when Rev. Frances Herron came as Pastor.

Penna. Arch. 5th Ser. Vol. 6, p. 277, 288, 286, 311.

DANIEL CLAPSADDLE

Served as Captain of Cumb. Co. Militia during 1780-81. He mar. Mary, dau. of Michael Halms (Helms) of Washington Twp. Deed Book 2, p. 393, Chambersburg, Penna. shows Daniel Klebsaddle and wife, Magdalena selling land in Washington Twp., to Peter Beaker date 1791. His will recorded at Hagerstown, Md., was dated Sept. 24, 1805, recorded Oct. 27, 1807. He names wife Anna to whom he gives one cow, 2 shep, household furniture, my haus and half a lot in Stull's addition to Elizabeth town; the interest of 600 lbs. current money as long as she remains my wito; To Raberd McCall 200 lbs., To my five Step-daus. of my second wife: To Elizabeth Shank, wife of Andrew Shank, 40 lbs; To Chatarine Cushwaugh 40 lbs.; To Mary Barktoll, wife of Peter Barktoll, 40 lbs.; To Susanna Barktoll, wife of Jacob Barktoll, 40 lbs.; To Esther Lantz, wife of Christian Lantz, Jr., 40 lbs.; 5 legacies: Joseph Clapsaddle, my grand Nevey, a son of Michael Clapsaddle. Said Joseph shall be larned to reet, rid, and siefer to the rool of three, when he comes to age of 21 yrs.; Michael Clapsaddle, son of my brother Michael and Elizabeth, sister of before mentioned Joseph shall have &c.; Exrs: friends, Geo. Nigh and Thomas Sherman, Wash. Co., Md. Some years ago I subscribed 15 lbs., current money for the use of the Charmen Lutheran Congregation in Hagerstown, and have pd. 5 lbs. toward it. Executors to pay remainder after my death. The body of Daniel Klepsattel, born 1734, d. Aug. 1807, was removed from Graveyard of St. John's Lutheran Church, Hagerstown, Md., to Rose Hill Cemetery and is marked No. 13.

Penna. Arch. 5th Ser. Vol. 6, p. 69, 92, 94, 115, 117, 614.

GEORGE CLAPSADDLE

Served under Capt. Walter McKinnie, 1780-81-82, the 4th Batt. Cumb. Co., Militia. In 1781, George Clapsaddle was a freeman in Peters Twp. Under St. John's Lutheran Church records, Hagerstown, Md., is recorded the marriage of Jacob Clapsaddle to Elizabeth Brooks, Nov. 15, 1812.

Penna. Arch. 5th Ser. Vol. 6, p. 266, 299, 301, 306.

JOHN CLAPSADDLE

A freeman in Peters Twp., served 1781-82, under Capt. Walter McKinnie. His will, dated and prob., Apr., 1810. He states that "all money and the ½ of the bonds, notes, book accounts between myself and the heirs of Michael Clapsaddle, decd., to my brother George and sisters, the heirs of my brother Michael, decd., and the heirs of sister Elizabeth, decd.; grist mill and saw mill not to be sold"; Exrs: George Clapsaddle and Daniel Ridenour.

Penna. Arch. 5th Ser. Vol. 6, p. 298, 300, 305.

MICHAEL CLAPSADDLE

Of Peters Twp., served as a pvt., with Capt. Walter McKinnie 1781-82. Letters on his estate were granted to Barbara Clapsaddle and Daniel Ridenour, Apr. 6, 1810. In 1781, the above man was taxed in Peters Twp., on 2 mills, 350 ac. of land, 4 horses and 5 cattle and as a freeman.

Penna. Arch. 5th Ser. Vol. 6, p. 297, 300. 304, 305.

GEORGE CLARKE

Served as pvt. 1780-81-82, under Capt. Thos. Johnson. In 1796 he was both Store and Innkeeper, with 420 ac. of land; 100 ac. land, 40 pounds in rents, 8 lots, 4 Horses and 4 Cows. In 1791 George Clark advertises in the "Carlisle Gazette," a tavern in which he lives in the town of Greencastle, at the Figure of General Green. In 1791, James McClanagan and wife, Isabel; John Allison and wife Elizabeth, all of Antrim Twp., sell to John Gebby, George Clark, Andrew Reed, John Coughran and James Crooks of same, Trustees for the Asso. Reformed Congregation in and about Greencastle, now under the pastoral care of the Rev. Matthew Lind for five shillings to each of above, they sell 1 acre, 32½ pchs. of land. Under Sept. 11, 1821, the "Repository" gives the death in Greencastle, on Wednesday last in the 69th year of his age. George Clarke, Esq., Collector of the U. S. Revenue of this District. His will names Dau. Mary Young and Dau. Jane Patterson and her husband (Dr.) Thos. Patterson of the City of Washington. Deeds show there were 2 sons, Matt. St. Clair Clarke and John X. Clarke; the father, George, had a "Memorandum of property." There was a plantation at Conococheague Creek, valued at $12,000.; A Mansion in Greencastle; A corner Lot and the plantation in Westmoreland Co. Penna., named "Sloan place." It is probable that the wife of George Clarke was Margaret, dau. of Matt. St. Clair, who signed the petition to have Greencastle made the County Seat. It is also probable that Mary (Clarke) Young, had a dau. Margaret St. Clair C. Young, who mar. Rev. John Lind. A Plan of the early Church is in existence. Undoubtedly George Clarke was buried beside his wife, who lies in the graveyard of the Asso. Reformed Church (known as the White Church), East Balto. St. Greencastle,— "Christian Reader here on the lap of earth are laid the remains of Mrs. Margaret Clark, the late beloved consort of George Clark, who on the 12th of February 1810, in the 59th year of her age closed a most useful and exemplary life of Gospel Faith and Piety; of conjugal and Maternal duty and affection. In memory of which, this tribute is paid by her sorrowing and affectionate husband."

"When marble monuments shall all decay
Rocks turn to dust and mountain melt away,
Her sainted form shall o'er their ruins rise
To meet her Savior thru the opening skies."

Penna. Arch. 5th Ser. Vol. 6, p. 76, 84, 114, 115.

JAMES CLARK

During the French and Indian War, Capt. James Burd of Lancaster Co., Penna., raised a regiment of foot soldiers, May 10, 1757. Among these who served was "James Clark, enlisted May 10, 1757, for three years, aged 36 years, born in Ireland," one Daniel Clark, Lieut. was in the same company. The above man is thought to have been the James Clark who came to the vicinity of Mercersburg where he bought a tract of land, known as "Clifton Hall." It was part of the Kyle tract which Thos. Kyle had received from his father, Samuel Kyle, an early settler from Lancaster Co., Penna. Thomas Kyle sells for 2275 lbs., Gold or Silver money paid by James Clark, Sr., Thomas Clark and James Clark, Jr., dated June 26, 1787. Here James Clark lived, and under date of May 15, 1821, the "Repository" states, "Died on the first inst., James Clark, Sr., of Montgomery Twp., having nearly attained his one hundredth year, and leaving behind him upwards of sixty great-grandchildren, forty-two grandchildren, five children and an aged widow," Under May 6, 1823, "James Clark of Montgomery Twp., in his 16th year, being the third generation bearing the same name to die in five years." James Clark had mar. 1st Nancy Reed, about 1754. He mar. 2nd Esther, in 1784, (late Esther Renick, widow and relict of Alexdr. Renick), shown in Deed Book 2, p. 39. James Clark left a will dated Apr. 15, 1820, prob. May 23, 1821. He names wife Esther; son James (decd), and grandsons James, George, John; son Thomas; sons-in-law, Charles Kilgore, David Humphrey, John Taggert. Of his children, David mar. Hannah Baird; Thomas mar. Jane Caldwell; John mar. ———— McDowell; Rebecca mar. John Taggert; Mary mar. 1st Jeremiah Rankin; 2nd Chas Kilgore; Nancy mar. David Humphrey; Esther mar. Josiah (Joseph) Smith; Jennie mar. David Elden. Esther Clark died Aug. 12, 1823. In 1790 Census the family of James Clark consisted of 3 men, 1 boy, 3 females and a slave. He is said by descendants to be buried in the Slate Hill graveyard.

Penna. Arch 5th Ser. Vol. 1, p. 93.

JOSEPH CLARKE

Of Guliford Twp., served as pvt. under Capt. Saml. Royer 1779-80-81. His will dated 1797, was prob. March, 1804. He named loving wife Margery; son Thomas and daus: Elizabeth; Susanna; Mary and Margaret. Dau. Deborah Fitzgerald, and grandson James Fitzgerald. On April 13, 1775, Joseph Clark was mar. to Margaret Finley by Dr. Alex. Dobbin. In the will of Susanna Shilito, Oct., 1804, she gives to her present and beloved Husband John Shillito, all estate left her by her father Joseph Clark, late of Guilford Twp.

Penna. Arch. 5th Ser. Vol. 6, p. 90, 99, 113, 543.

JOHN CLAYTON

Served as Pvt. in 1780, and came to Green Twp., Franklin Co., Penna., where he was killed in 1797. He mar. Elizabeth Miller, May 13, 1789, leaving issue: Polly; Betsy; Beckie; John; James. The estate was admr. by his brother James and Col. Jos. Culbertson, Mar 6, 1797. John, son of John mar. Sarah Foster, lived and died at Waynesboro, Penna. John Clayton may have been a son of Henry Clayton, Sr., of Cumb. Co., Penna., In 1785 he sells his interest in a tract bought by Henry, Sr. and Jr., in 1780.

Penna. Arch. 5th Ser. Vol. 6, p. 219, 225.

THOMAS CLIVES

Served with Capt. Wm. Smith, 1780, as a private. Another unfamiliar name in the county.

Penna. Arch. 5th Ser. Vol. 6, p. 276.

MICHAEL COFFEE

Served as pvt. under Capt. John McConnell, 1781-82.

Penna. Arch. 5th Ser. Vol. 6, p. 302, 309.

ROBERT COFFEY

Of Southampton Twp., served as Sergt. and private in 1777-78-79-80-81-82. He was with Capts. Alexander Peebles and John Campbell. His will, prob., Jan. 15, 1811, names wife Nancy; brother Thomas; children to be schooled and sons to be bound out to trade.

Penna. Arch. 5th Ser. Vol. 6, p. 31, 34, 57, 395, 420, 432, 444, 590.

THOMAS COFFEY

Brother of Robert, served as pvt., under Capts. Alex. Peebles, Benj. Blythe and Noah Abrahm.

Penna. Arch. 5th Ser. Vol. 6, p. 18, 20, 21, 139, 152, 589.

CONRAD COFFROTH

Rev. Soldier and pensioner No. 19146, died Feb. 26, 1831, aged 68 yrs. 6 mos. 12 days. His wife Magdalena, died 1835, in her 69th year. In the "recollections" of G. G. Rupley of Mercersburg, who was born and raised in Greencastle, he says "On the square fronting East Baltimore St., was a two-story weather board house, used as a store room by John D. Work, and there was also a stone back building where Conrad Coffroth, another Rev. Soldier dwelt." He and his wife are buried in the graveyard of the First United Brethren Church, Greencastle, Penna.

Penna. Arch. 2nd Ser. Vol. 15, p. 717.

NICHOLAS COLEMAN

Served in 1780, under Capt. John Woods of Antrim Twp. He may have also been in the Cont. Line, but not proven. He was born in Scotland in 1731 (?). Came to the Conococheague Valley, mar. at Mercersburg, Penna., Jean McClelland, Dec. 22, 1772. Presbyterian Church records show baptisms of children. He and wife Jean are buried in Ebenezer Church yard Indiana Co., Penna. He left issue: William, 1774-1851, mar. Mary Lytle; John, 1776-1865, mar. Martha Katon; Elizabeth, mar James Matthews; Margaret, mar. 1st John Matthews, 2nd. James Oliver; Mary mar. Samuel Craven; Nancy mar. Moses Thompson; Jane, 1783-1875, mar. Alex. McGaughey; Archibald mar. Margaret Jamison; Robert mar. Elizabeth McLane; James, 1795-1857, mar Mary Campbell.

Penna. Arch. 5th Ser. Vol. 6, p. 76, 92.

DAVID COLLINS

Was a pvt., under Lieut. John Eaton, Oct., 1777. He was an early settler in the vicinity of Welsh Run, his patents in 1788. He died intestate in Dec. 1804, leaving a widow Ann, and John; Martha; Elizabeth and Ruth. The son John took the land, later selling to Rev. Robert Kennedy. The tracts were called "Single Trouble" and Drumhubbart."

Penna. Arch. 5th Ser. Vol. 6, p. 373.

COL. EDWARD COOK

The gallant Colonel was born in the Conococheague settlement in Franklin Co., Penna., the year 1738. Three members of the family came to America one settled in east Jersey, another in eastern Penna., and all trace of the third is lost. Col. Cook was among the few early settlers who clustered around Fort Bird immediately after the successful expedition of Forbes against Fort Duquesne in the summer of 1758. He became active in guiding the affairs of the western region. He was made magistrate of Bedford and also one of the first magistrates on the formation of Westmoreland County; a member of the Provincial Congress that convened in Carpenter's Hall in Phila., June 18, 1776, and drafted the Declaration of Independence presented to Congress June 26, 1776. Col. Cook was a member of the State Constitutional Convention and Sept. 28, 1776 was made the first Commissioner of Exchange and was appointed Sub-lieutenant of Westmoreland Co., March 21, 1777; later lieutenant to succeed Col. Archbd. Lochry who was killed by Indians; he was also commander of the Rangers and all thru the Revolution he served his country with exceptional valor. He later became Justice of Fayette County. At the close of the war Col. Cook retired to his mansion in Fayette County. He founded the Rehoboth Church and continued to serve his country as a representative to the General Assembly; a member of the commission that located the County seats, Nov. 1786; Justice of the Peace; Associate Judge of Fayette Co., in 1791; Chairman of the Mingo Creek meeting at Parkinson Ferry, Gallitin acting as Secretary at the meeting. The old Cook mansion is about a mile back from the Monongahela at Fayette City, fifty miles up from Pittsburgh, Pa., and is a fine specimen of colonial architecture, completed by Col. Cook in 1776 after four years of ceaseless labor. The walls of stone were three feet thick, the doors built double, the interior finished in cherry and walnut, with floors of oak. It is said that both Washington and Jefferson were frequent visitors at the Cook Mansion. In 1882 Hist. of Westmoreland Co., Penna. p. 203, adds to above that Edward Cook presided at the Court sitting at Hannastown when it was attacked and burnt by the Indians and Torries. In "Early Western Penna. Politics" by Dr. Russell J. Ferguson, he states that, "Edwd. Cook was a farmer, distiller, storekeeper and slave-owner; he had sprung from English parents in the Cumberland Valley in Penna., and had arrived in Westmoreland County in 1772; subsequently a frontier soldier, Justice of the Peace of Westmoreland and Washington Counties; Associate Judge in Fayette County; interested in establishing the Pittsburgh Academy in 1787, and agent in terminating the Whiskey Insurrection." Col. Edward Cook mar. Martha, dau. of Edward Crawford, Sr., of Fayetteville, Franklin County. She was born 1743, died 1837. His stone in Rehoboth Church Graveyard, shows dates 1738-1808. The will of Edward Cook of Fayette Co., Pa., names wife Martha; Son James to pay bequests to "Joseph Bryan who mar. my grandau, Mary Cook, and to Dorcas Cook and Eliza or Elizabeth Cook, my granddaus." To grandson Edward Cook; Dated Sept. 17, 1808; prob., Dec. 8, 1808.

Journal of Am. History Vol. 4, 1910 by Dr. Speers Gillette. Early Western Penna. Politics by Dr. Russell J. Ferguson. The 1882 His. of Westmoreland Co., Penna., p. 203.

MICHAEL COOK

Served as a pvt under Capt. Samuel Royer, 1778-79-80-81. He was born March 24, 1755, died April 27, 1839, aged 84 yrs. 1 mo. 6 days. His first wife was Rachel Frederick, born Dec. 12, 1758, died Dec. 12, 1798. (His second wife, Mary Beam died June 29, 1824). Michael Cook owned land, horses and cows. However, he died intestate, leaving issue: Elizabeth, mar. Francis Welsh; John and Jacob, living in Bedford County; Michael; Peter; Mary; Daniel living in Franklin County; Catherine mar. Abraham Secrist; Five grandchildren, issue of his son George who died prior to his father, viz: Michael; Rachel; Elizabeth; George and Selina, who resided in Ohio. Orphans' Court, August, 1841.

Penna. Arch. 5th Ser. Vol. 6, p. 74, 89, 112, 542.

WILLIAM COOK

Served as pvt. 1780-81-82 under Capts. John

Woods and James Poe, Antrim Twp. William Cook was a son of Joseph Cook and wife Elizabeth, dau of pioneer Thos. Brown, early settlers. Tax list of Antrim Twp., 1796 shows a William Cook under "young Freemen."

Penna. Arch. 5th Ser. Vol. 6, p. 91, 103, 575.

WILLIAM COOK

Died in 1830 in Union Twp., Erie Co., Penna. Quoting from "Soldiers of the American Revolution" issued by the Erie County, Penna., Chapters is the following: William Cook died in 1830 in Union Twp., of which he was one of the first settlers; He was of Cumberland Co., in the 1790 Census, with one male over 16 in his family, two under 16, and one female. He mar. Margery Watts of Carlisle, dau. of David and they had five children, of whom there is record of John, born about 1784, who mar. 1803, Rachel Gray, aged 22 years, sister of Matt. and Wm. Gray. John Cook died 1835 aged 51 years. The son David mar. Sarah Gray, b. 1783, dau. of Wm. Gray, Sr., of Union Twp.; they moved to Indiana where David died soon after; she came back and lived with her brother Robert Gray, dying in 1873, aged 90 years. Margery Watts, widow of the Wm. Cook, lived with a dau. at Oil Creek, and died there.

Penna. Arch. 3rd Ser. Vol. 23, p. 452.

RICHARD COOPER

Was a pvt. with Capt. Samuel Patton, in 1779 as a Ranger on the Western frontiers. In 1781, he was in the Company of Capt. Wm. Huston.

Penna. Arch. 5th Ser. Vol. 6, p. 602, 610, 643.

ROBERT COOPER

Served as pvt. under Capt. John Jack 1778, and under Capts. Beryhill, Johnston and Poe, 1780-81-82. From the pen of M. A. Foltz, in a Kittochtinny Magazine, we quote," "Robert Cooper was a native of Chester, coming into Antrim Twp., Franklin County prior to the Revolution, and settled in Antrim Twp.; Robert Cooper had a son James who mar. Mary Clugston, and they had a son, John M. Cooper, the well known Journalist and historian. As an apprentice he was the proud purchaser of the first copy of "Border Life" a few hours after it left the bindery.

Penna. Arch. 5th Ser. Vol. 6, p. 79, 114, 129, 169, 575, 583, 599, 600.

ANDREW COOVER

Chambersburg, Penna. Orphans' Court, Vol. F, p. 176, Estate of Andrew Coover, Hamilton Twp., who died intestate April 17, 1849, leaving issue: Mary mar. Joseph Gipe; Jacob Coover of Wyandot, Ohio; Elizabeth mar. John Snyder, living near Tiffin, Seneca Co., Ohio; Martha mar. David Knouse, Franklin Co., Penna.; Catherine mar. Jonathan Whitmore, Franklin Co., Penna.; Violetta mar. Jacob Picking, Franklin Co., Penna. Two Grandchildren, being his son Andrew Coover's who died before the intestate: Jacob and Elizabeth, minors in Franklin Co., Penna. Susanna mar. David Foust, Franklin Co., Penna. Mansion farm in Letterkenny Twp., 123 acres. Patented land, 2 story stone dwelling house, a Switser barn, also 115½ acres Hamilton Twp., Patent; 2 story log house &c.

JOHN CORBIN

Penna Artillery, Cont. Line, Capt. Thos. Proctor, 1776 Matross, killed at Fort Washington. His widow received a donation from the Supreme Executive Council, later pensioned by State of Penna. When Mr. Shippen laid out Shippensburg, Feb., 1763, John Corbet bought Lot No. 37.

Penna. Arch. 5th Ser. Vol. 3, p. 948. Colonial Records, Vol. 12, p. 34

MARGARET CORBIN —MARGERY CORBET

Pvt., Col. Lewis Nicola, Cont. Line. Invalid Regt. as discharged, 1783.

Penna. Arch. 5th Ser. Vol. 4, p. 90, 40, 59, 65, 79. D. A. R. Magazine, August, 1936, p. 778, 779.

ADAM COULTER AND JAMES COULTER

Served as pvts., August the 27, 1781, under Capt. Thos. Askey, commanded by Col. James Dunlap.

Penna. Arch. 5th Ser. Vol. 6, p. 423.

RICHARD COULTER, LIEUT.

The inhabitants of Fannett Twp., signing petitions, May, 1778, June, 1778 and Feb., 1779. "Our Militia has received orders for four classes to be in readiness to march Immediately to Camp." What moves us to supplicate for rifles is, because muskets is of very little use in the woods against Indians." In the second petition they state: "Our harvest is hastening, and we are not able to Man the forts we intend to build and reap the Grain at the same time." "We have an ardent desire to maintain our Ground and think we could if we have had Guards sent to us to join our people, either to reap the Grain, Guard our forts or scout the woods beyond us."

Penna. Arch. 5th Ser. Vol. 6, p. 51, 53. Penna. Arch. 2nd Ser. Vol. 3, p. 167, 186, 320.

SAMUEL COULTER

Served as pvt. 1781 under Capt. Thos. Askey. He was of Fannett Twp., his will dated 1793, was prob., 1794. He names wife Margaret; son James; son Samuel; dau. Elennor Ardry; Dau. Elizabeth Holliday; sons Samuel and Matthew; Daus. Margaret and Margery; Grandson Samuel Ardrey;

Matthew and Margaret to get more schooling; Exrs: wife Margaret and Brother-in-law John Moor.
Penna. Arch. 5th Ser. Vol. 6, p. 424.

HENRY COW (COWE)

Served wth Capt. John Orbison, 1780-82. He is shown with 137 ac. land, Horses and Cattle. The name Cowe is frequently seen on old papers in Montgomery Twp. Records of St. John's Lutheran Church of Hagerstown, Md., show the mar. of Henry Cow, to Mary Zimmerman, Oct. 27, 1797.
Penna. Arch. 5th Ser. Vol. 6, p. 274, 307.

JACOB COWE

Was in Service 1780-81, under Capt. John Orbison. Deeds show that in 1801, Philip Davis and wife Jean, sell land to Jacob Cowe, who with his wife Susan, sell to George Rutter, 284 acres, by land of Mrs. McPherrin, by Henry Cowe and by Henry Angle.
Penna. Arch. 5th Ser. Vol. 6, p. 273, 293.

PAUL COW

Served in 1780 under Capt. John Orbison.
Penna. Arch. 5th Ser. Vol. 6, p. 273.

PHILLIPY COW

Served 1780 under Capt. John Orbison.
Penna. Arch. 5tht Ser. Vol. 6, p. 274.

BENJAMIN COWAN

Was in service 1777, with Capt. Williams, Cumb. Co., Penna.
Penna. Arch. 5th Ser. Vol. 6, p. 244.

DANIEL COWAN

Was in service 1780-82, under Capts. James Young, John Rea and Terrence Campbell.
Penna. Arch. 5th Ser. Vol. 6, p. 77, 82, 126.

DAVID COWAN

As Sergt., 1779-80-81.
Penna. Arch. 5th Ser. Vol. 6, p. 77, 82, 106, 111, 543, 584.

HENRY COWAN

Served 1778, with Capt Isaac Miller.
Penna. Arch. 5th Ser. Vol. 6, p. 37, 39, 68.

JAMES COWAN

Was serving with Capt. James Patton, 1780.
Penna. Arch. 5th Ser. Vol. 6, p. 271.

ROBERT COWAN

Appears in 1781-82, in service with Capt. Samuel Patton.
Penna. Arch. 5th Ser. Vol. 6, p. 287, 311.

THOMAS COWAN

Was serving during 1778-79-80-81, with Capts. Wm. Findley and John Rea.
Penna. Arch 5th Ser. Vol 6, p. 73, 78, 106, 527, 530, 544, 585.

WILLIAM COWAN

A private 1777-79-81-82, with Capts. Samuel Patton and Alexander Peebles.
Penna. Arch. 5th Ser. Vol. 6, p. 58, 287, 311, 449, 590.

WILLIAM COWAN

Served as First Lieut., 1779-80, under Capt. Alexander Peebles, command of Col. James Dunlap.
Penna. Arch 5th Ser. Vol. 6, p. 135, 385, 394.

WILLIAM COWAN

Served first as a pvt., under Capt. Alexdr. Peebles, "Shippensburg, June 13, 1777," and as 1st Lieut., 1779-80-81-82. His wife was Isabel, dau. of Wm. McConnell of Lurgan Twp., who died about 1796. The plantation of William McConnell of Lurgan Twp., of 217 ac. was sold by the seven heirs to Samuel Cox, as follows: Mary McConnell, spinster of Shippensburg; William and wife Mary of Shippensburg; William Cowan and wife Isabel, of Shippensburg; Robert McConnell of Shippensburg; James of Lewistown, Penna.; John Henry and wife Esther and Ennis King and wife, Ann, were of Westmoreland Co., Penna. One William Cowan was in James Dunlap's Dist. and another man of the same name is shown in Robert Donavin's Dist., of Middle Spring Church, 1776. William Cowan was born 1749, day and month not shown, in Chester Co., Penna. The names of his parents are not stated. While residing at Mt. Rock, near Carlisle, Cumb. Co., Penna., William Cowan was commissioned Apr. 19, 1775, Capt. of a Company of foot in the Third Batt. of Associates of Cumb. Co., Penna. In June, 1776 he was called out and marched with his company under the command of Major John Davis to Amboy, New Jersey, where he remained for two months; a few days after his return home, he was again called out and marched with his company under Col. Gurney to the Jersey coast and was engaged in protecting the inhabitants against the Tories, length of service, two months; in December following, he was requested to recruit a company in Cumb. Co., Penna., was engaged in this work until after Christmas, when he joined his company in Phila., was engaged for a time guarding the Hessian prisoners taken at Trenton, then marched into New Jersey under Major Davis and Col. Gurney and served two months in all; in April, 1777, he moved from Mt. Rock to Shippensburg, in same country, and was out in the fall of that year and in 1778 on four or five tours of two months each, as Capt. under Maj. Davis, Penna. Troops. He stated that his entire service amounted to sixteen months. In 1781, Capt. Wm. Cowan moved to Westmoreland Co., Penna. He was allowed pension on his application executed Nov. 20, 1832, while residing in Robbetown, Huntingdon Twp, Westmoreland, Co., Penna. The soldier mar., Nov. 15, 1785, near Chambersburg, Penna. Mary Wilson, a widow. They were mar. by the Rev. James Lang. The date and place of birth, names of her parents and name of her former husband are not shown. He died Sept. 19, 1838, in Westmoreland Co., Penna., and she died Aug. 4, 1839. In 1850, three children only were living, as follows: Susan Bigger of Allegheny Co., Penna.; Willianne Lewis, of Allegheny Co., Penna., and Maria M. Morgan, of Pittsburgh, Allegheny Co., Penna. The dates of birth of the above named daus. of Capt. Wm. Cowan are not shown, nor are the names of their husbands stated. In 1850, Edgar Cowan an attorney at law, of Greensburg, Penna., stated that he was a grandson of Capt Wm. Cowan and that he had been reared by his grandparents and lived with them until they died. He did not give the names of his parents nor his age. In 1833, one Hathew or Mathew Wilson, of Harrisburg, Pa., in a letter to a friend whose name is not shown, stated, "We are all well here please give my love to Mother and all the family and tell her I would be glad to see her here." No relationship of Hathew or Mathew Wilson to the wife of Capt. Wm. Cowan was stated.

Penna. Arch. 5th Ser. Vol. 6, p. 58, 135, 385, 394, 590. Veteran's Administration, Washington, D. C. R. 2388.

JOHN COWDEN

Is shown in service 1780-81, under Capt. Jas. Young. John Cowden bought a tract of land in 1762, which his Exrs., John Andrews and John Reynolds, sold to John and Martin Wingert. One Patrick Alexander left a will at Carlisle, dated 1777, in which he names sons Joseph; Patrick; James; John; Samuel. He was of Guilford Twp., and his first wife Margaret, and second wife Martha, are thought to have been daus. of John Cowden, a neighbor.

Penna. Arch. 5th Ser. Vol. 6, p. 82, 110.

MANASSAH COYLE

Is shown from Westmoreland County, Penna., serving in Cont. Line. In 1796, the family of Wm. Ewing consisted of his wife Ellanor, Adam and Isabel. They were in District 5 of the "upper West Conococheague" Presby., Church of Mercersburg, the Presiding Elder over that District being Major Wm. Maxwell. Wm. Ewing had baptized, a son Robert, May 27, 1770; a son Alexdr., Nov. 18, 1771. The family appears later in Western Penna., where Manassah Coyle born 1759, mar. in 1785, Isabel, dau., of Wm. and Eleanor (Thompson) Ewing. Manassah Coyle a pvt., with Capt. Robert Orr, was taken prisoner, escaped from Captivity, and returned Dec. 1782, to Westmoreland County, Penna. "Manassah Coyle, Fayette; in 1781 in Capt. Orr's Company, on expedition down the Ohio, on Aug. 24, 1781, taken prisoner by the Indians."

Penna. Arch. 5th Ser. Vol. 4, p. 433. Penna. Arch. 2nd Ser. Vol. 14, p. 698.

MARK COYLE

Franklin County in 1813. Scharf's History Western Maryland states: "Dec. 7, 1840, near Clearspring, Mark Coyle, aged 86, Soldier in Rev. War, in battles of Monmouth, Princeton and other important ones, a Penna. pensioner," aged 85 in 1840.

Penna. Arch. 2nd Ser. Vol. 13, p. 45.

JOHN CRAFT

Probably the son of Ludwick Crafft, of Chambersburg, is shown as pvt. in 1780-82 under Capt. Conrad Snider, and in the First Batt. Cumb. Co., Militia. Under the "German Settlement" George O. Seilhamer states that John Krafft (of Frederick) enlisted in Capt. William Heyser's company in the German regiment of Continental troops, July 27, 1776, discharged July 26, 1779. John Craft mar. Christiana Smith. They had one son and five daughters. In his will, prob., 1793, he names the son John and son-in-law Samuel Raudebaugh. The husband of the dau. Anna Mary is unknown; Catherine mar. John Stearny; one dau. mar. John Shook; Barbara mar. Jacob Seiner; Susan mar. Samuel Braizon. Christiana, widow of John Croft, became the second wife of Daniel Reisher.

Penna. Arch. 5th Ser. Vol. 6, p. 87, 123.

JOHN CRAIG

Quoting from "Five Typical Scotch-Irish Families," by Mary Craig Shoemaker, we find that John Craig's wife was the 3rd daughter of Benj. Boyd and Janet Elliott; she was left a widow in 1801, aged 31 years, with five young sons, and in 1814 left Derry Church and came to Lower West Conococheague Congregation. (Welsh Run). In 1813, Wm. and Benjamin Craig signed the deed for land. Original Grant to the tract was from the state of Maryland to Nathaniel Alexander, Feb. 17, 1741. It was called "The Three Cousins," 1000 acres, part of the Manor of Conococheague and was in Prince George County, Md. Nathaniel Alexander sold to Allen Killough, who sold to Moses Murphy, who sold 190 acres to William Craig. In a resurvey Nov. 3, 1752, the number of acres is given as 498 in "Three Cousins" and

"Locust Hill," the farm joining on the East, also known as the "Three Cousins" Tract.

JOSHUA CRAIG

Under pension applications Joshua Craig states that he enlisted with Captain Cluggage of Bedford Co., for one year and with him marched to Boston. He re-enlisted, a year later, with Capt., Wm. Rippey of Shippensburg, for one year and marched to Quebec. Taken prisoner there—paroled—later exchanged. He again enlisted at New York with Capt. Thos. Campbell of York County for five years and was discharged at the end of that time. Was in the Battles of Bunker Hill, Quebec, Long Island, Battle of New York, Trenton, Brandywine, Germantown, and at the taking of Cornwallis.

Penna. Arch. 5th Ser. Vol. 4, p. 519, 525.

JOHN CRAIGHEAD

Princeton, 1763, pastor at Rocky Spring Church, Franklin County, Pa., 1768-98, raised a company of Penna. Militia from among his parishioners, commanded it in the battle of Long Island, and was taken prisoner at the fall of Fort Washington. P. G. C.

Fithian's Journal, p. 33.

THOMAS CRAVEN

Served as pvt. under Capts. Robert Dickey and Walter McKinney in 1781. John Craven served in the same Company. D. A. R. Lineage Book 102, p. 66, shows Thomas Craven (1756-1832) born in Bucks Co., Pa., died in Indiana. He mar. 1st Eleanor Adams. In 1784 Thomas and Eleanor Craven were admitted to membership in the "Upper West Conococheague" Presby. Church of Mercersburg, Pa. Under marriages by Rev. John King are: Wm. Dickey and Mary Craven, July 31, 1781; Samuel Ferguson and Anna Craven, July 31, 1781; Joseph Craven and Polly Adams, Apr. 1, 1784. Under baptisms were: John Craven and Anne Ferguson, Adults; In Oct., 1782 Mary was baptized for ———Craven; a child for Samuel Ferguson, Dec. 8, 1782; a child for Thomas Craven, Oct. 3, 1784; John for Wm. Dickey, Apr. 6, 1788.

Penna. Arch. 5th Ser. Vol. 6, p. 285, 300, 315.

GEORGE CRAWFORD

Served as Capt. of Militia, 1777-78; as a pvt. under Capt. Wm. Long, 1778-79; also with Capt. Conrad Snider and Capt. John Orbison, 1780-81-82. He died intestate Apr. 17, 1813. His eldest son James had died, presumably 1789, leaving two sons, George and James Crawford; dau. Margaret mar. William Duffield; dau. Martha mar. William Davis; Dau. Elizabeth mar. James Duffield; son William Crawford, and dau. Polly lately mar. to Henry Gardner. He left 200 acres of land in Montgomery Twp. A George Crawford mar. Martha Van Lear, Apr. 7, 1808, and it is probable he was the son of James Crawford, and the grandson of the above Capt. George Crawford. In the will of Joseph Van Lear, prob., 1819, he names daus. Ann Crawford; Elizabeth Crawford; Martha Crawford. (Franklin Repository, April 13, 1830, died the 31st of March, Mrs. Martha Crawford, consort of Major George Crawford.) One Esther Crawford and George Crawford were pew-holders in the Welsh Run Church.

Penna. Arch. 5th Ser. Vol. 6, p. 87, 108, 118, 537, 545. Penna. Arch. 5th Ser Vol. 6, p. 274, 294, 307, 367, 370, 376, 608.

JAMES CRAWFORD

Of Montgomery Twp., served under Capts. Wm. Huston and Walter McKinnie, 1780-81-82. He is shown with 266 acres of land, Horses and Cattle. In his will, dated and prob. 1789, he names his wife, Jean to whom he gives one third of real and personal estate, "as long as she remains my widow, but should she change her estate by marriage, then I allow her 150 pounds and to clear-off from said plantation"; two sons George and James residue of estate and to be made good English Collers. Exrs: loving Uncle William Lowry, trusty friend John Worke; Wit: George Crawford; William Meers; Wm. Duffield. The wife Jean was probably the dau. of Wm. Lowry, Sr.

Penna. Arch. 5th Ser. Vol. 6, p. 265, 270, 276, 283, 306.

JAMES CRAWFORD

Served as Sergt., First Call, 1777, with Capt. James Poe; he served, also, under Capt. Berryhill and Findley, 1778-80-81-82. The Hon. Watson R. Davison, in "Reiminiscences of Greencastle" states that James Crawford first comes to our notice as a school teacher, in a school house "just this side of Squire Rankin's mill." He appears in 1777, under Capt James Poe, and was still in service in 1782. As a surveyor, James Crawford assisted Col. John Allison in laying out Greencastle and in point of time, the second schoolhouse was that of James Crawford, as above.

Penna. Arch. 5th Ser. Vol. 6, p. 79, 102, 520, 523, 527, 530, 571 575, 582.

JOSEPH CRAWFORD

Is shown in 1776 under Capt. Saml. McCune, and in 1778-81 with Capts. Adam Harmony and Conrad Snider. His estate was admr. Nov., 1793, by Henry Work and John Crawford. One Joseph Crawford is shown in Guilford Twp., under tax lists of 1786, as a freeman.

Penna. Arch. 5th Ser. Vol. 6, p. 87, 119, 538, 587.

ROBERT CRAWFORD

Served as pvt., 1778-80-81-82 under Capts. Walter McKinnie and Wm. Huston. Robert Crawford is shown in 1781 as a "freeman" in Peters Twp. An early Robert Crawford was located on or near, Welsh Run, about 1742, will dated 1777, prob. 1778, naming grandson Robert Blackford; son John and daus: Esther; Ann; Rebecca; with Geo. Crawford and Thos. Cellars as Executors. The land called "Newry," later to Henry Angle and John Rush.

Penna. Arch. 5th Ser. Vol. 6, p. 266, 298, 300, 306, 382, 643.

LEONARD CROBARGER

Of Peters, Twp., Franklin Co., Pa., said to be 90 years old in 1840, states the following in his will,—"Of Sound mind and health, but conscious that the disolution of my body is not far hence and ear long my soul will have to appear before that God in whose hands my breath is, do therefore make this my last Will and Testament. Wife Mary; Son John; dau. Susuanna and her two children, namely John Wever and Sarah Weaver; dau. Elizabeth's children; The Executor was Henry Hawbecker. Wit: Geo. Cook, Christian Wilhelm. Prob., July 18, 1844.

Census of Pensioners, Oct., 1840

JAMES CROOKS, SR.

Served 1780-81, under Capt. Daniel Clapsaddle. He was of Washington Twp., his will dated and prob., 1805; His wife Ann to be maintained by son Robert;; 3 sons: Robert; John; James; dau. Alice McCrea; The Executors, son Robert and David McCrea. James Crooks is shown in the Cont. Line entitled to Depreciation Pay.

Penna. Arch. 5th Ser. Vol. 6, p. 72, 94. 117.

JAMES CROOKS, JR.

Served under Capt. Daniel Clapsaddle 1780-81. Under records of Dr. Dobbin, who served both Greencastle and Gettysburg, Pa., are the following marriages: James Crooks and Ann Ambrose, June 31, 1794. James Crooks and Sarah Dunwoody, Apr. 5, 1798. John Crooks and Elizabeth Jenkins, Feb. 11, 1800, Franklin, Co.

Penna. Arch. 5th Ser. Vol. 6, p. 93, 107, 116.

JOHN CROOKS

Of Washington Twp., appears under Capt. Daniel Clapsaddle 1780-81, and he is also shown in the Cont. Line of Cumb. Co., as entitled to Depreciation Pay. In the will of John Crooks, dated 1783, prob. 1805, he names a son John; dau. Rachel Wallace; grandsons Robert and John Crooks, sons of James; also grandchildren; Wm.; James; and John Crooks, Rachel, all of my son John. Alice Crooks dau. of son James; Thomas and James Johnston were the witnesses.

Penna. Arch. 5th Ser. Vol. 6, p. 94, 97, 117.

WILLIAM CROOKS

Is shown under Capts. Wm. Long and Wm. Finley as a Corporal, 1777-78, and in 1780-81 under Capt. Daniel Clapsaddle.

Penna. Arch. 5th Ser. Vol. 6, p. 93, 116, 520, 524, 529, 596.

JAMES CROSS

Private served 1780-81 under Capt. Wm. Huston. A deed at Chambersburg, shows James Cross as son of pioneer William Cross. His wife Jane was a dau. of Alexander Miller, who was killed by Indians near Conococheague. William Cross, Jr., mar Agnes, also a dau. of Alexander Miller.

Penna. Arch. 5th Ser. Vol. 6, p. 270, 276. 283.

ROBERT CROSS

Served as private under Captain William Berryhill, 1780-81. In 1802 Robert Cross and wife Agnes sell to Daniel Stahl, for 876 pounds a tract of land in Antrim Twp., 106 acres, called "Crosses purchase," a gift from his Father, William Cross, who also conveyed 106 acres to his dau. Rebecca Cross, part of above tract; Rebecca sold to Daniel Stahl.

Penna. Arch. 5th Ser. Vol. 6, p. 79, 101, 107. Survey Book 1, p. 429, 506, 525.

SAMUEL CROSS

Served under Capt. James Poe 1777 and 1782, under Capt. William Berryhill 1780-81. One Samuel Cross was an Indian Trader, August, 1745 and Dec. 1747.

Penna. Arch. 5th Ser. Vol. 6. p. 79, 101, 107, 521, 571.

JAMES CROTTY, SERGT.

Under Capt. James Young, 1779, 8th Batt. under the command of Col. Abhm. Smith.

Penna. Arch. 5th Ser. Vol. 6, p. 547.

THOMAS CROTTEY

Appears in 1779, in the Company of Capt. Samuel Patton, in service on the Western Frontiers as Rangers, the Command of Col. Wm. Chambers, Mustered at Legonere, June 22, 1779. A man of the name appears in the 2nd Regt. Cont. Line. One Thomas Crotte enlisted by James Burd at Fort Granville, one of 39 men, each advanced 7 shillings "Sealed up and Directed to Lieut. Coll. John Armstrong, Esq., at Carlisle and delivered by Major Burd at the Camp at Harriss 3rd June, 1756."

Penna. Arch. 5th Ser. Vol. 6, p. 601 608, 610. Penna. Arch. 5th Ser. Vol. 1, p. 64.

WILLIAM CROTTY
Pvt. Aug., 1782, under Capt. Terrence Campbell, First Batt. Cumb. Co. Militia.
Penna. Arch. 5th Ser. Vol. 6, p. 125.

JAMES CROW
Served under Capt. Noah Abraham 1779-80.
Penna. Arch. 5th Ser. Vol. 6, p. 86, 383, 393.

MATTHIAS CROW
Served as pvt. under Capt. John Orbison, 1780-81-82, vicinity of Welsh Run. He had 100 ac. land, horses and cattle.
Penna. Arch 5th Ser. Vol. 6, p. 274, 294, 308.

JOHN CRUNKLETON
May 19, 1735. John Crunkleton 200 ac. On a Small run on the North side of Conococheague about a mile from the said Creek and about seven miles Westerly from Edward Nichols,—N. S. Blunston Licenses

JOSEPH CRUNKLETON
Served under Capts. Thos. Johnston and Wm. Berryhill, 1780-81-82 as a pvt., from Antrim Twp. He was a son of pioneer Robert Crunkleton and wife Margaret. Joseph Crunkleton left a will dated Jan. and prob., Feb. 1803; wife Magdalene; Executors to build a dwelling house and stable at the upper end of the spring near where the school house now stands, size to be 26 x 24 feet for wife; children to be kept at an English School and if my two sons be thought capable to receiving a Classical Education they are to be put to a Gramer School until they read the Roman Classick Authors; daus. Margaret and Mary after they receive their schooling, to be put one year to a sewing school; Books to be divided: Russell's History of Modern Europe in five Volumes, the first volume of Henry's Exposition of the New Testament to son Robert, and Wesley's Natural Philosophy in five Volumes and travels works in one volume to younger son Abraham; Tract of land in Somerset County, Penna., to be sold.
Penna. Arch. 5th Ser. Vol. 6, p. 84, 101, 114, 130.

ROBERT CRUNKLETON
Son of Robert, served under Capts. John Jack and Wm. Berryhill, 1777-80-81-82. On June 25, 1782, Robert Crunkleton was married by Rev. Alexdr. Dobbin to Anne Morhead of Washington Twp. Robert Crunkleton, whose will was prob., March 10, 1787, appears as the father of the Rev. Soldier above. His wife was Margaret and he names sons, Robert; Joseph; Samuel; 6 daus: Rebecca, who mar. ———— Miller; Mary; Martha mar. Jas. Finney, Apr. 20, 1774; Susan who mar. John Cellar of Antrim Twp., Jan. 2, 1776, Elizabeth; Sarah, who mar. Alexdr. McCutchen, June 27, 1780, the marriages by Rev. Alexdr. Dobbin. In the year 1734, Joseph Crunkleton obtained his license, and in 1735, he, Jacob Snively, James Johnston and James Roddy made settlements.
Penna. Arch. 5th Ser. Vol. 6, p. 79, 101, 123, 317, 321, 586.

CAPTAIN ALEXANDER CULBERTSON
"Officers of the Provincial Service," 1755, Capt. Alexander Culbertson, "Lurgan Twp. Cumb. Co.," killed by the Indians near McCord's Fort, April, 1756.
Penna. Arch. 5th Ser. Vol. 1, p. 31, 46.

COLONEL JOSEPH CULBERTSON
Son of Joseph, lived and died in the "Row," Greene Twp., Franklin Co., Penna. In 1777-78, he appears as Captain, with John Barr and Wm. Cessna as Lieutenants and Hugh Allison as Ensign. He was also in service in 1780-81, and was under the Command of Lieut. Col. Saml. Culbertson. As to his wives there is a stone in Rocky Spring Graveyard as follows: "In memory of Mrs. Mary Culbertson, Consort of Joseph Culbertson, and daughter of James Finley, Esq., who was born Jan. 13, 1781 (?) and died Apr. 2, 1817." Another Stone, with Rev. marker shows the three names as given: "In Memory of Elizabeth Culbertson, who died 1802. Joseph Culbertson died Nov. 6, 1818. Margaret Culbertson died Aug. 11, 1838." In the will of Colonel Joseph Culbertson dated Oct. 9, 1817, and prob. Nov. 17, 1818, he names Joseph; John; Margaret, wife of John Breckenridge of Franklin Co., Penna. Elizabeth (unmarried); Sarah (unmarried); Martha (Mrs. Duncan) and issue two; Hugh born 1792, d. 1876; Col. Joseph mar. 2nd., Mrs. Margaret Finley, d. 1839, who had a son Wm. A., when she mar. Col. Culbertson. It appears that the eldest son Joseph Culbertson, mar. Jean (?), presumably Thompson, as they and Elizabeth Thompson, of Fannett Twp., receive land left by their father, Andrew Thompson, 260 acres in Hopewell Twp. Joseph later lived in the "Row," died intestate with John Johnston as Admr., Jan. 1831.
Penna. Arch. 5th Ser. Vol. 6, p. 279, 280, 289, 290, 369, 377, 396.

COLONEL ROBERT CULBERTSON
Of Greene Twp., appears in a deed dated Dec. 4, 1779, from Captains Joseph and Robert Culbertson of Letterkenny Twp., and James Breckenridge of Lurgan, for land bounding Daniel Duncan. There was a 2nd Deed made 1798, by Samuel Nicholson to Capt. Robert Culbertson, the land at Greenvillage at crossing of Chambersburg and Strasburg Roads, and sold by Admrs. of Capt. Robert Culbertson, of Capt. Joseph Armstrong's

Batt. (5th) of the Cumb. Co., Penna. "Flying Camp" was in Phila. Aug. 16, 1776, where he drew knap-sacks and 50 cartridges boxes for his company. This regiment took part in the Battles of Trenton and Princeton. Col. Robert Culbertson mar. May 6, 1778, Annie Duncan of Middle Spring, Franklin Co., Penna. They had issue: Joseph, b. 1779, d. 1858; William b. 1780, d. 1785; Robert b. 1782, d. 1864; Alexander b. 1784, d. 1809, unmar.; Samuel Duncan, Dr. b. 1786, d. 1865; William b. 1787, d. 1824; Stephen b. 1790, d. 1854; John Craighead b. 1791, b. 1860; Mary b. 1793, d. 1852; Daniel b. 1795, d. 1808; Anne b. 1797, d. 1867; James b. 1799, d. 1873. Col. Robert Culbertson was in service as Captain and Wagon Master, 1777-1782. He was born 1755, died July 26, 1801, the son of Joseph Culbertson and wife, Mary Breckenridge. Letters on the estate were granted the widow, Ann (Duncan) Culbertson, and Joseph Culbertson a son, Aug. 19, 1801. The sureties were Col. Saml. Culbertson and Saml. Brackenridge.

Penna. Arch. 5th Ser. Vol. 6, p. 4, 15, 598, 384. The Culbertson Genealogy, by Lewis R. Culbertson, M. D. Revised Edition, 1923, p. 266, 267, 268.

CAPTAIN SAMUEL CULBERTSON

Armstrong's Batt., under Col. Joseph Armstrong, Dec. 8, 1776. Lieut. John Culbertson; Robert Culbertson; James Culbertson. Rev. John Craighead is shown in this group.

Penna. Arch. 5th Ser. Vol. 6, p. 316.

HUGH CULL

Pvt. under Capt. Wm. Rippey enlisted Jan. 24, 1776, in 6th Penna. Batt. On Jan. 20, 1777, under Capt. Alex. Parker in 7th Penna. Cont. Line. Transferred to Commander in Chief's Guards, shown under Pennsylvanians in Chief's Guards. Entitled to Dep. pay. He received 200 ac. Donation land. The will of Hugh Cull, recorded at Chambersburg, Penna., Dec. 20, 1808, gives to dau. Peggy Cull, a tract of 200 ac. land in Butler County, Penna. No. 423, called Munmouth. Exr: friend David Kennedy.

Penna. Arch. 2nd Ser. Vol. 10, p. 187, 632, 646. Penna. Arch. 5th Ser. Vol. 2, 3 and 4.

JAMES CUMMINS

Served as a pvt., 1780-81, under Capt. Alexander Peebles. His estate was admr., March 24, 1789.

Penna. Arch. 5th Ser. Vol. 6, p. 136, 396, 406, 422.

THOMAS CUMMINS

Served as pvt. under Capt. Alex. Peebles, 1780-81-82. He was of Southampton Twp., his will prob., Sept., 28, 1810, names wife Mary; To son John a Quarter Section of land in Ohio, purchased by Robert McConnell, the South-west of Section No. 1 in Twp., No. 1, Range No. 7, in the District of Lands office at Zanesville, also money coming from Peter Creamer; son James; all my children,—some minors.

Penna. Arch. 5th Ser. Vol. 6, p. 396, 421, 433.

HUGH CUNNINGHAM

Appears as a private 1780-81, under Capts, Jas. Patton, Robert Dickey and Thomas McDowell. He was a son of John Cunningham, whose wife Susanna King, was killed by Indians. Hugh Cunningham mar. Elizabeth Dunlap, May 20, 1784. They had baptized Susanna, June 19, 1785, and Elizabeth, Dec. 8, 1788. His only sister Elizabeth mar. John McCullough, Mar. 4, 1788.

Penna. Arch. 5th Ser. Vol. 6, p. 272, 285, 315.

JAMES CUNNINGHAM

Son of John, served as private under Capt. Robert Dickey and Thos. McDowell in 1781, and an undated roll.

Penna. Arch. 5th Ser. Vol. 6, p. 285, 315.

JOHN CUNNINGHAM

Was in service under Capts., James Patton, Robert Dickey and Thos. McDowell, presumably a son of John Cunningham. The marriage of John Cunningham and Agnes Prescott took place Nov. 17, 1789, and the baptism of a child in 1791. The above John Cunningham probably died May 1801. The heirs of John Cunningham late of Peters Twp., agreed to sell the real estate of their decd., brother John Cunningham,—"I, Hugh Cunningham of Robison Twp., Washington Co., Penna., appoint John McCullough of Peters Twp., as Atty.," Apr. 28, 1802. They sell to James Adair and John McMillan, land which was granted to Rev. John King.

Penna. Arch. 5th Ser. Vol. 6, p. 271, 284, 314.

JOHN CUNNINGHAM

Of Montgomery Twp., served under Capt. John Orbison, Aug. 24, 1780, also in 1781-82. He is shown with land, horses and cattle in 1781. It is probable that the above John Cunningham mar. Catherine, dau. of James and Gwin Davis, early Welsh settlers near the Welsh Run. James Davis' will, dated and prob., 1789, names a dau. Catherine, wife of John Cunningham, also a dau. Martha who mar. Thos. Meek of Kentucky. A dau. Mary mar. Joseph Shannon (of John) and went to Kentucky and a dau. (Probably Margaret) mar. Rowland Hanna, "Steat of Kentucky." Philip Davis d. intestate leaving a dau. Martha, wife of Philip Cunningham, and a dau. Gwin wife of Richard Cunningham. John Wilson mar. Rebecca Cunningham, Jan. 13, 1842, with desc., of this marriage in California. License at Hagerstown shows Matty Davis to Philip Cunningham 6-10-1808. The above John Cunningham was a pew-holder in the Presby., Church at Welsh Run. Penna. Arch. 5th Ser. Vol. 6, p. 274, 294, 308.

ROBERT CUNNINGHAM

Was in service under Capts., James Patton, Robert Dickey and Thos. McDowell, 1780-81. He was a son of John Cunningham, and a freeman in Peters Twp., 1781.
Penna. Arch. 5th Ser. Vol. 6, p. 272, 281, 286, 316.

WILLIAM CUNNINGHAM

Served under Capts., Thos. McDowell and Robert Dickey, 1781, and an undated roll. There appears to have been a 3rd Cunningham line in this vicinity. The marriage of John Irwin to Mary Cunningham, Lower Tuscarora, Sept. 4, 1775; also, James McConnell to Janet Cunningham (Great Cove), Nov. 21, 1781. Wm. Poak to Jean Cunningham, Feb. 24, 1773.
Penna. Arch. 5th Ser. Vol. 6, p. 285, 314.

JAMES CURREY

May 15 1776, for the war; in Parr's Co., 1777, in McClelan's in 1780. Samuel & Wm. Curry appear in the same Company. It is probable he is the James Currie whose marriage to Katherine, dau. of Joseph Armstrong, Sr., of Hamilton Twp., is recorded in St. James Prot. Episcopal Church of Lancaster, May 31, 1758. "Owing to the Indian incursions the settlement had fled," largely to Lancaster County. In the will of Joseph Armstrong, Sr., he gives "to my beloved daughter, Katherine Courey the sum of 20 pounds over and above what she has received."
Penna. Arch. 5th Ser. Vol. 2, p. 649, 674, 715.

GEORGE DAVIS

Served as pvt., in 1781, under Capt. Wm. Berryhill of Antrim Twp. He is shown as a freeman in 1781, Antrim Twp., taxables. He mar. Susanna, dau. of Andrew Geary (Garry). His will prob. May 5, 1808. He had minor children,—Issue: George; Andrew b. Dec. 25, 1785, d. May 31, 1872, Mt. Zion Churchyard near Quincy, Penna.; Margaret Elizabeth b. Nov. 10, 1788, d. June 5, 1856, mar. ———— Barnett; Christina; Susanna; Catherine mar. Jacob Fisher; Hannah; Nancy b. June 10, 1802, d. Oct. 8, 1874, mar. David Freeman; John b. Mar. 29, 1806, d. Nov. 4, 1852, mar. Julianna. Issue of Andrew Davis, Mar. Rachel Pinchon (?) or Howell (?): Susan, b. Nov. 21, 1815, d. Mar 15, 1876, mar. George Anderson; Catherine mar. Philip Spidel; Sarah Ann b. June 5, 1819, d. June 12, 1900, mar. Aug. 22, 1843, Levi C. Kepner. Hannah mar. Reuben Bowman; Geo. Washington, b. 1824, Soldier in Mexican war;

Elizabeth mar. Mr. Lane; John d. young. George Davis took up 100 acres land in Cumb Co., May 31, 1762 and more in 1769.
Penna. Arch. 5th Ser. Vol. 6, p. 102. Penna. Arch. 3rd Ser. Vol. 20, p. 394.

HENRY DAVICE

Pvt., in a Company of Militia "that has served" as stated by Capt. Thos. Davies, of Bedford Co., Penna. Henery Davies of Warren Twp., is shown in 1799, with 400 acres of land, horses and cows.
Penna. Arch. 5th Ser. Vol. 5, p. 111, 329.

JOHN DAVIS

Orphans' Court Jan. Term, 1849—The petition of George Heck stating that he is guardian for Thomas Davis; Wm. Davis; David Davis; and Mark Davis, minor children and sons of John Davis, late of Chambersburg. The said John Davis at the time of his death was an enlisted Soldier in Co. (B) 11th Regt. of U. S., Inf., serving in Mexico and that under the provisions of the Act of Congress passed 11th day of Feb., 1847, a warrant, No. 14831 for 160 acres was issued in name of the ward or minors &c. The petitioner prays that he may be empowered to sell aforesaid Certificate.
Chambersburg, Penna. Orphan's Court records Vol. F, p. 101.

JOHN DAVIS

And Mary M. Davis Pension Certificate 18,349, issued Aug. 14, 1833, at $80. per annum. He applied Sept. 17, 1832, from Kittaning Twp., Armstrong Co., Penna. Service, private; age 69; volunteered April, 1778, at Marchand's Fort on Sewickley Creek, 6 miles from Greensburg, to serve until the fall of 1778, under Capt. Nehemiah Stakely. Under an order from Sergt. Riley he went about 3 miles to his father's and remained there until Apr., 1779, when a notice was served by Sergt. Wm. Gibson to attend at Kennerer's Fort, about 2 miles from Marchand's Fort, and there remained that summer with Paul McLean, Peter Gross a man by the name of Reile and 6 or 7 others. In the fall they returned home—in April 1780, ordered by Sgt. Gibson to go to Walton's Fort on Burch Creek and was there that summer; in June 1780, they were attacked by the Indians 2 of whom were killed, and 2 of their men, Peter Williard, Sr., and Peter Williard, Jr., both belonged to his Co.; a girl named Catherine Williard was taken prisoner and never returned. Mar., 1781, he was called to Garret Pendegrass' Fort. March 18 or 19 his father's house was attacked by Indians and he (Nicholas Davis) and his brother, David Davis, were killed. Affiant and his brother Henry were taken prisoners and taken to Fort Niagra where the Indians delivered them to the British on Lake Ontario. Col. Lewis Williams was also a prisoner at that time. In the Spring of 1782 the said Williams, Henry Davis, two brothers, called Franklin, and the affiant were exchanged at Saratoga. He was born in 1763, near where Greencastle, Penna., stands, lived in Westmoreland County, when he enlisted, and also 10 or 12 years after the close of the Rev. War, then moved to Kittanning Twp. In June of 1853, Samuel Davis, resident of Armstrong Co., Penna., declares he is a son of heir of John Davis, decd., and U. S. Pensioner &c. Said pensioner died in Armstrong Co., leaving a widow, Mary M. Davis.

National Genealogical Society Quarterly, March 1930, p. 7.

JOHN DAVIS

Was 1st Lieut. under Capt. Wm. Crawford, 1779-80-81-82, Lancaster Co., Penna. He was John Davis of Big Spring, Earl Twp., Lancaster County, Penna. He inherited from his parents David and Hannah Davis, 297 ac. land, which he sold and came to Montgomery Twp., Franklin Co., Penna., where he bought from Henry Work a tract known as the "Blue Spring" farm. They are buried there, as were also a son Daniel, his first wife, and two small children,—originally a large graveyard, but now reduced to four panels of iron fence. John Davis mar. Mary Cornog, Nov. 4, 1766, from Chester Co., Penna., early Welsh. They had issue: David Davis, who was in Green Co., Ohio in 1810; Thomas Davis, late of Munroe Co., Va., and his five children; John; Mary; Lucinda; Malinda nd Sarah, minors; John Davis, mar. June 11, 1812, Rebecca, dau. of Col. John Work, she died and he went west; Daniel mar. 1st Dorcas Davis, 2nd Mary Miller Bowles, 3rd Mary Elliott Shannon; Geo. Washington Davis, left a widow, Rachael in Montgomery Co., Ohio; Hannah, mar. Alex. Caven.

Penna. Arch. 5th Ser. Vol. 7, p. 993, 469, 474, 492.

JOHN DAVIS

Served as pvt., under Capts. Wm. Long and John Jack, 1777-79-80-81-82. John Davis left a will, prob., Aug. 3, 1802; naming Sisters Isabella Robb; Jean Cummins; Mary Brown; Brother Joseph Davis' children, also names various nieces and nephews; Wm. Mulling, child of my sister Betsy; Betzy Grimes, &c. Rupp gives John and Thomas Davis among the 1751 taxables for Antrim Twp. The will of Thomas Davis was prob. 1795.

Penna. Arch. 5th Ser. Vol. 6, p. 84, 115, 130, 519, 524, 540, 557.

JOSEPH DAVIS

Served as pvt., under Capts. Wm. Long and John Jack, 1777-79-80-81-82. In the will of Wm. Baker, of Antrim Twp., he names his brother-in-law Joseph Davis. Will dated 1792.

Penna. Arch. 5th Ser. Vol. 6, p. 84, 114, 130, 519, 524, 540, 557.

PHILIP DAVIS

1736-1749 Tax List, West Hopewell paid 4 lbs. 19s, 3d. Collector; Patriot; Welshman; Member of the Presbytery of Newcastle; Collector of Taxes, was granted a Commission for his land, Jan. 11, 1733. One tract was called "Philipsburg" another was called "Wales."

Rupp's Hist. of Cumberland Co., Penna. p. 359.

PHILIP DAVISS, CAPTAIN

Wm. Duffield, Jr. was his Lieut. and Samuel Dougherty, Ensign, Cumb. Co. Militia,—under Lieut. Col. Patrick Jack and Major John Holliday. In several old records the above is called "Major" Philip Davis. His wife was Margaret and they lived in what was known as the "Major North" property in Mercersburg, N. Main St. His will dated 1825, was prob., 1828, David and Philip Blair and their heirs, "sons of my nephew John Blair" were legatees. The above was a grandson of pioneer Philip Davis of Welsh Run.

Penna. Arch. 1st Ser. Vol, 10, p. 599.

ELIAS DAVISON

Was Capt. of Militia, serving 1776-77-78 and as a pvt., 1780-81. He was mar. by Mr. Lang, to Agnes McDowell, March 19, 1771. Agnes was a daughter of John McDowell who built the early Fort. The will of Elias Davison was prob. Apr. 23, 1806. He names son John McDowell Davison, land both at home and in Westmoreland Co., on Loyalhannon Creek. To his son Elias, "the farm I now live on" and two tracts in Westmoreland County, the one on the head of beaver, the other on the mouth of the Kishaminitas, also a lot in the city of Washington. Son-in-law Lazarus Brown 5 pounds; dau. Elizabeth Davison, now Elizabeth McDowell 650 pounds; Dau. Mary Davison 1000 pounds; negroes, Jin and Rose; Exrs: Son John McDowell and Elias, as soon as he shall arrive at age of 21 years, and Dr. John King. Wit: Wm. Allison; Abhm. Prather; Allen Herper. Elias Davison is probably buried at Moss Spring Graveyard.

Penna. Arch. 5th Ser. Vol. 6, p. 6, 513, 533, 80, 101.

HUGH DAVISON

On Feb. 2, 1778, Sub-Lieut., of Bedford Co. Penna., wrote an interesting letter to the supreme Executive Council in reference to the prospect of Defense against the enemy "when one part of the Country is attacked, the Danger may be apprehended thro' the whole." He was later Lieut. Col. Davison. He was one of the Antrim Twp., family, early settlers, and on Nov. 21, 1774, married Catherine, dau. of John McDowell, of Fort McDowell, near Mercersburg. In 1776, he was admitted to the Presby. Church at Mercersburg, and appears in Bedford Co., Penna., in 1777. Hugh Davison, Esq., of Huntingdon Co., Penna., and wife Catherine, had an agreement in 1787, with Stephen Bayard of Pittsburg for certain land on which said Bayard was about erecting on Reardon's Run, a Saw Mill &c. The conveyances were in 1803-04-08-09. In 1814, Hugh and Catherine sell to Elias Davidson and Christian Latshaw, merchants of Pittsburgh, 338 ac., of land. The issue of Col. Hugh and Catherine Davison: I. John Davidson, wife not known. II. Nancy mar. Robert King, March 15, 1797, by Dr. John King. III. Margaret Davison mar. John King, Feb. 9, 1804, by Dr. John King, Mercersburg, Penna. IV. Catherine Davison mar. Christian Latshaw, 1804, by Rev. A. A. McGinley, D. D., Fannett Twp. V. Mary Davidson mar. March 12, 1807, Thos. McDowell, by Dr. John King of Peters Twp., Franklin Co., Penna. VI. Elias Davidson is said to have mar. Martha Meanor. VII. Elizabeth Davison mar. James Ramsey, Huntingdon Co., Penna. VIII. Annabella Davison mar. Wm. Armstrong, Plum Twp., Allegheny Co., Penna. The John King line went to Columbiana Co., Ohio. Burials from the old Laird Cemetry, which is about 15 miles N. E. of Pittsburgh, near Plum Creek Church and a small village called New Texas and first named Ebenezer Church. The monument to Col. Hugh and Catherine Davidson is of brown granite or marble and is in perfect condition: Col. Hugh Davidson, died July 3, 1820, in the 75th year of his age. Catherine M. wife of Col. Hugh Davidson, died Feb. 10, 1818, in the 65th year of her age. Elias Davidson and Martha M., died Mar. 28, 1840 and May 1, 1840, aged 40 and 60 years.

Penna. Arch. 2nd Ser. Vol. 3, p. 147, 148. Penna. Arch. 5th Ser. Vol. 5, p. 49-85.

JOHN DAVISON

Father of John and Elias, had purchased 3 warrants. Land in Antrim Twp.; Caveat Feb., 1767. Surveyed Apr. 1, 1749 by Thos. Cookson for John Davison. Said John Davison died intestate leaving a widow Margaret and 6 children, to-wit: John and Elias, Robert, Hugh and James Davison and Mary Owen. Orphans' Court at Carlisle adjudged the tracts to the Eldest son John Davison who secured the shares of the Widow and other Children to the satisfaction of the said Court.

Penna. Arch. 3rd Ser. Vol.1, p. 195.

DAVIDSON

James L. Graham, Trustee, to William K. Armstrong,—1859. "Whereas at an Orphans Court for the County of Allegheny, held at Pittsburgh on the twelfth day of February in the year of Our Lord One thousand Eight hundred and fifty nine, a certain Robert King presented to said Court a Petition in Substance and effect as follows to wit: "To the honorable the Judges of the Orphans Court of the County of Allegheny, the Petition of Robert King, cousin and one of the heirs of Susannah Davidson, late of Plum Township, Allegheny County, respectfully represents that Susanna Davidson, the deceased above named lately died intestate, and unmarried and without issue, leaving neither Father nor Mother nor Sisters, nor Brothers nor Uncles nor Aunts of the blood of her Father, John Davidson, from whom the Estate hereinafter described descended to her, but leaving as her next kin and heirs the children of her said Father's deceased brothers and sisters as hereinafter named,viz: The children of Nancy Davidson, deceased sister of said intestates father, and intermarried in her lifetime with Robert King, Viz: Catherine King intermarried with William Armstrong; Isabella King; Hugh D. King (whose interest in said estate has been purchased at Sheriff's Sale by John Mellon, Esq.); Robert King, your Petitioner; Parthenia G. King, intermarried with Josiah M. Junkin and Mary C. King, intermarried with Archibald Coon. 2nd. The children of Margaret Davidson, deceased sister of Intestates father intermarried in her lifetime with John King, Viz: H. D. King; William King; Robert King; Elias King; Thomas King. Mary Ann King, intermarried with James McMath; Margaret D. King; Annabella C. King; and Obadiah J. King. 3rd. The children of Catherine Davidson, deceased sister of Intestates father intermarried in her lifetime with Christian Latshaw, viz: Mary Latshaw and Henrietta Latshaw. 4th. The children of Mary C. Davidson, deceased sister of Intestates father, intermarried in her lifetime with Thomas McDowell, Viz: Mary McDowell, intermarried with Rev. A. K. Nelson; Catherine McDowell, intermarried with Rev. N. G. White and William D. McDowell. 5th. The children of Elias Davidson, deceased brother of Intestates father, Viz: Catherine Davidson (whose Committee or Trustee is John Hamilton); Hugh Davidson; Elias B. Davidson; Josiah Davidson; James Davidson; Samuel Davidson; Martha Davidson; and Mary Davidson. 6th. The son of Elizabeth K. Davidson, deceased sister of Intestates father intermarried in her lifetime with James Ramsey, Viz: Elliott D. Ramsey. 7th. The children of Annabella M. Davidson, deceased sister of the intestates father, intermarried in her life-time with William Armstrong, Viz: Eliza C. Armstrong intermarried with Robert Leech; James Armstrong; Rebecca L. Armstrong, intermarried with H. M. Little and Mary A. Armstrong, intermarried with Samuel Scott. (There is a long description of the lands. They were in Plum Township, and a tract granted to John Davidson by patent, March 13, 1839, on whose death his property descended to his two daughters—Eliza and Susannah; and upon the death of Eliza to Susannah, but the partition was made and the petition granted and recorded March 3, 1860.)

Allepheny County, Penna. Deed Book 143, p. 126. Deed Book 43, p. 406.

ABRAHAM DEAN

Served 1780-81, under Capt. John Woods. Official Roster Rev. Soldiers of Ohio, states the above man died May 10, 1806, Ross Co., Ohio, buried, South Salem.

Penna. Arch. 5th Ser. Vol. 6, p. 91, 103.

WILLIAM DEAN

Pvt. under Lieut. John Barr, January, 1778. He was killed at Crooked Billet, as shown in records of the Presby. Church of Mercersburg. Wm. Dean was married to Martha McNutt, of Hanover, Dauphin Co., Penna., on June 16, 1763. Chambersburg, Penna., Orphans' Court records, Book A, p. 12: The petition of Martha Dean, widow and relict of Wm. Dean, late of Peters Twp., in the said county, was read, stating that her said husband was lately killed by the enemy when serving as a Militia man in the Army of the United States and that she was left with five orphan children &c., prayed the Court to make an order agreeably to the law passed March 20, 1780. Granting her a certain annuity as they might think proper for the support of her and her children. The Court being satisfied by a certificate under the hand and seal of Abram Smith, Esq., the commanding officer of the Regt. to which he belonged certificate from overseers of the poor and two Freeholders that such support is necessary the sum of fifty pounds, six shillings, and three pence be paid said Martha in lieu of half pay since the death of her husband and the further sum of fifteen pounds annually during her life or widowhood,—June 19, 1788. On pages 31, 57, 81, 114, 135, 164, 190, 224, 233,—till the year 1807 the support is continued. In Deed Book 5 p. 416, on Oct. 29, 1795, Martha Dean and her children, Joseph; John; Jean; Elizabeth and Mary of Armstrong Twp., Westmoreland Co., Penna., sell land in Peters Twp., to Richard Bard. The land, 100 acres, had been conveyed to Wm. Dean by John McMath. In 1809, Martha, widow of Wm. Dean, late of Peters Twp., Franklin Co., applied to Indiana Co., Orphans' Court for a pension, stating that her husband was killed on May 1, 1778 at the battle of Crooked Billet as a soldier under Capt. Robert McCoy. In her behalf James Calhoun of Armstrong Co., swears before Robert Beatty, June 1, 1809, that he was present as a Soldier at the battle of Crooked Billet under Capt. Robert McCoy and saw Wm. Dean killed.

Penna. Arch 5th Ser. Vol. 6, p. 382.

JACOB DEARDORFF

Served as pvt., in 1783, in Lancaster Co., under Capt. John Shonhower; Jacob Deardorff was born Aug. 15, 1764, and his wife Catherine Zug was born Oct. 6, 1765. She was a dau. of Johannes Zug, and a grandau of Ulric Zug of Canton Zug, Switzerland, who came to America in 1727. They came to Franklin Co., from Lancaster Co., Penna., in 1802,—issue: Abraham b. Feb. 6, 1788; Jacob b. Feb. 1, 1789; Anna b. Oct. 24, 1791; Henry b. Oct. 13, 1792; John b. July 15, 1794; Christianna and Catherine b. Aug 11, 1796; Magdalena b. Jan. 20, 1798; Susanna b. Sept. 27, 1799; Mary b. Sept. 29, 1801; Elizabeth b. Oct. 10, 1803; Isaac b. Dec. 17, 1805; Hannah b. Dec. 1, 1807. When Jacob Deardorff came to Franklin County, he bought land adjoining the Wm. Stover homestead. He was the son of Abraham and grandson of Henry, who settled in Lancaster Co., Penna., in 1746. His grandfather Hendrick Dirdorf, and great-grandfather Anthony Dirdorff, Sr., were naturalized in New Jersey in 1730, native of Germany. Jacob Deardorff, and wife Catherine Zug, are said to be buried on the old Stover Homestead near Shady Grove, Franklin Co., Penna.

Penna. Arch. 5th Ser. Vol. 7, p. 609.

JOHN DEEDS

Was a pvt., under Capt. Saml. Patton, 1780-81 -82. He bought a tract of land in Hamilton Twp., from Thos. Shirley. The Admr. of Adam Deeds, 1805, at Hagerstown, Md.

Penna. Arch. 5th Ser. Vol. 6, p. 278, 287, 311.

JOHANN LUDWIG DETRICH

Arrived at Phila., ship Minerva, Nov. 7, 1767. He was born in Germany 1740, and died 1819. His wife Julia Ann Gushert born 1746, died 1832. He served from Lancaster Co., Pa., as pvt. under Capt. Huey, at Sunbury in 1780, and in 82 and 83. He and his wife lie buried on a plot of the old homestead, along Back Creek on what is known as the Teagarden farm. Their children were: George, b. Jan. 29, 1778, unmar.; Catherine b. Jan. 26, 1780, mar. John Lesher; Christian b. Nov. 4, 1781, mar. Susan Stotler; Elizabeth b. May 16, 1784, mar. Daniel Wolf; David b. Oct. 6, 1785, went west; Ellen b. May 24, 1787, mar. George Clapsaddle; Lewis b. Nov. 30, 1788, mar. Maria Frontz; Samuel b. Dec. 9, 1789, mar. Sarah Brindle; Mary b. May 28, 1792, mar. George

Schafer; Emanuel b. July 4, 1794, mar. Catherine Christman; John b. July 2, 1796, mar. 2nd. Mary A. Brazier.

History of the Detrich Family, by C. M. Deatrich. Penna. Arch. 5th Ser. Vol. 7, p. 1117, 67, 80, 82.

JAMES DEVOR

Of Southampton Twp., left a will dated and prob. 1794, in which he names wife Elizabeth; son John a certain piece of land, to make 100 acres; Dau. Jane Sturges; son James 20 pounds; dau. Rebeckah Snodgrass 20 lbs. Sons George and Wm. all the land whereon I now dwell; son Wm. a legacy left us by our Uncle Francis Moor, Kingdom of Ireland. Exrs: wife Elizabeth and sons Geo. and William. The widow, Elizabeth Devor, left a will dated 1800, prob. 1802. "Money coming to me from Samuel Brindle in April, 1804." She names sons Wm.; James; dau. Rebecca Snodgrass; dau. Mary Moore; grandau. Jean Devor, dau of Wm. Devor; Wit: Samuel Moore, John Steel.

JOHN DEVER

Serving in 1778.

JOHN DEVOAR

In 1781, with Capt. Thos. Askey, Col. James Dunlap. Deeds show in 1775, John Devir of Hamilton Twp., and wife Jean selling 226 acres land, it being the tract, now in the occupation of said John Devir and whereon he dwells. For 450 pounds, to John McKeamy and Joseph McKeamy (Mekeamey) of Letterkenny Twp., by lands of Wm. Lyons, Isaac Patterson. Patk. Knox, Joseph Armstrong's other land, by John Elliott's land North, and Matthew Patton. The same tract John Devir bought from James Armstrong, dated Oct. 24, 1770, granted to Jas. Armstrong, by Patent Feb. 13, 1765. Witness: Robert Stockton and Mary McKnight. Before John Rannells.

Penna. Arch 5th Ser. Vol. 6, p. 424, 608.

MICHAEL DEWALT

Penna. Pensioner,—S-43489, Michael Dewalt, Apr. 30, 1819, Franklin Co., Penna., aged 62 yrs., stated he enlisted 1775 in Penna., commanded by Capt. Prowell regiment of Col. Patton, served until 1783, discharged at Winchester, Va.; was in battles of Monmouth, Eutaw Springs, Guilford C. H. Camden, Ninety six. Signed by mark, made before Archibald Bard, Judge. John Findlay prothonotary, certified Bard was Judge. David Fullerton, member of H. of Rep., certified Dec. 23, 1819, that interlineation in the Certificate of Bard was in his own handwriting. Aug 21, 1820, Michael Dewalt, aged 63, resident of Franklin Co., Penna., stated he was enlisted by Henry Brimat, Abbott's Town, York Co., Penna., early in spring of 1778, whence was taken to Valley Forge and Joined the army in Capt. Joseph Prowell's Comp., in regt. of Col. Patton, in which Comp. he remained until next spring when he was transferred to Capt. Oldham's Comp. in Regt., commanded by Col. Campbell in State of Va., where he continued until end of the war and was discharged in Shenandoah Co. in Va., near Battletown in 1783; that he was in Battles of Monmouth Court House, in N. J.; Guilford Court House in N. C., Eutaw Springs and Camden and had filed declaration to obtain a pension about 13th of April 1819, and placed on pension list and certificate No. 16271 was issued to him. Was a resident citizen of U. S. 18th March, 1818. Has followed occupation of a labourer which his age has rendered him unable to pursue as in his younger days. That he has a wife aged 43 yrs., and one child living with him aged 6 years, real property none, personal property none but a few pots &c. necessary for cooking.

Sworn before John Findlay, Prothy., who certified the value of the personal property to be $2.00, 26th Aug. 1820. 29th April 1826, Augusta Co., Va., application for transfer from pension roll of Penna. to Virginia, in that his daughter removed to this state and he wished to accompany her. Before John C. Somers, J. P., April 29, 1826 Augusta Co., Va. John Wile made oath he knew Michael Dewalt, had known upwards of 20 years, knew him to be the person who formerly resided in Penna., and is now in Va. Erasmus Stribling, Clerk of Augusta Co. Court, certified John C. Somers was an acting Justice of the Peace. Wayne County, Ohio, 11th March, 1835, before Wm. Sarwill, Notary, Michael Dewalt declared he was pensioner in Penna. and then Virginia, from which State he has lately removed, that he now resides in Wayne Co., Ohio, where he intends to remain, and wishes his pension to be payable at Pittsburgh, Penna. For the last eleven years the deponent and his wife have resided in the family of John Wile, the son-in-law of deponent's wife and that Wile having determined to remove to Ohio and deponent's wife was not willing to be separated from her daughter, so deponent agreed to move to Ohio with said Wile.

Franklin Co., Penna., 27th March, 1819. Before John Flanagan, J. P. of Franklin Co., Penna., came John Noll, Sr., who swore he knew Michael Dewalt, now of the township of Washington, Franklin Co., that he first knew him in the American Army at Valley Forge, that he knew him in the army for three years. Franklin Co., 29th Nov., 1819. Samuel Rogers, Sr., Esq., on solemn affirmation, said he had known Michael Dewalt of the township of Washington, Franklin Co., for upwards of forty years and that some time after Dewalt enlisted in the U. S. service, Dewalt came home, that is, into the part of the country now known as Washington Twp., and came to home of deponent in uniform and on furlow and showed his furlow. 23rd. Nov., 1819, Before Wm. Bleakney, Justice of the Peace for Franklin Co., come Benjamin Bitter (?) who swore he was acquainted with Michael Dewalt, an old Rev. Soldier, who served in the first Penna. Regiment commanded by Col. Menges in Capt. Prowell's Comp., then in Capt. Oldham's Comp. Franklin Co., Feb. 16, 1819. Before John Flanagan J. P. came Henry Brim who swore that in April 1778 at Abbotts Town in Penna., he enlisted Michael Dewalt and he Michael belonged to Comp. of Light Infantry commanded by Capt. Joseph Prowell, in Col. Patton's Regiment and he, Michael, enlisted for 3 years.

Letter, June 11, 1826, Staunton, Va., from John C. Somers, transmitting request for transfer. Jacket cover, 16271, states Michael Dewalt served five years, placed on roll 30 April, 1819, $8 per month, Cert. of pension issued 23 Dec., 1819, delivered to Hon. David Fullerton, notification sent Nov. 7, 1820 to A. Colhoun, Chambersburg, Penna. 43489, Invalid, Oct. 18, March, 1818. In the will of Henry Pensinger, prob. 1821, he names a dau. Rosanna, wife of Michael Dewalt. He is said to have been in Franklin Co., Va., 1820.

Penna. Arch. 2nd Ser. Vol. 13, p. 55. Vol. 3, p. 126.

ANDREW DICKEY

Served as Lieut., under Capt. Jas. Patton in 1780 and under Capt. Robert Dickey in 1781 and in 1777 as a pvt. Andrew Dickey mar. Martha Wier and he had baptz., at Mercersburg, Penna., by Dr. John King: Wm. Wier, Sept. 2, 1781; Elizabeth, Apr. 21, 1783. Presumably he moved later to Washington Co., Penna., then to Clermont Co., Ohio, where he bot 100 acres land from Robert Dickey near Williamsburg. He died prior to 1830, leaving issue: Wm.; Thomas; John; Isaiah; Margaret; Robert; Elizabeth and Isabella. Thomas b. July 4, 1790, mar. Isabella Spence; Wm. Wier Dickey b. 1781, mar. Margaret Spence in Clermont Co., Ohio; they removed to Fayette Co., Ind.

Penna. Arch. 5th Ser. Vol. 6, p. 262, 271, 284, 315, 373.

JOHN DICKEY

Served as pvt. under Capt. Thomas McDowell and under Capt. Robert Dickey in 1781.

Penna. Arch. 5th Ser. Vol. 6, p. 262, 271, 284, 285, 315, 314, 368 370, 377, 379.

PETER DICKEY

Private appears on undated rolls under Captain Charles Maclay. Deed Book Vol. 5, p. 362, shows that Peter Dickey married Mary, widow of William Walker. Deeds at Chambersburg show that Peter Dickey, late of Shippensburg (1794) died intestate, leaving issue: Thomas and John, his sons and only children. Thomas Dickey and wife Margaret; John Dickey and wife Susanna, on Jan. 22, 1793, sell land to Martin Hammond, who sold to Jacob Rotz.

Penna. Arch. 5th Ser. Vol. 6, p. 148, 150.

ROBERT DICKEY

Chambersburg Penna., Court records show in Deed Book 5, p. 312, Dec. 1, 1801, "Robert Dickey on the North Western Territory to James Dickey of Newmills, Township of Peters, County of Franklin, State of Penna. Said Robert Dickey for $2916. U. S. money paid by said James Dickey all that land in Twp., and County aforesaid, 159 acres, 104 perches, surveyed Dec. 16, 1753, on Warrant granted to John Dickey, dated May 25, 1753, surveyed by Daniel Henderson, Nov. 28, 1797, &c.; it being the same tract of land devised by said John Dickey to his son Wm. by his last will, dated May 25, 1773, and by said Wm. Dickey to his son Robert, (above mentioned) by his last will, dated Aug. 24, 1793, with houses, barns &c." The will of the above Wm. Dickey of Peters Twp., names issue: Robert; Wm. Mary; John; Andrew; Hugh and a dau. Jean, wife of David Ross; prob. June 3, 1797, with son Robert as an Executor.

ROBERT DICKEY

Pvt. in 1777 and as Capt. in 1781, 7th Co., 4th Batt., Cumb. Co. Militia.

Penna. Arch. 5th Ser. Vol. 6, p. 284, 373, 375, 272, 285, 314, 615.

ROBERT DICKEY

S. 2174 was born in 1751, in Cumberland (that part which was later Franklin) County, Penna. The names of his parents are not shown. While residing in Cumb. Co., Penna., Robert Dickey volunteered about Sept. 1, 1776 or 1777, and served two months as a pvt., in Capt. James Campbell's Penna. Co.; he enlisted the latter part of Sept., 1777 or 1778, and served three months in Capt. Saml. Patton's Penna. Co.; in the spring of 1779, he went to the Falls of the Ohio, where Louisville now stands, and while residing there went on an expedition to Chillicothe in Capt. Wm. Harrod's Co., Col. Bowman's Virginia Regt.; was in the engagement with the Indians at Chillicothe, where he was wounded by a large ball which entered his right shoulder, passed through the joint and lodged against the backbone, where it remained for two years before it was extracted. On the retreat from Chillicothe, he was in another small engagement with the Indians. He stated that he rode a horse to the Ohio River and went down to the falls in a boat. He remained at the falls until September, year not shown; then returned to Franklin Co., Penna., where he lived for 8 or 10 years; then moved to Williamburg Twp., Clermont Co., Ohio. He was allowed pension on his application executed Nov. 6, 1832, while residing in Williamsburg Twp., Ohio. He died April 18, 1842, place not shown. It was not stated that soldier was ever married. In 1832, soldier referred to his sister, Mary Hunter, and in the same year, one Mary Hunter made affidavit in Cremmont Co., Ohio, in support of soldier's claim. In 1842, John Dickey and David Hunter were admrs., of the estate of Robert Dickey.

WILLIAM DICKEY

Served as pvt., under Capt. Robert Dickey, Lieut. Andrew Dickey and Ensign John Dickey, Cumb. Co. Militia. James, Robert, John and William Dickey, being privates in the above Company. Wm. Dickey mar. Sarah McClelland at Mercersburg, Penna., Nov. 23, 1786. They had John baptized Apr. 6, 1788; Nancy, May 10, 1802; a child in Oct., 1807 and one in Sept., 1808, with John and Maria Dec. 16, 1812. Wm. and Hugh Dickey were assessed in Scott Co., Ky., in 1793, about 4 miles N. W. of Georgetown, on McConnell's Run. William Dickey died March 10, 1848, aged 91 yrs., 6 mos., 18 days. Sarah, wife of Wm. Dickey, died Oct. 6, 1819, aged 53 yrs., 8 mos. They are in a private graveyard near Harrisburg, Fayette Co., Ind.

Penna. Arch 5th Ser. Vol. 6, p. 272, 286, 315.

ANDREW DICKSON

The will of Andrew Dickson of Antrim Twp., is recorded at Carlisle, Penna., his widow signs as Agnes and they are buried in Antrim Twp., Franklin Co., Penna. He names sons, George; James; Daus: Hannah; Jean; Easter; Sarah; Son Andrew; Dau. Agnes; Son John under age. The will was dated Oct. 5, 1770; prob. June 11, 1783. The above 3 sons served in the Rev. War from Antrim Twp., Franklin Co., Penna. The tract of land in Antrim Twp., was sold to Andrew Dickson in 1768 by Robert Love and Wife Jennet, which tract he willed to sons George and James.

ANDREW DICKSON

Served as pvt., in 1780-81-82, under Capt John Orbison. It is probable that he was the son of Andrew Dickson of Antrim Twp. Family records give his birth as May 21, 1748, and state that he died in the Rev. War.

Penna. Arch. 5th Ser. Vol. 6, p. 273, 293, 307.

GEORGE DICKSON

Pvt., served 1780-81-82, Cumb. Co. Militia under Capt. John Woods and Capt. James Poe. He mar. 1770, Rachel, dau. of James McKee, of Antrim Twp., Franklin Co., and they moved to Washington Co. Penna. They had issue: James Dickson, b. 1772, mar. Miss Frazer; Andrew Dickson b. 1775, mar. Miss Frazer; Anges Dickson b. 1777 —unmarried; Mary Dickson b. 1780, mar. Joseph Burnside; Rachel Dickson b. 1782, mar. Solomon Irons; Hannah Dickson b. 1785, mar. Andrew Henderson; Elizabeth Dickson b. 1789 mar. James Stewart; William Dickson b. 1791 mar. Margaret Glenn, 2nd Margaret Astin. The will of George Dixon of "Phiate" Twp., is recorded in Allegheny Co., Penna. He names sons: James; Andrew; Wm., land the family now lives on, a stone dwelling house &c; 2 daus. Mary and Hannah the use of the chimney room; Dau. Esther wife of Solomon Irons; To James Stewart $2.00. It was dated Feb. 12, 1815. George Dixon died in 1817, and he and wife Rachel are buried 12 miles from Noblestown, Penna.

Penna. Arch. 5th Ser. Vol. 6, p. 92, 104, 76, 576, 583.

JAMES DICKSON

Served as Ensign under Capt. James Poe in 1777-78 and under Capt. John Woods 1780-81-82. He was a son of Andrew and Agnes Dickson of Antrim Twp., and family records state that he went South. His birth is given as Apr. 20, 1739. Under a deed dated May 1, 1792, James Dickson and wife Martha are shown selling the Antrim Twp., tract of land to Peter Brubaker of Hamilton Twp., Franklin Co., Penna.

Penna. Arch. 5th Ser. Vol. 6, p. 91, 103, 137, 512, 532, 575, 582.

JOHN DIXON

Orphans Court, Carlisle, Penna., June 3, 1761; no wife named. Children John; Margaret; Samuel, over 14 yrs., of age; Joseph and David under 14 years. Guardians appointed were John Holliday and Wm. Swan.

JOHN DICKSON

Died in Chambersburg, Penna., intestate, leaving 8 children, to-wit: James; Wm.; Robert; John; Samuel; Joseph; David and Margaret. In 1771, Joseph Dickson, farmer, of Bedford Co., Penna., son of John, decd., and wife Jane, appear to be selling to Wm. Dickson, another son of John, decd. John in his lifetime possessed land in Hamilton Twp., adjoining lands of Chas. and Michael Campbell. Thomas McDowell had a Patent for the land in 1737, which he transferred to John Dickson. In 1774, James Dixon, oldest son of John Dixon, with Ann his wife, sells to

Wm. Dixon; the said James Dixon, as eldest son is entitled to 2 parts. The Tract of 173 acres, now in Hamilton Twp., was from the Proprietors of Penna., to John Dixon, dated Dec. 7, 1737. In 1773, Samuel Dixon, Tanner, and David Dixon, joiner, sell to Wm. Dickson, as legatees of a certain John Dixon. John Dixon in Washington's District, Province of Virginia left a will, dated and prob., 1777, recorded at Carlisle, Penna. He names eldest brother James Dixon and his oldest son James. Next eldest brother Wm. Dixon, my part in the place where he now dwells in Hamilton Twp., Cumb. Co., Penna. 3 brothers: Joseph; David; Samuel; 4 brothers, Wm.; Joseph; Samuel; David; Exrs.: Samuel and Joseph. Joseph Armstrong, a witness, with John Hackett, John Irons.

Deed Book 3, p. 530, Chambersburg, Penna.

JOHN DIXON

Served under Capt. Samuel Patton, 1780-81-82. The above John Dixon is probably the son of Robert Dixon, whose will was probated 1796. Robert names a grandson Robert, son of John Dixon.

Penna. Arch. 5th Ser. Vol. 6, p. 278, 286, 311.

ROBERT DIXON

Pvt., Capt. Joseph Armstrong's Co., Cumb. Co., now Franklin Co., Aug. 7, 1755. In Nov. 1790, Robert Dickson says in his will "being weak and infirm in body." He names James McNaught, Sr., and James McNaught, Jr. To son John Dickson 25 pounds and large Bible. To Margaret Graham, dau. of John Dickson; To John Walker mar. to Catherine Hill (or Hile); Grandson Wm. Lather; Catherine Dickson, dau. of Wm., Dickson, Decd.; To Robert Dickson, son of above John Dickson; Lands joining John McCamey and heirs of Wm. Dickson, decd. The will was prob. Dec. 12, 1796.

Penna. Arch. 5th Ser. Vol. 1, p. 37.

WILLIAM DIXSON

Pvt., Capt. Joseph Armstrong's Company, Aug. 7, 1755. One William Dickson of Hamilton Twp., died Nov. to Dec. 18, 1784, leaving a will, naming wife Margaret; Daus., Katherine and Rachel, who were minors. The Plantation to be held for seven years. In 1806, Katherine had become the wife of Humphrey Fullerton and they were in Ohio; with Rachel Dixon, they sold 367 ac. land, Margaret Dixon having sold to John Brown.

Penna. Arch. 5th Ser. Vol. 1, p. 37.

WILLIAM DIXON

1743-1812, miller, served as pvt., under Capt. Samuel Patton, 1780-81-82. Wm. Dickson of Hamilton Twp., left a will dated Oct. 1811 and prob. Nov., 1812. He names beloved wife Agnes, who was a dau. of Andrew Dunlap of Bedford Co., Penna., 1736-1829. Their sons Samuel, 1768-1835; David 1786-1849. After naming the sons, he mentions a dau. Mary Bratton; a dau. Margaret; a son Wm., and children of dau. Agnes. He also speaks of "what land falls to my share of my brother David Dickson's estate." In the line of William Dixon, Miller, Will dated 1811; prob. 1812, in addition to children named in the will, descendants add the following: Margaret b. 1772, mar. John Falls; Mary mar. Robert Bratton. They add a son James mar. to Jane Bratton.

Penna. Arch. 5th Ser. Vol. 6, p. 279, 281, 288, 312.

WILLIAM DIXON

In a paper dated Oct. 5, 1805, the statement is made by Capt. Patrick Jack, that William Dixon was a sergeant in Col. Joseph Armstrong's Company, in the 2nd Batt., Commanded by Col. Asshur Clayton. Hamilton Twp., Tax record—1786 William Dixon owned 174 acres of land, one Negro, two horses and two cows. To each of his heirs he left 2 lbs., 6s, 6d.

History of the Cumberland Valley, p. 337.

WILLIAM DIXON

Served under Capt. Samuel Patton, 1780-81.

Penna. Arch. 5th Ser. Vol. 6, p. 279, 287.

JOHN DINE

In 1840 the age of John Dine of Green Twp., Franklin Co., Penna., is given as 96 years. John Dine, Sr., of Green Twp., says he is sick and weak of body; Dau. Polly to have maintenance as long as she lives; To James Irwin my son-in-law; Exr.: David Coldsmith; Wit: Samuel Thomson and William Youst who believed John Dine, Sr., to be of sound mind &c., prob. March 31, 1843. The Census of 1790 Franklin Co., Penna., shows John and James Dines as men with families. From the Valley Spirit, Chambersburg, Penna., Aug. 31, 1864,—"On the 18th inst. by the Rev. S. McHenry Mr. David Dine of Fayetteville to Miss Margaret Jane Aikers of Guilford Township."

Census of Pensioners, Oct., 1840.

SAMUEL DINSMORE

Pvt., roll of Capt. John McClellan's Co., 6th Batt., Cumb. Co., Militia. From Deed Book 1, p. 26, Chambersburg, Penna., dated Oct. 27, 1783, —Samuel Dinsmore, of Mecklenburg Co., N. C., sells to James Lammon (Lamon) of Montgomery Twp., Samuel Dinsmore late of Peters Twp., (now Montgomery) bought an improvement in Peters Twp., of a certain John Craig the first settler thereon, and said Samuel Dinsmore, in his last will bequeathed this to his son Samuel, who now sells for 200 pounds, to James Lammon,

199 acres. In 1769, Samuel Dinsmore and wife Mary, with Agnes and Mary, were living in District 5 (Montgomery Twp.) as members of the "Upper West Conococheague" Presby. Church. John Craig, above named, appears in same vicinity in 1769. Samuel Dinsmore had Moses baptized May 3, 1773.
Egle's Notes and Queries, Vol. 1896, p. 204.

ABRAHAM DITCH

Appears in service 1780-81, with Capt. Daniel Clapsaddle, a son of Henry and Eve Ditch.
Penna. Arch. 5th Ser. Vol. 6, p. 71, 94, 117.

DAVID DITCH (DETCH)

Son of Henry, served 1780-81, under Capt. Daniel Clapsaddle. Marriages of Dr. Robert Kennedy show: Jacob Ditch and Catherine Mowen, June 16, 1808. Peter Ditch and Betsy Hull (?) Apr. 3, 1809.
Penna. Arch. 5th Ser. Vol. 6, p. 71, 94, 117.

HENRY DITCH (DETCH)

Is shown as a private in 1780-81, with Capt. Daniel Clapsaddle. He was a 1751 taxable in Antrim Twp., and left a will dated Oct., 1782, prob. Nov., 1783. His wife was Eve, and he named issue: Henry; Abraham; John; David; Eve wife of Ullery Bluketterfer, and Ann, wife of Henry Thomas. The sons Henry and David Dutch were taxables in Washington Twp., in 1786, including Quincy Township. St. John's Lutheran Church Hagerstown, Md., Marriages: Joh. Powles and Juliana Deutch, May, 1805. Henry Deutch, and Elis. Junes, Apr. 1805. James McCoush and Susanna Ditch, Nov., 1810. James Young and Elizb. Deitch, Mar 17, 1811.
Penna. Arch 5th Ser. Vol. 6, p. 94, 116.

ANDREW DODDS

Served with Capt. Alexdr. Peebles, Third of the Sixth Batt. Cumb. Co. Militia, under Col. Dunlap, during 1779-80-81-82.
Penna. Arch. 5th Ser. Vol. 6, p. 58, 134, 136, 389, 396, 421, 433.

THOMAS DODDS

Served as private under Capt. Alexdr. Peebles, 1781-82.
Penna. Arch. 5th Ser. Vol. 6, p. 421, 433.

HUGH DONALDSON

Is shown as a pvt., in 1777, serving under Capt. Patrick Jack. In 1769, Wm. and Hugh Donaldson appear as the heads of a family in the vicinity of Ft. Loudon, the other inmates being Matthew Jameson, Jean Jameson and Wm. Bonor. Under the will of John Dickey of Peters Twp., prob. about 1775, Hugh Donaldson signs in Allegheny Co., Penna., Apr. 11, 1797.
Penna. Arch. 5th Ser. Vol. 6, p. 372.

WILLIAM DONALDSON

Served as pvt. 1781-82, under Capt. Pat. Jack. He left a will dated Sept, 1798, and prob. Sept., 1799. He was of Peters Twp., and he names wife Margaret; nephews, Andrew, John and Robert Donaldson, sons of Andrew Donaldson; Brother Hugh Donaldson's children: niece Jean Taylor; Nephew Robert Jamison; Niece Mary Hunter; Niece Sarah Jinkens; Step-dau. Mary Campbell; Nephew John Dickey; Nephew Matthew Jamison; The witnesses were John and Jas. Taylor. In will of John Dickey of Peters Twp., dated 1773, prob. 1775, he names as Exrs., "loving friends," Wm. Donaldson and Matthew Wilson.
Penna. Arch. 5th Ser. Vol. 6, p. 296, 313.

DANIEL DONAVAN

Pvt., Col. Wm. Irvine, Capt. Jeremiah Talbot, 6th Penna. Batt. Chambersburg, Penna. Court Records Will Book 1, p. 118: Late a Soldier in Penna. Line, afterwards an inhabitant of Washington Twp., lived at Jacob Tridle's in Guilford Twp. His last sickness Apr. 1787. He left his wearing apparel to his Comrade Thos. Patton. He appears to have died at the house of John Harmony,—other bequests. On Jan. 13, 1777, Daniel Dunevan swears to be True to the United States of America &c., &c. Voluntarily enlists into Col. Wm. Irvin's Regt. of foot, belonging to the 7th Regt. of the State of Penna., &c.
Penna. Arch. 5th Ser. Vol. 2, p. 246. Penna. Arch. 5th Ser. Vol. 3, p. 210.

ROBERT DONAVAN

Served as pvt., under Capt. Alexdr. Peebles and Capt. Chas. Maclay, 1780-81-82. He was mar. 1767, by Rev. J. C. Bucher, to Martha Turner; he was an Elder in the Middle Spring Presby. Church, near Shippensburg, and is said to have lived near Centre Square, Franklin County. In his will he gives to his son John land in Ohio, to reserve a privilege for James Smith in the N. W. Corner of the run to make his milldam about 5 or 6 perches up the run in my land. Son Robert 1/2 of the above tract. To my dau. Sarah Smith, wife of Jeams Smith, Esq., land in Fairfax Co., Ohio xx. To my dau. Jean Willson, wife of Robert Willson land in Penna; to son Joseph and dau. Martha the plantation I now live on, 159 acres. The silver table spoons and tea spoons to be divided equally between my four daughters except the soup ladle, which I give to Martha. Lots in Shippensburg; lots in McKeesport, and my lot over the river, opposite McKeesport; bank stock &c. Shares to be divided as follows: Son John; Son Robert; Dau. Sarah; Dau. Jean; Son Joseph; Dau. Martha; Son Wm.; Dau. Frances; Son Jeams' share to be put to interest until he comes home and if Son Jeams should not come home in the course of twelve years, I allow my Executors to divide it among my children. Mr. A. B. Dunlap gives the following: Frances mar. John Colhoun; Sarah mar. James Smith, (?); Martha b. Dec. 25, 1770, died at Greenfield, Ohio, in 1847; John lived and died near Urbana, Ohio; Jean mar. Robert Wilson, Lancaster, Ohio; William b. 1779; Robert mar. Rachel Cox; James, residence unknown in 1822; Joseph mar. Miss Beatty, inherited home farm near Shippensburg.

Penna. Arch. 5th Ser. Vol. 6, p. 148, 150, 395, 421, 432.

JAMES DOUGHERTY

Appears in service, 1780-81-82, with Capts. Wm. Huston and Saml. Patton. Deeds show the following: John Dougherty, late of Peters Twp., now Montgomery Twp., had issue of son John, who died intestate in minority. The right of property devolved on and in James Dougherty, The eldest son of the oldest brother of first named John Dougherty. Land surveyed and granted said Dougherty June 3, 1762, by land of John Davy Richard, Geo. Brown, 70 ac., 74 Pchs. James Dougherty sells to Andrew Dicson, for 40 Shillings per acre.

Penna. Arch. 5th Ser. Vol. 6, p. 277, 284, 287, 311.

JOHN DOUGHERTY

Served in 1776, with Capt. Geo. Matthews and in 1780-81, as Ensign with Capts. Samuel Patton and Walter McKinnie.

Penna. Arch. 5th Ser. Vol. 6, p. 261, 277, 298, 318.

MOSES DOUGHERTY

Is shown in service under Capt. John Orbison, 1780-81-82. In 1781 he was taxed in Montgomery Twp., with 288 acres land, 2 Horses, 4 cattle and negroes. John Dougherty of Peters Twp., left a will, at Carlisle, dated 1777, naming wife Lilly and to son Moses the plantation; Dau. Sarah wife of David Maughan; Dau. Mary wife of John Kerr; son Samuel decd., who left issue, sons James and Samuel and a dau. Mary; son John; Exrs: Wife and son Moses. Letters of Admr., on estate of the Widow, Lillie, Aug., 1777, were issued to John Kerr, and David Maughan. (The above John Kerr laid out Kerrstown, a part of Chambersburg.) Deeds show that in 1785, Moses Dougherty and wife Sidney sell a tract in Montgomery Twp., that was left by the will of his father John Dougherty, on Licking Creek, then called Lick Run. In the will of John Patton of Peters Twp., July, 1767, John and Moses Dougherty are two of the witnesses. The will of Andrew Blair, 1787-1796, names daughters Sussanna and Eleanor Dougherty, his plantation being on the Penna. and Md. Line, Carlisle, Penna. Will of John Dougherty; land to his son John; Wife and dau. Lilly, on his death bed, Jan. 13, 1764.

Penna. Arch. 5th Ser. Vol. 6, p. 273, 293, 307.

ENSIGN SAMUEL DOUGHARTY

Served under Capt. Philip Davis (6th), Lieut. Wm. Duffield, Jr., Aug. 18, 1782. In 1789, one Samuel Dougherty and wife Sarah sold to James Lawson 104 acres, 27 perches of land.

Penna. Arch. 1st Ser. Vol. 10, p. 599.

THOMAS DOUGHERTY

Of Cumb. Co. served as a Ranger on the Frontier,—John, James and Wm. Dougherty appear with him on the above page. Thomas Dougherty of Hamilton Twp., left a will dated 1789, prob. 1790, naming wife Mary; Dau. Agnes wife of James Thorn; Dau. Margaret wife of John Rogers; Dau. Sarah wife of Jas. Matthews; Dau. Eleanor wife of Hugh Caldwell; other children, James; Alexdr; Martha; Robert; Thomas; Jean. Witnesses: Geo. and Jas. Matthews, Alexdr. McConnell.

Penna. Arch. 3rd Ser. Vol. 23, p. 263.

ANDREW DOUGLAS, SR.

Is shown serving under Capt. Noah Abrahm July, 1777. The other references are for Andrew Douglas, 1779-80-82, and may refer to a son of Andrew Douglass, Sr.

Penna. Arch. 5th Ser. Vol. 6, p. 85, 127, 141, 383, 428, 515.

EZEKIEL DOWNEY, SURGEON

Sept. 11, 1757, drowned at York River, Va., July 1, 1781, 6th Penna. Cont. Line; Letters of Admr. on estate of Ezekiel Downey, (Doctor) granted to Wm. Downey, Oct. 10, 1785. Ezekiel Downey is also shown as a Ranger on the Frontier.

Penna. Arch. 5th Ser. Vol. 2, p. 598. 5th Ser. Vol. 3, p. 168. 5th Ser. Vol. 4, p. 624. Franklin Co., Penna., Will Book A, p. 46.

WILLIAM DOWNEY

The will of William Downey of Antrim Twp. Cumb. Co., Penna., was dated Sept. 28, 1784; prob. Feb. 19, 1785. To dear wife Jennet Downey her living and sustenance, viz: 2 back rooms down stairs for her and the Girls to live in during her life. All furniture that usually was kept in the fire room, together with such necessaries as may inable her to keep house or live by herself if she is so minded. 40 bus. of grain, two hundred weight of meat and ten pounds in cash yearly, 2 cows, a mare and a negro wench; Son John a tract of land made over to him by Deed together with Twenty Shillings, sterling; daughter Mary Downey 160 lbs. in cash; dau. Margaret McCulloch 130 lbs. in cash; Son Robert 300 lbs., cash; dau. Jennet 200 lbs., cash, also negro child called Hanna; Sons Wm. and Samuel balance of estate divided equally between them; Exrs.: Sons William and Samuel; Abraham Smith overseer in the settlement; Wit: Wm. Scott, James McLenahan and David Scott. The will above is from Vol. A, page 19, Chambersburg Court records. The following notes were given by a descendant: Issue: (1) Mary Douglas, b. in Penna., 1749, unmar. (2) Margaret, b. 1750, Penna., mar. Samuel McCulloch. (3) John b. 1753, d. 1825, Jefferson Co., Va. mar. 1st Ruhanna Stocksdale, 1784. mar. 2nd Mary Douglas, 1797. mar. 3rd Elizabeth Owings, 1800. (4) William, b. 1755, d. 1786, unmar. Will in Franklin Co. Penna. (5) Ezekiel, b. 1757, d. July 1, 1781, drowned in York river in Rev. War July 1, 1781. Under a list given at Trenton Jan. 20, 1781, Signed, Anthony Wayyne, B. G. (6) Samuel b. 1760 d. unmar. 1828 (?) (7) Ruth, b. 1762. (8) Robert b. 1765, mar. Rachel or Rebecca Stockdale of Baltimore Co. Md.; moved to Batavia, N. Y. (9) James, b. 1769.

WILLIAM DOWNEY

Served as a pvt., under Capt. William Berryhill, 1780-81-82. His will probated Aug. 12 1786, naming sister Mary Downey and brother Samuel Downey.

Penna. Arch. 5th Ser. Vol. 6, p. 79, 101, 123.

BARNABAS DOYLE

Pvt. in Thos Askey, 1779 to 1782. Barnabas Doyle an early settler in Path Valley, d. 1797, aged 43 yrs., buried in the Catholic Cemetery at Doylesburg. His wife was Mary McElhenny, —they had seven sons and two daus.,—Edward W.; Thomas; John; James; Wm.; Felix.; Barnabas. Judith mar. John Skinner; Margaret of Warren Twp., mar. Bivens (Beavens).

Penna. Arch. 5th Ser. Vol. 6, p. 61, 132, 394, 409, 412, 424, 442.

SAMUEL DUFFIELD

Of Welsh Run, served as a pvt., under Capt. John Orbison in 1781. He was later Dr. Duffield. He mar. Eleanor, dau. of Johnston and Rebecca (Mayes) Elliott. Dr. Duffield's estate was settled in 1810,—leaving a widow Eleanor; Wm.; Johnston; David; George; Eleanor; Rebecca; Robert; John and Susanna, the last 7 minors. Eleanor Duffield, widow of Samuel, is buried in the Presbyterian Church graveyard at McConnellsburg, Penna.. She died May 2, 1839, aged 70 years, the daughter of a Rev. Soldier Ranger.

Penna. Arch. 5th Ser. Vol. 6, p. 288, 293.

WILLIAM DUFFIELD

Of Welsh Run was Armourer for Capt. John Orbison's Co., 1780. William Duffield, 1727-1799, is said to have been in the Provincial Service under Col. Bouquet for the defense of the frontiers. He was a Delegate to the Convention of 1776. Delegate to Convention of 1776 from Cumb. Co. Penna. He left a widow, Susanna, a dau. Susan mar. to Samuel Bell, and sons; Wm.; John; David; James; Samuel; the will of Susanna Duffield was prob. in 1804.

Penna. Arch. 5th Ser. Vol. 6, p. 273. Penna. Arch. 2nd Ser. Vol. 3, p. 596. Frontier Forts of Penna., Vol. 1, p. 541.

WILLIAM DUFFIELD

Son of William of Montgomery Twp., served under Capt. John Orbison in 1780-81-82. It is thought he mar. a Miss Crawford. He left issue: George; Susan mar. Mr. Harris of Ohio; Elizabeth; Jane mar. James Walker; James; Orphans' Court records show under estate of George Crawford, 1813, that Margaret Crawford mar. Wm. Duffield; Martha Crawford mar. Wm. Davis; Elizabeth Crawford mar. James Duffield and by 1824, Polly Crawford had mar. Henry Gardner.

Penna. Arch. 5th Ser. Vol. 6, p. 273, 293, 303, 307.

HENRY DUGAN

Under Pension applications is the following: Henry Dugan came from Ireland 1760 resided in Cumberland Co., Penna. Went up to Mongohala County with wife and three children where they were killed by Indians. In Spring of 1777 he went to Kentucky to improve lands, was driven off by Indians. On return home joined the Army, beat Indians at mouth of Kanawa River. Crossed Ohio River, joined Lord Drumore at Chillicothe. Next Spring enlisted with Capt Michael Crissup in Old Town, Md., in Company of Riflemen for one year. Shortly after, the Company marched to Boston and at expiration of term was discharged at Staten Island. Later re-enlisted in Col. Malcom's Regt., of N. Y. troops for a short time and was discharged. About 1780-81, he enlisted with Capt. John Boyd, in his Company of Penna Rangers, and at the Battle of Frankstown with the Indians, Capt. Boyd and he were taken prisoners and received very hard treatment. They reached New York on Christmas Day 1782. Henry Dugan was discharged as First Sergeant from the above Company July 18, 1783, is eighty-two years of age. Under Bedford County service it is stated that Sergeant Henry Dugan, "captured by the Indians, escaped January, 1782"; of Capt. John Boyd, "in captivity, Dec., 1782."

Penna. Arch. 5th Ser. Vol. 4, p. 237, 519, 775. Penna. Arch. 5th Ser. Vol. 5, p. 80, 101, 102, 108, 109.

ALEXANDER DUNCAN

Was in service as a pvt., 1780-81, under Capt. James Young, Command of Col. Jas. Johnston. In 1782 with Capt. Terrence Campbell of Chambersburg. Under Taxables, Alexdr. Duncan appears as a hatter in Guilford Twp., in 1779-80-81-82.

Penna. Arch. 5th Ser. Vol. 6, p. 82, 110, 125.

ALEXANDER DUNCAN

Was a private in the Penna. Line; he died Apr. 2, 1822. He was a pensioner.

Penna. Arch. 3rd Ser. Vol. 13, p. 507.

DANIEL DUNCAN

Appears as a pvt., under Capt. Alexdr. Peebles 1777-79-80-81-82, command of Col. Jas. Dunlap. A certain tract of land in Southampton Twp., was granted to Wm. and Arsbald Mahan, in 1762; then to Daniel Dunckan, who with Dinah his wife conveyed in 1779 to Robert Ramsey, who conveyed in 1780 to James Dunn. In 1795 Capt. James Dunn conveys 275 acres, called "Duncan's Delight" for 1411 pounds, 10 shillings, to Christian and Geo. Charles and Fredk. Moore. Under May 28, 1790, Daniel Duncan, of Shippensburg, Merchant, and Dinah, his wife, sell land in Fannett Twp., to Wm. McClelland of Fannett Twp. Orphans' Court records May 14, 1804, show that Daniel Duncan, late of Cumb. Co., Gentleman, died intestate, leaving land in Fannett Twp., and issue: 5 sons, 4 daus., Joseph; Arnold; Samuel; John; and Jesse; Ann Elliott; Sarah Campbell; Eleanor Duncan and Mary Duncan. Ann Eliott, above, was the second wife of Robert Elliott, Adjt. of the 7th Penna. Regt., Cont. Line. He was killed by Indians in Ohio, leaving the widow, Ann, and a large family of children, then living in Hagerstown, Md. The Thomas Duncan who left a will at Carlisle, dated 1766, prob. June 13, 1776, named wife Jane, and sons: Wm.; John; Stephen; David; Samuel; Daniel. Middle Spring Church records show under membership: Wm's. heirs: Samuel; David; John and James Duncan.

Penna. Arch. 5th Ser. Vol. 6, p. 58, 136, 389, 396, 421, 433, 590.

JACOB DUNKLE

Served as pvt. under Capt. Walter McKinnie in 1781. His estate was Admr., Nov. 27, 1809. Orphans' Court shows he died in 1809 intestate, leaving a widow Susannah and issue: Jacob; Michael; Henry; John; Peter; George; Daniel; Elizabeth, also a grandson Daniel Grible, a minor child of Levi Grible, and Susannah Dunkle, who d. prior to her father. 200 ac. land in Metal Twp., taken by oldest son, Jacob Dunkle. Dunkle graves in Spring Run Graveyard.

Penna. Arch. 5th Ser. Vol. 6, p. 281, 299, 301.

COL. JAMES DUNLAP

Is shown in Command of the Sixth Batt., of Cumb. Co. Militia, in 1777-78-79-80-81-82, also Lieut. Col. 10th Penna., Cont. Line, from Major of Sixth Batt., resigned Jan. 23, 1777. James Dunlop of Shippensburg is shown as "Overseer of the King's Pastures" between 1744-1765. The following family notes are contributed by a descendant, John S. Summerville of Bellefonte, Penna.: Col. James Dunlap was born in Ireland in 1727, died at Bellefonte, Dec. 15, 1821; married to Jane Boggs, by license dated, March 6, 1762 and who died in 1812. He was the son of Wm. Dunlap of Shippensburg, came with his parents to Penna., studied Law and practiced in Cumb. Co., and was also interested in the Dunlap Furnaces in Path Valley. He went with Anthony Wayne in the Canadian Campaign; was in active service in Penna.; was at Camp White Marsh; at Chestnur Hill and the Battle of Germantown; he preferred to serve in the Field work. In 1784 he was Commissioned Judge of Common Pleas and Justice of the Peace. In 1796 he joined his son John and others in building Harmony Forge near Bellefonte. With his son-in-law James Harris he laid out the County seat, Bellefonte, where his house was the first to be erected and where he lived until his death in the 94th year of his age. They had issue: (1) William b. 1763, died unmarried. (2) Andrew born 1764, admitted to the Bar of Franklin Co., 1783; represented that County in the Legislature 1796-1800. Admitted to practice in Centre County in 1800. He was married to Sally Chambers, Nov. 18, 1790, by Dr. John King of Mercersburg. She was a dau. of Genl. James Chambers of Loudon Forge, and a grandau. of Pioneer Benj. Chambers of Chambersburg, Penna. (3) Anne, born 1768, died 1844, mar. 1790, Senator James Harris, founder of Bellefonte. (4) John, born, 1770, mar. 1797, Eliza Findlay, a cousin of Gov. Wm. Findlay. He was the most extensive land owner and energetic iron-master in Centre Co. and was killed by a fall of earth in one of his ore mines in 1814. (5) Jane, born 1772, d. in Gettysburg, 1862; mar., 1794 Rev. Wm. Paxton, D. D. who was Pastor of the Lower Marsh Creek Church for fifty years. (6) Elizabeth, born 1774, mar. 1st James Smith; mar. 2nd Michael Simpson. (7) Debora, born 1776, mar. James Johnson of Franklin County. (8) Rebecca, born 1778, mar. 1st Robert McLanahan of Franklin County; mar. 2nd Robert Steele. (9) James, born 1780, admitted to the Bar of Centre Co., 1801. Later went to Natchez,

Miss., and engaged in Cotton raising; mar. a Mrs. Dunbar and died in 1824. (10) Mary, born 1784, died 1827, mar. in 1809 Robert Templeton Stewart of Pittsburg, Va. (11) Joseph, born 1786, died unmarried.

Penna. Arch. 5th Ser. Vol. 6, p. 9, 10, 19, 56, 60, 96, 138, 150, 384, 408, 412, 429, 608. Penna. Arch. 5th Ser. Vol. 3, p. 469. Penna. Arch. 5th Ser. Vol. 1, p. 348.

ROBERT DUNN

Appears as a private in 1781, under Capt. William Strain, also in the Cumb. Co., Militia. He is shown Apr., 1833, Nov. 1835, under Penna State Pensioners.

Penna. Arch. 5th Ser. Vol. 6, p. 642. Vol 4, p. 285.

ADAM DUNWOODY

Pvt., under Capt. Walter McKinnie, 1781. Deed Book 27, Chambersburg, Pa., shows releases from the heirs of David and Esther Dunwoody; John Dunwoody, District of York, S. C.,— Henry Killen, Evan S. Harris &c of Rutherford Co. Tenn., James B. Henry of Shelby, Ill., Elias Garrison &c Dist. of York, N. C. 1836, Abigail Davis, heir of Susan Henry, Carwell Co., Tenn., James Dunwoody, Gibson Co., Tenn. in 1835, James Dunwoody, Greene Co., Tenn., 1854, James C. Baird, Lincoln Co., N. C., for Nancy and Mahala Baird, 1834, Exr. of Samuel Dunwoody, Gibson Co., Tenn., 1854, Moses Henry, Weakly Co., Tenn., heir of Susan Henry in 1837.

Penna. Arch. 5th Ser. Vol. 6, p. 281, 299, 301.

JAMES DUNWOODY

Pvt., under Capt. Walter McKinnie 1780-81, Capt. Wm. Huston, 1781. There were two (2) men of this name, one the only son of Thomas Dunwoody and wife Agnes. Their farm was sold to James Buchanan, Sr., and later sold by President Buchanan to Hon. Jeremiah Black. The second James Dunwoody was the son of Wm. of Montgomery Twp., who had sons John; Adam; Samuel; Joseph; David; and "James who has been paid his full share." The Wm. Dunwoody family attended Church at Welsh Run. The Thomas Dunwoody family attended the Mercersburg Church. Deeds at Chambersburg show the following: James Dunwoody of Franklin Co., Penna., sold to John Irwin of the town of Pittsburg, County of Westmoreland, merchant, all my tract, 310 acres, being in Peters Twp., Franklin Co., Penna., adjoining Wm. Dunwoody, James Woodson, Samuel Findlay, on the east side of the West Conococheague. John Irwin has this day became Special Bail in a action against me depending, Samuel Sample of Plaintiff, in County Court of Westmoreland. Said John Irwin to be saved harmless, Aug. 23, 1792. Signed: James Dunwoody. Before George Wallace, a Judge of Common Pleas, Nov. 1, 1792. Roll of Capt. John McClellan's Company, 7th Comp., 6th Batt., Cumb. Co. Militia 44 names shown and certified by Capt. McClelland—Return for 1779,—Thos. Dunwoody; Adam Dunwoody; James Dunwoody; James Dunwoody (son of Thos).

Penna. Arch. 5th Ser. Vol. 6, p. 226, 299, 301, 643. Egles "Notes and Queries" Vol. 1896, p. 204.

JOSEPH DUNWOODY

Pvt. under Capt. Walter McKinnie, 1782. He was a son of Wm. and Esther (Rankin) Dunwoody. He died unmar., in 1824. He had an unmar. Sister Esther who died in 1838.

Penna. Arch. 5th Ser. Vol. 6. p. 306.

SAMUEL DUNWOODY

2nd Lieut., May, 1778. His Captain was Robert McCoy who was killed at Crooked Billet in 1778. Samuel Dunwoody served in 1780-81-82, as a pvt., under Capt. Walter McKinnie. He was a son of David and Esther Dunwoody.

Penna. Arch. 5th Ser. Vol. 6, p. 266, 298, 300, 305, 378, 643.

THOMAS DUNWOODY

Pvt., under Capt. Walter McKinnie, 1781-82. He died June 1782, leaving a widow Agnes; Son James and daus. Anne; Sarah; Agnes. Anne Dinwoddie mar. James Steritt, Sept. 12, 1788; Sarah Dunwoody mar., Wm. McClelland. The will of Agnes, widow of Thos. Dunwoody was probated Jan. 26, 1826. The legatees were her dau. Sarah McClelland and her children, John; Ruth; Nancy; James; Sidney.

Penna. Arch. 5th Ser. Vol. 6, p. 298, 300, 305.

WILLIAM DUNWOODY

Pvt., 1778. The Presbyterian Church records at Mercersburg, Penna., show that Wm. Dunwoody was killed at Crooked Billet in 1778, where he was serving under Capt. Robert McCoy.

Penna. Arch. 5th ser. Vol. 6, p. 375.

SAMUEL DREADEN (DRYDEN)

Served as pvt., in 1780-81, under Capts. James Young and Joseph Culbertson. Leaving Chambersburg, his will shows him to have removed to McConnellsburg, his will probated Apr. 15, 1816. He names wife Martha, and Son Samuel; Daus: Mary, wife of John Little; Elizabeth, wife of John McClintock; Martha; Margaret; Rebeckah; and Hannah not yet eighteen; Son James, and requests that the family go to Pittsburgh. Under the date of Dec. 16, 1834,—The Franklin Repository gives: Died on 10th inst., at the house of her son-in-law,

OF FRANKLIN COUNTY PENNSYLVANIA

John Little, in Pittsburgh, Mrs. Martha Dryden in her 78th year.
Penna. Arch. 5th Ser. Vol. 6, p. 82, 290.

THOMAS DRENNIN

Was in service as Sergt., 1777-78, with Capt. William Findley and John Jack, command of Col. Abraham Smith. William and Thomas Drennan were freemen in Washington Twp., in 1780.
Penna. Arch. 5th Ser. Vol. 6, p. 518, 527, 596.

WILLIAM DRENNON

Appointed Corporal, Oct. 25, 1776. Hugh and Thos. Drennon enlisted as privates in the same Company. William Drenan was in service 1778, under Capt. Wm. Findley and he and Thomas Drennon were freemen in Washington Twp., in 1780. William and David Drennan were in the Cont. Line, from Cumb. Co., Penna.
Penna. Arch. 5th Ser. Vol. 2, p. 231. Penna. Arch. 5th Ser. Vol. 6, p. 527, 530, 596. Penna. Arch. 5th Ser. Vol. 4, p. 285, 624, 845.

ALEXANDER DRUMMOND

Was in service 1780-81, under Capt. Thos. Askey, also in the Cont. Line from Cumb. Co., Penna. Court records in Franklin Co., Penna., fail to show data on Drummond, but one William Drummond left a will in Allegheny Co., 1785, naming wife Margaret; son Alexander "if he ever returns;" in case he fails to return the property to go to "sister's son James Wright."
Penna. Arch. 5th Vol. 6, p. 131, 394, 424. Penna. Arch. 5th Ser. Vol. 4, p. 285, 624.

JAMES DRUMMON

Appears as Ensign with Capts. John Jack and James Poe, 1777-78-79, also in service in 1781-82, under Capt. Thos. Johnston. James and Samuel Drummon were taxables in Antrim Twp., each having 100 acres of land and horses, 1778-82.
Penna. Arch. 5th Ser. Vol. 6, p. 114, 129, 511, 520, 523, 525, 532, 539.

SAMUEL DRUMMON

Was in service 1777-79-80-81-82, with Capts. John Jack and James Young, a taxable in Antrim Twp., commmand of Col. Jas. Johnston and a freeman over a period of years.
Penna Arch. 5th Ser. Vol. 6, p. 83, 113, 129, 520, 539.

BENJAMIN DYSART

Is shown in service with Capt. Wm. Moorhead, 1779-80-81-82. Benj. Dysart and Mary Dysart are shown in the list of members of Middle Spring Church and in Thos. McClelland's District, in 1776.

Penna. Arch. 5th Ser. Vol. 6, p. 66, 401, 405, 414, 440.

JAMES DYSART

Gave service as a pvt., 1779-80-81-82, with Capts. Wm. Moorhead and Thomas Askey.
Penna. Arch. 5th Ser. Vol. 6, p. 66, 405, 401, 414, 440, 631.

DANIEL EARLY

Served as pvt., 1777 under Capt. Geo. Crawford. In 1780-81-82 under Capts. James Young and Terence Campbell. In Deed Book 9 p. 157 is a deed showing land in Letterkenny Twp., Torrence land, from Thos. Cowan and wife Jean to Daniel Early in 1783; In 1785 Daniel Early and wife Ann sold to Robert Lee. In 1787 Robert Lee and wife Elizabeth sell the tract to Gabriel Gordon of Letterkenny Twp. Franklin Repository, Chambersburg, Penna., Sept. 16, 1817. Died at his seat in Green Co., Georgia, on 15th ult., Peter Early, late Governor of that State.
Penna. Arch. 5th Ser. Vol. 6, p. 81, 109, 110, 125, 371.

DAVID EARLE

Pvt., served under Capt. John Campbell and Lieut. Wm. Strain.
Penna. Arch. 5th Ser. Vol. 6, p. 143.

JOHN EARLY

Served as pvt., 1779-80, under Capts. John Rea and Joseph Culbertson. Dr. Denny of Chambersburg married Samuel Early to Polly Crocket, June 28, 1810, and John Nixton to Eliza Early, Oct. 27, 1812. The following Earleys are buried in Zion Reformed Graveyard, Chambersburg, Penna.: Thomas J., 1804-1869; Sarah, 1805-1868; Robert, 1834-1865; Nancy, 1835-1867; Thomas J., 1846-1848; Louisa, 1851-1857.
Penna. Arch. 5th Ser. Vol. 6, p. 72, 78, 290, 544.

WILLIAM EARLY

Served under Capt. John Rea, as Corporal, undated rolls.
Penna. Arch. 5th Ser. Vol. 6, p. 584.

JOSEPH EATTON

1756-1832, Penna. Rifleman at seige of Boston. Battles, Long Island, Brandywine, Germantown, Valley Forge, Monmouth,—born in Franklin Co., Penna., died in Guernsey Co. Ohio, mar. Jeanet Ramsey. Served as pvt. under Capt. Samuel Patton, 1780-81-82.
Penna. Arch 5th Ser. Vol. 6, p. 277, 286, 288, 311. D.A.R. Lineage Book Vol. 66, p. 5.

ANDREW ECKLES

Served as pvt. under Capt. Patrick Jack, 1781-82. He was a son of Charles Eckles who died 1781. Andrew mar. Mary dau. of James Crow and wife Catherine, all of Hamilton Twp.; he was in Franklin Co., in 1807, and in Bedford as an innkeeper in 1808. Mary (Crow) Eckles had a sister Janet, who mar. John Hamilton. The widow of James Crow mar. James Morton.

Penna. Arch. 5th Ser. Vol. 6, p. 293, 297, 313.

ARTHUR ECKLES

Pvt. in Col. Wm. Thompson's Batt of Riflemen in 1775. He re-enlisted and resided in Cumb., Co., in 1809. He married Ruth, dau. of George Jordan, an early settler in Antrim Twp., whose estate came before Court at Shippensburg in 1763. Arthur Eckels is shown in the Cont. Line from Wash. Co. Penna., entitled to Deprec. Pay, also Capt. Nehemiah Stokely's Co., 8th Penna. Regt.; Col. Daniel Brodhead, Corp. Arthur Ackles 3 years; Oct., Nov., Dec., 1778 and Jan., 1779 on guard at Block House.

Penna. Arch. 5th Ser. Vol. 2, p. 28. Penna. Arch. 5th Ser. Vol. 4, p. 389, 698. Penna. Arch. 5th Ser. Vol. 3, p. 338, 342.

DANIEL ECKLES

Served as a pvt., under Capt. Patrick Jack in 1780-81. He occupied pew 6 in the old Log church at Rocky Spring, with Joseph Henderson and Robert Caven. In 1800 when Rev. Francis Herron took the charge, Daniel Eckles is shown in pew 53 with Joseph Eaton. He, also was a son of Charles Eckels.

Penna. Arch. 5th Ser. Vol. 6, p. 313, 296.

JAMES ECKLES

Son of Charles Eckels, served as pvt. under Capt Thomas McDowell and Capt. John Jardon. Mr. H. E. Eckles of Chicago states that perhaps all the Eckles family of today in Cumberland Co., Penna., descended from the early Nathaniel and Francis Eckles.

Penna. Arch. 5th Ser. Vol. 6, p. 200, 316.

WILLIAM ECKELS

Served as pvt. under Capts. Samuel Patton and Patrick Jack, in 1780-81-82. William Eckels mar. Mary, late widow of Thomas Armstrong, decd., so shown on June 11, 1782. In 1796, she had become Mary Satimore. Wm. Eckels was a son of Charles Eckels. He moved to Bedford, and is said to have had issue: Thomas; Samuel; James and John.

Penna. Arch. 5th Ser. Vol. 6, p. 278, 311.

THOMAS EDMONDSON

Was a pvt., under Capt. John Orbison in 1780-81-82. Deeds show the following,—Oct., 1793 Thomas Edmiston (farmer of Burben Co., Ky., appointed the Atty., of Robert Edmiston of above County and State,) of one part; and Thos. Edmiston, Sr., of Franklin Co., Penna. The said Thos. Edmiston, Jr., for 110 pounds to him paid by Thomas Edmiston, Sr., confirms to Thos, Sr., a certain plantation in Montgomery Twp., Franklin County, 111 acres, 19 pchs., (being part of 2 tracts of land, one in right of Nathaniel Alexander, name of "Three Cousins," formerly thought to be in County of Frederick, State of Md., but now in Penna. The other part in right of Elias Alexander). Thos. Edmiston later sells above to Wm. Davis. Thomas Edmiston, pvt., P. M. appears as a pensioner, Gerrard Co. Ky., aged 73, Jan. 31, 1834.

Penna. Arch. 5th Ser. Vol. 6, p. 274, 294, 307.

ABRAHAM ELDER

Served 1777-79-81-82, under Capts. Noah Abraham and Thomas Askey. He is probably the Abraham Elder who mar. Susanna Ardery of Fannett Twp.; her sister Elizabeth mar. George Armstrong.

Penna. Arch. 5th Ser. Vol. 6, p. 140, 383, 408, 423, 429, 441, 515.

DAVID ELDER

Two men named David Elder were serving from Fannett Twp.; David of the Mountain and David of the Creek during 1777-78-79-80-81, in service with Capts. Noah Abraham and Thos. Askey. David is said to have been in one of the expeditions against the Indians in the Western territory. He mar., Jane, dau. of Andrew Boggs, an early settler in Bald Eagle Valley, leaving 5 sons and three daughters. Robert, eldest son, was the only one who located in Indiana Co., Penna. From the History of the Presbyterian Church of Path Valley, Franklin Co., Penna.: "A Deed from John Penn for 4 acres of land joining David Campbell, and James Montgomery, including part of the Spring Run, in Fannett Twp., for a meeting house of religious worship and for a burial yard. Patent to John Blair, Randall Alexander, David Elder and James Montgomery and their heirs in trust for use as above," June 21, 1765. Survey June 9, 1768.

Penna. Arch. 5th Ser. Vol. 6, p. 34, 384, 394, 409, 515.

JOHN ELDER

Mount, appears in a "Class Roole" of Capt. Thos. Askey's Company, also with Capt Noah Abraham, during 1778-80-81-82, command of Col. Jas. Dunlap.

Penna. Arch 5th Ser. Vol. 6, p. 41, 423, 441, 408, 620.

ROBERT ELDER

Came to America from Ireland about 1750, located in Path Valley, Franklin Co., Penna., with his wife Elizabeth Watt. He had two sons David and Abraham, and his wife dying, he mar. a second time; they had sons: John; Matthew; Robert; Samuel; and Joseph. Joseph died in the Ligonier Valley in 1858. David and Abraham removed to Half-Moon Twp., Centre Co., Penna. Abraham dying there about 1825. David removed to Spruce Creek, Huntingdon County in 1796, dying in 1823. In the will of Robert Elder of Fan-Twp., yeoman, dated Oct., 1799, prob. Apr., 1807, he gives to sons Joseph and Samuel "the plantation I now live on"; dear wife Mary to be maintained by son Samuel and when she has grown to a frail state, said Samuel is to provide a girl, at his own expense, to attend her with sufficient firing &c.; son David all my wearing apparel and 40 pounds in cash; son Abraham of Huntingdon County 40 pounds; son John 30 pounds; son Robert 5 pounds; son Matthew 13 pounds, 5 shillings; Exrs: sons Joseph and Samuel.

Caldwell's Hist. of Indiana Co., Penna. p. 460.

ROBERT ELDER

Of Fannett Twp., died Aug., 1804; wife Susanna; children to be supported; oldest son Robert; second son William; Exrs: John Elder, John and James Alexander. Wit: Joseph and Matt. Elder and John Campbell.

Chambersburg, Penna., Will Book B, p. 207.

SAMUEL ELDER

Shown in service with Capt. Noah Abraham, 1777-78-79-81-82, in the first Call, July 31, 1777. Samuel Elder and Robert McQuire appear repeatedly side by side, true "buddies," in modern terms, the only exception, under the First Call, where they were listed alphabetically.

Penna. Arch. 5th Ser. Vol. 6, p. 36, 42, 407, 121, 128, 141, 384, 515, 658.

WILLIAM ELDER

Served as Ensign, with Capt. Thos. Askey, from 1777 to 1782, Command of Col. Jas. Dunlap. In the Will of Thos. Barr of Lurgan Twp., 1797, he names three daus.: Sarah Elder; Elizabeth Walker and Mary Patterson; Sarah Elder, wife to Wm. Elder, Esq., decd., declines to admr., on the estate of her husband March 14, 1797; Witnesses were Sam. Thompson; T. Barr, and letters of Admr. were granted to David Elder, March 16, 1797. Sureties: Samuel Patton and James Jack.

Penna. Arch. 5th Ser. Vol. 6, p. 27, 43, 60, 62, 131, 387, 408, 422, 441.

May 18, 1778, June, 1778 and Feb., 1779, A Petition from the Inhabitants of Path Valley, to the Executive Council of Penna., To contribute to our assistance by sending us some quantity of Rifled guns and amunition because M'skets is of very little use in the woods against Indians. This, our petition, we commit to our very trusty friends, Capt. Noah Abraham and James Elder, in whom we very mutch Confide,—Signers: Wm. Elder, Ens'n; David Elder; David Elder, Jr.; John Elder. The 2nd petition, of a similar nature, was signed by John Elder; David Elder; David Elder, Jr.; Robert Elder. The 3rd Petition in 1779 had about 140 signers and was signed by John Elder; John Elder, Jr.; David Elder; Wm. Elder; Robert Elder; Abraham Elder; Tho. Elder; David Elder, Sr. The 2nd Petition is ended as follows: This is to sertify that ye Inhabetens of Fannett Twp., has Intrusted this Pittishen to ye bearer, David Elder, James Ardery, Robert Elder, Richard Coulter, Lt.

Penna. Arch. 2nd Ser. Vol. 3, p. 166, 167. Penna. Arch. 2nd Ser. Vol. 3, p. 185, 186. Penna. Arch. 2nd Ser. Vol. 3, p. 319, 320.

COMMODORE JESSE D. ELLIOTT

Born, Hagerstown, Md., July 14, 1782; appointed a midshipman, Apr. 2, 1804, by President Jefferson; promoted to a lieutenancy, April 10, 1810. In 1812, he was attached to the command of Commodore Isaac Chauncey at Sackett's Harbor. On the declaration of war against Great Britain he was sent to the upper lakes to purchase naval vessels and make preparations for the creation of a naval force on those waters. In October, 1812, while at Black Rock, he commanded a boat expedition which, in the night, boarded and captured two British brigs lying under the guns of Fort Erie. For this he received the thanks of Congress, $12,000. for himself and his men, and a sword which was presented to him by the President of the United States. In July, 1813, he was promoted and in command of the Niagara. At Perry's victory, September, 1813, he was second in command and received for his gallantry a gold medal from Congress. In October, 1813, he succeeded Commodore Perry in command on Lake Erie. In 1815, was in command of the Ontario on the Mediterranean Squadron. March 17, 1818, he was promoted to the rank of Captain, and till 1842, was engaged in locating light-houses, dockyards, and fortiforcations on the coast. As a commodore he commanded the West India squadron, the Charlestown navy yard, the Mediterranean squadron and the navy yard of Philadelphia. His home was for many years in Carlisle, Penna. He died in Philadelphia, Dec. 18, 1845.

Centennial Memorial Presbytery of Carlisle, p. 343.

Fannett Township, formed in 1761, originally embraced the territory now within the township of Metal. Path Valley was in old times called the "Tuscarora Path" and the Indian title was only extinguished by the treaty with the Six Nations, at Easton, Oct. 23, 1758. It was here at "Elliotts," a Fort was erected, with an Officer and 20 men, for the winter season of 1764. "Three or more lovely springs come gushing up here and there, and Marsh run sends its curves through the entire farm." An old stone wall survives to tell the tale; as yet, no Tablet to mark the spot. Survey Books show a warrant to John Elliott for 150 acres May 14, 1755, also a warrant to John Elliott, Jr., for 176 acres which he conveyed to John Elliott, Sr., June 5, 1762, with William and Robert Elliott as neighbors. A Deed gives the following: John Elliott, Sr., of Fannett Twp., and Francis, his wife, sold to James Morton of Bedford Co., Penna., for 50 pounds, 100 acres land granted to John Elliott, June, 1762, between the burnt Cabbins and the road that goes from Path Valley to the "Shades of Death" at the foot of Tuscaroro Mountains.

WILLIAM ELLIOTT

Son of Robert of Hamilton Twp., served as First Lieut. under Captains Joseph Culbertson and William Huston 1777-78. He served as private 1780-81-82. In 1769, William Elliott was living with his brother Johnston within the bounds of the "Upper West Cononocheague" Presby. Church of Mercersburg. He mar. Ruth Crawford, born Nov. 11, 1754, dau. of Edward Crawford of near Fayetteville, Pa. Baptisms for William Elliott by Dr. John King: Eleanor, Apr. 19, 1778; Betsy, June 10, 1781; Child, Feb. 13, 1783; Rebecca, Oct. 25, 1800; child for Mrs. Elliott, March, 1802. Mr. J. V. Thompson, of Uniontown, Penna., has a list of eleven children which he credits to the above William Elliott. William Elliott moved to Western Penna., where he was killed by the limb of a tree falling on him. A Westmoreland County Hist., states: John C. Plummer, b. 1788, mar. 2nd Dec., 1828, Maria Elliott of Fayette Co., Penna., whose parents Col. William and Ruth (Crawford) Elliott removed from Franklin County and settled near Brownsville, Penna. The youngest dau. Miss Ruth Elliott owns and lives in the old home in W. Newton. In Rohoboth Church Cemetery Rostraver Twp., are the graves of Capt. Wm Elliott, d. March 20, 1804, aged 54 years, his wife Ruth d. July 2 1830, aged 76 years.

JOHNSON ELLIOTT

Served as a private under Capt. William Huston, 1780-81. He was a Viewer of fences in Hamilton Twp., in 1768, a Grand Juror in 1770, and Constable in 1775. Johnston Elliott died Dec. 1802; his wife was Rebecca, dau of Andrew Mayes of Lancaster Co., Penna.; she died April 1813 at the home of Mrs. Shannon. They had issue: Rebecca Elliott mar. David Duffield; Andrew Maise Elliott, Mary Elliott mar. Samuel Shannon in 1805; James Elliott, Johnston Elliott, Barbara Elliott, William Elliott, Susanna mar. Samuel Davies, Elinor mar. Dr. Samuel Duffield, Jane mar. James Wilson.

Penna. Arch. 5th Ser. Vol. 6, p. 275, 282.

JOHN ELLIOTT

Quarter Sessions Docket, Carlisle, Penna., John Elliott Constable in Fannett Twp., in 1765. John Elliott was in Fannett Twp., in 1755, as shown in surveys, and he appears to have gone there with Richard Childerstone (Chillison) where they jointly took up land in 1761. St. Paul's Church Phila. records the marriage of Richard Childerstone to Frances Knot, July 27, 1764. The first wife of John Elliott is said to have been Patience Quigly (?) and he married as second wife, Frances, widow of Richard Chillison, as he gave it in his will. After years of search and study on the line of John Elliott above, the following is considered as authentic: To wife Frances the third of all my movable property, and one mare to be chused by her out of all I have &c. My dau. Margaret. She appears to have married Garrett Pendergrass, the younger, "late of Bedford Co., who was killed at Harrodsburg, Ky., March 28, 1777. Bedford Co., Penna., May 18, 1779, Letters of Admr. on estate of Garret Pendergrass, late of Bedford Co., Penna., were granted to James Elliott, highest creditor. They had a son Jesse, born prior to 1777, who mar. Patsy Moore, in Shelby Co., Ky., Apr. 24, 1797. (2) Garrett Elliott Pendergrast, b. 1776 at Harrodsburg, died 1850 at Louisville, Ky. (3) Patience Pendergrast mar. in Shelby Co., Ky., Sept. 18, 1797, Thomas Theobald. Her brothers Jesse and Garrett Pendergrast were her witnesses: (4) Polly Pendergrast, no record. Margaret Pendergrast, after the death of her husband Garret, about 1782 or '83 mar, a man named Wilson, and the Wilson-Elliott descendants say he was William Wilson, brother of Capt. Robert Wilson who had mar. Jane Elliott. Court records of Jefferson Co., Ky., show that Jesse Pendergrass, an infant son and heir of Garrett Pendergrass, decd., made proof by the Oath of Margaret Pendergrass, widow, of said decendent, that the said Garrett acted under a warrant or brevet as second in command of a company of guides to the Armies Commanded by General Forbes, in the year 1758, and by General Stanwix in 1759. That he was engaged in the said service by Col. Adam Steven and continued therein till he was regularly discharged. "To my son James Elliott." Under Provincial Officers for Cumb. Co., Penna., James

Elliott appointed Justice of the Peace, May 9, 1767. "To my son John Elliott." The data which follow were obtained from the papers on file in pension claim, S42701, based upon the Revolutionary War service of John Elliott: The date and place of birth and the names of the parents of John Elliott are not shown. While a resident of Cumberland County, Penna., he was commissioned Jan. 3, 1777, Lieut. in Capt. Benjamin Burd's Company, Colonel Cadwalader's and Lieut. Col. William Butler's Fourth Penna. Regt.; was in the battles of Brandywine, Paoli and Germantown and served to March or April, 1778. He was allowed pension on his application executed August 12, 1818, while a resident of Allegheny Co., Penna. On Aug. 8, 1820, he was a resident of Canton, Stark Co., Ohio, and aged seventy-five years, eight months and seventeen days. His wife, Catherine, maiden name not given, was then aged about fifty-five years. There are no further family data. The soldier, John Elliott, died in August, 1826, place not stated.

"To my son William Elliott," I bequeath my silver watch. This is William Elliott, Esq., who married Rosanna Craig. It is proven by a deed from John Elliott, Township of Fannett, Farmer, to "my son William Elliott, 200 acres, land in the Northermost end of my tract of land." This was in 1768 and doubly interesting as it bears the signature of both Patience and John Elliott. VI. "To my dau. Mary." No data. VII. "To my dau. Barbara." She appears to be the wife of William Elliott of the Bullock Penns. William Elliott of Path Valley was recommended for a Magistrate, Cumb. Co., in 1771. William Elliott, a Cumb. Co., Delegate to the Provincial Conference, Carpenter's Hall, Phila., June 18, 1775. Account of the Treasurer of Penna., Paid per order of Council to William Elliott, Esq., for 8 days attendance in Conference of Committee, 1776, 11 pounds, 7 shillings, 8 pence. William Elliott, Esq., was married to Rosanna Craig, Feb. 4, 1774, by Rev. John King, Mercersburg, Penna. They had issue: Ephriam Elliott; John; William; Elizabeth; Benjamin; Patience; Samuel; Martha; Rosanna; Alexander. VIII. "My son Benjamin," having received a sufficiency of my substance xx. This undoubtedly is Benjamin Elliott of Huntingdon Co., Penna., who, heretofore, has been confused with Benj. son of Robert Elliott of Peters Twp. (See records of Benj. and George Elliott of Peters Twp., Franklin Co., Penna.) The will of Benj. Elliott of Bedford Co., Penna., of 1791, added confusion, by reason of his houses, lands and the like. He names William Elliott of Path Valley as a nephew and Executor. Benjamin Elliott, son of John of Fannet Twp., mar. 1st Mary Carpenter, of Lancaster, Apr. 9, 1776; issue: Martha; Mary and James. He mar. 2nd at Mercersburg, Penna., Oct. 27, 1785, Sarah Ashman, and had issue: Eleanor; Harriet; Matilda. He mar. 3rd Susan Haines and had issue: Patience; Louisa; Benjamin and John. He is said to have been born in 1752 and died March 13, 1835. The above interpretation fulfills the statement that Benj. Elliott left home because a stepmother came into family. From Vol. 3, of the Penna. Magazine, p. 325, we quote: Benjamin Elliott of Huntingdon, chosen to Penna. Constitutional Convention from Bedford Co., July 15, 1776. Sheriff of Bedford Co., Oct. 31, 1785, Commission signed by Benj. Franklin. Sheriff Huntingdon Co., Oct. 22, 1787. Delegate to Fed. Constitutional Convention, Nov. 20, 1787. Lieut. of Huntingdon Co., Nov. 23, 1787. Treasurer, Huntingdon Co., 1789 and 1799. Member of Supreme Executive Council, Dec. 29, 1789. Justice of Court of Common Pleas under Constitution of 1776. Associate Judge of Huntingdon Co., Aug. 17, 1791. Brigadier-general of Militia, 1796. County Commissioner, 1800.

Penna. Arch. 2nd Ser. Vol. 9, p. 808. 1st Ser. Vol. 4, p. 409. 2nd Ser Vol. 3, p. 594. 3rd Ser. Vol. 7, p. 225. 2nd Ser. Vol. 9, p. 809.

ROBERT ELLIOTT

Was Commissary in the service of the United States and employed to take supplies to the Army of General Wayne during his Indian Campaign in Ohio, 1792-1794. He was killed by a party of Indians near Fort Washington, Ohio (now Cincinnati) Oct. 6, 1794, while enroute with supplies for the Army at Fort Recovery, Ohio, or as stated in some accounts, Fort Wayne, Indiana. In Feb. of 1804 Congress granted the sum of $2000. to Ann Elliott in recognition of the loss of property incurred by her husband employed on Government service at the time of his death. He was Chief Quarter Master of General Wayne's Army. Robert Elliott was the son of John Elliott and wife Patience of Fannett Twp., Franklin Co., Penna., whose will was dated Oct. 5, 1781. Robert Elliott mar. 1st Jean Wilson, July 6, 1773, at Mercersburg, Penna., by Rev. John King. He mar. 2nd "Anne Duncan, First Baptist Church of Phila., March 16, 1781, Robert Elliott, Merchant, he of Phila. and Ann Duncan, she of Shippensburg, Cumb. Co., Penna." Robert Elliott left issue: Robert; Patience, who mar. Callender Irwine, Esq.; Wilson; William; presumably above four to first wife. He left also Daniel; Harriet, who mar. Stephen Duncan; John; Jesse Duncan; St. Clair; Williams, a minor. In the estate of Daniel Duncan of Cumb. Co., Penna., a dau. Ann Elliott was named, who later mar. Daniel Hughes. Mrs. Ann Hughes, widow of Robert Elliott, died Aug. 31, 1825, aged 65 years, buried in the Presbyterian Graveyard, Hagerstown, Md. A monument to Robert Elliott, erected by his son Commodore

Jesse Duncan Elliott is in Spring Grove Cemetery, Cincinnati, Ohio, in a badly broken condition in 1936.

Office of Naval Records and Library Navy Department.

WILSON ELLIOTT

On Oct. 26, 1802, the "Franklin Repository" carries the notice that William Drevish and Wilson Elliott had dissolved partnership, but Wilson Elliott continues the Store in the house of Jacob Heyser. Under Nov. 30, 1802, New Store,— Wilson Elliott—A Handsome Assortment of Fall Goods, for cash or Country Produce &c, &c. In 1809, Wilson Elliott was admitted to the Bar at Chambersburg. Deeds in 1810, show that Robert Elliott of Adams Co. Mississippi Territory gives Power of Attorney to Wilson Elliott, Esq., of same, to collect from estate of the late Robert Elliott "of whom I am an heir." St. Clair Elliott of the Navy of the U. S. to John Hamon of Metal Twp., land in Metal. William Elliott, heir of Robert, of the town of Sandwich, Province of Upper Canada; Daniel D. Elliott, Adams Co., Miss., sells. Patience and Callender Irwin sell from Phila. in 1808. Elie W. (Williams Elliott) of Washington Co., Md. sells. John Elliott of Allegheny Co., Penna., sells to Edward Dunn.

Jane Elliott Wilson, widow of Capt. Robert Wilson, in a sworn statement says she was married to Robert Wilson at Hagerstown, Md., by Rev. Mr. Young, on Nov. 2, 1777 (License gives Nov. 4). Before marriage she resided with her father John Elliott, who lived in Penna., about 30 or 40 miles from Hagerstown. Her husband's home was about 3 miles from her father's. Shortly after her marriage her husband took her back to her father's house; he then rejoined the army at Valley Forge. In 1820 Robert Wilson testified he was 66 yrs. old on Nov. 13th, and gives his wife's age as 59. Both testify to their emigration to Kentucky soon after 1790. Excerpts from the "Louisville Courier Journal" June 5, 1898, "Capt. Robert Wilson and wife sought a new home in this state." Capt. Wilson mar. Jean (dau. of John Elliott who was a sister of Margaret Elliott Pendergrast. Collins History of Kentucky states that Garret Pendergrass was killed by the Indians at or near the Fort at Harrodsburg in March, 1777, and a Margaret Pendergrass, probably his widow, was living at Harrodsburg between Dec., 1777, and Oct., 1778. One note states she mar. 1st Garrett Pendergrass, the younger, mar. 2nd William Wilson.

JOHN ELLIOTT

This John Elliott, to date, has been uncertain, except for one reference furnished by the late Mr. Mattern, who had spent years in searching for Penna. Pensioners. His note from Washington, D. C. follows: "I have found a reference here to a Capt. John Elliott of Cumberland Co., who volunteered from Path Valley." There was a warrant of 176 acres to John Elliott, Jr., which he conveyed to John Elliott, Sr., June, 1762, with Robert and William (brothers) as neighbors; in 1778, John Elliott, Jr., owned 48 acres land. X. "My daughter Jane." She married a neighbor, Robert Wilson, presumably at the home of her brother Robert Elliott in Hagerstown. Pension record of Robert Wilson, who died in Jefferson Co., Ky. XI. "My dau. Hannah," who is now young, and to my son Right (Wright) and my step-son or son-in-law Richard Chillison and to his sister Frances Chillison. Hannah and son Right were the issue of the 2nd wife. Hannah mar. at Mercersburg, Ephriam Harris, Sept. 20, 1791.

BENJAMIN ELLIOTT

Served as private under Captains Samuel Patton and Walter McKinnie, 1778-81-82. Under the Quarter Sessions Docket No. 2, page one at Carlisle, before John Armstrong, in the first year of the reign of King George, July 1, 1761, Robert Elliott and John Huston are recorded as Supervisors of Roads for Peters Twp., and in 1766, Robert Elliott is again on record as supervisor. On March 2, 1768 Robert Elliott of Peters Twp., made his will naming his wife Martha (who was the widow of James Barnet) his 2 sons Benjamin and George, 3 daughters, and 4 step-children named Barnet. As executors he appoints his "dearly beloved brother Benjamin," James Maxwell, Esq., and his wife Martha. The two (2) sons of Robert Elliott (of Peters) continued to live on the land left them by their father, Robert, they were taxables there and sold land left them by their father, as in 1787 Benjamin Elliott sold to Patrick Maxwell the tract on which he lived. George Elliott and wife Susanna sell in 1790. The 1790 Census places them there: Benjamin's family composed of one man, five boys, and one female. In 1791 Benjamin and George Elliott each had 170 acres land, Horses and cows and the same in 1794. Benjamin, in 1796, sells 50 acres to Matthew Spear, both of Montgomery Twp. (Deeds 4, p. 88) Benjamin then disappears from our records.

Penna. Arch 5th Ser. Vol. 6, p. 297, 300, 305, 380.

GEORGE ELLIOTT

Is shown serving in the Cont. Line, a Soldier of the Revolution. He was a son of Robert Elliott, of Peters Twp., who made his will in 1768. He was also a Ranger on the Frontier. The 1790 Census shows the family of George with

two men, one boy and three females. In May, 1798, Susanna Elliott, widow of George, renounces her right to administer on her husband's estate, and in 1803, Archibald Irwin was appointed Guardian for Peter; Hannah; George; Betsy and James, minor orphan children of George Elliott. (See marriage of James Barnet of Conococheague and Martha Rogers of Hanover, Oct. 13, 1747, Stoever's Records). The above Martha became the 2nd wife of Robert Elliott of Peters Twp. One John Elliott, born 1776, lies at Welsh Run in an early graveyard, and is said to have been a son of Benjamin. Old Ledgers show them as Cabinet makers. The name continues to this day.
Penna. Arch. 5th Ser. Vol. 4, p. 285, 625.

JOHN ELLIOTT

John Elliott was pensioned on Certificate No. 2935, issued Sept. 24, 1818; rate $20. per month; act of March 18, 1818; Pennsylvania Pension Agency; transferred to Ohio Pension Agency. He alleged that he was commissioned on January 3, 1777, Lieut., in Capt. Benj. Burd's Company, Col. Cadwalader's 4th Pennsylvania Regt.; was in the Battles of Brandywine, Paoli and Germantown; encamped at Valley Forge; left the service in March or April, 1778, when he was designated Supernumerary Officer. Date and place of birth were not stated. His age was given on August 8, 1820, as 75 yrs. 8 mos. 17 days. Names of his parents not shown. John Elliott's wife Catherine, was aged about 55 years in 1820. The date and place of her birth, names of parents, her maiden name and date of marriage to the veteran are not shown. It is not stated whether or not they had children. During his service, John Elliott resided in Cumberland Co., Penna., and returned to that county after he left the service. In 1818, he was living in Allegheny Co., Penna. In 1820, he had moved to Canton, Stark Co., Ohio. He died in August 1826, place not given.

WILLIAM ELLIOTT

The Committee of Observation for that part of Augusta County that lies on the West Side of the Laurel Hill, at Pittsburgh, May 16, 1775, William Elliott was one of a Committee of twenty-eight. This was William Elliott of the Bullock Pens. He mar. Barbara, dau. of John Elliott of Fannett Twp. They had issue: Patience; Mary; Jane; Barbara; Margaret; John; William; Robert; George; Archibald. In August, 1765, "permission" was given by Lieut. Colonel Reed, Commandant of Fort Pitt, to Wm. and Daniel Elliott to settle a tract of land located at "Seven Mile Spring," about seven miles east of what is now Pittsburgh, Penna. Daniel later sold his interest to William, who named the tract "Bullock Pens," settling there in 1766, and lived there until his death in 1807.

He is buried in Allegheny Cemetery, Pittsburgh and was aged 68 years.
Penna. Arch. 2nd Ser. Vol. 14, p. 747.

NICHOLAS ELLIS (ALLIS)

Served in 1780, under Capt. John Orbison. In 1781, he is shown under taxables as a freeman. He appears in 1786, in Mercersburg, with one improved Lot and a cow.
Penna. Arch. 5th ser. Vol. 6, p. 274.

CHRISTOPHER ELMS, DRUMMER

May 17, 1758, a full Company for the Campaign in the lower Counties by Capt. McClugham, Conococheague, Penna. In 1767, John Elms died intestate, Antrim Twp., eldest son, Christopher Elms—large tract of land—the widow, afterwards called, Catherine Thompson obtained a warrant made over to son Christopher. In the will of John Moorehead, Antrim Twp., 1775, he names a dau. Ann Elms. Deeds shows an agreement by and betwixt Christopher Elms leat of Anteetam Settlement in Cumb. County and Daniel McCurdy of the seam County, for 116 pounds I gave him an Artickle, which is lost, March ninteent, 1770.
Penna. Arch. 5th Ser. Vol. 1, p. 142.

LUDWICK EMERICK

Was in Service in Lancaster Co., Penna., 1778-79-81, with Capt. Wm. Laird, Col. John Rodgers. In 1812 Ludwick Emerick and wife Susanna sell to John Funk, Sr., for $2243.20, part of a tract of land called "Fathers Good Will," in Washington Co., Md., to a white oak sapling standing by the spring that issues out of George Menser's part of Fathers "Good Will," stones marked E. H. and E. C., 48¼ acres. Patent to Fredk. Howard, who with his wife, Catherine conveyed in 1796 to Ludwick Emerick.
Penna. Arch. 5th Ser. Vol. 7, p. 558, 942.

JAMES ENDSLEY (ENSLOW)

Served as pvt. under Capt John McConnell, 1778-82. Orphans' Court records show his death July 9, 1806, with land in Letterkenny Twp. He left a widow Mary who mar. John Knox; and 8 children: John; James; David; Andrew; Jane mar. Peter Foreman; Polly mar. Wm. Barnhill; (which last four have sold their shares in the estate to John Gilmore, Esq.); Martha mar. Samuel Little (who sold their share of estate to John Mish) and Isabella mar. Cornelius Hagerty. James Ensley occupied pew No. 20 in the old Rocky Spring Church.
Penna. Arch. 5th Ser. Vol. 6, p. 310, 375.

JAMES ERWIN

Pvt., under Capt. Geo. Crawford in 1777. This service has been accepted by N. S. D. A. R. He

is probably the same James Erwin, or Irwin, who served under Capt. Wm. Huston, 1780-81. He was known as "Clerk." On Oct. 2, 1786 he was granted land, 200 acres, on West branch of Conococheague Creek, by Pat. Campbell, James Stuart, Robert McFarland. He was b. 1742, died Apr. 14, 1819, "James Irwin, Clerk." He mar. Olivia Bard and left issue: Sons John and James; Dau. Martha mar. Wm. Rankin; Daus: Catherine; Mary; Olivia. His land is now (1934) owned by the Spangler heirs, near Mercersburg, Pa. Warm Spring road.
Penna. Arch. 5th Ser. Vol. 6, p. 367.

JOHN ERVEN

Was a pvt under Capt Thos. Johnston 1780-81. He was a son of John Erwin (Ervin) of Antrim Twp., whose will was prob., Feb. 2, 1796. He left to his son John (above) all real estate.
Penna. Arch. 5th Ser. Vol. 6, p. 84, 115.

ROBERT ERWIN

Was a pvt., under Capt. John Jack in 1778-79, and Ensign in 1780-81, under Capt. Thos. Johnston. He was a son of John Erwin (Ervin) of Antrim Twp., who had mar. 2nd, Mary, widow of James Ramsey, her two children being John Ramsey and Mary, wife of David Agnew. In the will of John Erwin, Sr., he named his two sons as: my son Robert Ewin, and my son John Erwin.
Penna. Arch. 5th Ser. Vol. 6, p. 535, 539, 83, 113.

NICHOLAS ESHWAY

Served as Sergt. in Lancaster County Militia, under Capt. Wendel Weaver. He signed the Test Oath in Lebanon Twp., May 6, 1778. Deeds at Chambersburg, show that in 1792, Stephen Caldwell sold land to Nicholas Eshway of Daffin Co., Penna., yeoman. The will of Nicholas Eshway of Letterkenny Twp., was dated Apr. 20, 1813, prob. May 7, 1813. He named issue: Barbara mar. Michael Stump; Maria Elizabeth; Sarah mar. Leonard Walborn; John; Ann Catherine; George. Ann Catherine later mar. David Schlichter. See Upper Strasburg Union Cemetery.
Penna. Arch. 5th Ser. Vol. 7. p. 140, 161, 182.

JAMES EVANS

Served as pvt, under Capts. James Poe and John Woods, 1780-81-82.
Penna. Arch. 5th Ser. Vol. 6, p. 92, 99, 104, 138, 576, 583.

CAPTAIN MICHAEL EVERLY

1st Penna. Cont. Line, 1781, of the 10th Penna. Regt., Apr. 1, 1780, retired Jan. 1, 1783; resided in Franklin County, 1787; D. A. R. Lineage Book Vol. 94, p. 71, shows he married Mary Stuart in 1781. Michael Everly was an original member of the State Society of the Cincinnati of Penna.; he had no successor and the line has not been continued. To Pres. Reed,—Head Quarters, Morris Town, 11th of May, 1780. Sir: It has been represented to me by Brig. General Irvine, and by Lt. Col. Hay of the 10th Penna Regt., that Michael Everly, a Sergeant of that Regt., was promised an Ensigncy by Col. Humpton for his extraordinary exertions in inducing the Soldiers to reinlist, and upon many other services. From the above consideration, and from the want of Subaltern Officers in the Regt., I would recommend Mr. Everly to the promotion which has been promised to him, and which, if confirmed, is to bear date the 1st of October, 1779. I have the honor to be with great respect Sir, yr. Excellency's most obt. Servant. G. Washington. Appointed May 16, 1780. Michael Everly died in Franklin County, and his estate was administered in 1794. Orphans' Court shows Martin Mercle and wife Catherine, late widow of Michael Everly, late of Chambersburg, six minor children, the eldest under 15 years. Martin Markley admr., as a Taylor and Habit maker, Apr. 18, 1797. Deeds show that in Dec. 1792, James Riddle and wife Elizabeth, sell to Michael Everly, Waggon-maker, all of Chambersburg, a Town lot for 32 pounds, also Jacob Smith of Hamilton Twp., Carpenter, and wife Christina sell to Capt. Michael Everly, for 90 pounds, Lots in Chambersburg, Numbers 15 and 16. Records of St. John's Lutheran Church, Hagerstown, Md., show the marriage of Joseph Miller and Marg. Everly, Apr. 1808.
Penna. Arch. 1st Ser. Vol. 8, p. 240, 41. Penna. Arch. 2nd Ser. Vol. 10, p. 334.

ALEXANDER EWING

Is shown serving under Capt., John McConnell, 1780-81. Alexander Ewing and Jene Anderson were mar. by Rev. Alexdr. Dobbin, Nov. 28, 1775, of Hamilton Twp., she being a dau. of Thos. Anderson.
Penna. Arch. 5th Ser. Vol. 6, p. 267, 302.

DANIEL FALLOON

Served as pvt., 1778-79-80-81-82, under Capts. Moorhead, Askey and Strain. Under Capt. Askey on guard at Frankstown. Daniel Falloon died in Wheatfield Twp., Indiana, Penna., shown in Orphans' Court in March 1809. His wife is said to have been Elizabeth Lauther (Luther) of the Fannett Twp., Lauthers. The widow states her husband left issue 12 children, minors under 14 being,—David; Margaret; Elizabeth; Robert; Mary; Sarah and Anne; Jennet and John Falloon above the age of 14, asked that Archbd. Lathers and William Fallon be appointed their guardians. In 1819 Wm. Jourdan and wife Jane released their right in estate of Daniel Falloon to William Falloon, as did, also, David Falloon; Margaret, wife of Jonathan Louther; Jennett, wife of Robert Jurden; Sarah Falloon; Ann Falloon; Elizabeth; James; Robert. Ann Falloon mar. Thos. R. Elder. A descendant adds to above list: James D.; Mattie; William.

Penna. Arch. 5th Ser. Vol. 6, p. 37, 66, 135, 401, 405, 411, 414, 431, 440. Penna. Arch. 5th Ser. Vol. 4, p. 286, 625.

JOHN FALLOON

Served as pvt., under Capts. Brady and Moorhead 1777-1779, undated rolls and under Capt. Thos. Askey. In 1785 John Falloon took out a warrant for 300 acres land in Westmoreland Co., Penna., and in May, 1786 he appears there as a taxable. His will states he was of Ligonier Twp. Names his wife Hannah and 3 youngest children, viz: James; Sarah; Ann and Isaac Sharp under 14 yrs.; Dau. Elizabeth; real estate to sons John and David; son William; daus.: Mary Laughlin; Margaret Louther; Jane Shields; Agness Piper; Martha Louther. This will was prob. Feb. 23, 1825. William (son of John Falloon) was decd. in 1837—when Margaret Louther petitioned the Court of Westmoreland County that her nephew John Fagan Falloon was a minor under 14, but he had money from the estate of his father Wm. Falloon. David Falloon's wife was Clarissa (probably Carpenter) and John's wife was Margaret. John Shields and wife Jane emigrated to Ohio. The names Falloon, Lauther and Fegan suggest Fannett Twp., Franklin Co., Penna.

Penna. Arch. 5th Ser. Vol. 6, p. 65, 8, 133.

WILLIAM FARRALL

4th Penna., Cont. Line, Apr. 1, 1777; reinlisted in artillery 1781; discharged July 13, 1783, in battles of Trenton, Brandywine and Paoli; wounded in head and arm at Paoli; resided in Mercersburg, in 1818. Nancy Farrell mar. Geradus Wyncoop, Dec. 3, 1822, at Mercersburg, Penna. John Brumbaugh mar. Margaret Farrell, Apr. 7, 1814. Wm. Farrell (Ferrell) was a pvt., in Penna. Line, was a pensioner and died June 27, 1828.

Penna. Arch. 5th Ser. Vol. 2, p. 1062.

PHILIP FAUST

The Franklin Repository, Mar. 31, 1835,—"Died on the 10th inst., in Lurgan Twp., Mr. Philip Faust, aged 75 years. Mr. Faust was one of the fast vanishing soldiers of the Revolution and took part in the battle of Long Island." The will of Philip Faust was dated 1829, prob. Mar. 14, 1835. He names wife Susanna; ten children: Catherine Binkley, eldest dau.; sons Daniel and Philip; To Lydia Nead, dau. of Mary Nead, her brothers and sisters; Dau. Elizabeth Myers; John; Susanna; Peggy; Lydia; Philip; Sally; Mary; Elizabeth; Exrs: sons John and Daniel.

JAMES FEAGAN

Born 1748 of Fannett Twp., served under Capt. Thos. Askey 1779-81-82. Capt. Askey states that he "made out the class role in yere eighty, but it was not compleat." James Fegan dying intestate, the estate was Admr., Nov. 23, 1791, leaving a widow Honour (Timmons) born 1750, and issue ten: John; Peter; Catherine mar. ———— Harkins; Thomas; Elizabeth; Mary mar. Victor Graham; Barnabas; Eleanor mar. Robert Scott Rhea; Nancy; James. In the will of Barnabas Clark, Fannett Twp., (1821). Honora Fegan is named with others, as a legatee.

Penna. Arch. 5th Ser. Vol. 6, p. 62, 132, 407, 410, 424, 442.

THOMAS FEALS (FIELDS)

Served in 1781, under Capt. Patrick Jack. He was under the Elder Samuel Templeton of the 10th District of the Presbyterian Church, near Mercersburg, and had baptized David, Sept. 1769, and a child on Apr. 3, 1774.

Penna. Arch. 5th Ser. Vol. 6, p. 293, 292.

JAMES FERGUSON

Served as pvt., under Capts. Pat. Jack and Samuel Patton, 1780-81-82. He is shown in Franklin Co., Penna., as a pewholder, "Capt. James Ferguson," in the new Brick "Rocky Spring Church in 1794. James, Joseph, Thomas and Wm. Ferguson are shown as serving in the Cont. Line. James Ferguson's parents said to have been James and Rachel (Walker) Ferguson; he mar. abt., 1776, Margery Denny; issue: James; Margaret; John; Rachel; and Creaghead. He died Sept. 11, 1806, and is buried Grandview Cemetery, Chillicothe, Ohio.

Penna. Arch. 5th Ser. Vol. 6, p. 292, 279, 312. Penna. Arch. 5th Ser. Vol. 4, p. 286, 436, 625, Official Roster Rev. Soldiers of Ohio.

JOHN FERGUSON

Served under Capt. John Jack, John McConnell and Samuel Patton, 1777-80-81-82. This is probably the John Ferguson of Hamilton Twp., who was a freeman 1780-81 and pewholder 1784-1800 in the Rocky Spring Church.

Penna. Arch. 5th Ser. Vol. 6, p. 20, 139, 278, 302, 309, 517, 519, 584.

JOSEPH FERGUSON

Served as a Sergt., 1777-79-81, under Capts. Thos. Askey and Noah Abraham.

Penna. Arch. 5th Ser. Vol. 6, p. 10, 59, 416, 603.

MATTHEW FERGUSON

Served under Capt. Samuel Patton, 1781-82. Parents James and Rachel (Walker) Ferguson. In 1779 James and Matthew each had 100 acres land in Hamilton Twp., which increased to 225 acres with Matt., and James as freemen in 1782. Thos. Ferguson occupied Pew No. 4, in the old Log Church at Rocky Spring,—John Ferguson Pew 30; Matthew Ferguson, with John Chestnut, Pew 41, Hugh and John Ferguson Pew 21 in the new Brick Church, and Capt. Matthew Ferguson, pew 47 in the new brick church, with Hugh and John showing in 1800 when Rev. Herron arrived.

Matthew Ferguson mar. Ann Chestnut, 1782; issue: John; James; Rachel; William; Catherine; Matthew; Ann; Margaret; James. Died Nov. 2, 1848, near Kingston, Ohio, buried Mt. Pleasant Cemetery. He was aged 99 yrs., and said to have been a brother of James Ferguson buried at Chillicothe.

Penna. Arch. 5th Ser. Vol. 6, p. 287, 311. Official Roster, Rev. Soldiers of Ohio.

WILLIAM FERGUSON

Was in the Cont. Line from Cumberland County entitled to Depreciation pay, also under Capt. Thomas McDowell, undated roll. A Deed shows a conveyance from Wm. Ferguson, Executor of Wm. Dickson, to the two (2) daus., of William Dickson. A deed in 1791 shows Margaret Dickson (presumably widow of Wm.,) Wm. Ferguson and wife Sarah, James Ferguson and wife Margaret. One James Ferguson died leaving issue,—Margaret; Wm; James Ferguson. Margaret Ferguson mar. Wm. Dickson; Wm. Ferguson mar. Sarah Ligget; James Ferguson mar. Margery Denny.

Penna. Arch. 5th Ser. Vol. 6, p. 315. Penna. Arch. 5th Ser. Vol. 4, p. 286, 625.

ROBERT FILSON

Pvt., served under Capts. Adam Harmony, Samuel Patton and Terrence Campbell, 1778-80-82. He was a taxable in Guliford Twp., the Census of 1790 showing him with two (2) boys and five (5) females. He died in 1819 aged 60 years. Elizabeth Filson, consort of John Kuhn and dau. of Robert and Elizabeth Filson, died Oct. 21, 1848, aged 28 years and 2 months. Samuel Filson died Sept. 11, 1863, aged 45 years, 2 months. The above are lying in the White Church Graveyard at Marion, Franklin Co., Penna. The son Robert Filson, left a will, prob., 1839, his wife Elizabeth, was a dau. of Capt. Conrad Snider of Chambersburg, Penna.

Penna. Arch. 5th Ser. Vol. 6, p. 538, 278, 125.

ANDREW FINLEY

Independent Chronicle and Boston Patriot, Aug. 8, 1829. At South Huntingdon, Penna. Andrew Finley, aged 79 years one of the remaining few who had command from Washington in regular service in the Revolution. The parents of Andrew Finley were John, b. Ireland 1713, mar. Martha Barclay, Middle Spring Church. In 1757, John Finley was killed by Indians while at work in his fields. Andrew, b. 1750, d. July 3, 1829, was Lieut., 8th Penna. Regular Cont., Line, mar. Jane, dau. of John Jack, of Westmoreland Co., Penna. Penna. Arch. 5th Ser. Vol. 4, p. 162.

MICHAEL FINLEY

1683, mar. Anne O'neill July 12, 1712, came to Phila., 1734, with 7 children. Archbd. Finley, a brother and family came same time. Michael and Anna had: (1) John; (2) Rev. Samuel of Princeton 1761-1766; (3 and 4) Andrew and Wm., twins; (5) Michael; (6) Martha; (7) Rev. James. (1) John, son of Michael, b. County Armagh, Ire., May 13, 1713, mar. Martha Barclay, was member of Middle Spring Pres. Church. In 1757, while at work in fields in Lurgan Twp., Cumb., County, Penna., he was killed by Indians. He left 9 children,—(1) James; (2) Clement 1735-1775; (3) Mary; (4) Michael; (5) Anna; (6) Elizabeth; (7) Andrew; (8) Samuel who served in Rev. War, and a General in War of 1812; (9) John, Captain in the Rev. War. Andrew, son of Michael, the 7th child, b. 1750, d. July 3, 1829, mar. Jane Jack, was Lieut. 8th Penna., Regular Cont. Line. He was a Squire in South Huntingdon Twp., Westmoreland Co.

Hist. of Penna., by Dr. Donehoo, p. 96. Penna. Arch. 5th Ser. Vol. 4, p. 162. Hist. of Penna., Geo. P. Donehoo Vol. 4, p. 1879. Mercersburg settled by Scotch-Irish in 1730. Peters Twp., settled by Scotch-Irish 1714-20, p. 1878.

WILLIAM FINDLEY

Grandson of a native Scotchman, born in Ulster, Ire., in 1741; he came to Penna., 1763, taught school for some years in what is now Franklin County, moving to Westmoreland Co., in 1782 and settled near Youngstown. He was a member of the State Legislature; of the Constitutional Convention of 1790, and member of Congress 1791-99 and 1803-'17. He sided with Gallatin in his opposition to the United States Constitution. In the Hist., of the Bard Family, by Geo. Seilhamer, he states that Wm. Findley settled near Waynesboro, mar. Mary, dau of John Cochran, by Dr. Cuthbertson, Mar. 21, 1769. That he was on the County board of assessors Captain of a Company of the 8th Batt., Cumberland County Associators, 1777-80, and in active service in 1778. A member of the Penna., Convention that ratified the Federal Constitution of 1787; member of the Supreme Executive Council of Penna.; of the convention that framed the State Constitution of 1790. The History of Westmoreland County states that "Wm.

Findley was a descendant of one of the old signers of the Solemn League and Covenant in Scotland; that his farm was between Latrobe and St. Vincents; a weaver by trade, he set up his loom in one of the low rooms of his first log cabin; elected to the Assembly; one of the Council of Censors." Dr. Russell J. Ferguson says, He was "of his people," a fact which endeared him to the Westmoreland pioneers; he fought for the interest of his region. "A large, beardless man with a florid complexion tasteful in garb, and wearing a large white beaver hat, he visited the mills, the stills and the sessions of the Court to converse upon current political questions." Under May 1, 1821, the Rutland Vermont Herald announces "In Greensburg, Penna., Hon. Wm. Findlay, a hero of the Revolution and many years a member of Congress,—died April 5th, 1821." The will was prob., June 15, 1821, in which he names grandchildren, the children of his son David; Mary; Nancy; Wm.; John; David; grandau., Martha; Nephew James Clerk, raised from a child; children: John Findley; Elizabeth Patterson; Elinor Carruthers; Mary Black; son-in-law John Black is named. From the Grave Stone in Unity Church yard: "The Venerable William Findley Departed this life April 5th, 1821, In the 80th year of his age."

Penna. Arch. 2nd Ser. Vol. 4, p. 41. Hist. of Bard Family by George Seilhamer. Hist. Westmoreland Co., Penna. Early Western Penna. Politics by Dr. Russell J. Ferguson, Rutland Vermont Herald.

NICHOLAS FIRESTONE

Served as a pvt., in 1781, under Capts. Robert Dickey and Patrick Jack. In 1785, Samuel Holliday and wife Sarah of Wayne Twp., Cumb. Co., Penna., sold land to Nicholas Firestone, warranted to Samuel Holliday, in 1743-1752-1768. On May 8, 1786, Nicholas Firestone and wife, Eve, of Peters Twp., sold this land to Joseph Fleeginger of Lancaster Co., Penna.

Penna. Arch. 5th Ser. Vol. 6, p. 285, 291.

CONRAD FISHBORN

Of Southampton Twp., served under Lt. Strain. His will dated 1800, prob., 1802, names wife Mary "who is to live in my house in any of the rooms she pleases and to have one of the back rooms to her own;" sons Frederick and Conrad; son Philip; dau. Barbara; dau. Elizabeth wife Benj. Kooney; dau. Mary wife of John Writ.

Penna. Arch. 5th Ser. Vol. 6, p. 142.

FREDERICK FISHBURN

Served in 1782, under Capt. Wm. Strain.
Penna. Arch. 5th Ser. Vol. 6, p. 431.

ADAM FLACK (FLECK)

Is shown in service 1779-80-81, with Capt Samuel Royer.
Penna. Arch. 5th Ser. Vol. 6, p. 90, 98, 113, 543.

FREDERICK FLACK (FLECK)

Appears in service 1778-79 under Capt. Samuel Royer.
Penna. Arch. 5th Ser. Vol. 6, p. 538, 541.

JACOB FLACK (FLECK)

Was in service 1779-80, under Capt. Samuel Royer. Letters of Admr., on estate of Jacob Fleck were granted, Dec., 1813, to Maryann Fleck. Jacob Flack of Fannett Twp., left a will, prob. Aug. 17, 1821, in which he names: Bro. Philip's dau. Elizabeth Flack. Bro. Philip's dau. Rebecca Flack. Bro. Philip's son John. Exr.: John Flack. In the will of Christian Stouffer, Taylor, of the falling spring in Guilford Twp., 1798, he gives: "to John Flack of the falling spring, of the friendship he has manifested toward me, all my real and personal estate, wearing apparel and household furniture; Exrs.: John Flack and William Bently of the falling spring.

Penna. Arch. 5th Ser. Vol. 6, p. 89, 542.

JAMES FLECK

Served as private in 1777, with Capt. Thos. Askey.
Penna. Arch. 5th Ser. Vol. 6, p. 7, 10.

ROBERT FLECK

Served in 1778, as a private with Capt. Thos. Askey.
Penna. Arch. 5th Ser. Vol. 6, p. 52.

ANDREW FLANAGAN

Was a pvt., under Capt. John Orbison, 1780-81-82.
Penna. Arch. 5th Ser. Vol. 6, p. 274, 294, 307, 308.

ELIAS FLANAGAN

Son of John, served as a private under Capt. John Orbison 1780-81-82. He mar. Mary Dunlap, Apr. 20, 1779. He was a son of John Flanagan, and in 1809, he and his wife were living in Green Co., Penna.

Penna. Arch. 5th Ser. Vol. 6, p. 264, 274, 294, 307, 308.

JOHN FLANAGAN

Son of John Flanagan of Montgomery Twp., served under Capt. John Orbisno in what appears to be a Welsh Run Company, 1780-81-82. John Alexander Flanagan is named first in the will of his father John Flanagan.

Penna. Arch. 5th Ser. Vol. 6, p. 274, 294, 307, 308.

WILLIAM FLANAGAN

Served as Ensign under Capt. Geo. Crawford, in 1777-78, and as pvt., under Capt John Orbison (Welsh Run) in 1780-81-82. He was a son of John Flanagan of Montgomery Twp. He and his wife Elizabeth were living in Washington Co., Penna., in 1809.

Penna. Arch. 5th Ser. Vol. 6, p. 274, 294, 307, 367, 376, 373, 383.

JOHN FLEMING

Served in 1780-81, under Capts. John Orbison and Wm. Smith. In 1769, he is shown with wife Agnes, and had a dau. Janet baptized in 1770; a son Samuel in 1772.

Penna. Arch. 5th Ser. Vol. 6, p. 275, 294.

MATTHEW FLEMING

Served in 1780, under Capt. Walter McKinnie. The Widow Margaret Fleming, in 1778-1782, was in Peters Twp., with 340 ac. land, Horses and Cattle.

Penna. Arch. 5th Ser. Vol. 6, p. 275.

SAMUEL FLEMING

Served in 1781-82, under Capts. John Orbison and Wm. Smith. Samuel Fleming a taxable in 1781 in Montgomery Twp. He had a child baptz., in 1773; a son Samuel in 1775; a son James in 1777.

Penna. Arch. 5th Ser. Vol. 6, p. 298, 300, 306.

JOHN FLICKINGER

Served as a pvt., under Capt. Joseph Gehr, 1781-82-83, Lancaster Co., Militia. he died March, 1833 in his 75th year, was a son of Joseph and Esther Flickinger of Cocalico Twp., Lancaster Co., Penna. John Flickinger was married to Anna Handschly by Rev. John Waldschmidt, March 30, 1784. She died in 1830, in her 65th yr., was a dau. of Henry Henchi who also served and who came to Franklin County from Lancaster County. John and Anna Flickinger had issue: John, b. Oct. 31, 1787, mar. Mary Alexander in 1815; Henry, b. May 21, 1792, mar. Elizabeth Snively in 1818; Mary b. Sept. 10, 1805, mar. Henry Stouffer, Mar. 14, 1827; Joseph b. Oct. 22, 1789, mar. 1st Elizabeth Foltz, who died May 1, 1815, aged 20 years. He mar. 2nd, Nancy Stotler; Elizabeth mar David Bare. They are buried in the old Flickinger graveyard in Fannett Twp. John Flickinger b. 1787, d. Mar. 31, 1876, mar. 1815, Mary Alexander, b. 1790, d. Oct. 19, 1849. She was the dau. of Robert and Margaret (McConnell) Alexander. They had issue; I. Jacob b. 1816, mar. Lavina Klippinger, Mar. 21, 1839. II. Margaret Ann, b. 1819, mar. David Steiner. III. Barbara Ellen, b. 1820, unmar. IV. Martha b. 1822, d. July 11, 1823. V. Susan Pym, b. 1823, mar. David Shoemaker in 1843. VI. Alexander b. 1826, d. Mar. 27, 1852. VII. Mary Jane b. 1829, mar. Hewit Wilson in 1849. VIII. Elizabeth Jane, b. 1831, d. in 1833. IX. Hetty Catherine b. 1832, d. in 1833. The above Jacob Flickinger died Nov. 11, 1884; his wife Lavina d. Apr. 13, 1901; she was the dau. of Anthony and Mary (Hess) Klippinger.

Penna. Arch. 5th Ser. Vol. 7, p. 263, 270, 295, 297, 614.

John Flickinger b. Dec. 10, 1763, d. April 23, 1821, mar. Elizabeth Ober, b. Sept. 26, 1763, d. April 1, 1848. Issue: (1) John b. Oct. 26, 1789. (2) Catherine b. March 21, 1791, d. Feb. 4, 1872, mar. Peter Reed b. June 2, 1786, d. Oct. 14, 1861. (3) Anna b. Aug. 9, 1792. (4) Henry b. Sept. 24, 1793, d. Nov. 20, 1863, mar. Sarah Bucher b. Dec. 24, 1798, Jan 9, 1879. (5) Barbara b. Oct. 20, 1795, d. 1846, mar. John Bitting b. 1785, d. Aug. 7, 1858. (6) Elizabeth b Mar. 10, 1797, d. ———— mar. David Lichty b. Feb. 18, 1796, d. Mar. 29, 1838. (7) Jacob b. April 16, 1799. (8) Samuel b. Oct. 4, 1800, d. Jan. 1, 1879, mar. 1st Anna Bomberger, b. May 8, 1805, d. Jan. 27, 1844, mar. 2nd Elizabeth Haffley b. June 9, 1811, d. Jan. 24, 1887. (9) Benjamin b. Nov. 7, 1802, d. ———— mar. Catherine Payne, b. Dec., 1813, d. Oct. 9, 1880.

Presented to Mrs. V. S. Fendrick by Mrs. Willis Flickinger.

ABRAHAM FLORA

Is shown in service 1779-80-81, under Capt. Samuel Royer, of Washington Twp. In 1786 he appears with 200 acres of land, four horses and three cows.

Penna. Arch. 5th Ser. Vol. 6, p. 89, 112, 542.

JOHN FOOSE

Served under Capt. Walter McKinnie in 1781.
Penna. Arch. 5th Ser. Vol. 6, p. 289.

NICHOLAS FOOSE

Served under Capt. Walter McKinnie in 1781. As Nicholas Fouce he was a taxable in Peters Twp., in 1781. He had a son Benjamin, baptized May 30, 1778.

Penna. Arch. 5th Ser. Vol. 6, p. 298, 300.

JOHN FORREST

Is shown as a private with Capt Wm. Huston, 1780-81. On Jan. 27, 1779, he was mar. by Rev. Alexdr. Dobbin, to Agnes Hart of Antrim Twp.

Penna. Arch. 5th Ser. Vol. 6, p. 269, 275, 282.

JACOB FORE

Served as a pvt., with Capt. Walter McKinnie in 1781-82. He was of Montgomery Twp., and had 100 acres of land, Horses and Cattle. The 1790 Census shows him in Bedford Co., Penna.,

—one man, one boy and 2 females. There was also a George Fore there with a family.
Penna. Arch. 5th Ser. Vol. 6, p. 299, 306.

DANIEL FOREMAN
Served as pvt., under Capt Samuel Royer, 1779-80-81-82.
Penna. Arch. 5th Ser. Vol. 6, p. 89, 112, 123, 542, 585.

FREDERICK FOREMAN, SR.
Served under Capt. Wm. Findley and Samuel Royer, 1779-80-81. Deed show that on Nov. 25, 1805, he left the following heirs,—Nancy Foreman, widow of Frederick renounces, letters granted to Son Frederick Foreman; Son Frederick; Susanna Mentzer; Daniel Foreman; Martin Markle and wife Elizabeth; David Foreman and wife Susanna; Elias Horn and wife Marie; lawful heirs of Fredk. Foreman. They sell to Fredk. Foreman 50 acres land in South Mountain.
Penna. Arch. 5th Ser. Vol. 6, p. 74, 89, 530, 542.

FREDERICK FOREMAN, JR.
Served under Capt. Samuel Royer, 1778-79-80. Probably the son of Frederick, who died in 1805. In a deed Apr. 1, 1812, Fredk. Foreman and Maria, his wife of Washington Twp., convey Lot No. 217, in the town of Chambersburg. Article of Agreement Jan., 1817, Fredk. Foreman, Sr., to his son Fredk. Foreman, Jr., certain land in Washington Twp., off which said Fredk., Sr. and his wife, Priscilla are to have their maintenance during their natural lives. Orphans' Court records, Aug., 1823, Petition of Ferdk.Foreman and Sarah Foreman, on Est. of Fredk. Foreman, Esq., decd., died intestate, leaving a widow Sarah and six minor children: Susanna; Jacob; Nancy; Daniel; George; Frederick. The will of Fredk. Foreman, late of Washington Twp., dated and probated March, April, 1835,—Daniel Snowberg and wife Mary; Fredk. Foreman's heirs; David Knepper and Esther Knepper; Grandson Wm. Knepper, son of Solomon Knepper and Elizabeth Knepper, decd.; Great grandchildren, James Sanks Knepper, son of Jacob Knepper, decd. Two great grandchildren Daniel and Anna Burger, heirs of Samuel and Betsy Burger, his wife. Exr.: Jacob Snowberger of Daniel.
Penna. Arch. 5th Ser. Vol. 6, p. 75, 90, 113, 542.

JACOB FOREMAN
Served as First Lieut. under Capts. Samuel Royer and John Jack 1777-78-79, and as pvt. 1780-81-82. One Jacob Foreman and wife, Hannah conveyed in 1838, certain land to John Stouffer, the land in Guilford Twp.
Penna. Arch. 5th Ser. Vol. 6, p. 541, 535, 531, 168, 124, 112, 89.

PETER FOREMAN
In Franklin Co., 1826. He was a pvt., in Penna. Militia and was a pensioner. He was 79 in 1833. The heirs of Andrew Foreman who died intestate in Franklin Co.: Peter Foreman; Geo. Waggoner and Wife Mary; Thomas Douglass and wife Catherine; John Johnston and wife Susanna; Robert Douglas and wife Rachel; Amos Moore and wife Sarah; Heirs appoint Robert Douglass as Atty., all sign Jan. 2, 1817. Peter Foreman bought and sold land in Fannett Twp. Esther, was a pensioner in 1843, the widow of Peter.
Penna. Arch. 2nd Ser. Vol. 13, p. 73.

ROBERT FOREMAN
Served as pvt., 1778-79-80, under Capts. John Rea, James Young and Wm. Long.
Penna. Arch. 5th Ser. Vol. 6, p. 528, 537, 548, 557.

WILLIAM FORSYTHE
Served in the Cont. Line from Cumb. Co., and in 1780-81-82 under Capt. Walter McKinnie. In 1781, he is shown in Montgomery Twp., as a freeman, and on Oct. 30 1781, he was mar. to Mary Brady, by Rev. John King of Mercersburg. Wm. Forsythe had baptized: John, July 25, 1784 and Ezekiel, in March, 1786.
Penna. Arch. 5th Ser. Vol. 6, p. 281, 299, 301, 306, 615. Penna. Arch. 5th Ser Vol. 4, p. 286, 625.

SERGEANT, HUGH FOSTER
6th Penna. Cont. Line, Ap. Feb. 2, 1776, under Capt. Abraham Smith. Hugh Foster mar. Mary McCullough, dau. of James and Martha McCullough, they were mar. Jan. 5, 1779 by Rev. John King. Mary McCullough had brothers, John the famous Indian Captive, and Hance, also a sister Jean McClelland. Hugh Foster had baptized at Mercersburg, by Dr. King: James, Nov. 1, 1779; Daniel, May 6, 1781; William, Apr. 25, 1784.
Penna. Arch. 5th Ser. Vol. 2, p. 230.

WILLIAM FRAME
Served in 1781 under Capt. Robert Dickey; little is known of him. He had baptized here Ann in March, 1781, and Elizabeth in July, 1782.
Penna. Arch. 5th Ser. Vol. 6. p. 285, 315.

AIRS FRENCH
Is shown serving under Capt. Geo. Crawford, July, 1777. He had a child baptized Aug., 1778, and a son Hugh, May 4, 1783, by Dr. John King. In 1786, he was taxable in Derry Twp., Westmoreland Co., Penna.
Penna. Arch. 5th Ser. Vol. 6, p. 371.

ALEXANDER FRENCH
Served under Capt. Thos. Askey in 1781, and as a Ranger on the Frontiers.
Penna. Arch. 5th Ser. Vol. 6, p. 410, 631.

ARTHUR FRENCH
Served under Capt. Thos. Askey in 1781, and as a Ranger on the Frontiers.
Penna. Arch. 5th Ser. Vol. 6, p. 412, 631.

SAMUEL FRENCH
Is shown as a private with Capt. Thos. Askey, the Command of Col. Samuel Culbertson, 1780-81-82. Also in the Cont. Line in Cumb. County Militia. He was of Fannett Twp., dying intestate in Jan., 1816. He left a widow Rebecca and eleven children: Andrew; John; Polly wife of John Taylor; William; Sarah; Jane; Else; Robert; David; Peggy and Elizabeth. Adam and George Piper were witnesses when the widow renounces and were neighbors. Samuel French had 2 tracts of land in Amberson Valley, 120 acres and 100 acres of mountain land. They joined the McVittys, Herman Myers and others.
Penna. Arch. 5th Ser. Vol. 6, p. 394, 409, 424, 442.

ANDREW FRICKER
Is shown as a pvt., in the Cont. Line, from Berks Co., Penna. In 1787 he buys land in Letterkenny Twp., Franklin Co., Penna., from John Nelson, Jr.,—signature Andreas Friker. In 1796 Andrew Fricker of Letterkenny Twp., and Maria, his wife, sell to Abraham and Jacob Crotzer, yeoman, for 800 pounds the land sold him by John Nilson and wife, Margaret, 800 pounds in gold and silver, 100 acres land—Andrew Freaker left a will in Dublin Twp., on record at Bedford, naming wife Mary and Issue: Philip; Sophia Pottorf; children of dau. Molly Deafabough; Fanny; Andrew; Mary Reed; Barbary Stake; Catherine McCalmont; children of dau. Elizabeth Rogers. $14.00 to the Lutheran Church, near Strawsburgh, Franklin Co., Penna.
Penna. Arch. 5th Ser. Vol. 4, p. 617.

ANDREW FRIDLEY — FREAGLEY
Served 1779-80-81, with Capt. Samuel Royer, Cumb Co. Militia. Andrew Freedly of Washington Twp., left a will dated and prob. 1786, naming beloved wife,—my best cow, bed and bed clothing, my stove &c.; Son Andrew the plantation, whereon I live, joining Fredk. Foreman, John Price and Andrew Snowberger,—to pay the rest of my children; Son John; Son Ulery; dau. Rosa; dau. Mary's children. The widow Catherine renounces her right to administer and Letters of Admr. were granted to Andrew and John, sons of said Andrew Freedly, Jan., 1787. Under "Valuations" 1799, Son Andrew has Land, log house and barn; Smithshop; spring house; horses and cows. Son John Land; log house and barn; Horses and Cows. Son Uly, Land; log house; Half stone barn; Stone Spring house; Horses and Cows.
Penna. Arch. 5th Ser. Vol. 6, p. 89, 112, 542.

CHRISTLY FRIDLEY
Appears in 1779, as a pvt., with Capt. Saml. Royer.
Penna. Arch 5th Ser. Vol. 6, p. 542.

JOHN FRIDLEY
Is shown serving 1779-80-81, with Capt. Samuel Royer.
Penna. Arch. 5th Ser. Vol. 6, p. 89, 112, 542.

ABRAHAM FRY-FREY
Served as private in the Militia of Cumb. County under Capt. Charles Maclay and Capt. Alexander Peebles, 1778-79-81-82.
Penna Arch. 5th Ser. Vol. 6, p. 36, 42, 58, 136, 406, 422, 433.

CONRAD FRY
Is shown in service with Capt. Alexdr. Peebles in 1779, also an undated roll.
Penna. Arch. 5th Ser. Vol. 6, p. 58, 136.

GEORGE FRY
Is shown in Shippensburg, 13th June, 1777, a member of the Company of Capt. Alexander Peebles.
Penna. Arch. 5th Ser. Vol. 6, p. 589.

GEORGE FRY (FRYE)
Was in service under Capt. Alexdr. Peebles, 1777-79-81-82, the name appearing under various spellings.
Penna. Arch. 5th Ser. Vol. 6, p. 23, 25, 28, 57, 395, 421, 433, 587.

JACOB FRY
In service June 13, 1777-78, Shippensburg under Captain Alexdr. Peebles, showing Dr. John Colhoon, Daniel Duncan, Jacob Trush. George Fry, Samuel Rippey and many others of interest in this company.
Penna. Arch. 5th Ser. Vol. 6, p. 590.

JOHN FRY
Was in service in 1780, under Captain Samuel Royer.
Penna. Arch. 5th Ser. Vol. 6, p. 89.

MICHAEL FRY
Is shown in service 1779-80, under Capt. James Young, command of Col. James Johnston. He appears with Peter Fry, as trustees in the Lutheran

Church of Chambersburg. Court records fail to throw any light on the above man.
Penna. Arch. 5th Ser. Vol. 6, p. 82, 547, 586.

PETER FRY

Appears in service with Capts. Conrad Snyder, John Rea and Wm. Long, 1778-79-80-81. On the 28th of June, 1784, Benj Chambers and wife, Jane, conveyed a lot on West Washington St., Chambersburg, to Daniel Poorman, John Immel, Peter Fry, Matt. George, John Bussard, and Michael Fry "as trustees for building a Lutheran Church in the town of Chambersburg," for one pound, ten shillings, lawful money also reserving to the grantors and their heirs "annually forever one Rose in June which is to be the annual yearly rent." In Aug., 1799, John Stump and Henry Etter admr. on the estate of Peter Fry, and under date of Apr., 1804, the heirs are shown in a deed as follows: Henry Fry; Peter Fry, Jr.; Henry Etter and wife Mary; Martin Strein and Wife Christina; Daniel Cook and wife Magdalena; all of Franklin Co., Penna.; Joseph Cox and wife Susanna of Fyet Co., Penna., and Jeremiah Wilt and Elizabeth, his wife of Franklin Co., Penna., all selling land to John Bowman, the Wararnt to Peter Fry was dated July 5, 1762. On Nov. 7, 1823, Letters of Admr. were granted to Geo. Florry on the estate of Peter Fry; Philip Berlin and Barnard Wolff as sureties.
Penna. Arch. 5th Ser. Vol. 6, p. 88, 98, 118, 528, 537, 539, 546.

WILLIAM FULLERTON

Was a pvt., under Capt. Walter McKinnie in 1782. Two (2) men of the name occupied pews in the Rocky Spring Church. The above William was probably the son of Humphrey Fullerton of Antrim Twp., who willed to his son Wm., a tract of land in Westmoreland Co., called "Sugar Creek." In June of 1799, William Fullerton and wife Barbara of Westmoreland Co., Penna., sell to Geo. Roch, Jr., land in Guilford Twp., 99 ac., 67 pchs., part of a larger tract called "Springfield," which Joseph Clarke and wife Margery had sold to Wm. Fullerton.
Penna. Arch. 5th Ser. Vol. 6, p. 305.

REV. JOHN FUNK

The Franklin Repository, Dec. 2, 1823, Another soldier of the Revolution has taken his departure to a world of Spirits. The Rev. John Funk died at the residence of his son in Washington Twp., on Monday the 16th ult., aged 64 years. In the days of 76 when our bleeding Country lay prostrate at the foot of oppression he was among the first to raise the cry of liberty and independence although only in the 17th year of his age and was actively engaged in the war about five years. His later days were profitably spent in the service of God. His will, probated Jan. 20, 1824 names a dau. Esther mar. to Henry Nicodemus; Sons Henry and John Funk; Dau. Elizabeth mar. Abraham Rowland; Sons Jacob and Tobias; Dau. Susanna mar. Jacob Zigler. Bible Record: John Funk, born Sept. 27, 1759; Prudentia Miller, his wife, born Nov. 12, 1759. On the 5th of August, 1781, they were united in marriage. Issue: Esther, b. June 12, 1782, mar Henry Nicodemus; Henry b. Feb. 4, 1784, mar. Elizabeth Good; John b. Mar. 25, 1786, mar. Alice Barr; Elizabeth, b. Sept. 5, 1788, mar. Abraham Rowland; Jacob, b. Oct. 31, 1790, unmar.; Christian, b. Apr. 9, 1794; Tobias, b. June 13, 1796, mar. Mary; Susanna, b. Dec. 16, 1802, mar. Jacob Zigler. From a Christopher Sauer Bible, printed in Germantown, 1776, now in possession of Miss Bessie Rohrer, Waynesboro, Penna.

SAMUEL FUTHEY

Is shown on the Cont. Line of Cumb. County troops—and in service under Capt. Thos. Askey in Apr., 1781, "on guard at Frankstown" under Col. James Dunlap, Apr., 1781. The name is shown in Fannett Twp., 1778-79, as Robert and Samuel Futhey signed several petitions.
Penna. Arch. 5th Ser. Vol. 6, p. 406, 411.
Penna. Arch. 5th Ser. Vol. 4, p. 287.

JACOB FYOCK

Served under Capt. Samuel Royer, 1779-80, Cumb. Co. Militia. Jacob Fyock had a 1773 warrant for land which he sold in 1777 to John Riddlesberger. One Jacob Fiock was under Capt. Andrew Long in Col. Miles Penna. Rifle Regiment. The Fyocks are buried in the Nunnery Graveyard: David; Mary; Elizabeth; Susannah and Catherine, wife of Peter Fyock.
Penna. Arch. 5th Ser. Vol. 6, p. 90, 542.

ABRAHAM GABRIEL

Served 1777-78-80-81, with Capts. John Jack, Wm. Berryhill and Samuel Royer. Deeds in Allegheny Co., Penna., Book 11, pages 322, 323, show that in Apr., 1769, a Location was entered in the Office of the Surveyor General of Penna., in the name of Abraham Gable for 300 acres, on the east side of the Allegheny river, in Pitt Twp., No. 1450. On March 7, 1773, they surveyed 312½ acres for the aforesaid Abraham Gable, then in Westmoreland Co., Penna., which he sold to Hugh Davidson on May 10, 1774, for 100 pounds. On July 1, 1802, Abraham Gable came before Robert Galbreath, at Huntingdon, Penna., and acknowledged the above instrument of writing to be his act and deed. Hugh Davidson and wife Catherine sold in 1803, the above tract to Michael Kuhn of Plum Township.

Penna. Arch. 5th Ser. Vol. 6, p. 79, 101, 107, 169, 514, 517, 535, 580.

WILLIAM GABRIAL

Was a private in the Continental Line, also a Ranger on the Frontier, from Cumberland Co., Penna.
Penna. Arch 5th Ser. Vol. 4, p. 287, 626.

HUGH GAFF

Antrim Township, private, served in 1778 under Capt. Wm. Findley, and in 1780-81, under Capt. Wm. Berryhill. His wife was Mary, dau of John Rule. The will of Hugh Gaff, prob. 1825, shows a son John Gaff; a dau. Elizabeth Martin; a dau. Poly Greogry; a son Wm. Gaff; son James Gaff; a dau. Sarah, wife of Phineas Eachus.
Penna. Arch. 5th Ser. Vol. 6, p. 80, 101, 536.

JOHN GAFF

Private, served 1778-80-81, under Capts. Wm. Findley and Wm. Berryhill. The old Ledger of Samuel Findlay shows a charge against James Johnston, Aug. 11, 1775, for Broadcloth and silk for John Gaff. His wife was Sarah, dau. of John Rule. John Gaff left issue: Son John; Dau; Mary Ann, d. unmar.; Dau. Jane mar. Alexdr., Latta; Dau. Elizabeth mar. John Scott; Dau. Sarah; dau. Margaret.
Penna. Arch. 5th Ser.Vol. 6, p. 73, 80, 102, 527.

JAMES GALBREATH

In 1769, James Galbreath was living in District 6, of the "Upper West Conococheague" Presbyterian Church of Mercersburg. His wife was Martha, dau. of John McClelland, an early settler in Peters (now Montgomery) Twp. His children were: Rhoda; Robert; John; William; James; Patt.; Samuel; and Joseph was baptized by Rev. John King, Sept. 10, 1769. James Galbreath, born about 1741 is said to have been a soldier of the Penna. Line in the Rev. War and pensioner. Probable line: James mar. Mary Bell; Robert; Joseph; John; Patrick; Wm. mar. Mary Holliday; Samuel, born May 5, 1767, mar. Ann Morrison; Ephriam; Rhoda d. 1804. James Galbreath left a will in Allegheny Twp., Huntingdon Co., Penna. To his sons Robert and Joseph he leaves 557 acres land in Allegheny Twp., subject to the payment of ten dollars ground rent on each half, yearly and every year to his dau. Rhoda; To son John 240 acres, subject to the ground rent to Rhoda. To son Wm. 252 acres, subject to the ground rent to Rhoda. To son Samuel 251 acres also subject to ground rent to Rhoda. To son Ephriam 227 acres, subject to ground rent to Rhoda. To friend John Blair, in trust, for son James Galbreath, his wife and children, 241 ac. land &c. To dau. Rhoda $80. per annum from the lands bequeathed to her 8 brothers, also 400 pounds to Rhoda. To son Patrick 100 pounds. Will dated July 6, 1801. Ruth McClelland, dau. of Capt. John and Sydney McClelland of Peters Twp., Franklin Co., Penna., mar. June 19, 1798, Robert Galbreath, Esq., by Dr. John King. She is buried in the old McClelland graveyard with her parents. She left a will, dated and prob. 1823. She made bequests to her brothers and their children. To a niece Sidney Irwin, $60.00, the sum allowed to be given her by her uncle Robert Galbreath.

JOSEPH GALLEDY

Served as pvt., in 1780, from Antrim Twp. He left a wife Elizabeth; Son Jacob who was to have the free use of the plantation for eight years. Dau. Susanna Unger; and Elizabeth; John; Martha; Catherine; Abraham; Rebackah; Mary; Anne; Esther; and Isaac. His will was prob. June 13, 1785. Joseph Gallady had a warrant of 60 acres in 1763; he was chased by Indians, hid in tall corn and escaped, tho' he was among those reported killed by Indians. Joseph Gallady and wife had sold in 1767, 100 acres land to Joseph McGrew, land which he acquired from Abraham Gabriel. The various children of Joseph Gallady released to Jacob. The Michael Birely will shows his dau. Caty, wife of Abraham Gallody, and a deed in 1795, shows Katherine Gallady as the wife of Henry Miller, both of Rockbridge Co., Va.
Penna. Arch. 5th Ser. Vol. 6, p.73.

SAMUEL GAMMEL (GAMBLE)

Served as pvt., with Capt. Thos. Askey 1779-80-81. He was of Fannett Twp., and his will prob., Feb. 1797. His wife was Elizabeth and he named sons Samuel; William; James. Daus., Jean Kennedy; Polly Morton; Shusana Elder; Peggy Elder.
Penna. Arch. 5th Ser. Vol. 6, p. 61, 393, 424.

GEORGE GANS

Served as pvt., under Capt. Daniel Clapsaddler, 1780-81.
Penna. Arch. 5th Ser. Vol. 6, p. 93, 116.

JOHN GANS

Served as private under Capt. Daniel Clapsaddler, 1780-81.
Penna. Arch. 5th Ser. Vol. 6, p. 94, 116.

JOSEPH GANS

Served as pvt., under Capt. Daniel Clapsaddler, 1780-81.
Penna. Arch. 5th Ser. Vol. 6, p. 94, 117.

JACOB GANS

Served as pvt., under Capt. Daniel Clapsaddler,

1780-81; In the History of Franklin Co., page 277 by McCauley, a tract of land is described as partly in Maryland, which the Proprietor of Maryland, on Aug. 10, 1753, deeded to Jacob Gans, who sold to John Miller, June 22, 1784. Tract "Antietam Home." Jacob Gans of Washington Twp., died leaving a widow Susanna and issue: Elizabeth and David. Deeds show Jacob Gans selling land to John Miller "by John Stoner's Mill," and his estate shows land by David Stoner and John Gans, Sr. Letters of Admr., on Jacob Gans were granted Aug. 2, 1808 to Robert Crooks and Fredk. Mero.

Penna. Arch. 5th Ser. Vol. 6, p. 94, 117.

ABRAHAM GANSINGER

Served as pvt., under Capt. Wm. Berryhill in 1780-81-82. The will of Abraham Gansinger of Belfast Twp., Bedford Co., dated 1812, prob. 1813, states he was "late of Antram Twp., Franklin Co., Penna." He names son Daniel; son Abraham, decd.; who left sons John and Abraham; daus: Esther Stale (Stall, Stoll); Magdalene Crunkleton; Elizabeth Byers. His plantation in Antram Twp., was sold to John Wolford. The executors were: grandson Henry Stall, and Jacob Stall, Sr. The tracts in Bedford Co., were on Morrison's Cove, and on the Waters of Clover Creek.

Penna. Arch. 5th Ser. Vol. 6, p. 79, 101, 123.

FRANCIS GARDNER

Appears in service as pvt., later as Ensign, with Capts., James Young, Terrence Campbell, Patrick Jack and Samuel Patton, during 1777-78-81-82. Francis Gardner was a taxable in Guilford Twp., 1780-81-82, with land, horses and cows. He is shown several times in Militia rolls as Francy or Francis Garner.

Penna. Arch 5th Ser. Vol. 6, p. 82, 110, 125, 368, 372, 376, 383.

JOHN GAUDY (GOUDY)

Served in 1780 under Capt. William Smith, who later (1786) laid out the town of Mercersburg, Penna. John Gaudy was married by Dr. John King to Mrs. Davison, Feb. 22, 1798. Mrs. Goudy died Jan., 1803.

Penna. Arch. 5th Ser. Vol. 6, p. 275.

HENRY GEIGER

Enlisted March 1, 1814, as a pvt., in Capt., Gordon's Co., 5th Regt., (Fentons), Pa., Militia. Services ended Aug. 24, 1814. He was allowed bounty land for services in the war of 1812. Henry Geiger, III was the son of Lieut. Charles Geiger, 1750-1828, and wife Anna Maria Dilbon, (Trinity Luth. Ch. Reading, Pa.) Charles Geiger was the son of Valentine Geiger b. 1685, in Germany, died 1762 in the present Montgomery Co., Penna., and buried in New Hanover Luth. Ch. Cemetery. The first wife of Valentine Geiger was Johanna Frederika Henckel; the 2nd wife, mar. in America, was Maria Elizabeth ———? Henry Geiger, III, was a tailor by trade and came from Montgomery Co., Penna to Franklin County, where he settled in Antrim Twp.; he appears in the tax list as a single freeman 1813-14-15. He is later shown with a house and lot, but in 1832, he left Greencastle, going to Somerset County, then to Lisbon, Ohio,; to Holmes County finally to Urbana, Champaign Co., Ohio. He lived in Greencastle for nineteen years, and nine of his children were born there. III. Henry Geiger, born May 7, 1789, (Mertz Ch. records-Berks Co., Penna.) died Apr. 7, 1862, buried at Fern Cliff Cem. Springfield, Ohio. Married March, 1816 to Julia Ann Rudebush, probably Roudebush, born Oct. 11, 1796 at Mercersburg, Penna. or Hagerstown, Md., died Aug. 31, 1854, at Urbana, Ohio, buried in Fern Cliff Cem., Springfield, Ohio. Children: (1) Albertus Geiger mar. Catherine Sophia Bartges; (2) Henry Dilbon Geiger; (3) Hezekiah Rudebush Geiger; (4) Jeremiah Geiger; (5) Levi Geiger. (6) John Geiger; (7) Charles Cline Geiger; (8) Andrew Milton Geiger; (9) George Lemual Geiger; (10) Washington Franklin Geiger; (11) Urilla Melvins Geiger; (12) Francis Marion Geiger.

NOTE: by V. S. Fendrick: Leonard Schnebley, of Frederick Co., Md., (Wash. Co.) made his will in 1766, naming a wife Margaret (and wife) and oldest dau. Elizabeth, who later mar. Daniel Miller. He mentions 4th dau. Christina, who in April of 1817, was Christina Roudebush, which was in connection with settlement of the estate of Susanna Schnebly, decd. As Albertus was a Miller name, that fact and others point to a Miller Roudebush connection. Under records of Dr. Robert Kennedy, Welsh Run and Greencastle, Penna., 1803-1816, are the following: John Kean, Polly Roudebush, March 6, 1806. John Crouch, Catherine Roudebush, Aug. 21, 1806. Col. Robert Parker of Mercersburg left an account Book, 1799, in which John Roudebush is listed as owing a balance to the estate of Col. Parker.

GEORGE GEISEMAN

Was in service in Lancaster Co., Penna., 1781-82, with Capts., Baltzer Orth and John Stone. George Geeseman of Lurgan Twp., (Blacksmith) left a will in Franklin County, dated and prob. Jan.-Feb., 1815, naming wife Catherine; sons: George; John; Peter; William; 4 daus: Catherine; Mary; Elizabeth; Margaret. Wit: Thos. McClelland, Wm. Boggs.

Penna. Arch 5th Ser. Vol. 7, p. 146, 179

HENRY GEISMAN
Served in Lancaster Co., 1781, under Capt. Baltzer Orth.
Penna. Arch. 5th Ser. Vol. 7, p. 147.

HUGH GELVIN
Was in service 1781-82, as private with Capt. Alexdr., Peebles. John Gelvin occupied Pew No. 3, in the old Log church at Rocky Spring, with Robert Mitchell and others. In 1800 Matthew Gelvin appears alone in Pew No. 25. Matthew Gelvin, Sr. and wife Hannah are buried in the Graveyard at the church.
Penna. Arch. 5th Ser. Vol. 6, p. 421, 432.

JAMES GELVIN
Of Letterkenny Twp., served as pvt., under Capt. Joseph Culbertson, 1780-81. His father Jeremiah Gelvin left ten pounds to the trustees for Rocky Spring Church. James Gelvin had sisters, Hannah mar. to John Scott; Margaret mar. to John Ralstone; Mary mar. to James Walker; also brothers Joseph; Jeremiah; John and Matthew.
Penna. Arch. 5th Ser. Vol. 6, p. 279, 289.

JEREMIAH GELVIN
Of Letterkenny Twp., in his will, dated 1803, prob. 1804, states "being old and stricken in years." To the trustees of the congregation of Rocky Spring, 10 pounds; Dau. Hannah; sons James; Joseph; Jeremiah; John and Matthew. Dau. Margaret, the wife of John Ralstone; Mary wife of James Walker; she to share with her children; Mary Walker, Wm. Walker, Jeremiah Walker and Isabella Walker. Caveat entered by John Scott intermarried with Hannah dau. of Jeremiah Gelvin. The will established by Court. One John Galvin was in the 10th Penna. Regt. Cont. Line. A deed shows John Ralstone and wife Margaret (Gelvin) in 1809 in Crawford Co. Penna.

ADAM GEORGE
Son of Matthias George, of Grindstone Hill Settlement, served as pvt., 1777-78-79-80-82, under Capts., John Jack, Adam Harmony, Wm. Long, Conrad Snider and James Poe.
Penna. Arch. 5th Ser. Vol. 6, p. 87, 517, 519, 538, 546, 572, 586.

STOPHEL GEORGE
Served as pvt., 1779-80-81, under Capts., William Long and Conrad Snider.
Penna. Arch. 5th Ser. Vol. 6, p. 74, 88, 119, 546.

JOHN GEYER
Col. Samuel Miles, Penna. Rifle Regt., drummer boy (11 yrs. of age), son of Peter Geyer; wounded in the heel at Germantown; discharged Jan. 1, 1778 at Valley Forge; was a stone mason living in Metal Twp., Franklin Co., in 1821. From Pension Dept., Washington. Pension claim, S.-41567, that John Geyer or Gier, enlisted near Pittsburg, Penna., in March 1776, served 21 months as drummer in Capt. Irwin and Carnaghan's Company Cols. Miles and Stewart's Penna. Regt., and was in the battles of Fort Washington, Trenton, Princeton, Brandywine and Germantown, where he was wounded, the nature of wound not stated. He was allowed pension on his application executed Aug. 18, 1824, while a resident of Metal Twp., Franklin Co., Penna., aged sixty years. He died May 24, 1854, place not stated. Soldier had eleven children, seven of whom were living in 1824. His mother Mary was aged eighty-nine years and living in Franklin Co., Penna., in 1824. His father was a soldier in the Revolution, his name and details of service not stated, and the date of John Geyer's birth and names of wife and children are not given.
Penna. Arch. 5th Ser. Vol. 2, p. 392.

PETER GEYER
Private, served under Capt. Joseph Erwin; enlisted at Hannestown; discharged at Valley Forge, Jan. 1, 1778; wounded by a bayonet in the groin and by a ball in the leg at Germantown. His wife Mary went with his company as washerwoman, and accompanied the regiment in all its marches; she was 86 years of age in 1821, then living in Cumberland Co.; she had 3 other children, Jacob, Mary and Catherine. See data on John Geyer, her son, who was a drummer in same company at age of 11. Engagements were: Long Island, White Plains; Trenton; Princeton; Quibbletown, Brandywine and Germantown. We the undersigned citizens of Cumberland Co., do certify that the bearer of this, Mary Geyer, the widow of Peter, deceased, who she says, and alloweth to be able to prove, has been in service of the U.S.A., state of Penna., war of Revolution, as an enlisted soldier, as a rifleman under the troop of Penna., and which Mary Geyer now resides in Mifflin County, and has no property or means of support in her old age, and that we allow her to be entitled to such a pension as is allowed by the law for pension Widows of the Rev. War. Signed Aug., 1820, by at least thirty names, two of which were John Johnson and James Huston.
Penna. Arch. 2nd Ser. Vol. 10, p. 235.

DAVID GIBBS
Is shown 1777181, with undated rolls, serving with Capts. Abraham, Maclay and Miller, under Col. James Dunlap.
Penna. Arch. 5th Ser. Vol. 6, p. 19, 139, 149, 151, 406.

HUGH GIBBS

Served under Capts. James Young and Terrence Campbell, 1780-81-82. In the will of Hugh Gibbs, dated and prob. Oct., 1788, he names wife Rachel, to whom he gives "the house I now live in and formerly willed to her by Robert Jack, deceased;" sons William; Samuel; Hugh; dau. Rachel Gibbs a 1/5 part of my estate. The Executors were Josiah Crawford and James Jack. Under date of 1768, Deed Book 6, page 46 shows the heirs of Robert Rush, (an Indian victim), one being Rachel, wife of Robert Jack. McCauley's History states that Hugh Gibb kept a tavern in a small two-story log house which stood where the National Bank now stands. From the "Repository," Oct. 16, 1821 is this: Died Wednesday last, in this Boro,' at an advanced age, Mrs. Rachel Gibb.

Penna. Arch. 5th Ser. Vol. 6, p. 81, 110, 125.

ROBERT GIBBS

Is shown serving in 1776 under Capts. Samuel McCune, Charles Maclay and others. He was residing in Westmoreland Co., Penna., in 1825.

Penna. Arch. 5th Ser. Vol. 6, p. 39, 41, 149, 151, 587. 2nd Ser. Vol. 13, p. 81.

ANDREW GIBSON

Served with Capt. James Poe in 1782, in the 8th Batt., of Cumb., Co., Militia. His will was dated 1782, prob. March 1783, naming a wife Elizabeth; dau. Margaret Parkes (?); dau. Jane Long; sons John and Thomas; dau. Elizabeth. The witnesses were James Dickson, James Smith and James Poe. John Gibson, Jr., is shown in the same company.

Penna. Arch. 5th Ser. Vol. 6, p. 576.

HUGH GIBSON

Appears serving under Capt. George Crawford in 1777, probably other years. In Deed Book 7, pp. 229, 231, Hugh Gibson is shown selling land in 1788, to Daniel Erb of Warwick Twp., Lancaster Co., Penna. In 1789 Hugh Gibson and wife Eleanor are again selling land, for which Daniel Erb paid 1600 lbs. An order of Survey by James Waddle, in 1766, later surveyed for the Rev. James Waddle in Peters Twp., by lands late of Robert Waddle, Andrew Bigger, Wm. McElhatton, 247 acres. James Waddle in 1773 sold to Robert Waddle, who sold to Hugh Gibson. Hugh Gibson later appears of Providence Parish, Rockbridge Co., Va., yeoman.

Penna. Arch. 5th Ser. Vol. 6, p. 371.

JOHN GIBSON

Served as pvt., 1778-80-81, under Capts., Robert Dickey, Thos. McDowell, James Patton. On May 15, 1781, he was mar. to Sarah McDowell, by Rev. John King of the Presby., Church of Mercersburg. They had a dau. Mary baptized May 11, 1783. The line as verified by the N.S.D.A.R. shows John Gibson wounded at Brandywine. They had a son Hugh who mar. Elizabeth Rutledge.

Penna. Arch. 5th Ser. Vol. 6, p. 266, 272, 285, 315, 375.

JOHN GIBSON

Served as pvt., in 1777-80-81-82, under Capts., James Poe and Thomas Johnson. His will was probated May 26, 1789. He left a wife Mary and son James. He was of Antrim Twp.

Penna. Arch. 5th Ser. Vol. 6, p. 84, 114, 521, 523, 571, 586.

THOMAS GIBSON

Appears in service 1780-82, with Capt. James Poe. In the will of Andrew Gibson of Antrim Twp., wife Elizabeth, he names sons, John and Thomas, and a dau. Elizabeth, and two married daughters. The will noted was dated 1782, prob. in 1783.

Penna. Arch. 5th Ser. Vol. 6, p. 76, 92, 276, 576, 583.

EDWARD GIDENS

Was in service 1779, under Capt. Thos. Askey, from Fannett Twp., "a Class Roole" the command of Col. James Dunlap.

Penna. Arch. 5th Ser. Vol. 6, p. 61.

JAMES GIDDENS

Was in Service 1779-80-81-82, and was also under Capt. Thos. Askey of Fannett Twp.

Penna. Arch. 5th Ser. Vol. 6, p. 61, 150, 393, 409, 423, 442.

JOHN GIDDENS

Was serving 1779-81, under Col. Thos. Askey.

Penna. Arch. 5th Ser. Vol. 6, p. 62, 407, 409.

RICHARD GIDDENS

Of Fannett Twp., served 1779-81, with Capt. Thos. Askey, undated Roll.

Penna. Arch. 5th Ser. Vol. 6, p. 61, 131, 409, 423.

ADAM GIFT

Is shown in service in 1781, under Capt. John Rea, Col. James Johnston.

Penna. Arch. 5th Ser. Vol. 6, p. 106.

GEORGE GIFT

Drummer, was in service 1779, with Capt. Wm. Long, and in 1781, as a private under Capt. Conrad Snider. George Gift a taxable in Guilford Twp., in 1796. George Gift of Guilford Twp., left a will dated and prob., March-April, 1813, naming wife Catherine; 2 sons, Adam and John, and five daus.; Catherine; Magdalene; Elizabeth;

Sophia and Peggy. To the three last named as much household furniture as any of my other daus., received from me at their intermarriage and to live with my sons until they get married, the exrs., being wife Catherine and son Adam Gift. Deeds later show that Catherine mar. Ephriam Colby, and Peggy mar. Frederick George.
Penna. Arch 5th Ser. Vol. 6, p. 119, 545.

MATHIAS GIFT

Served with Capt. Wm. Long, in 1779, command of Col. Abraham Smith. In 1796, Mathias Gift of Guilford Twp., was taxed on 188 acres of land and a cow. Under Nov. 23, 1812, Letters of Admr., on the estate of Mathias Gift were granted to George Gift and George Helman. A Deed of 1798 from Mathias Gift of Guilford Twp., to George Gift of same; land joining Adam George, Robert English and John Thorn, being a grant to John Harmony in 1762. Signed by Mathias Gift and Margaret Gift. Deeds show an agreement dated March, 1798, from Mathias Gift to George Gift, both of Guilford Twp. Mathias conveys the plantation he now lives on with 1 wagon, windmill, log chain and 4 hogs to George Gift and for and in consideration of above articles George Gift binds himself unto Mathias and wife during their natural lives, the mantion house, garden, to plow the garden, cut and holl the firewood, 20 bushels Rye, wheat, corn or buckwheat, Pork, flax, 5 appletrees, take their grain to mill &c. At the death of Mathias and wife George to pay 400 pounds to such legatees as Mathias shall please to designate.
Penna. Arch. 5th Ser. Vol. 6, p. 546.

ALEXANDER GILCHRIST

Served as private under Capts., John McConnell and William Huston, 1778-80-81. He was mar. by Dr. John King, Oct. 28, 1782, to Peggy Hutcheson. They had baptized Alexander, Aug., 1784 and Robert in April, 1787. They probably came here from Paxtang and moved to Westmoreland Co., Penna.
Penna. Arch. 5th Ser. Vol. 6, p. 270, 276, 284, 374.

ROBERT GILCHRIST

Served as private under Capt. Wm. Huston, 1780-81. He had children baptized by Dr. John King: Anne in Jan, 1774; Robert in 1777.
Penna. Arch. 5th Ser. Vol. 6, p. 269, 275, 282.

REUBEN GILLESPIE (GELLESPIE)

A Lieut, under Capt. Joseph Culbertson, 1780-81 82. Reuben Gillespy occupied Pew No. 21, in Rocky Spring Church. Greenvillage was laid out by Samuel Nicholson, 1793, he having bought of Reuben Gillespie 45 acres "at the intersection of the Chambersburg and Strasburg roads." On May 19, 1801, Margaret Gillespie, widow, renounced her right to administer on estate of Reuben Gillespie and Matthew Duncan was appointed. Deeds show Reuben Gillespy formerly of Green Twp., Franklin County, Penna., now of Knox County, Tenn., revokes the appointment of Matt. Duncan and appoints S. Nicholson. The family as shown in Census of 1790, consisted of 1 man, 1 female.
Penna. Arch. 1st Ser. Vol. 10, p. 599. 5th Ser. Vol. 6, p. 261, 290.

JOSEPH GLASSGO

Served as pvt., 1777, under Capt. George Crawford. He was a witness on the will of John Glasgow of Peters Twp., Cumb. Co., Penna., 1779, with James Neely and Mary Arter. John Glasgow named his wife Ann, and three children: dau. Lates Glasgow; Agnes Glasgow and son Joseph Glasgow.
Penna. Arch. 5th Ser. Vol. 6, p. 371.

ALEXANDER GLENDENING

Served as a pvt., in 1781, under Capt. Walter McKinnie, he calls himself "yeoman" of Peters Twp. He died Feb., 1812, leaving by will his plantation to the two sons, Robert and Adam, of his niece Jane McKinnie and also naming their brothers Josias and James. He had a beloved sister Mary Rusk. A deed in the family shows a Patent to Alexdr., Clindinnan, tract called "Petersburg," Peters Twp., by Wm. McClelland, Richard Bard &c., surveyed Feb. 17, 1773.
Penna. Arch. 5th Ser. Vol. 6, p. 300.

PETER GOOSEHEAD

Served as pvt., in 1780, under Capt. James Young.
Penna. Arch. 5th Ser. Vol. 6, p. 77, 82.

PHELTY GOOSEHEAD

Served as pvt., under Capt. James Young in 1780-81.
Penna. Arch. 5th Ser. Vol. 6, p. 83, 100, 111.

PHILIP GOOSEHEAD

Served under Capts. James Young and Terance Campbell, 1777-78-79-80-81-82.
Penna. Arch. 5th Ser. Vol. 6, p. 82, 111, 126, 523, 527, 548.

VALENTINE GOOSEHEAD

Served as pvt., in the "Flying Camp" Cont. Line. Deed Book 6, p. 462, in Nov., 1804, shows Valentine Cussard of Green Twp., and wife Mary selling to Joseph Waddle, of Guilford Twp., 174 acres, 2 Roods, 30 perches land, for 720 pounds. The will of Michael Reifsnider, weaver, of Guil-

ford Twp., Franklin Co., Penna., names wife Mary; sons John and Henry; a dau., wife of Falentine Cusard, and a dau. Gertrude, wife of Michael Rhine. The will dated 1794, prob., 1796. Official Roster, Rev., Soldiers of Ohio, states Valentine Coosard born at Chambersburg, Penna., 1745. In battle Fort Washington, taken prisoner and confined in Sugar House 2 months, Pensioner.
Penna. Arch. 5th Ser. Vol. 4, p. 229.

JACOB GOOSHORN
Served as a private May 1, 1781.
Penna. Arch. 5th Ser. Vol. 6, p. 497.

NICHOLAS GOOSHORN
First Lieut., in Captain Andrew Farrier's Co., 1780, Cumb. Co. Militia.
Penna. Arch. 5th Ser. Vol. 6, p. 481, 497

GEORGE GORDON
Private, served under Capt. John Jack and Lieut., Richard McLene in 1778-79-80-81-82. George Gordon is said to have moved to Missouri. Family records give his birth as April 17, 1758. He married Mary Prather, born Oct. 31, 1760, d. Sept. 26, 1805. Miss Susan Snively has an old Bill which "Bindeth us, George and Mary Gordon of Franklin Co., Penna., unto Abraham Prather," &c., dated Apr. 1, 1800.
Penna. Arch. 5th Ser. Vol. 6, p. 84, 114, 129, 169, 535, 540, 599, 600.

GEORGE GORDON
Deeds at Chambersburg, Penna., show George Gordon of Antrim Twp., dying intestate, Orphans' Court at Shippensburg, March 8, 1763, Son Henry to hold plantation &c. Heirs: Mary, wife of John Laurence, Sarah, wife of Geo. Dement, 1778; Arabella, wife of Joseph McGrew, 1779; Rachel wife of Wm. Matthews, 1781; James; Prudence; Ruth, wife of Arthur Eckles; Elizabeth Crunkleton. George Dement and wife Sarah had issue: Wm., born, 1768; Ruth; George Gordon Dement; Elias; Sarah; Henry; Rachel; Samuel; Anna. Deeds at Frederick, Md., to and from Geo. Dement are dated 1768-1775. He was a Rev. Soldier, verified by N.S.D.A.R.

HENRY GORDON
Served as a private from Antrim Twp., in 1779-1780, under Capt. John Jack and Lieut. Richard McLent. Henry Gordon, born Jan. 8, 1734, died Aug. 10, 1809, was a son of George Gordon, 1698-1763, an early settler in Antrim Twp. Henry Gordon mar. Sarah Johnston, born July 10, 1736, died June 18, 1819, they had issue: George, born Apr. 17, 1758, Rev. Soldier; William, born July 20, 1760; Susannah born Nov. 7, 1763 (Laurence); Elizabeth born Dec. 4, 1765 (Smith).; Alexander, born March 10, 1768; Sarah, born March 28, 1770, (Smith); Mary, born July 8, 1772 (Mason.)
Penna. Arch. 5th Ser. Vol. 6, p. 85, 99, 541.

MATTHEW GORDON
Served under Capt. Wm. Berryhill, and Capt. John Jack, 1778-79-81. Deeds in 1773, show Margaret Gordon as the widow of John Gordon; she and her son Matthew Gordon sell a tract of 245 acres, "where the Gordons dwelt," to Edward and John Wishard.
Penna. Arch. 5th Ser. Vol. 6, p. 102, 537, 541.

ROBERT GORDON
Was a pvt., under Capt. John Woods, 1780-81-82. From Orphans' Court Nov. 18, 1816, is found a petition from Edward Gordon, a son of Robert Gordon, of Montgomery Twp., who d. intestate leaving 3 children: Wm. Gordon; Edward and Elizabeth, mar. to Joseph Martin; said Elizabeth has since died leaving 4 children; Robert G.; Anne; Isabella; William, all minors. Said Robert died in Jan. last, seized of land in Montgomery Twp.
Penna. Arch. 5th Ser. Vol. 6, p. 91, 104, 138.

WILLIAM GORMAN
Franklin County, with Wayne in his campaign against the Indians Chambersburg, Penna., Deed Book 3, p. 266. William Gorman, Labourer, of Fannett Twp., sells land to William McClelland of Guilford, in 1823, land being in Fannett Twp.
Penna. Arch. 2nd Ser. Vol. 15, p. 766.

JOHN GOSSARD
Of Lancaster Co, served 1777, under Col. Philip Greenawalt, as 2nd Lieut., 1st Batt., 7th Company, Associators and Militia. He came to Franklin County where he mar. Mary Kieffer of Leitersburg. John Gossert, his wife and one son are buried on what is known as the Harry Dougherty farm. His will, dated Oct., 1832, was prob., Aug., 1834, in which he wills to son George and heirs a plantation in Cambria Co., Penna., south of the yellow spring and rocky run to its mouth near a popular tree, about 100 acres. To son Christian and heirs 100 acres off the same tract; my son George to enjoy the full right of the waters of rocky run. Balance of said farm to be sold, proceeds to be divided; To sons George; Christian and John; to my daughters Catherine, wife of Peter Springer; Nancy, wife of Daniel Angle; Margaret, wife of John Frederick; and to their heirs, 1/7 part each of Nett proceeds. To my dau. Mary, wife of Peter Tallhelm and William Logan, the 1/7 part to said dau., and her son; son Jacob, and dau. Elizabeth, wife of Philip Replogle and my dau. Barbara, wife of John Yeager, $1.00 each. Money kept in hands to maintain my wife comfortably.

Under records of Rev. John Casper Stoever, will be found baptisms of the children of John Jacob Gassert, of Atolhoe. Under Reformed Church records, Greencastle, John and Maria Gossert were confirmed 1819, and Mary Jane in 1840. John Gastert and wife Anna Maria had a son Christian baptized Jan. 22, 1798, under records of Jacob's Lutheran Church. In 1804 John Gossert and wife buy lots 15 and 16 in Waynesboro and sell the same to Martin Motz. Deed Book 1, p. 155, shows the following: Peter Gozett and Eve, his wife of Guilford Twp., Cumberland Co., Penna., to Valentine Gozet and Phillipe Gozet of same; Warrant to said Peter Oct., 1763, land adj., Fredk., Craft, John Irwin and others, was surveyed at a hickrey joyning Saml. McCrea, Jacob Snively, Conrad Freeman's Improvement, 326 ac. 159 perches; for 450 pounds Peter and Eve Gozet grant to Valentine and Philipe Gozet.

his
Peter P. K. Gozett
mark

JOHN GOULDING

Was a private under Capt. John McClelland, 1779, under lieut. John Eaton in 1777, and under Capt. Walter McKinnie, 1781-82. He was living in Montgomery Twp., and was mentioned in the wills of John Jerrit (1801) and James Maxwell, Esq., who says "John Goulden and wife shall have the use of the buildings, the meadows and two fields." Letters on estate of John Goulden were granted to Moses Murphy Oct. 28, 1806.

Penna. Arch. 5th Ser. Vol. 6, p. 298, 300, 305, 373.

FRANCIS GRAHAM (GRIMES)

Is probably the son shown in the will of Mary Graham of Lurgan Township, June 29, 1787. His wife Margaret, dau. of Wm. Reynolds. In his will prob. March 26, 1840, he names the following children: Mary Maciben; Margaret Williamson; Nancy Dickson; Sarah Vanderbolt; Elizabeth; John. There appear to have been men named Francis Graham, the above probably having served under Capt. Thos. Askey. See pension record of same name. You are advised that it appears from the papers in the Rev. War pension claim, S.8622, that Francis Graham was born in Franklin County, Penna., date not stated. While living in Franklin County, Penna., between eighteen and nineteen years of age, he enlisted about Jan. 1, 1777, and served at various times as a private in the Pennsylvania troops, amounting in all to six months and eleven days, under Capts. Charles Maclay, Isaac Miller, Lieut. Samuel Walker and Major McCalmont. He was allowed pension on his application executed Jan. 30, 1834, at which time he was a resident of Roxbury, Franklin County, Penna., aged seventy-seven years. In 1834 he stated that his father had died and there were no persons at home besides himself except his mother and sister whose names were not given. It is not stated whether soldier was ever married and there are no further family data.

Penna. Arch. Ser. Vol. 6, p. 200, 406, 411, 436, 450.

JOHN GRAHAM

Was a pvt, under Capt. Isaac Miller, 1782, undated rolls. This John Graham appears to be a son of John Graham of Lurgan Twp., whose estate was administered July 4, 1761, and a distribution made (from Carlisle) in 1764. The wararnt was in 1755 for 200 acres. He left a widow Elizabeth, and issue four: William died in minority; Hannah mar. John Allison of Armstrong Twp., Westmoreland Co., Penna., and Jennet mar. James Caldwell of Robinson Twp., Allegheny Co., Penna., and John Graham, who sold the land in 1791, to Thomas McClelland of Hopewell, Cumb. Co., Penna.

Penna. Arch. 5th Ser. Vol. 6, p. 435, 450.

ROBERT GRANT

Served in the Cont. Line, 11th Penna. Regt. One Robert Grant mar. Margaret, dau. of Alexander McConnell, at Mercersburg, Oct. 15, 1783. He was murdered in Kentucky.

Penna. Arch. 5th Ser. Vol. 4, p. 178.

GEORGE GREASING

Of Chambersburg, served as pvt, under Capt. James Young, in 1779-80-81, and under Capt. Terrance Campbell in 1782. His will prob. Jan. 31, 1797, names wife Catherine; dau. Elizabeth Greasing; dau. Catherine, wife of William Kelly, and her children. Lots in town of Chambersburg and other real estate.

Penna. Arch. 5th Ser. Vol. 6, p. 548, 82, 110, 126.

NATHANIEL GREEN

Served under Capt Walter McKinnie and others, 1781, undated rolls. He had baptized Catherine, May, 1799; Elleanor, Apr. 8, 1781; David, May 4, 1783; William Clark, June 19, 1785; Jenny, June 3, 1787. Nathaniel Green was living in Peters Twp., during the above period, but he may not have owned land.

Penna. Arch. 5th Ser. Vol. 6, p. 285, 300, 315.

NICHOLAS GREENAWALT, PRIVATE

P L., Bankson's Company, July, 1778, afterwards Col. Murray's; resided in Franklin Co., 1835, aged 79. p. 221—Nicholas Greenawalt, May 29, 1776, transferred to Capt. Moore's Company, reenlisted in Col. Stewarts Regt. Enlisted Spring 1776 under

Capt. Shade, continued there until Battle of Long Island. Re-enlisted under Col. Stewart for 3 yrs. Kicked by a horse, but returned to the army at West Point. In army until Jan., 1779, unfit for service. In Battles of Long Island, White Plains, Germantown, Brandywine. He was a pensioner; in Southampton Twp., taxed 1796 with 2 acres land. Nicholas Greenawalt testified to the service, under Col. Stewart, of Benj. Long; also of Thos. Sulivan, Balser Meeze, Louis Houser, and Benj. Beever, all applicants for pensions from Franklin Co., Penna. Census of 1790 shows the family as 1 man, 1 boy, 1 female.

Penna. Arch. 2nd Ser. Vol. 10, p. 431.

THOMAS GREER

Served in the Cont., Line, entitled to Depreciation Pay, as well as in Cumb. Co. Militia, 1777-1780-82. He died intestate March 30, 1813, leaving a widow and ten (10) children. Isaac was the oldest son and there were Margaret mar. to John Culbertson; Mary mar. to Samuel Smith; Isaac; Thomas; William; Michael; Martha; Elizabeth; Hugh; Jane. There were over 400 acres land, a 2 story stone house, log houses, barns and small houses.

Penna. Arch. 5th Ser. Vol. 6, p. 371, 397, 428, 430. Vol. 4, p. 288, 627.

ROBERT GREY

Served under Lieut., David Shields, 1778, and under Capt. Samuel Patton, 1781-82. The "Repository," March 20, 1821, gives: "Died on the 9th inst. Mr. Robert Gray, of Hamilton Twp., in the 91st year of his age." In the will of Isaac Patterson of Hamilton Twp., he names among others, a dau. Agnes, wife of Robert Grey, and grandchildren, Isaac, Mary and Jane Grey. Isaac to receive lands, plantation, when of age. This will was dated 1783, prob. 1787.

Penna. Arch. 5th Ser. Vol. 6, p. 286, 288, 311, 379.

HENRY GRINDLE

Served as pvt., under Capts., James Poe and John Woods, in 1780-82. On June 5, 1784, Henry Grindle of Antrim Township is shown transferring to Fredk., Fisher his right in about 80 acres of Rye in the ground, on Widow Hart's plantation; 1 dark bay mare; a baldface red cow; 2 beds and bedding, furniture &c. The witnesses: Arthur McGill and David Fullerton.

Penna. Arch. 5th Ser. Vol. 6, p. 91, 124, 137, 575, 583, 586.

JACOB GRINDLE

Served as pvt., under Capts. James Poe and John Woods, 1780-82.

Penna. Arch. 5th Ser. Vol. 6, p. 76, 92, 138, 169, 576, 522, 583, 599.

JOHN GRINDLE

Served as pvt., under Capts. James Poe and John Woods in 1780-82.

Penna. Arch. 5th Ser. Vol. 6, p. 91, 137, 576, 583.

DETRICK GUSHERT, PENSIONER

S 22804, Penna. Franklin County, Penna., June 12, 1833. Detrick Gushert of St. Thomas Twp., aged 83 on March 5th last. Born in Germany on March 5, 1750 and brought to Philadelphia, Penna., in 1768; his age recorded in his father's Bible, now in his possession. He was living near New Holland, Lancaster Co., when he enlisted and resided there about 30 years. Aug., 1776, he volunteered in the Company of Capt. Andrew Bear, for 3 months, from Lancaster to Phila.; Trenton; Princeton; Brunswick; Woodbridge; Blayington; in 1778 he was in Militia with Capt. Alexdr. Martin; Major Henry Nansbright (?); Col. David Jenkins. He was also under Col. Ferree; Major John Boyd and discharged at Blayington. When he enlisted he left a wife and small child 3 weeks old, having been married about one year. After the war he came to St. Thomas Twp., Franklin Co., Penna., where he has resided ever since. Dietrik Gushert (Gossert) private Penna., Militia, aged 85 yrs. in 1833, a pensioner. Index at Chambersburg gives Detrich Gushert (Revolutioner). Letters of Admr., to Jacob Gushert, July 27, 1840. The "Repository and Whig" Thursday, July 23, 1840. "Died on Monday last, Mr. Dietrich, Gushert, a soldier of the Revolution, aged upwards of 90 years, and for a long time a citizen of this country. His remains were committed to the earth with Military honors."

Penna. Arch 3rd Ser. Vol. 13, p. 530.

ISAAC GUSHERT

Of Southampton Twp., Franklin Co., Penna., a brother of Detrick Gushert, states that he resided in Montgomery Co., Penna., at the time of the Revolution and when he heard his brother had enlisted, he volunteered in the same Company. He is aged 81 years, and 4 months and is now blind, June 21, 1833.

JAMES GUTHERY

Private, 1778-79, under Capt. James Young. The Rev. Laurence R. Guthrie gives the following: James Gutherie was in the Company of Col. Joseph Armstrong, which was included in Col. John Armstrong's 700 men who attacked the Indian town of Kittanning and drove them out with great slaughter. His land was on Back Creek in Hamilton Twp., and he had surveys in 1762-1763. He signed a petition in 1755; executor of the will of John Burns of Hamilton Twp., in 1760; he sold his homestead on Back Creek in 1777 and moved to Chambersburg. In 1780 he removed to Westmoreland County. His wife was Jennet Culbertson and they had issue: James; Wm.; and Elizabeth who mar. Isaac Parr.

Penna. Arch. 5th Ser. Vol. 6, p. 209, 548

JOHN GUTHERY

Was a private under Capt John Rea and Col. Abraham Smith 1780-81. On page 188 of the Guthrie History by Rev. Laurence R. Guthrie, the above John is given as a presumptive son of Robert Guthrie of Chester Co., Penna. Referring to John, James and William, he says, "each of them lived for a time on Back Creek, in Hamilton Twp., now Franklin County and may properly be referred to as the Back Creek Guthries."

Penna. Arch. 5th Ser. Vol. 6, p. 73, 106, 78, 585.

WILLIAM GUTHRIE

Pensioner, applies from Westmoreland Co., Penna. Served in the Penna. Line one year and nine months, Capt. Irwin's Company, under Col. Walter Stewart. In Battles of Germantown, Brandywine, taken prisoner at Long Island and held eighteen weeks. Was discharged by Col. Stewart at Valley Forge. His discharge was stolen, on his way home at the Burnt Cabins also money and papers. Served under Capt Jack against the Indians. He served two months in Cumberland County Militia under Col. Culbertson. In 1771 Thomas Barnet of Hamilton Twp., named his son-in-law William Gothery and wife, a witness being John Gothery. To further identify William Guthrey, pvt., who applied for a pension, he served in Capt. Joseph Erwin's Com., Rifle Regt., Col Saml. Miles, encamped near King's Bridge Sept., 1776; with Capt. James Carnaham at Red Bank in 1777.

Penna. Arch. 5th Ser. Vol. 4, p. 439, 588, 743. Vol. 2, p. 393, 395, 551, 552.

WILLIAM GUTHRIE

7th Penna. Cont. Line, Seventh Penna. Regt., May 27, 1777-1781; died Aug. 1, 1829, in Westmoreland Co., aged 84 years. The above William Guthrie does not appear to be the man who applied for a pension, but rather as the pvt., May, 1777, under Capt. Wm. Alexander, Seventh Penna. Cont. Line, Col. Wm. Irvine.

Penna. Arch. 2nd Ser. Vol. 10, p. 647, 626.

JOHN HACKET

Clerk, served under Capt. Patrick Jack, July 1, 1781. In the will of Wm. Peebles of Letterkenny Twp., prob. at Chambersburg, Penna., May 7, 1799, he names his 2nd dau. Ann Hacket. Ann Peebles had first mar. Moses Swan, who, dying 1787, left one child, Moses H. Swan. In 1803, James Swan, of Knox Co., Tenn. was guardian for Moses H. Swan. Ann, the widow of Moses Swan, mar. John Hacket and deeds show that in 1791 "John Hacket of the Western territory South of Ohio sold land in Hamilton Twp., Franklin Co., Penna., called Hackets borough," to Joseph Grimes." The children of John and Ann Hackett were: Elizabeth b. Feb. 22, 1791; Cynthia b. Dec. 18, 1792; Ann b. Oct. 11, 1794; Wm. Peebles b. June 21, 1796; Samuel Ramsey b. March 31, 1798; Margaret Peebles b. July 4, 1800; Harriet Holmes b. March 14, 1804; James Henderson b. Oct. 20, 1806; The marriage date as given Nov. 5, 1789. John Hackett is said to have been decd., in 1812. The Census of 1850 showed Ann Swan Hackett living in Washington, Rhea Co., Tenn., aged 87 and her birthplace given as Penna. From letters by Mrs. P. J. Kruesi, 4th St. Chattanooga, Tenn.

Penna. Arch 5th Ser. Vol 6, p. 293

JOHN HAGER

Is shown in 1780-81, in service under Capts. Joseph Culbertson and Wm. Berryhill.

Penna. Arch 5th Ser. Vol. 6, p. 80, 102, 290.

HANS HAMILTON

Appears in the Provincial Service, as Capt., 1755, with Rev. John Steel, Alexdr. Culbertson, Benj. Chambers and others. He had as Lieut. Jacob Sneider and Ensign Hugh Crawford, "Ensign Wm. McDowell was a Sergt. in Capt. Hance Hamilton's Company, at the capture of Kittanning." "Capt. Hanse Hamilton, late Lieut. Col. Resigned March, 1759." Hans Hamilton late from Ireland and now residing in Chambersburg, will dated and prob. Oct.-Dec., 1788. Brother William in the town of Goetree, County Dunnigall in Ireland, all real and personal estate both in America and Ireland; friend Josiah Crawford, Jr., of Franklin County my horse, saddle and bridle; beloved sister Martha Woods; sister Jennet Ralston, niece of Mary Crawford each one English Guinea; Exrs.: John Calhoun and Josiah Crawford, who renounce their rights to admr., and special letters of Admr., with the will annexed, were granted to James Roddy, Dec. 23, 1788.

Penna. Arch. 5th Ser. Vol. 1, p. 31, 44, 62, 89, 105, 106, 107, 115, 120, 122, 128, 178, 185, 230, 280, 264.

JAMES HAMILTON

Was a Sergt. under Capt. Noah Abraham 1777-78-79. One James Hamilton was living in the family of Janet Barr, widow of Thomas Barr in 1769, under Mercersburg Presby. Church records; vicinity of Ft. Loudon.

Penna. Arch. 5th Ser. Vol. 6, p. 18, 53, 59.

JAMES HAMILTON

Surgeon's Mate, d. in Franklin Co., 1820, age 59. Letters of Admr. were granted Jan. 2, 1824.
Penna. Arch 3rd Ser. Vol. 23, p. 397.

WILLIAM HAMILTON

Aug. 13, 1776, later of Indiana Co., Penna., served in Capt. Samuel McCune's Company of the Flying Camp; took sick at Fort Lee. William Hamilton, Sr., William Hamilton, Jr., as well as Sergt. George Hamilton are shown in the company of Capt. McCune.

Penna. Arch. 5th Ser. Vol. 6, p. 587. Penna. Arch. 2nd Ser. Vol. 15, p. 766.

JOHN HAMILTON

School Mr., served 1781-82, as a private under Capt. Thos. Askey. He signed a petition from Fannett Twp., in 1779.

Penna. Arch. 5th Ser. Vol. 6, p. 409, 424, 442.

NATHANIEL HAMMEL

Of Bedford Co., Penna., served in the Cont. Line. He was mar. to Martha Bickett, June 13, 1775, by Rev. John King of Mercersburg, Penna. A descendant furnishes the following: Nathaniel Hamil, b. Sept. 7, 1737, in Ireland, came to America 1760-61, lived in Ayr Twp., Bedford Co., Penna.; served with Penna Troops in Rev. War; mar. "a young widow with red hair," who was born 1740, Ulster, Ireland, d. Apr. 20, 1817 and buried in Bethel Cemetery Enon Valley, Lawrence Co., Penna. Nathaniel Hamil was killed by wolves Jan. 6, 1789, in Ayr Twp. The wolves were after his cattle and in spite of a terrific blizzard he took his gun and powder horn, and was never seen again, tho' his gun with name on it, and his powder horn were found twenty years later. Issue of above: I. Nathaniel, Jr. b. 1776, Ayr Twp., died Enon Valley Nov. 1, 1843, buried in Bethel Cemetery, mar. 1st Dec. 16, 1806, Katherine Lackey; mar. 2nd Anna Johnson. II. John b. Ayr. Twp., Apr. 17, 1777, d. Sept. 5, 1850, at Bethel, mar. March 30, 1807, Rosanna Davidson b. Aug. 16, 1783, in Ulster; died 1864, Keokuk, Iowa, while visiting her son, Smith Hamil. III Martha mar. Robert Smith. IV. Jannette b. 1782, d. 1852, mar John Smith (brothers). V. Sarah b. Sept. 14, 1780, died Nov. 6, 1872, unmar. Rosanna Davidson was a dau. of Wm. Davidson, 1752-1820, and Mary Ramsey, b. 1757, d. 1831. It is probable there were three Hamil brothers: John, Robert and Nathaniel, and perhaps a Joseph. Robert settled in Fayette Co., Penna. Some moved to Xenia, Ohio; his first wife was Mary Bickett, a sister of Martha; Robert left a will in Fayette Co., dying there in 1799.

Penna. Arch. 5th Ser. Vol. 4, p. 240, 605.

ROBERT HAMEL

Is shown in service 1777-79, with Capts. Noah Abraham, Alexdr. Peebles and John Jack. They probably were connected with Middle Spring Presby. Church, as Elizabeth Hammel appears in James Dunlap's District. Contributed to the Building Fund for the old Stone Church of 1781. Robert Hammell signed the Oath of Allegiance Oct. 22, 1777, before John Creigh, J. of P at Carlisle, Penna. Middle Spring Church Records near Shippensburg, Penna.—Marriages by Rev. John Moody: Geo. Hammil, Molly Rippey, Aug. 6, 1812; Wm. Hammil and Dorcas Galbreath, Oct. 1, 1812. Baptisms, Apr., 1821, For Geo. Hammil: Charlotte; Elizabeth; George Washington; Mary; Samuel Rippy; Wm. Cromwell. Wm. Hammill had baptized: Geo. Abraham, 1813; Robert, 1816. One Wm. Hammill was mar. to Rebecca Ashman, by Rev. A. A. McGinley, in 1818. George Hammill and wife Mary of Shippensburg, Penna., sell to George McGinnes, Esq., of same, land conveyed by James Hamill and wife Mary to Geo. Hamill, Apr., 1818.

Penna. Arch. 5th Ser. Vol. 6, p. 21, 57, 18, 139, 540, 589.

BARNETT HAMSHER

Served as pvt. in the Northampton Co. Militia, 1782, under Capt. John Deter, and Lieut. and Ensign Adam Hamsher, (Humsher) his brother. Daniel Hamsher was shown in the same company. Barnett Hamsher, of Lurgan Twp., left a will dated April, 1815, and prob. May of same year. He named his children: Peter; John; Catherine; Margaret; Mary; Susannah; Adam; Jacob; Elizabeth; Martha; Lydia; Hannah. Jacob, son of Barnard and Catherine Hamsher, is lying in the Graveyard at Pleasant Hall, born Sept. 17, 1803, died May 19, 1837, aged 33 yrs., 8 mos.

Penna. Arch. 5th Ser. Vol. 8, p. 288.

JOSEPH HANCOCK

Was born July 21, 1758, place of birth and names of parents are not shown. He enlisted in the state of Pennsylvania, Aug. 20, 1776, and served as a private in Capt. Andrew Mann's Co. Col. Mackey's 8th Penna. Regt., was wounded in a skirmish at New Brunswick, Mar. 16, 1777, by a musket ball in his right shoulder, and was discharged April 3, 1780. The soldier was allowed pension on his application executed Aug. 25, 1828, while a resident of Wayne County, Indiana, having served 3 years. In 1828, he referred to his wife, Diana, her maiden name not stated, aged about 46 years, and to three children—Enoch, aged fourteen years; Simeon, aged twelve years; and Philip aged ten years. Soldier died in 1834, aged 77 years, leaving a widow, who he married in 1816 or 1817; she was alive in 1846. There are no further family data shown. The arrears of pension due the decedent, covering the period from March 4, 1834 to September 2, 1834, were paid on November 29, 1834, at the Pension Agency in Corydon, Indiana, to I. W. Kintner, as attorney for the widow. One Joseph Hancock was admitted to membership in the Presbyterian Church of Mercersburg, Penna., in the year 1786.

Penna. Arch. 5th Ser. Vol. 3, p. 339, 342, 368.

CORNELIUS HANLINE

Served as pvt., under Capt. Daniel Clapsaddler in 1780-81. He was living in Washington Twp., 1782, with 150 acres land, 4 Horses and 5 Cattle. The Hon. Benj. Focht descended from the Henline family which settled on the Big Antietam Creek, Franklin Co., Penna. One branch went to Huntingdon Co., in 1800 where the Congressman's father was born. Two of his brothers were born in Chambersburg. The first charge of Rev. D. H. Focht covered Chambersburg, Marion, Fayetteville, Scotland and Grindstone Hill churches.

Penna. Arch. 5th Ser. Vol. 6, p. 71, 117, 94.

SAMUEL HANLINE

Served as pvt., under Capt. Findlay, undated, and in 1782. One Casper Hanline is also shown as a taxable, 1782, with Horses and Cattle.

Penna. Arch 5th Ser. Vol. 6, p. 122, 586.

TOBIAS HANLINE

Served as pvt., under Capt. Daniel Clapsaddler in 1780-81. Tobias Hanline had in 1782, 140 acres land, 3 horses, 2 Cattle.

Penna. Arch. 5th Ser. Vol. 6, p. 93, 116.

WILLIAM HANNAH

Served as pvt., under Capts. Wm. Berryhill and Joseph Culbertson 1777-78-80. He was a son-in-law of John McDowell or Antrim Twp. In 1782 Wm. Hannah had 100 ac. land, 3 Horses and 4 Cattle, in Antrim Twp.

Penna. Arch. 5th Ser. Vol. 6, p. 80, 382, 589.

WILLIAM HANNAH

Of Antrim Twp., served in 1780 under Capt. Wm. Berryhill. He left a wife Elizabeth and son John his whole estate; if John died without issue, sons-in-law, James and Henry Morrows to divide estate between them. Son-in-law John Wherry; son-in-law Samuel Adams; will prob. Nov. 25, 1785; Exrs.: Son-in-law James Morrow and John Hannah.

Penna. Arch. 5th Ser. Vol. 6, p. 80.

JOHN HARMONI (HERMAN)

Served as Sergt. under Capt. Thomas Askey, 1777-78-79-81. John Ludwig Harmoni, born March, 1734, died November 23, 1831. He married Elizabeth Lowe in 1772. She was born Oct. 14, 1752, died Aug. 17, 1831. John Harmoni was born in Germany, Principality of Nassau-Dillinburg town named Herborn. He landed in America in 1765; settled in Fannett Twp.; and is buried in the Stake graveyard at Amberson. Letters of Admr. were granted Jan. 9, 1832. He left issue one son Henry, and the children of his dau. Elizabeth who had mar. John McGee, viz: Mary; Elizabeth; Jane and George McGee. From Franklin Telegraph and Democratic Advertiser: Tuesday, Feb. 28, 1832. Died on Nov. 1, last, at his residence in Fannett Twp., John Harmony, Esq. The deceased in early life emigrated to this country from Germany and on the breaking out of the American Revolution served several tours in the militia. After the revolutionary struggle had subsided on the organization of the government of Pennsylvania he received from Gov. Mifflin, a commission of Justice of the Peace which some years since on account of his age, he resigned—was an industrious and valuable citizen enjoyed good health until within four days of his death.

Penna. Arch. 5th Ser. Vol. 6, p. 7, 60, 423, 605, 637. Penna. Arch 2nd Ser. Vol. 15, p. 766, under Applicants for State Annuities. Penna. Arch. 2nd Ser. Vol. 15, p. 621.

ADAM HARMONE (HERMONY)

Served as First Lieut. First call in 1777, under Capt. James Poe, later under Capts. Wm. Long and Conrad Snider to 1782. He was a son of John Harmon of Guilford Twp., whose will was prob. 1801.

Penna. Arch. 5th Ser. Vol. 6, p. 523, 520, 525, 533, 512, 87, 536, 537, 544, 571, 581, 119.

PETER HARMONY

Served as pvt., 1780-81, under Capt. Conrad Snider.

Penna. Arch. 5th Ser. Vol. 6, p. 87, 108, 118.

PHILIP HARMON (HARMONY, HERMONY)

Served as pvt., under Capts. Wm. Long and Conrad Snider, 1778-79-80-81-82.

Penna. Arch. 5th Ser. Vol. 6, p. 87, 118, 123, 538, 546, 586.

LUDWIG HERMAN

Served as a private under Berks Co. Cont. Line, Capt. John Ludwig, 1780-81. Ludwig Herman, born 1720, d. 1790, buried Grindstone Hill Graveyard. Orphans' Court Vol. A, pp. 44, 46, 47, 1793, estate of Ludwig Harmon; Eberhart Ena, the widow; son Philip; dau. Fredrika, wife of Nich. Coleman; dau. Catherine, wife of Henry Stouffer; dau. Elizabeth, wife of John Flack; son William. Gravestone states issue as 6: Philip;

William; Ebernardina; Catherine; Elizabeth and Jeremiah.

Penna. Arch. 5th Ser. Vol. 4, p. 260.

PETER HERMANY—HERMAN—HARMONY

Private 1st Batt., Cumb. Co., Militia. Chambersburg Will Book D, page 237, Peter Harrmon of Guilford Twp.; Son John; Dau. Anna Maria Harmon; Dau. Elizabeth; Son Peter; Dau. Rebecca; wife Elizabeth Harrmon. Dated May 28, 1832; prob. Sept. 3, 1832. Peter Hermany, 1760-1832, is buried in the Grindstone Hill graveyard. His wife, Magdalena died Dec. 7, 1815.

Penna. Arch 5th Ser. Vol. 6, p. 108, 118.

GEORGE HARRIS

Served as a pvt., in Capt. John Nelson's Co., of Independent Riflemen, under Col. Philip DeHaas, First Penna. Batt., at Ticonderago, 1776; George Harris in the Fifth Penna Regt., Cont. Line, in 1781. He was born 1756, wife Elizabeth Coxen; the estate of Geo. Harris was administered by Elizabeth and George Harris, Oct. 14, 1811 in Franklin Co., Penna.

Penna. Arch. 5th Ser. Vol. 2, p. 76 Penna. Arch. 5th Ser. Vol. 3, p. 38, 79.

RICHARD HARRIS

Son of Rowland Harris, served as pvt., 1780-81, under Capts. James Patton, Robert Dickey and Thomas McDowell. In 1802 Richard Harris of Peters Twp., and wife, Mary, sell land to James Chambers.

Penna. Arch. 5th Ser. Vol. 6, p. 272, 286, 315.

ROWLAND HARRIS, SR.

Of Peters Twp., lived in the Gap above Fort Loudon, an early settler. He gave service under Capt. Robert Dickey and James Patton 1780-81. In 1769, his family consisted of wife Rebecca and James; Richard; Hannah; Sarah; Rowland. His wife Rebecca died Apr. 4, 1772 and he mar. Elizabeth as named in his will; sons Richard; Rowland; Ephriam; the heirs of his son James; daus: Sarah Armstrong; Mary Childerson; Anna Ewalt. Ephriam Harris mar. Hannah Elliott, Sept. 20, 1791 by Dr. John King. She was a dau. of John Elliott of Path Valley and his 2nd wife Frances (Knott) Childerstone. The Census of Penna, 1790 shows "Rollen" Harris' family with 3 men, 3 females.

Penna. Arch. 5th Ser. Vol. 6, p. 272, 285.

ROLLAND HARRIS, JR.

Served under Capt. Thos. McDowell. He mar. Mary, dau. of John and Jane Ramsey of Dublin Twp., Jane being a dau of George McConnell of Cumb. Co., Penna. From "Biographical Annals" by Seilhamer, we have the issue of Rowland and Mary Harris: John; Rowland; Benj.; Susanna; Charlotte; Rebecca; mar. James Austin; Hannah mar. John Stewart; Sarah mar. John Noble; Mary mar. Mr. Shannon; Jane mar. Joseph Brown, and Catherine Margaret Harris. Baptisms of above by Dr. John King: a child, Feb. 2, 1793; a child, Apr. 1, 1797; John, Oct. 1799; Child, Dec. 1802; Rowland, Nov. 24, 1805; Benjamin, Jan. 4, 1807; Cath. Margaret, July 1, 1810. Rowland Harris and Mrs. Harris were admitted to membership in the Presbyterian Church, Mercersburg, 1791. Under 1790 Census, his family shows 1 man, 1 female.

Penna. Arch. 5th Ser. Vol. 6, p. 315.

BENJAMIN HARRISON

Settled in Virginia in the 17th Century. In the fifth generation Benj. Harrison represented his people in the Continental Congress; was chairman of the Committee of the Whole, presiding over the debates, for a year and a half, which led to the adoption of the Declaration of Independence. He is designated among all the Harrisons in American affairs as "The Signer." Later he presided over the debates on the Articles of Confederation, assisted Washington and Adams in organization of the first State, War and Navy Departments, and then went home to serve three terms as Governor of Virginia. It was his son William Henry, who became the first Harrison in the Presidency, and he came up by way of the army. First as an aide to Anthony Wayne in Ohio wars with the Indians, he later served as Secretary for the Northwest Territory and was its first Delegate to Congress. Appointed Governor of Indian Territory, he served in that capacity for twelve years, treating with the redskins for land grants and defending with whites against Indian attacks. It was his battle with Tecumseh's Shawnees at Tippecanoe Creek in the Wabash Valley that gave his friends later their stirring political battle cry of "Tippecanoe and Tyler too." In 1836, he was a candidate for President but lost to Van Buren. Age was wearing him down, but he was a doughty warrier and came back at the age of 68 to enter the presidential lists four years later, and was triumphant with Tyler, after the eclipse of Webster and Clay. His age and the strenuous campaign were too much for him; pneumonia cut him down shortly after he became President. His son Wm. Henry Harrison, 1802-1838, mar. Feb. 18, 1824 at Mercersburg, Penna., the marriage by Dr. David Elliott, Jane Irwin, 1804-1846, dau. of Archibald and Mary (Ramsey) Irwin. When General Harrison became President his son's widow accompanied him to Washington and was mistress of the White House during his brief administration. His sister, Elizabeth Irwin, mar. John Scott Harrison, Aug. 12, 1831. Their son Benjamin

Harrison was elected President of the United States in 1888.
From Article by Charles W. Duke in Phila. Ledger.

JAMES HARROD, CAPTAIN

A list of Capt. James Harron's Company in the Fincastle County Batt. 29 privates, which includes Thomas and James Harrod.
Annals of Southwest Virginia 1769-1800. By Lewis Preston Summers, p. 1414.

COL. JAMES HARROD

Elizabeth Madox Roberts in "The Great Meadow" states "In the past summer season of the year, in June, a mighty man of valor, James Harrod, and thirty men, made a town in the Caneland, the beginnings of a nation. I came to this place and I saw men felling trees and building houses, James Harrod and his thirty." In the Ledger of Samuel Findlay of Mercersburg, Penna., the father of Governor Wm. Findlay, Rev. War period, was a store account against Col. James Herrod; "Col. James Herrod, Land to be taken up for my use on Cain Tuskee or Cumberland River, or where the Colonel pleaseth, it being situate for trade."

JOHN HERROD (HARROD)

Was one of the early Welsh Settlers in the Little Cove and Connallaways (Bedford Co., Penna.) According to Draper, John Harrod came to America, in 1734, name of wife unknown. They had issue: Thomas; John; James, b. 1761; Levi; Samuel; Josiah; Lucinda; Hannah; Polly wife of Steven Montgomery; Jane wife of Wm. Groom; Betsy wife of John Touch; Leah wife of Wm. McCallister. John Harrod mar. Rachel Shepherd; John b. 1736, d. 1781; Rachel b. 1739, d. Nov. 10, 1806. They had issue: Sarah b. 1759; Thomas b. 1761, mar. Jane Bowen; Mary b. 1763; Wm. b. 1765; Catherine b. 1767; Elizabeth b. 1769, mar. Robert Stinson, whose dau. Rachel mar. Benj. Boone; Rachel b. 1771; John b. 1773; Levi b. 1776. If dates as given are authentic, it is probable that the above John and Col. James Harrod, b. 1742, were brothers. The Census of 1790, shows Rachel Herred, a family of two females, Bedford Co., Penna. In 1770, the will of James Balla was dated and prob. naming a grandson Jonathan Shelby; a dau. Elizabeth, and the witnesses Wm. John; Evan Shelby; John Harrod, Ayr. Township.

LEVI HAROD

Appears in Washington Co., Penna., Militia, 1782-85, and earlier years. In 1781 he is shown in Washington County with 300 acres land, horses, cattle and sheep. Levi Harrod, Knox Co., Ohio, Ranger on Frontier. Levi Harod, Sergt., Washington Co., Penna., Militia in the Cont. Line entitled to Depreciation Pay. He was born Jan. 22, 1750, Bedford Co., Penna. (Little Cove) died Oct. 2, 1825, in Pleasant Twp., Knox Co., Ohio; buried Union Grove Cemetery. His father was James Harrod (?). Levi Harrod mar. Rachel Mills, b. Oct. 22, 1752, d. Sept. 28, 1834,—issue: Levi; Michael; James; Wm.; Samuel; Jemima; Rachel; Elizabeth; Sarah.
Penna. Arch. 2nd Ser. Vol. 14, p. 751, 760, 765.
Penna. Arch. 5th Ser. Vol. 4, p. 402, 403, 711, 712.
Official Roster, Rev. Soldiers in Ohio.

THOMAS HARED—HERROD

Appears as an Ensign, with Capt. Thos. Paxton's Ranging Company, Bedford Co. Militia, and as a Ranger on the Frontier, "Along the Province line to the North Mountain, including all the inhabitants of the little Cove, then on Licking Creek to place of Beginning." In an undated roll of Thos. Davies, Capt., he adds "Thomas Herrod, Ensign and hes served." Survey Books show the Harrods in Little Cove, now Warren Twp., Franklin Co., Penna. "The Widow Herrod" neighbor to Jacob John warrant to Enoch Williams in 1755; Wm. Harrod and James Balla as neighbors. The Thos. Hearod tract of 107 acres, with John Anderson and David Carlisle adjoining. Thomas Herrod mar. Jan. 13, 1785, Jane Bowen, a dau. of Samuel Bowen and a grandau. of David Bowen of Montgomery Twp., Franklin Co., Penna., whose will was dated Jan. 25, 1794. He named his son Samuel and his family; the widow; son David; Elizabeth Davis; Rebeccah Bowen; Jane Hared; Hannah Evans; Mary Denham.
Penna. Arch. 3rd Ser. Vol. 23, p. 236, 269.
Penna Arch 5th Ser. Vol. 5, p. 53, 56, 62, 63, 83, 111. Penna. Arch. 5th Ser. Vol. 4, p. 240, 605, 606.

WILLIAM HARROD

1737-1801, born in Big Cove (?) Valley commanding a Company in the Illinois Expedition under Gen. Geo. Rogers Clarke, died in Bracken Co. In Sept., 1769, Wm. Herrod had baptized a son Samuel by Rev. John King, of the Mercersburg Church. In 1773 Wm. Herod appears as a taxable in Air Twp., Bedford Co., Penna. Also James, Levi, John and Samuel Herod. In 1783 James Herod, Single freeman was in Air Twp. with land, horses, cattle and sheep.
D. A. R. Lineage Book 94, p. 144.

CHRISTOPHER HARHSBARGER

Served under Capt. Samuel Royer, in 1780, in Cumb. Co., Militia.
Penna. Arch. 5th Ser. Vol. 6, p. 89.

JACOB HERSHBERGER

Of Washington Twp., served 1780-81 as a pvt., under Capt. Samuel Royer. His will, dated 1782, was prob. Nov., 1791. He was of Washington Twp., and names wife Mary, who was to live with son Samuel; sons, Christian and Jacob; to Samuel the plantation I now live on, joining John Johnston, James Moor and others, also land in South Mountain. The Executors were the three sons; the witnesses: Adam Pritz and Samuel Royer.

Penna. Arch. 5th Ser. Vol. 6, p. 89, 108.

SAMUEL HERSHBERGER

Is shown in 1780-82 serving in Militia with Capt Samuel Royer.

Penna. Arch. 5th Ser. Vol. 6, p. 89, 123.

CHARLES HART

Served under Capts. Wm. Long, James Young and Wm. Huston, 1777-78-80-81. He was a freeman in Antrim Twp., and was married to Jennet Dale, of Peters Twp., July 6, 1780, by Rev. Alexdr. Dobbin.

Penna. Arch. 5th Ser. Vol. 6, p. 269, 275, 283, 520, 524, 601.

JAMES HART

Served under Capts. Thos. Johnston and Daniel Clapsaddle, 1778-80-81, as a private. Two men of the name are shown, one having removed to York Co., Penna. In 1778 the Widow Hart, Rodger Hart and James Hart were taxables in Antrim Twp.; John and James were freemen.

Penna. Arch. 5th Ser. Vol. 6, p. 94, 97, 528, 537.

JOHN HART

Appears as a Lieut., later as a pvt., 1777-78-80, with Capts. Wm. Findlay and James Young, with a group of Washington Twp., men.

Penna. Arch. 5th Ser. Vol. 6, p. 71, 94, 513, 521, 525.

JOHN HART

Was in service the spring and summer of 1779, as a Ranger on the Frontiers of Bedford and Westmo. Counties, in Capt Samuel Patton's Company. He also served with Capt. Thos. McDowell.

Penna. Arch. 5th Ser. Vol. 6, p. 314, 601, 610.

LUDWICK HART

Is shown serving in 1780-81 as a pvt., under Capt. Wm. Berryhill. He is also given as a pvt., in the Cont. Line, Cumb. Co., Militia with Daniel, John and Matthew Hart.

Penna. Arch. 5th Ser. Vol. 6, p. 79, 101, 107.

MATTHEW HART

Appears as a pvt., in the Cont. Line, Cumb. Co., Penna. and was a taxable in Washington Twp., in 1779, with 50 acres land, a horse and cattle. The Harts and Hopkins are known to have gone to West Virginia from Franklin Co., Penna.

Penna. Arch. 5th Ser. Vol. 4, p. 289.

WILLIAM HART

Served as pvt., with Capt Daniel Clapsaddle 1780-81. By 1782 the widow Hartt, John and Ludwick are the only taxables of the name of Hart in Antrim Twp.

Penna. Arch. 5th Ser. Vol. 6, p. 94, 97, 117.

JOHN HART

Served as a pvt., 1780-81-82 with Capt. Thos. Johnston. In Old Congruity Cemetery, Westmoreland Co., Penna., are buried John Hart, Sr., died March 18, 1817, aged 64 years, and Martha, relict of John Hart, d. Aug. 23, 1831, aged 79 years. No definite data on above John Hart and wife.

Penna. Arch. 5th Ser. Vol. 6, p. 114, 130.

PATRICK HARTFORD

Province of Penna. A Roll of Soldiers enlisted by James Burd, at Fort Granville, Patrick Hartford appears as No. 33, and delivered by Major Burd at the Camp at Harriss, 3rd June, 1756. When James McCalmont of Letterkenny Twp., made his will in 1772, he named his wife Jean; To Dau. Jean, now the wife of Patrick Hartford; To my grandchildren, the children of my dau. Jean, wife of Patrick Hartford. The will of Major James McCamont, prob. 1809, names the above Hartford children. Two men named Patrick Hartford, and two families are shown in 1790, in the Census of Bedford Co., Penna.

Penna. Arch. 5th Ser. Vol. 1, p. 64.

JACOB HARTLEIN

Armand's Legion, residing in Franklin Co., 1835, aged 80. You are advised that it appears from the papers in the Rev. War pension claim, S. 39640, that Jacob Hartline enlisted in the fall of 1781 in Shepherdstown, Virginia, and served until October, 1783, as a private in Captain Baron de Uechtritz' company under Major Shaffner in Armand's Legion. He was allowed pension on his application executed Nov. 24, 1823, at which time he was a resident of Franklin Co., Penna., aged sixty-six years. In 1823 he stated that his family consisted of a wife and five children, and that the only ones at home were a girl aged about twenty-one years and a boy about seventeen years of age; the names of wife and children are not given and there are no further data.

Penna. Arch. 2nd Ser. Vol. 11, p. 155.

GEORGE HARTSOUGH

Of Guildford Twp., served as pvt., under Capt. Wm. Long in 1779; Col. Abraham Smith Commanding. His will was prob. Apr. 18, 1789, naming a wife Judeah; daus., Caterene and Mary; sons, George; Henry and Anthony.

Penna. Arch. 5th Ser. Vol. 6, p. 545, 580.

CHARLES HARVEY

Served in 1777, with Capt. Noah Abraham.
Penna. Arch. 5th Ser. Vol. 6, p. 515.

HENDERSON HARVEY (HERVEY)

Served as pvt., under Capt. Noah Abraham, in 1777-79-80-81-82. A desc. states that his wife was Martha McConnell. He was in Franklin Co. Fannett Twp., in 1790, probably stopped in Ohio; going to Indiana in 1811. A son James was mar. in Union Co. Ohio Oct. 11, 1811, to Sarah Davis. Henderson and Martha (McConnell) Harvey were mar. by Rev. John Plummer; issue: Isabel, b. 1786; Robert, b. Feb. 29, 1788; James, b. 1791; Samuel, b. Aug. 29, 1801 in Penna. John, Henderson, Jr. Martha, unmar.; Anna; Francis; William.

Penna. Arch. 5th Ser. Vol. 6, p. 86, 121, 128, 141, 384, 393, 516.

JAMES HARVEY (HERVEY)

Of Fannett Twp., is shown under Capt. Thos. Askey, 1st Batt., 1st Marching Company, First Call, July 31, 1777. He served almost entirely under Capt. Noah Abraham, 1777-79-80-81-82. James Hervey signed several petitions from Fannett Twp., 1778-79. In his will prob. July, 1789, he names "My dear Mother"; sisters, Elizabeth Brice; Sarah Neely; Mary Randels; Brother Wm. Harvey; to Thomas, son to my brother Thomas Harvey, decd.; to Wm. Harvey, son to my brother Henderson Harvey; Brother John Harvey; Brother Henderson Harvey. On Apr. 16, 1793, Letters were granted to Hannah Harvey, on the estate of James Harvey, decd. Hannah sells in 1806 to a Kilgore. John Harvey (wife Elizabeth) is the oldest surviving brother to the decd., Robert Hervey and James Hervey.

Penna. Arch. 5th Ser. Vol. 6, p. 7, 10, 16, 17, 19, 120, 127, 131, 140, 383, 428, 626.

WILLIAM HARVEY

Served as pvt., under Capts. Patrick Jack, Noah Abraham and Chas. Maclay, 1777-78, the 8th Class of Cumb. Co. Militia, under Col. Abraham Smith. A Wm. Harvey of Metal Twp., left a will in 1809, naming minor children: Wm.; Ester; Sarah; Elizabeth; Margaret; son James.

Penna. Arch. 5th Ser. Vol. 6. p. 29, 516, 658.

CASPER HASSLER

Served as pvt., in 1778-79 under Capt. Joseph Gehr, Lancaster County Militia. Casper Hassler, son of Abraham Hassler, the emigrant and his wife Anna, was baptized Sept. 25, 1757 at Swamp Church, Cocalico Twp., Lancaster Co. Casper Hassler settled in Guilford Twp., Franklin Co., Penna., in 1802. Wife Elizabeth; they had issue: Catherine born 1779, mar. Jacob Omwake; Anna Barbara born 1780; Anna Elizabeth born 1782; John born 1785, had a large family; Anna Maria born 1786 mar. Joseph Everhart; George born 1787; Eva Catherine born 1789; Peter born 1792; Hannah; Jacob born 1799. Letters of Admr. on estate of Casper Hosler granted Dec. 8, 1807.

Penna. Arch. 5th Ser. Vol. 7, p. 879, 900.

JOHN HEATHERINGTON

Enlisted Jan. 1776, under Capt. Jeremiah Talbot, 6th Penna., Batt., Col. Wm. Irvine. He mar. Ruth, dau of Samuel and Mary Smith, early settlers in Antrim Twp., Samuel Smith dying intestate in Nov., 1763. John Heatherington died June 10, 1810; his wife Ruth died Oct., 1817, in the 62nd year. They had one child, Dr. Andrew Heatherington, b. Sept., 1778, who mar. Ruhamah Sterrett June, 1811. She was the dau. of John and Myrtilla (Irwin) Sterritt, and the grandau. of Cairns and Mary (Mayse) Sterritt, who came from Lancaster Co., prior to 1769, to Franklin Co., Penna.

Penna. Arch. 5th Ser. Vol. 2, p. 209, 211.
Penna. Arch 2nd Ser. Vol. 10, p. 185.

DAVID HEEFNER

Served as pvt., 1780-81, under Capt. Daniel Clapsaddler. David Hefner was of Washington Twp., his will dated and prob., 1791, in which he names wife Mary and his children: Veronica; Benjamin; Mary; Catherine; David; George; Miriam; Daniel; Esther; Samuel; Elizabeth and an expected child. In 1799, the Widow Heffner is taxed with Land, 1 Log House, Saw Mill and Smith Shop, Horse and Cow.

Penna. Arch. 5th Ser. Vol. 6, p. 72, 94, 117.

FELTY (VALENTINE) HEEFNER

Appears in Militia in 1781, but as a pvt., in the Cont. Line, and was a Ranger on the frontier, with the Cumb. Co. men. In 1799 Valentine Hifner was a taxable in Washington Twp., Franklin Co., Penna., as were also John Hifner; George Hefner; and Benj. Hefner.

Penna. Arch 5th Ser. Vol. 6, p. 107. Vol. 4, p. 289.

JACOB HEEFNER

Served as pvt., under Capt. Daniel Clapsaddler,

1780-81. 1790 Census shows the family as 1 man, 2 boys, 3 females.

Penna. Arch. 5th Ser. Vol. 6, p. 72, 94, 117.

JOHN HAFNER

"Born 1728, 13th day (parents were John and Elizabeth Hafner he mar. Barbara Metzgar, Nov. 16, 1748 and begat 4 sons and 6 daus., died Dec. 30, 1791. Maria Catharina Heefnerin b. 1735, Jan. 23, her father was George King and her mother Maria King. She mar. Albertus Heefner 1755." "Anna Maria Hufnerin 1769-1790." Albertus Heefner left a will dated 1804 and prob. 1809, naming wife Barbara, who was to have the privilege of the new dwelling house I now live in, and her dower; the heirs were: John Heefner; Jacob Valentine; Margaret; Elizabeth; Peter; Conrad; Catherine; Susanna.

Records of Jacob's Lutheran Church S. of Waynesboro, Penna.

CHRISTIAN (CHRISTLY) HEGE (HEGY)

Served as pvt., in Lancaster County in 1781-82-83. He was born in Lancaster Co., 1751, died near Marion, Franklin Co., Penna., May 13, 1815, a son of John and Elizabeth (Pealman) Hege. He mar. 1st Maria Stouffer, who died 1784, leaving issue: Anna mar. John Snively; John mar. Maria Lesher, Jacob mar. Martha Lesher, Christian mar. Elizabeth Bohn; Christian Hege mar. 2nd Maria Shank who died 1818, issue: Henry mar. Sarah Zent; Elizabeth mar. Samuel Zent; Barbara died young; Catherine mar. John Feighner; Martha mar. Philip Tritle; Peter mar. Mary Updegraff; Mary mar. Daniel Tritle.

Penna. Arch. 5th Ser. Vol. 7, p. 442, 730, 765. McCauley's Hist. Franklin Co., Penna. p. 277, 278.

DANIEL HELMAN

Was in service 1780-81, with Capt. Samuel Royer. In 1791, Daniel Helman of Franklin Co. and wife Elizabeth, convey certain land in Washington Twp., joining lands of Daniel and George Helman, John Woolf and Peter Bonebreak. A deed of Apr., 1804, shows Daniel Helman and wife Elizabeth, selling 85½ ac. of land in Washington Twp., to Daniel Leab of same and in 1810, George Helman again sold land to Daniel Leib.

Penna. Arch. 5th Ser. Vol. 6, p. 89, 108, 112.

GEORGE HELMAN

Served as a Corporal under Capt. Samuel Royer in 1779 and under Capt. Conrad Snider in 1780-81. Letters of Admr. on his estate granted to Christian and George Helman, Apr. 13, 1787. In Feb., 1785, a deed shows George Helman, Sr., as decd., having owned certain lands in Washington Twp., joining Adam Cook, Daniel Poorman and John Stitt; in consideration of 250 lbs., paid by Geo. Helman, Jr. and Daniel Helman unto Catrin Helman and to John Sell and his wife, Susany, who release said George and Daniel Helman. In Jan., 1810, Daniel Hellman to George Hellman, both sons of George Sebastian Helman, decd., who had obtained, in his lifetime, surveys on 2 locations, abj. each other, in Guilford and Antrim Twp. The said George Sebastian Helman died intestate before the year 1794, leaving two sons, George and Daniel and two daus. Catherine and Susanna, said Susanna is now married to John Sell, which said Catherine and John Sell and wife convey to their brothers the aforesaid George and Daniel, alloting to said George 105¼ ac. joining Daniel Poorman. Geo. Sebastian Helman, decd., obtained surveys in the name of Sebastian Helman on which was surveyed 157 ac. It will be noted that Letters of Admr., on the estate of the above George Helman were granted to Christian and George Helman, Apr. 13, 1787. It is quite probable that Christian was the widow of George Helman. Mr. Wertz, whose ancestor came over with the Helmans, states that George Sebastian Helman requested that he be buried between two trees then standing in a woods on his farm. The Western Md. R. R. Co., about 1885, moved the stone "along the fence." It is of sand stone with inscription in German and deeply sunken, inscription partly buried,—Gerg Sebastian Helman, Jan. 1st, 1725?—Feb. 1st 1784 (?)

Penna. Arch. 5th Ser. Vol. 6, p. 87, 119, 541, 542.

GEORGE HELMAN, JR.

Was in service, 1780, under Capt. Samuel Royer. He was a son of Geo. Helman, Sr., of Washington Twp. In 1790, a deed shows his wife as Elizabeth, and they sell 85 ac. of land in Washington Twp., to John Wollf, Farmer, joining Fredk. Bonebrake, David Sellers and Ludwick Harmony. Under Jan. 28, 1832 is shown the Admr. of the estate of the above Geo. Helman, late of Guilford Twp., Farmer, who left to survive him children and grandchildren, viz: 3 grandchildren, being the issue of his eldest child, Susan, who was mar. to David Foreman, leaving to survive her; Betsy mar. to Saml. Hoover; Esther mar. to Christian Fried (Freet) and Martha, a minor. The 8 children were: Martha mar. Henry Baker; Betsy mar. Nicholas George; George Helman; Daniel Helman; Peter Helman; Michael Helman, who purchased the shares of Jacob and Samuel Hoover, and Betsy, his wife, late Betsy Foreman; Jacob Helman; Samuel Helman. The above Geo. Helman died owning 109 ac. land in Guilford Twp., a 2 story log dwelling house and a double log barn.

Penna. Arch 5th Ser. Vol. 6, p. 89.

MICHAEL HELMAN

Is shown in service with Capt. Samuel Royer in 1780-81. In the Grindstone Hill Graveyard there are nineteen Helman graves with stones. One Michael died 1861 in his 70th year; Nancy, his wife, died in 1876, in her 90th year. Another Michael b. 1823, d. in 1900, his wife b. 1832, d. 1909. There are no legible stones standing to the Helmans who gave service in the Revolution.

Penna. Arch. 5th Ser. Vol. 6, p. 74, 89, 112.

JOHN HENNESY

Died June 10, 1819 in Franklin Co. John Henise in 4th Penna. Cont. Line, Oct. 21, 1779; taken prisoner Apr. 25, 1780; d. June 10, 1819, aged 76 in Franklin Co. Letters Admr., Aug. 25, 1819. He was a pensioner.

Penna. Arch. 2nd Ser. Vol. 13, p. 100. Penna. Arch. 2nd Ser. Vol. 10, p. 525.

JOHN HENRY

Served under Capt. Wm. Rippey of Shippensburg, enlisting Feb. 5, 1776. On the death of Wm. McConnell of Lurgan Twp., 1796, a daughter Esther was the wife of John Henry. They were then of Westmoreland Co. Penna. Another dau. of Wm. McConnell was Ann wife of Ennis King, and also living in Westmoreland County, in 1796.

Penna. Arch 5th Ser. Vol. 2, p. 237, 239.

HENRY HENSHEE, SR.

Appears on Muster Rools of Lancaster Co., as pvt., under Capt. Joseph Gehr, 1778-79-81-83. He came to Antrim Twp., Franklin Co., Penna. and his will was prob. Jan. 10, 1795. His wife was Barbara; Son David not yet 21; Daus., Anna; Elizabeth; Catherine; Mary; dau. Barbara is dead; Son Henry; son-in-law John Fleckinger; Anna "Hanschly" was mar. to John Flickinger, Mar. 30, 1784. A descendant states that the above Henry Henshee came from Switzerland in 1740 at the age of four years, with his parents. Henry Henshing was taxed in Washington Twp., 1799, with 200 ac. land, Log House, Stone Barn, small Spring House, 3 Horses and 5 Cows.

Penna. Arch. 5th Ser. Vol. 7, p. 899, 878, 270, 263, 613.

HENRY HENSHEE, JR.

Served as pvt., in Lancaster Co., Penna., under Capt. Joseph Gehr, 1779-78-81. Deeds show that in 1810 Henry Henshey and Barbara were in Huntingdon Co., Penna.

Penna. Arch. 5th Ser. Vol. 7, p. 878, 899, 270.

DAVID HERRON

Served under Capt. Thos. Askey and as a Ranger on the Frontier. Under Orphans' Court, May, 1808, is shown the petition of Mary and James Pollock, Mary as eldest dau., of David Herron states that David lately died intestate, leaving seven daughters: Mary mar. to James Pollock; Sarah mar. to Wm. Montgomery, since died leaving 9 children, to wit: David; Humphrey; Martha; Wm.; Andrew; Elizabeth; Sarah; Richard and Jennet. Margaret mar. John Thomson; Hannah mar. Hugh Cochran; Elizabeth mar. John Wood; Rebecca mar. Robert Knox; Jennett mar. Jacob Porter. Blunston Licenses July 19, 1734,—David Heron, 200 acres, as near the Settlement of his father Francis as the Same Can Conveniently be had. N. S.

Penna. Arch. 5th Ser. Vol. 6, p. 411, 631.

JAMES HERRON

Served as pvt., under Capt. Wm., Strain, 1778-82. The "Franklin Repository" May 12, 1829. "Departed this life on the 24th ult., Major James Herron in the 75th year of his age. The last of the Herrons on that beautiful stream bear-the name of their great ancestor, a daring pioneer of the forest in early Times whose numerous progeny for a long while occupied the land which he had marked out for their inheritance xxx flourished 40 years ago on the banks of Herron's branch." In 1808 there is a deed from "Major" James Herron to John Herron, Esq.,—another in 1812 to Matthias Painter. In 1822 James Herron to David Herron and Samuel Davidson Herron, for natural love and affection which said James bears toward his sons. In the will of John Brackenridge of Southampton Twp., dated 1806; prob. 1810. he names dau. Elizabeth mar. with James Herron, Middle Spring Church Graveyard records show: James Herron, b. 1754, d. Apr. 24, 1829; Margaret, wife of James Herron born 1766, d. Sept. 16, 1801. Blunston Licenses July 19, 1734,—James Heron, 200 acres, as near to the Settlement of his father and Brother as the same can conveniently be had. N. S.

Penna. Arch. 5th Ser. Vol. 6, p. 34, 143, 431, 443.

JOHN HERRON ESQ.

Of Southampton Twp., served in 1778-81-82, undated rolls, under Capts. Thos. Askey, Conrad Snyder and Wm. Strain. When he made his will in 1815 he said he was in his 67th year. His first wife was Mary Jack. His wife Jane was the widow of John McMasters. His son was Rev. Francis Herron of Pittsburgh; Son John; Son David the plantation on which I now live on Herron's Branch, Merchant Mill &c.; Library, Silver watch, &c. to sons John and David; Dau. Eliza; the lawful issue of my son James decd., their mother Elizabeth &c.; Dau. Sarah, wife of

James Brice; Dau. Elinor, wife of David Maclay; John Herron Kennedy, heir of dau. Jane, decd. To Robert Peebles and John Herron Peebles, heirs of my dau. Kezia. To Mary Jane and Margaret Natcha (?) Culbertson, heirs of my dau. Margaret, decd. A Codicil names "My sister Mary Gilchrist." Dated Sept. 11, 1815, prob. Oct. 11, 1815. Middle Spring Church Graveyard records show: John Herron, b. 1750, d. Oct. 2, 1815; Mary, wife of John Herron b. 1753, d. Jan. 28, 1808 Charles Herron occupied Pew No. 9, in the old Log Church at Rocky Spring. Robert Herron, Pew No. 38, in the new Brick Church. Land entries in Southampton Twp., Dec., 1735, show Wm.; David; James; and Francis Herron.

Penna. Arch. 5th Ser. Vol. 6, p. 50, 52, 119, 143, 411, 431.

WILLIAM HERRON

Served as pvt., under Capts. Strain, Peebles and Jack, 1777-1778 and one William Herron served in 1780-81-82 under Capt. Jno. Hodge; Records of Rev. John C. Bucher show the marriage of Wm. Herron to Agnes Brown, Oct. ye 26th, 1767. Deeds show William Herron and wife Agnes selling land, and the will of Wm. Herron of Southampton Twp., is dated Jan. 15 and prob. Dec. 5th of 1828. He names: Son Francis Herron; Dau. Jane Herron; Dau. Agnes Herron; Dau. Martha Nevin; Matthew Shields, son of deceased dau. Sarah. The Exrs., were David Shields and Wm. Herron. Blunston Licenses July 19, 1734: Francis Herron 200 acres On a Branch of Conococheague on the South side of Edward Nichols. N. S. Rev. Francis Herron came as pastor of Rocky Spring Church in 1800.

Penna. Arch. 5th Ser. Vol. 6, p. 23, 25, 28, 34.

ANDREW HERSHEY (HARSHAW)

Appears serving in the Militia of Cumb. Co., Penna., Cont. Line. One Andrew Hershey of Washington Twp., Franklin Co., Penna., left a will dated 1837, prob. 1839, in which he names a son Joseph; Sarah mar. Philip Laymaster; Jacob; John; Andrew; Elizabeth and Isaac. Court records at Hagerstown, Md., show the will of an Andrew Hershey in 1823, and of Barbara in 1845.

Penna. Arch 5th Ser. Vol. 4, p. 289, 627.

FREDERICK HESS

Sergt., served in Northampton Co. Militia. He may be the man who was in Franklin Co., and who bought a tract of land from Andrew Hamilton of Fayette Co., Penna., in 1787. It is not proven, but possible, and in the estate of Peter Benedict, 1798, a dau. Catherine is shown as the wife of Fredk. Hess.

Penna. Arch 5th Ser. Vol. 8, p. 350, 361.

JACOB HESS

Was in service as a pvt., 1779-80-81, under Capt. Saml. Royer. "'Valuations" in 1799 show him with land, log house and barn, horses, cows, &c. In 1822, Jas. McCullough and wife, Margaret of Peters Twp., sell land to Jacob Hess of Washington Twp.; in 1824 Jacob Hess of Peters Twp., farmer, and Betsy, his wife, sell to George Shade of Mercersburg. He left no estate in Franklin County. One Phebe Hess was mar. to Benj. Chestnut, March 19, 1811, by Dr. Robert Kennedy. Under records of St. John's Lutheran Church, Hagerstown, Md., are the following: Church Articles—1770—Signers: Jacob Hoss and Peter Hoss, The death of Mrs. Hoss, Sept. 6, 1838. Under Jan. 24, 1850, the death of Mr. Jacob Hess, 88 yrs., 2 mos., 19 days. In 1851, Mr. Hess. Marriage: Michael Baker and Motlina Hess, March 17, 1795. Baptisms: Jacob Hoss and wife Magdalene had Peter J. Baptized, July, 1774, also had George baptized, 1778. Peter Hoss and Salome had baptized Peter, Apr.. 1775; Mary, Apr., 1778,; William, June, 1806. The name Hess will be found in Court records at Hagerstown, Md., both Wills and Admrs. and the 1790 Census, Washington Co., Md., shows the Jacob Hess family as 3 men, 2 boys, 5 females.

Penna. Arch. 5th Ser. Vol. 6, p. 90, 98, 113, 543.

PETER HESS

Was in service 1780, under Capt. Wm. Berryhill. There is a Hess Family Graveyard near Waynesboro, which John Hess, 1797-1868, is lying with his three wives: Catherine; Fanny and Barbara. There are also Hess burials in Price's Graveyard. The 1790 Census, for Antrim Twp., shows the family of Peter Hess as,—1 man, 1 boy, 2 females.

Penna. Arch. 5th Ser. Vol. 6, p. 80.

ALBRIGHT HICKMAN

Served as pvt., under Capts. James Young and Terance Campbell, 1779-80-81-82. He was of Guilford Twp., dying intestate in 1804; no widow named, but issue: Margaret mar. Wm. Huston, Michael, eldest son; Elizabeth mar. Samuel Overdeer (?); Henry, Philip; Catherine mar. John Ralphsnider; Mary mar. Geo. Piper; All of full age.

Penna. Arch. 5th Ser. Vol. 6, p. 77, 82, 111, 126, 548.

ALEXANDER HILL

Served as pvt., under Capt. Samuel Patton and Capt. George Matthews, 1776-81-82.

Penna. Arh. 5th Ser. Vol. 6, p. 287, 211, 318.

JAMES HILL

Pvt., 1781-82, under Capt. Thos. Askey. James Hill mar. Isabella, dau. of Wm. Wallace, Sr., of Fannett Twp. James Hill also served in Westmoreland County.

Penna. Arch. 5th Ser. Vol. 6, p. 408, 441, 429.

SAMUEL HILL

Appears in service with Capt. Jas. Poe, in 1780-81-82. He was a taxable over that period in Antrim Twp., and Michael Stover names a son David, who mar. Mary Hill. Samuel is said to have been born 1755, and mar. Constance Brimley.

Penna. Arch. 5th Ser. Vol. 6, p. 92, 99, 576, 583. D. A. R. Magazine, Aug., 1924.

JAMES HINDMAN

Served as pvt., under Capt. Geo. Matthews in 1776, and under Capt. Samuel Patton 1780-81. He was of Hamilton Twp., and his will prob. Aug. 15, 1805, he names wife Mary and 3 youngest sons: Samuel; James; William; Son John and his son Joseph; Dau. Agnes wife of Davidson Filson and her 2 sons, Robert and James. Dau. Martha, wife of George Wilson. One Robert Hindman, late of Antrim Twp., left a wife Jean. Letters on estate of Robert Hindman were granted to Alexander Armstrong, Nov. 21, 1794.

Penna. Arch. 5th Ser. Vol. 6, p. 264, 279, 287, 312, 318, 643.

JOHN HINDMAN

Served as pvt., under Capt. Samuel Patton 1781-82. Both John and James Hindman are shown as taxables 1780-81-82, with land, horses and cows, in Hamilton Twp., Franklin Co., Penna.

Penna. Arch. 5th Ser. Vol. 6, p. 288, 312.

THOMAS HINDMAN

Served as pvt., under Capt. Conrad Snyder in 1780.

Penna. Arch. 5th Ser. Vol. 6, p. 74, 88.

CASPER HOCKENBERRY

Served 1781-82 under Capt. Thomas Askey as private.

Penna. Arch. 5th Ser. Vol. 6, p. 409, 423, 441.

HENRY HOCKENBERRY

Served as a pvt., under Capt Thos Askey in 1778-81. The name occurs under many spellings. Undoubtedly Henry, John and James were sons of Peter Hockenberry who died 1811.

Penna. Arch. 5th Ser. Vol. 6, p. 24, 55, 132, 409.

HENRY HOCKENBERRY, JR.

Served under Capt. Thos. Askey, 1779-82, as private.

Penna. Arch. 5th Ser. Vol. 6, p. 61, 442.

JAMES HOCKENBERRY

Served as pvt., under Capt. Thomas Askey, 1779-81-82.

Penna. Arch. 5th Ser. Vol. 6, p. 61, 131, 408, 429, 423.

JOHN HOCKENBERRY

Of Fannett Twp., served as a pvt., under Capt. Thos. Askey, 1779-81.

Penna. Arch. 5th Ser. Vol. 6, p. 61, 132, 409, 423, 441.

PETER HOCKENBERRY

Of Fannett Twp., served as pvt., under Capt. Thomas Askey, under the first Call, July 31, 1777, also in 1779-81-82, with some undated rolls. His will made in 1810, was prob. Feb. 19, 1811. He names wife Alice; eldest son Henry; 2nd son John; who gets land and Mills; two (2) daus., Mary and Margaret; 3rd son James' children land west of the creek; son Peter land which I now live on; daus., Catherine and Nancy; son Samuel; son Jeremiah; son Robert and son Samuel to be bound to a trade.

Penna. Arch. 5th Ser. Vol. 6, p. 7, 10, 61, 131, 408, 423, 441.

PETER HOLLER (HOLLAR-HALLER)

Served in the Militia of Lancaster Co., Penna., 1782-83, with Capt. John Lutts. Peter Hollar was born in Switzerland, Sept. 18, 1762 and died in Monguel, Franklin Co., Penna., May 12, 1851. He was buried in German Ref. Churchyard, later removed to Spring Hill graveyard, Shippensburg. He settled first in Lancaster County, Penna.; mar. Katherine Sweigert in 1778, who was born 1767 and died 1846. They had issue: I. Peter born 1790, d. 1869, mar. 1812, Nancy Waggoner, born, 1785, d. 1868. II. Henry b. 1794, d. 1863, mar. Catherine Carmony, b. 1799, d. 1877. III. Elizabeth mar. Abraham Stump. IV. Susanna mar. John Clippinger. V. Mary mar. David Bowers. VI. Catherine mar. Henry Alleman.

Penna. Arch. 5th Ser. Vol. 7, p. 501, 864.

PHILIP HOLLINGER

Served as pvt., Lancaster Co. Militia, 1781-82-83, under Capt. Andrew Boggs and Col. Lowery. He was born May 20, 1762 in Lancaster Co., Penna., died Sept. 5, 1821 in Franklin Co., Penna.; mar. Elizabeth Hess in 1779. He was buried on the Hollonger Farm, on Roadside road near Waynesboro, Old Sandstone marker with P. H. on it. They had issue; Susannah mar. Jacob Bonebreak. Samuel mar. Elizabeth Royer; Christine mar. David Walter; Motlena mar. Michael Holm; Mary mar. Abraham Grove; Peggy mar. Jacob

Wishinger; Nancy mar. John Shank; Hannah mar. ——— Sadler; John mar. Elizabeth Grove.
Penna. Arch. 5th Ser. Vol. 7, p. 690, 737, 752, 772.

GEORGE HOLSINGER

Served as pvt., 1780-81, under Capt. Daniel Clapsaddle. George Holsinger, 1762-1813, mar. 1st Rosanna Friedly; mar. 2nd Elizabeth Reichard. He died in Bedford County and certain releases on record in Franklin County show the following heirs: Dau. Mary, wife of Andrew Biddle; Son Jacob; Son John; Dau. Susanna, wife of Wm. Mikesell; Dau. Catherine, wife of Daniel Ulrich.
Penna. Arch. 5th Ser. Vol. 6, p. 71, 94, 117.

JACOB HOLSINGER

Was a pvt., 1780-81 under Capt. Daniel Clapsaddle. His will shows him of Washington Twp., and is dated Apr., 1810, prob. Mar, 1817. He names sons: Jacob; George; John; David; a dau. Nancy, who mar. Andrew Baker. The above man, born 1731, died 1817, mar. Susanna Yeakel.
Penna. Arch. 5th Ser. Vol. 6, p. 93, 94, 107, 116.

JACOB HOLSINGER, JR.

Served under Capt Daniel Clapsaddle in 1781. He is undoubtedly the son of George or Jacob Holsinger. There are Holsingers buried in Price's Graveyard near Waynesboro, Penna.
Penna. Arch. 5th Ser. Vol. 6, p. 117.

JOHN HOOD

Served as pvt., under Capts. Wm. Huston and Walter McKinnie 1780-81-82. He was also a Ranger on the Frontiers.
Penna. Arch 5th Ser. Vol. 6, p. 265, 270, 298, 306, 615, 643.

ROBERT HOOD

Served as pvt., 1780-81 under Capts. James Patton, Robert Dickey and Thos. McDowell. In the 1790 Census, the family of Robert Hood consisted of three men. The land of Robert Hood joined the early tract of John Holliday.
Penna. Arch. 5th Ser. Vol. 6. p. 272, 285, 315.

ADAM HOOPS

Appointed Coroner, Oct., 1750 and Justice of the Peace, Oct., 1764. In 1755-56 Adam Hoops appears as Commissary with Dr. Mercer, Col. Benj. Chambers, Rev. John Steel and others. Deed Book 2, p. 173, shows William Moorehead selling to George Chambers, his right to a piece of land on the west side of Conococheague Creek, in Hamilton Twp., opposite Adam Hoop's old Mill, about 90 acres; George Chambers hath it in contemplation to purchase of the representatives of said Adam Hoops, since decd., the tract of land whereon the old Mill stood, xxx for the purpose of erecting Water works thereon, which will drown the lands of Moorehead. In the will of Humphrey Fullerton he mentions a tract of land along the Great Road, to Adam Hoops Line. Under date of Oct. 16, 1775, Elizabeth Hoops of Phila., widow, and Exrx.; Robert Hoops of Hunterdon Co., N. J., gentleman and David Hoops of Virginia, gentleman, Exrs. of the will of Adam Hoops, late of the Falls, Bucks Co., gentleman, decd., to Wm. Long of Lancaster Co., Penna. This Grant to Adam Hoops was dated Mar. 11, 1763, and was in Antrim Twp., and is under Court records of Franklin County, Penna.
Penna. Arch. 2nd Ser. Vol. 9. p. 806, 808.

PHILIP HOOVER

Served in 1782 under Capt. Wm. Strain. Letters on his estate, 1804, were granted to Col. Joseph Culbertson and George Johnson and the widow Sophia Hoover.
Penna. Arch. 5th Ser. Vol. 6, p. 431.

JOHN HOPKINS

Served as Sergt., under Capt. James Poe, 1782, undated rolls.
Penna. Arch. 5th Ser. Vol. 6, p. 575, 582.

MATTHEW HOPKINS

Served under Capts. James Young, Adam Harmony and Conrad Snyder, 1778-79-80-81.
Penna. Arch. 5th Ser. Vol. 6, p. 74, 88, 119, 538, 548.

RICHARD HOPKINS

Served as private under Capts. John Woods nad James Poe, 1780-82. The Census of 1790 shows the family as 1 man, 3 females.
Penna. Arch. 5th Ser. Vol. 6, p. 91, 576, 583.

JOHN HORN

Served as pvt., under Capt. Daniel Clapsaddler in 1780; Orphans' Court records, May 16, 1803, John Horn died intestate; a widow since decd., (Knepper records show that Wilhelmus and Veronica Knepper had a dau., Catherine who mar. John Horn,) and issue: Elias Horn; Beniah Horn; Sulimet Horn mar. Daniel Foreman; Lydia mar. Samuel Burket; Bosmer Horn, yet single; Tertzee mar. Jacob Rheseman; Elizabeth (now decd.) mar. David Foreman and left issue: 4, Abraham; Susanna; Royer and Catherine, all yet living. Land in Washington Twp., 191½ acres warranted to John Horn. Deeds show that Susanna (of Elizabeth) mar. Dewald Bonebrake.
Penna. Arch. 5th Ser. Vol. 6, p. 93, 586.

LOUIS HOUSER

From Strasburg, Franklin Co., Penna., moved to

the Western Country. Nicholas Greenawalt testified that the above served in same Company and Regiment as he did. The Census of 1790 shows Ludwick Houser's family as one man and four females.

Penna. Arch. 5th Ser. Vol. 4, p. 523.

DANIEL HOUSTON

Served as 2nd Lieut., in Capt., Slaymaker's Company, Lancaster Co., Militia from 1777 to the close of the War. He was the son of John Huston, and was born in Pequea in 1754. His name is on the Pension list, July 3, 1834, aged 80 years. He was then living in Washington Co., Penna. By his father's will he was left a tract known as "Lowdon Land," and the ½ of what I have on Octorara Hill to the south, about 30 acres." Daniel Houston mar. Hannah Johnston (her brother Thomas mar. Anne Houston). They moved to the vicinity of Greencastle, where some of their children were born and where they lived eight or ten years. Court records show various transactions in Guilford Twp., 1810, 1811 over the settlement of the estate of Thomas Johnston of Lancaster Co., whose will was dated 1758, whose son John died without heirs. Daniel Houston and wife, Hannah Johnston being the legal heirs. Their children were: I. John b. 1777, mar. Rebecca Black, died in Newark, Ohio. II. Hannah b. 1786, mar. Wm. Buchanan, in 1808, lived in Chambersburg, moved to Washington Co., Penna., 1812. III. Daniel b. Greencastle, 1782, mar. Elizabeth Clark. IV. Nancy, unmar. V. Lydia b. 1788, mar, Nathan Patterson. VI. Polly, mar. John Buchanan. VII. Martha mar. ——— Dickson. Chambersburg, Pa. Will Book "B," p. 394. Letters of Admr. estate of Wm. Buchanan were granted to Hannah Buchanan and Daniel Houston, Jr., Mar. 17, 1810. Sureties: Daniel Houston, Sr. and John Brown. Daniel Houston and family moved to Washington Co., Penna., near Cross Creek village, where he bought a farm and built a substantial log house on it, which he left his dau., Nancy. It was built with regard to danger from Indians, the door being made of double planks, thickly studded with nails. This house was a land mark in the country, known as the "Nancy Houston place." Daniel Houston died in 1837, and is buried in Mt. Hope Churchyard, near West Middleton, Penna.

Penna. Arch. 5th Ser. Vol. 7, p. 58, 93, 648.

DANIEL HUSTON

Carroll Co., Ohio, July 31, 1833, Daniel Huston, resident of Washington Twp., Carroll Co., Ohio, age 78, enlisted Aug. 7, 1776, drafted, Capt. Scott's Company, Lt. Wm. Scott, Ensign John Underwood. At the time of enlistment was resident of Lancaster Co. Penna. Marched under Col. James Crawford, Maj. Fullerton. At Philadelphia, Trenton, Perth Amboy, N. J., New York City. Discharged Sept., 1777 drafted Lancaster Co. at a place called Horse Shoe Road under Capt. John Rowlins, Lt. Davis, Ensign John Ross. Bucks Co. under Gen. Potter. He was discharged Nov., returned home. Again drafted, served as Sergt. (July, 1778) under Command of Capt. Matheas Sheymaker, etc., in New Jersey, served as wagoner. Soon after left service he moved across the mountains to Washington Co., Penna., and served in Company of Capt. Ringland, Lt. Abraham Fry, as 2nd Lieut. Daniel Huston was born in County Antrim, Ireland in 1755. There is no record of birth. He came to this country in 1775, then about twenty years old. In Guilford Twp., 1791, Daniel Huston is taxed with 150 acres of land; four horses; five cows; one servant, a negro, 75 years old; four tablespoons. Washington Co., Penna., June 19, 1832, Daniel Huston, Nottingham Twp., age about 80. Same application as the one made in Carroll Co., Ohio. Last paid Sept., 1839 Carroll County, Ohio.

Rev. War Pension claim No. S-7055.

JAMES HUSTON

Pensioner. It appears that James Huston was born Apr., 16, 1758, on the Delaware river near Marcus Hook, which was later in Delaware Co., Penna. While living in Centre Twp., Washington Co., Penna., (which was later the part that was in Indiana Co.) Penna., he enlisted Apr. 5, 1777, and served four months as a pvt., in Capt. Samuel Dixon and Andrew Lower's Co. of Rangers, Penna. Troops, and was in an engagement at Wallace's Fort, Westmoreland Co., Penna. He then moved to Conocacheague (which was later in Franklin Co.) Penna., where he enlisted late in August 1781, and served two (2) months as a pvt., in Capt. John McConnell's Co., under Thomas Johnston in the Penna., Troops. After the Revolution he returned to Centre Twp., Ind. Co., Penna. where he was allowed pension on his application executed March 25, 1834. He died Sept. 16, 1841 in said Township. Soldier mar. Nov. 20, 1793, Mary, maiden name not stated, and who was allowed pension on her application, executed Aug. 2, 1844, while living in Centre Twp., and still living there in 1870. James Huston, a son, living in Centre Twp., in 1844, aged 49 years. In the will of above Rev. Soldier he names wife Mary; James; Nancy; Emily; Wm., also Mary, dau. of Samuel Reed.

Rev. War Pension claim No. W-273.

JAMES HUSTON

Was a pvt., 1781-82, under Capt. Patrick Jack. The above was probably a brother of Capt. Wm. Huston.

Penna. Arch 5th Ser. Vol. 6, p. 289, 291, 295, 313.

JAMES HUSTON

Served as pvt., under Capt. Wm. Huston, 1780-81. His wife was Susanna Teagarden. James Huston d. intestate, June 30, 1802, leaving a widow Susanna Teagarden and seven children: I. Elizabeth mar. Andrew Work, and had James; Andrew and Elizabeth Work, then minors. II. Wm. Huston mar. Mary Ann Bell, Jan. 17, 1815. III. Ann mar. Wm. Maxwell, Apr. 11, 1805. IV. John. V. James Johnston, mar Sarah, sister of Pres. James Buchanan, Oct. 14, 1818. VI. Susanna, unmar. VII. George, since died, no issue. James Huston, dying 1802, left 13 tracts of land: "Fortune"; "St. James Park"; "Generosity"; "Joy"; "Fairfiels"; "Oxford"; "Dundee"; "Flat Richland"; "Fat Ridge"; Lot No. 52 in Mercersburg, Mt. Land; and 2 not named. From the "Repository" and Church records we have: John Huston died Apr. 30, 1822. Died Sept. 24, 1822, Mrs. Ann Maxwell, wife of Wm. Maxwell. Died Sept. 27th, 1822, Miss Susan Huston. On Oct. 5th Susanna Huston, Sr. Some of the above were removed from the old Shannon Graveyard, to Fairview Cemetery, Mercersburg, Penna.

Penna. Arch. 5th Ser. Vol. 6, p. 269, 275, 282, 288.

JOHN HOUSTON

Of Pequea. The Immigrant. Born 1705, in the north of Ireland, came to America 1725-30 and settled in the Pequea Valley, Lancaster Co., Penna. At his death his estate amounted to over one thousand acres of land, along the old Phila. road, from the old "Hat Tavern" to the Pequea Creek. He mar. Martha, dau of George Stewart, a neighbor, who was the mother of eight children; John Houston died in 1769, his issue as follows: John; Jane; Daniel; James; Wm.; Anne; Thomas; Samuel.

WILLIAM HOUSTON

Son of John, entered the Army near the beginning of the war, in active service in 1777, from Lancaster Co. He was in the battle of Brandywine, one of the rear guards who stood at the crossing covering the retreat. He was taken prisoner at Long Island, confined in the prison-ship "Dutton" for seven months. He never recovered from the hardships, but was a sufferer as long as he lived. In 1781, Wm. Houston mar. Jane Watson and in 1789 he sold his land started with his family, his cattle and his two negro slaves, Andy and Sally, for the far west, traveling by wagon. They stopped first in Penn's Valley and then on the Conococheague Creek between Chambersburg and Mercersburg, Penna., where they lived eight years; then to "Brush Run" and in 1802 to Coitsville, now Mahoning Co., Ohio, where they settled. He died Dec. 28, 1834, and is buried in Deer Creek Churchyard, near New Bedford, Penna. His Epitaph: "In memory of Wm. Houston, who departed this life Dec. 28, 1834, aged 77 yrs., 7 months, after devoting his early life in the defense of his country, and in later years in the service of his God." His wife died Jan. 23, 1841 and is buried beside her husband. They had issue: John; David died in infancy; Patty; Peggy; Jane; Anne; Wm.; Betsy.

"The Houstons of Pequea" by Margaret E. Houston.

SAMUEL HOWARD

Is shown as a private in the company of Capt. Samuel Patton, on the Frontiers of Bedford and Westmoreland Counties, 1779. In 1780-81, he appears in Capt. Joseph Culbertson's Third Company, Cumb. Co. Militia.

Penna. Arch. 5th Ser. Vol. 6, p. 279, 288, 289, 601, 610.

FREDERICK HOWART

Served as pvt., 1780-81 under Capt. Daniel Clapsaddle. The Plum Graveyard, in a field, between Chambersburg and Williamson, shows the old Stone: "In memory of Catherine, wife of Frederick Howard, born Apr. 11, 1754, died Nov. 18, 1837, aged 83 yrs., 7 mos., 7 days. The will of Frederick Howard was dated and prob. 1805. He names wife Catherine; Two youngest children: Susanna and Abraham to be given a good schooling; Two eldest daus., Elizabeth and Hannah and oldest son John to be paid their legacies at once; residue of my children to be paid as they become of age. They were all of Washington Twp. The will of Catherine Howard of St. Thomas Twp., dated March, 1836, prob. Nov., 1836. She states she is "old and weakly." She names: Dau. Hannah Bartle, husband George; Dau. Esther, widow of David Yockey; Son Fredk. now living in the West. Grandchildren: Elizabeth Fisher; Esther Fisher, wife of Jacob Potter; Susan; Jacob; John; Abraham; Daniel; Samuel and Fredk. Fisher, issue of my dau. Elizabeth Fisher, decd.; Fredk. Fisher, decd., his two (2) children Hiram and Mary Ann Fisher; Catherine Howard wife of John Hafer; Hannah Howard, wife of Daniel Gallentine; Barbara Howard, dau of son John; David; Jacob; John; Catherine; Eliza and Hannah; Martha wife of Jacob Avey, children of dau. Catherine Snider, decd.; Christina Howard, dau of my son Jonathan, decd.

Penna. Arch. 5th Ser. Vol. 6, p. 71, 94, 117.

RUDOLPH HUFFER

Served as pvt., with Capt. Wm. Berryhill, in 1781, command of Col. James Johnston. In 1783, Rudolph Huffer and his wife Catherine of Antrim Twp., sell to Daniel Poorman of said County and State; Patent dated Mar. 22, 1773, to Rudolph Huffer and Daniel Poorman for a tract of land called "Success," in Washington Twp., then Antrim; joining Sebastian Hellman, Geo. Helman, Ludwick Herman and Adam Cook.

Penna. Arch. 5th Ser. Vol. 6, p. 102.

HENRY HUMBARGER (HUMBURGHER) (UMBERGER)

Appears in Cumb. Co., Penna., in 1780, "summoned by Capt. James Bell according to orders Red, that is to say the 5th, 6th, and 7th," Classes of the 3rd Batt. Cumb. Co., Militia. Court Records Chambersburg, 1786, show a deed from Mary Turner, widow of Adam Turner, of Westmoreland Co. Penna., late of Cumb. Co., Penna., to Henry Hambersburger of Lurgan Twp., Franklin Co., Penna. Land in Lurgan Twp. Henry Humbarger of the town of Strasburg, yeoman. Will dated July 1802, prob. Aug., 1802; wife Katharine $60, per year; 1/2 part of my lot No. 19, in the town of Strasburg and 2 rooms on the lower floor of the house I now live in, on Lot No. 11. 3 sons: Peter; Henry and Benj., two tracts in Lurgan of 172¼ acres, also a tract of 70 acres called Duncansburg, joining various persons. Son John and dau. Christina who is married to Jacob Right, all the ground rents which I own in Strasburg; son Adam lots Nos. 11-12-19-20, situate in Strasburg, and a small piece of land, late the property of George Lucas, also all the stock now on hand in the tanyard, he to pay son Jacob 400 lbs, specific, when he arrives at the age of twenty-one years.

Penna. Arch. 5th Ser. Vol. 6, p. 218: 222, 224.

JOHN HUMPHREY

It appears that John Humphry (pensioned as John Humphrey, Senior) was born in 1752 near the New London Cross Roads, Chester Co., Penna. While a resident of the Cannochocheague Settlement, Cumberland Co., Penna., he enlisted in Dec., 1776 and served as orderly Sergt. two months in Capt. Patrick Jack's Co., Col. John Allison's Penna. Regt. In Dec., 1777 he enlisted and served as orderly sergt. two months in Capt. John Orbison's Co., Col. White's Penna. Regt. In the summer of 1778 and 1779 he enlisted and served two months as a pvt., in Capt. John Taylor's Co. The next fall he was elected Capt. and served one year in Col. James McDowell's Penna. Regt. The following fall he enlisted and served two months as Sergt., in command of a guard of Penna. Militia. After the war he moved to Ohio Co., Virginia, and in 1800 went to Jefferson Co. Ohio. He was allowed pension on his application executed Nov. 18, 1833, while a resident of Warren Twp., in said Jefferson Co. John Humphrey, Certificate No. 25785, Rev. War, Ohio Agency, you are advised that the records of this office show that he died on June 30, 1841, in Warren Twp., Jefferson Co., Ohio, leaving surviving him no widow, but children whose names are as follows: Robert Humphrey of Scott Co., Iowa Territory; John Humphrey, Jr.; David Humphrey; Elizabeth McElroy; Mary Trimble of Jefferson Co., Ohio, and George Humphrey of Fulton Co., Ill. The County Clerk at Wheeling West Va., furnishes the fact that George, Robert and John Humphrey all received land grants in the Panhandle of Virginia, prior to the close of the Rev. War, surveyed in the three names as above.

Rev. War Pension Claim, S 8744.

WILLIAM HUMPHREY

Served as a pvt., under Capt. Wm. Huston, in 1780-81. He was a son of David Humphrey. He died in Warren Co., Ohio, will dated May 15, 1823,—the legatees were David and Samuel Anderson, "Sons of my sister Jane, formerly the wife of Oliver Anderson, decd.;" 225 acres of military land on the left fork of Sciota Brush Creek to the children of my brother John Humphrey; other land to the children of my brothers George and Robert Humphrey and sister Jane Anderson's children; 450 acres to the children of my sister Anne McChesney, formerly wife of John McChesney.

Penna. Arch 5th Ser. Vol. 6, p. 276, 283.

ALEXANDER HUNTER

Is shown as serving 1780-81, under Capt. Wm. Huston. In 1769 Alexdr. Hunter was living in the family of Wm. Hunter and wife Rhoda, presumably a brother, and in 1781, he owned land, horses, and cattle, in Peters Twp. His Warrant was dated June 1786 and Apr., 1787, which he appears to have sold to Wm. Johnston, the Patent to David Campbell, referred to, as the "Briggs Farm" and located between Mercersburg and the Gap. A Hist. of Allegheny Co., Penna., states that Alexdr. Hunter mar. Elizabeth Anderson of Franklin Co. and removed to Westmoreland Co. Penna. One Capt. Alexdr. Hunter served 1747-48 in Bucks Co., Penna.

Penna. Arch. 5th Ser. Vol. 6, p. 269, 276, 283.

DAVID HUNTER

Served in 1780 under Capt. Wm. Smith. One David Hunter married at Mercersburg, Penna. Elizabeth Galloway, Feb. 27, 1776. Greensburg,

Penna., Court records show a long will of David Hunter, in 1818, naming wife Jane.

Penna. Arch 5th Ser. Vol. 6, p. 276.

GEORGE HUNTER

Served under, Capt. Samuel Patton, June 22, 1779, then at Legonere. He also gave service 1778-1781, under Capt. Robert Dickey. He may have been the son of James and Mary Hunter, of District 8, Presby. Church of Mercersburg, Penna.

Penna. Arch. 5th Ser. Vol. 6, p. 601, 610, 382, 285.

JAMES HUNTER

Served 1780-81 under Capt. Wm. Huston. He is probably the James shown in District 8 with wife Mary, son George and dau. Elizabeth and the James of Peters Twp., who had land, horses and cattle in 1781. There was another James of Peters who was a weaver. James Hunter and wife Elizabeth left wills at Greensburg, Penna. James names sons Ephriam and William. Elizabeth's will, 1809, names 2 daus.; Sarah Brandon and Mary Wilson.

Penna. Arch. 5th Ser. Vol. 6, p. 265, 283, 643.

JOHN HUNTER

Son of William Hunter, mar. at Mercersburg, Apr. 1, 1800, Miss Mary Johnston, dau of Thos. Johnston. John Hunter left a will at Bedford, Penna. prob. 1811,—"I desire that my body may be laid as near my late brother William and sons William and Thomas and daughter Rhoda as may be in the dust. Four hundred dollars to the permanent fund of the Theological Seminary in the city of New York, under the care of the Rev. J. M. Mason. Ten dollars annually to the Rev. John Linn, pastor of the Reformed Congregation in this place, while he remains the pastor. Wife Mary the yearly interest on forty shares in the Union Bank of Maryland and also half of my personal estate as well as one third rent of my lands and house in McConnellsburg. Sister Elizabeth Gallaway one hundred and fifty dollars. Sister Agnes Gallaway one hundred dollars. Brother David the watch given me by my late brother William and also certain books. Brother Alexander six of my books. Honored Father my Margin Bible and other books. Sister Rhoda a legacy. Dau. Mary Ann Hunter is not of age and is in the care of her mother. Exrs.: Father-in-law Thomas Johnston and brother David Hunter."

JOHN HUNTER

Served with Capt. Thos. Askey under the first Call, 1777. It is possible that he was the John Hunter who later served with Capt. Alexdr. Peebles.

Penna. Arch 5th Ser. Vol. 6, p. 7, 10, 24.

JOHN HUNTER

Served as pvt., later as Ensign, under Capt. Alexdr. Peebles, 1779-81-82.

Penna. Arch. 5th Ser. Vol. 6, p. 57, 135, 395, 420, 432, 589.

ROBERT HUNTER

Under Wise's Oil Mill, Mr. John G. Orr states that Jacob Wise in 1822, purchased a farm in Lurgan Twp., and later included the farm of Robert Hunter, who had served in the Rev. War, and lies buried on his farm.

Kittochtinny Magazine Vol. 9, p. 473.

ROBERT HUNTER

Appears as Corporal Jan., 1776, under Capt. Jeremiah Talbott of Franklin Co., as Sergt., Nov., 1777, Seventh Penna. Regt. Cont. Line. It is possible there were two men of the name as one Robert Hunter of Capt. John Finley's 8th Penna. Co., states he was wounded at Bound Brook and at Paoli, residing in Westmoreland Co., Penna., in 1808. In the will of Robert Hunter of East Huntingdon Twp., Westmoreland Co., Penna., Dated Feb. 1, prob. March 1810,—Brother David Hunter sole heir and Executor, all my claim on the public as a Soldier.

McCauley's Hist. of Franklin Co., Penna. Penna. Arch 5th Ser. Vol. 3, p. 235, 238, 239, 240.

WILLIAM HUNTER

Served 1778-79-80, under Capt. Patrick Jack. In 1769 Wm. Hunter and wife Rhoda were living in District 2 near Mercersburg, Penna. His will recorded in Bedford County, Penna., is dated 1824 and prob. 1826, of Air Twp. He names wife Rhoda, sons Alexdr. and David; a dau, Elizabeth Galloway; dau. Rhoda; heirs of son John Hunter and dau. Nancy Galloway. John Galloway had mar. Nancy Hunter July 5, 1785, at Mercersburg. William and Alexander Hunter are shown as signing the Oath of Allegiance, at Carlisle, Jan. 20, 1778, under John Creigh, Justice of the Peace.

Penna. Arch. 2nd Ser. Vol. 14, p. 479. Penna. Arch. 5th Ser. Vol. 6, p. 30, 32, 64, 95, 96, 145, 147.

WILLIAM HUNTER

Served under Capt. Noah Abraham and Thos. Askey, 1779-80-81-82. He may be the Wm. Hunter who mar. Mary Dickey in 1778. The Ledger of Samuel Findlay, father of Gov. Wm. Findlay, shows store accounts over the Rev. War period. The following were shown for vicinity of Mercersburg:

Wm. Hunter ------ (Weaver)
Wm. Hunter ------ (Shoemaker)
Alexdr. Hunter; John Hunter; David Hunter.
Penna. Arch. 5th Ser. Vol. 6, p. 61, 86, 121, 128, 392, 393, 409, 424, 442, 620.

CORNELIUS HUTCHISON

Pension application, Huntingdon Co., Penna.,—John Campbell of Franklin Co., Penna., states that Cornelius Hutchison of Indiana Co., Penna., formerly lived in Cumb. Co., and was in Capt. Mathius Scott's Co., in Walter Stewart's Regt. for 3 years. He was in the 2nd Regt. Continental Line. Cornelius Hutchison and Elinor, his wife, of Fannett Twp., sell land warranted to Philip Hutchinson, father of said Cornelius, whereon Cornelius now lives, Nov. 24, 1795. From a descendant we have: Cornelius Hutchinson b. 1743, d. 1832, mar. Elinor McGuire, 1786. They had a son Robert, 1789-1877 who mar. Nancy Steel in 1810. A history of Indiana Co. Penna., shows above man there in 1840, pensioner aged 84 yrs.
Penna. Arch. 5th Ser. Vol. 6, p. 423, 409, 442. Penna. Arch. 5th Ser. Vol. 2, p. 837. Penna. Arch. 5th Ser. Vol. 4, p. 532.

JOHN HUCHESON

Of Hamilton Twp., served as pvt., under Capt. Patrick Jack in 1781. His will prob. Nov. 29, 1788, names wife Esther; Son William; Dau. Esther; Sons James; George; John and Robert.
Penna. Arch. 5th Ser. Vol. 6, p. 296.

JAMES INNES

Served as pvt., under Capt. Walter McKinnie in 1781. He had served earlier under Capt. John McClelland, as shown on Return for 1779. In 1809, Thos Ennis, and wife Lydia of Mercersburg, sell Lot 23 in the town, for $759. Vol. 6, of the 8th Ser., Penna. Arch., contains many references to James Ennis, Sr. and Jr., (1759) going express to Sundry Places with Dispatches to General Forbes; to New York with Dispatches from the Governor, and the like. Tax lists of 1799, show James Innis (Ennis) as a School Master in Montgomery and Peters Twps.
Penna. Arch. 5th Ser. Vol. 6, p. 289, 299.

JOHN IRELAND

Appears first, 1776, with Capt. Saml. McCune, later under Capt. Patrick Jack, some undated rolls.
Penna. Arch. 5th Ser. Vol. 6, p. 64, 145, 147, 403, 407, 420, 438, 587.

SAMUEL IRELAND

Served under Capts. James Patton, Thos. Mc Dowell and Robert Dickey, 1780-81, an undated roll. He was a taxable in Peters Twp.
Penna. Arch. 5th Ser. Vol. 6, p. 272, 285, 315.

WILLIAM IRELAND

Served 1780-81 under Captains Patton, McDowell and Dickey as above.
Penna. Arch. 5th Ser. Vol. 6, p. 271, 284, 314.

JAMES IRVINE

Private Penna. Militia, aged 76 in 1832, was a pensioner. He was allowed pension on his application executed August 29, 1832, at which time he was living in Franklin Co., Penna. He stated that his father served in the Quartermaster Department under Col. Archibald Steel. He died Nov. 9, 1843 in Cincinnati, Ohio. The widow Margaret, was allowed pension on her application executed Jan. 24, 1844, while a resident of Mercersburg, Penna., aged seventy-eight years. White Church Graveyard near Mercersburg, Penna.: Margaret Irwin, wife of James Irwin, born Apr., 3, 1765, died Feb. 20, 1852. Jane Irwin, their Daughter, born June 30, 1803, died Apr. 12, 1852. Inseparable in life they sleep side by side in death. A. Irwin b. Feb. 13, 1772, d. March 3, 1840. Matthew Irwin b. Sept. 5, 1800, d. Nov. 22, 1869. James Irwin, born Apr. 14, 1758, died Nov. 9, 1843, son of Archibald and Jean (McDowell) Irwin. He married Margaret (Piper) Smith, widow of Wm. Smith, Jr., who laid out the town of Mercersburg. They were Married Dec. 5, 1787, and had Issue: Archibald Irwin, 1788-1797; Mary Smith, 1790-1863, mar. James McClelland; Wm. born 1791; John, 1794-1838; James, 1797-1798; Archibald James born 1798; Matthew born 1800; Jane, F., 1803-1852.
Penna. Arch. 3rd Ser. Vol. 13, p. 530. Biographical Annals of Franklin Co. Veterans Administration, Bureau of Pensions.

JAMES IRWIN, SR.

Served in 1781-1782, under Capt. Walter McKinnie. He was a son of James Irwin, pioneer, and wife Jean, early settlers. The above James is in tax lists as "Uncle" to distinguish him from his nephew, James, son of Archibald. The will of James Irwin of Peters Twp., names wife Rebecca; son John, a child; Brothers and Sisters named: John Irwin; Archbd., Irwin; Elizabeth Torrence; Martha Neely; Margaret Patton; Mary Nesbit; Lidea Porter. Exrs: My brother's son James Irwin, son of Archibald, and James Maxwell. Dated June 5, 1784; prob. Jan. 7, 1785. This widow Rebecca, of James Irwin, Sr., married May 8, 1787, John Hoge, by Dr. John King.
Penna. Arch. 5th Ser. Vol. 6, p. 297, 299, 305.

JOSEPH IRWIN

Served in 1777, as First Lieut., under Capt. Robert McCoy. He served in 1781-82, under Capt. Walter McKinnie, Capt. McCoy having been killed at Crooked Billet May, 1778. Joseph Irwin, died Aug. 28, 1803, his wife Violet (Porter) dying at the home of her son-in-law Genl. Wm. Young, Oct. 9, 1823, at an advanced age. They had issue: Son Joseph; Myrtilla mar. John Sterrett; Jean mar. Nathan McDowell; Mary mar. Capt. Wm. Young; Elizabeth mar. Robert McDowell; Rebecca mar. John Gamble. Joseph Irwin, Jr., son of above, also served in 1782, under Capt. McKinnie. From an old Bible, printed by Matt. Carey, Phila., 1801, is the following: Joseph Irwin born Aug. 15, 1736; Violet Irwin Born March 7, 1739; Elizabeth Irwin born June 23, 1771; James Irwin born June 8, 1773; Jane Irwin born Aug. 20, 1766; Myrtilla Irwin born March 26, 1765.

Penna. Arch. 5th Ser. Vol. 6, p. 299, 301, 306, 369.

WILLIAM IRWIN

Served under Capt. Wm. Strain 1780-81-82. A deed shows Martha as widow of Wm. Irwin of Southampton Twp., in Sept. of 1790. Sons Wm. and John Irwin; Mary wife of John Mitchell, Jennet wife of Wm. Strain; Martha wife of David Simmeral; Margaret Irwin; Ann wife of John Ogilby; Grandchildren,—Wm. Irwin Hunter, Martha Hunter; by his dau. Elizabeth Hunter.

Penna. Arch 5th Ser. Vol. 6, p. 72, 406, 431.

BENJAMIN ISHMAEL

Served under Capt. Daniel Clapsaddle 1780-81, when it is shown that Benj. Ishmael moved to Bedford Co., Penna. McCauley's Hist. of Franklin County, shows Benj. Ishmail to have enlisted under Capt. Abraham Smith in 1776, a company of ninety three officers and men. In 1780 Benj. Ishmail is shown as a freeman, in Washington Twp., Franklin Co., Penna. Under pensioners living in Nicholas Co., Ky., Benj. Ishmail appears as a pvt., in the Penna., Line, was 83 years of age on Jan 15, 1822 and died July 10, 1822.

Penna. Arch 5th Ser. Vol. 6, p. 94, 97.

CAPTAIN JAMES JACK

The bearer of the Mecklenburg Resolves of May, 1775, to Philadelphia. Capt. James Jack was of Irish descent, born in Penna., in 1739, whence he removed to North Carolina, and settled in Charlotte eight or ten years before the commencement of the Revolutionary War. He mar. Margaret Houston, and was long a popular hotel keeper in Charlotte. He took a decided and active part in the Rev. War. He probably served under Col. Thomas Polk on the Snow Campaign in 1775. His large acquaintance with the people enabled him to raise a company of men whom he led forth on Rutherford's Cherokee campaign in 1776. He was with the troops embodied who opposed Cornwallis when he entered Charlotte in Sept., 1781, and also led his Company in General Polk's brigade in April 1781, joining General Greene at Rugeby's Mills. In 1783, Capt. Jack removed to Georgia, settling in Wilkes County. Capt. Jack's Certificate: He states "I was then solicited to be bearer of the proceedings to Congress." xx "I then proceeded on to Philadelphia and delivered the Mecklenburg Declaration of Independence of May, 1775, to Richard Caswell and Wm. Hooper, the Delegates to Congress from the state of North Carolina." "I am now in the 88th year of my age, residing in the County of Elbert, State of Georgia." James Jack. Signed this 7th Dec. 1819 befor Witnesses.

"The Mecklenburg Declaration of Independence, May 20, 1775" p. 137, 178, 179, 180.

PATRICK JACK

In sketches of Western North Carolina" is given the will of Patrick Jack May 19, 1780. He names: Beloved wife; Five Married daus.: Charity Dysart; Jane Barnet; Margaret mar. Saml. W. Wilson; Mary mar. Capt. Robert Alexander (from Penna., to N. C. about 1760); Lillie Nicholson.

CAPT. JOHN JACK

Appears first in July, 1776, later under Lieut. Col. James Johnston. His service covers 1777-78-79-80. The will of John Jack of Huntingdon Twp., Westmoreland Co., Penna., names wife Eleanor; son Patrick Jack; Daus.: Anna Robertson; Elizabeth Marklin; Rebecca Jack; Grandsons: John Clark; Andrew Thompson; John Finley; Three sons-in-law: Andrew Finley; John Robinson; John Marklin. To my other children, not before named, one dollar if called for. Son Thomas J. Jack. Exrs.: Sons-in-law, Andrew Finley and John Robertson. Wit: John Carnahan and Charles Hunter, Apr. 23, 1808.

Penna. Arch 5th Ser. Vol. 6, p. 6, 69, 168, 511, 517, 518, 532, 535, 539, 598, 599, 609.

JOHN JACK

Served as pvt., 1779-80-81-82, under Capts. James Young and Patrick Jack. Letters on his estate were issued to James Orbison, March 28, 1806, in Franklin Co. Penna. Under a deed dated Dec. 10, 1784, John Jack of York Co. Penna., and Margaret, his wife, sell to James McLanahan of Antrim Twp., Franklin Co., Penna., certain land in Antrim Twp., joining Wm. Stover, John and James Johnston. The Warrant dated Sept. 28, 1750, was to James Jack of Antrim Twp., Cumb. Co., Penna., who with Anne his wife, sold to John Jack of aforesaid County and state in 1767.

Penna. Arch. 5th Ser. Vol. 6, p. 82, 110, 292, 296, 313, 548.

MATTHEW JACK PENSIONER

W2809, BLWT 2483 300. The 8th Penna. Regt., under authority of a resolution of Congress dated July 15, 1776, for the defense of the western frontier, to garrison the posts of Presqu' Isle, Le Boeuff and Kittanning. Matthew Jack, First Lieut., Aug. 9, 1776, under Capt. Saml. Miller, Matt. Jack, states in his pension application, "marched to Kittanning, Quibbletown, joined General Washington, attached to Genl., Lincoln's division xx" and further, Capt. Matt. Jack says "they were stationed at Bound Brook, N. J. in the winter and spring of 1777, where the British attacked and defeated it, losing a number of men. In the year 1778, it was sent to Pittsburgh, to guard the frontier and placed under the command of General McIntosh. They went down to the mouth of the Beaver, and there built Fort McIntoch; then to the head of the Muskingum, and there built Fort Laurens. In 1779 went up the Allegheny, on Genl. Brodhead's expedition, attacked the Indians, defeated them and burned their towns." Matthew Jack lost his left hand by the bursting of his Rifle gun, at Bound Brook, New Jersey; promoted captain Apr. 13, 1777, in defense of a Redoubt. Court records at Greensburg, show the will of Charles Wilson, Apr., 1800, in which he names sons-in-law, Wm. and Matthew Jack. To grandson Matt. Jack, he gives his sword; to grandson Samuel Jack, his case of pistols; to grandson Robert McMahan, his gun. The pension paper shows the marriage of Matt. Jack and Nancy (Wilson (?) about Feb. 15, 1782 at Hempfield twp., before John Guthrie, Esq., J. P. Robert Shields had known them 40 years; Elizabeth McMahon, age 75, was present at the marriage; the children named Wm. Samuel; Elizabeth; Matthew; Mary. Matthew Jack died Nov. 2, 1836. Nancy Jack died Nov. 20, 1840. In 1854 Samuel Jack and Polly (Mary) Shields are the only two children living. Matthew Jack, Jr., left issue: Isabella who mar. John McCulloch; Wm.; Matthew; Agnes; Richard; Mary; Jane; Samuel Jack. Heirs of Elizabeth (Jack) Woods: 4—Matthew Woods; Ann Woods, wife of Thos. Wilson; Mary Woods; Margaret Woods. From Congruity cemetery, near New Alexandria, Westmoreland Co.: Capt. Matthew Jack d. Nov. 26, 1836, in 82nd year of age; Nancy, wife of Capt. Matthew Jack d. Sept. 20, 1840, aged 80 years. Matthew Jack d. Feb. 10, 1817, in 51st year.

Penna. Arch 5th Ser. Vol. 3, p. 307, 309, 314, 315, 323, 320, 327, 328, 336, 376.

LIEUT. COL., SAMUEL JACK

Served under Col. Wm. McAlvey, in the 3rd Batt., of Bedford County Militia, Dec., 1777. Deeds show that in Feb., 1771, Samuel Jack, son of James Jack, Blacksmith, of Guilford Twp., Cumb. Co., Penna., sells to his brother Patrick Jack, of Hamilton Twp., 200 acres land, adjoining John Holliday and others in Peters Twp. The Order No. 2952, in 1767, was granted to Samuel Jack. Patrick Jack had surveyed in same place 221 acres, 153 perches. "Samuel Jack to Martha Heran, Dec. Ye 29th, 1766" by Rev. John C. Bucher. Samuel Jack died Oct. 16, 1814, aged 82 years. He is buried in the St. Clair Cemetery at Greensburg, Penna.

Penna. Arch 5th Ser. Vol. 5, p. 72.

WILLIAM JACK

Under pension applications in Westmoreland County, Penna., William Jack Lieut., in Capt. Moorhead's Company, 8th Regt., testifies to Richard Hackley's enlistment into the above company. Wm. Jack further states that he, Wm. Jack, continued therein about two years and was discharged by General Irwin at Pittsburgh after the War. In the will of Charles Wilson, of Franklin Twp., Westmoreland Co., Penna., he names sons-in-law Wm. and Matthew Jack. From the Hist. of Westmoreland Co., Penna., 1882: The ground for the St. Clair Cemetery at Greensburg was deeded by Wm. Jack (old Judge Jack) in 1803. Burials: Samuel Jack died Oct. 16, 1814, aged 82 years; William Jack died Feb. 7, 1821, aged 69 years; Margaret, wife of Judge Jack, died May 3, 1818, aged 63 years.

Penna. Arch 5th Ser, Vol, 4, p. 588, 590, 592.

GEORGE JACOBS

Served as a private under Capt. Daniel Clapsaddle 1780-81. He died 1790. His wife Madalena renounced her right and Martin Jacobs acted as Admr. To widow 1/3 and to son and only child the residue of estate. He is buried in Jacob Lutheran Church Graveyard, near Waynesboro, Penna. George Jacobs was born March 14, 1763, died Nov. 16, 1790.

Penna. Arch. 5th Ser. Vol. 6, p. 94, 116.

MARTIN JACOB

Served under Capt. Daniel Clapsaddle in 1780, undated roll. His will was dated 1789, prob., 1803. His dearly beloved wife Anna Barbara to have six hundred weight of flour for bread, 100 lbs., of pork, a good milk cow, 2 lbs. of coffee, 2 lbs., of tea, 6 lbs., of sugar, 1 bushel of salt, 2 pairs of shoes yearly and peaceable house room and fire wood in the old house. 3 sons, George, first born, Henry and Michael, all my lands. To George, one English Shilling for his first Birth.

Penna. Arch. 5th Ser. Vol. 6, p. 72, 94.

ENOCH JAMES

Served as pvt., 1780-81-82 under Capts. Huston and Orbison. He was a son of Meseck James.

who died prior to 1771 and who settled on the site of the village of Fort Loudon. On Sept. 30, 1748, Thos. and Richard Penn granted to Mesech James 370 acres land in Heidelberg Twp., Lancaster Co., now Peters Twp., Franklin Co., Penna. Here he built the house that was burned by the Indians Nov., 1755. It is thought that two sons, Isaac and Wm., were carried into captivity, as an instrument of writing in Aug. of 1771, shows that Isaac and Wm. each had a right to a share in the estate if he came to claim it. The heirs of Mesech James: Owen David (Davis) wife Hannah; David Bowen, wife Sarah; and Mary Owens, granted part of said land to Enoch James, son of Mesech, by Conococheague Creek, by Robert Barr, by James Barr, 179 acres. In 1774, Enoch James and wife Sarah sold to John Walker, who, with wife Mary, sold in 1787 to Wm. Withrow of Hamilton Twp. In the will of David Bowen, Montgomery Twp., old and frail, he names 4 daus., now living: Mary John; Gwen Denham; Sarah James; Rebecca Ross; dated 1794; prob. 1802. These heirs are shown in Deed Book 3, p. 169 as: Wm.; Isaac; Enoch; Jean; Hannah; Sarah; Mary. Jean mar. John Ross; Hannah mar. Owen Davis; Sarah mar. David Bowen; Mary mar. Samuel Owen. The Blunston Licenses show Samuel and Thomas Owen in June, 1735, with 500 acre tracts, at a branch called Lick Run, a northern branch of the Conococheague, a Sandy Spring.

Penna. Arch. 5th Ser. Vol. 6, p. 264, 274, 294, 308, 643.

HENRY JAMES

Served as pvt., 1781, under Capts. Walter McKinnie and Robert Dickey, an undated roll.

Penna. Arch. 5th Ser. Vol. 6, p. 285, 299, 315.

JESSE JAMES

Is shown serving 1780-81-82 under Capts. Patton, Dickey and McDowell. He was a taxable 1781 in Peters Twp., Benjamin James is shown as a 1781 taxable, with 50 acres of land in Peters Twp., but the name disappears in the County by 1790.

Penna. Arch. 5th Ser. Vol. 6, p. 271, 284, 304, 314.

JAMIESON

"Another woman named Jamieson, was missing, supposed to be carried off." In 1784, twenty years later, Dr. John Ewing in passing across the Cumberland Valley, stopped at Rev. John King's at McDowell's Mill, and on the next day, June 16, he writes: after proceeding up the Valley 10 miles, we came to Jamison's Tavern, where we dined." If the report that a woman named Jamieson was taken was correct, it might explain the fact that Bouquet brought back a Betsy Jamison with his other prisoners.

Hist. of the Cumb. Valley, Donohoo, p. 336. Gordon's Hist. of Penna. p. 625.

JOHN JEFFERY

Served under Capt Patrick Jack, as pvt., 1781-82. In his will prob. Jan. 9, 1810, he names these legatees: Isaac Jeffery; Thomas Menich; Betsy Burns, dau. of James Burns, decd.; Easter Burns, dau. of James Dyer; my sister Betsy Burns the residue of my estate.

Penna. Arch. 5th Ser. Vol. 6, p. 289, 291, 295, 313.

BENJAMIN JENKINS

Served as pvt., under Capts. Robert Dickey and Thos. McDowell, 1777-81. He mar. at Mercersburg, Penna., Sarah Hutcheson, Dec. 29, 1778. He appears as a freeman in Peters Twp., in 1782. One Thomas Jenkins also appears under Capt. Wm. Huston, as pvt., in 1781. Baptisms of children for Benjamin Jenkins were: Agnes, in 1780; John 1782; Ezekiel—one in 1785.

Penna. Arch. 5th Ser. Vol. 6, p. 284, 314, 372.

EVAN JENKINS

Is shown in the Cont. Line, and in the Militia of Peters Twp., where he appears as a freeman. He served under Capts. Jas. Patton and Wm. Huston 1780-81. He mar. Elizabeth Griffith, May 30, 1780. One Evan Jenkins, living on Licking Creek, Bedford County (Now Warren Twp.,) gave service there in 1777-79, and it is probable the service was all given by one man.

Penna. Arch. 5th Ser. Vol. 4, p. 629. Penna. Arch. 5th Ser. Vol. 6, p. 265, 272, 283, 615, 643.

DAVID JOHN

Appears serving in Bedford Co., Penna., with Capt. Thos. Davies, undated rolls, also as a Soldier in the Cont. Line, from Bedford County. Deeds show that David John of Franklin Co., Penna., on Jan., 1810, sold to Jacob Zimmerman of same a tract of 341 acres 52 perches, in the Little Cove, under 3 Patents. Whereas Jacob John Sr., decd., of Little Cove, died owning a tract in Little Cove, by his last will leaves the estate to his children, viz.: David; Margaret; Jacob; Daniel; Joseph; Benjamin; by an act of assembly passed in 1806, David Bowen, Jr., and David Bowen of Samuel, appointed trustees for the minor children. On the farm sold to Jacob Zimmerman by the Johns, is a small graveyard in the corner of a field, in which the early Johns are buried.

Penna. Arch. 5th Ser. Vol. 4, p. 242, 607. Penna. Arch. 5th Ser. Vol. 5, p. 96, 103, 111.

GIDEON JOHN
First appears in 1778 with Capt. Saml. Patton, and in 1781, under Capt. Patrick Jack.
Penna. Arch. 5th Ser. Vol. 6, p. 292, 296, 380.

JAMES JOHN
Served as Lieutenant from Bedford Co., Penna., under Capt. Thomas Davies, who attests "and hes served." James John, Lieut., appears from Bedford County in the Cont. Line.
Penna. Arch. 5th Ser. Vol. 5, p. 82, 111. Vol. 4, p. 242, 607

LEMUEL JOHN
Appears with Capt. Thos. Paxton's Ranging Company, of Bedford Co., in 1776, with undated rolls. He was also a Rev. Soldier in the Cont. Line, of Bedford Co.
Penna. Arch. 5th Ser. Vol. 5, p. 62, 63, 91, 111. Vol. 4, p. 242, 607

SAMUEL JOHN
Served in 1776, in Capt. Thos. Paxton's Company of Rangers, of Bedford Co., Penna.
Penna. Arch. 5th Ser. Vol. 5, p. 53, 56.

THOMAS JOHN
Is shown in the "Class Role of Capten Davee Company of Militia of Bedford County, Penna." He also appears as a Rev. Soldier, in the Cont. Line, from Bedford Co. The Ledger of Samuel Findlay, Rev. War period, shows six men named John,—John John (Neighbor); Thomas John (Cove); Jacob; Wm.; David; James. In the will of David Bowen of Montgomery Twp., "old and frail," he names "all of my daughters now living, viz: Mary John; Gwen Denhan; Sarah James; Rebecca Ross.
Penna. Arch. 5th Ser. Vol. 5, p. 111. Vol. 4, p. 242, 607

BENJAMIN JOHNSTON
Under date of Jan. 8, 1845, the "Mercersburg Visitor" gives the following: "Mr. Benjamin Johnston died at Collinsville, Madison Co., Ill., on the 6th inst., in the 87th year of his age. Mr. Johnston served under Capt. Charles Maclay during 1779-80-82, and was a Soldier and a Patriot of the Revolution."
Penna. Arch. 5th Ser. Vol. 6, p. 62, 150, 149, 397, 430, 428.

MAJOR JOHN JOHNSTON
Appears in the First Batt., in service Jan., 1778, of Cumb. Co. Militia, with Col. Saml. Culbertson; they were "ordered back from Lancaster." He was Major of Col. Abhm. Smith's Eighth Batt., in 1777-78. He appears with a Company of Light Dragoons in 1781, for twenty five days, under the Command of James Culbertson. John Johnston, 1747-1826, Mar. Nov. 3, 1772, Rebecca, dau. of pioneer Wm. Smith of Mercersburg. He mar. 2nd Anna belle, dau. of Major James McDowell. The Franklin Repository—from the Pittsburg Gazette, of Nov. 3, 1826. Died at the home of Major Thomas Johnston of Indiana, on the 21st, Major John Johnston, formerly of Franklin Co., aged about 80 yrs. From D. A. R. Lineage Book 93, p. 65,—John Johnston, 1748-1826, Capt. of Light Horse and Major 8th Batt., Cumb. Co. Militia, mar. 1st Rebecca, dau. of Wm. Smith, Sr., of Mercersburg, Penna. He mar. 2nd Annabelle, dau. of Major James and Jane (Smith) McDowell. Married by Rev. John King, John Johnston to Rebecca Smith, Nov. 3, 1772. "The Old Burial Ground is situated on the southern limit of the borough, (Saltsburg, Penna.,) on the bank of the Conemaugh river. When this spot was chosen probably about 1810, it was a pleasant and convenient place for the dead. In the course of years, the surveys for the Pennsylvania canal traversed the bank of the river, and the final location of the improvement penetrated the sacred spot, resulting in the exhumation of some of the bodies, and rendering the place no longer tenable. But two graves of all who were interred there have been preserved with any indications of care, and they are surrounded by a small enclosure. There is a plain stone tablet over each of the graves, each bearing an inscription. The first and oldest is erected: "In memory of Mrs. Jane Boggs, Consort of Andrew Boggs, Esq., who departed this life June 3, 1821, aged 36 years." The second is: "Sacred to the memory of Major John Johnston, who departed this life Oct. 21, 1826, in the 79th year of his age." Andrew Boggs mar. Jane Johnston, dau. of John Johnston, Sept. 10, 1805. Dr. Robert Kennedy.
Caldwell's Hist. Indiana Co., Penna., 1880, p. 383. Penna. Arch. 5th Ser. Vol. 6, p. 30, 511, 531, 614, 640.

WILLIAM JOICE
Pvt., under Capt. John McConnell in 1778 under Capt. James Patton in 1780 later under Capt. Thos. McDowell. William Joice left a will at Greensburg, Penna., Court records. He states he was of Westmoreland County. He names a wife Mary; sons Wm. and Henry; a dau. Mary. His will was dated July 25, 1798, prob., Sept. 10, 1798.
Penna. Arch. 5th Ser. Vol. 6, p. 272, 315, 374.

JOHN JONES
The will of John Jones of Metal Twp., Franklin Co., Penna., states, "being now in my natural and common senses, knowing well what I am about to doo, throughe the marcy of Almighty

God Amain." Beloved wife Elizabeth Jones; if my wife lives single till the youngest child is of age; wife is not to "wantingly" destroy any Timber. Sons Samuel; Joseph; Jesse; Daus.: Polly and Sally. Jesse and Sally schooling equil with the rest of my children; Sons John; Jacob; James; Dau. Betsy Rutter; Dau. Nancy Rutter; dated May 17, 1806; prob. Nov. 18, 1840. In 1799 John Joans of Metal Twp., was taxed on 213 acres land, 70 acres being improved; he had one Cabin; 2 Horses and 4 Cows. Repository and Whig Thursday July 2, 1840. Died at his residence in Metal Township in this county on Wednesday the 24th untimo Mr. John Jones Sen'r aged 110 years and 6 months. He was born on the 24th of December, 1729. The place of his nativity was Worcestershire England but he resided in the City of London for many years from which place he was impressed on board a British man of war that was aiding on the blockade on the American coast during the war of the revolution from which he made his escape and entered the American army in the Company of Capt. Alexander. He was subsequently taken prisoner by the British, but not being recognized was exchanged and again entered the service where he remained until honorably discharged. He resided fifty-seven years on the property he obtained when he came to this country and left a widow now 85 years of age, 10 children, 100 grandchildren and about the same number of great grand-children.

Census of Pensioners, Act. 1840.

DAVID JORDAN

Served as a pvt., under Capt. John McConnell in 1781-82. He mar. Jean, dau. of Francis and Mary Graham of Lurgan Twp. They moved to Westmoreland Co., Penna., where he left a will. David Jordan of Derry Twp., wife Jennet; son Francis the use of my cooper tools. 3 sons: Samuel; David; John. 6 daus: Margaret; Mary; Elizabeth; Jannet; Easter and Sarah. The Executors were: wife, son Francis and Robert Barr of Salem Congregation. Dated Sept. 11, 1795; prob. May 15, 1796.

Penna. Arch. 5th Ser. Vol. 6, p. 302, 309.

JOSEPH JUNKIN

Served under Capt. John Trindle, as First Lieut., 1777-78. He was the son of Joseph Junkin and Elizabeth Wallace, and was born Jan. 22, 1750. Joseph Junkin enlisted early, leaving his intended bride unwedded until the storm of war was should pass; he enlisted and went to the front. In the battle of Brandywine, Sept. 11, 1777, he commanded a company. In the sharp skirmish near White Horse Tavern, on the 16th, his arm was shattered by a musket ball. He finally made his way home, a distance of ninety miles, in three days, where, with good care, his wound healed. In May, 1779, he was married by Dr. Dobbin to Eleanor Cochran by whom he had fourteen children. Eleanor, dau. of John Cochran of Waynesboro, born 1760, was baptized Apr. 30, 1761, by Rev. John Cuthbertson. In the spring of 1806, Joseph Junkin and family removed to Hope Mills, Mercer Co., Penna., where he died Feb. 21, 1831, his wife Eleanor died in 1812. Issue of Joseph and Eleanor Junkin: Joseph died young. John; Joseph; George; William; Benjamin; Wm. Findley; Matthew; Oliver; David X; Elizabeth; Eleanor; Mary; Agnes. The Hist. of the Bard Family by G. O. Seilhamer gives much of interest on the above family.

Penna. Arch. 5th Ser. Vol. 6, p. 202, 204, 211, 213, 609.

ROBERT JUSTUS

Enlisted in Penna., Line, in Capt. Scott's Co., Col. Stewart's Regt., transferred to Capt. Campbell's Co., in same Regt., during War. Served until peace in 1783, later applied for a pension from Franklin County.

Penna. Arch. 5th Ser. Vol. 4, p. 531.

GEORGE KAHL

In 1840 George Kahl gives his age as 82 years. George Kahl of Green Twp., being old and weak in body, but of sound mind, memory and understanding (Praised be God for it) considering the certainty of death, and the uncertainty of the time thereof, &c.; Oldest dau. Catherine (who had been his housekeeper), balance between nine (9) children or their heirs; Dau. Polly mar. James Beaty and is long since decd., her share to her children; my sons, Jacob, John, Henry and other daus.: Sarah, Elizabeth who mar. Peter Spence and Susanna. Wit: Jacob Heysinger and John Schmidt. Prob. Sept. 30, 1845.

Census of Pensioners, Act of 1840.

ANDREW KAUFFMAN

Served in Lancaster County, 1782-83, under Col. Fredk. Zeigler, Captain Jacob Brand.

Penna. Arch. 5th Ser. Vol. 7, p. 427, 447, 965.

CAPT., SAMUEL KEARSLEY

Served under Col. Hartley, 1777, in the 11th Penna. Regt. He appears as a First Lieut., promoted to Captain, Feb. 18, 1778, and served under Capt. John Steel. He is also shown in 1781, serving in the New Eleventh Penna. Regt. Capt. Kearsley died March 22, 1830, aged 80 years, and is buried in Middle Spring churchyard, Franklin Co., Penna. (?)

Penna. Arch. 5th Ser. Vol. 3, p. 611, 631, 642, 665.

JOHN KEASY

Appears in Cumb. Co. Militia, Cont. Line, also in service with Capt. Wm. Huston. He was of Metal Twp., and left a will prob. Nov. 6, 1801, in which he names wife Mary; Son John and daus.: Barbara; Elizabeth; Nancy; Mary, he also named Wm. Stinger as the first husband of his dau., Barbara; a son-in-law, Barnet Shetler. John Keasy, son of above John and Mary was mar. by Dr. David Denny to Barbara Hammond, Sept. 11, 1798, Barbara was born May 5, 1780 and died in 1826. John died 1850 and their issue follows: I. John, b. 1799, mar. Jane McCurdy, 1830. II. Jacob, b. 1800, mar, Jane Bigler. III. Henry, b. 1803. IV. Philip b. 1805. V. Barbara b. 1807, mar. Daniel Wolff, 1830. VI. Mary, b. 1809 mar. Jacob Willet. VII. David b. 1811. VIII. Susan b. 1815, mar. Anthony Klippinger b. 1848. IX. Solomon, b. 1818, mar. Margaret Hammond. X. Jane Filson b. 1821, mar. John Richardson. XI. James b. 1826. John Keasey b. July 31, 1799. d. Feb. 8, 1866, mar. Apr. 7, 1831, Jane McCurdy, b. Oct. 15, 1808, d. Nov. 2, 1882. They had issue: 1. Mary Ann b. Jan. 7, 1833; died Jan. 10, 1915, mar. 1st Edward M. Rice; Mar. 2nd James McCurdy Rankin. 11. James McCurdy b. June 13, 1834, d. in infancy. III. James Alexander, b. May 18, 1835, d. in infancy. IV. Barbara born, died March, 1837. V. John b. July 5, 1838, d. Feb. 14, 1926. VI. Margaret Susan, b. Oct. 19, 1841, d. Aug. 14, 1883, mar. John Chambers Flickinger, Nov. 1, 1866; he was born Jan. 18, 1840, d. Sept. 7, 1869.

Penna. Arch. 5th Ser. Vol. 6, p. 643. Penna. Arch. 5th Ser. Vol. 4, p. 629.

FREDERICK KEEFER

Of Warren Twp., age given as 78 yrs. in 1840. His will, prob. March 18, 1852, names wife Barbara; Son Frederick; Daus.: Elizabeth; Catherine; Sons John; David; Michael; Samuel; Daniel; Jacob; Dau. Sarah Miller and Benjamin Miller. Wit: Geo. Conrad Boehler and A. S. McCullough. Census of Pensioners, 1840 Act.

RICHARD KEEN (KANE)

Served as a pvt., under Capt. Wm. Long in 1777, First Call and under Capt Thomas Johnston in 1780. His will was prob. Nov, 1, 1785. His legatees were John Ervin, Jr.; James Brotherton; Jacob Wider and Jin Bea.

Penna. Arch. 5th Ser. Vol. 6, p. 84, 519.

EDWARD KELLEY (KELLIAH)

Was a Sergt., under Capt. Thos. Askey, 1777-79-81-82.

Penna. Arch. 5th Ser. Vol. 6, p. 27, 60, 131, 423, 441.

JOSEPH KELLEY

Served as pvt., under Capt. Patrick Jack, Thos. Askey and Noah Abraham, 1778-79-81-82. From the Franklin Repository, June 24, 1805, we have the following: "For Sale,"—That Capital Plantation late the property of Joseph Kelley, decd. Situate in Cumberland Valley, Bedford County, 18 miles from town of Bedford, and 12 miles from Fort Cumberland, 228 acres, 140 cleared and 40 in meadow; never-failing Springs, 2 story dwelling house. Inquire of the subscriber, near the premises. Thomas Kelley.

Penna. Arch 5th Ser. Vol. 6, p. 32, 61, 95, 96, 132, 393, 409, 424, 442, 620.

WILLIAM KELLEY

B. Smith, served as pvt., under Capt. Thos. Askey, 1781-82.

Penna. Arch 5th Ser. Vol. 6, p. 409, 424, 442.

WILLIAM KELLEY

Served as a pvt., with Capt Thos. Askey, 1778-79-80-81-82.

Penna. Arch 5th Ser. Vol. 6, p. 62, 132, 407, 410, 412, 424, 428, 442, 631, 605, 620.

WILLIAM KELLEY

Served as pvt., under Capt. James Patton, 1780.
Penna. Arch. 5th Ser. Vol. 6, p. 271.

WILLIAM KELLY

Served as a pvt., from Fannett Twp., 1779-80-81-82, an undated roll, under Capts. Thos. Askey, Noah Abraham and James Patton.

Penna. Arch. 5th Ser. Vol. 6, p. 62, 407, 409, 410, 412, 424, 428, 442, 271, 132, 620, 631.

THOMAS KENNEDY

Served as pvt., under Capt. John McConnell and Wm. Huston 1778-81-80. He was a pew holder in Welsh Run Presby. Church and gave the land for the Mt. Pelior Schoolhouse. In 1793, he sold 30 acres land "whereon there is a Schoolhouse erected now, and forever hereafter." Tract called "Retrext" (?) and also a tract "Impoling" to Jacob Nafe (or Nase). Deed signed by Thomas and Diana Kennedy. Penna., Marriages gives this: Thomas Kennedy and Dianna Percal, Oct. 28, 1767. The Franklin Repository, Apr. 4, —11th, 1804: The subscriber will engage to carry any quantity of flour that may be delivered at his WARE-HOUSE before the last day of April next, at one dollar per barral of Flour, and in proportion for other produce, including all changes till delivered on any Wharf in George-Town.

THO. KENNEDY

Williamsport, Mar. 20, 1804, N. B. Flour delivered after the above time will be carried at the current rates.

Penna. Arch. 5th Ser. Vol. 6, p. 276, 281, 284, 374.

ROBERT KERR

Served as pvt., 1778, under Capt. James Patton; he mar. Agnes Elder in 1784. Quoting from her printed Obituary by Rev. Naylor, Pisgah, Ohio: "Agnes (Elder) Kerr, born March 17, 1763, in what was then called Shippensburg Station, Franklin Co., Penna., joined (about time of her marriage) the Upper Path Valley Presby., Church. They had 12 children and removed in 1826 to Ross Co., Ohio, where she died, near Pisgah, Apr. 15, 1859, Robert Kerr having died in 1817 in Penna. Both her parents lived over 100 years." A grandau, Martha Hughes McCord, states she had heard Agnes speak of having been born in a fort, whither all had fled during an Indian raid. The father, on his return from a trip, found his house in flames and the family gone. The will of Robert Kerr of Fannett Twp., was dated and prob. 1817, naming issue: Alexander; James Elder; Wm.; Agnes; Robert; Elizabeth; Andrew; Thomas; Esther; Matthew. The marriages are from the Hist. of the Presby Churches of Path Valley: Mr. Simeson—Miss Kerr, 1811; A. Kerr—S. Peoples, 1814; Mr. Kennedy—Nancy Kerr, 1815; Wm. Kerr—Elizabeth Elder, 1818; Robert Kerr—Martha Elder, 1821; Andrew Kerr—Margaraet Campbell, 1821; Wm. Swan—Betsy Kerr, 1822; Continuing family Notes: "Alexander mar. Sally Peoples; James Elder mar. Nancy; Robert mar. Patsy; Nancy mar. John Simmerson; Andrew mar. Margaret, a dau. of David Campbell. Esther mar. Samuel Ross; Martha mar. Daniel Hughes."

Penna. Arch. 5th Ser. Vol. 6, p. 381.

JOHN KEYSER

Appears as a private in the Second Penna. Cont. Line. It is probable that the above soldier is the man who came to Franklin County, as three or four men from the Second Penna., came here after the Revolution. This John Keyser was of Antrim Twp., and left a will dated and prob. Aug.—Oct. 1814, naming a beloved wife Susanna to whom he left 1000 pounds. To sons Benj. and Jonathan all the tract on which I now live, bought of Andrew Coover, appraised at $25,000. Son Jacob the 1/5 part of estate, having already received &c. Dau. Sally mar. Adam Club 1/5; Dau. Catherine mar. Michael Reed 1/5; Sons Benjamin and Jonathan each 1/5; Two grandsons Leonard and William Keyser (sons of John Kyser, decd.) 518 pounds, 15 Shillings each. Exrs.: Son Jacob, Son-in-law Michael Reed and Son Benjamin.

Penna. Arch. 5th Ser. Vol. 2, p. 877.

BENJAMIN KIDD

Appears under Capt. John Jordan, in Col. Flower's Regt. of Artillery Artifices, 1778-79-80 as a Carpenter. The following items were contributed by Miss Hannah M. Spangler from old papers in her possession: Know all men by these presents that I Benjamin Kidd of Petters Township, Cumberland County and Province of Penna., carpenter, in consideration of the Sum of Twenty pounds lawful money of said Province to me in hand paid before the Insealing hereof the Right whereof is hereby acknowledged have granted, Bargained and Sold, and by these presents do bargain and Sell unto George Elder of Hopewell Township, Bedford County and Province afforesaid yeoman his heirs and assigns the one half or equally undivided Share of the following Described Tract of Land lying and being in Petter's Township afforesaid adj. James Wilkey, Francis Patterson and Archbd. Scott as also the Title in proportion the Right of which I bought of Samuel McMachan as aforesaid, a Conveyance bearing Date the tenth day of Jany., 1776 Reference thereunto being had may more fully show and at large appear by a location bearing date at Philla. to have and to hold this described tract of land in manner afforesaid with its title in proportion—appurtenances and improvements thereunto belonging unto the said George Elder his heirs and assigns to the only use and behoof of the said George Elder his heirs and assigns forever—Subject to the proportionall part of the purchase money Interest and quit Rent due and to be Come Due thereon to the lord of the Sayle (?), Sois (?) and the afforesaid half or equal undivided half share of the afforesaid Tract of Land afforesaid to the afforesaid George Elder his heirs and assigns the said Benj. Doth from his heirs Extrs. and Admr's warrant forever Defend in Witness whereof I have hereunto Set my hand and Seal this 13th day of August., 1778. Sealed and Delivered in the presents of Joshua Davis, Lewis Foster (?)   Benj. Kidd   (SEAL) This 27th Day of Novr., 1779. Know all men by these presents that I Beng Kidd Carpenter in the States Sarvis in Carlisle have constituted Made and appointed xx do constitute Make and appoint my trusty and loving Friend George Elder of Hopewell Township Bedford County and State of Pennsylvania yeoman my true and lawful attorney for me and in my name xxx to sue for levy Recover and receive all such Damages received from Joseph Roberts or eny Other person xx that land in partnership between the said George and Me. James Young, John harris.   Benjamin Kidd.

JOHN KILGORE

Signed the Oath of Fidelity, Oct. 9, 1777, in Westmoreland Co., Penna., before Hugh Martin, Esq His wife was Rosanna, dau. of Francis and Margaret Jamison. The Kilgores are said to have gone to Kentucky at an early date.
Penna. Arch. 2nd Ser. Vol. 3, p. 31.

JOSEPH KILGORE

Is shown as a pvt., under Capt. Noah Abraham, 1777-81-82, with undated rolls. There was an order of survey to Joseph Kilgore, for 200 acres land in Metal Twp., June 30, 1767, No. 4090. "Joseph Killger" signed a petition from Fannett Twp., in 1779.
Penna. Arch. 5th Ser. Vol. 6, p. 120, 127, 140, 147, 516.

NEAMIAH KILGORE

Served as Pvt., 1781-82 under Capt. Noah Abraham.
Penna. Arch. 5th Ser. Vol. 6, p. 121, 128.

PATRICK KILGORE

Served in 1776, in the Company of Capt. Samuel McCune. He also served in 1778-80 under Capt. Patrick Jack.
Penna. Arch. 5th Ser. Vol. 6, p. 32, 95, 96, 588.

JOHN KINCAID

Appears as Sergt., in 1779 with Capt Samuel Patton on the Western Frontiers, and in 1781-82 in continued service with Capt. Patton.
Penna. Arch. 5th Ser. Vol. 6, p. 286, 288, 311, 601, 609.

GEORGE KING

Penna. State Library, Harrisburg, Penna. The State Treasurer is hereby authorized and required to pay to Eve Diehl of York Co., widow, of George Diehl, a soldier of the Revolution, to xxx to George King of Franklin County xxx Rev. Soldiers, a Gratuity of $40 each, as full compensation for their respective claims against the Commonwealth xxx in conformity to existing Laws.
Laws Of Penna., 1834-35," page 36, Section 5.

THOMAS KING

Served under Capt. Samuel Patton, 1780-81-82. He had two (2) children baptized by Dr. John King, on March 3, 1805, and a child Apr. 26, 1807. He is shown in Tax lists, and Deeds of 1795,—"Wm Smith and wife sold a lot, No. 11, in Town of Mercersburg, to George Teagarden. George Teagarden of Lexington, State of Kentucky, now sells to Thos. King of Mercersburg for 37 lbs., 10 shillings, specie." Wit: James Irwin and James Speer.
Penna. Arch. 5th Ser. Vol. 6, p. 278, 287, 311.

PETER KINGERY

Served in Lancaster County Militia, 1781-82, under Capt. Daniel Bradley. Under deeds at Chambersburg, Peter Kingery and wife Mary of Hamilton Twp., are shown selling a tract of land to James Guthery of Chambersburg, 284 acres. Jost Hungery had obtained a warrant from Penna., in 1753. In the will of Henry Pensinger, prob. 1827, he names, among others a dau. Caty Gingry, wife of Peter Gingry.
Penna. Arch. 5th Ser. Vol. 7, p. 916, 941, 961.

WILLIAM KINNARD (KINNAIRD)

Served under Capt. Samuel Patton, 1780-81-82, 4th Batt., Cumb. Co., Militia, under Col. Samuel Culbertson; In 1807, Tax lists show him as a weaver in Hamilton Twp., with Horses and Cows, and in 1809 he bought from Thos. Campbell and wife Mary a lot in St. Thomas known as No. 42. William Kinnard died July 30, 1822, his wife Sarah Hanagan, dying Feb. 3, 1830. Their children were: John, died Feb. 7, 1837; James died Dec. 14, 1838; Catherine died Jan. 29, 1844; Margaret, born Aug. 28, 1784, died Aug. 2, 1845, mar. John Bossart. They had issue Elizabeth; John; Wm.; Sarah; Catherine Bossart. Descendants state that the Kinnards are buried in Rocky Spring Graveyard. Sarah Kinnard had a sister Catherine Hanagan b. Feb. 6, 1776, d. Dec. 19, 1831.
Penna. Arch. 5th Ser. Vol. 6, p. 278, 287, 311.

BENJAMIN KIRKPATRICK

Served as pvt., under Capt. Wm. Huston, 1780-81. The will of Benj. Kirkpatrick of Westmoreland County, Penna., wife Jane," all the moveables she brought with her when she became my wife. All monies to be got from the estate of Alexdr. Scott and Joseph McKean, decd., late of Franklin Co., arising to her out of the estate of Thomas McKean, her former husband." He names Dau. Polly Craig; Son Benjamin; Son Samuel of Ohio; Son John, decd. Issue of decd. dau. Jane Harris; Grandau. Sally Cochran; 4 surviving children; Samuel Kirkpatrick of Ohio; Rebecca wife of Robert Larimore; Polly wife of John Craig; Benj. who lives with me. Dated March 1826, prob. Aug., 1826. Benj. Kirkpatrick was married to Mrs. McKean, by Dr. Denny, June 11, 1807. Franklin Repository, Feb. 7, 1837, Chambersburg, Penna. Died in Westmoreland Co., Penna., on the 13th of January, Jane Kirkpatrick, widow of Benj. Kirkpatrick, late Jane McKean of Chambersburg, Penna., aged 92 years. (She was probably a dau. of Alexdr. Scott, Silversmith, of Chambersburg.

V.S.F.). The marriage of Robert Larimer and Rebecca Kirkpatrick, May 16, 1797, was performed by Dr. John King, Mercersburg, Penna., also the marriage of Samuel Kirkpatrick and Nancy Johnston, Apr. 5, 1798, also Joseph Harris to Jane Kirkpatrick, March 4, 1802.

Penna. Arch. 5th Ser. Vol. 6, p. 270, 276, 284.

JOHN KIRKPATRICK

Served under Capt. Wm. Huston and Wm. Smith, 1780-81. Orphans' Court records show that John Kirkpatrick, late of Mercersburg, Merchant, died intestate, Aug. 31, 1809, leaving a widow Catherine, and 6 children: Rachel McKee, formerly Rachel Kirkpatrick, whose husband Alexdr. McKee is now decd.; James; Sarah; Isabella; John; Alexander. Alexander McKee mar. Rachel Kirkpatrick, Dec. 7, 1802, by Dr. John King, of Mercersburg. John Kirkpatrick owned 4 certain Lots of ground in the Town of Mercersburg of much interest. The Court appointed Moses Kirkpatrick, Esq., of Letterkenny Twp., Guardian over the person and estate of John, minor son of John Kirkpatrick aged 14 yrs. and upwards. The Auditors appointed by the Court were: Major John Brownson, James Buchanan and Robert Smith, Esq.

Penna. Arch. 5th Ser. Vol. 6, p. 276, 284.

PETER KISHNER

Was a pvt., under Capt. Patrick Jack in 1780.
Penna. Arch. 5th Ser. Vol. 6, p. 95.

GEORGE KISHTATER

Served as Corporal, 1782, under Capt. Saml. Patton, command of Col. Samuel Culbertson.
Penna. Arch. 5th Ser. Vol. 6, p. 311.

YERRACK KISHVATER

Is shown as a Corporal, 1781, with Capt. Saml. Patton.
Penna. Arch. 5th Ser. Vol. 6, p. 286.

NICHOLAS KLINE

Orphans' Court Book A. p. 298, Chambersburg, Penna., Nicholas Kline of Guilford Twp., died intestate, since 1794; widow Elizabeth; 9 children all yet living: David; Susanna mar. Jacob Staley; John; Michael; George; Dorothy mar. John Wallace; Nicholas; Wm.; Jacob; Catherine mar. James McAnulty. Nicholas Kline died in Franklin Co., 1827, Admr., 1805.

Penna. Arch. 2nd Ser. Vol. 13, p. 123.

JAMES KNOX

Served as pvt. under Capt Walter McKinnie, 1778-81-82. In 1769, he and his wife were living in district 7 of the Presby. Church of Mercersburg, Penna. His family in 1769 consisted of Charles Neely and wife Lettice; also Lettice McClelland. In his will dated Apr. 7, 1794, prob. Apr. 16, 1794, he requests that he be buried beside his wife; eldest dau. Lettice; Son Thomas, land; Dau. Hannah; Dau. Elizabeth; Dau. Jean; Brother Thomas and his son James. Elizabeth Knox died Nov. 13, 1786; John Crisswell mar. Lettice Knox, March 3, 1789.

Penna. Arch. 5th Ser. Vol. 6, p. 266, 289, 300, 306, 382.

THOMAS KNOX

Brother of James Knox served under Capt. Matthews in 1776; under Capt. Noah Abraham 1777-78-79. He was at Legonere June 22, 1779. Dr. John King Presby., pastor at Mercersburg baptized William for Thomas Knox, Apr. 3, 1774. There were some church admissions.

Penna. Arch. 5th Ser. Vol. 6, p. 18, 53, 59, 318, 603.

PETER KOON (KOONS)

Appears as serving under Capt. John Wood and James Poe, 1780-81-82. Letters on the estate were granted to Samuel and Peter Coon. Sureties John Smith and John Shoup, under date Apr. 2, 1804. The above man is probably the Rev. Soldier, tho' another man of the name is shown Apr. 14, 1808 when letters on the estate of Peter Coon were granted to Margaret and Philip Hammon. The Sureties were John Keasy and Martin Hammon. Under Path Valley marriages are the following: W. Shetler—Mary Coons, 1811; Jacob Coons—Lydia Bear, 1818; Martin Coons—Jane Wallace, 1821. The German Evangelical Reformed Zion's Church, Greencastle, Penna., Membership List: Samuel Kuhn, Catherine Kuhn, 1818; John Kuhn, Conf., 1819; Peter Kuhn, Conf., 1821; Samuel Kuhn, Conf., 1827; Catherine Kuhn, Conf., 1827; Elizabeth Kuhn, Conf., 1831; John Kuhn, Conf., 1832; Martha Kuhn, Conf., 1832; Juliana Kuhn, Conf., 1832; Charlotte Kuhn, ..., 1849; Esther Kuhn, Conf., 1851; Margaret Kuhn, Conf., 1851; Jacob Kuhn ...., 1853; John W. Kuhn, Conf., 1854; Jesse Kuhn, Conf., 1858; Leah Kuhn, Conf., 1858.

Penna. Arch 5th Ser. Vol. 6, p. 92, 99, 576, 583.

JOHN KREMER

Pleasant Hall Graveyard: John Kremer, 1753-1836. Pioneer; Ensign Revolutionary War. Enlisted spring of 1776, 5th Battalion of Associators in Berks County, Pennsylvania. One of the Founders of this church. Erected by descendants in 1911. John Kremer, Pensioner, June 30, 1834, Franklin Co., Penna. John Kremer of Letterkenny Twp., aged 80 on 29th of last October, lived in Berks Co., Penna., during the Rev. War. About six years after the Revolution he moved to Franklin County, where he has resided ever since. He was commissioned an Ensign of a company of Foot in the 5th Batt. in Berks Co. by John Morton, Speaker of the Assembly—Company of Capt. Henry Shoemaker—Major Samuel Arly—Col. Philip Gehr—to Easton—to Brunswick — to Amboy — discharged. Affidavit Abraham Keefer—knew him during the Revolution. Aff. John Kremer—age 80 on Oct. 29, 1834—record of birth in Church, Berks Co., Penna. In 1893 Matilda (widow of Samuel Kramer, Chaplain in U. S. Navy) In 1893 Mary W. (dau. of Samuel Kramer) asked for bounty land of his father John or John Jacob Kramer. John Kremer enlisted in the Rev. War in the spring of 1776 for six months as an Ensign in the 5th Batt. of Associators in Berks County, Penna., and served under Capt. Henry Shoemaker and Col. Philip Gehr. Date of Application for Pension—June 30, 1834. This claim was allowed for conformity with the law of the U. S., of the 7th of June, 1832. John Kremer of the State of Penna., who was an Ensign during the Revolutionary War is entitled to receive $60. per annum during his natural life, commencing on the 4th of March, 1831, and payable semi-annually, on the 4th of Mar. and 4th of September in every year. Given at the War Office of the U. S. this 22nd day of July, 1834.

Signed: B. F. Butler, Acting Sec. of War.
Rev. War Pension Claim No. S-7120.

DAVID KYLE

Served as pvt., 1780-81 under Capt. Samuel Patton. He was not a brother of the Kyles of Montgomery Twp.

Penna. Arch. 5th Ser. Vol. 6, p. 264, 278, 287.

JAMES KYLE (KYLL)

Served as pvt., 1780-81, Cumb. Co. Militia under Capt. Wm. Huston. James, John and Samuel Kyle are also shown in the Cont. Line, and one John was a Captain in Westmoreland County. The deeds quoted show that Thos. Kyle became possessed of his own, and the share of James Kyle, decd. Miss Kyle thinks that James Kyle mar., left a family, dying in Mississippi, date unknown.

Penna. Arch 5th Ser. Vol. 6, p. 269, 275, 282, 288.

JOHN KYLE

Son of Samuel, served as Capt., of Rangers from Westmoreland Co., Penna., also as Capt. in the Cont. Line. In 1769, John Klye and wife Hannah were living near his father Samuel Kyle, in District 4, over which his brother-in-law, Robert Fleming was then the Elder. They had Anne and Samuel; Mary in 1771, and John in 1773. Miss Etta M. Kyle, a descendant kindly furnished some family notes,—John Kyle was living at Elizabeth, Rostraser Twp., where he bought 400 acres land in 1778 from his brother-in-law, John Wilson. His will was dated May 14, 1782, and he is said to have died 1787, leaving nine children. Miss Kyle failed to locate positively the grave of John Kyle at "Round Hill Cemetery," tho' there was part of a stone, illegible, with a foot stone marked J. K.; and next ot it a foot stone with an H and balance defaced. She also searched the "Belle Vernon" and found much of family interest, but the Wilsons were buried in the "Rehobeth Presby., Ch. Cemetery." Capt. John Kyle and wife Hannah are said to have had issue: Samuel; Joshua; Mary; John; Anne; Sarah; Robert; Jane; Hannah. His will is on record at Greensburg, Penna.

Penna. Arch. 5th Ser. Vol. 4, p. 444. Penna. Arch. 3rd Ser. Vol. 23, p. 330.

JOSEPH KYLE (ALSO JOSIAH)

Was a 1st Sergt. 1780-81, under Capt. Wm. Huston. Court records show that Joseph Kyle "hath sold his share, or part of land to Joseph Boagle for 487 lbs, 10 shillings in Speacy in hand paid, what was called Wm. Kyll's part, now Baltzer Gull's land by Widow McCalmash's—106¾ acres," signed by Joseph and Cathren Kyll, Jan. 19, 1785. Joseph, said to have been born 1749, mar. Catherine, a dau. of Rowland Chambers. Joseph Kyle had baptz. at Mercersburg, Penna., three children: Samuel in 1777; Anne in 1780; Wm. in 1782. Joseph Kyle is said to have died 1821 at Cedarsville, Ohio, Greene Co., leaving sons Samuel and John and four daughters.

Penna. Arch. 5th Ser. Vol. 6, p. 265, 270, 275, 283.

ROBERT KYLE

Was Ensign 1777-78 under Capt. Wm. Huston. He also served 1780-81. Under Jan. 12, 1793, is shown Robert Kyle and wife Sarah, of Montgomery Twp., selling to James Boagle of Newton Twp., Cumb. Co., Penna., a tract called "Clifton Hall," 349 acres, by land of Wm. Shannon, David White and Robert Black. Patent to Samuel Kyle, decd., Oct. 30, 1771, made over to son Robert one divided tract of 100 acres. Robert Kyle and wife Sarah sell for 750 lbs., to James Boagle. The Census of 1790, shows Robert Kyle in Franklin Co. with one man, 3 boys, 3 females. Robert Kyle had baptized at Mercersburg three children, Samuel Bell in 1782; Jean in 1784; Thomas in 1788. "Robert Kyle, b. 1751, settled in Covington, Ky., where he was Justice of the Peace and Probate Judge for over 20 years. He mar. Sarah Pierce, and died in 1825, leaving 4 sons and 4 daughters, his eldest son Samuel Bell

Kyle having died prior to his father. He left a long and important will. 1000 acres land near Covington, 1000 acres near Tobasco, Clermont Co., Ohio."

Penna. Arch. 5th Ser. Vol. 6, p. 270, 276, 283, 369, 378.

SAMUEL KYLE

Served as pvt., 1780-81, under Capt Wm Huston. By a deed, June 11, 1786, Samuel Kyll and wife Mary sell to Rowland Chambers all of Montgomery Twp., Samuel Kyll, now decd., and father to the above Samuel Kyle was xx possessed of land in Township, aforesaid which said tract he purchased of and from the reverend Richard Peters of the City of Phila., on the 2nd day of June in 1763; he the said Richard Peters having purchased the said Tract from Thomas McClure who had it surveyed and laid out under a warrant, under the sale of the Land Office, bearing date Nov. 1, 1745, cont. 250 acres. The decedent on Jan 31, 1781, assigned all his right &c to his 3 sons,—Samuel; Joseph and William Kyll, to be held by them xx division lines by him made before that time and also by his last will &c. Said Samuel, since deceased of his Father, had his own part surveyed, by lands of Baltzer Gull, Joseph Boagle, heirs of Wm. Morrison, David Humphrey, 93 acres, 20 perches. For 465 lbs, 12 shil and 6 pence in specie. Samuel Kyle and wife Mary sell to Rowland Chambers. Miss Kyle states that Samuel Kyle was pensioned while living in Fayette Co., Kentucky—and living in 1833-34.

Penna. Arch. 5th Ser. Vol. 6, p. 269, 275, 282, 288.

THOMAS KYLE

Served as pvt., under Capt. Wm. Huston, 1780-81. Under date of June 26, 1787, deeds show that Thomas Kyle and wife Elizabeth of Montgomery Twp., sell land to James Clark, Sr., Thomas Clark and James Clark, Jr., of the same. A Patent to Samuel Kyle, Oct. 30, 1771, a tract known by the name of "Clifton Hall," 349 acres. Samuel Kyle, in his life time, conveyed to his son Robert Kylle a part of said tract of land on the West side of tract, 100 acres, xx Thomas became possessed of his own and a share of James decd., for 2275 lbs., Gold or Silver money as it passeth in the Com. of Penna., paid by James Clark, Sr., &c., after the conveyance made to son Robert, by decedent, adj. heirs of Wm. Shannon, decd.; heirs of Dougel Campbell. decd.; to Robert Kyle. Thomas Kyle b. 1756, d. 1828, at Kyle, Butler Co., Ohio. His first wife Elizabeth Chambers; 2nd wife Sarah Patterson; issue:—7 —Sarah; Isabel; Mary; Ann; Jean. From a descendant the following: "Thomas Kyle with 3 of his sons came to Ohio in 1802, and took over a portion of the old Symmers Patent for homesteading. The sons were Samuel Jr.; Roland; James. There were two daus., Jean and Ann who remained in Penna." "Thomas Kyle owned a mill 1789 near Perryopolis and Fayette City, Fayette Co., Penna., and in 1803 at Kyle's Butler Co., Ohio, where he died in 1828.

Penna. Arch. 5th Ser. Vol. 6, p. 276, 283.

SAMUEL KILL (KYLE)

Of Montgomery Twp., in his will names a dau. Ann Fleming; her son Samuel Bell Fleming; Dau. Mary Wilson and her dau. and Jean Orbison; Dau Isabella Garretson, her son Samuel Kyle Garretson (Garrison); Son John Kyle and his son Samuel Kyle; Grandson Samuel Kyle, son of my son Joseph; Son Samuel, his daughter; Son Joseph; Son Robert; Son Thomas; Son James, land bounded by Wm. Shannon; Wm. Newell; Exrs.: Sons Samuel and Thomas; dated July 23, 1784; prob. June 16, 1785.

NOTE: Thomas Orbison came to America about 1740. Settled near Welsh Run and died March, 1779. His 1st wife was Elizabeth Miller; issue 6 children. He mar. 2nd Mary Kyle and had issue Jean, born July 5, 1776. Mary (Kyle) Orbison mar. 2nd _____ Wilson.

WILLIAM KYLE

Served as pvt., 1780, under Capt. Wm. Smith. He is probably the William Kyle who was 2nd Lieut., 1777 in the Seventh Penna. Cont. Line, as Major Jeremh. Talbot recruited in this vicinity. Letters of Admr. on the estate of William Kyle of Franklin Co., Penna., were granted to Thomas Kyle, Dec. 24, 1785.

Penna. Arch. 5th Ser. Vol. 6, p. 275. Penna. Arch. 5th Ser. Vol. 3, p. 218, 228.

ISAAC LACY (LEACY)

Served as a pvt., under Capt. Noah Abraham and Thos. Askey, 1777, First Batt., 3rd Marching Company, under command of Col. Jas. Dunlap, undated rolls.

Penna. Arch. 5th Ser. Vol. 6, p. 18, 21, 131, 139, 151.

THOMAS LEACY

Served under Capt. Thomas Askey, Col. James Dunlop, undated rolls. They were in Fannett Twp., Thos Lacy signing a petition there in 1779. Job. Lacy, G. A. R., also George and Catherine Lacy lie in the Concord Union Graveyard in Path Valley. A tract of land, 152 ac. held by Location of Thos. Lacy, No. 784 and was conveyed to Elizabeth Sacket by deed bearing date March 16, 1782.

Penna. Arch 5th Ser. Vol. 6, p. 132.

DANIEL LADY

Was a private under Capt. Daniel Clapsaddler in 1780. He owned a dwelling Plantation Called "Lady's Delight." He left a widow Anna and a son Henry; Dau. Barbara Summers; Dau. Elizabeth Summers; Dau. Mary Shiver (of John); Dau. Margaret Sharrot, decd.; Dau. Rosanna Bamgarner; His will was prob. March 25, 1809. "Daniel Ladi" was an Elder in the old Salem Reformed Church, near Waynesboro.

Penna. Arch. 5th Ser. Vol. 6, p. 93.

HENRY LADY

Served as a pvt., under Capt. Daniel Clapsaddler, 1780-81. Henry Lady mar. Elizabeth, dau of Henry Miller of Washington Twp. He died intestate in 1822, leaving a widow and nine children: Daniel; Elizabeth mar. John Amwick; Henry; Joseph; Susanna; Catherine; Samuel; Molly and Barbara, a minor.

Penna. Arch. 5th Ser. Vol. 6, p. 94, 117.

GEORGE LAMB

Is shown serving under Capt. Wm. Long, Conrad Snider and Samuel Patton, 1778-79-80-81. At Legonere, June, 1779, with Capt. Samuel Patton as a Ranger on the Western Frontier.

Penna. Arch. 5th Ser. Vol. 6, p. 87, 119, 536, 546, 581, 601, 610.

JAMES LAMB

Was a Sergt. in 1779-80-81 with Capts. Wm. Long and Conrad Snider.

Penna. Arch. 5th Ser. Vol. 6, p. 87, 118, 108, 545.

JOSEPH LAMB

Served in 1778, as a pvt., under Capt. Charles Maclay.

Penna. Arch 5th Ser. Vol. 6, p. 42.

MICHAEL LAMB

Is shown serving under Capt. Daniel Clapsaddle, in 1780-81, as a private.

Penna. Arch. 5th Ser. Vol. 6, p. 94, 97, 117.

MOSES LAMB

Served as a pvt., 1781, under Capt. Conrad Snider, the Command of Lieut. Col. James Johnston. He was a Merchant of Franklin County. He names 3 brothers: James; George; Joseph. Wearing apparel to brother James and his son Moses, as follows: "my surtout, brown coat with stuffed collar, gray coat, white marsails and striped waistcoats and brown thick waistcoat, all my small cloaths, two shirts and my hat and my boots to brother James; my snuff colored cloath coat, nankeen Cotee, black silk and barred marsails and scarlet waistcoats, a pair of white marsails, a mixed broad cloath, and a pair of mixed cassimer pantaloons, the residue of my shirts and my best shoes to my nephew Moses; brother George my watch; brother Joseph my saddle, bridle and spurs; sister-in-law, my brother James wife, calico material for a dress, one green shawl and a shawl of larger size; stockings to be divided among my three brothers; residue of estate to two nephews, Moses and James, sons of brother James." The will of Moses Lamb was dated March 1804, and prob. Apr. 18, 1804. The Census of 1790 shows his family consisting of 5 men, 1 boy and 2 females.

Penna. Arch. 5th Ser. Vol. 6, p. 119.

DANIEL LANEY

Appears under Capt. Patrick Jack, 1781-82 as a pvt. The name is shown in the records of Dr. Robert Kennedy, pastor at that period of the Presby. Churches at Greencastle and Welsh Run. The marriage of Robert Laney to Jane Vance, on Sept. 7, 1813. Also the marriage of James Edwards to Elizabeth Laney on Sept. 16, 1813.

Penna. Arch. 5th Ser. Vol. 6, p. 295, 304.

HUGH LANEY

Served in 1781, under Capt. Patrick Jack. Hugh Laney, Sr. and Jr. are shown as taxables in Hamilton Twp., 1778-82 with land, horses and cattle. Alexdr. Lainy was a Store keeper in 1796 in Letterkenny Twp.

Penna. Arch. 5th Ser. Vol. 6, p. 296.

PETER LANGINECKER

Is shown in service under Capt. Samuel Royer and Daniel Clapsaddle 1777-80-81. He was of Washington Twp., his will prob. Dec. 7, 1803. Wife Anna; Son Daniel; Sons and daughter not named. Deeds show Joseph Ellar selling 50 acres land to Peter Longnecker in 1790; the Hon. Proprietors of Penna., did grant a tract in March, 1789, Washington Twp., also one other tract adj. above, called "Brush Hill," 232¼ acres, for 2824 lbs., 1 shilling, 3 pence. The Executors of Peter Longnecker sell to Jacob Hollinger, Jr., Oct. 9, 1804. Letters of Admr., on estate of Anne Longenecker, Spinster, to Daniel Lonenecker, acting executor of estate of Peter Longnecker, decd.: shows 4232 lbs. and two pence half penny in his hands. In 1799 Peter had land, Stone House, a half-stone barn, Log House, Log Stable and Smith Shop, Horses and Cows. The known children were: Anna, wife of John Mack; Magdaline Bowman; Abraham of Bedford Co.,; Daniel; Joseph; Under marriage records of St. John's Lutheran Church of Hagerstown, Md., are the following: Abraham _____, Cath Langenecker, June 25, 1796; Jacob Gantz, Sus. Langenecker,

OF FRANKLIN COUNTY PENNSYLVANIA

Aug., 1799; Jacob Langenecker, Nanzi Ryneberger, Nov., 1801.
The 1790 Census shows the family of Peter Longenecker as, 3 men, 3 boys, 5 females.
Penna. Arch. 5th Ser. Vol. 6, p. 93, 116, 107, 517.

EPHRIAM LATTA

Appears as a pvt., under Capt. Samuel Royer in 1777. He was a freeman in Antrim Twp., in 1779. On Apr. 11, 1805, Dr. Robert Kennedy mar. Wm. Latta to Charlotte Harris. On Jan. 7, 1806, he married Alexdr. Latta to Jane Gaff, vicinity of Greencastle, Penna. Moses Latta and Polly Scott were mar. Nov., 1798 by Dr. John King of Mercersburg. Alexdr. Latta and Moses Latta appear in Antrim Twp., Taxables, 1796, as "young freemen."
Penna. Arch. 5th Ser. Vol. 6, p. 517.

WILLIAM LATTA

A taxable in Peters Twp., is shown in service, under Capt. Walter McKinnie, in the year 1782. A man of the name appears in Bedford Co., as a pvt., in the Cont. Line. One William Latta was mar. to Charlotte Harris, Apr. 11, 1805, by Dr. Robert Kennedy.
Penna. Arch. 5th Ser. Vol. 6, p. 306.

GEORGE LATTIMER

Served in Westmoreland Co. Militia. St. James Episcopal Church of Lancaster shows two marriages on Dec. 29, 1757. George Lattimer to Margaret Potter and Wm. Piper to Sarah McDowell, both representing the "Conococheague Settlement." Margaret Potter a dau., of Capt. John Potter, the first Sheriff of Cumb. Co. Sarah McDowell a dau. of pioneer Wm. McDowell. The Bard Hist., states that George Latimer, a native of Ireland, died in 1793. They had issue: John: Arthur; James; George; Thomas; Robert; Margaret and Martha.
Penna. Arch. 5th Ser. Vol. 4, p. 444.

ALEXANDER LAUGHLIN

Appears under Capt. Noah Abraham and Patrick Jack in 1777, with undated rolls.
Penna. Arch. 5th Ser. Vol. 6, p. 18, 19, 139, 145, 146, 592.

HUGH LAUGHLIN

Served with Capt. Patrick Jack in 1779, undated rolls.
Penna. Arch. 5th Ser. Vol. 6, p. 64, 145, 147.

JAMES LAUGHLIN

Is shown with Capts. Alex. Peebles and Patrick Jack in 1777-79, undated rolls. James Jr., also served.

Penna. Arch. 5th Ser. Vol. 6, p. 23, 28, 62, 64, 145, 147.

JOHN LAUGHLIN

Was an Ensign in service with Capt. Patrick Jack, 1778-79-81.
Penna. Arch. 5th Ser. Vol. 6, p. 44, 63, 144, 146, 407, 411, 658.

RANDLS LAUGHLIN

Is shown in 1780, in service with Lieut. Richard McLean, the command of Col. James Johnston. Caldwell's Hist. of Indiana County, Penna., shows Randall Laughlin first settling in Franklin County, prior to the Rev. War, later removing to a tract lying in Blacklick and Centre Townships, where he built a small cabin, then returned to Franklin County. He was married in the winter of 1777, again returning to his land, but the Indians took him captive with Charles Campbell, Dickson, John Gibson and his brother; the first station they reached was Kittanning where they had to run the gauntlet and undergo drill to the great amusement of the savages. The captives were then taken to Detroit where they were delivered to the British, and thence conveyed to Quebec, where they passed a severe winter. Mrs. Laughlin had made her way to Franklin County as best she could, and in eighteen months after his capture Randall Laughlin returned to the same place, and found her well cared for with their first born son over a year old. Ramsell (?) Laughlin was married to Elizabeth Warnack, March 10, 1777, by Rev. John King, Presbyterian Pastor at Mercersburg. Joseph Warnock is the only one of the name who served in Franklin County, in 1782, with Capt. Walter McKinnie. The name is found in Lancaster and Chester Counties, showing service in the Rev. War. Randall Laughlin, who died Jan. 6, 1818, aged 75 years, and his wife Elizabeth, who died Jan. 30, 1838, aged 80 yrs., are buried in the old Bethel Cemetery, Westmoreland Co., Penna. Congruity Cemetery, Westmoreland Co., Penna.,—one Robert Laughlin, Sr., d. July 26, 1809, aged 80 yrs. Will of Randall Laughlin, Blacklick Twp., Indiana Co., Penna.—names wife Elizabeth; issue: James; Martha Mitchell; Jane McComb; Elizabeth Rankin; John; Thomas; Joseph; grandsons: Randall, son of John Laughlin; Randall, son of John Mitchell; Exrs.: Thomas and Joseph Laughlin, Sons; Dated Nov. 28, 1817; Prob. Oct. 15, 1818; Wit: John M. Rankin, Zachariah Leard.
Penna. Arch. 5th Ser. Vol. 6, p. 75, 84.

THOMAS LAUGHLIN

Served in 1780, under Capt. John Woods. Letters on his estate were granted unto Joseph Snively, July, 1803. He died unmar., and without issue, but left interesting relatives in Ireland, His mother, Jane Laughlin, a widow, sisters, a brother John and nephews and nieces. One Thos. Laughlin is shown serving under Capt. John Mc-Clelland, under date of 1779, and probably the above man.

Penna. Arch 5th Ser. Vol. 6, p. 91.

JAMES LAUTHER

Served as Lieut., under Capt. Chas. MacClay 1779-80-81, also in the Cont. Line. In 1779, Wm., James and Robert Lauther, as freeholders, petition from Fannett Twp. Deeds show that in 1782, Barnabas Clark, farmer of Fannett Twp., sold 190 acres of land to James Lauther, Blacksmith; and in 1791 James Louther, sold 100 acres to James Alexander, warrant to Samuel Parker in 1767. James Lauther sold the Barbabas Clerk tract to Thos. Shields in 1782. James Lauther is thought to have gone to Westmoreland Co., Penna.; he does not appear in Fannett as a taxable after 1793. James Lauther, Franklin Co., served 3 tours in the Militia, died 1826. James Lauther mar. Jane McMath, June 5, 1794, by Dr. David Denny, Path Valley. James Lowther mar. Margaret Freeman, Concord, Penna., they had a dau. Rebecca Bell, a widow who mar. John Unckles, born 1787, she was his 2nd wife.

Penna. Arch. 2nd Ser. Vol. 15, p. 767. Penna. Arch. 5th Ser. Vol. 6, p. 36, 41, 60, 131, 387, 408, 422, 620, 658. Penna. Arch. 5th Ser. Vol. 4, p. 292.

ROBERT LAUTHER

Served as pvt., under Capt. Thomas Askey, 1779-81-82. His name is shown as a taxable in Fannett from 1788 to 1807.

Penna. Arch. 5th Ser. Vol. 6, p. 37, 41, 62, 132, 424, 442.

WILLIAM LAUTHER

Pensioners, Westmoreland Co. Penna., William Luther, pvt., P. M. Oct. 21, 1816, d. Nov. 13, 1831. (Lauther) (?) William Lauther of Fannett Twp., is shown in the Company of Capt. Chas. Maclay, under Col. Abraham Smith. On March 5, 1806, Letters of Admr. on the estate of William Lauther were granted to Robert Lauther, with John Campbell and Richard Morrow as sureties. Randall Alexander of Fannett Twp., conveyed 167 ac. of land to Wm. Louther in 1787, and in 1791, Wm. Louther, Sen, sells part of the tract to Wm. Taylor. It is probable that children of the above Wm. Lauther continued to live in Fannett, as Wm. Lowther left Letters of Admr., 1821, minors being Margaret; Mary; Catherine; Elizabeth and Wm., children of Wm. Lathers, decd.

Penna. Arch. 5th Ser. Vol. 6, p. 658. Penna. Arch. 5th Ser. Vol. 4, p. 292. Penna. Arch. 3rd Ser. Vol. 23, p. 489.

JOHN LAWRENCE

Served as a pvt., under Capt. John Jack in 1779, under Capt Thos. Johnston in 1780-81, as a Clerk and Sergeant. He married 1st Mary, dau of George Gordon (proven by a deed in 1778). John Lawrence Mar. Rebecca Long, June 3, 1807, By Rev. Rohauser. The will of John Lawrence of Greencastle, names a wife Rebecca; son John; dau. Rachel Long; dau. Margaret Hutcheson; a grandson, John Lawrence McClean; also grandson John, the son of George Lawrence. This will was prob. Aug. 2, 1809. Moss Spring graveyard shows a stone to John Lawrence, no dates. Anna, wife of John Laurence, and Elmira J. Laurence, aged 11 years.

Penna. Arch. 5th Ser. Vol. 6, p. 539, 83, 114.

ANTHONY LAWSON

Served in 1781, under Capt. Walter McKinnie. He was a Freeman. Under Taxables Anthony Lawson is shown in 1779, in Ayr Twp., Bedford Co., Penna.

Penna. Arch. 5th Ser. Vol. 6, p. 300.

CASPER LAY

Of Southampton Twp., served as a pvt., under Capt. John Campbell. His will was prob. Sept. 12, 1796, naming wife Sophia; Sons: George; John; Philip; Christian; Dau. Sophia and her four children; Daus: Barbara, Elizabeth and Magdalena.

Penna. Arch. 5th Ser. Vol. 6, p. 143, 406.

DANIEL LEAP

Private First Batt. Cumb. Co. Militia. Daniel Leap is buried at Grindstone Hill graveyard, dates on stone 1761-1823. The will of Daniel Lape, Washington Twp., Franklin Co., shows wife Mary; dau. Mary, wife of Saml. Lear. Dau. Christina, wife of Peter Heckman. Dau. Elizabeth Lape. Dau. Susanna Lape. Dau. Matty Lape. Dau. Peggy Lape. Dau. Nancy Lape; Dau. Sally Lape. Son-in-law Geo. Brandhefer. Grandchildren named Myer. Dated Feb. 16, 1821. Prob. May 29, 1824.

Penna. Arch 5th Ser. Vol. 6, p. 108.

JACOB LEAR

Of Montgomery Twp., served as pvt., under Capt. John Orbison in 1782. His will was dated 1794, prob. May 1807. He names son Philip with whom he had an Instrument of writing, March 10, last, giving the children's shares. Son Jacob and his 2 sisters. The 2 sisters were probably Nancy and Susanna who died unmarried. Grandson David Leer, son of Philip. xx Daniel Leer bequeaths to brother Jacob, his share in his father's plantation in 1818. xx Estate of Philip Lear in 1807, widow Frances now decd.; Philip having died "since 1794," and leaving issue: Elizabeth mar. Johnston Ray; Catherine mar. ———— Kean or Kane; Mary mar. Wm. Harden; Hannah mar. ————Beamer; Philip; Jacob; Delilah. Land in Blairs Valley. The marriage of Jacob Lear to Fanny Blair, 9-27-1801, is under Licenses at Court House, Hagerstown, Md. Jacob died leaving a widow Frances and issue: Catherine; Philip; Jacob; Delilah and Mahala (?) all under 14 yrs., except Catherine and Philip (date 1828). David, son of Philip, died 1819, leaving a wife Margaret, issue: Daniel; John; Elizabeth, minors and 250 acres land left by Philip Lear. Deeds at Hagerstown, may help clear the Lear line, as Lydia, first wife of Jacob Lear appears to have been a dau. of Stephen Ulrick.

Penna. Arch. 5th Ser. Vol. 6, p. 308.

JOHN LEAR

Served from Berks Co., Penna., in 1781, with Capt. John Robinson, and in the Cont. Line, also from Berks County. One John Lear of Southampton Twp., dying Aug. 12, 1793, left 243 acres of land, a widow Mary and eleven children, viz: Henry; Eve, wife of Philip Young; Katherine, wife of Jacob Philips; Margaret, wife of Wm. Philips; Susanna wife of Geo. Zigler; Barbara Elizabeth, wife of John Lindsay; Martha Sarah; John; Abraham; They sell the land to Benj. Blythe, July 27, 1801. Deeds show the following: Jacob Lear of Fannettsburg, yeoman, sells to Henry Lear and John Lear, both of the Twp. of Amity, County of Berks, Penna. He sells goods and chattels, household stuff, implements and furniture, horses, cows, pigs, tenplate stove, Dictionary, Bible, &c &c; Said articles are now being and remaining on and in a certain lot of ground and house in Fannettsburg, where Jacob Lear now lives.

Penna. Arch. 5th Ser. Vol. 4, p. 262. Penna. Arch. 5th Ser. Vol. 5, p. 279, 282.

ROBERT LEEPER

Served as pvt., 1777-81-82, under Capt. Patrick Jack. In the will of James McRoberts, dated 1800, prob., Aug. 1804, he gives to son-in-law Robert Leeper one Crown; a grandson James Leeper to have one-fourth part of residue of the estate.

Penna. Arch. 5th Ser. Vol. 6. p. 291, 295, 304, 313, 372.

JOHN LEMMONS

12th Penna. Cont. Line, private John Lemmons, from Tuscarora Valley, Harris' Co., Feb. 2, 1777; wounded in head and left leg at Monmouth; transferred to 3rd Penna.

Penna. Arch. 2nd Ser. Vol. 10, p. 781.

ELISHA LEWIS

Served in 1780-81-82 as a pvt., under Capt. John Orbison. He was on or near the Welsh Run, and was one of that early Welsh Colony. He names a daughter Kittura, who mar. Wm. Wilson; Elizabeth mar. Robert Dunn; Mary Davis Lewis, and her dau. Mary Lewis. His will was prob. Aug. 30, 1813. A desc. of Elisha Lewis and his wife states that Mary Davis Lewis mar. Robert Mackey.

Penna. Arch. 5th Ser. Vol. 6, p. 274, 294, 308.

ROBERT LIGGETT

Appears as a pvt., in the Flying Camp. In 1780-81-82 he was serving under Capt. Samuel Patton, as Ensign in 1782. The will of Samuel Liggett of Hamilton Twp., dated 1805, prob. Jan., 1812, names son Robert, grandson Samuel, son of Robert; eldest dau. Sarah Ferguson; dau. Martha Liggett, "boarding and living in the family." Son Robert and family to live on my farm while unsold. Robert Liggett appears in Franklin County as Director of the Poor in 1808-09, and as Coroner in 1812. Deeds show Robert Liggett and wife Florence of Hamilton Twp., selling in 1813, a lot in Chambersburg and the estate of one Robert Liggett was administered in Hagerstown, Md., in 1817. Under a list of Rev. Soldiers gives "Robert Liggett, residing in Franklin Co., Penna., 1829." It is possible that he went to Indiana Co., Penna., as Caldwell's Hist. (p. 473) refers to Margaret Mabon, dau. of Robert Liggett.

Penna. Arch. 5th Ser. Vol. 6, p. 277, 286, 288, 310. Penna. Arch. 5th Ser. Vol. 4, p. 229. Penna. Arch. 2nd Ser. Vol. 13, p. 130.

JACOB LIGHT, SR.

Jacob Light, the son of John, and Jacob Light, son of Martin Light, all were in service in 1782 under Capt. John Stone. One Jacob Light is shown in Franklin County later in an exchange of land to straighten lines. "Know ye that Henry Butterbaugh and wife Susanna did sell to Philip Sword, decd., 74½ acres, called Flaggy Meadows, Montgomery Twp., by deed dated Aug. 5, 1815. The said Philip Sword or (Schwardt) died, leaving seven heirs still living; said heirs did exchange 2 ac. 93½ perches with Jacob Light (to straighten lines) xxx by Daniel Wolff's land, near Jacob Light's dwelling house, by Light's land east, David Cushwa on the south, by xxx 74¼ acres. Deeds 20, p. 292-293. By a white Oak corner of Benjamin Elliott, thence by same, thence by land of School lot to David Wolff's line, to Daniel Zuck's line, xxx to Jacob Sword's post corner xxx thence by lands of James Buchanan, 150 ac. 140 perches, being a tract of land which Nicholas Martin died seized; title became vested in Henry Swart in right of his wife Hannah, late Hannah Martin, one of the daus. of decd., dated Apr. 28, 1832. Deed Book Vol. 20, p. 264, 265, 266, 267, Franklin County, Penna. records.

Penna. Arch. 5th Ser. Vol. 7, p. 159, 179, 180.

DAVID LIKENS

Pvt. in Col. Wm. Thompson's Batt. of Riflemen, under Capt. James Chambers, March 7, 1776. He was also under Capt. James Grier, First Penna. Regt., Cont. Line. The 1790 Census shows him in Antrim Twp., with 1 man, 1 boy, 3 females. David Lackens appears in W. Wheatfield Twp., Indianna Co., Penna., as an early settler.

Penna. Arch. 2nd Ser. Vol. 10, p. 17.

JAMES LINN

Born Oct. 17, 1761, died in Lurgan Twp., May 28, 1835; served in Militia under Genl. Armstrong at Germantown, ordained a Ruling Elder of the Church at Middle Spring, Sept. 22, 1822; mar. Feb. 3, 1786, Griselda Patterson, born June 8, 1759, died Aug. 1, 1839. They had issue: Wm. born 1787, mar. Mary Galbreath; Mary, born 1790, mar. Robert Patterson; Jane, born 1793, mar. James Rodgers; Elizabeth, born 1799, mar. Robert Cochran; Andrew P., born 1800, mar ———— Walker.

Egle's Penna. Genealogies, p. 374.

JOHN LINN

Born, Lurgan Twp., now Franklin Co. Penna., Apr. 2, 1754, d. March 18, 1809, buried Presbyterian Cemetery, Buffalo X Roads, Penna. "Did a tour," received depreciation pay, Northunberland Co. Militia. He mar. 1780, Ann Fleming, born Sept. 6, 1761, died Sept. 4, 1841, dau. of John and Ann Fleming.

Mrs. Bartol's list Rev. Soldiers Shikelimo Chapter, D. A. R.

WILLIAM LINN

Pioneer, settled in Chester Co., Penna., 1732, having an only son Wm. Following the tide of emigration, they settled upon the frontiers of the Purchase of Oct., 1736, near what is now known as Roxbury, in Franklin Co., Penna. Wm. Linn, Jr., born 1722, in Ireland was an officer in the Middle Spring Church. In June 1755, he was in Phila., with his wagon and was pressed into service, with his team, to haul supplies to General Braddock's army, and was at the noted defeat. He died in 1812; mar. 1st Susanna Trimble and had issue: Wm. b. Feb. 27, 1752, mar. 1st Rebecca Blair. Wm. Linn b., Feb. 27, 1752, graduated Princeton, N. J., Class of 1772; studied theology under Rev. Robert Cooper, D. D.; appointed chaplain of Fifth and Sixth Penna., battalions, Feb. 15, 1776; pastor at Big Spring (Newville) Cumb. Co., Penna., until 1784; president of Wash. College, Md., 1784-85; pastor of Collegiate Dutch Ch. N. Y., 1786-1808; first Chaplain of the House of Representatives U. S., May 1, 1789. He died in Albany, N. Y. Jan. 8, 1808. He had issue by his first wife; by his second wife Catherine Moore and by his third wife, Helen Hanson. "I find on a sermon of the chaplain of the regiment, Rev. Wm. Linn xx and chaplain of the First Congress, this endorsement: "Preached before the regiment when about leaving Carlisle, March 14, 1776."

Kittochtinny Magazine Vol. 3, p. 137. Penna. Genealogies, Dr. Egle. Penna. Arch. Vol. 2, p. 167.

DAVID LINSEY

Capt. Wm. Rippey of Shippensburg, Sixth Penna. Batt., Col. Wm. Irvine, David Linsey enlisted, Jan. 18, 1776.

Penna. Arch. 5th Ser. Vol. 2, p. 238.

FULTON LINDSAY

Is shown in service 1778-80-81, with Capts. Conrad Snider and Adam Harmony, the command of Lieut. Col. James Johnson. Fulton Lindsay left a will, dated June 17, 1788, prob., March, 1789, in which he names wife Jane Fulton, to whom he gives her Dowry as the law directs, a bed and bedding, a Rone mare and a cow. To son Fulton 1/6 part of real estate in Guilford Twp.; son Wm. 3/4 of real estate and son James 2/6 part of real estate in Guilford Twp. To daus: Elizabeth, Margaret, Jane, Martha, Susanna, each 36 lbs. The Executors were: James Lindsay, Batchelor and James Lindsay, farmer. Deeds show that in 1800 Fulton Lindsay of Kentucky sells to John Dickey of Guilford Twp., a tract surveyed, 1766 (No. 1111) to Fulton Lindsay, Sr., by lands of Wm. Lindsay, a post on the bank of the Falling Spring, John Andrew, Col. Benj. Chambers and Wm. Adams. By the will of Fulton Lindsay, Sr., dated June, 1788, he willed 1/6 part of his real estate to his son Fulton, who now sells for 100 lbs.

Penna. Arch. 5th Ser. Vol. 6, p. 88, 98, 119, 539.

Rupp gives the names of townships organized and tax paid prior to the erection of Cumberland County, in the North Valley, from 1736 to 1749. Both James and John Lindsay are shown as taxables in Guilford Twp., in 1751, and at a Court of General Quarter Sessions of the Peace, held at Shippensburg, July 24, 1750, James Lindsay was one of the persons sworn on the Grand Jury, with John Potter, John Davison, Adam Hoops and others. Rupp gives John Lindsay as Tax Collector in 1746 for Antrim Twp., which embraced a large section at that period; he probably served in that capacity until 1764, when James Lindsay, his son, appears as Collector and continued as such until 1770.

JAMES LINDSAY

Was in service 1778-80-81, with Capts. Conrad Snider and Adam Harmony. The Franklin Repository, Oct. 16, 1804 gives the following: "On Friday last at his dwelling on the Falling Spring, of the prevailing fever, Mr. James Lindsay. On Saturday his remains were brought to town and deposited in the burial ground of the Presbyterian Congregation, of which he was a worthy Elder." In the will of James Lindsay, dated Sept. 8, prob., Oct. 17, 1804, he requests the plantation be sold; wife Martha, 300 lbs.; residue between son James and six daughters: Elizabeth; Martha; Jane; Agnes; Sarah; Mary. Son John the residue of all land with the farming utensils; Exrs.: James Lindsay of Chambersburg and son John. Lindsay Family Record: James Lindsay, Sr., born Aug. 18, 1743, died Oct. 12, 1804. His wife Martha Breckenridge, born Apr., 1743, d. Sept. 7, 1833, married Jan. 4, 1770. Issue: (1) John Lindsay, 1770-1825, wife Frances Crawford, born 1781, mar. Apr., 16, 1805. (2) James Lindsay, born 1772. (3) Elizabeth Lindsay, born 1774. (4) Samuel Lindsay, born 1776. (5) Martha Lindsay, born 1779. (6) Jane Lindsay, born 1781. (7) Agnes Lindsay, born 1783. (8) Sarah Lindsay, born 1786. (9) Mary Lindsay, born 1788.

The above Frances was the daughter of Edward Crawford, farmer, and wife Elizabeth Reynolds. In his will 1801, he names his eldest dau. Frances, wife of John Lindsay. When Martha, widow of James Lindsay, died Sept. of 1833, she named her surviving children: Elizabeth Thompson; Mary Davidson; Martha Thompson and James Lindsay.

Penna. Arch. 5th Ser. Vol. 6, p. 74, 88, 119, 538.

JOHN LINDSAY

Presumably a pioneer with James Lindsay, left no will, but his estate was administered Nov. 9, 1799. The warrant from the Proprietaries to John Lindsay, the father, was dated July 10, 1752; survey Apr., 1767, No. 3302, for 350 lbs., xx by land of Wm. Lindsay, now of John, the son. On Nov. 4, 1806, the executors of John Lindsay, Sr., convey to Daniel Houston, in Guilford and Hamilton Twp., 500 acres of land early to John Mushitt, decd., which became vested in Paul Zantzinger, who in 1774 conveyed 200 acres to said John Lindsay Esq., by lands of George Cook, Leonard Stans and Andrew Gibson.

JOHN LINDSAY

Served as a pvt., under the First Call, and during 1777-78-79-80-81, he was with Capts., James Young, John Rea and Wm. Long.

Penna. Arch. 5th Ser. Vol. 6, p. 72, 74, 78, 105, 522, 526, 538, 544, 546, 585, 597.

SAMUEL LINDSAY

Appears as an Ensign, May 3, 1758, under Col. Hugh Mercer. Wm. Maclay was a Lieut., in the Company. Capt. Samuel Lindsay, July 13, 1763, had an Lieut., James Chambers, and as Ensign James Smith. It is stated Samuel Lindsay joined Col. Francis.

Penna. Arch. 5th Ser. Vol. 1, p. 329, 336, 131, 184, 265.

THOMAS LINDSAY

Is shown in service 1779-80-81, with Capt. John Rea, command of Col. Smith. Andrew Lindsay and wife Jane, of McConnellsburg, Pa., sell to Thomas Lindsay of Chambersburg, for $140. a lot in Chambersburg, No. 32, sold by Capt. Benj. Chambers to Matthew Wilson. The above Andrew Lindsay was the son of John Lindsay and Agnes Andrew, dau., of John Andrew, the Miller on the Falling Spring. Andrew Lindsay mar. Sept. 7, 1813, Jane, dau. of Joseph Davison, of Antrim Twp., and in 1827 was living in McConnellsburg, Pa.

Penna. Arch. 5th Ser. Vol. 6, p. 78, 105, 107, 543, 584.

WILLIAM LINDSAY

Appears first in 1777, under Capt. Noah Abraham, again under Benj. Blythe, and an undated roll. In June 1774, Wm. Lindsay and wife Margaret, sell to Samuel Rea, 300 acres land on Survey to Wm. Lindsay Sept. 9, 1766, No. 1118, by land of Benj. Chambers, Archbd. McCartey, John Andrews, John Miller and Samuel Lindsay. They sell for 900 lbs., both parties of Letterkenny Twp. The above William may be a son of Fulton Lindsay.

Penna. Arch. 5th Ser. Vol. 6, p. 21, 133, 152.

Marriages by Dr. David Denny, Chambersburg, Penna.: William Lindsay, Nancy McConnell—Oct. 29, 1799; Andrew McCulley, Eliza Lindsay—Apr. 21, 1801; James Black, Jane Lindsay—Apr. 19, 1804; John Lindsay, Frances Crawford—Apr. 17, 1805; John Vance, Nancy Lindsay—Oct. 26, 1809; John Davis, Polly Lindsay—March 26, 1812; John Palmer, Polly Lindsay—Aug. 18, 1812; Samuel Gillaspy, Rebecca Lindsay—March 27, 1823; Battlemen Jones, Ann Lindsay—Dec. 14, 1824; James L. Thompson, Martha Lindsay—Sept. 9, 1828; Samuel Bingham, Elizabeth Lindsay—Oct. 16, 1828; Dr. Joseph Lanston, Elizabeth

Lindsay—May 5, 1831; J. Smith Grier, Sarah H. Lindsay—Jan. 28, 1834. Robert McGregor, Ellen Lindsay—July 2, 1835; Frederick Byer, Jane Lindsay—Dec. 17, 1840.

JAMES LITTLE

Served under Capt. Thos. Askey, 1779-81-82, under the command of Col. James Dunlop. John Little requests land in Fannett Twp., 219 ac., date Dec. 1766. A second tract in 1787, in the name of Robert Little; a third tract in 1819 in the name of James Little and a fourth tract in the name of James Little, May, 1819.

Penna. Arch 5th Ser. Vol. 6, p. 61, 408, 423, 429, 441.

ROBERT LITTLE, JR.

Served under Capt. Thos. Askey, 1779, undated rolls, certified by Benj. Blythe, Sub. Lieut.

Penna. Arch. 5th Ser. Vol. 6, p. 61, 131, 151.

ROBERT LITTLE

Served 1781-82 as a private under Capt. Thos. Askey, Cumb. Co. Militia. He lived in Fannett Twp., where he mar. Rosannah, dau. of Col. Robert Baker, and his wife Frances. They had no issue. The will of Robert Little of Fannett Twp., was dated 1799, and prob. Mar. 13, 1813. His Exrs. were his wife and his nephew James Little.

Penna. Arch. 5th Ser. Vol. 6, p. 423, 441.

BENJAMIN LONG

Of Southampton Twp., Orphans' Court Book, C, p. 202, Benj. Long of Southampton Twp., died intestate in 1828. Issue: Benjamin; Elizabeth mar. Robert Hunter; Fanny mar. Jonathan Dice. Penna. Rifle Regt., Col. Samuel Miles, Benjamin Long, enlisted at Lebanon, Apr. 9, 1776; Discharged Jan 1, 1778, resided in Franklin Co., in 1827. He was a pensioner.

Penna. Arch. 2nd Ser. Vol. 10, p. 238.

DAVID LONG

Was an Ensign, in 1777 under Capt. Elias Davidson and in 1780-81 under Capts. Wm. Berryhill and James Poe. An old Deed shows him to have been a son of Thomas Long, whose will was dated Oct. 27, 1753. David Long's will dated 1805, was prob. Aug. 22, 1806, in which he names his wife Rebeccah and daus.: Mary; Rebeccah; Ester; Ruth and Jemima Long. The same old deed names as heirs,—George Lawrence; John Gaff; Rebecca Gaff; Easter Steele; and Ruth Long as selling land to Wm. Martin.

Penna. Arch. 5th Ser. Vol. 6, p. 80, 101, 513, 521.

PATRICK LONG

Served in 1780, as a pvt., under Capt. Wm. Smith. Of the Longs of Montgomery Twp., there were John, a freeman, also Conrod, George and William, but Patrick is unaccounted for in the vicinity.

Penna. Arch. 5th Ser. Vol. 6, p. 276.

CAPTAIN WILLIAM LONG

Is shown serving in the 8th Batt. 4th Co., First Call, Oct. 23, 1777, under the Command of Abraham Smith, Cumb. Co. Militia. He was in service during 1778-79-80, and his Lieuts., were Adam Harmony, James McWilliams, with Robert Snodgrass as Ensign. In 1775, Williaim Long and James Watson purchased from Elizabeth Hoops, widow, and her sons Robert and David Hoops, Executors of the will of Adam Hoopes, land in Antrim Twp., a Grant to Adam Hoops March 11, 1763, to Wm. Long of Lancaster Co., Penna. In 1787, Wm. Long of Guilford Twp., and Isabella, his wife, sell to James Watson, Tanner of Antrim Twp. Wm. Long is said to have mar. Isabella, dau. of Hugh Long of Chestnut level, Lancaster Co., Penna.

Penna. Arch. 5th Ser. Vol. 6, p. 512, 519, 524, 525, 533, 544, 556.

JOHN LOVE

Served as pvt., under Capt. James Patton, in 1780. John Love had baptized a son John, March 5, 1775. A son David June 28, 1781, church records, Mercersburg, Pa.

Penna. Arch. 5th Ser. Vol. 6, p. 271.

WILLIAM LOVE

Served under Capt. Noah Abraham, 1778-79.

Penna. Arch. 5th Ser. Vol. 6, p. 52, 593, 603.

ANDREW LOWERS (LOWARDS)

Served as a pvt., under Capt. John Orbison, 1781. His will recorded at Carlisle was prob. June 11, 1782. He was of Montgomery Twp., names his Mother, Isabel Stewart; his sister Mary mar. to Matthew Wilkins; his son Andrew and sisters.

Penna. Arch. 5th Ser. Vol. 6, p. 291.

In 1769 the Lowrys were living in District 5 of the Presbyterian Church of Mercersburg, under the Eldership of Major Wm. Maxwell; Wm. Lowry and wife Margaret had Sarah Trecy living with them. Another Wm. Lowry, with wife Rebecca, was neighbor to Patrick Maxwell. John McClelland mar. Sarah Lowry, Jan. 9, 1770. David Kelly mar. Martha Lowry, March 4, 1776. Under Church admissions: Rebecca in 1771; Robert and Joseph in 1785; Peggy in 1787; Polly in 1790. Deaths recorded: Wm. Lowry's

Rebecca and Charles Apr. 11, and 17 in the year 1777.

BENJAMIN LOWRY
Served as pvt., under Capt. Wm. Huston, 1780-81.
Penna. Arch 5th Ser. Vol. 6, p. 265, 270, 276, 283, 643.

CHARLES LOWREY
Served as pvt., 1781-82 under Capt. Walter McKinnie. He was a son of Wm. Lowry, Sr. of Montgomery Twp., whose will was prob., 1785. The Lowrys were members of the "Upper West Conococheague" Presby. Church of Mercersburg, Penna. In 1769 Charles Loury, wife Martha, with Wm.; Margaret and Robert were living in District 5. Charles Lowry had baptized Martha in 1770; Charles in 1772; a child in 1775.
Penna. Arch 5th Ser. Vol. 6, p. 297, 300, 305.

GEORGE LOWRY
Was a pvt., 1778 in the Eighth Batt. Militia with Capt. Wm. Findley.
Penna. Arch. 5th Ser. Vol. 6, p. 527.

JAMES LOWRY
Served as pvt., under Capt. Walter McKinnie, 1781-82.
Penna. Arch. 5th Ser. Vol. 6, p. 298, 305.

JOSEPH LOWRY
Served as pvt., under Capts. Wm. Long, James Poe and Thos. McDowell.
Penna. Arch. 5th Ser. Vol. 6, p. 315, 520, 576, 583.

PATRICK LOWRY
Pvt., in Major Jeremh. Talbot's Company Aug. 26, 1778, Sixth Regt. C. L.
Penna. Arch. 2nd Ser. Vol. 10, p. 601.

ROBERT LOWRY
Served as pvt., under Capt. Walter McKinnie, 1781-82. His father, Wm. Lowry, Sr., gives to his son Robert's eldest son, 20 shillings.
Penna. Arch. 5th Ser. Vol. 6, p. 298, 300, 305, 306.

SAMUEL LOWREY
Served in 1782, as a pvt., with Capt. Walter McKinnie.
Penna. Arch. 5th Ser. Vol. 6, p. 305.

STEPHEN LOWRY
Pvt., in the Cont. Line from Westmoreland County, Penna. One Stephen Lowry was mar. July 4, 1776, to Catherine Stephens by Dr. John King of Mercersburg, Penna.
Penna. Arch 5th Ser. Vol. 4, p. 445, 748.

THOMAS LOWREY
Appears as a pvt., 1781, under Capt. Walter McKinnie.
Penna. Arch. 5th Ser. Vol. 6, p. 300.

WILLIAM LOWRY, SR.
Served as pvt., 1781-82, under Capt. Walter McKinnie. In his will prob. 1785, he names son Wm. and his dau. Margaret; Grandson, Wm. Crawford; Son Charles, Son Robert Lourey's eldest son 20 shillings; Dau., Jean Crawford.
Penna. Arch. 5th Ser. Vol. 6, p. 299, 301, 306.

WILLIAM LOWRY, JR.
Served as pvt., under Capt. Samuel Patton in 1778-79 and under Capt. Walter McKinnie, 1781-82, presumably a son of Wm. Lowrey, Sr. Wm. Lourey was with Capt. Patton as a Ranger on the Frontiers of Bedford and Westmoreland Counties, the Spring and summer of 1779.
Penna. Arch. 5th Ser. Vol. 6, p. 298, 305, 380, 601, 610.

WILLIAM LOWRY
Served in 1781 with Capt. Thomas Askey.
Penna. Arch. 5th Ser. Vol. 6, p. 411, 631.

MICHAEL LOY
From Franklin County. Killed at Long Island, Aug. 27, 1776.
Penna. Arch. 2nd Ser. Vol. 13, p. 134.

BENET OR BENNET LUCAS
Served from Fannett Twp., 1780-81-82, under Capt. Noah Abraham.
Penna. Arch. 5th Ser. Vol. 6, p. 86, 121, 128, 393.

GEORGE LUCAS
Applied for pension from Bedford County, late a Sergeant in Penna. Line. He enlisted at Greencastle, Penna. in 1776, in 6th Penna. Regt., Capt. Abraham Smith. Marched to Canada; in defeat at Three Rivers; re-enlisted for 3 years in 7th Penna. Regt.; discharged Jan. 23, 1781. In battles of Monmouth and Stony Point. He had nine children.
Penna. Arch 5th Ser. Vol. 4, p. 503.

THOMAS LUCAS
New 11th Penna.; 1st Lieut.; Commissioned Jan. 23, 1777, died in Franklin Co., 1823. Letters Admr., March 20, 1824. Thomas Lucas enlisted in Philadelphia, Penna., in October, 1775, as a marine under Capt. John Welsh, served on the brig, "Cabot," commanded by Capt. John Hop-

kins, was at the taking of the "Iceland" off New Providence, in the battle with the British ship, "Glasgow," and was discharged in December, 1776. On his return to Phila., he was commissioned first Lieut. in Capt. James Calderwood's Company, Col. Daniel Morgan's Virginia regiment, was in the battle of Brandywine, at which time he was promoted to the rank of captain in Col. Wm. Malcolm's regiment, was in the battle of Germantown, was severely wounded Oct. 19, 1777, by a musket ball in his right thigh and was discharged in June, 1778. He was allowed pension on his application executed April 15th, 1818, aged sixty-one years and a resident of Franklin Co., Penna., where he had lived for forty years. In 1820 he was living in Franklin Co., Penna., and stated that he was a cooper by trade. He referred to his wife, Mary, then aged fifty-seven years, and to his son, John, aged twenty-eight years, with whom he resided. He also referred to the following children: Margaret; Martha; Mary; Eliza and Thomas, aged thirty, twenty-five, twenty-two, nineteen and seventeen years respectively. He died Nov. 3, 1823. "The Franklin Repository," Nov. 11, 1823. "Another of the patriots of 76 has descended to the republic of dust and ashes. Capt. Thomas Lucas of St. Thomas departed this life on Sunday the 2nd inst. He was an honest industrious man. He was a faithful officer during the greater part if not the whole of the Revolutionary War and at the time of his death enjoyed the bounty of a grateful Country. He has left an aged widow." From the Repository we also have the following: "May 30, 1820, died on the 15th Mrs. Baxter Carney, consort of John Carney one of the editors of this paper, and dau. of Capt. Thos. Lucas, of this county,—also, Nov., 1820, died at St. Thomas in his 17th year, Thomas McKean Lucas, son of Capt. Thomas Lucas; also, under Sept. 4, died on Wednesday, Mary Lucas, dau. of Capt. Thomas Lucas, of St. Thomas, in her 23rd year, Aug. 29, 1821. The Ledger of Matthias Nead, Esq., who had a Tannery in St. Thomas gives the following charges against John and Garret Lucas, 1821-27 and Margaret Lucas, Aug. 31, 1827, was charged "To 1 Crobet for her school, at 12½." Stoehr and Lucas were credited "By 722 ft., Blackoke Bark."

Penna. Arch. 2nd Ser. Vol. 11, p. 49.

THOMAS LUCAS

Appears in service under Capts., Walter McKinnie, William Huston and James Poe. He was in Peters, 1789, as were, also, Robert and Samuel Lucas.

Penna. Arch. 5th Ser. Vol. 6, p. 269, 275, 276, 282, 288, 297, 300, 284, 576, 583.

BERNARD LUTZ

Served as a pvt., under Capt. Wm. Crawford, 1780-82, undated rolls. In 1792, John Ritchey and wife Margaret of Green Twp., sell to Barnet Lutz of Mountjoy Twp., Lancaster Co., Penna., for 1395 lbs., two (2) tracts of land in Green Twp.,—264 ac. 143 pchs. The Executors of David McCreight sold in 1779. The Franklin Repository of December 23, 1828 refers to Bernard Lutz as an old and respected citizen of Green Twp. His will prob. Dec. 20, 1828, names son Christly, decd. "All my Mansion place, 267 acres, unto Elizabeth, John, Martin, Henry and Rebecca Lutz, children of son Christly 1/2 of my estate." Son John has gotten his share.

Penna. Arch. 5th Ser. Vol. 7, p. 470, 493, 915, 987.

JOHN LYTLE

Is shown in service on the Frontiers of Bedford and Westmoreland Counties in the spring of 1779,—in Capt. Samuel Patton's Company.

Penna. Arch. 5th Ser. Vol. 6, p. 601, 610.

ALEXANDER MACK (MOCK)

Is shown in service 1780-81, with Capt. Daniel Clapsaddler. Under "Valuations," 1799, in Washington Twp., Alexdr. Mack, Sr., son of Johannes, has 2 log houses; Half Stonebarn; Stone springhouse and cows. Jacob Mack Sr., son of Johannes, has 128 ac. land; Log house and barn; Spring house, horses and cows. Jacob, Jr., Alexdr., Jr., and John Mack have horses and cows. He removed to Bedford Co., Penna., where he left a will, dated Nov. and prob. Dec., 1811. He had already given portions to his children at the time of their marrying. Eldest son John; Eldest dau. Elizabeth, wife of John Gerber; Sons Alexdr. and Jacob; dau. Sarah, wife of Daniel Longacre; Dau. Ann, wife of Samuel Gerber; "I live with my son Jacob and his wife who attend to me." Exrs.: Sons John, Alexdr. Jacob, all of Woodberry Twp. A descendant states that the above Alexdr. Mock was a son of Johannes, and a grandson of Alexander Mack who founded the Church of the Brethren and a church History, by Brumbaugh, shows that Johannes went to the "Antitum" country. One George Mock, also left a will in Bedford County, dated and probated 1810. To his wife Eve "all wool which is now clipt of the sheep and one third of my estate during widowhood." Peter Mock, St. Clair Twp., Bedford Co., Penna., left a will dated 1815, prob. 1817, leaving many children and grandchildren.

Penna. Arch. 5th Ser. Vol. 6, p. 71, 94, 117

WILLIAM MACK

Son of Alex. Jr., appears with Alexdr. Mack, son of Johannes, both serving, 1781, with Capt.

Daniel Clapsaddle. In Sept. 1729, the Ship Allen brought the Macks and Kneppers: Johannes Mack; Alexdr. Mack, Sr.; Johannes Valentine Mack; Alexander Mack, Jr.; Velten Mack; Feltes Mack; Anna Margaretta Mack; Wilhelmus Knepper and Ferina Knipper.

Penna. Arch 5th Ser. Vol. 6, p. 117.

ROBERT MACKEY

Served as a private under Capt. John Orbison, 1780-81-82. Mrs. Harriet (Mackey) Balsbaugh, states that Robert Mackey was mar. 3 times. By first wife he had a dau. Sally. He mar. 2nd Harriet Mackey and had Wm.; James; Robert; Elizabeth; Mary. He mar. 3rd Mary Davis Lewis, dau. of Elisha Lewis, and they had Rebecca; Elisha Lewis; Eleanor Jane, who mar., Wm. Lackens; Daisy T. mar. Susan Taylor; Rebecca mar. Josiah Keefer and had 10 children. Mary Mackey (above) was the 2nd wife of Wm. Wilson; her sister Elizabeth mar. Frank Dunn, who had issue, Robert Mackey Dunn, Samuel Nye Dunn, Nancy Elizabeth and Frank Dunn. Letters of Admr on estate of Robert Mackey taken out in 1833 by Wm. Mackey and F. Dunn. The widow, Mary Davis (Lewis) Mackey, born Feb. 11, 1776 died Feb. 1858, aged 82 yrs., and was buried in the old Welsh Graveyard, near Welsh Run.

Penna. Arch. 5th Ser. Vol. 6, p. 273 293, 307.

CHARLES MACLEY

Born 1748, recruited a company of Militia, 1777-78. At the battle of "Crooked Billet" he was killed with most of his company. He was the son of John Macley, born 1721, and Elizabeth McDonald. His sister Elizabeth mar. Col Samuel Culbertson and his sister Martha mar. John Irwin. The Archives show an appraisement bill of blankets, knapsacks &c., belonging to Capt. Chas. McClay's company, commanded by Col. Abraham Smith, and they also show him as Captain, 1776-77-78.

Egle's Penna. Genealogy, p. 409.

CHARLES McCLAY, JR.

Served 1778-80-82 under Capt. Isaac Miller. This appears to be the Charles Maclay, born 1739, died 1834. He mar. 1762, Mary Templeton (1742-1812) but left no issue.

Penna. Arch. 5th Ser. Vol. 6, p. 37, 390 435, 450.

DAVID MCCLAY (MACLAY)

Served under Capt. Isaac Miller in 1782, undated roll. He was born 1762 and died 1839. He is said to have operated the well-known Maclay Mill in Lurgan Twp. He mar. 1st in 1785, Eleanor Maclay and 2nd Eleanor Herron, dau. of John and Mary (Jack) Herron. They had issue: John Herron; David; Jean Elinore; Charles Templeton; Francis Herron; James Herron; Mary Ellen.

Penna. Arch. 5th Ser. Vol. 6, p. 435, 449.

JOHN MACLAY

Born 1748, mar. Eleanor Maclay. Orphans' Court records show Admr., of Estate Feb. 13, 1813. On Nov. 15, 1813, John Maclay, eldest son of John Maclay, late of Franklin County, Esq., states the intestate died Jan. 11, 1813, leaving a widow Eleanor and issue: Margaret Maclay and John Maclay legal heirs of Charles Maclay, 2nd child of John Macley, decd., who died in the lifetime of Intestate, under 21 years, Daniel Henderson, guardian; and nine children: Elizabeth mar. to Wm. Reynolds; Eleanor mar. to Jacob Smith; John, the petitioner, Robert; Samuel; James; Mary mar. David Edgar; Wm. and Kitty, all over age. One Charles Maclay died 1805 and left John and Margaret minors as above. One Mary, widow of Charles is shown in 1814.

JOHN MCCLAY, JR.

Served 1778-80-82, under Capt. Isaac Miller.

Penna. Arch 5th Ser. Vol. 6, p. 37, 390, 435, 450.

JOHN MACLAY

Born 1734, died Apr. 4, 1804, in Lurgan Twp. A Provincial Magistrate in 1760, member of Provincial Conference at Carpenter's Hall, Phila., June 18, 1776; member of Penna., Assembly, and a Ruling Elder in Dr. Cooper's Church at Middle Springs. His wife was Jean Dickson and they had issue: Charles b. 1757, mar. Susannah Linn; Catherine b. 1760, mar. Wm. Irwin; David b. 1762, mar. 1st Eleanor Maclay; mar. 2nd Eleanor Herron; Wm. b. 1765, mar. Margaret Culbertson; Samuel b. 1767, mar Margaret Snodgrass; Eleanor b. 1769, mar. Capt. David McKnight; Jane b. 1774, d. unmar.; John, b. 1776, mar. Hannah Reynolds.

Egle's Penna. Genealogies.

SAMUEL MACLAY

Served as pvt., 1780-81-82 under Capt. Wm. Strain. Further data in Bates History of Franklin Co., Penna., 1887.

Penna. Arch. 5th Ser. Vol. 6, p. 398, 406, 430.

SAMUEL MACLAY

Born June 7, 1741, in Lurgan Twp. He was chosen Lieut., Col. of Northumberland County Associators, and was in active service; member of Congress; State Senator; U. S. S. Senator. He mar. in 1773, Elizabeth Plunkett and had issue nine children. He died in Buffalo Valley, Oct. 5, xx 1811 and is buried on his farm, (now Green farm) in Buffalo Valley, and later buried in Dreisbach Church. In March, 1769, Samuel Maclay for Wm. Maclay, surveyed 8000 acres of the grant in Buffalo Valley (now Union Co.,) the greater part on Bald Eagle Creek.

Egle's Penna. Genealogies. Mrs. Bartol's list Rev. Soldiers Shikelimo Chapter D. A. R.

WILLIAM MACLAY

Born 1737, died 1804, his boyhood days spent on the paternal farm in Lurgan Twp. He is shown as a Lieut., of Capt. John Montgomery's Company, in Col. Hugh Mercer's battalion, May, 1758. He is shown in the Penna. Regt., as Capt., 1758-59, and under Capt. Asher Clayton in 1763; on Boquet's expedition in 1763; in the fight at Bushy Run, on the line of the stockade forts on the route to Fort Pitt as lieutenant commanding the company and assisted in surveying the Provincial grants of land to the officers connected therewith. Mr. Maclay mar. Mary McClure, dau. of John Harris, founder of Harrisburg. They had nine children.

Eagle's Penna. Genealogies, p. 411.

CHARLES M'GILL

Blunston Licenses Apr. 5, 1737, Charles M'Gill 300 ac., where he is already settled at the round meadow, On the Old Waggon road to Potomac, about three miles Beyond Falling Spring. Charles Magill served as Lieut., under his brother-in-law, Capt. Benj. Chambers, 1747-48, with Robert Mull as Ensign, "over the River Susquehanna." He was a taxable in Guilford Twp., (now Franklin County) 1751, and Collector of Taxes for Antrim Twp., 1748. He died in Bedford Co., Penna., and letters of Admr., were issued to his widow, Jane Magill, Oct. 16, 1779. In 1764 Charles McGill entered a Caveat against the acceptance of a Survey for John Jack for 300 acres, claims a prior title having made improvements thereon upwards of fourteen (14) years ago.

Penna. Arch. 5th Ser. Vol. 1, p. 25.

DR. WILLIAM MAGAW

In 1775 was Surgeon of Col. Wm. Thompson's Batt., of Riflemen. In 1781 transferred from the 1st to the 4th Penna. Regt. Dr. William Magaw, Surgeon, was an original member of the Penna., Society of the Cincinnati. His Grandson was admitted in 1852. His greatgrandson in 1885, another in 1924. He resided many years after the war at Mercersburg, Penna., where he mar. his second wife Polly McDowell, Oct. of 1790. After her death he mar. Martha, widow of James Crawford. Franklin Repository notice: Necessity induces me to call on all those that are indebted to me, particularly such as have long standing accounts, to come forward and make immediate payment. I have lately received a general assortment of medicine, likewise paints, all which I will sell for cash on very moderate terms. I will continue to practice Physic, and will pay particular attention to those who may please to put confidence in me. William Magaw—Mercersburg, Nov. 10, 1802. He removed, late in life, to Meadville and died there May 1, 1829, aged 85 yrs.

Penna. Arch. 5th Ser. Vol. 2, p. 16, 631, 700. Penna. Arch. 2nd Ser. Vol. 10, p. 694.

ROBERT MAGWIRE

Of Fannett Twp., served as a pvt., under Capt. Noah Abraham in 1777-79-81. He names his father, Philip Magwier and his wife Mary; Son John's two children; other children not named. Friends and brothers-in-law James Hervey and John Walker. His will was prob. March 27, 1786. Deed Book 5, p. 57. Indenture Sept. 2, 1799. Matthew Ewing and wife Mary of Metal Twp., refers to will of Robert Maguier, 1786. Matthew Ewing in right of marriage to Mary Maguier was entitled to a share of estate. They sell to John Maguier. Thomas Cisna had mar. Margaret Maguier.

Penna. Arch. 5th Ser. Vol. 6, p. 141, 384, 407, 516.

ARCHIBALD MAHON

Of Southampton Twp., served as pvt., under Capt. Chas. Maclay, 1778 and later some undated Rolls. His will was dated 1798, probated, Jan. 6, 1802. He named wife Jean; a dau. Jean mar. to Robert Mahan and a dau. Mary; Grandau. Margaret, dau. of his son John, decd. His trusty friends were John Brackenridge, Sr., and John Herron, Esq. One Archibald Mahon mar. Sarah, dau of John Brackenridge, whose will was prob. Nov., 1810. He names dau. Sarah's children: Sally; John; Jean; David.

Penna. Arch. 5th Ser. Vol. 6, p. 36, 40, 149, 151, 435, 450.

ALEXANDER MACHON

Is shown in 1778-82, serving under Capt. James Adams, stationed at Bald Eagle Creek, Jan. 22, 1778.

Penna. Arch. 5th Ser. Vol. 6, p. 563, 597.

DAVID MAHAN

Served as pvt., under Capt. Chas. Maclay, 1778-1781. He was of GreenTwp., and his will was dated and prob., in 1800. He and wife Agnes made a joint will. He names his eldest brother Archibald Mahon; brother Henry Mahon; our sister Ann mar. to Samuel Clark; then they name the brothers of Agnes: James, John, Wm., and Archibald Mahon then the sisters of Agnes: Jean

Mahon; Elin Foreham; Rachel Right; Mary Kelly; balance of estate to Robert Mahan, son of Robert Mahan, decd.

Penna. Arch. 5th Ser. Vol. 6, p. 36, 40, 406.

DAVID MAHAN

1744-1813, served as a pvt., under Capt. Alex. Peebles and Capt. Wm. Strain 1777-79-80-81-82. He was a merchant of Shippensburg.

Penna. Arch. 5th Ser. Vol. 6, p. 58, 62, 396, 422, 430, 433, 590. Biographical Annals of Franklin County, p. 156.

HENRY MAHAN

Served as pvt., under Capt. Wm. Strain.
Penna. Arch. 5th Ser. Vol. 6, p. 143.

JAMES MAHAN

Served in 1780-82 under Capts. John McConnell and Isaac Miller.

Penna. Arch. 5th Ser. Vol. 6, p. 267, 435.

JOHN MAHON

Served under Capts. Noah Abraham, Thomas Askey and Wm. Strain, the years of 1777-78-80-82, presumably a son of John Mahon who died in 1805.

Penna. Arch. 5th Ser. Vol. 6, p. 18, 15, 142, 397, 430.

ROBERT MAHON

Served as pvt., under Capts. Thos. Askey and Wm. Strain, 1778-1780-1782.

Penna. Arch 5th Ser. Vol. 6, p. 50, 142, 430, 397, 416.

WILLIAM MAHAN

Served as pvt., under Capts. Noah Abraham, Alex. Peebles and Wm. Strain. He is shown in 1777-1782, with several undated rolls.

Penna. Arch. 5th Ser. Vol. 6, p. 18 ,58, 21, 139, 396, 397, 389, 430, 590.

WILLIAM MAINS

Pensioner, S-2721, Pennsylvania. Franklin Co., Penna., Nov. 7, 1832. William Mains (Means) of Lurgan Twp., aged 75 years on May 16, last. He was born in Bucks Co., Penna., May 16, 1757, record of birth now in his possession, which is a record of his father's family. At the time of the Revolution he was living in Bucks Co., a member of his father's household. He volunteered in the first call under Capt. Nich. Patterson, marched to Amboy and served 2 months; discharged and again enlisted with Capt. Patterson; at Trenton under Lieut., Wm. Mains; joined Capt Jameson's Company under Genl. Washington, 3 months; Capt. Wm. Irwin, Bristol below Phila. (details of battles). The Spring after the Revolution he moved to Shippensburg, in that and adjoining Co. of Franklin; in Franklin County 35 years. William Means served as Lieut., and Ensign, 1777-80-81, under Capt. Nich. Patterson and Capt. Wm. Erwin, 1st Regt., of Foot in 1781, also undated rolls. The above Wm. Mains of Lurgan Twp., left a will dated Jan. 11, 1839; prob., July 26, 1843, in which he named wife and "all my children," Richard Morrow being appointed as Executor.

Penna. Arch. 5th Ser. Vol. 5, p. 334, 367, 395, 439, 445.

JOHN MARDIS

Served in the Cont. Line from Bedford Co., Penna., and was also a pvt., in Company of Capt. Thomas Davies. On March 26, 1787, Ann Mardis was married to Joshua Phillips, by Dr. John King at Mercersburg. They were from that part of Bedford which later became Warren Twp., Franklin Co., Penna. A note taken from a book kept by Joshua M. Philips: Old inhabitants,—Grandmother's (Ann Mardis); Grandfather's name is George Cheeks—German; Eleanor Cheeks mar. to John Mardis or T. Mardis. Thomas Mardis, brother of Ann died Dec. 21, 1857 aged 89 years and 5 mos. He was buried on his own land. Cousins of Joshua M. Philips: Samuel L. Mardis, lived at Strongstown, Indiana Co., Penna.; Mardis Thomas lived in Salt Lake City, Utah in 1877; John H. Thomas, whose grandmother was a Mardis, died July 9, 1879, buried at St. John's Church. Feb. 10, 1886 Jasper Mardis of Indiana, Penna., paid grandfather a visit.

Penna. Arch. 5th Ser. Vol. 4, p. 609. Penna. Arch. 5th Ser. Vol. 5, p. 111, 245.

PETER MARKS

Is shown as a pvt., in the Cont. Line, from York Co., Penna. He is probably the man whose will follows, but not proven. Peter Mertz (Martz) of Peters Twp., left a will dated January 1804, prob., February, 1804, naming wife Mary; eldest son Peter to remain with his mother and to be sent to school for one year. Son John; younger sons Jacob and David; 3 daus., Mary; Catherine and Elizabeth to be left under the care of their mother. My father's property to which I am entitled, to be sold. Wit: Conrad Stenger and Thomas McDowell. John Miller married Mary Marks, June, 1811, by Rev. John King. Early Land Warrants in Peters Twp., show the following: "Peter Martz, Aug. 25, 1791, 50 acres, adjoining lands of Wm. McDowell and Henry Work." Again on Oct. 26, 1818, Peter Martz of Peters Twp., buys land in Peters Twp. Mr. Finafrock was told that Peter Martz wished to be buried near the Pike, "where he could (as an old waggoner) hear the teams and herds go by."

The place is marked by a group of lilac bushes, on the Chambersburg-Bedford Pike, the road having been built too late for the first Peter Martz. There are descendants living today, (1939) in Mercersburg.

Penna. Arch. 5th Ser. Vol. 4, p. 473.

ANDREW MARSHALL

Served from Hamilton Twp. as pvt., in 1780-81-82, under Capt. Samuel Patton. His will was prob. Nov. 17, 1789, naming wife Mary, and issue: Joseph; Wm; Samuel; John; Katherine; Martha and Andrew; Son Andrew to be kept, schoold, clothed and maintained.

Penna. Arch. 5th Ser. Vol. 6, p. 278, 287, 311.

HENRY MARSHALL

Was a ranger on the Western Frontiers, under Samuel Patton in 1779. He also served, 1778-1780-81 with Capt. Wm. Huston.

Penna. Arch. 5th Ser. Vol. 6, p. 269, 275, 282, 380, 601, 610..

JOHN MARSHALL

Served as a pvt., 1780-81 under Capt. Thos. Johnston. The will of John Marshall dated May, 1804, was prob. October of the same year. He requests his executor to have him decently buried. Wife Agnes all property, and named 3 children; son Robert; dau. Gennet McCoy and dau. Mary Jones.

Penna. Arch. 5th Ser. Vol. 6, p. 75, 115.

WILLIAM MARSHALL

"A plan for the defence of the Frontier of Cumb. County." "Let five men be constantly at Philip Davies's, Wm. Marshall's and Thos. Waddle's xxx ten men sent from the chief quarters xx to go by Wm. Marshall's to Philip Davies's and return in the afternoon." In 1769, Wm. Marshall was living in District 4 of the "Upper West Conococheague" Presby., Church near Mercersburg. His wife was Mary, and the children John; Elizabeth; Martha; Henry; Wm. The Presiding Elder of this District was Robert Fleming. Henry Anderson, in his will names "nephew Henry Marshall, son to my brother-in-law, Wm. Marshall." The 1790 Census shows the family as 3 men, 1 boy, 3 females. On Aug. 13, 1802, Letters of Admr., on the estate of Wm. Marshall were granted to son John. Surety Oliver Anderson. Oliver Anderson mar. Elizabeth Martial. March 14, 1770.

Rupp's Hist. of Dauphin, Cumb., Franklin and other Counties, p. 78.

JOHN MARTIN

3rd Penna. Cont. Line. John died in Franklin Co., June 13, 1824, aged 80 years. Armand's Legion, 1780-83. John Martin, S-40123. The data which follow were obtained from papers on file in claim for Rev. War. The date and place of birth of John Martin are not given, nor are the names of his parents shown. He enlisted in "Fredericktown," Maryland, in the year 1780, served as a private in a company commanded by Baron de Uechritz in Col. Armand's Legion; he was in the battle of Camden, and was discharged in the year 1783, in York, Penna., where he had been stationed about one year. He was allowed pension on his application executed April 28, 1818, at which time he was a resident of Berkeley County, Va., aged about sixty-three years. The soldier, John Martin, had moved to Chambersburg, Franklin Co., Penna., in 1819, was still there in 1821 and 1823. His wife, Catherine was about seventy-four years of age 1821. John Martin died June 13, 1824. The last payment of pension due John Martin, a pensioner of the Rev. War, Certificate No. 9459, Penna., Agency, covering the period from Sept. 4, 1823 to Mar. 4, 1824, was made March 15, 1824, at the Pension Agency in Phila., Penna., to Joseph Boyd, as attorney for the pension. On March 9, 1824, the pensioner was residing in Franklin Co., Penna. John Martin kept tavern in a low two-story log house about twenty by twenty five ft. in size, where Mrs. Watson now resides (1876). One John Martin was appointed the first Post Master at Chambersburg, June 1, 1790.

Penna. Arch. 2nd Ser. Vol. 10, p. 481. Penna. Arch. 2nd Ser. Vol. 11, p.155. McCauley's Hist.

JOHN MARTIN

Served under Capt. Wm. Huston, 1780-81, in the Fifth Company Fourth Batt., Cumb. Co. Militia. John and William Martin were taxables in Montgomery Twp., with land, horses and cattle.

Penna. Arch 5th Ser. Vol. 6, p. 265, 270, 276, 283.

WILLIAM MARTIN

Served 1780-81, as pvt., under Capt. Wm. Huston. The will of Wm. Martin of Montgomery Twp., dated and prob., June—Aug., 1810. My wife Jane; my dau. and my dau-in-law (Mary Martin and her children); dau. Sally Martin 2/3 part; 1/3 to my three grandchildren, that is Wm. (son of Dr. Martin) and Culbertson and John Martin (sons of John Martin, decd.) Exrs.: James Clark, Jr, and Wm. McClelland. From the Repository, Feb., 1827: "Died on the 17th, Mrs. Jane, widow of Wm. Martin, late of Montgomery Twp., aged 107 years."

Penna. Arch. 5th Ser. Vol. 6, p. 265, 270, 276, 283.

GEORGE MATTHEWS

Of Hamilton Twp., was a Captain under Col. Joseph Armstrong, Fifth Batt. 1776-77. He died in Hamilton Twp., the estate, in Orphans' Court in 1799, and undoubtedly is buried in Rocky Spring Graveyard. He left a widow Isabella; Dau. Abigail mar. Josiah Nash; Dau. Jean mar. Isaac Eaton; Dau. Margaret mar. John Wilkerson; Dau. Elizabeth; and Isabella; George; James; John; Agnes; Mary; Samuel; Wm. George died since, of full age and unmarried. Isabella, widow of above George, left a will dated and prob. 1801, in which she named grandchildren, four unmarried daughters who were young, and ten pounds each to Sons Samuel and William.

Penna. Arch. 5th Ser. Vol. 6, p. 5, 318.

GEORGE MATTHEWS

Served as a pvt., under Capt. Samuel Patten 1780-81-82. In his will prob. March 27, 1798, he names: Sister Jean, wife of Isaac Eaton; Sister Margaret, wife of John Wilkinson; Brother John my horse, watch, Shoebuckles &c.; Brothers and Sisters, James; Samuel; Wm. Matthews; Abigal wife of Josiah McNash; Elizabeth; Isabella; Agnes; and Mary Matthews.

Penna. Arch. 5th Ser. Vol. 6, p. 278, 287, 311.

JOHN MATTHIAS

Weaver, served during years 1778-79-81-82, with Capt. Samuel Patton. On the Western Frontier in 1779 as a Ranger, the Command of Col. Wm Chambers.

Penna. Arch. 5th Ser. Vol. 6, p. 286, 309, 380, 602, 610.

ALEXANDER MAXWELL

Sept. ye 23, 1777, Alexander Maxwell took the Oath of Fidelity before Hugh Martin, Esq., in Westmoreland Co., Penna. A list of 94 persons who subscribed is given by James Kinkead, Recorder. Alexander Maxwell served first in Cumb. Co., Militia, in the Cont. Line, later serving from Westmoreland Co., Penna. He appears first in 1772, as a communing member of the Presby. Church of Mercersburg. Thomas Maxwell in 1771. A Jean Maxwell, and John, compose a family in 1769.

Penna. Arch. 2nd Ser. Vol. 3, p. 31. Penna. Arch. 5th Ser. Vol. 4, p. 298.

JAMES MAXWELL, CAPTAIN

Son of Major Wm. Maxwell, appears as an Ensign in the Provincial service. He was in Braddock's Expedition against Fort Duquesne; a Justice of the Peace for Cumb. County; a member of the Committee to erect the Court House and Jail; Govnr. Mifflin appointed him Associate Judge of the Courts; in addition to above he gave service during 1780-81-82, with Captain Walter McKinnie. He died Dec. 10, 1807. He was an Attorney wrote many of the early wills in his vicinity. To his nephew James Maxwell he left his plantation; nephew James Maxwell Reynolds; to his nephew Wm. M. Brown his riding horse, saddle and bridle; to nephew Wm. Maxwell his sword and pistols; to niece Eliza Maxwell a negroe girl; Pompey, Joe, black Grace and Mulato Grace to be set free.

Penna. Arch. 2nd Ser. Vol. 2, p. 484. Penna. Arch. 3rd Ser. Vol 1, p. 178. Penna. Arch. 5th Ser. Vol. 6, p. 266, 298, 300, 305.

PATRICK MAXWELL

Served as pvt., under Capt. Walter McKinnie, 1780,-81-82. He was a brother of James Maxwell, Esq. He was married Oct. 19, 1769 to Hannah Whitehill, at Lancaster. Patrick died Sept. 14, 1786, his wife, May 18, 1805. They had 4 sons: Wm.; James; Patrick; John; 3 daus.: Rachael; Susanna; Elizabeth. John Davison mar. Rachel Maxwell, Apr. 16, 1793. Susanna Maxwell mar. James McClelland Dec. 29, 1802. Elizabeth Maxwell died prior to her mother. The will of Hannah Maxwell, widow of Patrick, dated and prob. 1805, bequeaths to dau. Rachel Davidson "my Silver cream pot; son Wm., my clock; son James large looking glass, Son Patrick silver table spoons; Son John a chest of drawers."

Penna. Arch 5th Ser. Vol. 6, p. 266, 298, 300, 305.

MAJOR WILLIAM MAXWELL

Provincial Service, appears with Col. Benjamin Chambers under "Officers of the Associated Regt., of Lancaster County, over the River Sasquehanna" 1747-48. Wm. Maxwell an early settler in the present Montgomery Twp., applied for land Nov. 12, 1745. A Patent was granted by the Penns, Feb. 12, 1749, for land on Conococheague Creek, in Rath Mullen Twp. Lancaster Co., Penna. His neighbors were the widow Davis, Aaron Alexander's heirs, Thomas David, the Welsh Settlement and Philip David. The will of Major Wm. Maxwell was dated Oct. 10, 1772, and Church records show the death of Wm. Maxwell as Sept. 27, 1777. The death of Susanna as Dec. 30, 1781. He left to wife Susanna, 10 lbs., yearly, household goods, riding horse and saddle, a cow &c. My Negro wench called Nell to my wife, after her death to son James. To son James that part of my Original Dwelling Plantation whereon I now live. To son Patrick that part whereon he now lives. Also to Patrick and James a small tract in the Barrens adj., Archbd., Irwin xx a tract in Virginia called the Swanpons xx a tract in the Great Cove. To son Patrick the negro girl Chloe. To son-in-law Wm. and Nathan McDowell my right and title to a tract of land at Augwick for which I have Warrants in their names. To sons-in-law George Brown and Wm. Reynolds that tract of land in Virginia near Sleepy Creek. To Wm. McDowell, aforesaid, I bequeath my coat and silver buttons, upon which buttons he is to get engraved my name, and also his own. To his wife Mary, I bequeath the negro girl Dina and to his son John 10 lbs., out of my personal estate. To dau. Catherine McDowell, the negro child Fanny and to her son John 10 lbs. To dau. Ruth Reynolds the negro child Phillis and 10 lbs. To 2 grandaus., Susanna and Sarah Brown 1/3 part of the price of the tract of land their father sold for me to Phillip McGuire; residue to sons James and Patrick. Signed: Will Maxwell. It is probable that the Maxwells were buried in the John McClelland Graveyard. At least two stones were standing, in recent years, to the Maxwells, of a later generation.

Penna. Arch. 2nd Ser. Vol. 2, p. 438, 439.

ANDREW MAYS (MAYES)

Served as pvt., under Capts. Walter McKinnie and John Orbison, 1781-82. His will was prob. Oct. 3, 1804. He named a son Andrew, who was to care for sons James and Nesbit, also a dau. Rebecca. He was related to the wives of Cairns Sterrett, Johnston Elliott and Joseph Bogle. Andrew "Maze" was a pew-holder in the Welsh Run Church and is probably buried there. Wm. Mees was also a member as were Nathaniel and John Nesbit.

Penna. Arch. 5th Ser. Vol. 6, p. 301, 307.

JAMES MAYS (MAISE-MEES)

Was a private under Capt. John Orbison, 1780-81.

Penna. Arch. 5th Ser. Vol. 6, p. 273, 293.

JAMES MEARS

Served 1780-81-82, under Capt. Noah Abraham and was a son of Samuel Mears. Mrs. Henderson states that James Mears mar. Mary Bear, and in 1826-27 she found them in Derry Twp., Westmoreland Co., Penna., and may have moved to Kentucky.

Penna. Arch. 5th Ser. Vol. 6, p. 85, 121, 128.

JOHN MEARS

Served as pvt., under Capt. Noah Abraham, 1779-80-81-82. He mar. Ann Baldridge about 1783 and they had issue: Samuel d. young; James mar. Mary Steel; John mar. Martha Ann Young; David mar. Margaret Patterson; Wm. mar. Elizabeth McKee; Joseph mar. Mary Smith; Rebecca mar. James Dunn; Margaret mar. Samuel Kell.

Penna. Arch. 5th Ser. Vol. 6, p. 85, 120, 127, 383, 516, 626.

SAMUEL MEARS

Served as pvt., 1777-79-80 under Capt. Noah Abraham. Letters of Admr. were granted May 2, 1793, to Samuel and John Mears. Under date of Dec. 1, 1792, Samuel and John Mears offer for sale a Plantation of 150 acres, in Fannett Twp., Path Valley, a good dwelling house, with 2 Stone Chimneys &c. From the Mears Hist. by Helen Welsh Henderson we quote: Samuel Mears, Sr., mar. Mary or Mollie Blair. Known children were Samuel; James; John; Sarah, who mar. James Moore. In 1823 John Anderson of Derry Twp., Westmoreland Co., Penna., by will devised to Mary, wife of James Mears, 50 acres land.

Penna. Arch. 5th Ser. Vol. 6, p. 86, 384, 516.

ABNER MEEKS

Served under Capt Patrick Jack 1781-82 as First Sergeant.

Penna. Arch. 5th Ser. Vol. 6, p. 292, 295, 312.

GEORGE MEEK

Served in the Cont. Line, as a pvt., and entitled to Depreciation Pay, and also in the Militia of Cumb. Co. From family records it appears that Geo. Meek was from Cumb. Valley, later in Centre County, and that he was a son of Robert who came from Edinborough before the Revolution. In 1783, David Meek sells to Jacob Miller of Cumb Co., Penna., (son of Conrad) for 400 lbs., land lying in both Wash. Co., Md., and in Cumb. Co., Penna., 100 acres of land, part of a tract called "Meeks Ingenuity." David Meek was a pew-holder in the early Presbyterian Church at Welsh Run.

Penna. Arch. 5th Ser. Vol. 4, p. 298, 634.

HUGH MEEK

Served under Capt. Patrick Jack in 1781-82 as Second Sergeant.

Penna. Arch 5th Ser. Vol. 6, p. 291, 295, 312.

JAMES MEEK

Served under Capt. Patrick Jack, 1781, as Drummer. In 1804, James Meeks appears as a taxable in Franklin Twp., shown as a Saddle Tree Maker.

Penna. Arch 5th Ser. Vol. 6, p. 295.

JOHN MEEK

Was in service as a pvt., in 1780-81-82, with Capts. Patrick Jack and Wm. Huston. John Meek born Feb. 14, 1753, mar. Euphemia Hill, Dec. 12, 1787, in Chambersburg, by the Rev. Christopher Faber. He bought land in Chambersburg, Nov. 6, 1786, and sold the land Oct. 20, 1789. Deeds show "John Meek and Euphan, his wife, of Hamilton Twp., sell to Charles Cochran, a lot in Chambersburg, Oct. 20, 1789." John Meek probably went to Ohio, and he and wife Euphemia had issue: Jean; Sarah; Abner; Martha; Hannah; Mary; Hugh; Cynthianne; John; Alexander, the births ranging from 1788 to 1809.

Penna. Arch. 5th Ser. Vol. 6, p. 292, 265, 296, 313, 643.

THOMAS MEEK

Served as pvt., under Capt. John Orbison 1781, vicinity of Welsh Run.

Penna. Arch. 5th Ser. Vol. 6, p. 293.

Deeds at Chambersburg show that Alexdr. Meek of Washington Co., Va., farmer, sells land to Jacob Miller, son of Conrode, of Cumb. Co., Penna. Thomas Meeks, Senr., decd., formerly of Frederick Co. Md., by his will dated Oct. 29, 1776, bequeathed to his son Alexander Meek land called "Mullens Delight," also a certain tract called "Needlewood Forrest," all said land patented in Md. Beginning on line of land called "Richland" originally granted to Evan Shelby, Sr., "Mullens Delight" Patented to Thos. Meek. All tracts vested in said Thomas Meek who disposes of them by will to son Alexander Meek. Since the establishment of the Provincial line, between Maryland and Pennsylvania, said land is on the north side of Provincial line in Cumb. Co., Penna. Originally granted to Col. Thos. Cresop, by land called Rich-land. When Daniel Miller (son of Conrad) made his will, March 2, 1812, he gives to his sons Samuel and Henry "my lands called Meek's Ingenuity, Mullens Delight and Need Wood Forest to be divided by them xx when Henry arrives at the age of 21 years." Daniel Miller also refers to ":he lands which I purchased lately from my brother Jacob Miller."

HENRY MENNER

(Son of Geo. Minor) is shown in service 1780-81, under Capt. Daniel Clapsaddle. A Deed in 1798, from Solomon Segrist and Jacob Snowberger, Exrs., of Geo. Minor, show Joseph Menner, now of the State of Virginia. One part of the tract was granted to Henry Neaf in 1763, who sold to David Stoner, who in 1771 sold to George Menner; said George, by will, appointed as Exrs., Sol. Segrist and Jacob Snowberger. Henry Meenah was married to Polly McCumsey, June 25, 1811 by Dr. Robert Kennedy.

Penna. Arch. 5th Ser. Vol. 6, p. 97, 94, 117.

ISAAC MENOUGH

Served 1780-81 under Capts. Wm. Smith and Wm. Huston.

Penna. Arch. 5th Ser. Vol. 6, p. 270, 284.

ISAAC MINOR

Served under Capts. Chas. Maclay and Noah Abraham 1778-79, undated rolls. They were under the Command of Col. Wm. Chambers, and on June 22, 1779 were then at Legonere, signed by Col. John Thompson. Letters on the estate of Isaac Minor were granted to Mary Minor, Apr. 4, 1794.

Penna. Arch. 5th Ser. Vol. 6, p. 47, 49, 59, 148, 150, 603.

JOHN MANNER

(Son of George Minor) of Washington Twp., was in service 1780-81 under Capt. Daniel Clapsaddle. In the will of his father, George Minor, dated Apr., prob., May 1791, he names wife Susanna 20 lbs out of my personal estate and to have a house built "18 ft. in linth, and 16 ft. in Brenth with a well Shildled Roof and every part to be fully finished, near a spring"; Son John one Shilling and to share equally with the rest of my children: Mary, Elizabeth and Henry; Son Joseph 10 lbs.; daus: Eve; Catherine and Esther and youngest dau. Susanna being the children of my second wife were left a legacy by their grandfather George Minor.

Penna. Arch. 5th Ser. Vol. 6, p. 71, 94, 117.

JOHN MENOUGH

Served 1780-81.

Penna. Arch. 5th Ser. Vol. 6, p. 269, 276, 282.

SAMUEL MENOUGH

Served in 1781, under Capt. Huston.

Penna. Arch. 5th Ser. Vol. 6, p. 283.

WILLIAM MENOUGH

Served under Capt Wm. Huston 1780-81. In the will of James Scott of Montgomery Twp. 1787, he names daus., Mary & Elizabeth Meanough.

Penna. Arch. 5th Ser. Vol. 6, p. 275, 282.

ABEL MENSER (MENTZER)

Served as pvt., 1781, in Capt. Daniel Clapsaddler's of the First Batt., Cumb. Co. Militia. A Deed shows the issue of George Menzer: Joseph; Abel; Daniel; Jonas; Japhet; Lea, wife of Joseph Keller; Thecla, wife of Fredk., Fuhrman; and the widow Elizabeth (of George).

Penna. Arch. 5th Ser. Vol. 6, p. 117.

JONAS MENSER (MENSURE)

Served under Capt. Wm. Findley in the 2nd Class of 8th Batt., an undated roll.

Penna. Arch. 5th Ser. Vol. 6, p. 586.

JAPHET (JEPHA) MENSER

Served in 1781 under Capt. Daniel Clapsaddle.

Penna. Arch 5th Ser. Vol. 6, p. 97, 117.

JOSEPH MENSER

Served under Capt. Daniel Clapsaddler 1780-81. Joseph Mensor and wife Barbara Seachrist are buried in the Menser graveyard near Waynesboro. A descendant writes that they are lying under the branches of a beautiful pine tree, and two fine old boxwoods are nearby. She also states that a Rev. Soldier named Sechrist is buried there, as well as Jacob Gossert of the War of 1812. The will of Joseph Mentzer is dated June 10, 1827. In commending his soul to Almighty God, he adds, "My body to earth on my plantation." He names and bequeaths: To son David; to the children of son Abraham, decd.; To dau. Katherine intermar. to Andrew Snowberger; to dau. Susannah; dau. Elizabeth intermar. to Jacob Gossert land adj. Solomon Seachrist, Peter Harbaugh and others; to Jonathan Mentzer 75 acres land now left of the old tract where I now live, with buildings and improvement, I am to have the privilege of one room in the house for myself.
Penna. Arch. 5th Ser. Vol. 6, p. 71, 94, 117.

GENERAL, HUGH MERCER

This distinguished soldier was by profession a physician. He was born at Aberdeen, Scotland, in 1721, educated at the university of that city and studied medicine. Having served as surgeon's assistant in the army of the young pretender at the battle of Culloden in 1745, he emigrated to America and settled in the neighborhood of Davis' Fort, south of where the town of Mercersburg now stands, and here he practiced his profession. Having a taste for military life he was, early in 1756, appointed a captain in the provincial service, in which he continued for some years, rising to the rank of Colonel. On the 13th of July, 1757, he was appointed and commissioned by the Supreme Executive Council, one of the Justices of the peace for Cumberland County. During the wars with the Indians he became a comrade and friend of the immortal Washington. He was severely wounded on one of these expeditions, and reached the settlements after much suffering. When the provincial forces were re-organized in 1758, Mercer was made lieutenant Colonel and went with General Forbes to Fort Duquesne. With two hundred provincials he was left in command of this post for the winter. Lancaster, Nov. 17, 1756. Hugh Mercer again urges that Dr. Blair be ap., Surgeon "of our Batt.",—"I intend to joyn, next week, my Company at Shippensburg (my Wound being in a fair way of being Cured) tho' it will be a considerable Time in healing up and rendering me fit for much Duty." To Col. James Young, Esq., Commissr. Genl. of the Musters. In Philadelphia. By Favour of Dr. Blair. Capt. Hugh Mercer to Gov. Denny, Camp at Loyal Hanning, Dec. 3, 1758. He later settled at Fredericksburg, Va., where he practiced his profession. On the outbreak of the Rev. War, he warmly asserted the rights of the Colonies and in 1775 raised three regiments of Minute Men. In 1776 he was made Colonel and organized the Virginia Militia, Congress appointing him brigadier general, June 5, 1776. He led the attack at Trenton, Dec. 25, 1776, and suggseted the night march on Princeton. Commanding the advance he met a large body of British troops, Jan. 3, 1777, and in the ensuing action was mortally wounded, dying later at Princeton, New Jersey. "Jan. 16, 1777, All the officers and men of the City guards not on Duty to parade under the market house at two o'clock, in order to attend the Funeral of the late Gen. Mercer. All the Regular Troops and Militia in the City to parade at two o'clock this afternoon, in Walnut Street, to attend the Funeral." It is said that his body was followed to the grave in Philadelphia by more than 30,000 persons. Provision was made by Congress for the education of his youngest son. General Mercer was a member of the St. Andrew's Society of Phila., and his body was removed in 1840 to Laurel Hill Cemetery, and reinterred in the burial lot purchased for the purpose by that Society. Mrs. Isabella Mercer, wife of Gen. Hugh, d. May 27, 1791 aged 51yrs., buried in Norriton graveyard.
Penna. Arch. 1st Ser. Vol. 3, p. 27. Penna. Arch. 1st Ser. Vol. 5, p. 222.

JOHN MILHOUSE

Served as pvt., under Capt. John Orbison, 1780-81-82. He appears to be in a company from Welsh Run. The will of Fredk. Tefern of Conococheague Hundred, in Wash. Co. Md., names his beloved wife Barbara, and dau. Margaret, mar. to John Millhouse. The will is dated Oct. 21, 1778, and prob. Nov. 24, 1778.
Penna. Arch. 5th Ser. Vol. 6, p. 273, 293, 307.

ALEXANDER MILLER

Was a pvt., 1778 under Capt. Joseph Culbertson, and under Capt. Wm. Huston in 1780-81. In 1786 he sold a tract of land in Montgomery Twp., to James Ramsey, which joined Wm. McCune, Sr. and Jr.; Wm. Campbell, Alex. White and Joseph Miller from Wm. McCune, Sr., in 1777, showing the Meeting house land, the Spring &c., &c.
Penna. Arch. 5th Ser. Vol. 6, p. 270, 276, 283, 382.

ANDREW MILLER

Served as pvt., in 1779-80-81-82, under Capt. Thos. Askey, Cumb. Co., Militia. An order of survey in Fannett Twp., was dated Dec. 3, 1766, No. 2053, in the name of Andrew Miller, 158 acres, 98 perches part of a tract of 200 acres. In 1784 John McClure and Andrew Miller, both of Fannett Twp., sell one Cabin and Improvement situate in the head of the Path Valley between Jacobus Hawkenbury and Edwd. Batton, to Wm. Richardson. In 1790 Miller sells to Amos Moore, both of Fannett Twp. It appears that there were three men of the name in Franklin County over the period of the Rev. War.

Penna. Arch. 5th Ser. Vol. 6, p. 61, 95, 96, 132, 393, 409, 412, 423, 442, 513, 520, 524, 534, 631.

ANDREW MILLER

Of Antrim Twp., served as Second Lieut., 1777-78, under Captain Elias Davison, and Capt. Wm. Long. A deed in 1791, shows "Andrew Miller, formerly of Green Co., N. C., but now of Washington Co., Md., transfers a tract of land to the heirs of Henry Prather which he had previously bought from Henry Prather."

Penna. Arch. 5th Ser. Vol. 6, p. 513, 520, 524, 534.

ANDREW MILLER

Served as pvt., with Capt. Patrick Jack, in 1778. Penna. Arch. 5th Ser. Vol. 6, p. 29, 32.

DANIEL MILLER

Was a private under Capt. Wm. Berryhill, 1780-81-82. He was born 1742, died March 7, 1812. His wife was Elizabeth Schnebley, (of Leonard) b. 1752, d. 1839; they are buried at Mason & Dixon, in the Samuel Miller graveyard, and have stones. They had issue: Daniel Miller mar. Catherine Rench, Mary Miller mar. 1st Samuel Boles, 2nd Daniel Davis; David Miller mar. Margaret Brenner; Albertus—unmarried. Elizabeth mar. Jacob Barnet, Jr.; Otho mar. Margaret Rummel; Arawine mar. Jane Williams; Samuel mar. Catherine Elliott; Henry mar. Eliza Davis; Nancy mar. Samuel Spiegler.

Penna. Arch. 5th Ser. Vol. 6, p. 101, 79, 123.

HENRY MILLER

Orphans' Court Chambersburg, Book C; Henry Miller of Lurgan Twp., Letters of Admr., 1825,—was living in Franklin Co., in 1823. Widow Elizabeth and nine children: Elizabeth wife of John Speice; Susan wife of Jacob Shoemaker; Margaret wife of Philip Shoup (Shoaf); Henry, Samuel, Thomas, David, Mary and Jacob, who petition, March 9, 1830. Henry Miller had land, with a Two story Log Tavern Stand, and stabling thereon erected.

Orphans Court, Chambersburg, Pa., Book C. Penna. Arch. 2nd Ser. Vol. 13, p. 162.

HENRY MILLER

Served as Sergt., 1780-81 under Capt. Wm. Berryhill. The Hist., of Leitersburg District shows Henry Miller as a resident of Antrim Twp., 1773, and a founder of Salem Reformed Church. The will of Henry Miller was dated 1812, prob., 1817. He named Son Henry; Dau. Elizabeth wife of Jacob Heifner; Dau. Barbara wife of Valentine Heifner; Dau. ———— wife of Henry Lady; Heirs of Mary, wife of Henry Jacobs; Dau. Catherine, wife of Jacob Heilman; Of the above, Henry Jacobs born 1764, d. 1821, wife Anna Maria born 1770, died 1809; George Jacobs mar. Susan Bell.

Penna. Arch. 5th Ser. Vol. 6, p. 79, 101.

HENRY MILLER

Son of Conrad, served as Sergt., under Capt Wm. Berryhill, 1780-81.

Penna. Arch. 5th Ser. Vol. 6, p. 79, 101.

JACOB MILLER

Son of Conrad, served from Antrim Twp., under Capt. William Berryhill, 1780-81-82. He mar., a dau. of Peter Rench of Washington Co., Md. Jonathan Hager and Peter Rentch came to America on the same boat, Sept., 1736. Peter Rentch, in 1771, wills to his son-in-law Jacob Miller a tract of land called "The Wooden Platter" of 320 acres, more or less. Jacob Miller and wife had issue: Peter; John; Susanna mar. Jacob Orendorff; and one who was the widow of Jacob Shimer.

Penna. Arch. 5th Ser. Vol. 6, p. 79, 101, 123.

JOHN MILLER

Son of Conrad, served as pvt., 1780-81, under Capt. Wm. Berryhill. John Miller dying, Letters of Admr., were granted Oct. 26, 1804, to Margaret Miller, Daniel Miller, Jr., and Michael Tice.

Penna. Arch 5th Ser. Vol. 6, p. 79, 101.

ISAAC MILLER

A Lieut. with Capt. Charles Maclay. Later as Captain Miller, appears in service 1777-78-80. In 1776 he is shown as a member of the Middle Spring Church, and in Thos. McClelland's District. Under Taxables of Lurgan Twp., 1799, Isaac Miller appears with 192 acres of land; a Midling good log Barn; 1 Good log House; 3 horses; 4 Cows and 50 acres Mt. Land.

Penna. Arch. 5th Ser. Vol. 6, p. 14, 37, 38, 40, 45, 143, 148, 386, 609.

ISAAC MILLER

Private, appears in service with Capts. Wm. Strain and Wm. Moorhead, 1780-81-82.

Penna. Arch. 5th Ser. Vol. 6, p. 388, 398, 400, 404, 414, 440.

PETER MILLER

Lebanon Twp., Feb. 21, 1778, Peter Miller signed the "Oath of Allegiance," a Patriot. He was born March 5, 1747, and taxed in Lebanon Twp., 1771-72-73-79-82, with deeds on record 1789-1794. Tradition states that he was a teamster in the Rev. War, and that he was a miller. In 1795 he bought from Samuel Beltzner, Sen., of Green Twp., Franklin County, and wife Maria, certain land in Green Twp., as "Peter Miller of Dauphin County, Pa." He is taxed in Green Twp., 1796-99-1804-1807, with land, horses, cows, Grist Mill, Merchant Mill &c. Barbara Jungin is thought to have been his first wife. He mar. 2nd the widow Christina Jumper (nee Shirk) and they had issue: Peter; Christina; Susanna; and Magdalina who mar. John Wilson, who died 1824 aged 77 yrs. In the will of Peter Miller, dated 1819, prob., 1824, he names Wife Christine; Sons Tobias and Christian; 3 children to my wife Christina; Son Peter; daus.; Christina and Susanna; Dau. Barbara in a frail state; names dau. Elizabeth wife of Christian Eagle. Births as follows: Elizabeth b. Dec. 24, 1767, mar. Christian Eagle; Jacob b. Nov. 9, 1770, d. Aug. 23, 1781; Barbara b. Aug. 8, 1774; Peter b. Apr. 9, 1778, d. March 26, 1779. Tobias b. Apr. 26, 1782, d. Nov. 23, 1840, mar. in 1804, Susan Lehman; Christian b. Feb. 13, 1788, d. 1873, mar. Mary Elizabeth Jumper; Anna b. March 13, 1790, died July 15, 1884, mar. Jesse Ferree. Peter Miller is known to have been buried in the Methodist Graveyard, Greenvillage, Penna. Jesse Ferree, b. Feb. 20, 1766 mar. Ann Miller, Oct. 10, 1814. Ann Ferree and a number of her children lie buried in the above graveyard with stones. The Blankneys are also buried as above. The Ferree, Blankney and Miller Bibles in Possession of Miss Ailie Smith of Mercersburg, Pa.

Penna. Arch 2nd Ser. Vol. 13, p. 413.

JAMES MITCHELL

Served under Capt. John McConnell 1780-81-82. He was of Letterkenny Twp., and probably the pioneer of the name. He had a son James and two grandsons named James. He left a will dated 1796, prob., 1797, and refers to land sold to Abraham Keeker. He names sons James and John; a dau. Elizabeth, now the wife of Robert McConnell; a Dau. Margaret now the wife of James Anderson; dau. Sarah now the wife of John Cochran; sons, Jesse; Nathaniel and Joseph. He names Margaret the wife of Son Joseph and their son James Patterson. The witnesses were John, Robert and James McConnell; In the will of Thos. Anderson, Hamilton Twp., 1792, he names a dau. Agnes, wife of James Mitchell.

Penna. Arch. 5th Ser. Vol. 6, p. 267, 302, 309.

JESSE MITCHELL

Served as pvt., and Ensign, 1777-80-81-82 under Capt. John McConnell. He was a son of James Mitchell of Letterkenny Twp. His brothers were James; John; Nathaniel; Joseph, all giving Rev. War service.

Penna. Arch. 5th Ser. Vol. 6, p. 6, 263, 267, 302, 309.

JOHN MITCHELL

Of Antrim Twp., Franklin Co., dated Jan. 9, 1756; Wife Elizabeth the plantation; Daus: Jane; Elizabeth; Margaret; Martha; Mary Ann; Mary E.; Son Robert the plantation at the Coper Spring 250 acres; Son John 5 shillings; Dau. Rachel 1 shilling.

Signed: John X Mitchell
Elizabeth X Mitchell

The Will of Elizabeth Mitchell, Apr. 26, 1765, names a son Thomas.

Carlisle Court Records.

JOSEPH MITCHELL

Served as pvt., 1780-81-82, under Capt. John McConnell, and was a son of James Mitchell.

Penna. Arch. 5th Ser. Vol. 6, p. 267, 268, 302, 303, 310.

NATHANIEL MITCHELL

Served as pvt., under Capts. Pat. Jack and John McConnell, 1776-77-78-80-81-82, Cumb. Co. Militia. He was a son of James Mitchell of Letterkenny Twp., who died 1797.

Penna. Arch. 5th Ser. Vol. 6, p. 302, 309, 267, 317, 318, 372, 380.

ROBERT MITCHELL

Served during 1778-79-80-81-82, with Capt. Wm. Moorhead and others. There were two (2) men of the name serving as above, one marked "Mountain"; also one Samuel with "Mountain" attached. Under Deeds dated Oct. 8, 1800, Robert Mitchell of Letterkenny Twp., gives "for love and affection which I bear to my children"; all named Mitchell; Christian; Isabella; Jencey; Ann; Gavin; John; George; Robert; Hannah; Matthew; hath granted to them; 1 Wagon; 2 stears; 2 feather beds; walnut cupboard &c. Robert Mitchell, late of Ohio Co. Va., decd. Gavin Mitchell, one of the Exrs., releases to John Gilmore, Esq., under date of Apr. 22, 1809. Deeds show that Robert Mitchell, son of John Mitchell, late of Antrim Twp., decd., for 5 lbs., paid to him by Wm. Beatty sells to Wm. Beatty and his heirs or assigns forever., all my estate, Interest in and to the Shears of Elizabeth late the wife of Francis Inglish, and of Margaret, late the wife of Isaac Steel, both decd., they being heirs and legatees of the said John Mitchell, decd. Witnesses: Robert

Robyson and David Carson. Before David Carson, Dec. 4, 1794. Date of transfer March 29, 1786. In 1791, John Mitchell, of Lexington Co., Planter, State of South Carolina, sells to Vallentine Keller, of Antrim Twp., Franklin Co. Penna. for 500 lbs., 104 acres, part of a tract of 254 acres 114 perches, granted to me by warrant from the Hon. Proprietors, then of Hopewell Twp., Lancaster Co. Pa., on March 21, 1737, Surveyed 1739, adjoining lands of Wm. Beatty and others. Valentine Keller sold the tract to Saml. McCulloch.

Penna. Arch. 5th Ser. Vol. 6, p. 66, 134, 401, 405, 414, 440, 605.

WILLIAM MITCHELL

Served as pvt., 1777-78, under Capt. Patrick Jack; 2nd Lieut., was John Welsh; Wm. Mitchell, John Welsh and Robert Campbell were witnesses to the will of Matthew Patton, Aug. 1776. The following men gave service in what is now Franklin County, largely under Capts. John McConnell and Patrick Jack: Mitchell,—Andrew; Alexdr; Ebinezer; Ezekiel; James; James 3rd; Jesse; John; Robert; William.

Penna. Arch. 5th Ser. Vol. 6, p. 372, 380.

ANDREW MIVALE

Served as a pvt., in 1780, with Capt. Wm. Smith. No further record found.

Penna. Arch. 5th Ser. Vol. 6, p. 276.

PATRICK MONEY

Private under Capt. Daniel Clapsaddle, 1781. He was born March 26, 1748, died Dec. 28, 1814, aged 66 yrs. 9 mos. 2 days. He is buried at Blue Ridge Summit, close to the Right of Way of the W. M. R. R. on George D. Buddeck's property. He left sons,—Wm.; James; Daniel; John; estate divided into five parts, perhaps a daughter. He is shown with 414 acres land; 2 log Houses; 2 Barns; Tan-House; Spring House; Horses and Cows. Lots in Waynesboro, Penna. Deeds show Daniel Mouney of Washington Twp., in 1813, selling to David Benchoff of same place; granted by the state of Maryland in 1755 to George Craft, who with his wife Catherine in 1771, sold to Patrick Mowny, who conveyed to his son Daniel in 1802. In 1782 the Commonwealth granted to Robert Cunningham a tract in Washington Twp., 188¼ acres. In 1788 Robert Cunningham conveyed to Dr. Robert Johnston, who with his wife Eleanor conveyed to Patrick Mooney Apr. 24, 1788 and from Patrick to his son Wm. Each heir of Patrick sells his 1/5 share of tracts.

Penna. Arch. 5th Ser. Vol. 6, p. 117.

HUMPHREY MONTGOMERY, SR.

Is shown in service with Capt. Isaac Miller 1777-78-80-81-82 and in the Company of Capt. John Campbell. Surveys show a tract of land in Southampton Twp., of 241 ac., on Warrants 1755-1766, surveyed to Humphrey Montgomery in 1767. "Umphrey" Montgomery, Jr., also appears in service.

Penna. Arch. 5th Ser. Vol. 6, p. 15, 31, 41, 142, 143, 428, 627.

JAMES MONTGOMERY

Appears as a pvt., 1777-78-81, under Capts. Noah Abraham and Thos. Askey.

Penna. Arch. 5th Ser. Vol. 6, p. 18, 20, 21, 52, 53, 423, 516.

JAMES MOUNTGOMORY

Of Path Valley was a signer to a petition, May 18, 1778, asking for "Rifled guns and amunition, what active men is of use here is entirely Defenceless, for want of arms and amunition if our men is marched to Camp our women and children will fall a sacrifice to savage Cruel Barbarity &c." James and John Montgomery were both serving under Capt. Noah Abraham in 1777. James in the Third Marching Comp., called Sept. 26, 1777. He also served, 1778-81, under Capt. Thos. Askey. One John Montgomery of Lurgan Twp., left a will dated and prob. 1779, all estate left to a minor dau. Eliabeth; the Exrs., being Robert Peebles, Esq. of Shippensburg and James Smith of Lurgan. "Should dau. Elizabeth die under age, then Jas. MtGomery, son to James Montgomery, a half part." "The other half part into 6 equal shares; my brothers Thomas; Robert William; Humphrey, and sister Elizabeth Smith, wife of James Smith, is to have two shares.

Signed: John Mt.Gomery.

Penna. Arch. 5th Ser. Vol. 6, p. 18, 20, 53, 423, 516. Penna. Arch. 2nd Ser. Vol. 3, p. 167.

ROBERT MONTGOMERY

Appears as a pvt., in 1778, undated roll, in service with Capt. Isaac Miller. It is probable that Robert was the son of Humphrey Montgomery of Lurgan Twp. Robert Montgomery and wife Jane; Wm. Montgomery and wife Sarah; Humphrey Montgomery and wife Mary, sell land to John Haine of Berks Co., Penna., a tract partly in Lurgan Twp., the same parcel of land granted in 1767 to Humphrey Montgomery, Sr., and which he conveyed by deed in 1773, to the above three sons. One Robert Montgomery received a Patent Sept. 17, 1746, and a residue later both being conveyed to Wm. Montgomery, Feb. 7, 1772. The said William had died July, 1814, leaving a widow, Mary and issue seven: Robert; John; James; Campbell; Martha; Jane mar. to Erasmus Cooper in 1802; Martha mar. Hugh Cooper Nov., 1819. This land was in St. Thomas

Twp., the son Thomas and wife Sarah, son Campbell and wife Mary, all join in selling the land to David Brandt of Dauphin Co., Penna., and a tract of 67 acres in 1831 to Philip Laymaster.
Penna. Arch. 5th Ser. Vol. 6, p. 37, 41, 143.

SAMUEL MONTGOMERY

Is shown as a Volunteer in Col. James Burd's Company and as Ensign, 1758, with Col. Hugh Mercer. It is possible, not proven, that he was the man whose will follows: Samuel Montgomery of Hopewell Twp., Cumb. Co., Penna. Wife Hannah ½ of estate; nephew Thos. Montgomery; balance to Mary Moar; Martha Bratton; Rachel Williamson; Margaret Ramsey; Samuel Bratton; Elinor Linton; Samuel Sirels (Sewels) and a full brother and sister of my nephew Thos. MtGomery, if they come in from Ireland in ten years &c. Exrs: wife Hannah and Robert McComb. Dated Feb., 1766; prob. May, 1766.
Penna. Arch. 5th Ser. Vol. 1, p. 182, 185, 190.

SAMUEL MONTGOMERY

Appears in Service, 1778-80, with Capts. Isaac Miller and Wm. Strain. Deed show that James R. Montgomery, yeoman, of Southampton Twp., and Agnes, his wife, sell to John Sailhamer, singleman, a tract of land of 90 acres. The tract was granted to Samuel Montgomery, Nov. 7, 1790, by the Commonwealth; Samuel died leaving one child, a son, James R. Montgomery to whom the same "did descend and come."
Penna. Arch. 5th Ser. Vol. 6, p. 37, 41, 143, 391, 398.

THOMAS MONTGOMERY

Rev. Soldier living in Franklin Co., 1828.
Penna. Arch. 2nd Ser. Vol. 13, p. 165.

WILLIAM MONTGOMERY

Was in Service as pvt., 1780-81, under Capts. James Patton, Robert Dickey and Thos. McDowell. He was of Peters Twp., and in 1781 had a Tanyard, 220 acres land, horses, cattle and one negro. On Oct. 5, 1814, the estate of Wm. Montgomery was admr., by Mary and Robert Montgomery. Orphans' Court records show, in Oct., 1818, that Wm. Montgomery had died July 11, 1814, leaving a widow Mary and issue 7: Robert; John; James; Campbell; Martha; Jane mar. to Erasmus Cooper; and Thomas, all above 21 yrs. The Plantation joined Andrew Lemaster, Christian Ober, Henry Christman, Stephen Keefer, and Henry Heckman, with a 2 story log dwelling house and a double log barn. Jane Montgomery was mar. to Erasmus Cooper Feb., 1802. Hugh Cooper to Martha Montgomery (near St. Thomas) Nov. 23, 1819.
Penna. Arch. 5th Ser. Vol. 6, p. 272, 285, 315.

WILLIAM MONTGOMERY AND WILLIAM MONTGOMERY, SR.

Are shown serving with Capt. Isaac Miller and others 1778-80-81.
Penna. Arch. 5th Ser, Vol. 6, p. 40, 41, 143, 389, 396, 398, 400, 406, 413.

JAMES MOOR

Served from Fannett Twp., under Capt. Thomas Askey in 1779, some undated rolls. He bequeaths money and land to relatives in Ireland. States that John Moor, son to his brother John, was now in the back woods. His will was prob. May 2, 1786.
Penna. Arch. 5th Ser. Vol. 6, p. 62, 132, 139.

JAMES MOORE, JR.

Served under Capt. Patrick Jack in 1782.
Penna. Arch. 5th Ser. Vol. 6, p. 313.

JOHN MOORE

Served as pvt., under Capt. Samuel Patton, 1781-82.
Penna. Arch. 5th Ser. Vol. 6, p. 287, 312.

JOHN MOORE

Served as pvt., under Capt. Patrick Jack, 1777-81-82.
Penna. Arch. 5th Ser. Vol. 6, p. 296, 313, 372.

JOHN MOORE

Served as pvt., under Capt. Wm. Huston 1780-81. He appears with a group of Montgomery Twp., men. In 1781, a freeman in Montgomery Twp., Franklin Co., Penna.
Penna. Arch. 5th Ser. Vol. 6, p. 269, 282.

MOSES MOORE

Served under Capt. Patrick Jack 1781-82. Deed Book 12, p. 73, Chambersburg, Pa., Dec. 5, 1817. Moses Moore of Madisonville, Parish of St. Tammary, Louisana, and wife Jane appointed George Chambers of Chambersburg, their Atty., to receive from Executors of James Finley and Wm. Finley of Franklin County and of David Duncan of Cumb. Co., what may be due said Jane, late Jane Potter, Executrix of Stephen Duncan of said Parish in Louisiana, decd., &c; money owing to said Moses Moore as Admr. of Elizabeth Duncan, Decd. (James Findlay left a dau. Elizabeth wife of Stephen Duncan).
Penna. Arch. 5th Ser. Vol. 6, p. 296, 313.

SAMUEL MOORE

Served as pvt., under Capt. Patrick Jack, 1781-82. In the will of Isaac Moore of Hamilton Twp.; prob. Oct. 18, 1796, he names three elder brothers: Samuel; Moses; John Moore; Sister Isabella Poulk; Sister Deborah Welsh; brothers,—

David; Seth; sisters Elizabeth and Jean Moore.
Penna. Arch. 5th Ser. Vol. 6, p. 291, 295, 313.

SAMUEL MOORE

Served as a pvt., under Capt. John Jack in 1779 and under Capt. Thomas Johnston, 1780-81-82.

Penna. Arch. 5th Ser. Vol. 6, p. 84, 114, 129, 539.

AMOS MOOR (MOORE)

Served in 1781-82 with Capt. Thos. Askey, command of Col. James Dunlop. Under date of May, 1792, Amos Moor and Sarah his wife, of Fannett Twp., sell land to Peter Foreman, also of Fannett Twp. On Apr. 13, 1810, Peter Foreman and Esther his wife, sell to Samuel and Matthew Coulter. Sarah, wife of Amos Moor, was a dau. of Andrew Foreman who died in Franklin County.

Penna. Arch. 5th Ser. Vol. 6, p. 423, 442.

Peter Foreman record.

DAVID MOORE

Served as pvt., under Capt. Patrick Jack, 1781-82. He was of Hamilton Twp., and his will dated and prob., 1803, naming sister Elizabeth Moor and nephew James Welsh as legatees of his real estate. To nephew James Welsh, Sheridans Dictionary in 2 Volumes; The Spectator in 8 volumes and young Clerk's Magazine; Brothers and Sisters; Brother Samuel Moor, and brother-in-law Charles Gillespie; Sister Isabella Folk (Poulk).

Penna. Arch. 5th Ser. Vol. 6, p. 292, 297, 313.

JAMES MOORE

Served as a private under Capt. Patrick Jack. He was probably the James Moore whose will was prob. Aug., 1795, naming sons David, Seth and Isaac; daus. Elizabeth and Jean; Sons Samuel, Moses and John; dau. Deborah, who later mar. James Welsh. Letters of Admr., were issued to David Moore, 1798, on the estate of Seth Moore. The will of Isaac Moore was prob. in 1796, naming 3 elder brothers, Samuel; Moses and John Moore, also brothers David and Seth Moore; sister Isabella Poulk; sister Deborah Welsh; sisters Elizabeth and Jean Moore.

Penna. Arch. 5th Ser. Vol. 6, p. 265 292, 296, 643.

JAMES MOORE

There were probably several men of the name. It appears four times in Fannett Twp. 1779-80 in Fannett Twp., under Capts. Patrick and John Jack, Alexdr., Peebles and Noah Abraham 1777-78-79, wiht James, Jr., in 1782 under Capt. Patrick Jack. Under Orphans' Court Records at Chambersburg is found the estate of James Moore, who died intestate, Feb., 1803, leaving a widow, not named and issue seven: Samuel; Isabella mar. Wm. Ross; James; Agnes mar. Wm. McKinley; Elizabeth mar. Arnold Johns; Jane and Hamilton, minors. James Moore of Greencastle had a house and lot there taken by son James.

Penna. Arch. 5th Ser. Vol. 6, p. 62, 132, 139, 265, 313, 375, 394, 541, 589.

FERGUS MOORHEAD

Served as a private under Capt. John Orbison, 1780. His heirs sold land to James Buchanan in 1810—issue Sarah, wife of Samuel McCune. Polly who mar. Charles McCoy, Dec. 29, 1808; Catherine mar. George Johnston; Margaret mar. Isaac McCune. Ann, and 5 sons, John; Samuel; James; Fergus; Thomas. They were in Montgomery Twp. Samuel and Isaac McCune were sons of Samuel and Jean McCune. Fergus Moorhead was a pewholder in the Presby. Church at Welsh Run and is probably buried in the graveyard.

Penna. Arch. 5th Ser. Vol. 6, p. 264, 274.

EDWARD (EDMOND) MORAN

Was taxed, 1776-79 in Cumb. Valley Twp., Bedford Co., Penna., on land, Horses, Cattle Sheep, and one George Moran was taxed 1779, in Bethal Twp. Edward (Edmond) Moran served under Capt. Evan Cissna, in Bedford County Militia. In the will of Daniel Davis of Peters Twp., dated and prob. 1782, he names his brother-in-law Andrew Blair and his children: the children of niece Catherine (Blair) Moran, wife of Edmond Moran, viz: Susanna Moran; Elizabeth Moran; Blair Moran and Catherine Moran. A witness to will being Edmond Moran. Heitman states that Edmund Moran died in 1812. Where? From "Collections of the State Historical Society of Wisconsin," edited by Lyman C. Draper, Vol. VIII, pages 232-240, Madison, Wis., Pub. by the Society, 1908: Green Bay and the Frontier, 1763 65; the following letters, written by Edmond Moran and Lieut. James Gorrell, the former of whom was a trader at Green Bay, when the latter abandoned the fort at that place, in June, 1763—together with a brief letter from John Clark at Cumberland, Maryland, all relating to the frontier trade and difficulties of that period, and never before published. Moran's first letter, written at Green Bay, is so faded towards its close that it is impossible to decipher or restore some portions of it; but the sense is probably fairly conveyed by the aid of words in brackets. These documents were long preserved by the Shelby family in Kentucky, Capt. Evan Shelby referred to, having been the father of Gov. Isaac Shelby; and though they impart no important or detailed facts, yet as they relate to an interesting period of Wisconsin and frontier history, concerning which documents and reliable information is scarce, it is deemed advisable to publish them entire. It is possible that the trader, Edward Moran, may have descended from Capt. Moran or Morin, the early commandant at Green Bay, who so distinguished himself against the Sauks and Foxes in 1730. But this is only supposition. He was furnished with goods by the large mercantile establishment of Capt. Evan Shelby and Capt Samuel Postlethwaite of Frederick County, Maryland, who were largely engaged in supplying goods for the Indian trade. It is natural to suppose that Moran, having some knowledge of Green Bay, proposed to take a stock of goods there as a promising trading point; and this design was carried into effect apparently in the early part of 1762. It must have been a very respectable stock, amounting after a year's sales to between six and seven thousand dollars in value and among the sales, as shown by Gorrell's journal, published in the Socety's first volume of "Collections," were goods amounting to 935 pounds, 12 shillings, 2 pence, sold to Lieut. Gorrell for presents to the Indians. The very day, June 15, 1763, that Mr. Moran was to have started from the bay to Detroit, bearing despatches from Lieut., Gorrell to Major Gladwyn, intelligence was received from Capt. Ethrington of the capture of Mackinaw, and directing the abandonment of Fort Edward Augustus; when all his unsold goods were seized and appropriated by the Indians, Moran and the other traders then retired with Gorrell's party first to Mackinaw, and then down the Lakes. It would seem probable, as a portion of the goods lost by Shelby and Postlethwaite on the Monongahela, by the Indian outbreak of 1703 (?), was reimbursed by the British Government, this tacitly acknowledging the Justice of the claim, that the loss at Green Bay was also subsequently made good. We hear nothing further of Moran after the date of his Carlisle letter of Aug. 31, 1765 (?). Lieut. Gorrell was a Marylander, and had served in the 605 and 5 and 94 or Royal American regiment during the latter part French and Indian War, on the borders of New York, and in the conquest of Canada, having entered the regiment as an ensign, May 30, 1759. He was sent with a small force to establish a garrison at Green Bay, in October, 1761; was promoted to a lieutenancy March 2, 1762. After abandoning Green Bay, by order of Capt. Ethrington, in June 1763, he retired to Montreal, where he arrived in August following. On the reduction of the army, at the close of the war, Lieut. Gorrell was placed on half pay, till he was assigned as a lieutenant to the 70th regiment of foot, Mar. 18, 1767, stationed at the Caribbee Islands, in the West Indies, where he probably died in 1769, as his name last appears in the British Army List in that year, without transference, or replacement on the halfpay list.

L. C. Draper.

Fort Edward Augustus, or La Baye,
May 14, 1763.

Dear Sirs:—If you have rec'd every letter I wrote you last year which I believe you have, as I always sent them by good opportunities, you will before this know what I then thought would answer in the trading way for these posts—which scheme I hope has so far met with your approbation, that before this can come to hand, and before you will be at Detroit; at which place I hope to meet you about the last of June. The goods you bring, if there is not a good market at Detroit for them, keep them until I come; but by no means let you assortment be broken as you may be assured this place will afford good sale for them. I have sent most of my goods to a gentleman whom I fell in with, one Louis Constant, at Detroit on the out limits of Canada. They are expected here the last of the month, when I shall get off. I have done every thing in my power for the best, and am in hopes it will turn out well; as yet I have a good prospect of it's so doing. Lieut. Jas. Gorrell commands here, who has used me exceedingly kind ever since I have been with him, for which reason if you arrive at Detroit before me, and can in any way send him a ten gallon bag of spirits, I will pay for it myself. You may remember you desired me to engage goods to sell to the French, wholesale. I wrote you from Michilimackinac last fall, respecting my having engaged between two and three thousand pounds' worth to be delivered at Detroit. The men will have the pay ready, I understand; and they depend on the bargain (that is: rely on it's fulfillment).

I am in hopes I shall not be disappointed in it. The proposal of bringing cattle, I am assured, would be very advantageous, otherwise I would not so earnestly recommend it to you. I am very much surprised that I have never heard a word from one of you since I left home. It gives me no small uneasiness, for many reasons you very well know, I would inform you, however, that I hourly expect to hear from you now, as Lieut. Gorrell expects news from Detroit very soon. (They go) from here to Machilimackinac by Indian (canoes); but it's not safe going over the waves (in such small craft), as many (accidents occur). There has been no opportunity before this year; but (whether) any offers by (sail is a) question. I intend going as soon as Mr. Lottridge and Jimmy Daugherty arrive, which is expected soon. Enclosed is a letter to my wife, and one to Mr. Clallen, which I would be obliged to you (to deliver to them). The Indians seem well inclined if (it were not) for those d—d Canadians; they (appear to be as well) attached to the English (as any we) have yet had. Pray give my compliments to your families and all friends. I hope in everything I act to meet your approbation, as it is my wish (to do).

Dear Gentlemen, your much obliged and very humble servant. Edmond Moran

Ye 15th—This morning this Dennis Croghan arrived here from the Sauk country with no news. He has been there all winter, and has seventy packs of beaver with him; each weighing thirty pounds, French weight. Pray let me hear from you. This country affords abundance of peltry.

E. Moran

For Messrs. Shelby and Postlethwaite.

Tuscarowa, At Camp No. 13,
Oct. 21, 1764.

Dear Sir: Yesterday evening we arrived here. We were kindly received by Col. Bouquet, who was hold— a conference with the Indians, of whom there is a tolerable number, and some of them are the d—st rascels that now live. The speech the Colonel made co-operated with their character. I believe a peace will ensue; if so we must return without scalps; but if a peace, we may be assured it will be much to our advantage, etc. I wrote you from Fort Pitt, that I intended coming here in consequence of Col. Gladwyn's not being yet gone to New York. He is now with Col. Bradstreet, not above eighty miles from here. I could wish Lieut. Gorrell was here, then we might go to him and have our business settled at once. I hired nine horses to Mr. Elliott, who is to return them at Fort Pitt. I have ordered them to be sent home. I left the greatest part of our goods with Mr. Spears' clerk at Fort Pitt. Two small loads of goods, with one of tobacco, I have here and shall sell them. I believe we shall sell all our goods this fall to good advantage. I shall go twenty-five miles further, then will return; if Capt Postlethwaite should come up, he may proceed. Mr. John Gibson is here, given up by the Indians, with many other prisoners. The Indians are d—mnably scared, which you may believe on their seeing such an army in their country. I believe I shall see Col. Gladwyn before I return, and before I go home. At every opportunity I shall write you. Tomorrow we shall march with all the army. All the gentlemen send their compliments to you. My best respects to Mrs. Shelby and all friends, and believe me to be, with the utmost sincerity and kind regards, dear sir, Your most obedient, humble servant,

Edmond Moran

N. B. Please keep my horse until I come in, and take care of him with your own.

Capt. Evan Shelby, Frederick County, Md.

New York, May 27th, 1765

Dear Shelby:—

I have the pleasure to assure you, that I have got all the King's accounts passed, and the cash is now in the General's hands, who will pay it on the certificates, which you know are in the wido's Devisme's hands. As Mr. Moran lodged them with her brother Stillwell, in pledge of the sum which he borrowed of him, as well as the sum due to her by Stidman and Tayler, the whole not amounting to four hundred pounds, York currency, and as she is threatened by Stephen West, I was obliged to enter a protest against the cash being paid on these certificates, which the General approves of. Therefore, as I believe West is set off from this in order to get a later power of attorney than mine, you will set off as fast as possible the nearest way to this place; and you'll not only miss West but also by my giving you other certificates, as they have not lawfully a right to receive the cash by them without a power of attorney, and you know there are other things which will answer. I have been advised to this by the lawyers and other of my friends. You may come in the night from Dugle's (Douglas?) ferry to me at William Tayler's, who lives now at Crinling (?) wharf, known by the name of Peck slip. It is the best and remotest place in town, where I shall be glad to see you as soon as possible. As the post is just going you'll excuse haste. If you had Mr. Postthwaite with you, it would be so much the better, or at least have his approbation, as well as Mr. Moran's, in writing, and all will be well. Compliments to all friends, in particular to Mrs. Shelby. Don't fail in making all haste possible. As we shall not let above two or three friends know anything about the matter until all is finished, which will be done in two hour's time after your arrival here, and then I hope to have the pleasure of riding home with you. Which is all from your sincere friend and well wisher,

Jas. Gorrell

Capt. Evan Shelby, Frederick county, Md.
Lieutenant James Gorrell, to John Morin Scott, Dr.
To two different written opinions relating to the certificates of Moran and Co. at 40 shillings each
4-0-0
Perusing and amending a letter of substitution to Major Moncreif 1-9-p
Dr. Protest 19-9
Persuing the bonds to be executed by Messrs. Gorrell and Stearndel for indemnifying Mr. Stillwell and Mrs. Devisme 1-9-0
Attending and advising on incidental matters relating to the settlement of this affair, including two different conferences with Mr. Smith and Mrs. Devisme's council in all 18 attendances at 10 shil-

lings each	9-0-0
A fee on Mrs. Gorrell's first application to me	1-2-6
	18-10-3

New York, July 12, 1765, received of M. James Gorrell, eighteen pounds, ten shillings and three pence in full for the above bill.

John Morin Scott

New York, 12th July, 1765, received af Lt. James Gorrell two pounds, ten shillings, for my trouble in receiving the money of General Gage.

Jona Holmes

New York, 15th July, 1765, some time ago, I think in April last, Mr. Gorrell took my opinion relating to certain certificates to the General, and paid me for it, I think forty shillings.

Wm. Smith. Jr.

Carlisle, 31st August, 1765.

Dear Sir:

I am favored with yours of the 27th inst., which as I am at present very much hurried, on account of the bearer, I shall answer briefly. I am much surprised to hear that Mr. Stephen West should not have received that money, as Crohon (Croghan) told me he had; it is most certain that the money has come in to be paid. As for Lottridge's bond, I do assure you that I am very sensible we don't owe him anything; but on the contrary always imagined he was in our debt; and if I had time, would send you his account, and a paper from under his hand to oblige him to settle whatever amount should happen to be proved by me against that bond. The first opportunity I have, whichever day offers, I will send you the accounts and the paper or obligation I have from under his hand. The other account you make mention of, is one of Wm. Bruce's. It was in his custody I left them goods you heard me make mention of, at LaBaye, the amount of which was far above his account against us; and I am lately credibly informed that he arrived safe at Detroit with the proceeds of them, which must as I always allowed it, over pay him, so that I don't regard what West can do in that affair, and can assure you I can not charge myself with anything faulty, in any sense, towards you, since I commenced company with you, but in not giving you a particular detail of everything when I came in. However, in my next, when I send you Lottridge's accounts, which you shall have against Wednesday or Thursday next, I flatter myself you will acquesce with me in it. I am well satisfied to give you all my lands, warrants, etc, as nothing could render me more satisfaciton than to see you satisfied but would not allow that West should have them,

neither have I the warrants here to asign you-my wife is not yet come home. I am very sorry that it did not suit you to answer my request; as I know full when Ward and Crohon (Croghan) find that nothing will be done here for me, they will immediately fall upon you in Maryland (for which I should be exceedingly sorry), as would they all, knowing you are equally liable. All they do to me, is to keep me here, which I expect they will, perhaps as long as I live; and if that would satisfy them, I would willingly resign to it, though my fate will be (as it is very nigh now) to live upon bread and water. I shall enclose you an account of my sales to the northward, and which I expect will be satisfactory, and inform you who we are indebted to. I am, as I before mentioned, ready to comply with your request of the land, and shall write you more fully about it in my next. Please let me know what Capt Postlethwaite has done in regard to the re-survey on Janes' Run. I have opportunity almost every day to write to you, and shall embrace the first that offers, in which I enclose the papers you request, and those I mentioned above, which may perhaps be the last you will receive from me (as I am almost tired of writing) while I am here.

I am with the utmost respect,

Your ever devoted, humble servant,

Edmond Moran

If it would suit, do let West know what I say in regard to those debts he has industriously brought against me. I will write to him the first opportunity.

Capt. Shelby.

Hollidaysburg, Penna.
October 6, 1927

Dear Mrs. Priest:

About Edmund Moran, I am enclosing copies of some letters written by him to the firm of Postlethwaite & Shelby of Washington (Frederick) Co., Maryland. Saml. P. was formerly from Lancaster, Penna. and formed a fur trading firm with Evan Shelby, Jr., to exploit the trade in and around Northern Michigan, Canada, Minessota, etc. Edmund Moran was their agent in the field. This concern suffered greatly during the French and Indian War, Pontiac's Conspiracy coming right afterwards, they nearly went under—the letters towards the last indicate a fear of the "debtor's prison," so prevalent in those days. Evan Shelby finally left Maryland for the newly opened lands in North Carolina. (N. E. Tenn.); I do not know what became of Moran. Unfortunately I haven't anything on the latter that helps us genealogically, but will be glad to send you anything that I might run across if I do so. On inquiry I find his will is not on file in Carlisle, so he either left none, or did not die there.

The person who typed the Moran data is not an expert, but she got it all down, which is the main thing.

Very sincerely
Cass K. Shelby

P. S. About the oldest Church in Carlisle where records can be obtained, I do not know, but will enquire.

Information contributed by:
Mr. Cass K. Shelby
Mrs. Edgar Priest
Mrs. V. S. Fendrick

Penna. Arch. 3rd Ser. Vol. 22, p. 154, 163. 5th Ser. Vol. 5, p. 110.

RODGER MORNING

Served in Capt. Noah Abraham's Marching Company Sept. and Oct., 1777, several undated rolls.

Penna. Arch. 5th Ser. Vol. 6, p. 18, 21, 133, 152.

WILLIAM MORRISON

Served as pvt., under Capt. John Orbison, 1780-81-82. He was a son of Andrew Morrison, an early settler on the Welsh Run. The will of Andrew Morrison of Montgomery Twp., was prob. Feb. 17, 1807. He names daus., Elizabeth; Sarah; Margaret; Quinn; Mary; Agnes and children of dau. Jean: 3 sons, Wm.; John; Robert. Wm. Morrison of Peters Twp., left a will dated and prob. in 1771, of the same vicinity as the above Andrew Morrison. He names first brothers and sister in Ireland. Brother Samuel Morrison; Brother Robert's dau. in Md. To Rev. John Cuthbertson 10 lbs. To Rev. Mr. Rogers if settled in the Associate Cong. of Conococheague 5 lbs. To that Body of People called Seceders in West Conococheague, 15 lbs. for raising a meeting house. Nephew John Morrison; To David Humphrey 4 lbs. To Oliver Anderson 3 lbs. Wife Jennett the residue. Exrs. last three named. Wit: Andrew, Wm., and Matthew Willoughby.

Penna. Arch. 5th Ser. Vol. 6, p. 273, 293, 307.

In Dr. George P. Donehoo's Hist., of the Cumb. Valley, he records the Settlement at Shippensburg, in 1730. In June of that year these persons built the first Cabins: Alexdr. Stein, Robert Morrow, John Culbertson, John Strain, John McAllister, John Johnston, John McCall, Gavin (Gawn) Morrow, Hugh Rippey, Alex. Askey, David Magaw,—later came Benj. Blythe, John Campbell, Robert Caskey.

CAPT. CHARLES MORROW

Officers of the Assos. Regt., of Lancaster County over the River Susquehanna, 1747-48, Capt. Charles Morrow, Lieut. James Dyssart, Ensign John Anderson. The will of Charles Morrow is No. 55, Carlisle Court Records. Dated June 7, 1758. "Exhibited and Proved," Sept. 7, 1758. He states "being in perfect health and sound memory Blessed be God for it But Being Lawfully called to Enter into the field of Battle and Calling to mind the mortality of my Body and knowing that it is Appointed for all men once to Die, xxx I have no heirs of my own Issue; I give to my Eldest Brother's Son Gawn Morrow Seven Shillings and sixpence; To my Eldest brother Wm. Morrow five shillings and to Wm. Morrow my Brother John's Son, I allow to be given to him seven pounds or a horse of that Value. To my Well Beloved Wife Mary Morrow xx my Lands and Tenements my whole estate Real and Personal By her freely to be possessed and enjoyed and Disposed of as She thinks proper" x x x x Wit: John McKee; Francis Campbell; Joseph Bready.

Penna. Arch. 5th Ser. Vol. 1, p. 25.

GAWN MORROW

Of Lurgan Twp., served under Capt. Chas. Maclay. His will was dated 1796, and prob. Feb. 5, 1805. He names wife Margaret, providing for her most quaintly and liberally,—a Case of Ten Drawers, one Walnut Cubbord, Dinah to be at her command at any time; a son William; Son-in-law James Henderson; Dau. Elizabeth wife of Grier McIlvain; Dau. Margaret, wife of John Bratton; Grandau. Jane Morrow Henderson; Brother-in-law Andrew Murphy. In 1776, Gawn Morrow was in the Subscription list, James McKee's District, in Middle Spring Church. In the will of John Hannah of Antrim Twp., 1785, he names sons-in-law James and Henry Morrow, also sons-in-law John Wherry and Samuel Adams.

Penna. Arch. 5th Ser. Vol. 6, p. 148, 150.

JOHN MORROW

On Feb. 1, 1779, John and Thomas Morrow signed a petition from Fannett Twp. John Morrow appears as a private with Capt. Thos. Askey, 1777-79-81-82. Marriage records of Dr. David Denny show some Morrow marriages: Samuel McCune and Jane Morrow, Apr. 19, 1796; Samuel Gammel and Kitty Morrow, June 4, 1799; Rev. A. A. McGinley records show: Stephen Skinner and Nancy Morrow—1805. R. Clymans and B. Morrow—1807; R. Morrow and Margaret A. Irwin—1809.

Penna. Arch. 2nd Ser. Vol. 3, p. 320. Penna. Arch. 5th Ser. Vol. 6, p. 24, 61, 131, 417, 423, 441.

RICHARD MORROW

Served under Capt. Thos. Askey, 1782, and probably in the Cont. Line. His will, dated and prob., 1813, states he is of Fannett Twp., names wife Agnes, to live in the "Mention" house. Sons

Andrew; Thomas; Dau., Catherine Gamble; To sons Richard and Daniel ½ Section of land in Cumb. Co., State of Ohio, East half of Section 35 of Twp. Twelve and Range Eight to be divided betwixt them &c. Son Michael Morrow forever, all this tract I now live on &c.; Dau. Margaret Conner; Dau. Agnes Skinner; Dau. Jean Morrow horse and much else; china Tea ware, Silver teaspoons, Copper Tea Kettle; Puter dishes, plates &c. Witnesses: John Elder, John Price, William Gamble.

Penna. Arch. 5th Ser. Vol. 6, p. 442, 658.

THOMAS MORROW

Served as pvt., under Capts. Thomas Askey and Chas. Maclay, 1779-81. Deeds in Court records, Chambersburg, Pa., show Thomas Morrow of Shirley Twp., Bedford Co., Penna., Millwright, buying land in Fannett Twp., Apr. 20, 1787.

Penna. Arch. 5th Ser. Vol. 6, p. 36, 62, 132, 408, 412, 424.

WILLIAM MORROW

"In ye Light Dragoons," served 1778-79-81, some undated rolls, under Capts. John and Patrick Jack and James Young. From Geo. Seilhamer we have the following: Wm. Morrow was born in Lancaster Co., and died in Pittsburgh, Sept. 22, 1817, "an Innkeeper, at an advanced age." He settled in Chambersburg before the Revolution and was an original purchaser of four lots, in 1778 and 79. He kept the stone tavern on the west side of Main Street at which President Washington lodged when he was on his way to quell the Whiskey Insurrection in 1794. He removed to Pittsburgh in 1795 where he kept "The Green Tree" on the bank of the Monongahela. His wife was Barbara Zantzinger of Lancaster. Their children were: Paul and Thomas; Alexdr.; Mary wife of John McDonald and Nancy wife of James Grossan.

Penna. Arch. 5th Ser. Vol. 6, p. 64, 109, 110, 145, 147, 169, 535, 544, 547, 580, 599.

WILLIAM MORROW

Served as Pvt., with Capt. Samuel McCune in 1776, and in 1780 undated rolls. In the will of Wm. Morrow of Lurgan Twp., dated 1830, he states "I want no Vendue to be made of my moveable effects, but all my three houses that join togehter xx I leave to my beloved wife Mary Morrow and children." 3 sons: Wm. Morrow; James Boyd Morrow; John Boyd Morrow. Oldest dau. Margaret Morrow exclusive of her uncle John Boyd's bequeath; Dau. Agnes Boyd Morrow; Dau. Mary Morrow; Dau. Jane McCune Morrow; Dau. Elizabeth McIlvaine; youngest dau. Bathsheba McCune Morrow. To oldest son Wm. my Rifle gun, Sworn, Silverwatch, Silver Sleve buttons, and Silver Shoe Buckles, and my set of Silver Tea Spoons having the inicials of my name engraved on them; To son James Boyd Morrow my Eight day clock and Silver Knee buckles; To son John Boyd Morrow my Desk and Book case and my father's Silver buckles. Younger branches to have sufficient education equal to those of greater age. Wit: James Henderson, Jr.; James Henderson; Wm. Morrow, late Capt. U. S. Army, resident of Pittsburgh.

Penna. Arch. 5th Ser. Vol. 6, p. 220, 223, 226, 558.

JAMES MORTON

Served as pvt., under Capt. Patrick Jack, 1781-82. Penna. Arch. 5th Ser. Vol. 6, p. 292, 313.

THOMAS MORTON

Served as an Ensign under Capt. Noah Abraham, 1777-78-80-81-82. He also signed several petitions from Fannett Twp. He left no will in Franklin County. He was probably a brother of John Morton of Bethel Twp., Bedford Co., Penna., whose will was dated June 15, 1781. He named his children,—Wm.; John; Thomas; Mary; all minors; his sister Frances Morton and as Executor, "brother Thomas Morton."

Penna. Arch. 5th Ser. Vol. 6, p. 12, 16, 43, 46, 55, 140, 626.

BALSOR MOWEN

Served as a private under Capt. Wm. Berryhill, 1780-81. He went to Ohio, and is buried in the old cemetery, North Lima. Born 1759, d. 1845, married Matlena (1776-1838).

Penna. Arch. 5th Ser. Vol. 6, p. 80, 101. Official Roster, Rev. Soldiers in Ohio.

DANIEL MOWAN

Appears in Antrim Twp., 1779 to 1782, as a taxable with land, horses and cattle. His sons, Balser, Ludwick and Stephen also held land over the same period. Daniel Mowan left a will dated Apr., 1786, prob. March, 1787. To wife Catherine ⅓ of personal estate and to live in a house my son Ludwick is to build before harvest, coming by the spring on my plantation to be two story high with a good room in the upper story, and the under story to be for a still house; son George (being blind) to live with his mother in the new house xx son George my still, xx also a tract bought of Jacob Snyder; son Stephen; sons John, Baltzer, Ludwick, Daniel and Peter, and daus., Elizabeth Hartley, Catherine Stuff and Mary and Molly Mowans the rest of my estate. Exrs: Elias Davison and John Johnston. Catherine, widow of above Daniel Mowan, left a will 1789-1798, naming son George "my undivided equal third of the plantation, left me by the will of my husband." To dau. Molly Mowan my riding mare and saddle; one cow; red teapot; cups and saucers and ½ of my clothes; dau. Mary Mowan ½ of my clothes; grandau. Elizabeth Hess all my wearing caps, one silk handkerchief and other items; balance of estate among all my children.

LUDWICK MOWEN

Served as a private under Capt. John Jack, Sept. 16, 1778. Lodowick Mowin, Widdower, of Greenfield Twp., Bedford Co., Penna. His will was dated Apr. 23, and proven Aug. 24, 1803. He directs that his five sons shall learn trades, viz: Peter; Daniel; John; David; Ludowick, and his two daughters Molly and Prudy to have Schooling, "as is proper for girls to have." His Executors were his brothers Steven and Daniel Mowin of Franklin Co., Penna., farmers.

Penna. Arch. 5th Ser. Vol. 6, p. 599-600.

STEPHEN MOWEN

Served as a private under Capt. Wm. Berryhill, 1780-81.

Penna. Arch. 5th Ser. Vol. 6, p. 80, 101.

PHILIP MUHLHOF (MILLHOFF)

Came to America in 1753, settled near Chambersburg for awhile. The ship Edinburgh, Capt. James Russell, qualified Sept. 14, 1753, with Philip Jacob Muhlhoff, also a passenger. After service in the Rev. War from York Co., Philip Muhlhof is said to have settled in St. Thomas Twp., where he died 1831-40, leaving a will at Chambersburg. He named wife Barbara and issue: John; Jacob; Daniel; Philip; Henry, the plantation; Barbara; Christiana; Susanna; Catherine and AnMaria. A deed from Detrich & Jacob Gushert, 1838, "have sold a Tract in St. Thomas Twp., by lands of Henry Hoffman, Philip Milheof," and others. In March, 1840, Philip Millhoff and wife Margaret were "of Donogall," Westmoreland Co., Penna.; they appoint John Coble, Jr., of St. Thomas their Atty to collect moneys &c for them. Philip Millhost (?) took the Oath of Allegiance before John Creigh, J. P. at Carlisle, Penna., June 8, 1778. There are descendants living in Fort Loudon and in Johnstown, Penna.

Prowell's Hist. York Co., Penna. Vol. 1, p. 268. Encyclopedia of Westmoreland Co. by John M. Gresham, p. 549. Penna. Arch. 2nd Ser. Vol. 14, p. 483.

HENRY MULL

Served under Capt. Daniel Clapsaddle, 1780-81. The name was early in Franklin Co., as Ensign Robert Mull served, 1747-48 under Capt. Benj. Chambers and Lieut. Charles McGill.

Penna. Arch. 5th Ser. Vol. 6, p. 93, 116.

ANDREW MURPHY

Served as pvt., under Capts. Noah Abraham, Chas. Maclay and Isaac Miller. In the will of Gawn Morrow he names his brother-in-law Andrew Murphy. He was in Robert Donavan's District of Middle Spring Church.

Penna. Arch. 5th Ser. Vol. 6, p. 19, 20, 21, 139, 148, 150, 435, 449.

PATRICK MURPHY

Appears as a pvt., with Capt. Thos. Askey, 1778-79-80-81-82. Patrick and William Murphy sign early Petitions from Fannett Twp.

Penna. Arch. 5th Ser. Vol. 6, p. 61, 132, 393, 409, 423, 442, 620.

PATRICK MURPHY

Is shown as a pvt. 1781-82, under Capt. John McConnell.

Penna. Arch. 5th Ser. Vol. 6, p. 302, 310.

CHARLES MURRAY

Served as pvt. under Capt. Jeremh. Talbot, having enlisted 1776 from vicinity of Chambersburg, Penna. He was in the 6th Penna. Batt., under Col. Wm. Irvine.

McCauley's Hist. Franklin Co., Penna. p. 83. Penna. Arch. 5th Ser. Vol. 2, p. 210. Penna. Arch. 5th Ser. Vol. 4, p. 635.

PATRICK MURRAY

Pvt., enlisted Capt. Jeremh. Talbott's Co., Jan. 9, 1776, discharged 1782, born county Donegal, Ire. Mar. Mary Brereton Beatty, 1786, issue: James; Edward; Catherine; Patrick; Susannah; Wm.; John; Mary; Elizabeth; Alice Ann; Sarah; Rebecca; George; Anna Hill; Hugh; Died July 23, 1854 Orange Twp., Ashland Co., Ohio. Worn moss-covered marble slab, name and dates. Clothier & Fashioner, as was Thos. Murray of Chambersburg, Penna. The name was also known for many years in Mercersburg, Penna.

McCauley's Hist. Franklin Co., Penna. p. 83, 84. Official Roster Rev. Soldiers of Ohio.

THOMAS MURRAY

Pvt., 3rd Penna. Cont. Line. Thomas Murray resided in Franklin County. Will probated Oct. 6, 1824; late of Chambersburg; Names children: Anna; Patrick; James; Washington; John; Polly McAllor (decd). From Franklin Repository Apr. 5, 1803, we have an advertisement of Thomas Murray, for three or four Journeymen Taylors to whom generous wages and constant employment will be given, on Queen Street, opposite the Buck

Tavern. Signed: Thomas Murray, also under Feb. 18, 1805, "Thomas Murray informs his friends he has opened a Tavern in Queen St., at the sign of, General Wayne. He solicits the patronage of his friends and a generous public, &c. He carries on his Tayloring business as usual."
Penna. Arch. 2nd Ser. Vol. 13, p. 169. Penna. Arch. 5th Ser. Vol. 2, p. 1008.

HERMAN MYERS

Served as pvt. in Capt. Henry Bicker's, Jr. Company 4th Penna. Regt. Cont. Line. He died in Letterkenny Twp. Franklin Co., Penna., his will dated 1810, and prob. Jan. 30, 1826. Wife Odilla; dau. Elizabeth mar. Peter Piper; dau. Annie mar. Peter Stake; Son Michael mar. Elizabeth Foust; Anna Maria Myers mar. Simon Shearer in 1811. There may have been more children.
Penna. Arch. 5th Ser. Vol. 2, p. 1100. Penna. Arch. 2nd Ser. Vol. 13, p. 170.

JOHN MYER

Pulaski's Legion, Cont. Line died in Franklin County, Sept. 6, 1828, aged 79 yrs.
Penna. Arch. 2nd Ser. Vol. 11, p. 161.

JOHN MCADOO

Served as pvt., in 1780-81-82 under Capt. John Wood and James Poe. In the will of John McMath, of Antrim Twp., prob. 1785, he names wife Ann, all estate. The legatees were Archibald Thompson 20 shillings; John McDoo, bay mair and colt; John McMath McAdoo, 20 lbs.; Mary and Ann McAdoo, (children of John McAdoo,) 10 lbs. each. The executors were wife Ann and Wm. Rankin. A McAdoo descendant gives: John McAdoo 1778 to 1781 in Antrim Twp.; in 1780-81-82, a pvt., in the Rev. War from Cumb. Co., and in 1791 he was in Moon Twp., Allegheny Co., Penna.
Penna. Arch. 5th Ser. Vol. 6, p. 91, 103, 109, 137, 575, 582.

JOHN MCANULTY, JR.

Served as pvt., under Capt. Wm. Berryhill 1780-81. The Caldwell Hist., of Indiana Co., Penna. p. 336, gives: John McAnulty, born in Franklin Co., Penna., served in Rev. War, mar. Isabella McLane, of Chambersburg, and with their goods and chattels on pack horses, they migrated to Indiana Co., Penna. They had: Michael; Margaret mar. Philip Rice; Mary mar. Daniel Stanard; Martha mar. Peter Sutton Jr.; Patrick in War 1812, never returned; Isabella mar. Peter Sipher; John mar. Rachel Templeton and Anna. (Isabella McLane was probably a dau. of Patrick and Margaret McLane of Antrim Twp.) Deed Book Vol. 3, p. 314,—In 1783, John McAnulty and wife Isabella of Antrim Twp., Franklin Co., Penna., sell to George Clark 130 ac land for 30 pounds, one Waggon and Team of four horses, 1 lot in Hagerstown, and 1 tract of land in Westmoreland Co., Penna.
Penna. Arch. 5th Ser. Vol. 6, p. 80, 102.

ROBERT MCANULTY

Private in 1782, under Capt. Richard McLane. The will of Michael McNaulty of Franklin Twp., probated May 7, 1799, names his son Robert to whom he gives his "lot No. 10, in Greencastle, which he now lives on;" wife Mary ½ of lot 10 in Chambersburg, &c. He also names dau. Mary Stuard, as a son Hugh; Son John having received his full and part, is given but one Crown. (See John and wife Isabella McLane).
Penna. Arch. 5th Ser. Vol. 6, p. 129.

DAVID MCBRAYER

Served in 1777-81-82 under Capt. Patrick Jack, Orphans' Court records show the above man as the son of William McBrayer of Hamilton Twp., who died intestate Oct., 1795, leaving a widow Rebecca and issue: James; Samuel; William; Sarah; who mar. Andrew Taylor; and David, all of full age. An earlier David McBrayer had died in Antrim Twp., in 1771, leaving a wife Elizabeth (Campbell) and five married daughters. Deeds show that in 1796, Samuel and Wm. McBrayer, both of the County of Rutherford, N. C., sold their interest in a tract of land in Franklin Co., Penna., for 69 pounds, 10 shillings to David McBrayer. The map shows 137¼ acres, much attested. The tract granted to William McBrayer, by patent, in 1788, was sold by David McBrayer of Hamilton Twp., and wife Agnes to Daniel Leman, March 31, 1806. It is probable that David McBrayer and family removed about this period to Westmoreland Co., Penna., where he died in Mt. Pleasant Twp., Sept.-Oct., 1816. To his wife Agnes he left $1000. cash. It is thought that Agnes, wife of David McBrayer, was Agnes Dickson, which, owing to the similarity of given names, is quite probable. Eldest son, William; Andrew; Samuel; James; John; David; a dau. Hannah Killgore; Sons Isaac; George; Henry; Dau. Betsy McBrayer; Son Robert, rifle gun; Dau. Rebecca McBrayer; son Matthew; youngest dau., Nancy McBrayer; youngest children by last wife. Henry to have books and large family Bible. Of the above children, Samuel "Brier" mar. to Betsy Campbell, Jan. 26, 1804 by Dr. Robert Kennedy, of Welsh Run and Greencastle, moved to Fountain Co., Ind. John mar. Daminen West, Oct. 31, 1809, Champaign Co., Ohio; Isaac, b. June 29, 1787, in Franklin Co., Penna., mar. Mary West, Oct. 31, ———, Champaign Co., Ohio; George, b. 1790, mar. Letitia Mitchell; David mar. Elizabeth Jacobs, Miami Co., Ohio. James "Brier" and wife Mary, who was the dau. of Benjamin Lodge, were of Montgomery Co., Ohio, on Sept., 1815. In Jan., 1814, Ezekiel Kilgore of Cincinnati, Ohio, appoints Wm. "Brier" of Cincinnati as his attorney. Ezekiel was son and heir of David Kilgore, Westmoreland Co., Penna. In 1818, Orphans' Court records show that Anges, widow of David McBrayer, had mar. Samuel Coyle and guardians were appointed for the minor children, Matthew, Nancy, Robert and Rebecca McBrayer.

Penna. Arch. 5th Ser. Vol. 6, p. 292, 296, 313, 373.

NATHANIEL MCBRIER, BREYER, BRAYER

Served as private with Capt. Patrick Jack, 1781-82, the command of Lieut. Colonel Saml. Culbertson. He was a taxable in Hamilton Twp., 1777-82, with land, horses and cattle. He was in Hempfield Twp., Westmoreland Co., Penna., in 1783, with land, and in 1809, had pending a land grant from the government for services in the Rev. War. Deeds show that in June, 1812, Nathaniel McBryar and wife Agnes sell to Malachia Brindle of Peters Twp., Franklin Co., Penna., a tract in Hamilton Twp., 218¼ acres. He had previously sold a tract to Samuel McCutcheon. Nathaniel McBrier and wife Jane (Watson) widow of Alexdr., Thompson, are buried in Poke Run Cemetery, Westmoreland Co., Penna. As Court records show the second wife as Margaret the previous statement is open to question. Nathaniel McBrier settled in Washington Twp., Westmoreland Co., Penna. He had a grist and saw mill on Beaver Run and his will dated July, 1820, was prob. Jan., 1835. The son James received from his father the "Poke Run Meeting House Plantation" in 1811, also other tracts; his wife Elizabeth Dickie. The son David received the "Mill Place on Beaver Run" from his father in 1814, and Dr. Egle states his wife was Elizabeth Lochry. There were other children, but the grandsons named in the will the sons of David, who appear to be, James McBrier, Jr., wife Nancy Livingston; Polly mar. John Duff; David; Nathaniel Watson who mar. 1st Mary Ann———; 2nd——— Duvall; John mar. Hannah.

Penna. Arch. 5th Ser. Vol. 6, p. 292, 296, 313. 2nd Ser. Vol. 13, p. 143.

The Franklin Repository, Chambersburg, Penna. Aug. 20, 1805. Died in Hamilton Twp., on Monday the 12th inst., one of the first settlers, and it is supposed the oldest inhabitants of this County, Mrs. Rebecca McBrier, relict of the late Wm. McBrier, aged 101 years. A native of Ireland, emigrating to this County about 1737, soon after which her husband purchased and settled on a tract within about seven miles of this town xxx On Tuesday her remains were deposited by the side of those of her husband, in the old burial ground near Mr. Brown's Mill.

JAMES MCBRIDE

A Kentucky pioneer, was killed by Indians in 1789, on the Dryridge, Kentucky, near the trace then leading to the mouth of the Licking. In 1779 his name was 20th on a list of 25 men who founded Lexington; from list in John D. Shane's handwriting in the Draper Collection of Kentucky. The 25 men mentioned were from Harrod's Fort. In 1780, he purchased 500 acres of land at the Elkington and Licking. 400 on Kentucky River. In 1781, among the first lot holders of Lexington, when the plan of the town was adopted, and lots disposed of, was James McBride. In 1782, a young man at Lexington Station. 1782, "The Bloody year." He fought bravely in the battle of Blue Licks when "Col. John Todd and his brave fellow Kentuckians suffered terrible defeat at the hands of the British and Indians, Aug. 19, in what has been called the Last Battle of the Revolution." In 1783, Rev. David Price settled at Mr. McBride's on Dick's river a few miles southeast of Harrodsburg. In 1784 James McBride built the first water grist mill located at a large spring on a branch of South Elkhorn Creek. Kentucky Court, Woodford estates James McBride of Antrim Twp., Cumb., Co., Penna. Legatees were: Sister Mary's two sons, James and Henry McBride, land in Antrim Twp.; Sister Jean's children, pre-emption right in Kentucky; Sister Hannah's children all other claims in Kentucky. The Executor to be James Poe of Cumb. Co., Penna. Written Apr. 3, 1783. Wit: Joseph McClean and John Maxwell. Prob. Nov., 1790, Woodford Co., founded from Fayette in 1788. Following the making of above will, dates unknown, James McBride returned to Franklin County, Penna., where he married Margaret, dau of James McRoberts, of Antrim Twp. Their son, James McBride (of Hamilton, Ohio) was born in 1788, near the town of Greencastle, and the will of his mother, Margaret 1808, names first: To son James McBride all bedding and furniture and all my share of my Father's estate. She also names Sisters Jane and Mary McRoberts and Eleanor Law; Nephew James Law, my cow. Exrs., were Friend David Fullerton and "my son James McBride." She was buried in Moss Spring Graveyard, near Greencastle, Penna. Of the two nephews named in the Kentucky will of 1783, by 1798, Henry had died, and James of Westmoreland Co., Penna., sold the lands willed them in Hamilton and Antrim Twps., to Richard Bard. The late James McBride, of Hamilton, Ohio, was, at the time of his death, one of the oldest and best known pioneers of Southern Ohio, having gone there in 1806, then in his eighteenth year.

He gave much time to the monuments and Indian fortifications of Southern Ohio and Indiana. He was connected with Miami University, and truly devoted to the interest and improvement of the State of Ohio. He survived his wife but ten days, dying Oct. 3, 1859, aged seventy years.

Draper Collection of Kentucky Hist., M. S. S. at Madison, Wis. M. S. S. 12CC65, Calendar of Kentucky papers 1925, p. 268. Collins Hist. Fayette Co., p. 172. Willard Rouse Jillson.

WILLIAM MCCACHLEN

Sir: After my compliments to you and your family, I would remember you of that Tower of Duty I searved in your Company in the year 1781 for which Tower I have received no recompense as yet. I was Informed that some of the Melishy was paid in paper money and same in Dewbills Bearing Interest, and some none, as I have no opportunity of seeing you I hope you will send me one of the best kind if possible by the Bearer of my letter James Moroson. Remember my kind Compliments to your Brother Robert McConald and Desire him to pay James Moroson five shillings on my account the Ballance Dew for a sythe, and you'll oblidge Sir your Hum. Servt., William McCachlen, Robertson Township, Washington County. Oct. 18, 1787. To Capt. John McConald, Cumberland Co.

Penna. Arch. 5th Ser. Vol. 6, p. 639.

ZACHARIAH MCCALEY

Clarana McCaley, widow of above, states that her husband was killed by Indians when serving his own tour in the militia as a private in Capt. John Craig's Company from Westmoreland Co., Penna., in May 1791, leaving the above widow, son John aged 18 months, and Betsy about 4 months old. This application appears in the Orphans' Court records of Chambersburg. She remained a widow and is shown receiving pay from 1791 until Aug., 1821. Clarana McCalla occupied a pew in Rocky Spring Church in 1794.

Penna. Arch. 5th Ser. Vol. 4, p. 531.

JOHN MCCALISTER

Chambersburg, Penna. Court Records Will Book B, p. 9. The will of John McCalister of Chambersburg, dated Dec. 31, 1789; prob. Apr. 18, 1796; To John Scott, Esq., and Samuel Dryden, all my lands due and owing to me from the State of Penna.; also all the lands due me for my services in the army of the United States, to be equally divided between them.

JOHN MCCALL

Served under Capt. James Patton 1780, also under Capt. Thos. McDowell. One John McCall was mar. to Elizabeth, dau. of Capt. James Patton, March 25, 1790. John Dickey, who lived and died in McConnellsburg, Penna., mar. Betsy McCall Nov. 20, 1781. Among the 1730 settlers, who built the first Cabins at Shippensburg, was John McCall. Thomas & Josiah McCall enlisted Jan., 1776, under Capt. Wm. Rippey of Shippensburg.

Penna. Arch. 5th Ser. Vol. 6, p. 271, 315.

JAMES MCCALMASH

Was a pvt., under Capt. Patrick Jack in 1777. They were pewholders of the Presby. Church at Welsh Run. His widow, Rebecca secured a tract called "Fidelity in Trust," and in May, 1802, the widow and children sold 185 acres to Jonas Troutman, who with his wife Catherine sold in 1803 to Matthias Maris. The children of James McCamish were: Thomas; James; John; Anna wife of James Kelly; Margaret wife of Allen Speedy; Rebecca McCamish; One Thomas McCamish mar. Polly Alexander, March 13, 1804, by Dr. John King. The land now (1937) in possession of E. S. Myers.

Penna. Arch. 5th Ser. Vol. 6, p. 372.

ALEXANDER MCCALMONT

Was in service 1779-80-81-82, with Capt. Wm. Moorhead, who stated his list was in "Classical order."

Penna. Arch. 5th Ser. Vol. 6, p. 66, 134, 388, 401, 414, 440.

WILLIAM MCCAMMON

Is shown in service 1777-80-81, with Capts. Robert Dickey, Thos. McDowell and James Patton. He was taxable in Peters Twp., in 1781.

Penna. Arch. 5th Ser. Vol. 6, p. 271, 284, 314, 371.

THOMAS MCCAMMOT

Is shown in Service July, 1782, with Capt. Alexander Peebles.

Penna. Arch. 5th Ser. Vol. 6, p. 432.

JOHN MCCAMEY

Served Dec., 1776, under Lieut. John Culbertson, Armstrong's Battalion. The Rev. John Craighead was in the same company. John McCamey, Sr., did by will dated March 4, 1765, give to his 3 sons the whole of his real estate; Robert; John; Joseph. John McCamey, Sr., names wife Margaret; beloved dau. Margaret Alexander, my plantation in N. C. on Sugar Creek Settlement, ajoining James Norris and James Campbell. Will dated 1766. Robert McCamey, formerly of Green Twp., and wife Rosanah and John McCamey, formerly of Letterkenny Twp., sell to Robert Beard. Joseph and wife, Mary did sell Dec. 11, (?) his share to his brother John for 402 lbs. Robert McCamey occupied Pew No. 5, in the early Log Church at Rocky Spring.

Penna. Arch. 5th Ser. Vol. 6, p. 316.

JOSEPH MCCAMEY

Served as a private under Capt. Samuel Patton 1781. Orphans' Court gives the following: Joseph McCamey died intestate before Apr. 19, 1794, leaving a widow Mary afterwards mar. John Warden) (said Mary is since decd.) and their children: Elizabeth mar. Charles Culbertson; Margaret mar. Henry Cotton (Collon?); James, since decd., leaving a widow Martha and issue one child, Joseph Allison McCamey, a minor. Joseph McCamey left land in Hamilton Twp. The above Martha was probably a dau of Capt. Joseph Allison and wife Ann, buried at Falling Spring.

Penna. Arch. 5th Ser. Vol. 6, p. 286, 288.

WILLIAM CARTY (MCCARTY)

Served as private under Capt. Noah Abraham 1777. He mar. Ann, dau. of William Wallace, Sr., and wife Margaret of Fannett Twp. In the will of William Wallace he names dau. Ann, and son David as his youngest children. The estate of above William Carty (or McCartney) was admr., by his sons William and James, May 13, 1808.

Penna. Arch. 5th Ser. Vol. 6, p. 18, 21.

ARCHIBALD MCCAUGHRAN

Served as pvt., under Capt. Patrick Jack, 1781-82. A descendant of the above, Vicksburg, Miss., states that Archibald McCaughran, Jr., mar. Jane Mercer.

Penna. Arch. 5th Ser. Vol. 6, p. 296, 313.

WILLIAM MCCAUSLAND

Served 1778-80-81 under Capts. Joseph Culbertson, Patton, Dickey, Houston and McDowell. Baptisms for the above were: Jane, April 23, 1782; Child, Oct. 3, 1784; John, Oct. 12, 1788. Andrew McCausland was a 1781 taxable in Peters Twp., with land, horses and cattle. James McCasland, Adult, was admitted to the church in 1781.

Penna. Arch. 5th Ser. Vol. 6, p. 265, 272, 285, 315, 382, 615, 643.

JAMES MCCLACHEY

Private under Capt. John Jack 1779, and under Capt. Thomas Johnston and Lieut. Richard Mc Lane, 1780, Cumb. Co. Militia. In the will of John Noble of Fannett Twp., dated 1794, prob., 1799, he refers to a plantation formerly occupied by Robert McClatchey.

Penna. Arch. 5th Ser. Vol. 6, p. 84, 540.

ROBERT MCCLACHEY

Private under Capt. John Jack in 1779 and under Capt. Noah Abraham in 1782. The 1790 Census of Penna. shows Robert McClotcheys with 1 man, 2 boys, 3 females, presumably in Fannett Twp. The following notes are from a family Hist., written 1876 by Alexander Donaldson, D. D. founder of Elder's Ridge Academy: "The McClatcheys came from Ulster in 1767 and settled in Franklin Co., near Path Valley. The names were James and Robert, the latter our ancestor. He mar. a Scotch wife and they had 3 children, Robert, Mary and James, before coming to America, and at least two later, as Charles and Elizabeth were born July 26, 1769. James mar. 1st Margaret Glenn, 2nd Catherine Davis, 3rd name unknown. In 1798 the McClatcheys moved to Armstrong Co., Penna., near Kittanning. Mary mar. Daniel Killen; issue 12, names unknown. Charles mar Betsy Crawford, issue: Samuel; John; Robert; Wm.; Jane; Margaret; Sarah; Betsy. John, born 1800 mar. Susan Brown of Scotch descent, lived near Brookville, Jefferson Co., Penna., and was frozen to death, Feb., 1832, while enroute to town to make the last payment on his farm. The contribution of these notes is a G. G. G. Grandau., of Capt. Samuel Craig, Sr., who was killed by Indians near Ligonier in 1777. The above Samuel Craig and family, in their journey from New Jersey to Western Penna., tarried for a year or more in Franklin Co., where two daus., married, one Rosanna to Wm. Elliott, Esq., Feb. 4, 1774.

Penna. Arch. 5th Ser. Vol. 6, p. 127, 540.

HUGH MCCLELLAND

Col. Hazen's Regiment, "Congress' Own," 1776-1783. Hugh McClelland entered the service Nov. 24, 1776. He was a son of Hugh McClelland, who was one of the Elders of Donegal Presbytery in 1740, dying prior to 1768, leaving a widow and at least four children: Robert; John; Sarah; Hugh. Mr. Emmons gives the service of Hugh as above, the Regt., called "Congress Own" and also the Canadian Old Regiment. By June of 1793, Hugh McClelland had married Sarah Armstrong, dau. of Thomas Armstrong. Hugh McClelland of Franklin Co., Penna., and wife Sarah deeded her 1/6 to Joseph Armstrong. Hugh McClelland and wife Sarah, removed to Stark Co., Ohio, their issue as given: Sarah; Wm.; James; Nancy; Eliza; Lillian. Hugh McClelland applied for a pension Aug. 8, 1820, giving his age at that time as 67, his wife Sarah's as 52 years.

Penna. Arch. 5th Ser. Vol. 3, p. 769, 772, 774.

JAMES MCCLELLAND

In 1769, James McClelland and wife Martha (dau. of Robert McCoy), were living in District 2 of the Presbyterian Church of Mercersburg. James McClelland was enrolled in Capt. William Huston's Company, Cumb. Co. Militia, in service

1780-81. They appear to have had sons William and Robert, when baptisms begin with Martha in 1773; James in 1776; John in 1778; a child July 4, 1781; a child in 1784 named Thomas. One of above was Joseph who died Nov. 1, 1806. The father, James McClelland Sr., died 1802. Martha, the widow, and her children sold the land in March, 1811, to Jacob Stover. This land was part of a 1740 grant to John Black, 341 acres; Blacks sold to Samuel Carrick, who sold to Jonathan Smith in 1774, 162 acres, Jonathan Smith sold 62 acres to James McClelland. The deed mentions the 2nd son, Robert and states that one of the sons had previously purchased Robert's interest at Sheriff's sale. William McClelland, the oldest son, became a prominent citizen of Butler Co. Ohio. He was the first Sheriff and was elected the second time. When the deed was given the where-abouts of the son Robert were probably unknown to his family in Franklin County. In 1810 he had been trading far up the Missouri. Of the goods which he recovered from the Indians, he distributed among his men, then dropped down the River 200 miles, and in December he came to the place where Astors' expedition was wintering in preparation for the great overland expedition. Robert, now a partner of John Jacob Astor, was busied with more than fifty other men in making the final preparation for that famous journey. By January 1814 he was in business at Cape Girardeau with a stock of goods furnished by a merchant of St. Louis. His last days were spent at the house of Abraham Gallatin and he finally was laid to rest on the farm of his old friend, General Wm. Clark, who became Governor of that Louisiana Territory that he had explored. The Clark farm is near Normandy, Missouri, and on this farm, was a lonely grave at the foot of an oak tree. On the grave lay a slab on which was inscribed: "To the Memory of Captain Robert McClellan. This stone is erected by a friend who knew him to be brave, honest, and sincere an intrepid warrior, whose services deserve perpetual remembrance, A. D. 1816."

PATRICK MCCLELLAND

Presbyterian Church records, Mercersburg, Penna., Patrick McClelland died 1777, near Phila., by illusage of enemy. He was a grandson of John McClelland and wife Ruth, early settlers near Mercersburg, Penna. John McClelland and a son Patrick, born 1734, died Apr., 1757, in (then) Peters Twp. On Apr. 23, 1757, Patrick was wounded in the shoulder, near Maxwell's Fort, by Indians and died a few days later. He left two sons, William and Patrick, the son Patrick being the above who died in 1777, near Phila.

ROBERT MCCLELLAND

From Deed Book 3, p. 88, Chambersburg, Penna., and from articles prepared by Prof. John L. Finafrock for the Kittochtinny Society, on the life of Robert McClelland of the "Upper West Conococheague" settlement and Church Records.

DANIEL MCLENE

Served as 2nd Lieut. 1777-78-80-81 under Capts. James Johnston, John Jack and William Long. On June 2, 1795, Daniel McLene was mar. by Dr. John King to Sarah McDowell. His estate was administered by his widow Feb. 13, 1809. The will of Sarah McLene was dated & prob. 1828, naming seven children: Jane mar. Joseph Dunlop; Phanuel mar. John Graham; Mary; Anabella; James; Sarah and Robert.

Penna. Arch. 5th Ser. Vol. 6, p. 114, 511, 532, 557, 525, 532.

JOHN MCCLENE (MCLENE)

Appears first in 1777 as a Lieut. with Capt. Patrick Jack, and again in 1781. He was of Hamilton Twp., and is shown with wife Isabel, 1769, as members of the "Upper West Conococheague" Church of Mercersburg. Rev. John King baptized James for John McClean, Sept. 2, 1770; and John for John McClean on Aug. 2, 1772. A deed shows that John McClene died intestate, Dec. 28, 1789. He was a brother of James McLene and Patrick McLene of Antrim Twp., these three early and prominent men having come from Chester Co., Penna., to what is now Franklin County. In May, 1796, Jeremiah McLene and Isaac McLene were both of Franklin Co., Penna. Their father died owning 236 acres land, the younger children being Hacket; James; John; Patrick. As the name Hackett belonging in that vicinity at that period it is quite possible that John McLene mar. ———— Hackett. From 1778 to 1781 John Hackett had land, horses and cattle in Hamilton Twp., but in 1782, is shown with land, only,—probably had gone south. Of the children, Jeremiah was born 1767 and about 1790 settled in Chillicothe, Ohio; a representative in the State Legislature 1807-08 and Secretary of State 1808-31. He removed to Columbus, Ohio in 1816; a democratic elector from Ohio in the Electoral College of 1833, until March 1837. He died in Washington, D. C. March 19, 1837. Deed Book 9, p. 200, gives the following: State of Ohio, Madison County; Be it known that I, Patrick McLene of lawful age, citizen of that County and State aforesaid for divers good causes xxx doth constitute and appoint my brother John McLene lite of the said state of Ohio my true and lawful Attorney &c, to ask, receive &c all monies or property &c to which I have right or title in the state of Penna., I, Patrick McLene Citizen,

Oct., 6, 1810. In a deed of 1811, Isaac McLene was in Fairfax Co., Va. John Hackett and wife Ann, gave Power of Atty., in 1803, in Knox Co., Tenn., later in Rhea Co., Tenn.

Penna Arch. 5th Ser. Vol. 6, p. 292. 2nd Ser. Vol. 14, p. 409.

RICHARD MCLEAN

Served as Lieut., 1777-80-82, under Col. James Johnston. He was the only son of Patrick McClane of Antrim Twp. Will dated 1776. He, Patrick, names wife Margaret; son Richard; Dau. Mary, wife of Benj. Gass; Daus: Jean; Isabella; Martha; 3 grandchildren: Margaret, Wm. and Patrick Gass. He names "my brother John McClane and my brother James McClane." Richard McLean sold the land left him by his father to Alexander McKeehan, May 2, 1792. The Census of 1790 shows the family of Richard McLean to consist of 3 men, 2 boys, 3 females.

Penna. Arch. 5th Ser. Vol. 6, p. 83, 129, 514, 580. p. 70, 113, 539.

DANIEL MCCLINTOCK

Served as pvt., under Capt. John Rea, 1779-80. He died in Chambersburg, his will prob. Feb. 6, 1790, naming a wife Mary; daus: Agnes; Margaret; Mary; Jane. Smith tools to be sold. The "Repository" gives the following, under Dec. 30, 1828. "Died in this boro' on Friday last in her 75th year, Mrs. Mary McClintock, widow of Daniel McClintock." She is buried in Falling Spring Graveyard and has a stone. An unmarked grave, beside her, is undoubtedly that of her husband Daniel McClintock.

Penna. Arch. 5th Ser. Vol. 6, p. 78, 97, 544, 585.

JOHN MCCLOSKEY

Was a pvt., in 1782, under Capt. Terrence Campbell. Letters of Admr., on his estate to Dennis McCloskey, October 31, 1801. One John McCloskey appears in 1796, as a shoemaker in Antrim Twp.

Penna. Arch. 5th Ser. Vol. 6, p. 126.

JAMES MCCOMB

Light Horse, is shown serving 1778-82 under Capt. Thos Askey. He was probably the son of Robert McComb (1) and brother to Robert and Wm. McComb. McCauley's Hist., of Franklin County, shows on p. 81, James McComb as a private in the Company of Capt. Wm. Rippey, Jan. 9, 1776.

Penna. Arch. 5th Ser. Vol. 6, p. 39, 52, 428.

LIEUT. JOHN MCCOMB

Of Lurgan Twp., served with Capt. Wm. Strain, 1780-82. He left a will, dated and prob., 1803, giving to wife Martha the privilege of one third of his mansion house. A dau. Margaret, wife of David Johnston, and 3 sons; Thomas; David and George who are to have "all my lands on which I now live." Under application for land (undated) John Lee applies for land in Southampton Twp., 50 acres, part of a larger tract on Warrant July 10, 1752 to John McComb. John Stevenson and wife Jean (dau. of John McComb), of Cisel Twp., Wash. Co., Penna., yeoman, sell to Robert Scott their interest in in tract of land surveyed to John McComb in 1783, on warrant to John McComb, July 10, 1752 in Lurgan Twp.

Penna. Arch. 5th Ser. Vol. 6, p. 143, 386, 397, 429.

ROBERT MCCOMB

Served under Capt. Alexdr. Peebles, as 2nd Lieut., 1777-78-79, having been under Capt Samuel McCune, Aug. 13, 1776, as a private. Recd., Nov. 12, 1777, of Timothy Matlock, Esq., Commissions for Alexander Peebles, Archbd. Elliott, Robert McComb and Wm. Elder, of the first Battalion, John Brooks, Major. The above Robert McComb is probably the 4th child of Robert McComb (1) and his wife Janet, born 1753, died 1827 in Cross Creek Twp., Wash. Co., Penna. He mar. Elizabeth McCune, b. 1760, d. 1835. They had issue: Margaret b. 1781, d. 1796; Robert b. 1783, d. 1866, mar. Isabella Chidester; Elizabeth b. 1785, d. 1834, mar. ——— Smith; Jean b. 1788, d. 1859, mar. ——— Dickey; Mary mar. 1st Wm. Patterson; 2nd Robert Forsman; Sarah b. 1793, d. 1834, mar. ——— Byers; James, mar. Griselda Hill; Abigail mar. Edward Daugherty; Rebecca, b. July 28, 1801; Martha b. July 28, 1801, twins; Margaret b. 1803; never married.

Penna. Arch. 5th Ser. Vol. 6, p. 8, 12, 22, 24, 24, 54, 62, 51, 142, 588 596.

THOMAS MCCOMB

Served under Capt. Noah Abraham, rolls undated. George; John; Robert and Thomas McComb are shown as serving from Washington Co., Penna., in the Cont. Line, entitled to Depreciation Pay.

Penna. Arch. 5th Ser. Vol. 6, p. 20, 139, Vol. 4, p. 410, 718.

WILLIAM MCCOMB

Served as private 1777-80-82, undated rolls, under Capts. Noah Abraham and Isaac Miller. William McComb, enlisted under Capt. James McConnell July 20, 1776. At the fall of Fort Washington he was taken prisoner Nov. 16, 1776, paroled in March; as a prisoner he was confined on board the prison ship "Jersey." His application, in 1833, for a pension was allowed, as was also the application of his widow, Rebecca McComb, in 1839. Quoting from a Hist. of the McComb Family by P. H. K. McComb, is the following: William McComb 5th child of Robert McComb and his wife Jean; Born Jan. 10, 1757 in Cumb. Co., Penna.; died Feb. 10, 1835 at his home in Truro Twp., Franklin Co., Ohio, mar. Rebecca Kearsley, Dec. 16, 1779; b. 1762; died Nov. 20 1848 at Truro. She was the 9th child of Jonathan Kearsley of Carlisle. Resided on a farm in Lurgan Twp.; removed first to Washington Co., Penna., later to Ohio. They had issue fifteen children: Jane mar. Wm. Patterson; Catherine died in infancy; Thomas mar. Ann McCormick; Jonathan mar., Lucretia H. Beeler; Eliza mar. Wm. Forbes; Maria mar. Samuel Morrow; Martha mar. Adam Turner; John mar. Charlotte Chambers; William mar. 1st. Elizabeth Ramsey, 2nd ———; Samuel mar. 1st Elizabeth Turner; 2nd Anne W. Gibson; 3rd N. J. Gyer; Margaret mar. John Turner; Rebecca mar. Wm. Turner; David b. 1802, d. Dec. 29, 1840; Robert Cooper mar. Ann S. Kemper; Sarah mar. Robert C. Henderson.

Penna. Arch. 5th Ser. Vol. 6, p. 18, 152, 390, 435, 450.

ALEXANDER MCCONNELL

Served in Cumb. Co., Militia. As one man of the name served from Path Valley, another from Hamliton Twp., the above is offered with the following authentic data. In 1769, William McConnell, wife Margaret, children Mary and Sidney were living in District 2 of the Presbyterian Church of Mercersburg. His son Alexdr., wife Martha, and son James McConnell, lived nearby. Martha was the dau., of James Wilson. Of the issue of Alexdr. McConnell,—I. Margaret mar. 1st Robert Grant, removed to Kentucky, where he was murdered. She mar. 2nd,——— Taylor, Kentucky. II. James mar. Jennie Cunningham. III. Alexdr., b. 1767, d. 1846, mar. Jennie Warden. IV. Robert b.——— d. 1850, mar. 1st Mary Caldwell; mar. 2nd, Prudence Coleman; V. William mar. Margaret Johnson. VI. Martha b. 1772, d. 1858, mar. Andrew Henderson, b. 1769, d. 1831, they had issue: Alex; Betsy; Mattie; Andrew; James; Matthew; Wm; Samuel; John; Mary. VII. Mary mar. 1st Joseph Mathers; mar. 2nd Alexdr. Smiley. Mattie, dau. of Andrew and Martha Henderson, mar. John Carnahan.

Penna. Arch. 5th Ser. Vol. 4, p. 295.

JAMES MCCONNELL

Served under Captains Robert Dickey and Walter McKinnie, 1781 an undated roll. He was a weaver and had land horses and cows. He is said to have been born about 1759, and he was married by Rev. John King to Janet Cunningham (Great Cove) Nov. 21, 1781. Under baptisms for the above are Martha in 1788; Samuel in 1789.

Penna. Arch. 5th Ser. Vol. 6, p. 281, 286, 316, 301.

MATTHEW MCCONNELL

Served as 1st Lieut., March 7, 1776, under Col. James Chambers of Chambersburg, in Col. Wm. Thompson's Batt. of Riflemen, later promoted to Captaincy and transferred to Hazen's Regt. Capt. Matt. McConnell had his leg broken at the battle of Brandywine and was transferred to the Invalid Corps. Capt. McConnell was born in 1748, Chester Co., Penna., son of Matt. McConnell, Sr., and wife Mary Wilson. He mar. Nov. 2, 1780, Ruth, dau. of John Hall and Sarah Parry, his wife, of Oxford Twp., Phila. Co., Penna. Court records at Chambersburg, Deed Book 1, p. 510,— April 12, 1782, Matthew McConnell, late of the County of Cumberland, now of Phila., a merchant, and wife Ruth, sell Lot No. 84, in Chambersburg, to Walter Beatty of Chambersburg. In 1784 Mr. McConnell, Merchant, was on the south side of Hight St., actively engaged in financial matters; was one of the auditors of the estate of his friend Robert Morris. In 1790 he became an original member of the Hibernian Society of Phila. The Third Troop of Phila. Light Horse or the "Volunteer Greens" was organized July, 1794, with Mr. McConnell as first Captain. In 1800 he became the first President of the Phila. Stock Exchange. He was an active member of the Penna., Society of the Cincinnati and was on the first Standing Committee. He died in Phila. Nov. 11, 1816. He had issue Robert; Matthew; Juliana; Dr. Benj. Rush McConnell. Mrs. McConnell d. in 1832.

Penna. Arch. 2nd Ser. Vol. 10, p. 15, 328, 344. Vol. 11, p. 104, 274.

ROBERT MCCONNELL

Served as Sergt. and Ensign under Capts. Thos. Askey and Noah Abraham, 1777-1780, some undated rolls. D. A. R. Lineage Book gives Robert McConnell, 1750-1800. His estate was admr., in Franklin Co., Penna. in 1805. Orphans' Court, Vol. C, pages 32 to 223. He is said to have mar. Agnes Wilson. There may have been an earlier Robert, who mar. Agnes Wilson. In 1824, Francis McConnell was bound to the heirs for payments to Joseph McConnell; Paul Geddis and wife Elizabeth; David Walker and wife Isabella; Jane McConnell; Robert McConnell; Samuel Walker and wife Martha; Mary McConnell; John McConnell. Joseph Sherard of Metal Twp., died in 1816, widow Catherine, settlement showed, among others a dau. Martha who had mar. Robert McConnell, both since decd., leaving issue, as given above, in 1819 all of age except Molly, Martha and John, minors, last three named. From this the wife of Robert McConnell appears to have been Martha Sherrard. Capt. John Walker of Fannettsburg stated that Robert McConnell was buried in the Presby. Church graveyard at Fannettsburg, Penna. The above Joseph McConnell mar. Sarah Job, in 1798 and their daughter Nancy mar. John Reynolds.

Penna. Arch. 5th Ser. Vol. 6, p. 7, 141, 387, 515.

ROBERT MCCONNELL

Was in service as a pvt., 1780-81-82 under Capt. John McConnell. Robert, John and James McConnell were early taxables in Letterkenny Twp. Under pewholders in the Rocky Spring Church, pew No. 39, was occupied by Robert; James; John and Donald McConnell. In 1794, pew 52, in the new brick church shows both Robert and John McConnell. James Mitchell, Letterkenny Twp., left a will, dated 1796, naming a dau. Elizabeth, the wife of Robert McConnell.

Penna. Arch. 5th Ser. Vol. 6, p. 267, 288, 301, 309, 639.

ROBERT MCCONNELL

First Batt. First Marching Company, First Call, July 31, 1777. Robert McConnell appeared in 1777, as Sergt. under Capt. Thos. Askey; as Ensign in 1780, and under Capt. Noah Abraham as Sergt. 1779-80-81. In 1778, Isabella McConnell was a taxable in Fannett Twp., with land, horses and cattle, and in 1779, taxed as Widow McConnell, probably the mother of above Robert McConnell. A deed shows Robert McConnell and wife Martha, of Fannett Twp., selling land to Wm. Hervey. Robert McConnell pvt., enrolled in 1777, in addition to the man who was sergeant.

Penna. Arch. 5th Ser. Vol. 6, p. 7, 120, 141, 384, 387, 515.

DAVID MCCORD

Served as private under Capt. Wm. Strain 1780-82.

Penna. Arch 5th Ser. Vol. 6, p. 398, 430.

MARK MCCORD

Served as private, 1782, under Capt. Wm. Strain. Penna. Arch. 5th Ser. Vol. 6, p. 431.

SAMUEL MCCORD

Served as private under Capt. John McConnell, 1780-81-82. He was born 1757, died 1837, wife Mary Hendricks, born in New Jersey. They had issue: Margaret mar. ——— Sample; Mary mar. ——— Jenkins; Jane mar. ——— Hubley; Nelly mar. ——— Knox; Sons, Robert, John Samuel.

Penna. Arch. 5th Ser. Vol. 6, p. 268, 303, 310.

WILLIAM MCCORD

Fort McCord a private fort built 1755-56 by Wm. McCord, a settler before 1745, on what was later Bossert land. William McCord occupied Pew No. 19 in the old Log Church at Rocky Spring. In 1773 David McCreight sold 38 ac. land to Wm. McCord for 5 shillings and again in 1773, Wm. McCord sold 224 ac. land to Thos. Lindsay and in 1790, Wm. McCord and wife Sarah sold 290 ac. to Andrew Harshman, the latter a tract from the Proprietors, Jan. 6, 1775. Wm. McCord, Sr., and Wm. McCord, Jr., are shown as serving under Capt. Wm. Strain, 1782. William McCord served as above, 1780, undated rolls. Dr. A. R. Johnston, New Bloomfield, Penna., in his family History states, that Wm. Anderson and wife Margaret McCord probably came to Perry County, Penna., about 1766. "I think that he and his wife and her father and brother, (both named Wm. McCord), came here from the neighborhood of Chambersburg, Penna.," letters, papers and public records point to that conclusion. The Orphans' Court, Chambersburg, shows one Samuel Bell, who died, Oct.,1823, leaving a sister Rosanna, wife of Andrew McCord.

Penna. Arch. 5th Ser. Vol. 6, p. 430. Penna. Arch. 5th Ser. Vol. 6, p. 143, 390, 398.

ELEXANDER MACCOY OR MCCOY

Alexander MacCoy or McCoy was pensioned on Certificate No. 26,348, issued May 9, 1834: rate $20 per annum; act of June 7, 1832; Ohio Pension Agency. He alleged that he enlisted in April 1782; served on different tours in the Pennsylvania Troops under Captains Swearingin, Builderback, Shannon, Major Scott, Cols., "McClelan," Crawford, Williamson and Gibson; was in the Battle of Sandusky; served as Private. His alleged service totaled 6 months. Alexander McCoy was born in 1764, in Scotland. He came to America in 1772. Names of his parents not shown. It was not stated whether or not he married. During his service the veteran was a resident of Washington Co., Penna. He lived there until he moved to Brown Co., Ohio, about 1814. In 1834, he was living in Brown Co., Ohio. The veteran died August 12, 1837, place not stated.

DANIEL MCCOY

Of Washington Twp., served as private under Capt. Samuel Rogers (Royer) 1779. His will was prob. 1798, naming wife Agnes; sons James and William; a dau. Mary McCoy; Daniel Irvin, son to Robert Irwin and his wife Martha.

Penna. Arch. 5th Ser. Vol. 6, p. 542.

JAMES MCCOY

Private. He was killed at Fort Washington, Nov. 16, 1776. He was a brother of Capt. Robert

McCoy and member of the Presbyterian Church of Mercersburg, Penna.

Penna. Arch. 5th Ser. Vol. 6, p. 297, 299, 305.

JOHN MCCOY

Served as private under Capt. Walter McKinnie, 1781-82. John McCoy and wife Rebecca were early members of the Presbyterian Church at Mercersburg. He died intestate May 28, 1801, and his wife, Rebecca died Nov. 18, 1805. Orphans' Court records show they had 4 children: James; who lately died intestate leaving a widow Elizabeth and 2 minor children: John and Mary; Isabella; John, the petitioner, and Robert since deceased, intestate and unmarried. 2 tracts of land, one 300 acres and one of 350 acres.

Penna. Arch. 5th Ser. Vol. 6, p. 297, 300, 305.

CAPTAIN ROBERT MCCOY

A member of the Presbyterian Church, Mercersburg, Penna., was killed at Chooked Billet, May 1, 1778. Orphans' Court Book A, p. 187,—A petition of John McCoy, eldest son of Robert McCoy, of Montgomery Twp., who died intestate in 1778, leaving a widow Sarah and issue: John, the petitioner; 2 daus: Alice, mar. Patrick Long; Jane mar. John Long; Rebecca McCoy; (Jane died, leaving 3 children: Cynthia, Bella, Robert.) Captain Robert McCoy left 165 acres land, which son John takes, p. 194-28. Petition of Sarah McCoy, widow and relict of Capt. Robert McCoy, late of Peters Twp. Robert was killed when serving as Capt., in a Batt., of Militia, commanded by Col. Abraham Smith, in the service of the United States, leaving 4 children, the eldest at that time not seven years old, and the youngest unborn, no support except from a small farm in Montgomery Twp., in said county, which has not yielded then annually more than 6 or 7 pounds, the personal property of decd., having perished by the rapid depreciation of Continental money, prayed the Court to make an order agreeably to the 55th Section of a law, passed March 20, 1780, granting her a certain annuity as the Court in their discretion might think proper for the support of her and her children. The Court being fully satisfied by a Certificate under the hand of Abraham Smith, Esq., the Commanding officer of the said Regiment, and also by a Certificate from the overseers of the poor of said Twp., of Peters, and four Freeholders that such a support is necessary do adjudge that an order be made for the sum of 607 pounds, ten Shillings, being the half pay of her Husband during her Widowhood for support of her and orphan children aforesaid, agreeably to the said law.

Penna. Arch. 5th Ser. Vol. 6, p. 369, 378.

MCCREA

Chambersburg, Penna., Deed Book Vol. 2, p. 408, show that in 1772, Samuel McCrea, farmer, and wife Elizabeth, of Antrim Twp., transfer certain land to their son Thomas McCrea, farmer, on the Waters of Antietam, under Patent of 1769. Later Thomas McCrea and Susanna sell the above land.

ADAM MCCREA

6th Penna. Batt., Col. Wm. Irvine, Capt. Abraham Smith, Private Adam McCrea enlisted Feb. 4, 1776. Records at Hagerstown, Md., show, under the heirs of John Brewer, 1835, a dau. Elizabeth, mar. to Adam McCrea.

Penna. Arch. 5th Ser. Vol. 2, p. 232, 235.

JAMES MCCREA

Private under Capt. John Woods, John Rea and John Reed in 1778-1782. James McCrea of Washington Twp., Franklin Co., Penna., names in his will his Sister Susanna McNeal; Sister Jean Armstrong; children of my brother Robert, Margaret, Mary and John McCrea; To children of Sister Elizabeth Black, wife of John Black; To Brothers, Wm., and David McCrea. This will was prob. June 1808. James McCrea as a son of Samuel McCrea, and as Executor, sold in 1806, 6 acres from a tract called "Aberdeen," to Fredk. Nicodemus.

Penna. Arch. 5th Ser. Vol. 6, p. 138, 528, 537.

JOHN MCCRAY

Private under Capts. Joseph Brady, Thomas Askey and John McConnell in 1778-1781. From Egle's "Notes and Queries," we have: Col. Robert Baker, Provincial Service 1747-48, lived in Path Valley, he died 1768 and his widow Francis Beaker left a will prob. 1791. Their dau. Anne (or Nancy) mar. John McCray, who was a son of Samuel. It is probable, from will abstracts, that one of the McCreas settled in Erie Co., Penna. In 1790 the Census of Franklin Co., shows for John McCre, 1 man, 3 boys, 4 females. Deeds Vol. 3, p. 466, Nov. 17, 1795, Chambg., Court House,—Ann McCrea, in place of her husband John McCrea, now delerious, they being now of Bald Eagle, Mifflin Co., Penna., and Barnabas Doyle of Fannett Twp., for 250 pounds formerly paid her husband John McCrea, and her the said Ann (Orphans' Court held at Carlisle, Feb. 18, 1779) the 1/9 part of a Plantation in township of Fannett, 300 acres. ("It being the tract of land whereon Robert Baker, father to said Ann McCrea lived and died possessed of "). Ann now releases for herself and Husband John McCrea,— Received 250 pounds.

Penna. Arch. 5th Ser. Vol. 6, p. 39, 41, 132, 374, 424.

ROBERT MCCREA

Private under Capt. Daniel Clapsaddler, Capt. Wm. Long and Capt. James Young in 1777-1778-1781. Robert McCrea, son of Samuel, is named in the will of Wm. Allison, of Antrim Twp., dated 1777, thus: "Dau. Agnes, wife of Robert McCrea." Robert McCrea was one of three men appointed to mark out the boundary lines between Cumberland and Bedford Counties. In 1793 Robert McCrea was in Woodford Co., Ky., as witness to a Power of Atty. to Benj. Ramey of Hamilton Twp., Franklin Co., Penna.

Penna. Arch. 5th Ser. Vol. 6, p. 71, 94, 117, 520, 522, 548.

SAMUEL MCCREA

6th Penna. Batt., Col. Wm. Irvine, Capt. Abraham Smith, Private Samuel McCrea, enlisted Feb. 12, 1776, d. Aug. 10, 1776. The above Samuel McCrea left a will at Carlisle, Penna. recorded March 25, 1778; he names wife Elizabeth, sons, Robert, Thomas, John, James, William, Isaac, David, a dau. Jean Armstrong, and daus., Shusana and Elizabeth. They were of "Entrim" Township. Elizabeth McCrea, d. 1777, was a dau. of Robert McClelland and his 2nd wife Elizabeth Ewing. James Ewing of Hunterdon County, N. J. and Robert McClelland were founders of the Middletown Twp., Presby., Church, now Elwyn, Delaware Co., Penna. one of the oldest in that part of the State. Deeds show that Samuel McCrea sold land in 1769 to James Wishard, "on the Waters of Antietam and Thomas McCrea sold land in 1775 to John Wishard. The will of John Wishard, Nov. 1777 at Carlisle, Penna.

Penna. Arch. 5th Ser. Vol. 2, p. 232, 235.

THOMAS MCCREA

Private under Capt. Daniel Clapsaddler in 1780-1781. He mar. Dec. 20, 1770, by Rev. John King, Susanna Coil. He appears in Bedford Co. Penna., and gave service there in militia. He was a son of Samuel McCrea of Franklin Co., Penna. His will is recorded at Greensburg, Penna., dated and prob. 1804. He names wife Susanna, Grandson Thomas Trimble; Grandson George Trimble; son-in-law Wm. Trimble. The Executors and witnesses were old Franklin County men,— Michael and Charles Campbell and Alexdr. Moorhead. In Cross Creek Graveyard, Washington Co., Penna.: William McCrea d. Sept. 3, 1841, aged 85 yrs. Sarah McCrea d. March 3, 1825, in 49th year. One James McCray left a will at Erie, Penna., recorded 1840. John Allen left a will at Erie, Penna., in which he named McCreas, Wards, and many others, prob. 1838.

Penna. Arch. 5th Ser. Vol. 6, p. 93, 116.

WILLIAM MCCRIGHT

Was a pvt., in Capt John Jack's Company in 1778, a probable son of David McCreight. Court records at Carlisle give the will of David McCreight, of Letterkenny Twp., May 10, 1774. He names a son William; Daus.: Margaret and Sarah McCreight; Grandau: Kethrin Shields; 4 children: Mary; Wm.; Margaret; Sarah.

Penna. Arch. 5th Ser. Vol. 6, p. 169.

GEORGE MCCULLOUGH

Was in Air Township, Bedford County, Penna., Jan. 29, 1789, subject to Militia duty. George McCullough, son of Archibald, came to America, presumably from Derry, Ireland. He landed in Newcastle County, Del., where he mar. Mary Crosby about 1770. They had John b. June 28, 1771; 2nd child was Rebecca. George McCullough mar. 2nd, Mary Eynon, dau. of Wm. Eynon, issue: Eynon McCullough. He mar. 3rd, Sarah, dau. of Evan and Catherine Phillips of what is now Warren Twp., Franklin Co., Penna. They had issue: Evan; Samuel; Mary; Catherine; Hannah; Rachel and Jane. George McCullough later came to the vicinity of Upton, a taxable in 1786, a tanner by trade. He was a cousin of Archie McCullough, who was in the Enoch Brown massacre. Of the above issue, John McCullough mar. Elizabeth McCune in 1795, who was born 1772. They had issue: Archibald Scott b. 1797; Rebecca b. 1799; Mary Ann b. June 5, 1803; Isabella b. Sept. 2, 1805; Eleanor b. 1808; Elizabeth b. Nov. 26, 1810; Margaret D. b. Feb. 8, 1814; John Free b. Dec. 18, 1816; John McCullough d. Jan. 4, 1851. His wife Elizabeth McCune McCullough d. June 4, 1847.

Penna. Arch. 6th Ser. Vol. 3, p. 36.

HANCE MCCULLOUGH

Served as Lieut. in the Cont. Line, and as Lieut. in 1780-81-82 under Capt. Walter McKinnie. He was a son of James McCullough of Peters Twp., and a brother of John, the Indian Captive. Letters of Admr., on the estate of Hans McCullough were granted Aug. 20, 1789.

Penna. Arch. 5th Ser. Vol. 4, p. 295. Vol. 6, p. 263, 297, 304.

JAMES MCCULLOUGH

The Company of Capt. William Rippey, made up largely of Franklin County men, Jan. 1776, James McCulloch, Corp. James McCullough of Peters Twp., died Dec. 19, 1781, naming the following heirs: Wife Martha to have the use of the following books, viz: my large Bible, Whatsens body of devinity and Browns Explanation of the Romons, during her life, then to the use of son Hance. To brother Archibald McCullough my white Coat and Jacket; sons John and Hance;

Dau. Jean McClelland; Dau. Mary Foster; Grandson James McClellan; (Hugh Foster to Mary McCullough, Jan 5, 1779). The above James McCullough may not fit the service given. It is open to question.
Penna. Arch. 5th Ser. Vol. 2, p. 236. McCauley's Hist., of Franklin County, p. 80.

ROBERT MCCULLOUGH

Private in 11th Penna. Regt., C. L. b. in Scotland about 1732, mar. Miss McCartney in 1753. They had issue Janet, b. 1754, mar. Ephraim Wallace Apr. 25, 1774; Agnes mar. Joshua Marlin, March 25, 1776; Sarah mar. Hugh Barclay June 19, 1777. The above marriages were by Rev. Alex. Dobbin and they were from "Canigogig."
Robert McCulloch also had a son Samuel who probably mar. Margaret Downey (of William). Deeds show Robert McCulloch, (Miller) of Antrim Twp., conveying land to his son-in-law Hugh Barkley of Balt., Md., also shows Samuel McCullough and wife, Margaret selling land given him by his father Robert McCullough.
Stewart's Hist., of Indiana Co., Penna., p. 674.

ROBERT MCCUNE

Served in 1778 under Captain Patrick Jack. His will dated 1810 was prob., May, 1815. He was of Hamilton Twp., and names a son-in-law Josiah Allen, wife Susanna. Dau. Mary Ritchey's children and land where John Ritchey now lives. Dau. Susanna Allen.
Penna. Arch. 5th Ser. Vol. 6, p. 32.

SAMUEL MCCUNE, CAPTAIN

Is shown with his company, Phila., Aug. 13, 1776. Through the years 1778-80-82, Capt. Samuel McCune, Esq., appears in service as a private with Capts., John Campbell and Wm. Moorhead. He is regarded as one of the Rev. Soldiers of Middle Spring Presby., Church. Mr. John G. Orr, in his interesting article on "Early Grist Mills of Lurgan Township" states that a stone grist mill was built about 1775 by Samuel McCune, and the picture given is a fine example of the period; the land was an original grant to McCune from the Penns. An old account book of Capt. Samuel McCune, was used in his business as a Miller, distiller and farmer. The initial entry in this account book is the roll of Capt. McCune's Company of revolutionary service, made by his own hand, dated Aug. 13, 1776. Under Orphans' Court, May, 1803, is shown a petition from two sons-in-law of Samuel McCune, Esq., decd., to wit: Robert Sterrit mar. Rosannah McCune; John Campbell mar. with Elizabeth McCune; the widow Eleanor and seven children: John; Elizabeth mar. John Campbell; Rosannah mar. Robert Sterritt; Margaret mar. George Ritchey; Kesiah; Eleanor; Maria; Said Maria born since the death of said Samuel McCune, her father.
Penna. Arch. 5th Ser. Vol. 6, p. 31, 34, 134, 135, 388, 400, 440, 443, 587.

ALEXANDER MCCURDY

In 1776 was serving under Capt. Wm. Peebles, Penna., Rifle Regt., Col. Samuel Miles. In 1780-81, he was with Capt. John McConnell as 2nd Lieut. in Militia, and he appears in Westmoreland Co., Penna., under Pension applications, where he testified to the service of Wm. Waddle.
Penna. Arch. 5th Ser. Vol. 6, p. 267, 302. Penna. Arch. 5th Ser. Vol. 2, p. 358, 361, 364, 369, 371. Vol. 4, p. 594.

ARTHUR MCCURDY

Born in Scotland, moved to County Antrim, Ireland and immigrated to America prior to the Revolution, with sons John; James; Robert and Hugh. James and Hugh settled in Franklin County, Penna., John in Virginia and Robert in Adams Co., Penna.

HUGH MCCURDY

Appears as a pvt., with Capt. Noah Abraham, 1777-79-81-82. He is also shown signing two petitions in May and June of 1778. His will states he is of Fannett Twp., advanced in age, dated May 23, 1808; prob. Apr. 14, 1813. Wife Catherine certain lands, sons James and John McCurdy. Son Hugh to be raised and educated. Dau. Jane Johnston. Son Thomas; dau Nancy Moore. Exrs.: Wife Catherine, James Dougal and James McCurdy, son of my brother James.
Penna. Arch. 5th Ser. Vol. 6, p. 120, 128, 384, 516.

JAMES MCCURDY

Served with Capts. Noah Abraham and Patrick Jack, 1781-82, witih undated rolls. James McCurdy of Metal Twp., left a will dated June 1806, prob. July 1806. He names wife Ann; sons James and John to maintain her. Daus. Nancy Farmer and Polly Adams; Son Robert; Son William's children, Eliza and James; Exrs: Sons James and John. Ann, wife of above James, died in 1312. James McCurdy, b. 1770, d. Sept. 24, 1822, mar. Apr. 23, 1801, Mary (Polly) Brown, b. Oct. 17, 1772, died Oct. 15, 1847; the dau. of Allen Brown and his 2nd wife Margaret Oliver. They had issue: (1) Anna McCurdy b. Mar. 22, 1802, mar. John Alexander, 1822. (2) Margaret McCurdy b. Sept. 19, 1803, mar. James H. Rankin, 1823. (3) Joseph Brown McCurdy, born Apr. 21, 1805. (4) James McCurdy, born Oct. 15, 1808, mar. Eliza Klippinger, 1831. (5) Jane McCurdy b. Oct. 15, 1808, mar. John Keasy, Apr. 7, 1831. (6) Stephen Oliver McCurdy b. May 8,

1810, mar. Mariah Klippinger, 1835. From Bible records. Marriages by Dr. David Denny, Fannett Twp., Franklin Co., Penna.: James Turner, Nancy McCurdy, Apr. 2, 1799; Wm. McCurdy, Ann Coyle, May 29, 1800. Dr. David Denny, Chambersburg, Penna. Pastor Falling Spring Church. John Johnstone, Jane McCurdy, Mar. 3, 1801; James McCurdy, Polly Brown, Apr. 23, 1801. Rev. A. A. NcGinley, Fannett Twp. J. McCurdy, B. Evert, 1811; Ed. Johnson, Ann McCurdy, widow, 1821; John Alexander, A. McCurdy, 1822; James H. Rankin, Margaret McCurdy, 1823; Wm. Gaston, Mary McCurdy, 1830.

Penna. Arch. 5th Ser. Vol. 6, p. 120, 128, 144, 146.

HUGH MCCUTCHEON

Is shown in 1781-82, in service under Capt. Wm. Kerr, and he probably came from Cumb. Co., to Franklin Co. where he mar. Eleanor, dau of Samuel and Catherine McCutcheon; they were mar. by Dr. John King, May 30, 1780. James McCutcheon, of Washington Twp., Westmoreland Co., Penna., left a will dated Sept. 25, 1814, naming wife Margaret, also sons Samuel and Alexander; youngest sons William and Andrew; Five daus., not named. Exrs.: Wife and sons Samuel and William. Wit: Benj. Bunnell and Jean Murray.

Penna. Arch. 5th Ser. Vol. 6, p. 357.

ALEXANDER MCDOWELL

Served as private 1780-81, under Capts. James Patton, Thomas McDowell and William Huston. The following is from Deed Book 1, at Chambersburg: Alexander McDowell, appointed Deputy Surveyor of Donation Lands on the West side of the Allegheny river within this Comonwealth according to an Act of General Assembly xxx from directing the mode of Distributing the Donation lands, promised to the troops of this Commonwealth. Bond of Wm. McDowell and James Maxwell, Esq., of Franklin County and Alexander McDowell of Peters Twp., in said County, June 15, 1785. He was agent for the Holland Land Company at Franklin, and died in Venango County, Penna., leaving a wife and children.

Penna. Arch. 5th Ser. Vol. 6, p. 265, 271, 272, 285, 314, 315, 615, 642.

ANDREW MCDOWELL

Son of William and Mary (Maxwell) McDowell served under Capts. Robert Dickey and Conrad Snider. Dr. Andrew McDowell was mar. to Nancy McPherson, May 9, 1793, by Dr. John King, of Mercersburg. He was for many years a prominent physician of Chambersburg. In his will prob. Jan., 1846, he names four children: Dr. John McDowell of Mercersburg; Dau. Ann M. Williams near Williamsport; Dr. Robert McDowell in Ohio; Dr. Andrew N. McDowell in Pittsburgh; some namesakes are remembered; to son John my gold sleeve-buttons; my gun; clock and stand. To Ann M. Williams my silver snuff box &c; Son Robert my wearing apparel and my carpet bag. To Andrew my gold and silver spectacles. Dr. Andrew Nathan McDowell of Pittsburgh was mar. July 13, 1824, by Rev. Mr. Woods, at Lewistown, to Jane Denny Porter. They had a dau. Jane, born Dec. 10, 1829, who mar. June 1, 1850, Stephen Collins Foster, born Apr. 17, 1826, died Jan. 13, 1864, the celebrated song-writer, author of "My Old Kentucky Home" and other famous songs. They came to Mercersburg on their wedding trip. The parents of Stephen Collins Foster were married in Chambersburg by Dr. David Denny,—William Foster and Eliza Tomlinson, Nov. 14, 1807.

Penna. Arch. 5th Ser. Vol. 6, p. 119, 284.

ROBERT MCDOWELL

Served as private under Capts. James Patton and Robert Dickey, 1780-81. Robert McDowell mar. Betsy Irwin, Nov. 24, 1789; she was a dau. of Joseph Irwin and wife Violet Porter. In his will dated Oct. 3, 1806, prob. 1808, he directs that his land be sold, and to purchase a "Plantation back to the Westward," for the family to live on until the youngest child becomes fifteen. He names "Wm. and James McDowell my brothers; Wm. Young, Thos. Campbell, John Johnston and Daniel McLene, my brothers-in-law." Robert McDowell died Oct. 10, 1806.

Penna. Arch. 5th Ser. Vol. 6, p. 272, 285.

THOMAS MCDOWELL

Served as Captain with Lieut. John Holliday, under Capt. James Patton and Col. Samuel Culbertson in 1777-78-80. In 1769 he and his wife Annabelle were living near Fort Loudon. Robert McDowell, presumably his brother, was living with him. Annabelle was a dau. of pioneer William McDowell. They had no issue, but the will of Thomas shows bequests to nephews and nieces; "to John McDowell my nephew, son of my brother Robert; all residue and heirs of my brother John, decd., now living in Kentucky."

Penna. Arch 5th Ser. Vol. 6, p. 314, 368, 372, 377, 382, 615.

JAMES MCDOWELL, SUB-LIEUT.

Quarter Sessions Docket at Carlisle, Penna., Court House shows in 1768, Constable, James McDowell and John Anderson. James McDowell (vice McCoy decd.) from Nov. 29, 1777 to Apr., 1780; (Capt. Robert McCoy, killed at Crooked Billet). The accounts of James McDowell, Esq., Sub-Lieut., Cumb. Co., Penna., March, 1777 to March, 1780,—"In March, 1777, the Supreme Executive Council created the office of County Lieutenant, a most arduous and responsible position. With the aid of his sub-Lieutenants, he was required to district the county, enroll the militia and organize them into Companies, hold elections for officers, collect fines, purchase arms, munitions and supplies, and represent generally the State government in Military matters."

Penna. Arch. 2nd Ser. Vol. 3, p. 281, 282, 662. 3rd Ser. Vol. 6, p. 663, 664, 671, 699, 700, 701.

The will of Major James McDowell was dated 1804, and prob. 1811. To Robert his eldest son he gives land on a warrant of 1753, and part of another of 1773. To sons Wm. and James the plantation "on which I now live," farming utensils, Smith tools in the Shop and a small tract of Woodland (location of Francis Waddal) &c. To all my daughters as Tenants in Common, my right in a tract in Westmoreland County, near Greensburg; 1/6 part to each of my five Daughters, and one to my son-in-law Thomas Campbell, because of trouble and expense in a suit of ejectment xx the use of the Plantation, only to give me my living in the manner that took it heretofore, I being then rendered unfit by the rheumatism, and since by accident, unable to manage the affairs of the Plantation, Stock, and family. Exrs.: Thomas Campbell, Daniel McLean, Robert McDowell. Bible Record: James McDowell mar. Jane Smith, daughter of William Smith, Sr., June 17, 1761. Mary b. Apr. 5, 1762 d. Aug. 7, 1821; Anabell b. Dec. 24, 1763, d. Dec. 22, 1807; Robert b. June 13, 1766, d. Oct. 10, 1806; James (1st) b. June 5, 1768, d. Nov. 4, 1770; Jane b. Feb. 13, 1771, d. Jan. 23, 1847; Sarah b. Oct. 13, 1773, d. May 18, 1828; William b. Oct. 20, 1776 d. Jan. 23, 1834; Margaret b. June 8, 1779, d. Dec. 8, 1819; James (2nd) b. Dec. 6, 1782, d. Apr. 8, 1861; The dear partner of my life died Aug. 28, 1784; James McDowell the maker of the above words died Feb. 5, 1811, aged 83 yrs. From: Miss Katherine Huber.

MATTHEW MCDOWELL

Served as a private under Capt. John Jack and under Capt. Thos. Johnston, 1780-81-82. In 1769 he, wife Anne and son Robert were living in Hamilton Twp., members of the Presby., Church of Mercersburg. He later married Jean Boreland, moved to Westmoreland Co., Penna., dying about 1799. He names in his will, dau. Polly; son David; Robert; Matthew; John; James; Allen; Catharan; Agnes; Joseph. The widow Jean, b. 1758, moved to Mercer Co., Penna., where she died July 23, 1834, aged 76 years. A descendant gives the following: Issue of Matt. McDowell,—Robert Mar. a Cunningham, or Margaret Uber; Polly mar. a McMichael; Nancy (Anne) mar.

James Brandon; David born Aug. 21, 1777, d. Jan. 18, 1860, mar. Hannah Anderson, Feb. 21, 1804; she was b. Aug. 12, 1782, d. Aug 26, 1873. John mar. Susan Whan; Matthew mar. 3 times—a Jolley and two named Kerr; James mar. Sarah Brandon, he d. 1836, aged 46 yrs. Sarah d. 1855, aged 60; Allen mar. a Ghost; Catherine mar. Thos Courtney. Catherine b. Apr. 6, 1792. She was probably a 2nd wife, as 2 children were born to Thos. Courtney in 1812 and 1814. He mar. Elizabeth Robison June 29, 1809, Antrim Twp., by Dr. Robert Kennedy. Thomas Courtney was a son of Anthony and Sarah Courtney and was born Apr., 1771. Sarah Courtney d. 1802, aged 62 yrs., is buried in Browns Mill graveyard, Franklin Co., Penna. Joseph McDowell (a minister) mar. Esther Newman. Sons of Matthew McDowell,—John, Matthew, Allen and Joseph went to Iowa, and their descendants are scattered all through the west.

Penna. Arch. 5th Ser. Vol. 6, p. 84, 114, 124, 129, 586.

JAMES MCELHANEY

Is shown serving as Sergt. 1776-1779-80-81-82, under Capts. Abraham Smith, Samuel Patton and Wm. Long. James McElheny, pvt., appears in the Cont. Line from Cumb. Co., Penna.

Penna. Arch. 5th Ser. Vol. 6, p. 277, 286, 311, 318, 545. Vol. 4, p. 296, 632.

JAMES MCFARLAND

Served as a private 1780-81, under Capt. Wm. Huston. When James Wilkins of Peters Twp., made his will 1773, he named his brother-in-law James McFarland as an Executor, the other being his wife Jean, a sister to James McFarland.

Penna. Arch. 5th Ser. Vol. 6, p. 270, 276, 284.

ROBERT MCFARLAND, JR.

Served in 1780, under Capt. Wm. Huston.

Penna. Arch. 5th Ser. Vol. 6, p. 270.

HENRY MCFERRAN

Born 1764, died 1834, mar. Susanna Knepper, born 1757, died 1832. He served under Lieut. John Stitt, 1781. They had issue: John; Jacob; Henry; George; Peter; Mary; Susanna.

Penna. Arch. 5th Ser. Vol. 6, p. 113.

MATTHEW MCFERRAN

Served, also, in 1781.

Penna. Arch. 5th Ser. Vol. 6, p. 112.

SAMUEL MCFERRAN (MCPHERRIN)

First Lieut., a prisoner, the report being made by Col. Grier, following their return from Ticonderago, 7th Penna. Cont. Line; taken prisoner June 21, 1776, at Isle Aux Noix. In 1769, Samuel

McFerran was a member of the family of Jonathan Smith (Presiding Elder) and wife Jean, of the "Upper West Conococheague" Presby., Church near Mercersburg. There is a possibility that Jean Smith was the widow of Samuel McFerran, (died 1753) in Antrim Twp. Samuel McPherrin was mar. to Margaret McMullin, May 22, 1781, by Dr. John King. They had baptized Alexander, Oct. 20, 1786, and Jean, Feb. 25, 1784. The Samuel Findlay Ledger shows Samuel McFerran charged for a pair "Briddle Bitts" 7 shillings, 6 pence in 1774, and on April 10, 1775, he was credited with 2 lbs., for "one month's attending the Store last spring." He next appears buying lots 12-13-27, from Wm. Russel in the town "commonly known by the name of Williams or Hancocks town," in Wash. Co., Md., Aug., 1789, and his estate was administered Jan., 1791. Under Warrant No. 2640, 200 acres bounty land was issued Apr. 5, 1794 to Margaret McFerren, on account of the services of Samuel McFarren, Lieut., in the Penna. Line. The son Alex. McFerran (Admr. 1824) mar. Priscilla Thomas, buried in Hancock, Md., and they had issue: Daniel; Johnson; James B.; Alexander.

Penna. Arch. 5th Ser. Vol. 5, p. 200, 226.

DUNCAN MCGEE

Served as pvt. in the Cont. Line, from Bedford County, Penna. In 1769 he was living in District 4 of the Presby. Church of Mercersburg, Penna.

Penna. Arch. 5th Ser. Vol. 4, p. 244, 609.

PATRICK MCGEE

b. 1741; served as pvt. under Capt. Thomas Askey, 1781-82. He was a petitioner from Fannett Twp. in Juune of 1778, to the Exec. Council of Penna., asking for arms, ammunition &c, to defend them from the Indians. He married Jane Hall, Dec. 24, 1765, Christ Church, Phila., and they settled in Path Valley. His will recorded Oct. 18, 1811, names wife Jane, Sons, Adam, John; Daughters Nancy Bickerstaff, Mary Murphy, Nickley McGee, sons James, George, William, Patrick, Alexander not of age. The son Adam died in Fannett Twp., in 1854, he was born 1766, mar. Martha Appleby. John McGee, b. 1768, mar. Elizabeth, dau. of John Harmoni and they had Mary, Elizabeth, Jane, George, Nancy, born 1770; Mary born 1772; James b. 1774, went to Allegheny Co.; Nickley born 1778; Alexander b. 1790, went to W. Va., later Butler Co., Ohio. William b. 1799, assisted in creating a great free state out of the Territory of Kansas. Patrick b. 1782, mar. Nancy Jane Fagan, lived in Mercer and Butler Counties; George, 1776-1854, mar. Agnes Appleby. These Magee descendants settled in Lawrence, Mercer, Butler, Juniata, counties of Penna.

Penna. Arch. 5th Ser. Vol. 6, p. 408, 423, 429, 441.

PATRICK MCGEE

Was born in Londonderry, Ireland, 1750, came to Franklin Co., Penna., at the age of 21 years. He joined the Cont. army and served 3 years under Capt. John Marshall, Col. Samuel Miles Rifle Regt. He fought in the battle of Long Island, was a prisoner in the Sugar House, N. Y. Patrick McGee lived in Antrim Twp., and served in Militia under Capt. John Woods, 1780-81. He moved to Westmoreland Co., and in 1794 to Black Lick Twp., Indiana Co., Penna. He mar. Esther Philson, Apr. 17, 1796, they had issue: James McGee, b. Feb. 14, 1797, mar. Mary Lyons. Robert McGee, b. Oct. 25, 1798, mar. Isabella Ross. John McGee b. May 19, 1801, mar. Margaret Lyon. Patrick McGee died 1818, buried in Hopewell Churchyard, about 4 miles from Blairsville, Penna. From Jessie McGee Geary (Mrs. J. R.) Patrick McGee was in Capt. Houston's Comp., Col. Watt's Regt., of Flying Camp, paroled Jan., 1777.

Penna. Arch. 5th Ser. Vol. 2, p. 344, 347, 355. 5th Ser. Vol. 6, p. 92, 99.

BERNARD MCGUIRE

Of Derry Twp., Westmoreland Co., Penna., states in his pension application that he served in First Penna. Regt., commanded by Col. James Chambers from July 1, 1775-1781. Was in Battles of Quebec, Germantown, where he was wounded, also wounded at Stony Point and on North River below Fort Lee. Also at many skirmishes, and finally in Battle of Green Springs, Va., after which was discharged, being unable to march. Was examined by Drs. Huchenson and Denny. Statement sworn to by Samuel Guthrie and eight others. The Census of 1790 shows Bernard McGuire in Westmoreland, the family consisting of one man, four boys, and two females. Barnabas McGuire, Sergt., died 1823, in Westmoreland Co., Penna.

Penna. Arch. 5th Ser. Vol. 2, p. 670, 728. Penna. Arch. 2nd Ser. Vol. 13, p. 154. Penna. Arch. 5th Ser. Vol. 4, p. 587, 591.

ALEXANDER MCKEAN

Served as private under Capt. John Rea, 1780-81. He was of Guilford Twp. His will prob. Feb. 14, 1817, names wife Elizabeth; sons Alex and William; a dau. Elizabeth Brown and children; a dau. Nancy McCreary and children; Dau. Ann Renfrew; son Robert, decd., who left wife Roseanna and 6 children; a grandau., Ruhamah. His widow, Elizabeth McKean left a will, prob. Oct. 15, 1825, naming as husbands of her daus., John Brown; Robert McCreary; Robert Renfrew, also

named son William and grandau. Ruhamah Douglas. The son Alex. left a will prob. 1820.
Penna. Arch. 5th Ser. Vol. 6, p. 72, 106.

ROBERT MCKEAN

Served as pvt. under Capt. Wm. Strain in 1782. Letters of Admr., on estate of Robert McKean were granted to Alex. McKean, Dec. 31, 1814.
Penna. Arch. 5th Ser. Vol. 6, p. 430.

THOMAS MCKEAN

Served as pvt. under Capts. James Young and Terance Campbell, 1780-81-82. Thomas McKean of Chambersburg, Penna., left a will prob. Apr. 16, 1806, naming wife Jane; Son Robert; Son Samuel C. McKean the lot his Currying shop now is on; Dau., Mary Scott; Sons, John and Joseph; Daus., Elizabeth and Nancy McKean; Grandchildren, Elizabeth and Thomas Scott. In the will of Joseph McKean of Peters Twp., (1815) he names his step-mother, Jane Kirkpatrick and names children of his decd. brother John.
Penna. Arch. 5th Ser. Vol. 6, p. 82, 110, 125.

WILLIAM MCKEAN

Was a private under Capt. Thomas Askey, 1781.
Penna. Arch. 5th Ser. Vol. 6, p. 424.

ALEXANDER MCKEE

Served as pvt., under Capt Wm. Huston, 1780-81. He was baptized as an adult Dec. 9, 1779, by Dr. John King; he had baptized Robert, July 28, 1782, and David, Aug. 4, 1783. He mar. Rachel Kirkpatrick, of John, Dec. 7, 1802. Letters of Admr., on estate of Alexander McKee were granted June 19, 1807. His widow Rachel requested that her father John Kirkpatrick and Moses Kirkpatrick, Esq., administer the estate. Surety being Benj. Kirkpatrick.
Penna. Arch. 5th Ser. Vol. 6, p. 269, 275, 282, 304.

HUGH MCKEE

Born near Greencastle, Franklin County; he engaged in Indian Fur trade; letter from Valley Forge:

In Camp on the Schuylkill, Dec. 12, 1777.

Dear Mother: My company came here yesterday and we are preparing for a long stay. We feel that we have a long gloomy winter ahead. The General does not think we will move before spring. My foot is still very sore and walking about in the cold and snow with it bound up in cloth does not help it any. God knows I do not complain when my comrades are also without shoes and without covering, and our country's liberties are in the balance. We laugh at our hardships and joke about the beef-fed Britons. Be brave, the God of Battles is with us. It is so cold, I can hardly write another word and what I have written with this poor quill and worse fluid may not be made out. Father and brother are out scouting toward Philadelphia.

Your loving son, Hugh

Hugh McKee became a Captain of Riflemen before the close of the War. He was also a Captain of the Congruity Rifles during the War of 1812. His wife was Elizabeth Thompson, born 1764 in Cumberland Co. He was buried in old Punxsutawny graveyard, 1st burial.

Geo. P. Donohoe—Hist. of Penna., p. 84.

HUGH MCKEE

Was a 2nd Lieut., in 1st Company, 6th Batt., Cumb. Co. Militia, July and October, 1777 and May and November, 1778. He was a pewholder in the Welsh Run Church, as were, also, Mary and Wm. McKee. His will, probated May 22, 1795, states he was of Peters Twp.; Wife Mary; Dau. Martha; Sons, James and Andrew; Daus., Isabel and Elizabeth; Mary Wilson and heirs; Sons Thomas and William; Son-in-law George Dickey. It is probable that he was related to James McKee of Antrim Twp., who left a dau. Rachel mar. George Dickson.
Penna. Arch. 5th Ser. Vol. 6, p. 367, 372, 376, 383.

HUGH MCKEE

Served as a private under Capt. Daniel Clapsadler, 1780-81. He is shown in Antrim Twp., tax lists in 1788-96-99, with land, horses, cows and a negro.
Penna. Arch. 5th Ser. Vol. 6, p. 93, 116.

JAMES MCKEE

Served as a private under Capt. James Poe, and Lieut. Daniel Smith in 1777-78.
Penna. Arch. 5th Ser. Vol. 6, p. 522, 526, 583.

JAMES MCKEE, JR.

Served as private 1780-81, under Capt. John Woods.
Penna. Arch. 5th Ser. Vol. 6, p. 76, 92, 104.

JAMES MCKEE, JR

Born about 1740, moved from Snyder County to the Cumb. Valley. James and two sons, Thomas and Hugh enlisted in a company of Frontier Riflemen, Regt., commanded by Col. Chambers. Took part in N. J. Campaign, wintered at Valley Forge. In 1783, James and his 8 children removed to Westmoreland County. He had mar. Susan, dau. of Thos Nesbit.

Hist. of Penna. Geo. P. Donehoo, Biographical, p. 84.

ROBERT MCKEE

Served under Capt. Wm. Huston, 1780-81. Tax list of 1796, Antrim Twp., shows Robert McKee, 94 ac land, Maryland and John McKee, Maryland line, also a young Freeman.

Penna. Arch. 5th Ser. Vol. 6, p. 269, 275, 283.

THOMAS MCKEE

Private under Capt. James Poe in 1782.
Penna Arch. 5th Ser. Vol. 6, p. 576.

WILLIAM MCKEE

Private under Capt. James Poe in 1782. William McKee is shown in Tax Lists for Antrim Twp. in 1788, with Patented and Warrented land, horses and cows.

Penna. Arch. 5th Ser. Vol. 6, p. 576, 582.

WILLIAM MCKIBBEN

Served as a private under Capt. Noah Abraham, 1777-81. He was married to Hannah, dau of John Blair, an early settler in Fannett Twp. William McKibben of Metal Twp. died intestate in 1808, leaving seven children: Elizabeth; John; Nancy; William; Margaret; minors being James and Catherine. He left 300 acres of land. Hannah, wife of Wm. McKibben died Feb. 10, 1808; her husband died 8 days later. Deeds show the children married: Margaret mar. David Ferguson; Agnes (Nancy) mar. Levi Gribble; William mar. Nancy Wagoner; Catherine mar. Alex. Nelson; James mar. Esther (?) John mar. Mary (?) Elizabeth, no date. John Mckibben, eldest heir, took the real estate, stone house, log barn, 2 tenements; later selling to Richard Childerstone. Dr. Thos. Ferguson was told by his father that James and John McKibben moved near Pittsburg to A TOWN CALLED Cross Keys. The above Wm. McKibben was probably a son of James and Lettice McKibben (Will of 1786) of Lurgan Twp.

Penna. Arch. 5th Ser. Vol. 6, p. 120, 140, 417, 426, 516.

PETER MCKINLEY

Served under Major Jeremiah Talbott, 7th Penna. C. L. Peter McKinley mar. at Mercersburg, Penna., Jean Kinkade, Jan. 2, 1787. Deeds at Chambersburg, 1788 show: "I, Peter McKinley of Franklin County, appoint my trusty friends John McCoy and William Nesbit, of County aforesaid, Gentlemen, my true Attorneys &c, to recover from John Erawin of Chester County, near derby, a Patent which was granted to me by the Commonwealth aforesaid for 200 acres of land for my service in the first Batt., of the Penna., troops &c.

Penna. Arch. 2nd Ser. Vol. 10, p. 625.

JOHN MCKINNIE

Served as a private under his brother Capt. Walter McKinnie. In 1769, John McKinnie and wife Catherine were living near Church Hill. Agnes Thompson was a member of the household. Catherine McKinnie died Oct., 1785, and in 1814 John McKinnie, Sr., sold some land to John Wise. Deeds at Chambersburg, Penna., show that in Oct., 1794, John McKinney, Sr., of Rutherford Co., N. C. gives to his son John McKinney, Jr., and Jonas Bedford, Jr., state and county aforesaid, for love and affection which he beareth unto said John McKinney, Jr., his loving son and said Jonas Bedford, Jr., his son-in-law, confirms to them all that tract of John McKinney, Sr., by Heirship patent, in State of Penna., on Conococheague Creek (Now Franklin Co.,) warrant to John McKinnie for 200 acres, July 1, 1762. The will of John McKinney, Sr., Rutherford Co., N. C., prob., July, 1804, names wife Jean, sons John, James, Henry, Wm., George, dau. Diadeema, dau. Sally Camp and her dau. Lydia Camp, Wm., son of Henry, and sons-in-law John Roberts and Jonas Bedford. Witnesses: D. Camp and Wm. McKinney.

Penna. Arch. 5th Ser. Vol. 6, p. 297, 380.

JOSEPH MCKINNIE

The will of Joseph McKinnie of Hopewell Twp., dated and prob., 1785, names,—Eldest son Thomas; son David; Elizabeth, widow of decd. son Samuel; son Joseph; son-in-law John Macon; dau. Marey; son-in-law Wm. McCord; dau. Agnes now decd.; grandchildren: Joseph McCord; Samuel McCord; Grisell McCord; Andrew McCord; son-in-law John Campbell; son Wm. decd.; his widow Elizabeth and four daughters: Eleanor, Jean, Marey and Agnes McKinnie; grandchildren Jean and Grisel McKinnie.

WALTER MCKINNIE

In 1777-78, Walter McKinnie is shown as an Ensign under Capt. Robert McCoy (who was killed at Crooked Billet). In 1781-82, Capt. Walter McKinnie was in charge of the 8th Comp., 4th Batt. of Cumb. Co. Militia. He is also shown in the Cont. Line from Cumb. County. He appears as a Captain of Rangers on the frontiers with Jeremiah Rankin as Ensign, between 1778-83. Capt. McKinnie died intestate Apr. 20, 1806, leaving a wife Jane (Rusk) and five children: Josiah; Robert; James; Adam and Mary mar. to James McMullan, said Adam "is yet a minor" and James McCoy his guardian. He owned 300 acres of land, joining Nathan Brownson, John Wise, James McKinnie's heirs, and Wm. McClelland. The pioneer was Josiah McKinnie, who with wife Isabel settled at Church Hill very early. Their children were: Walter (Capt);

John; James; Mary; Elizabeth; Martha; Margaret; Isabel; Catherine; Anne.

Penna. Arch. 5th Ser. Vol. 6, p. 263, 297, 299, 304, 370, 378; Vol. 4, p. 296, 633.

BRYAN MCLAUGHLIN

Of Antrim Twp., enlisted Feb. 2, 1776, under Capt. Abraham Smith, Col. Wm. Irvine, 6th Penna., Regt. His estate was administered in Franklin Co., June 20, 1785.

Penna. Arch. 2nd Ser. Vol. 10, p. 179.

DANIEL MCMULLEN

Was a pvt. with Capt. Thos Askey, 1779-80-81-82. By an act of Genl. Assembly, passed Apr., 1835, to graduate the lands on which money is due &c, the Commissioners viewed these lands. The 51st was a request of Robert Campbell, for land in Fannett Twp., 104 ac. 132 pchs., held by Location of Daniel McMullen No. 1842, dated Nov. 8, 1766.

Penna. Arch. 5th Ser. Vol. 6, p. 61, 132, 393, 409, 423.

JAMES MCMULLEN

Served as a pvt., under Capt. Thos. Askey, 1779-81-82.

Penna. Arch. 5th Ser. Vol. 6, p. 61, 410, 412, 407, 442.

JOHN MCMULLEN

Is shown in Service 1779-81-82, as a pvt., with Capt. Thos. Askey. Eneas (Enos); Daniel; John; James; David and Laurence McMullen signed petitions from Fannett Twp., in 1778-1779.

Penna. Arch. 5th Ser. Vol. 6, p. 61, 131, 409, 412, 423, 442, 631. 2nd Ser. Vol. 3, p. 167, 185, 319.

JOHN MCMULLEN

Of Peters Twp., served as pvt., under Capt. Geo. Crawford and Lieut. David Shields in 1777-78, under Capt Walter McKinnie in 1781. He died July 10, 1822, an Elder in the Presbyterian Church of Mercersburg, Penna. He mar. Mary, dau. of Thos. and Mary Poe. Her first husband was Alex. Long. John McMullen and wife Mary had issue: Alexander; dau. Margaret mar. Wm. Waffle; dau. Rachel mar. Jeremh. Evans; son James Poe McMullan. His will dated Feb. 1, 1821, was prob. Aug. 21, 1822.

Penna. Arch. 5th Ser. Vol. 6, p. 279, 289, 297, 299, 371.

LAWRENCE MCMULLEN

Appears in service 1779-80, undated roll, as a pvt., with Capt. Thos. Askey.

Penna. Arch. 5th Ser. Vol. 6, p. 62, 132, 394.

THOMAS MCMULLEN

Served with Capt. Askey, 1781.

Penna. Arch. 5th Ser. Vol. 6, p. 424.

THOMAS MCMULLEN

Was a private under Capt. John Woods, 1782. In 1769 he was living in District 4, Presby. Church of Mercersburg, Penna., with Duncan McGee.

Penna. Arch. 5th Ser. Vol. 6, p. 424.

THOMAS MCMULLEN, JR.

Served as pvt. under Capt. Wm. Berryhill, in 1781.

Penna. Arch. 5th Ser. Vol. 6, p. 102.

HECTOR MCNEIL

Is shown in the Company of Capt. Alexander Peebles, at Shippensburg, June 11, 1777, and again in Feb., 1779. A man of the same name was in the Cont. Line from Bedford Co., Penna.

Penna. Arch. 5th Ser. Vol. 6, p. 58, 590.

JOHN MCNULTY

Appears in service, 1777-1780, with Capt. Wm. Long, Lieut. Joseph Patton, Daniel McClean, and others. A man of the name was in Hamilton Twp., early.

Penna. Arch. 5th Ser. Vol. 6, p. 524, 557.

WILLIAM MCNUTT, SR

Served with Capt Walter McKinnie, 1780-81-82. He was mar. to Jane McNutt, Paxtang, by license, Sept. 11, 1766. He was a brother-in-law of Wm. Dean who mar. Martha McNutt in 1763. The following children were baptized for Wm. McNutt at Mercersburg, Penna.: Samuel, May 20, 1770; James, Oct. ———, 1771; Robert, Nov. 7, 1773; Child, Oct. 6, 1782.

Penna. Arch. 5th Ser. Vol. 6, p. 266, 298, 300, 306.

WILLIAM MCNUTT, JR.

Served as pvt., 1781-82, under Capt. Walter McKinnie.

Penna. Arch 5th. Ser. Vol. 6, p. 281, 299, 301, 306.

LORANS MCREADY

Appears as one of Capt. Samuel Patton's Rangers, at Ligonier, under the command of Col. Wm. Chambers, April 27, 1779, to June 22, 1779. As "proof of the effective" Capt. Patton swears to one Captain, one Lieut., 2 Sergts., 18 privates.

Penna. Arch. 5th Ser. Vol. 6, p. 601, 610.

CROMWELL MCVITY

Served in Lancaster Co., Militia under Capt. Joseph Jenkins, 1782. Under Orphans' Court records, 1794, at Chambersburg we have: Petition of Edward McVitty, one of the sons of Cromwell McVitty late of Carnorvon Twp., Lancaster Co., Penna., decd., who lately died intestate owner of two tracts of Patented land in Fannett Twp., Franklin Co., Penna., leaving a widow Margaret and lawful issue to survive him: Wm.; Elizabeth; Edward; John; Ann; Sarah; Thomas; Margaret; Samuel. Edward was released by his older brother Wm. and sister Elizabeth and John paying shares to the widow and other children. Cromwell McVitie mar. Margaret Anderson, Apr. 4, 1763. Under records of St. James Prot. Epis. Church, Lancaster, Penna.

Penna. Arch. 5th Ser. Vol. 7, p. 499.

JAMES MCWILLIAMS

Is shown serving as Lieut., and pvt., in the Cont. Line of Cumb., County, and under Capts. John Jack, Wm. Long and Conrad Snider, Col. Thomas Gibson and Col. Abraham Smith, 1777-78-79-80-81-82. Henry McWilliams is shown with James in the Cont. Line. In a deed dated May, 1775, Wm. Gass, farmer, of Guilford Twp., and Mary, his wife, to James McWilliams of same place, blacksmith; consideration natural love and affection which Wm. Gass and wife, Mary bear unto said James McWilliams, their son-in-law. The land in Guilford Twp., and in case of the death of James McWilliams, the land is to go to Mary McWilliams, his present wife or to his lawful issue.

Penna. Arch. 5th Ser. Vol. 6, p. 87, 118, 123, 512, 533, 535, 545, 599. Vol. 4, p. 634.

SAMUEL MCWILLIAMS

Antrim Twp., Cumb. Co., Penna. Pennsylvanians from Col. Oliver Spencer's Regt., referred to as Fifth battalion, Jersey Line. Sergt. Samuel McWilliam, under Col. Henry Jackson, Cont. Line.

Penna. Arch. 5th Ser. Vol. 3, p. 761. Penna. Arch. 2nd Ser. Vol. 10, p. 812.

PHILIP NAGLE

The Musketry Batt., Col. Saml. J. Atlee, private Philip Nagle living in Guilford Twp., Franklin Co., in 1819, aged 67. Capt. Robert Grey's Co., Red Bank, May 9, 1777. 1st Lieut., Thos. Johnston, of the Flying Camp, later Col. Thos. Johnston. Private Philip Neagle, discharged at Annapolis, in Franklin Co., 1819. Chambersburg, Penna.. Court Records, Deed Book 8, p. 269, Philip Nagle and wife Mary Barbara, late Barbara Smith, one of the daus. of John Smith of Washington Twp., decd., sell to Jacob Smith their right in the estate of their father John Smith 1809.

Penna. Arch. 5th Ser. Vol. 2, p. 484. 2nd Ser. Vol. 10, p. 282, 256.

PHILIP NOGLE

Served in the Tenth Penna. Regt., Cont., Line, Apr. 25, 1777-1781; resided in Franklin County in 1835, aged 74 years, a pensioner.

Penna. Arch. 2nd Ser. Vol. 10, p. 753.

JOHN NAVE

Served under Capt. Daniel Clapsaddle, 1780-81. Deeds show that Michael Nave of Dauphin Co., sold to Jacob Detwiler 340 ac. land in Letterkenny Twp., formerly of John Irwin, who sold to Samuel Culbertson, Sr., in 1760, who conveyed it to his son John Cumbertson, who in 1786 conveyed to John Nave and John Nave and Sarah, his wife, to Michael Nave.

Penna. Arch. 5th Ser. Vol. 6, p. 94, 97, 117.

WILLIAM NEALL

Served as private under Capt. William Findlay in 1778, and Capt. William Berryhill, 1780-81, in Antrim Twp. On March 13, 1799, William Neall of Westmoreland Co., Penna., sold to George Clarke of Franklin County, two tracts of land in Antrim Twp., "laid out" to James Scott by 2 warrants in 1762-1763. William Niell died Sept. 5, 1813, and is buried in Bethel Cemetery, Indiana Co., Penna., aged 77 yrs.

Penna. Arch. 5th Ser. Vol. 6, p. 73, 80, 102, 527, 530.

DAVID NEEL (NEIL)

Served as private under Capt. Noah Abraham 1777-79-80-81-82. He was of Fannett Twp., his will prob. May 24, 1810. He named: Dau. Mary wife of Andrew Strovick; Dau. Sarah Neel; Dau. Letitia, wife of Adam Greene; Dau. Rhoda, wife of Wm. McElheny; grandson David, son of John Neel; grandson David, son of David Neel; Sons David and John; Wife Mary; To Rhoda McElhany my bell cow, and twelve dollars.

Penna. Arch. 5th Ser. Vol. 6, p. 86, 121, 128, 141, 384, 393, 516.

JAMES NEELY

Served as a private 1777-79-80-81-82, under Capts. Noah Abraham and Patrick Jack. In the will of Isaac Patterson, yeoman, of Hamilton Twp., he names a dau. Martha wife of James Neely; also a dau. Margaret, wife of Wm. Neely. The will is dated 1783, prob. Sept., 1787.

Penna. Arch. 5th Ser. Vol. 6, p. 85, 296, 313, 383, 516.

ELIAB NEGLEY

Served under Capts. James Collier, Henry McKinney and Samuel Cochran, 1778-79-82. He was born in Lancaster Co., Penna., in 1746, died in Franklin County Oct. 8, 1825. His wife was

Barbara, dau., of Stephen Poorman, and is buried beside him in the Hawbaker Graveyard near Welsh Run. David Martin and wife Rosanna sold their tract of land to Eliab Negley in 1806 and Eliab sold in 1823 to his sons, Christian and Joseph. It was land held by Daniel Davis, who sold to Samuel Davis, Samuel selling to Robert Chambers, who with wife Nancy sold in 1802 to David Martin. Issue of Eliab and Barbara Negley: John; Jacob, b. 1776, mar. Mary Bowermaster; Joseph, b. 1781, mar. Elizabeth Strickler; Christian, b. 1791, mar. Barbara Newcomer.; Elizabeth, b. 1793; Barbara ———.

Penna. Arch. Ser. Vol. 7, p. 373, 378, 390, 1040, 1146.

JOHN NELSON

Of Letterkenny Twp., served with Capt. Samuel McCune, Aug. 13, 1776, at Phila., serving in 1778-81-82, under Capts. Patrick Jack and John McConnell. He occupied Pew No. 45, in the old Log Church at Rocky Spring, with George and James Matthews, Martha Allen and John Poak. It is probable that there was a connection with the family of George and Isabella Matthews. Thomas Stockton, b. 1709, d. May 31, 1795, wife Margaret Fleming. Of the issue, Isabella mar. ——— Neilson. Under deeds at Chambersburg, Apr. 1797, John Nelson and Isabel, his wife, of Letterkenny Twp., sell land situated in Letterkenny to Martin Nisle of Lancaster Co., Penna. In 1787 John Nelson had sold land in Hamilton Twp., to John Hager of Antrim Twp., John Nelson a witness. Tax records show John Nelson (Neilson) in Letterkenny Twp., 1778 to 1782, with 310 ac. land, horses and cattle, and in 1796, he had 337 acres, 2 Horses, 4 Cows, 2 Houses and 2 Barns, and Joseph Neilson under "Having no trades."

Penna. Arch. 5th Ser. Vol. 6, p. 29, 32, 302, 303, 587.

JOHN NELSON, JR.

Was in Service, 1777-80, with Capts. John McConnell and Patrick Jack. In May, 1787, John Nelson Jr., of Letterkenny Twp., and Margaret, his wife, sell land in Letterkenny Twp., to Andrew Fricker of Tulpehocken Twp., Berks Co., joining Chas. Cummins and James Mitchell.

Penna. Arch. 5th Ser. Vol. 6, p. 267, 372.

JOHN NILSON (NEILSON)

Is shown in Service, 1779-80-81-82, with Capt. Noah Abraham. This was undoubtedly the man who signed the petitions from Fannett Twp., but he does not appear under Taxables in 1796. The earliest marriages were by Rev. David Denny who went from Path Valley as pastor to the Falling Spring Church of Chambersburg, in 1801. Samuel McCammon and Martha Nelson, Apr. 9, 1795.

Penna. Arch. 5th Ser. Vol. 6, p. 85, 120, 127, 383.

WILLIAM NESBIT

Of Antrim Twp., served as pvt., 1780-81-82, under Capts. John Woods, James Poe, and under the First Call of Oct., 1777, with Lieut Daniel Smith. He was the son of Thomas and Jean Nesbit. In addition to the name of Wm. Nesbit, of Antrim Twp., Thomas Nesbit names Dau. Mary, who mar. Hugh McKee; Dau Frances who mar. Wm. Sloan; Dau. Susanna, who mar. James McKee; Dau. Martha, who mar. James Dixon. This will was dated Apr., 1783.

Penna. Arch. 5th Ser. Vol. 6, p. 76, 92, 104, 138, 522, 576, 583, 623.

FREDERICK NICHODEMUS

Was appointed by Council of Safety of Maryland, Sept. 26, 1776, 1st. Lieut. of Capt. Daniel Clapsaddle's Co., of Militia in Washington Co., Md. Frederick Nicodemus died Oct. 26, 1816, aged 83 yrs. 8 mos. His wife Margaret died March 15, 1815, aged 67 yrs. 2 mos. They are buried in Salem Church graveyard near Waynesboro, Penna. Frederick Nicodemus mar. Margaret Ripple, early German settlers at Hoover's Mill, Washington Twp., Penna., a founder of Salem Reformed Church. Frederick Nicodemus and Henry Miller, Elders, Christopher Adam and Conrad Nichodemus, Deacons. They are buried at Salem. Sons Conrad and John; daus. Susanna, Catherine, Elizabeth; dau. Magdalene, who mar. Peter Adam; Conrad mar. Margaret Hartel; Susanna b. 1781; John b. 1783, mar. Margaret Potter; Catherine b. 1787 mar. John Oellig; Elizabeth b. 1789.

Maryland Archives Vol. 12, p. 301.

WILLIAM NICHOLAS (NICKLES)

Was a private under Capt. Daniel Clapsaddle in 1780-81. He died intestate leaving a widow and issue 9. A dau. Sidney mar. James Monahan. Orphans' Court records, Chambersburg give in Vol. C, pp. 94, 99, 101, Oct., 1826, William Nichols, late of the State of Maryland, decd., died intestate in June last; widow Barbara and issue 9: Susanna mar. Mase Duloser (?); Sarah mar. Collosin Birley (?) Matthias Nickoles; Margaret mar. Conrad Humberg; John Nicholes; Henry Nicholes; Elizabeth Nicholes; Sidney and Hetty (minors); 227 acres land in Washington Twp., Franklin Co., Penna.

Penna. Arch. 5th Ser. Vol. 6, p. 93, 107, 116.

JAMES NICHOLSON

Served under Capts. John Rea and William Long, 1777, 78, 79, 80, 81.

Penna. Arch. 5th Ser. Vol. 6, p. 78, 105, 520, 524, 544, 585, 597.

JOHN NICHOLSON

Capt. John Alexander's Company, Sergt., John Nicholson, 7th Penna. Regt., Cont. Line. John Nicholson served as Sergeant in 7th Regt., Regular Troops, and 2nd Regt., from Mar. 15, 1777, to July, 1783, received a wound in the leg; since served 2 tours in Militia of Penna., against Indians, and received a wound in the head. He was a pensioner. It appears from the papers in the Rev. War pension claim, S. 40208, that John Nicholson enlisted in 1777 and served as a sergeant in Capt. John Alexander's company in the 7th Penna. Regt. He was in the battles of Brandywine, Germantown, Monmouth, Stony Point and Yorktown and served until the close of the war. He was allowed pension on his application executed April 4, 1818, aged sixty-three years. He stated that he was a resident of Greencastle, Franklin County, Penna., but at that time was in the District of Columbia. John Nicholson, a pensioner of the Rev. War, certificate No. 58, Penna. Agency, you are advised the last payment of pension covering the period from Sept., 4, 1819, to March 4, 1820, was made to Roland and Ford, attorneys for the pensioner, at Philadelphia, Penna., on June 3, 1820 Franklin Repository—Chambg., Dec. 22, 1802. Three tracts of land—595 ac. 16 perches, patrimonial lands of John and Samuel Nicholson. Same lands which Samuel Nicholson of Green Twp., and Jane, his wife, by indenture, 28th of Dec., 1793, conveyed to John Nicholson in fee simple. William Nicholson (father of said John Nicholson) by his last will dated 24th of Oct., 1785, devised to son John Nicholson in fee, 1/3 part one other 3rd part to Samuel Nicholson and wife Jean to Daniel Henderson. 1/3 to Matt. Duncan and wife Elizabeth (Nicholson) conveyed to James Duncan &c. Above tracts seized by Joseph Ball against Hannah Nicholson, widow of John Nicholson, William, Seth, John, James, Samuel, Joseph, Anna, Maria and Sarah Nicholson, heirs of John Nicholson, decd.

Penna. Arch. 2nd Ser. Vol. 10, p. 630. 5th Ser. Vol. 4, p. 531.

SAMUEL NICHOLSON

In 1791 Samuel Nicholson was taxed on five tracts of land; 360-80-100-300-85 acres; Horse 1; Cows 4; Saw mill 1; Chair 1;

Penna. Arch. 5th Ser. Vol. 6, p. 78, 105, 106, 544.

SAMUEL NICHOLSON

Served as a pvt., 1779-80-81, under Capt. John Rea. There were two (2) men of the name, distinguished as William's son, and Sam's son, both serving in Class 3 of Capt. John Rea's Company, Aug., 1780.

Penna. Arch. 5th Ser. Vol. 6, p. 78, 105, 106, 544.

WILLIAM NICHOLSON

Served under Capt. Pat. Jack, undated roll. William Nicholson of Letterkenny Township; wife Sarah; issue: John; Samuel; Elizabeth; will dated Oct., 1785; prob. 1788; Vol. A, p. 128, Chambersburg Court records.

Penna. Arch. 5th Ser. Vol. 6, p. 145.

GEORGE NIGH

Served under Capt. Wm. Berryhill, 1781. His will was dated Sept. 1821, prob. Oct., 1822. He names his wife Elizabeth; Dau. Catherine Mitchell; son Samuel and as Executor his son Samuel.

Penna. Arch. 5th Ser. Vol. 6, p. 101.

JACOB NIGH

Served 1777-82 as Corporal with Capt. James Poe.

Penna. Arch. 5th Ser. Vol. 6, p. 523, 571, 520.

JOHN NIGH

Served in 1781 under Capt. Wm. Berryhill, Cumb,. Co., Militia. He was of Antrim Twp., his will prob. 1806. Sons John and George; Daus.: Christina; Elizabeth; Dorothy's issue to Peter Wolf, 6, namely Catherine; Elizabeth; Daniel; Madlina; Christian; Peter. Elizabeth, wife of my son George, my riding bay mare. Estate into 6 equal shares: sons John; George; heirs of dau. Barbara; Christina; Elizabeth; and dau. Dorothy's children. Executors: son George, George Nigh my brother's son and John McD. Davidson. The above John Nigh was a farmer. At present it is not possible to determine whether the service given belongs to the Innkeeper, or to the above man.

Penna. Arch. 5th Ser. Vol. 6, p. 101.

JOHN NIGH, INNKEEPER

Letters of Admr., on the estate of John Nigh, Innkeeper, were granted May 15, 1807, to George Nigh and Robert Robison. In May, 1809, it is shown that John Nigh died intestate, leaving a widow Catherine and issue 6: Catherine mar. Jacob Sites; Elizabeth mar. Fredk. Hochlander; Christina mar. Geo. Kyner; John; George and Polly, (last two minors over 14 years). The will of the widow Catherine states she is "old and infirm," dated Jan. and Prob. May, 1830. Polly had become Mary McCutchen; Christina is not named; son John and family; son George; Grandchildren of son John: John; George; Catherine. Exrs.: Friend Samuel Nigh and John B. McLanahan. From the "Repository," May 12, 1807. The death of Mr. John Nigh Innkeeper, in Greencastle on the 1st inst.

WILLIAM NOBLE

Served 1778-1781, as private under Lieut., Col. William Butler; and later as sergeant in Col. Gibson's regiment. He was killed at St. Clair's defeat. Elizabeth, dau of Anne Howe, testified she married William Noble in Path Valley, Franklin County, Pennsylvania, in 1788. They were married by Rev. Samuel Dougal, a Presbyterian clergyman. After her marriage her husband enlisted at Carlisle, Penna., and marched under Col. George Gibson of 2nd Regt., of levies to fight the Indians. He was mortally wounded and died a few days after. She moved from Path Valley to Washington, Penna., and applied for pension May 27, 1844, aged 73. She again testifies in 1848. In 1844 James Noble testifies he is son of William Noble, deceased, and his widow Elizabeht Noble. There are two letters written by William Noble, Bedford, Penna., June 8, 1791, to his wife in Path Valley; and from Camp Fort Pitt, Aug. 4, 1791, to his mother-in-law, Mrs. Ann Howe, care of James Howe, Blacksmythe, Path Valley, Franklin Co., Penna., Bounty land approved, Mar. 26, 1813, to Elizabeth Noble and children, wift and children of William Noble, late a Sergeant in the Rev. War. 100 acres were granted. She was granted a pension of $80 per annum from Mar. 4, 1836. Penna. agency.

Penna. Arch. 5th Ser. Vol. 2, p. 106. 2nd Ser. Vol. 10, p. 530.

MICHAEL NOUSE

Is shown serving under Capt. Daniel Clapsaddler 1780-81-82, the command of Col. James Johnston, included in a Class Roll of the male white inhabitants of Capt. Clapsaddler's Co.

Penna. Arch. 5th Ser. Vol. p. 72, 94, 81.

THOMAS NEIL

Appears as a pvt., 1781-82, serving with Capt. John Hodge. In May, 1785, one Thos Neil, of Washington Co., Penna., sells tract of land in Antrim (later Washington) Twp., to John Redelsperger, of Franklin Co., Penna., for 20 pounds, No. 1906, on application at Phila., Nov. 18, 1766.

Penna. Arch. 5th Ser. Vol. 6, p. 418, 428, 436.

RICHARD O'KANE (O'CAIN)

April 4, 1741. Under this date Richard O'Kane was appointed a Justice of the Peace. John O'Cain of Guilford Twp., left a will in which he names "My brother Daniel O'Cain, his first son Richard my plantation;" To my sister's children; to Mary McClean; to Margaret McClean; and to my sister Mary Ramsey's son James Ramsey at end of 3 years. The executors were John Rannells of Antrim Twp.; Brother Daniel O'Cean. Dated. Jan. 13, 1751; prob. Feb. 8, 1752.

Penna. Arch 2nd Ser. Vol. 9, p. 789.

CAPTAIN JOHN ORBISON

Born March 27, 1750, died 1827, mar. Elizabeth Lloyd Feb. 6, 1781. He was the son of Thomas Orbison and wife Elizabeth Miller, early settlers on the Welsh Run. John Orbison was 1st Lieut. of a Company July 31, 1777, of which George Crawford was Captain, Hugh McKee 2nd Lieut., and William Flanagan, Ensign, a strictly Welsh Run group. This was repeated in May 14, 1778, —John Orbison served as Captain 1780-81-82. Some time after the War the family moved to Maryland, thence to Rockbridge Co., Va., and about 1806 near Pequea, Ohio; seven years later to near Troy, Ohio, where Capt. Orbison died, Nov. 22, 1827, aged 77 years, his wife dying in 1833. They had issue: (1) Thomas b. Feb. 3, 1782. (2) Henry b. Sept. 22, 1783. (3) David b. Dec. 21, 1785, d. Oct. 15, 1820. (4) Elizabeth b. Nov. 24, 1787, d. Sept. 1, 1821. (5) James b. Oct. 27, 1789, d. Sept. 5, 1791. (6) Julia L. b. Apr. 24, 1791, d. 1830. (7) John b. Dec. 3, 1793, d. Aug., 1820. (8) Nancy b. Oct. 6, 1797, d. Mar. 1799.

Penna. Arch. 5th Ser. Vol. 6, p. 261, 273, 293, 307, 367, 371, 376, 379.

JAMES ORBISON

Born 1757, served under Capt. Alexdr. Peebles. Family records state that William Orbison, born 1745, died in Flying Camp service. The will of Thomas Orbison (born about 1715, died March, 1779, near Welsh Run, Penna.) names children: William born 1745; Thomas born 1747; John born 1750, died 1827; Susanna, born 1752; Bethiah born 1755, mar. Robert Waddell; James born 1757. Issue of 2nd wife, Mary Kyle; Jean born July 5, 1766.

Penna. Arch. 5th Ser. Vol. 6. p. 389, 396. Biographical Annals Juniatta Valley. Carlisle, Penna. Court Records, Will Book C, p. 145.

ADAM OTT

Is shown Jan 30, 1776 as Second Lieut., later as First Lieut in the Fifth Penna. Continental Line, under Col. John Philip De Hass. He appears later as a pensioner, in Washington County, Md., where he and wife Juliana had born a son Frederick, July 11, 1780. The date is from St. John's Lutheran Church records of Hagerstown, and Adam Ott is shown to be aged 73 years on July 30, 1821, and to have died Aug 10, 1827, the Admr. of estate July 28, 1829. St. John's Lutheran Church, Hagerstown, Md: Jacob Ott and Katherine had George born May 10, 1777; Margaretha b. Oct. 17, 1779; Katharina b. Feb. 15, 1782; Elizabeth b. June 23, 1785; Juliana b. Jan. 9, 1790. John b. Oct. 29, 1793.—Jacob b. May 24, 1795. One Michael Ott left an estate in 1781, and Julian Ott's estate was administered in 1829. There are other Otts shown in Court records at Hagerstown, Md., and the name is found today in Mercersburg.

Penna. Arch. 5th Ser. Vol. 2, p. 75. Vol. 3, p. 34. 3rd Ser., Vol. 23, p. 547.

JOHN OVER (OBER)

Served as pvt., under Capt. Joseph Gear in 1778-79-83. He came to Franklin County, Penna., from Lancaster County, buying in 1785, 272 ac. land from Samuel Smith. A warrant was granted in 1770 to Wm. Holliday who sold in 1778 to Samuel Smith, name written OWVER. He d. intestate in 1793, leaving issue: Mary mar. Michael Swaggert; Catherine mar. Peter Witter; Fanny mar. Henry Cryder; Christian Ober (Dauphin Co., Penna.); Jacob Ober; Henry Ober; Barbara mar. Henry Christman; Elizabeth mar. John Flickinger. (See Over graveyard).

Penna. Arch. 5th Ser. Vol. 7, p. 613, 878, 898.

SAMUEL OWENS

Samuel Owens, John Piery and two others are named with James Smith May 28, 1765, all under the Command of the aforesaid James Smith, who is referred to as "late Lieut., in the Pennsylvania Service." James Smith and Samuel Owens hold themselves firmly bound unto Lieut. Charles Grant xxx the condition being "that we shall disperse immediately from this Post, without xxx assault to any Person or Persons." An old deed shows Samuel Owen, and wife Mary, dau. of Meseck James, of near Fort Loudon. The will of Ezekiel Owens, weaver, dated 1752, prob. 1761, names as Exrs., uncle Thos. Owens and Philip Davis; sisters; and names his 2 half-brothers Owen and Samuel Owens. June 17, 1761, Cairns Sterrett, William Morrison and William Marchall enter a Caveat against the Representatives of Samuel Owen, decd., obtaining a Patent for a Tract of 588 acres of Lands in Peters Twp., now Cumb. Co.; surveyed to said Owens, under warrant dated Aug. 31, 1738; they alledging they have since made a purchase of said land. Samuel Owens is shown with a Survey in "Little Cove" or what is now Warren Twp., Franklin County of 37 acres, 57 perches, No. 3132, March, 1767, with Enoch Williams as neighbor. In 1773 the "Widow Owen" is shown in the Little Cove. She had a store account with Samuel Findlay, as had Wm. Owens.

Penna. Arch. 1st Ser. Vol. 4, p. 220, 221, 245. 3rd Ser. Vol. 2, p. 252.

WILLIAM OWENS, HATTER

Is shown serving as a pvt., in 1782, with Capt. Terrence Campbell, Command of Col. James Johnston. One Wm. Owens served in the Cont. Line from Westmoreland Co., Penna. Thomas Owens, pvt., in the Cont. Line, was living in Union District, S. C., on March 5, 1819, a Pennsylvanian.

Penna. Arch. 5th Ser. Vol. 6, p. 121.

ARTHUR PARK

Deeds show an Arthur Park of Shippensburg, Wheelright, who for 25lbs., sells to Robert Peebles, blacksmith, land in Lurgan Twp., Apr. 22, 1763. In 1825, Power of Attorney granted Hugh Wiley of Nicholas Co., Ky., by heirs of their uncle Wm. Wiley: Arthur Parks and wife Isabella; James McAnulty and wife Margaret; John and William Wiley appeared in Randolph Co., Ill. Kaskaskia Court, Sept. 19, 1825.

DAVID PARKS

Was a private under Capts. William Findley, John Jack and Daniel Clapsaddler, 1778-80-81. In 1787, David Parks of Dublin Twp., Bedford Co., Penna., sells to Jacob Hollinger in Washington Twp. Franklin Co., Penna., the 1/3 part of a Survey on which he had received 2 lbs.

Penna. Arch 5th Ser. Vol. 6, p. 72, 94, 117, 527, 530, 599.

GERARD PENDERGRASS

The petition of Gerard Pendergrass to Governor Penn, Phila., Oct. 10, 1766. He states he is of the Town of Bedford, Co. of Cumb., yeoman, that in the year 1752 he settled on the very land on which the Town of Bedford now is by virtue of your Honor's Warrant laid out; at his own proper cost and expense, did erect and build, a good and substantial round Log house, of 24 feet square well shingled and had cleared and enfenced 40 to 50 acres land. In the year 1755 he was obliged to fly before the Indian enemy xxx. That the King's Generals made the Fort Bedford on your Petitioners Improvements and an Inclosure for pasturing Horses and Cattle. He claims under that ancient and well known Right of Occupancy and Improvement xx they are intitled to the quiet possession of their Improvements, &c., &c.

Signed: Gerard Pendergrass
        Anne Pendergrass

Penna. Arch. 2nd Ser. Vol. 7, p. 306.

JAMES PARK

Was a private under Capt. Daniel Clapsaddler, 1780-81. In 1787 James Parks and wife Frances of Washington Twp., sell to John Steinman of same, land on which James Parks now lives, 113 ac. 146 pch., under 2 Proprietary warrants, one to Jacob Beesacker in 1750, who sold to Abel John. In 1788 James Parks of Peters Twp., yeoman, to David Parks of same, land from James Galbreath to Samuel White in 1771, who in 1777 sold to Henry Helm, who in 1787 sold to James Parks, who now sells for 100 lbs, 50 acres of above tract. In 1794 David Parks of Peters Twp., sells to James Parks of same, the above tract with James Buchman as witness. In 1794, James Parks of Peters Twp., and wife Frances, sell to Rev. Wm. Speer and James Buchanan, 275½ acres, for 1239 lbs, 15 shillings, it being part of the James Galbreath tract. In 1790 James Parks was taxed on Horses, Cows and 100 acres land in Peters Twp. James Parks had Thomas baptized at Mercersburg, Penna., Oct. 16, 1789 and a child baptized May 3, 1791. In 1801, John Linton and John Agnew mar. Ann Park and Elizabeth Park at the same time in Greencastle, Penna.

Penna. Arch. 5th Ser. Vol. 6, p. 71, 94, 117.

JAMES PARKS

Served as private under Capts. Wm. Strain and John Love, 1780-81.

Penna. Arch. 5th Ser. Vol. 6, p. 181, 198, 398.

JAMES PARKS

Served under Capt. Noah Abraham, 1777. In 1800 James Park and wife Rebecca of Fannettsburg to John Long of same; part of Lot No. 37 in the town of Fannettsburg, Penna.

Penna. Arch. 5th Ser. Vol. 6, p. 516.

JOHN PARKS

Is shown with Path Valley men, in 1781.
Penna. Arch. 5th Ser. Vol. 6, p. 407.

JOHN, JAMES, AND ROBERT PARKS

Served in Cont. Line in Wash. Co., Penna.
Penna. Arch. 5th Ser. Vol. 4, p. 723.

JOHN PARK

Served under Capt. Daniel Clapsaddler, 1780-81. In 1802 John Parks and wife Isabells of Washington Twp., sell a tract of land to Philip Reed for 500 lbs., warrant to Jacob Pesecker, 18 ac. 77 perches. They also sell to Michael Miller, 41 ac. 152 perches, also a Jacob Peesecker grant. One John Parks is known to have mar. Isabella McMullen, and one Isabella McMullen was admitted to the Presby Ch. of Mercersburg in 1772, and her sisters Catherine, Margaret and Jean later. An early John Park and wife Isabella are lying in an old Carlisle graveyard.

Penna. Arch. 5th Ser. Vol. 6, p. 94, 116.

JOSEPH PARKS

Served as private under Capt. Patrick Jack, 1778-79.

Penna. Arch. 5th Ser. Vol. 6, p. 32, 64, 145, 147.

ROBERT PARK

Served as private under Capt. John McConnell, 1780-81. In 1796 one Robert Parks of Antrim Twp., Storekeeper, was taxed with 2 Houses, 2 Lotts, 1 Horse and 1 Cow, and in 1799 with a House, Horse and Cow.

Penna. Arch. 5th Ser. Vol. 6, p. 268, 281, 303.

ROBERT AND SAMUEL PARKS

Were soldiers in the Cont. Line, entitled to Depreciation Pay, from Cumb. Co., Penna.

Penna. Arch. 5th Ser. Vol. 4, p. 300, 636.

SAMUEL PARKS

Was a private under Capts. Joseph Culbertson, Samuel Patton and William Huston, 1778-80-81-82.

Penna. Arch. 5th Ser. Vol. 6, p. 264, 311, 381, 643.

JOHN PARKER

Served with Capt. Samuel Patton the Spring and Summer of 1779, on the Frontiers, in Col. Wm. Chambers Battalion.

Penna. Arch. 5th Ser. Vol. 6, p. 601, 610.

JAMES PARKHILL

Private, Penna. Militia, was 83 years of age in 1833, and a pensioner. He was of Peters Twp., and his will prob. Dec. 4, 1838, names children: James; John; Andrew; Samuel; Nancy. His son John Parkhill mar. Susanna, dau. of John McCullough and his 2nd wife Elizabeth Cunningham.

Penna. Arch. 3rd Ser. Vol. 13, p. 530.

JOHN PASCO

Was a private 1781-82, under Capt. Thos. Askey. His estate was administered Nov. 27, 1802, by Catherine Pasco. The following marriages were by the Rev. A. A. McGinley of Fannet Twp.; Michael Pasco and R. Hudson—1807; J. Pasco and Polly Phetty 1810. In the will of Barnabas Clark of Fannett Twp., prob. 1821, he names as a legatee, Catherine Pasco, widow, and others.

Penna. Arch. 5th Ser. Vol. 6, p. 132, 424, 442.

JAMES PATTERSON

Served as private under Capts. Maclay, Culbertson and McConnell, 1780-81-82. He was probably a son of Isaac Patterson who died about 1787. James Patterson names his wife; Son Robert; Dau. Mary; Daus.: Sarah; Ann; Hannah; Son Francis G.; Grandau Jean White, "of my dau. Jean, decd." David Maclay an Executor and George Weir a witness, in 1811. In 1815, Margaret, widow of above James Patterson, states that dau. Mary had mar. ———— Sterrett, other daughters then unmarried. They were of Lurgan Twp.

Penna. Arch. 5th Ser. Vol. 6, p. 148, 150, 264, 290, 310.

JOHN PATTERSON

Served 1782, under Capt. Thos. Johnston.
Penna. Arch. 5th Ser. Vol. 6, p. 130.

JOSEPH PATTERSON

Served as First Lieut., May, 1778, under Capt. James Poe. Undoubtedly there was a Patterson line in Antrim Twp., during the period of the Revolution.

Penna. Arch. 5th Ser. Vol. 6, p. 532.

NICHOLAS PATTERSON

Served 1782, under Capt. John McConnell. He appears to be a grandson of Nicholas Patterson and wife Martha of Letterkenny Twp. In 1786 he was listed in Letterkenny Twp., as a Captain.

Penna. Arch. 5th Ser. Vol. 6, p. 309.

SOLOMON PATTERSON

Served 1782, under Capt. John McConnell, and was a son of Nicholas and Martha Patterson.
Penna. Arch. 5th Ser. Vol. 6, p. 309.

THOMAS PATTERSON

Served 1781-82, under Capts. John McConnell and Joseph Culbertson.
Penna. Arch. 5th Ser. Vol. 6, p. 290, 309.

THOMAS PATTERSON

Served 1782, under Capt. Thos. Johnston. John Patterson served in the same Company. One Richard Keene sold land in Antrim Twp., Apr. 4, 1783, to Thos. Patterson for 250 lbs. Thomas Patterson and wife Elizabeth, Feb. 10, 1786, sold the tract to Robert and John Clugston.

Penna. Arch. 5th Ser. Vol. 6, p. 130.

WILLIAM PATTERSON

Served under Capt. Wm. Findlay, 1778, as an Ensign, and several years with Capt. Saml. Patten. On the Frontiers of Bedford and Westmoreland Co., as a Ranger in 1779, and in service 1780-81.

Penna. Arch. 5th Ser. Vol. 6, p. 277, 286, 380, 534, 602, 610.

JAMES PATTON

Served as Captain in the 4th Batt. Cumb. Co. Militia, under Col. Samuel Culbertson 1777-78-80. His will probated 1821, names: Son Matthew; Dau. Elizabeth McCall; Dau. Margaret White; Dau. Mary McKinstry; Dau. Rebecca Patton; The wife of James Patton was Mary Newell.

Penna. Arch. 5th Ser. Vol. 6, p. 262, 271, 368, 377, 598.

JOHN PATTON

Served 1779 under Capt. Patrick Jack, and may have been a son of Matthew Patton. The sons of the pioneer Matthew were: Samuel; Robert; John; Matthew; Thomas.

Penna. Arch. 5th Ser. Vol. 6, p. 64.

JOSEPH PATTON

Served under Capts. Wm. Long, John Woods and James Poe, as a First Lieut. in 1777-80-82.
Penna. Arch. 5th Ser. Vol. 6, p. 91, 138, 519, 524, 525, 556, 575, 582.

MATTHEW PATTEN

The petition of Matthew Patten of Conegocheague, was presented to the House and read, setting forth, that in the year 1755, upon an Incursion of the Indian Enemy into the inhabited Parts of the Province being obliged to abandon his Dwelling, and retire with his Family to a neighboring Fort, for the Preservation of their Lives, the next Day his said Dwelling-house and Barn were burnt down by the Indians; and that some time after an Order being issued by the Government for erecting a Fort, on or near, the spot, where the Petitioner's late Dwelling stood, his Plantation had suffered, during the Building of said Fort, very great Damages, by the Destruction of his Fences, and Loss of several Stacks of Grain, besides the large Quantities of Timber cut from thence for the use of the Fort; by means whereof he hath ever since been kept from his said Plantation, to the great Inconvenience, Impoverishment and Distress of his poor Family; and praying such Relief in the Premises, as the House may think due to him. Sept. 19, 1759, John Holliday, for his and his two Sons, accounts of Sundries Building Fort Loudon. March 1, 1759, Matthew Patten attending the House, pursuant to order, in support of his Petition, answered such Questions xx Col. Armstrong answered such questions, the petitioner of Matthew Patten.

Penna. Arch. 8th Ser. Vol. 6, p. 4929. p. 5061. p. 4932.

ROBERT PATTON

Of Antrim Twp., served 1780-81-82, under Capts. John Woods and James Poe.
Penna. Arch. 5th Ser. Vol. 6, p. 91, 104, 138, 576, 583.

ROBERT PATTON

Son of the pioneer Matthew Patton and wife Elizabeth served as a private, 1778-80-81-82, under Capt. Samuel Patton, his brother. Robert Patton and Elizabeth Elder were mar. by Rev. John King,

May 4, 1775. In the will of John Patton of Peters Twp., (July, 1767) he names a wife Susanna and son William, also a dau. Mary Johnson. His "Buckskin Britches to nephew Robert Patton." To "Abigail Tassey a Grey mare." This John Patton was probably a brother to Matthew of the Fort, and the son William may have gone South.
Penna. Arch. 5th Ser. Vol. 6, p. 279, 287, 375, 312.

NATHANIEL PAUL
Served as a private under Capt. Thomas Askey in 1779-81-82. He died leaving a wife Mary; a son William (eldest son); Mary mar. to John Kelley; George; Samuel; Margaret mar. to Nehemiah Kilgore, of full age, and Jane, aged 20 yrs., and upwards. He was of Fannett Twp., and his Admr., was dated April 7, 1795. A deed shows John Kelly and wife Mary of Huntingdon, Penna., and Jean Paul, single woman, of Fannett twp., selling land to James Johnston in 1800.
Penna. Arch. 5th Ser. Vol. 6, p. 61, 131, 409, 423, 441.

JAMES PAXTON
Is shown in service, 1781-82, under Capt. Patrick Jack. He was a miller and was in that part of Southampton Twp., which was taken from Lurgan Twp. In the will of James Paxton dated and prob. 1810, he gives to "dear wife Jane three hundred dollars and to receive the interest of $2500;" the same amount to his son-in-law the Rev. James Ramsey, as trustee, the interest of which was to be paid to son Patrick; the interest of $900 to be paid to the nearest congregation of Associate Presbyterian belonging to the Assoc. Synod of North America, where any of my children may reside xxx fund for young Students of the Assoc. Synod the yearly sum of $18; Rev. James Ramsey, my son-in-law, of the Assoc. Church at Chartiers, Washington Co., Md.; residue to my daughters: Margaret; Martha; Esther; Jane; Mary; Anne; Rebekah; Euphemia; brother Andrew Paxton; brother-in-law Joseph Alexander; Exrs.: Marshall Mains; John Thompson; Andrew Thompson. The above James Paxton probably mar. the dau. of Patrick Alexander.
Penna. Arch. 5th Ser. Vol. 6, p. 292, 296, 313, 419, 438.

JOHN PAXTON
Served with Capts. Wm. Strain and Alexander Peebles, 1779-80-82.
Penna. Arch. 5th Ser. Vol. 6, p. 58, 398, 430.

NATHANIEL PAXTON
Appears in service in 1779, with Capt. James Young.
Penna. Arch. 5th Ser. Vol. 6, p. 548.

RICHARD PAXTON
Was in service, 1782, under Capt. John Hodge.
Penna. Arch. 5th Ser. Vol. 6, p. 437.

THOMAS PAXTON
Served in 1780-82, under Capt. Wm. Strain. He was a taxable in Lurgan Twp.
Penna. Arch. 5th Ser. Vol. 6, p. 390, 430.

PATRICK PEACE
Served as a pvt. in 1780, under Capt. William Smith, apparently a "bird of passage."
Penna. Arch. 5th Ser. Vol. 6. p. 276.

ABRAHAM PEACEACRE
Served as private under Capt. Daniel Clapsaddler, 1780-81. His estate was administered, 1795; he left a widow Elizabeht and issue: Elizabeth mar. Geo. Delnog; Hannah mar. Adam Horner; Jacob, David, Abram, Mary, Nicholas, Daniel, Catherine, Frederick.
Penna. Arch. 5th Ser. Vol. 6, p. 93, 107, 116. Ser. Vol. 6, p. 93, 107, 116.

ROBERT PEEBLES
Shown as Colonel of Militia, July, 1776. He is shown as First Lieut. 4th Penna. Regt. Cont. Line; continuous service, and transferred to the Third, Jan. 1st, 1783. He was entitled to Depreciation pay, and received it in cash at Carlisle, with others of the 4th Penna. Line, amount 128 lbs. His will shows he received 3 military Land grants. He names wife Sarah, and brother George; To his son Isaac he willed 2 tracts known in plots as Nos. 26 and 35, 100 acres in each, situate in Section 3 twp. 11 Second and Range 8 of the Military Dist. northwest of the river Ohio. To son Robert tract of land No. in the draft of same 826, situate in Mercer Co., the Shenango creek running through the same. To son John a tract in Erie Co., Penna., marked on plot of same No. 2129. Residue to six children: Arabella Peebles; Isaac Peebles; Robert Peebles; Sarah Peebles; Eliza wife of Hugh Peebles. This will was prob. May 12, 1813.
Penna. Arch. 5th Ser. Vol. 3, p. 207, 208, 218, 219, 228, 229, 241, 294. Vol. 2, p. 980, 1021, 1068, 1093. Vol. 6, p. 5.

ROBERT PEEBLES
Was in service as a private, 1777-78-81, with Capts. Alexdr. Peebles and Samuel Patton—undated rolls. The above man is probably "Robert of Southampton Twp., farmer" whose will was dated 1808, prob. Aug., 1809, giving to son Robert 150 acres of land, 1 full share of all my personal estate, also all my law books; other lands to be sold after son John comes to the age of twenty-one years; proceeds to sons Hugh, James, and

John; sons Robert, Hugh, James and John, my tract of land in Cumb. Co., South Mountain; dau. Sarah Donald 50 lbs.; grandau. Nancy Piper 10 lbs.; grandson Robert Porter a small field; son James to learn some mechanical trade; son John to be furnished with sufficient means to qualify him for a doctor of Physic; Exrs.: son Robert and friends James Lowery, Esq., and Thos. Cummins. A Codicil directs sons Hugh, James, John to give son Robert 100 lbs., out of their shares of the estate. In the will of Benj. Allsworth, 1782-84, he names, among others, a dau. Jane, wife of Robert Peebles.

Penna. Arch. 5th Ser. Vol. 6, p. 26, 34, 51, 54, 134, 143, 286.

WILLIAM PEEBLES

Penna. Rifle Regt., Col. Samuel Miles. William Peebles appointed Captain from Cumb. Co., March 9, 1776; captured Aug. 27, 1776; died in 1776. 2nd Batt. Rifle Regt., Capt. Wm. Peebles, Dead Prisoner. Col. Samuel Miles was also a prisoner.

Penna. Arch. 5th Ser. Vol. 2, p. 356-450.

JAMES PEEL

Served as private under Capt. Wm. Strain, 1780-82. An Admr., of his estate is shown in Orphans' Court, 1812. On October 13, 1813, Frederick, a son of James Peal, late of Southampton Twp., stated that his father, James Peal,, died intestate Feb., 1812, leaving a widow Catherine (Carr) and issue seven children: James; John; Barnhart; Jacob; Catherine wife of Oliver Reeves, now decd.; Samuel; and Frederick, the petitioner. Deeds show that Samuel Blythe had sold land in Franklin Co., to James Peal. Of the above, John mar. Mary McClintock; Bernard mar. Catherine Newman; Jacob mar. Elizabeth; Frederick; Samuel mar. Isabel Nesbit.

Penna. Arch. 5th Ser. Vol. 6, p. 143, 391, 431.

HENRY PENSINGER

Private, 4th Penna., Col. Anthony Wayne, wounded at Three Rivers and lost his leg at Ticonderoga from intense cold, in 1777. In Franklin County, 1820, aged 60 yrs. The will of Henry Pensinger of Montgomery Twp., was probated Apr. 23, 1821. He speaks of eleven children, but names the following only: Henry; Jacob; Polly mar. John Myers; Caty mar. Peter Gingry; Rosanna mar. Michael Dewald. (See Pension record of Michael Dewalt).

Penna. Arch 5th Ser. Vol. 2, p. 154.

DAVID PERRY

On Oct. ye 14th, 1777, David Parry signed the Oath of Fidelity before Hugh Martin, Esq., Westmoreland Co., Penna. He was a son of Samuel and Annas Perry, early settlers near Mercersburg, and who later removed to Westmoreland Co., Penna. David Perry mar. Sarah Dunlop and is said by descendants to have taken, with five other men, the first horses and cattle down the river into Kentucky.

Penna. Arch. 2nd Ser. Vol. 3, p. 31.

JAMES PERRY

Served as Sub-Lieutenant March 21, 1777, to June 21, 1780, Westmoreland Co., Penna. He and Edward Cook, both from Franklin County, were the Committee from Westmoreland Co., Penna., to the Provincial Conference, held at Carpenter's Hall, Philadelphia, June 18, 1775. James Perry was a Delegate to the Convention of 1776, from Westmoreland and he is also shown as a Sub-Lieut. in the Cont. Line. The will of John McMasters of Allegheny Co., names his niece Rebecca Perry and his beloved sister-in-law, Hannah, wife of James Perry, Merchant of Charlestown.

Penna. Arch. 2nd Ser. Vol. 3, p. 594, 596, 682.

JOHN PERRY

Commissioner of Purchases, Aug. 31, 1781, of the County of Westmoreland, Penna. John Perry mar. Violet Moore.

Penna. Arch. 2nd Ser. Vol. 3, p. 683.

SAMUEL PEARY

Col. John Armstrong to Gov. Denny, Nov. 8, 1756,—"a certain Samuel Peary left McDowell's Fort on Wed. afternoon, only going to put his horse to pasture xxx and had with him a little boy xx neither returning that night, men were sent from the Fort who found said Peary scalped and his body covered with leaves. In 1769, his widow Annas (Annis) Perry, with sons Samuel and David, were living within the bounds of the "Upper West Conococheague" Church, between Mercersburg and Cove Gap. A Deed in June, 1773, shows Annas Perry and her sons selling the land to Samuel Smith, Taylor, of same Township. The sons were: William; John; James; Samuel and David. The maiden name of Annas was Watson and her sons gave service in Western Penna.

Penna. Arch 1st Ser. Vol. —— p. 40.

WILLIAM PERRY

Appears in 1776, as a private with Col. John Proctor, later as Captain William Perry; as Sheriff, Nov. 18, 1777 and Nov. 28, 1786; as Treasurer of Westmoreland Co., and was Collector of Excise, Jan., 1778. He was a Lieut. in the Cont. Line. A History of Westmoreland Co., Penna., confirms the above records from Penna. Archives. One Robert McConnell applied for a pension in West-

moreland County, to William Perry, treasurer of said County.
Penna. Arch. 2nd Ser. Vol. 14, p. 689. 2nd Ser. Vol. 3, p. 680, 681. Vol. 4, p. 589.

JAMES PETTIGREW

New 11th Penna., from Ensign, retired 1781. Resided at Shippensburg, Dec. 24, 1831, aged 80 yrs. Tombstone shows, "a member of Associate Reformed 50 years." Mrs. Catherine Pettigrew died Oct. 26, 1823, in 38th year. "All bodies removed from Asso. Ref. Pres. Graveyard, Penn St. Shippensburg, Penna." Franklin Repository, Dec. 27, 1831. Died Saturday last at the residence of Philip Winter, Mr. James Pettigrew formerly of Cumberland County. Records of Rev. John Casper Stoever show the marriage of James Pettigrew to Jane Ainsworth, Sept. 6, 1762 at Hanover by license. James Pettigrew of Chambersburg left a will dated Nov. and prob. Dec., 1831, naming friend Philip Winters and his wife Elizabeth Winters; To the Seminary at Pittsburg of the Assoc. Ref. Church $100 for educating young men to the ministry to be paid to Rev. Alex. Sharp who is to apply it to said purpose. Friend Mrs. Jane Hays, wife of Samuel. Exr: Archbd. Fleming of Chambersburg. The National Genealog. Society Quarterly, Dec., 1937, p. 130,—under 1824, Feb. 7, is given the following: Died the 19th in Washington D. C. John Erskine, printer, aged 40, and also James Pettigrew, printer and pres. of the Columbia Typographical Society.

Penna. Arch. 5th Ser. Vol. 3, p. 643. 5th Ser. Vol. 2, p. 975.

CASPER PHILEY

Private 1st Penna. Cont. Line. In 1796, (Gasper) Casper Phily is shown as a Taxable in Montgomery Twp., with 150 acres land, 1 house and 4 acres, 1 Horse, 1 cow. Henry Phily, Sr., and Jr., also appear with land, horses and cows. Casper Phyly and wife Margaret of Montgomery Twp., sell to James Stephenson, of Washington Co., Md., the above land for 125 lbs. on Apr. 2, 1798. Official Roster Rev. Soldiers of Ohio, gives: "Casper Phyly died March 28, 1849, aged 86 years. Margaret, wife of Casper Phyley died March 19, 1836, aged 60 years.

Penna. Arch. 5th Ser. Vol. 2, p. 755.

EAVEN PHILLIPS, PATRIOT

Bedford County, I do hereby certify that Eaven Phillips Hath voluntarily taken and subscribed the Oath of Allegiance and Fidelity, as directed by an Act of General Assembly of Pennsylvania, passed the 13th day of June, A. D. 1777. Witness my hand and Seal the 18th Day of May A. D. 1778. No. 15K—Thomas Paxton Baltimore: Printed by M. K. Goddard. SEAL. He lived and died in Warren Twp. Franklin Co., Penna. Evan Phillips estate appraised 1787, his widow Catherine died prior to Feb. 23, 1791. They had issue: Lettie mar. Owen Davis, March 5, 1772. Martha mar. Thos. Mills; Hannah mar. John Clark; Sarah; Joshua mar. Ann Mardis, March 26, 1787. Evan killed in Rev. War. The Sureties on the estate of Evan Phillips were: Thomas Harrod; Thos. Davies; Theopeles Belle; John Owens; Thomas John; Joshua Phillips. Joshua Phillips b. July, 1763 in Va. died Oct. 22, 1849, mar. Ann Mardis, b. Feb. 21, 1771, d. Apr. 20, 1850. Issue: Catherine b. June 4, 1788; Eleanor b. June 2, 1791 mar. Jacob John; Thomas b. Sept. 6, 1793. Sarah b. Oct. 29, 1795, unmar. Elizabeth b. March 2, 1798 (Acres); Evan b. Apr. 9, 1802; William b. Sept. 28, 1804. Penna. Magazine, Vol. 21, p. 419. Owen Davis mar. Letitia Phillips, March 5, 1772; both families came from Wales about 1754 (?) settled in Little Cove, Penna., (Now Warren Twp., Franklin Co., Penna.) Under early Pennsylvanians in Franklin Co., Ohio; Philo Hopkins Ilmstead, born in Conn. mar. in 1817 Miss Sarah Phillips of Mercersburg, Penna. A prominent family in Columbus for many years.

PETER PICKING, PENSIONER

In Deed Book Vol. 5, p. 11, Peter Pinckney, in 1800, now of the County of Franklin, for $200, sells to Philip Foust xx two Stocking Looms, one other Loom and Tacklings, a bed and bedding one Chest, Two Iron Potts, Three Wooden Buckets, two Cheers, three Pewter Basons, two Pewter Plates, eight plates, eight spoons, one table, one frying pann, one cow, one heiffer, one spinning wheel, one Bedstead. Under Taxables of 1804, Peter Pinkney appears as a Stocking weaver in Lurgan Twp., and in 1817, Peter Picking buys land in the County of Franklin. Orphans' Court records, in 1835, state that Peter Picking, late of Hamilton Twp., died intestate in May last, leaving a widow Mary and five minor children: Susanna; Jesse; Jacob; Peter; Barney. The will of Andrew Coover of Hamilton Twp., 1849, names a dau. Violetta as the wife of Jacob Picking. In the Account Book of "Squire" Mathias Nead, Peter Picking is shown with suits against Joseph and John Pensinger. The Cashtown Graveyard has several stones to Pickings and the name continued in the County for a number of years.

WILLIAM PIPER

Served in 1780-81 with Capt. Samuel Patton. William Piper b. Oct. 31, 1735 in Cumberland Co., Penna., mar. Dec. 29, 1757, Sarah McDowell, the marriage being recorded under St. James Prot. Episcopal church of Lancaster Aug. 15, 1806. Letters of Admr., on the estate of William Piper granted unto James Irwin. The McDowell family fled during the Indian forays which explains the above marriage at Lancaster. William Piper, a captain in Col. Clayton's regiment in 1763-64, served in Col. Boquet's Expedition. In 1768 he settled on the West Branch of the Susquehanna, on a grant from the Province for his services in the French and Indian War. He died in Peters Twp., leaving a widow Sarah who died Sept. 5, 1805, and a dau. Margaret (known as Peggy Piper) who mar. 1st Wm. Smith and mar. 2nd James Irwin. William Smith and Margaret Piper had one daughter, Sarah who mar. John Brownson. By her 2nd marriage to James Irwin she had issue eight children.

Penna. Arch. 5th Ser. Vol. 6, p. 277, 286. Penna. Arch. 5th Ser. Vol. 1, p. 329, 337. Biographical Annals of Franklin Co., Penna., p. 84.

CHRISTIAN PLOUGH

Was in Service, 1779-81-82, in Lancaster Co., Penna., with Capt. Robert McKee, Col. Alexander Lowrey. Coming from Lancaster Co., Penna., they bought land in 1804 in Franklin County, and are buried in Salem Graveyard, near Rocky Spring. Christian Plough died Apr. 18, 1836, aged 73 years, 6 months, 17 days. His wife, Barbara Plough died Apr. 15, 1863, aged 88 years, 29 days. They had issue: (1)Henry mar. Mary Bosserman; (2) Mary mar. David Bechtel; (3) Barbara mar. John Grove; (4) Nancy, unmarried, in 1889; (5) Christian mar. Elizabeth Sorber; (6) Peter mar. Mary Johns of Lancaster County, Penna. (7) Ephriam mar. Cassie Stauffer; (8) Jacob mar. Mary Rife; (9) John; (10) David; (11) Daniel mar. Hannah Stouffer.

Penna. Arch. 5th Ser. Vol. 7, p. 221, 732, 767.

JOHN PLUMMER

Of Chambersburg, served as private under Capts. James Young and Terrence Campbell, 1780-81-82. Orphans' Court gives his children as minors, Elizabeth aged 14 years and upwards and Margaret; John; Thomas and Ann as minors in 1804.

Penna. Arch. 5th Ser. Vol. 6, p. 82, 110, 126.

SAMUEL POLAND

The Bureau of Pensions and General Accounting Office gives this: Samuel Poland (pensioned Pollard) S.40272, Rev. War enlisted in Shippensburg, Penna., pensioned while living in Montgomery Twp., Franklin Co., Penna. The last payment of pension covered Sept. 4, 1821, to March 4, 1822, made to Robert McKinstry at Phila., Apr. 3, 1822, as Atty. for pesioner. The Ledger of "Squire" McKinstry, Mercersburg, 1817-1820, shows Samuel Poland receiving a "Pention" of $20 for 1/2 year. From a descendant in Upper Sandusky, Ohio is this: Samuel Poland, born in Lancaster Co., Penna., in 1750, died near Greencastle, Penna., in 1822. He was twice married, his first wife being Margaret Ullinger. A son John Poland was born 1796, died 1865, was mar. to Rachel Cookson and had issue 3 sons, 3 daughters: Daniel; Samuel; Thomas; Hannah; Sabina; Caroline. Hannah mar. Jacob Stewart. Samuel Poland enlisted, 1776; Col. Moses Hazen; Captains Herron, John Tomson, ———— Muncher, Samuel Loyd. Battles engaged in, wounded in battle of Brandywine; Germantown, Siege of York. At time of application (1818), he was aged 68 years.

Penna. Arch. 5th Ser. Vol. 4, p. 531. Vol. 3, p. 780.

JOHN POMEROY

From the History of the Pomeroy Family, the first settler in Franklin Co., was George Pomeroy, whose wife was Margaret Galloway. They had a son John Pomeroy who went to Westmoreland County, Penna., where he became Lieut. Colonel of the First Batt. Westmoreland County Associators. He took command at Fort Ligonier, Oct., 1777, and in Apr., 1781, Col. Archbd. Lochry reported that he had just returned from burying a man, scalped and killed at Col. Pomeroy's house. He was one of the Commissioners to locate a County seat for Westmoreland County and was also a Justice of the Peace. He mar. Hannah Graham, dau of Francis and Mary Graham. Their issue appear as follows: (1) Francis went to Wooster, Ohio,—wife Margaret; (2) John removed to Mercer where he mar. Jane Porter; (3) George went to Wooster, Ohio,—wife Jenny; (4) Thomas went to Wooster, Ohio,—wife Anny; (5) Margaret; (6) Mary mar. James Gibson. John Pomeroy is buried in Salem Cemetery, Westmoreland County and his stone shows he died, Feb. 16, 1809, aged 64 yrs. Oct. 31, 1777, This day Lieut. Col. Pomeroy came to take Command of the Garrison xx Col. Pomeroy demanded from me the Continental Salt to have it in his own keeping xx Col. John Pomeroy, a prominent man in Indian affairs during all these times (1781). Col. Lochry to Col. Brodhead, Apr. 2, 1781: "I am just returned from burying a man killed and scalped by the Indians at Col. Pomeroy's house, one other man is missing and all Pomroy's effects carried off." The Pomroy Blockhouse was about a mile from Barr's Fort.

Penna. Arch. 5th Ser. Vol. 4, p. 452, 753. Caldwell's Hist. of Indiana Co., Penna., p. 103, 104. Frontier Forst of West, Penna., p. 243, 244, 286, 352, 354, 355, 371.

THOMAS PUMROY

Served as private under Capt. Charles McClay and under Capt. Isaac Miller 1782, also undated rolls. It is stated that his first wife and two children were killed by Indians. His 2nd wife was Mary Graham, born 1747, died 1815. The will of Thos. Pumroy of Lurgan Twp., was prob. Sept. 9, 1803. He names wife Mary; son Charles to have land, to enjoy full benefits until son James is 21, which will be in Feb. 1810; son Isaac; dau. Margaret Adams, wife of John Adams; Dau. Elizabeth Pumroy; Eldest son John; son Francis of Kentucky; Dau. Mary wife of John Caldwell of Ky.; sons George and Joseph of Kentucky; Grandson Thos. Pumroy, son of above John; The historian of the family states that including Thos. and Mary Pomeroy, five generations are buried at Middle Spring graveyard.

Penna. Arch. 5th Ser. Vol. 6, p. 148, 150, 427, 434, 449.

DANIEL POORMAN

Served as private, 1778-79-80-81, with Capt. Conrad Snider, Adam Harmony and Wm. Long.

Penna. Arch. 5th Ser. Vol. 6, p. 88, 98, 119, 539, 546.

MELCHOR POORMAN

Of Guilford Twp., gave service in Lancaster County, Penna., 1781-82, undated roll, under Capt. Abraham Scott. He left a will dated Jan. and prob. March, 1808; To wife Elizabeth household and Kitchen furniture and ninety dollars, also sufficient house room; sons Joseph and John, lands where they reside for 2 years; wife Elizabeth, son John and daughter Catherine to live together; son Joseph all that plantation in Hamilton Twp.; son John that plantation in Guilford and Hamilton Twps.; dau. Catherine Poorman $300 yearly; Exrs.: Son John and trusty friend Jacob Negley. Chambersburg, Penna., Deed Book Vol. 2, p. 361, May 25, 1790. From John Alexander and Mary, his wife of Franklin Twp., to Melchor Poorman of Lancaster County, Penna. Certain real estate which was conveyed to John Alexander May 28, 1777. In 1803, Robert Peebles of Hamilton Twp., sold land in Hamilton, Twp., to Melchor Poorman of Guilford Twp.

Penna. Arch. 5th Ser. Vol. 7, p. 703, 749, 776.

DAVID PORTER

Served under Capt. Wm. Strain, 1780-81-82, the command of Col. James Dunlap. In the will of James Porter at Carlisle, dated Sept., 1762, he names a nephew David, son of his brother John. The will of David Porter of Shippenstown dated and probated 1785, names wife Mary; oldest son Robert. To each of two (2) youngest sons, Washington Porter and David Porter; oldsey dau. Agnes Porter; youngest dau. Sarah Porter. Exrs.: Capt. Alex. Peebles of Shippenstown and Samuel Porter. Wit.: Wm. Rippey.

Penna. Arch. 5th Ser. Vol. 6, p. 143, 398, 406, 431.

JACOB PORTER

The Franklin Repository, March 4, 1828: Died at his residence in Lurgan Twp., on the 26th of February, 1828, Mr. Jacob Porter at an advanced age after an illness of several weeks leaving a wife and two daughters with many other relatives and acquaintances. The deceased was a soldier of the Revolution and fought and bled to secure to us the blessings of liberty and equality which we now enjoy. His scene of action lay in the South under General Green and Lafayette; he bore a conspicious part in the battle of Cowpens and of King's Mountain &c, in the latter of which he received a wound with a musket ball which he carried to his grave.

WILLIAM PORTER

Appears as a private under Capt. Samuel Patton, 1780-81, Command of Col. Saml. Culbertson.

Penna. Arch. 5th Ser. Vol. 6, p. 278-287.

JOHN POTTER, JR.

Served under Capt. Daniel Clapsaddler, 1780-81. His will dated and prob., 1821, names wife Barbara; Son Daniel; Dau. Catherine Baker; Dau. Polly Bashore; Margaret Nicodemus (John); Barbara Leady. Under July 3, 1821, the "Repository" gives the following: "Died at his residence near Waynesburg on Sunday the 24th untimo, Capt. John Potter, and on Monday the 25th his remains were interred at the Lutheran graveyard in Waynesburg in the presence of perhaps the largest concourse of citizens that ever assembled there on a similar occasion."

Penna. Arch. 5th Ser. Vol. 6, p. 94, 97, 117.

SIMON POTTER

Served as private, 1780-81, under Capt. Daniel Clapsaddler. The will of John Potter of Washington Twp., prob., 1792, names wife; Son Simon; Son John; Son George; Daus. Barbary; Margaret; Eve; Catherine; Elizabeth; Esther. No will nor Admr., of Simon Potter in Franklin County, but a deed shows his wife's name as Catherine.

Penna. Arch. 5th Ser. Vol. 6, p. 94, 97, 117.

ALEXANDER POTTS

Appears in service 1779-80-81-82, under Capt. Noah Abraham, a taxable in Fannett Twp., over the above years. John Potts was one of those early settlers in Path Valley, or "Tuscarora Path" who maintained most friendly relations with the Indians, but in 1744 they notified the colonial authorities that they objected to have their lands taken by the whites, in violation of former agreements. In May, 1750, Richard Peters, and a number of Magistrates, went to Path Valley, burned the cabins of the settlers, John Potts being one, brought them before court, tried and convicted each, and put them under bonds to remove at once with their families, "taking servants and effects" and to appear at Carlisle to answer charges made against them. When the land was purchased of the Indians, Oct. 23, 1758 some of the settlers returned and became permanent residents of the valley. Alexdr. Potts was a taxable in 1786, both John and Alexdr. Potts being freemen at that period.

Penna. Arch. 5th Ser. Vol. 6, p. 86, 121, 128, 384, 393.

JOHN POTTS, JR.

Appears in service, 1780-81-82, with Capt. Noah Abraham. He was of Fannet Twp., and had a Grist Mill, 300 acres land &c, 1780-81-82. Under Taxables, Peters Twp., 1807, is the following: Beaver and Pott, 450 acres land, 1 Forge, 1 Grist Mill &c.

Penna. Arch. 5th Ser. Vol. 6, p. 85, 120, 127.

THOMAS PREATHER

Served as private under Capt. William Berryhill, 1780-81. Thomas was the son of Henry Prather and wife Elizabeth Heickes of Antrim Twp., who married 1754 and had issue: Thomas Heickes; Abraham; Henry, Jr.; George Gordon and wife Mary; Eleanor mar. David Shannon. The above Henry Prather was appointed a Justice of the Peace May, 1770, and April, 1771; his will was dated Oct., 1775, naming the above children.

Penna. Arch. 5th Ser. Vol. 6, p. 80, 101.

JOHN PRICE

The Rev. John Price before removing from the homestead on the Indian Creek, appears to have been a personal friend of Christopher Saur, the noted printer, and wrote, at times, for Saur's paper. The land he acquired in Germantown from his grandfather, he sold, and in 1752, he took up land in the present Washington Township, Franklin County, Penna. The Patent to John Price from the Penn's was dated Oct. 31, 1765. It was a tract first granted, 1750, to John Leatherman; then to George Grubb of Chester County, who in 1752, sold to John Price, then of Philadelphia Co. Another warrant having been granted, in 1750 to Richard Ocain for 100 acres, became void, the said John Price later purchased the claim of Richard Ocain, and the survey included both warrants. John Wallace's land was on the east, other neighbors were John Whitehead, Wm. Blakely, Wm. Irwin, Foreman, Hollinger and John Crooks, 430¼ acres. He later secured part of a tract called "Dryberry" from Wm. Irwin, and Wm. Patterson granted him in consideration of 8075 lbs., another tract not named. During the years 1780-81, John Price was in service under Capt. Daniel Clapsaddle, as were also Daniel and Jacob Price. John Price was an Elder or Bishop in the Conococheague congregation of the Brethren which was organized not later than 1752, on land commonly called Price's Meeting. The Deed from John Price to Christian Royer and Andrew Freadly, Trustees of the First Day German Baptist Congregation in Antietam, was dated March 31, 1797, and recorded at Chambersburg, Penna. The Rev. John Price born about 1725, in Montgomery Co., Penna., died 1803 in Franklin Co., Penna. He came to the present Franklin County in 1752. Under Tax list of 1799, Rev. John Price appears with Land, 2 Log Houses, horses, cows, halfstone barn, and stone spring house. It is thought that the first wife of Rev. John Price died about 1792, name not known; the second wife was Mary Ann, and to her he left a "comfortable residence," ground for a garden, 2 cows, one horse of $60 value, house furniture, 200 lbs in Specie; to daughter Hannah xx to dau. Elizabeth Miller xx to the children of dau. Catherine Stover xx. To son Jacob tract on which he lives xx To sons John and Abraham real and personal property, part eventually going to Mrs. S. Catherine Bonebrake, through her father, the Rev. Benj. E. Price.

Penna. Arch. 5th Ser. Vol. 6, p. 93, 107, 116. The Price family by Wanger, p. 396 to 402.

JOHN PRICE

Of Washington Twp., served as pvt. 1780-81, under Capt. Daniel Clapsaddle. His will dated 1795, was prob. 1803, requested that his wife Mary be furnished with a comfortable residence, to be maintained out of the estate, also 200 lbs.; Dau. Hannah; Dau. Elizabeth Miller; children of dau. Catherine Stover; Dau. Susannah Stover; Sons Jacob; John; Abraham.

Penna. Arch. 5th Ser. Vol. 6, p. 93, 107, 116.

JOSIAH PRICE

First Lieut., June 22, 1778, under Capt. Evan Baker. Josiah Price, b. 1757, d. 1825, mar. 1st Jane Scott, dau. of Wm. Scott, who was a member of the Upper West Conococheague Presby. Church. Josiah Price and wife Jane Scott had issue: Sally; William; Ruhannah; Josiah; Benjamin; Washington; Jane Scott. Josiah Price was a pew-holder in the Church at Welsh Run, tho' he lived just across the line in Maryland. A beautiful Stone Bridge, known as "Price's Bridge," spans the creek at the Price plantation. Under Deeds at Chambg. May 25, 1805, John Bowles and James Wray were appointed and authorized by the Elders and Congregation of "Lower West Conococheague" Church to convey to Jacob Angle. In the year 1774 the Trustees and Elders of above

Congregation made a Deed to John Ulric, a lein on said land of 5 shillings per annum; the land was sold to David Martin and by said Martin to Jacob Angle, who wishes to extinguish such incumbrance &c, they release for $20. After the above was signed and sealed, the Elders and others of said Congregation have subscribed their names to express their approbation,—George Crawford—Josiah Price—John Work—George Eaker. Aug. 5, 1805.

Maryland Archives, Vol. 21, p. 145. Williams Hist. Washington Co., Md., p. 426. Records from Price Bible, dated 1712. Chambersburg Penna., Deed Book Vol. 6, p. 138.

ADAM PRITS

Served as a private, 1779, with Capt. Samuel Royer in the 8th Batt. Cumb. Co. Militia. In 1782 Adam Prits had 224 acres land, 3 Horses, 7 Cattle.

Penna. Arch. 5th Ser. Vol. 6, p. 542.

GEORGE PRITS

Served under Capt. Samuel Royer, 1777, and an undated roll.

Penna. Arch. 5th Ser. Vol. 6, p. 542.

JOSEPH PRITS

Is shown serving 1781, called upon to perform a Tour of Duty by an order of Council. The name, Joseph Pritts, is associated with early newspapers of Chambersburg, a Joseph Pritts from Cumb., Md., having removed to Chambersburg in 1820. In 1840 he purchased the Repository from Mr. Harper, uniting 2 papers under the name of the "Repository and Whig." Mr. Pritts died in 1884.

Penna. Arch. 5th Ser. Vol. 6, p. 405.

WILLIAM PYM (PIMM)

Served as a private in 1780, under Capts. James Patton and Thos. McDowell. There was an undated roll. He was a communing member of the Presby. Ch. of Mercersburg in 1776. In 1781 he had 300 ac. land in Peters Twp., and a horse. He probably mar. Rebecca, dau. of John and Jane (McConnell) Ramsey. Deed dated Dec. 31, 1804, William Pimm and Anne, his wife of Peters Twp., sell to Fredk. Shearer of same place. Land situate in Peters Twp. On Apr. 9, 1810, Ann Pym, widow, renounces her right to administer on the estate of her husband. Letters were issued to Wm. Pym, with sureties, Roland Harris and John Holiday. The second Wm. Pym, is possibly, the man who mar. Sept. 26, 1851, Mrs. Eloisa M. Trout. William Pym appears later in Bedford Co., Penna. Nicholas Snider, wife Catherine Stants, son Jacob, had wife Elizabeth Christiana Faber, b. 1771, d. 1850. Their dau. Eloisa mar. 1st. Jacob Trout, 2nd William Pym,—Sons Dr. Wm. F. Trout and Dr. Nich. C. Trout.

Penna. Arch. 5th Ser. Vol. 6, p. 272, 315.

CHARLES QUERY

Gave service in 1782, under Capt. Noah Abraham. On Sept. 26, 1770, he was mar. to Janet Ralston, by Rev. John King of Mercersburg, Penna. Deeds show that in 1787, John Queery of Mecklenburg, N. C., Eleanor Reagh of Cumb. Co., Penna., Wm. Queery of Mecklenburg Co., N. C., Elizabeth Queery and Charles Queery of Fannett Twp., Franklin Co., Penna., of the one part, sell to Joseph Noble of Fannett Twp., for 300 pounds, land in Fannett Twp., surveyed for John McConnell.

Penna. Arch. 5th Ser. Vol. 6, p. 127.

JAMES QUARRE (QUERY)

Enlisted 1776, in Franklin Co., Penna., under Capt. Jeremiah Talbot. He is shown in the 6th Penna. Batt., under Col. Wm. Irvine.

Penna. Arch. 5th Ser. Vol. 2, p. 210, 212. McCauley's Hist. of Franklin Co., Penna., p. 83.

JOHN QUEARY

A native of Scotland first migrated to Penna., and then to Mecklenburg some years before the Revolution. As early as January, 1770, we find Mr. Queary residing in what was called for a time Clear Creek, now Philadelphia, in the bounds of Rocky River, and was an elder in that church. He was a member of the Mecklenburg Convention of May, 1775; a man of strong and vigorous intellect, and a good scholar, especially in mathematics; died at an early period and is buried in what was once Mecklenburg, now Union County.

"The Mecklenburg Declaration of Independence, May 20, 1775," by George W. Graham, M. D. p. 124.

PATRICK QUINN

Served as pvt., in Captain Wm. Peebles Rifle Regt., encamped near King's Bridge Sept.; Oct.; Nov., of 1776. John Quinn appears in same. Patrick Quinn's estate was administered at Chambersburg, Oct. 19, 1801. John Kerr of Chambersburg, had a son Samuel, born 1778, d. 1823 in Ohio, who mar. Nancy Quinn. John Quinn was mar. to Katherine Guinn, Nov. 26, 1784 at Mercersburg, Penna., by Dr. John King. One Patrick Gwinn d. in Huntingdon on the 18th, aged 80 yrs., dated Aug. 6, 1839,—Newspaper.

Penna. Arch. 5th Ser. Vol. 2, p. 361, 364, 367, 369, 371.

ANDREW RALSTON

Is shown as private in the Company of Capt. Wm. Peebles, the second Batt. of the Penna. Rifle

Regt., commanded by Col. Daniel Broadhead, near Kingsbridge Sept. 1, 1776. Andrew Ralston re-enlisted in the 2nd Penna. In 1782 he appears in the Company of Capt. Wm. Strain. Under pension applications, in Westmoreland Co., Penna., Andrew Ralston states his service as above, his discharge was lost, but James Gageby verifies the statement. Under papers on the Whiskey Insurrection Secretary Dallas addresses a letter to Major Andw. Ralston of Franklin County. In 1794, Major Andrew Ralston occupied Pew No. 34 in the new Brick Church at Rocky Spring. He died Aug. 1, or 31, 1819, in Westmoreland County, Penna. His name is on a list of Soldiers buried in Congruity Cemetery.

Penna. Arch. 5th Ser. Vol. 2, p. 359, 360, 363, 366, 369, 371. Vol. 6, p. 431. Vol. 4, p. 592.

BENJAMIN RAMSEY

Served under Capt. Samuel Patton, 1780-81-82 as private Cumb. Co. Militia. Benjamin Ramsey, 1758-1810, mar. in 1795, Mary, born 1768, dau. of Matt. Shields. They left Franklin Co., in 1804, settled near Washington, Penna.

Penna. Arch. 5th Ser. Vol. 6, p. 279, 288, 312.

JAMES RAMSEY

Served under Capt. Wm. Smith in 1780. He built, near Mercersburg a mill, now known as "Hiester's Mill' and in 1799 was taxed on 148 acres, 1 Lot, 1 Grist and 1 Saw Mill; 6 horses; 1 cow; 2 slaves. He mar. Elizabeth Porter and had issue: Sarah mar. Rev. Wm. Speer; John mar. Jane Van Lear; Mary mar. Archbd. Irwin; Alice mar. Wm. Johnston; Elizabeth mar. Michael Campbell; Nancy mar. John Sutherland. James Porter who mar. 2nd, Jane, dau. of Rev. John Young of Greencastle and wife Mary Clarke. James Ramsey of Franklin Co., Penna., bought at Sheriff's sale, 1794, the "Ligonier Tract" of 660 acres, also 12 adjoining acres, the Indian field, and mill creek for 721 lbs. It had been the property of Thomas Galbreath, decd., who had, in 1777, bought 3 tracts from Genl. Arthur St. Clair, "one of which did embrace Fort Ligonier." From the Franklin Repository, March 15, 1803, we have: "James Ramsey offers at Public Sale, at Fort Ligonier, on May 10, that noted stand, containing 600 acres land, complete Merchant Mill, with two Water Wheels, one pair of country stones, and one pair of burrs. Saw Mill, orchard, large double barn, fall grain in the ground &c." John Ramsey is said to have kept a hotel in Pittsburgh, where he entertained General Lafayette in 1825. Under date of Sept 13, 1831, the Repository gives us: Died in Cincinnati, on the 28th in his 53rd year, Col. John Ramsey, late of Pittsburgh. He was a native of this county and a son of Mr. James Ramsey. He left a large family of children.

Penna. Arch. 5th Ser. Vol. 6, p. 275.

JOHN RAMSEY

Served as private under Capt. Samuel Patton and William Huston, in 1780-81-82. He was a younger brother of Benjamin, Thomas and William Ramsey. John Ramsey mar. Martha, dau. of Matthew and Mary (McKane) Shields who was born 1774, died 1856. They were mar. 1795, and went to Washington Co., Penna., where John died in 1814, leaving a widow and 8 children. The widow mar. 2nd John De France. From records of Jane E and Isabel R. Shields.

Penna. Arch. 5th Ser. Vol. 6, p. 264, 278, 287, 311, 643.

THOMAS RAMSEY

Served as private, 1776-77-80-81-82, under Capts. Geo. Matthews, Patrick Jack and Samuel Patton. Court records at Chambersburg, Penna., show "Thomas Ramsey of Woodford Co., Ky., appoints my trusty friend and Brother, Benj. Ramsey of Hamilton Twp. Franklin Co., Penna., as my Atty., to settle xxx a Mortgage on the land where I formerly lived in Hamilton Twp.," xxx Witnessed by Caleb Wallace, George McFall and Robert Mc Cray. Isaac Shelby, Esq., Governor of this State hath set my hand and seal and caused the Seal of the State to be affixed at Lexington, on the 23rd day of November, 1793.

Penna. Arch. 5th Ser. Vol. 6, p. 287, 278, 303, 311, 318, 372.

WILLIAM RAMSEY

Served as Ensign and private, 1776-77-78-80-81-82 as Ensign and private, under Capts. Geo. Matthews, Patrick Jack and Samuel Patton. A son of William Ramsey of Hamilton Twp., and members of Rocky Spring Church. He is said to have been born in Bucks Co., Penna., in 1755, mar. 1780 in Franklin Co., Penna., Martha, dau. of Josiah Allen. Records from the Bible of Ensign Wm. Ramsey follow. He died in Morristown, Ohio, in 1841. (Older records in his own handwriting,—later ones in that of Edwina Rodgers). Births: Wm. Ramsey b. January 1, 1756, (Ensign Wm.); Martha Allen b. December 25, 1760, (His wife); Wm. Ramsey, Jr. b. May 26, 1781; Josiah Ramsey b. December 4, 1783; Martha Ramsey b. Apr. 2, 1786; Benjamin Ramsey b. Aug. 16, 1788; Mary Ramsey b. January 25, 1791; John Ramsey b. June 28, 1797; Jinnie (Jenny) Ramsey b. May 31, 1800. Moriah (Maria) Ramsey b. April 3, 1805. Marriages: Wm. Ramsey, Sr. and Martha Allen were married Aug. 26, 1780. Josiah Ramsey and Catharine McElvaine married 1804; Wm. Ramsey, Jr. and Mary Trimble married

1812; Martha Ramsey and Wm. Eaton married 1813; Elizabeth Ramsey and David Carrick married 1817; Benjamin Ramsey and Isabella Ramage married 1817; Benjamin Ramsey mar. 2nd Isabella Hanna, 1821; Mary Ramsey and David Andrews married 1820; John Ramsey and Sarah Craig married 1832; Moriah Ramsey and Nicholas Rodgers married Nov. 17, 1853; Deaths: Jennet Ramsey, Oct. 28, 1815; Martha A. Ramsey, Sept. 28, 1837; Mary R. Andrews, Dec. 12, 1841; Wm. Ramsey, Jr. Josiah Ramsey, Mar. 16, 1835; Wm. Ramsey, Jan. 1, 1841; Dr. John Ramsey, Mar. 31, 1845; Wm. Eaton, Sr., killed, June 23, 1847. Mary McKelvy, July 29, 1847; Mary Jane Carrick, May 12, 1844; Tabitha W. Ramsey, Feb. 27, 1848; Nicholas Rodgers, Mar 24, (year obscure); Tabitha McKeever, Jan. 15, 1863; Jane Eaton, Feb. 11, 1863; Martha Eaton, Mar. 31, 1868; David Andrews, Jan. 14, 1869; Isabella R. Ramsey, May 18, 1820; Isabella H. Ramsey, April 2, 1846; Wm. M. Carrick, April 7, 1862, (at Pittsburgh Landing); Thomas McKeever, Dec. 3, 1861; Catherine Eaton, Mar. 1, 1863; David Stewart Carrick, Dec. 26, 1863; Benjamin Ramsey, April 17, 1869; Elizabeth R. Carrick, Nov. 15, 1873.

Penna. Arch. 5th Ser. Vol. 6, p. 278, 287, 303, 311, 318, 368, 372, 377, 380.

DAVID RANKIN

Is shown in 1780, as private under Capt. William Smith. The will of David Rankin of Montgomery Twp., was dated 1829 and prob. 1833. He names wife Molly and 2 children, James and Betsy. To Mary Elizabeth Sellars, only child of dau. Molly, who had married Alexander Sellars, Oct. 7, 1824. Miss Molly L. McFarland of Mercersburg stated that the above David was the son of William Rankin of Antrim Twp., who died, 1792. She further said that he came here and built the stone house and barn on what was later the Jordan (now Neely) farm.

Penna. Arch. 5th Ser. Vol. 6, p. 275.

JAMES RANKIN

Served under Capt. Wm. Huston, 1777-80-81. Penna. Arch. 5th Ser. Vol. 6, p. 275, 283, 373.

JEREMIAH RANKIN

Ranger on the Frontier, served in 1778, under Capt. John McConnell, and as Ensign, 1780-81, with Capt. Wm. Huston; a son of pioneer James Rankin of Montgomery Twp. He mar. Mary, dau. of James Clarke. His will was dated June, 1803 and prob. Aug, 1803, and only son James Clark Rankin and 3 daus.: Nancy; Mariah; Ester. The widow Mary later married Charles Kilgore. James, Jeremiah, David and William Rankin were Pewholders in the "Lower Conococheague" or Welsh Run Church. Nancy Rankin mar. John Imbrie, Beaver Co., Penna., 10 children Maria Rankin mar. Samuel Johnston, son of Thos. and Anne Houston Johnston. Esther Rankin mar. Alex. M. Johnston, son of Thos. and Anne Houston Johnston.

Penna. Arch. 5th Ser. Vol. 6, p. 262, 269, 274, 282, 374.

WILLIAM RANKIN

Of Antrim Twp., appears as a private under Capt. James Poe, 1782, and an undated roll. He married Mary Huston, daughter of Archibald, as shown by the will of Agnes Huston, widow of Archibald. The will of William Rankin of Antrim Twp., was dated Oct. and prob. Nov. of 1792. He names wife Mary. His children were Archibald, to whom he gives 200 acres land "off my Mansion place;" Sons James and William a tract in Penns Valley; Dau. Betsy; Son David the old Mansion place; Sons John and Jeremiah a tract on Spring Creek, Penn's Valley; Sons John and Jeremiah to be schooled, clothed &c, and Betsy to have maintenance until the three arrive at 21 years.

Penna. Arch. 5th Ser. Vol. 6, p. 576, 583.

WILLIAM RANKIN

Son of James, served as private, 1777, under Capt. Samuel Patton and in 1780-81 under Capt. William Huston. William Rankin mar. Ann Gillespie, at Mercersburg Nov. 5, 1771. His will dated 1797, was prob. 1802, naming wife Ann; Son James, unmarried; Dau. Elizabeth Ritchey; Daus.: Jean; Ann; Ruth; Mary Gillespie Rankin, to live on the plantation. Ann Rankin, widow of above William, died 1808 at the home of her son James Rankin. Ruth Rankin was married to Samuel Thompson, Nov. 12, 1807, by Rev. Robert Kennedy.

Penna. Arch. 5th Ser. Vol. 6, p. 269, 275, 282, 372, 373.

FREDERICK REEVES (REEVER)

Was serving 1780-81, under Capt. John Orbison. He is shown in Montgomery Twp. taxables, 1781, with 137 ac. land, horses and cattle.

Penna. Arch. 5th Ser. Vol. 6, p. 274, 294.

FREDERICK REED

Private in Penna. Militia, aged 75 years in 1833, was a pensioner. Of Letterkenny Twp., his will prob. March 17, 1847, names wife Elizabeth, and children: Polly; John; Jonathan; Lenard; William; Jacob. The 1790 Census shows the above family as: 1 man, 3 boys, 2 females.

Penna. Arch. 3rd Ser. Vol. 13, p. 530.

BERNARD REICHART (RIGHER-RIGER)

Served as private 1778-79, under Capts. Adam Harmony and William Long, commanded by Col.

Abraham Smith. A Deed at Chambersburg, dated Jan. 8, 1794, states that Bernard Reichart of Guilford Twp., died intestate, leaving a widow Hannah and issue: John, his oldest son; Hannah; Maria Eva and Bernard Reichart.

Penna. Arch. 5th Ser. Vol. 6, p. 537, 545.

MICHAEL REIGN (RAYNE)

Served as Corporal under Capts. Long and Berryhill, 1778-79-80-81. His wife was Gertrude, dau. of Michael Reifsnider of Guilford Twp.

Penna. Arch 5th Ser. Vol. 6, p. 77, 80, 82, 111, 545.

JOHN RENFREW

Is shown as a private under Capt. Conrad Snider in 1781. He was born Apr. 4, 1755, died Oct. 14, 1844, aged 91 years, 6 mons. 10 days, and is on the 1840 list of pensioners. He was mar. to Sarah Ray, dau. of Samuel Rea of Green Twp., Nov. 9, 1779, by Dr. Alex. Dobbin. He is buried in the old Covenanter Graveyard, Fayetteville, Penna., and his will dated 1841, was prob. 1844, and names the following: Sons Samuel; Robert; John; dau. Margaret; dau. Sarah mar. Jeremh. Burns; graudau. Sarah Andrew; grandson John (of Samuel); Son James. In the Historical Sketch of Franklin County, by I. H. McCauley, (page 246), we learn of John Renfew settling near Scotland, Penna., and eventually on a certain tract called "Boyne" in Guilford Twp. It was a tract surveyed in 1774, for James Crawford who conveyed it to Patrick Alexander. Following the death of Patrick Alexander, his son Joseph took the property, and on April 29, 1784, conveyed to John Renfrew, who had been a soldier in the Rebolution, and bore to his grave marks of wounds received in the great struggle for liberty. About 1807 John Renfrew bought from Jacob Gsell an additional tract, where he lived until his death in the fall of 1844. The son John became the next owner where he died in Sept. of 1863. The Boyne farm is located at Turkey Foot, where they have the original Patent, and the old Deeds from the Penn's.

Penna. Arch. 5th Ser. Vol. 6, p. 108, 118.

SAMUEL RENNIX (RENICK)

Was in service 1777-79, with Capts. James Poe and Wm. Long, command of Capt. Abhm. Smith. He was a taxable in Guilford Twp.

Penna. Arch. 5th Ser. Vol. 6, p. 521, 546.

ALEXANDER RHEA (WRAY)

Served under Capt. Wm. Huston 1780-81.

Penna. Arch. 5th Ser. Vol. 6, p. 269, 275, 282.

DANIEL RHEA

Served 1780-81, under Capt. John Orbison. Orphans' Court records in 1824 show minor children of Daniel Rhea, guardians for Eliza Ann, Thomas and Susanna (under 14) and of Jane Rhea above 14 years. In 1793 Daniel Wray and wife Elizabeth sell Lots 27-28 in the town of Mercersburg, to John Goudy and Robert Williams, Merchants. The Rheas attended the Welsh Run Church and are probably buried there. In the interesting will of Jane Wray, presumably the step-mother of above Daniel, she gives to Daniel her cow; to Daniel's dau. Jean, cash; to grandau. Jane Powell, her silver tea-spoons and to grandau. Jane Wray, dau. of John, her side saddle. She also names her brother David English.

Penna. Arch. 5th Ser. Vol. 6, p. 274, 277, 294.

JAMES RHEA (WRAY)

Served 1780-81-82 under Capts. Wm. Huston and John Orbison. In the will of John Rhea, Sr., dated 1806, prob. 1807, he directs son Daniel to maintain his wife Jane. He names son Isaac; Dau. Annie Powell; Son Henry; Dau. Elizabeth Taylor; Son James; Son John; In 1796, John Rhea, Sr., of Montgomery Twp., shows three (3) Tracts of patented land, one on which he lived called Rhea's Fancy; one called Rheasburg; one called Fayette, in all 665 acres, 96 perches.

Penna. Arch. 5th Ser. Vol. 6, p. 269, 293, 307.

GENERAL JOHN REA

Franklin Repository, Chambersburg, Penna.—Tuesday, Nov. 11, 1806, Married on Thursday last by the Rev. Mr. Herron, General John Rea to Miss Elizabeth Culbertson, dau. of Col. Samuel Culbertson, all of this County. Franklin Repository Feb. 10, 1829, No. 26, Vol. 33,—Died on the morning of the 6th inst. General John Rea, after a very short illness aged 74 years xx in less than a day and a half he breathed his last xxx. In the career of his life he was early found among those who were engaged in the defence of liberty and their country. He served several tours in the Militia during the Revolutionary contest and afterwards he was the uniform asserter of the rights of his country, xxx highly esteemed, member of State Legislature. (The mortal remains of General Rea were interred at Rocky Spring on Saturday last, they were escorted out of town by the "Franklin Blues," and the Washington Grays" with solemn music and accompanied by the first named Company and an unusual concourse of relatives and neighbors.) A Government Stone has been erected in the Rocky Spring Graveyard, by the Franklin County Chapter, Daughter of the American Revolution. Franklin Repository, June 21, 1836. Death of Mrs. John Rea, in her 52nd year, buried at Martinsburg, Bedford Co., Penna., at home of her son. She left 6 sons and 1 daughter.

JOHN REA

Lieut., Jan. 20, 1777, Captain 1780, years 1777-78-80-81.
Penna. Arch. 5th Ser. Vol. 6, p. 6, 69, 77, 78, 105, 328, 534, 584, 587.

ROBERT RHEA (WRAY)

Served 1780-81, under Capt. Wm. Huston.
Penna. Arch. 5th Ser. Vol. 6, p. 270, 276, 284.

SAMUEL REA

Served 1781-82, under Capts. Conrad Snyder and John McConnell, a tanner. His will dated 1807 and prob. 1811 names wife Martha; Dau. Ann, wife of Patrick Wright; Son Wm. Rea; Dau. Sarah Renfrew; Dau. Hannah Thomspon; Son James Rea; Grandau. Hannah Potts, dau. of Ann Wright; Son John Rea; Son Samuel Rea; Polly Edgar and Rosanna, daus. of Andrew Thompson. Exrs.: Son John Rea and Andrew Thompson of Green Twp. Sarah mar. John Renfrew, Nov. 9, 1779.
Penna. Arch. 5th Ser. Vol. 6, p. 119, 310.

SAMUEL REA, JR.

Served under Capt. John Rea, 1780-81. It is probable this is the man who died in Erie Co., Penna., 1813, aged 50 years. He went there from Franklin Co., Penna., wife Margaret Eaton, 1776-1832. He is said to have had nine children but four only are shown: (1) Samuel b. 1792, Washington, Penna., died 1883, mar, 1818 Elizabeth Ferguson, who died 1855. (2) A son who mar. Margaret Ferguson, sister of Elizabeth. (3) Johnston born 1805, mar. Susanna Porter. (4) Eliza, born 1808, mar. Joseph Ware, Jr., son of Joseph from Vermont.
Penna. Arch. 5th Ser. Vol. 6, p. 72, 78, 106.

WILLIAM RHEA

As Ensign under Capt. James Young, 1777-78.
Penna. Arch. 5th Ser. Vol. 6, p. 521, 526.

WILLIAM REA

Served as Sergeant under Capt. James Young in 1778, in 1779-80-81 under Capt. John Rea.
Penna. Arch. 5th Ser. Vol. 6, p. 72, 78, 106, 543, 584, 600.

JOHN REYNOLDS

Served as private under Capt. Alexdr. Peebles, 1780-81-82. John Reynolds, Esq., became lawfully entitled to four Plantations, and a house and Lot in Shippensburg, No. 78, "Subject to the yearly payment for ever of four Spanish dollars to the proprietor of the Soil" and on each of two plantations is a Grist or Merchant Mill; John Reynolds left issue six children: Sarah, now the wife of Wm. McPherson; Abigail the wife of John Shippen; George, since decd.; Benjamin; John and Hannah. George, as eldest son received a double share, but died intestate, leaving a Mother and the above Brothers and Sisters but no issue. The widow became Hannah Leeper, and the lands were sold—One was known as John Reynolds, Esq., new or lower Mill place; in the tenure of Wm. Leeper; another tract known as the old or upper Mill place; one tract of 300 acres in Franklin County, lately belonging to Samuel Blythe, known as Pine Meadow place; another known as Woodland Tract, and the house and lot in the town of Shippensburg. John Reynolds, Esq., born 1749, died Oct. 20, 1789, and is buried in the graveyard of Middle Spring Church, near Shippensburg.
Penna. Arch. 5th Ser. Vol. 6, p. 395, 421, 432.

JOHN RIDDETT (REDDART)

Appears in service with Capt. Alexdr. Peebles, 1780-81-82, command of Col. James Dunlap. In 1785, John Reydatt had a Tan yard in Shippensburg, also Horses and Cattle.
Penna. Arch. 5th Ser. Vol. 6, p. 421, 432, 395.

DAVID RIDDLE

Enlisted from what is now Franklin County, under Capt. James Chambers, and in June, 1775, they marched as a Company of Riflemen, to the siege of Boston, arriving there about the last of July. Capt. Chambers' company was the only one in the regiment that was raised within the bounds of our present Franklin County. They were stout and hardy yoemanry, the flower of Penna's frontiersmen, and according to Thatcher "remarkable for the accuracy of their aim." Under Col. Wm. Thompson, of Cumb. Co., this Command became, in January, 1776, the first regiment of the army of the United States, commanded by Genl. Geo. Washington.
Penna. Arch. 5th Ser. Vol. 2, p. 19. McCauley's Hist. Franklin Co., Penna. p. 71-72.

JAMES AND JOHN RIDDLE

Appear as privates in the Cont. Line, from Cumb. Co., Penna., as entitled to Depreciation Pay. One James Riddle of Chambersburg, left a will dated June 9, 1834, naming wife Ariana, and issue: Rebecca; John Stuart; Wm. M.; Horatio R.; and Edward.
Penna. Arch. 5th Ser. Vol. 4, p. 302.

MATTHEW RIDDLE

Was in service 1779-81-82, under Capts. James Young and Terrence Campbell. In 1779 his name appears in a list of "new recruits" which included Col. Chambers, Miller, Dr. John Calhoun, Jonathan Loveberry and others. The men were

JOHN RIDDLESBERGER

Served as 2nd Lieut. with Capt. Samuel Royer, 1777-78-79 and in 1780-81. The first deed of 1779 was from Daniel Royer of Bedford Co., Penna., to John Riddlesberger of Cumb. Co., the land in Antrim Twp., joining Wm. Beddy (Beatty), John Potter, Samuel McCrea and Christian Flougher. The 2nd deed of Oct. 17, 1782, James Potter, Vice President, to John Riddlesberger. Warrant to Jacob Fyock, dated Apr. 15, 1773, who sold to John Riddlesberger, Aug. 12, 1777. Situate in Antrim Twp., called "Fiascone" (Fyerstone). The will of John Riddlesberger of Washington Twp., was dated July 20, 1838 and prob. Aug. 12, 1844. He was then "weak in body;" He left a wife Elizabeth and a son John, who was Executor of the will. A John Riddlesberger who died in 1887, left a large family. From Family Records:

John Riddlesberger, b. Sept. 29, 1770, d. June 12, 1844. His wife Elizabeth, b. July 26, 1771, d. May 31, 1857. Their son, Rev. John Riddlesberger, Jr., b. March 4, 1813, d. Nov. 23, 1887. His wife Elizabeth b. Feb. 15, 1815, d. Aug. 30, 1885. They had the following issue: (1) Lydia Ann, b. Apr. 3, 1838, d. Dec. 1, 1893; Mar. William Geesaman. (2) Jacob b. Jan. 21, 1840, d. Jan. 16, 1850. (3) John b. Dec. 19, 1841, d. July 12, 1845. (4) Isaac b. Apr. 5, 1844, d. Aug. 15, 1917. (5) Abraham b. June 12, 1846, d. Oct. 13, 1848. (6) David b. March 1, 1848, d. Sept. 16, 1862. (7) Samuel b. Jan. 30, 1853, d. Sept. 15, 1862. (8) Elizabeth b. Jan. 30, 1855, d. Sept. 18, 1862. Orphans' Court, June, 1839, shows a petition of Jacob Riddlesberger, and his wife Hannah, late Hannah Foreman, dau. of David Foreman, who died intestate in April last, late of Quincy Twp., decd. There were many heirs living in Ohio, Kentucky, &c. Under a Release of Aug., 1830, estate of John Horn, Washington Twp., Franklin Co., Penna., Jonathan Foreman and Josephine Riddlesberger, late Foreman, heirs of Sally Foreman, decd., who was one of the heirs of John Horn. Under Deeds, Vol. 26, 1852, is shown Catherine Foreman of Franklin Co., Penna., to John Riddlesberger of Washington Twp. John Riddlesberger, Sr., and Elizabeth his wife were to hold said land during their lives, and at their death to their heirs. Elizabeth Foreman, decd., was mar. to Jonathan Foreman, and was one of the daughters of John Riddlesberger, decd., and mother of said Catherine Foreman, above.

Penna. Arch. 5th Ser. Vol. 6, p. 89, 112, 524, 532, 541, 511.

STEPHEN RIGLER

Served as a private 1780-81-82 under Capts. James Young and Terrence Campbell. Andreas and Stephen Reigler signed the Test Oath in Lebanon Twp. Lancaster Co., Penna., in 1778. In 1791 taxed with a house and Lot, a horse and cow and 6 teaspoons, and in 1796, as an Innkeeper. In 1795, Stephen Rigler built the stone house, long known as Noel's Hotel, later known as the Ludwig lot. The old tavern stand long known as Miller's Hotel, was the means of public entertainment offered in this part of town. A stone tavern, known as the "Golden Lamb" occupied the northwest corner of the square, and opposite the present location of the Central Presby. Church, Chambersburg, Penna. It was built in 1795 bq Stephen Rigler. A deed dated Feb. 1793, shows that Stephen Rigler had mar. Catherine, widow of Nicholas Snider. In Dec., 1793, under the estate of Nicholas Snider, the widow Catherine is again shown as the wife of Stephen Rigler, and on Oct. 3, 1804, Letters on the estate of Stephen Rigler, were granted to Jeremiah Snider, John Shyrock and Catherine Rigler. Oct 3, 1807. The Repository stated that he was buried in the English Presbyterian Graveyard. Catherine Rigler left a will in 1829, in which she names Mary Richardson and Catherine Strealy, each one bed and bedding. To Elizabeth and Margaret Gilchrist, furniture, waring Clothes equally between my four daughters. Property sold to me by Stephen Rigler, bill of sale to me in 1822. To Mary Rigler and to Stephen Rigler. Exr.: Jeremiah Snider.

Penna. Arch. 5th Ser. Vol. 6, p. 82, 110, 126.

ELIJAH RIPPEY

Served in the Cont. Line and was entitled to Depreciation pay. He is shown in the New 11th Regt. of Penna., under Capt. James Calderwood, raised principally in Cumb. Co., Penna., May, 1777. Capt. Calderwood died on the field of Brandywine Sept. 11, 1777. Elijah Rippey, who died 1794, was a brother of Capt. Wm. Rippey. He mar. Elizabeth Thompson, who died in 1826; they had issue: Samuel; Thompson; Isabel.

Penna. Arch. 5th Ser. Vol. 3, p. 190, 652, 663. Vol. 4, p. 181, 221.

JON RIPPEY

Served in 1755, under Col. Joseph Armstrong. He was a son of pioneer Hugh Rippey, an early settler at Shippensburg, and he was Administrator of his father's estate in 1750. John Rippey was a taxable in Lurgan Twp., in 1751, his wife Mary and brother Samuel, Executors of his will signed Oct. 7, 1758. He had issue: Hugh; Margery and Agnes, who died prior to her father.

Penna. Arch. 5th Ser. Vol. 1, p. 38.

SAMUEL RIPPEY

Served under Capt. Alexdr. Peebles, 1777-79-80. He was a son of Samuel Rippey and wife Rachl Armstrong, and was a Tanner. He died 1804, and his wife, Mary Finley died in 1836. They had issue: John; Armstrong; Isabella; Harriet; Mary; Elizabeth.

Penna. Arch. 5th Ser. Vol. 6, p. 23, 25, 57, 136, 589.

SAMUEL RIPPEY, JR.

Died 1829, served under Capt. Alexdr. Peebles, 1780-81-82. He was probably the son of Elijah and Elizabeth (Thompson) Rippey and was a Tanner. He mar. Jane Falkner, born 1791, died 1857, and they had issue: Elijah; Elizabeth; Mary Jane; John Thompson; Isabel; and Samuel.

Penna. Arch. 5th Ser. Vol. 6, p. 395, 421, 433.

CAPTAIN WILLIAM RIPPEY

Resided in Shippensburg, but most of the men composing his company were from Lurgan Twp. In the summer of 1776 they were sent to Canada under Genl. Sullivan, many captured at the Isle Au Noix, among them Capt. Rippey, who was so fortunate as to escape. They fell back to Crown Point and Ticonderoga, and wintered there. The company of Capt. Rippey consisted of ninety-nine officers and privates. Col. Rippey died Sept. 22, 1819, aged 78 years. His wife Margaret d. Jan., 1801 in her 59th year. Capt. Rippey mar. 1st, Margaret Finley; 2nd Elizabeth McCracken, who survived him; issue: (1) Ruth died prior to her father), mar. 1791, Joseph Duncan. (2) Samuel A. mar. Jane Finley. (3) Isabella mar. Joseph Kerr. (4) Jane, mar. Dr. Alexdr. Stewart. (5) Catherine mar. John Raum. (6) John C. became a physician. (7) Margaret b. 1768, d. 1820, mar. Joseph Chambers, son of Col. Benj. Chambers. (8) William died 1821, mar Lucy Piper. Further items of interest in Biographical Annals of Franklin Co., Penna.

McCauley's Hist. of Franklin Co., Penna., p. 80, 81.

JACOB RIPPLE

Was a private under Capt. Noah Abraham, Oct., 1777.

Penna. Arch. 5th Ser. Vol. 6, p. 19, 141.

LODOWICK RIPPEL

Signed a petition from Fannett Twp., and in 1782 he signed another petition, owning large tracts of land in Fannett Twp.

Penna. Arch. 5th Ser. Vol. 6, p. 141.

MATTHIAS RIPPEL

Is also shown in service with Capt. Noah Abraham an undated roll.

Penna. Arch. 5th Ser. Vol. 6, p. 141.

VALENTINE RIPPLE

Signed a petition owning large tracts of land in Fannett Twp.

Penna. Arch. 5th Ser. Vol. 6, p. 141.

MATTHEW RITCHEY

Appears as a soldier in the Cont. Line, entitled to Depreciation Pay, from Westmoreland Co., Penna. Dr. Alexdr. Dobbin served the Covenanter congregation near Greencastle for one fourth time until the union of 1782 (1774-1782) and his records show the marriage of Matthew Richey to Rachel Wallace, Oct. 13, 1778, Antrim Twp. Dr. Dobbin was pastor of the congregation of Rock Creek, now Gettysburg, 1774-1809. He maintained, 1788-99 a private classical boarding school in his own house, in which over sixty professional men were classically educated, of whom twenty-five were clergymen. He was regarded as one of the very best Latin, Greek and Hebrew Scholars in the country.

Penna. Arch. 5th Ser. Vol. 4, p. 453, 754.

JOHN ROATCH

Served as Sergt. under Capt. Noah Abraham, at Legonere, June, 1779, in the service of the United States, commanded by Col. Wm. Chambers.

Penna. Arch. 5th Ser. Vol. 6, p. 59, 603.

JOHN ROBINSON

Signed the Oath of Fidelity Oct. 13, 1777, in Westmoreland Co., Penna., before Hugh Martin, esq. His wife was Margaret, dau. of pioneer Francis Jamison and wife Margaret, early settlers in Franklin Co., Penna.

Penna. Arch. 2nd Ser. Vol. 3, p. 31.

GEORGE ROCK

Served as private under Capt. Samuel Royer, 1780-81. Deeds show William Fullerton and wife Barbara selling land in 1799, to George Rock, Jr. It was in Guilford Twp., and part of a tract to Joseph Clarke and wife Margery, called "Springfield," 99 acres and 67 perches. Another deed in 1802 shows Thos. Murray and wife Mary selling a tract in Guilford Twp., to Geo. Rock. George Rock died in 1803. In 1790 Census his family consisted of 1 man, 2 boys, 1 female.

Penna. Arch. 5th Ser. Vol. 6, p. 75, 90, 113.

HENRY ROCK

Served as private under Capt. Samuel Royer, 1780-81. Letters Admr., on the estate of Henry Rock were granted to Andrew Wagoner. 1790

Census shows: 4 men, 4 females. One Fredk. Rock of Washington Twp., died in 1804 naming a wife Molly and David Mann's son David, Jr., to share in the estate, the family consisting of 1 man, 1 female. There are Rocks buried in the Nunnery Graveyard,—Adam; Susan A.; Mary Alas and Leanah, Wife of Wm. Rock.

Penna. Arch. 5th Ser. Vol. 6, p. 90, 99, 113.

JOHN ROCK

Served 1780-81, under Capt. Daniel Clapsaddle.
Penna. Arch. 5th Ser. Vol. 6, p. 93, 106, 116.

MORRIS ROCK

Served 1781 under Capt. Wm. Berryhill.
Penna. Arch. 5ht Ser. Vol. 6, p. 81, 102.

BARTHOL ROHARTY

Enlisted March 9, 1776, as shown in the roll of Capt. Abraham Smith (Raised in Cumberland Co., Penna.) The will of Betholomey Rhoharty of Air Township, farmer; dated and proved April, 1807; To Ann Linn 50 acres on North side of my plantation, adjoining Lawrence Bulger up to John Davises lands. Lodowick Cunneham fifty acres to be laid off adjoining Erwin's line. Certain sum for the use of building a meeting house for the Presbyterian Congregation living in the great Cove, the meeting house to be built in McConnell's Town, Air Township. Executors: Wm. Patterson and James Nilson of Air. Wit: Abednego Stephen, Laurence Bulger, Philip Butner, Abraham Bulger, Ludwick Garnegain.

Penna. Arch. 5th Ser. Vol. 2, p. 233, 235. Vol. 5, p. 114.

ABRAHAM ROSENBURY (ROSENBERG)

Was a private under Capt. Samuel Patton in 1778-79, Ranger on the Frontier, and under Capt. John McConnell, 1780-81. He was born Feb., 1754, died Dec., 1821. He is buried in the graveyard on the Stephen Keefer farm in Horse Valley, Fannett Twp. As he had a dau. Rebecca, who mar. John Keefer, he probably lived with her. His estate was in Letterkenny Twp.; he left a widow Catherine, issue: Rebecca, wife of John Keefer; John; Joseph; Susan; Peter; Catherine; Abraham.

Penna. Arch. 5th Ser. Vol. 6, p. 267, 302, 380, 601, 610.

GEORGE ROSENBERGER

Appears in service 1780-81. Under Deeds June, 1789, George Rosenberger and wife Elizabeth of Letterkenny, sell land to Herman Myer of same Twp. The original grant was to Thomas Barnet Feb., 1744, who in 1751, conveyed to Michael Higgins, who in 1752, sold to Thos. Clark, now decd.; Thos. Clark, in his life tme, gave the land to his son Samuel, who in 1779, conveyed to John Gault, and they to Geo. Rosenberger on Jan. 13, 1789. In the Nunnery Graveyard, near Waynesboro, is the grave of Peter Rosenberger, who died March 29, 1832, aged 77 years, 3 mos.; there is also a much worn old Sand Stone marker with "Rosenberger" the only legible word.

Penna. Arch. 5th Ser. Vol. 6, p. 220, 236, 238.

WILLIAM ROSS

Served as private under Capt. Thos. Johnston, 1780, under Capt. Patrick Jack, 1781. He mar. Feb. 20, 1803, Esther, dau. of Andrew and Esther Reed of Antrim Twp. William Ross is said to have studied surveying under a Mr. Rankin at Greencastle. They moved to Westmoreland Co., Penna. William Ross, b. Londonderry, Ire. Nov. 25, 1762, mar. Esther Reed, b. in Franklin Co., Penna., Jan. 1, 1780. Issue: Esther, 1804-1890, mar. 5-15-, 1825, Hugh Douglass. Prudence, 1806-1887, mar. Apr. 11, 1826, Samuel Hill Joanna, 1808-1894, mar. March 26, 1828, Andrew White, Samuel Hopkins, 1812-1885, mar. 1st Elizabeth Leslie, May 30, 1836. Mar. 2nd. Margaretta McClerey; William Ross, 1814-1893, mar. Nov. 12, 1841, Martha (?) Martin Andrew Ross, 1816-1847; Martha (?) Ann Ross, 1819-1894, mar Sept. 16, 1845, Robert Caldwell, Mary Eliza Ross, 1821-1848. Andrew Ross in Mexican War, 2nd Lieut. 11th Inf. died on shipboard on his way home.

Penna. Arch. 5th Ser. Vol. 6, p. 84, 291, 295.

WILLIAM ROSS

Appears in 1781 under Capt. Wm. Huston, Lieut. Hance McColoch.

Penna. Arch. 5th Ser. Vol. 6, p. 643.

JOHN ROUAN

Third Penna. Cont. Line, enlisted 1780; discharged 1783; wounded in right knee and left leg; lived near Mercersburg, but died in Belfast Twp. Bedford Co., Penna. His fiirst wife was Margaret, dau of Andrew and Rebecca (McFarland) Mayes of Lancaster Co., Penna. In his will, dated June 20, 1822, he named a wife Corneliann and son-in-law Andrew Woods and family. They were to have the plantation in Bedford Co., at death of wife, also tract of land in Montgomery Twp. Franklin Co., Penna. Will probated Jan. 6, 1824. He was a pensioner.

Penna. Arch. 2nd Ser. Vol. 13, p. 197. 2nd Ser. Vol. 10, p. 485.

CHRISTIAN ROYER

Served as private in Lancaster Co., Penna., in 1778-79-82, under Capts. Duck and Volicks (Volck). Christian Royer bought land in Franklin Co. in 1792, from his cousin Samuel Royer, land which Samuel had gotten from the Penns in

1774. The tract called "Turnpitt" and part called "Jacks Spitt." In 1796 he bought the land known as "Jacks Line," the Old "Price Meeting House," but a mile away, where he is probably buried. His wife was Anna Stohler, born 1749, died 1811. In the will of Christian Royer, dated June, 1808, probated June, 1814, he names wife Anna; sons John and Christian; a dau. Maria Shank; a dau. Anne Hollinger; a dau. Catherina Zook; and a son George Royer. Catherina mar. David Zug (Zuck), born about 1780 in Washington Co., Md., who died at Welsh Run about 1824, youngest son of Jacob, a descendant of Ulrich Zug, who fled from Switzerland, landing in America in 1727.

Penna. Arch. 5th Ser. Vol. 7, p. 289, 291, 885, 890, 905.

WILLIAM RULE

Served 1780-81, as a private under Capt. William Berryhill, Cumb. Co. Militia. The above William Rule was a son of John Rule, whose will was probated May, 1794. John Rule names two daus.; Mary and Sarah Gaff, a grandau., Mary Ann Gaff, and a son William Rule.

Penna. Arch. 5th Ser. Vol. 6, p. 81, 98, 102.

GEORGE RUMMEL, SR.

Signed the Oath of Allegiance in Lancaster Co. Cocalico Twp., 1777-78. In the 1790 census, he and his wife Barbara were in Straban Twp., York Co., later Adams Co., where he left a will. (Will Book B, p. 100). He names the following children: Suffia, who mar. Jacob Maye; Jacob Rummel, George Rummel, Peter Rummel, Christian Rummel, John Rummel, Catherine, mar Conrad Loure; Elizabeth, mar. John Loure; Susanna, mar. Henry Ashbaugh; Barbara, mar. Christian Culp. Exrs.: John Semple and William Gilliland. Will prob. 1810.

Penna. Arch. 2nd Ser. Vol. 8, p. 467.

GEORGE RUMMEL, JR.

Born about the year 1762, was the son of George Rummel and wife Barbara, of Cocalico Twp., Lancaster Co., Penna. George Rummel, Jr. was a soldier in the American Revolution, serving from Cumb. Co. now Franklin Co., Penna.; serving in the Third Co. 1st Batt. under Capt. Wm. Berryhill. He served also under Capt. Daniel Clapsaddler, being listed on his roll of the first Batt., July 28, 1781. He came to Antrim Twp., Franklin Co., where he was a taxable in 1786. In 1787 he bought a tract of land called "Bath" from Christian Flaugher, in Antrim Twp. He married about 1786 Elizabeth Besore, dau of Daniel and Catharina (Rudy) Besore. Salem Church records show the following births of their children: Catharina, b. July 22, 1787; Magdalena, b. Dec. 4, 1789; Ann Maria, b. July 25, 1791; Johannes, b. July 14, 1794; Elizabeth, b. June 17, 1799; John George, b. Oct. 31, 1796.

Penna. Arch. 5th Ser. Vol. 6, p. 102, 116

GEORGE RUNYON

Served as Corporal in the Tenth Penna. Regt. Cont. Line. In 1818 he was in Greene Twp., Franklin Co., said to have been 74 years of age in 1819, and a pensioner.

Penna. Arch 2nd Ser. Vol. 10, p. 727, 755.

ANDREW RUSSEL

Is shown serving in Capt. John Rea's Company, 1779-80-81 and an undated roll, the Command of Col. Abhm. Smith. Andrew Russell of Lurgan Twp., left a will dated and prob. 1791. He names William, son of his brother Robert Russell, and Wm., son of his brother Joshua Russell, who are his legatees.

Penna. Arch. 5th Ser. Vol. 6, p. 78, 105, 543, 584.

ANDREW RUSSELL

Is shown as a private under Capts. John Jack and William Findley, 1777-82 and an undated roll.

Penna. Arch. 5th Ser. Vol. 6, p. 122, 517, 518, 519, 587.

DAVID RUSSELL

Appears as a private under Capt. Samuel Patton, 1777-80-81-82. In 1782 David Russell was taxed with 200 acres of land, horses and Cattle. He was a son of John Russell of Hamilton Twp., whose will was dated 1780, prob. March, 1789. In this will John Russell names Caleb as his oldest child. Eldest dau. Sarah, wife of Anthony McKnitt; dau. Elizabeth, wife of Joseph Fair; Dau. Eleanor wife of John Williams; sons William and John; 2 sons James and David all the plantation on which I now live; dau. Margaret, wife of Wm. Robison. Executors were son James and Francis Gardner.

Penna. Arch. 5th Ser. Vol. 6, p. 278, 287, 311, 373.

HENRY RUSSELL

Served as private 1781, under Capt. Joseph Culbertson.

Penna. Arch 5th Ser. Vol. 6, p. 290.

JAMES RUSSELL

Of Hamilton Twp., served as private under Capts. Noah Abraham, Samuel Patton and Alexdr. Peebles, 1777-78-79-80-81-82. He is shown as a freeman on Tax lists 1778-82.

Penna. Arch. 5th Ser. Vol. 6, p. 52, 57, 136, 20, 21, 53, 139, 287, 312, 395, 589.

JOSEPH RUSSELL

Served under Capts. Joseph Culbertson and John McConnell, 1780-81. Joseph Russell is also shown in the Cont. Line, Cumb. Co., Penna.

Penna. Arch. 5th Ser. Vol. 6, p. 267, 288, 302. Vol. 4, p. 302, 638.

AMOS SACKETT

Served as private under Capt. Thos. Askey, 1779-80-81.

Penna. Arch. 5th Ser. Vol. 6, p. 62, 409, 423.

AZARIAH SACKETT

Gave service as Sergt., 1777-78, under Capt. Robert Shannon, and in 1779-80-81-82, under Captains Thos. Askey and Noah Abraham. A freeman in 1779-80-81-82.

Penna. Arch. 5th Ser. Vol. 6, p. 16, 60, 120, 127, 48, 131, 408, 428, 55.

ELIJAH SACKETT

Served under Capts Thos. Askey and Noah Abraham, 1779-80-81. In 1778 he had 300 ac. land, horses and cattle, also in 1782. Deeds show the above man, May 1812, as of Toboyne Twp., Cumb. Co., Penna., with wife Catherine, selling land in Fannett Twp. to Philip Shoop. In May, 1778 Elijah and Azariah Sackett signed a petition from Fannett Twp. explaining the lack of arms and ammunition; and in 1779, Azariah, Joseph and Enos again signed a petition from Fannett Township.

Penna. Arch. 5th Ser. Vol. 6, p. 61, 394, 442, 620.

JOSEPH SACKETT

Served under Capt. Thos. Askey and others 1778-79-80-81-82; a freeman in 1779-80-81-82, 300 acres land.

Penna. Arch. 5th Ser. Vol. 6, p. 37, 39, 41, 62, 121, 128, 132, 409, 394 605, 620.

THOMAS SACKETT

1777-78, stated as persons in actual service during three several calls or times in the year 1778. All of above Sacketts were in Path Valley.

Penna. Arch. 5th Ser. Vol. 6, p. 605, 24.

PATRICK SAGERSON

Served as a private under Capt. Samuel Royer in 1779, and under Capt. Thomas Johnston in 1781-82. In 1790, the Census gives this family as: 1 man, 3 boys, 6 females. An old Article of Agreement, Andrew Snively and P. Sagerson, Apr. 1, 1793, Both of Antrim Twp., Andrew Snively Doth Lease and Let a parcel of Land, Being part of a tract Belonging to Margaret Crunkleton a Minor unto Patrick Sagerson For the Term of two years from the date hereof xxx P. Sagerman is to pay for the First year one pound or twenty Shillings pr. Acre, Second year sixteen Shillings and eight pence pr. Acre the Upland and Meadow Included and the sd. Sagerson is to build a house at his own Expense, and the afforsd. Andrew Snively Guardian of Margaret Crunkleton minor is to find two Gallons of whiskey for the sd. use of The sd. Sagerson is to have the Sole priviledge Orchard and Garden for the building of the house the Land that the sd. Sagerson has Cleared is to be under Sufficient fence with one Round Rail at the bottom and Six split Rails in each pannel with Stakes and Riders Sufficient and the said Sagerson is to have the priviledge of the Remainder of ye Timber. The Clearing for his own use after the fence is sufficiently made two trees Only Excepted No timber is to be cut for any Use off the Clearing nor any more to be cleared xx Each and both parties do bind themselves in the pennal Sum of Ffty Pounds xxx Wit: Wm. Newell.

Penna. Arch. 5th Ser. Vol. 6, p. 115, 130, 542.

ANDREW SANDS, PENSIONER

S40 383—Pennsylvania, applied for a pension from Franklin Co., Penna. In Aug., 1820, he was aged 66 years, then in Huntingdon Co. Penna., stating he enlisted June 7, 1777, in a company under Capt. Holliday, 1st Regiment, Penna. Line, under Command of Col. Chambers; served in said Regiment until discharged Aug. 13, 1783. In battles of Brandywine, Germantown, Monmouth, Stoney Point, Seige of York when Cornwallis was taken, and others. His family consists of wife Mary age about 43, and three children: the eldest in his 17th year; the second in his 11 year; the youngest in his 9th year. John Sands had a warrant in Metal Twp., of 207 acres, June 4, 1762.

Penna. Arch. 5th Ser. Vol. 2, p. 737.

SAMUEL SATTERLY

Served in 1780, under Capt. Alexdr. Peebles, Col. James Dunlap.

Penna. Arch. 5th Ser. Vol. 6, p. 395.

JOHN SAVAGE

Is shown in service under Capt. Thos. Askey, 1780-81. He was in Fannett Twp., with horses and cattle. The will of Robert Walker of Peters Twp., Franklin Co., Penna., names a dau. Elizabeth Savage. Under date of Jan. 11, 1831. The Chambersburg Repository gives: "Married the 29th at Mount Alto Furnace, by Rev. Robert B. Drane, of Hagerstown, Md., John Savage, Jr., Esq. of Philadelphia, and Miss Adelaide H. dau. of Samuel Hughes, Esq.

Penna. Arch. 5th Ser. Vol. 6, p. 79, 393, 409, 424.

PATRICK SAVAGE

Appears in service under Capt. William Huston and James Patton, 1780-81. He was of Peters Twp., and under a list of Freemen in 1781.

Penna. Arch 5th Ser. Vol. 6, p. 315, 265, 272, 285, 643.

RICHARD SAVAGE

Is shown in service 1779, with Capt. Wm. Long. Penna. Arch. 5th Ser. Vol. 6, p. 546.

JACOB SAYLOR

Served as Ensign with Capt. John Woods, 1777-81-82. His descendants have a tradition that he came with Lafayette. The "Franklin Repository" Aug. 25, 1829, gives the following: "Departed this life in Washington Twp., Monday 17th inst, in the 70th year of his age, Mr. Jacob Saylor; he left a desolate wife and three children to deplore the loss of a most effectionate companion and tender parent." Under Dec. 3, 1822, the "Repository" gives the marriage of George Seabrooke to Leah, only dau, of Mr. Jacob Saylor, on the 19th by Rev. Mr. Ruthrauff.

Penna. Arch 5th Ser. Vol. 6, p. 103, 137, 157.

PHILIP SCHOLL

Is shown giving service in 1775, in Bucks Co., Penna., Court records fail to show his arrival in Franklin Co., but McCauley (p. 123) states that Philip Scholl, at a very early period, carried on at Chambersburg, the manufacture of cards for fulling mills, and for all other purposes. The Repository" of July 26, 1814 gives the following: "Died on Thursday last in the 64th year of his age, Mr. Philip Scholl, a respectablr citizen of this Borough. On Saturday his remains were interred in the German Lutheran burial ground, the Rev. Mr. Moeller delivered an appropriate address. Under Jan. 12, 1830, is the marriage of George McFerron to Miss Elizabeth Sholl, on Thursday last, both of Guilford Twp.

Penna. Arch. 5th Ser. Vol. 5, p. 401.

ADAM SCOTT

Served as Lieut., under Capt. Chas. Maclay, 1777-78-81-82, several undated rolls. In 1794, in Deed Book 4, William Scott of Berkeley Co. Va., wagon maker, Brother and apparent Heir of Adam Scott late of Franklin Co., Penna., decd., sells land to Barnabas Doyle of Fannett Twp., Franklin Co., Penna.

Penna. Arch. 5th Ser. Vol. 6, p. 14, 31, 33, 45, 148, 390, 443, 631.

ALEXANDER SCOTT

In Franklin Co., Penna., Letters of Admr. in Chambersburg, Sept. 21, 1822. The Franklin Repository of Sept. 17, 1822 states, "Died Friday the 13th Alexander Scott, silversmith." He is thought to have come from Lancaster Co., Penna. Under date of Oct. 14, 1817, is this: "Oct. 14, 1817, married Tuesday evening, 7th inst., by Rev. Denny, Col. George Clingan of Union Co., Susquehannah, to Miss Eliza Scott, dau. of Alexander Scott, of this Borough." The "Repository," Feb. 13, 1821, gives the marriage of "William McGaughey, Jr., of Adams County, to Miss Martha, dau. of Alexander Scott of this place, by Dr. D. Denny."

Penna. Arch. 2nd Ser. Vol. 13, p. 201.

ARCHIBALD SCOTT

Served as private 1780-81 with Capt. Wm. Huston, 4th Batt. Cumb. Co. Militia, under Col. Samuel Culbertson.

Penna. Arch. 5th Ser. Vol. 6, p. 270, 276, 283.

DAVID SCOTT

Is shown in service with Capt. Daniel Clapsaddle, 1780-81-82, a son of David Scott, an early Tax Collector in Antrim Township, who moved to Air Twp., (Cove) and left will of May 25, 1779. David Scott, above, of Washington Twp., left a Will prob. Nov. 14, 1800; the legatees, "Sons and daus. of my father," brothers: William; McLure; Sister Mary Lowry; brother James and sister Martha Gaff; brother John. Exr. brother John. Bedford, Penna., Court records. Will of David Scott, Air Twp., May 25, 1779, 20 pounds to the support of the Gospel in the Cove. Son John (for the use of Son James' schooling 20 pounds.) Son William; Grandau. Martha Scott (dau. of Wm.); Son George; Dau. Mary Lowry; Grandau. Mary Lowry; daughter-in-law Rebecca Scott, relict of James Scott; Son Robert; Money from sale of balance of estate to be put in bank at Phila. Exrs.: My sons, John, Robert and George Scott. Wit: Wm. Gaff, Barthol Roharty and James White. My trusty friends Col. John Allison (of East Conococheague) and Rev. Patrick Allison of Baltimore to be guardians. David Scott is believed to have held the oldest proprietary title to land in the Great Cove, dated Nov. 6, 1749. He gave his bond to pay and maintain a body of twenty-seven Scouts for three months, during which time the Indians were repulsed, and the settlers were enabled to harvest their crops. It seems to have been during the summer of 1763, when the Indians fell upon the frontiers during harvest time, killing many settlers in sections of the Great Cove, tho' many were killed and taken prisoners in Jan., 1756, according to the Penna. Gazette of Feb. 12, 1756. Under Votes of the Assembly, 1766, David Scott was paid 169 pounds for paying and subsisting 27 Rangers.

Penna. Arch. 5th Ser. Vol. 6, p. 93, 116, 122, 580.

JAMES SCOTT

Of Montgomery Township, served under Capt. John Orbison, 1780-81-82. His will was prob. March 15, 1787; wife Jannet; Sons Samuel, William; Thomas; Dau. Jean McCune; Dau. Mary Meonough; Dau. Elizabeth Meanough.

Penna. Arch. 5th Ser. Vol. 6, p. 273, 293, 303, 307.

MATTHEW SCOTT

Is shown serving under Col. Samuel Miles, Penna. Rifle Regt. He was appointed First Lieut. March, 1776, under Capt. Wm. Peebles, captured Aug 27, 1776, exchanged Dec. 8, 1776, for Lieut. Cleveland of the Seventh British; promoted Captain, Apr. 18, 1777. Matthew Scott appears through 1780-81-82, in service with Capt. Alexdr. Peebles. He died May 20, 1798, at Shippensburg.

Penna. Arch. 5th Ser. Vol. 2, p. 356.

SAMUEL SCOTT

Served as private 1780-81, under Capt. Wm. Huston, Command of Col. Samuel Culbertson. Samuel Scott was married to Elizabeth Wilson, by Rev. Alexdr. Dobbin, Feb. 14, 1776, probably of Antrim Twp., and the "Cove."

Penna. Arch. 5th Ser. Vol. 6, p. 270, 276, 283.

WILLIAM SCOTT

Served as a private under Capt. John Orbison, 1780-81-82. William Scott had the fulling mill in Montgomery Twp. He died June 17, 1786, naming in his will wife Jean; sons John and Wm.; daus. Jean, Sarah; a brother John Scott; Sisters, Sarah, Rebecca, Mary, also two sisters-in-law, Martha and Mary Scott, and Rebecca Parkhill each to receive a morening gown. The two daughters, Jean and Sarah Scott became the 1st and 2nd wives of Col. Josiah Price.

Penna. Arch. 5th Ser. Vol. 6, p. 274, 294, 307.

TIMOTHY SCYHAWK

Served in the Continental Line, Cumb. Co. Penna. In the Concord Union Graveyard, Path Valley, Penna., are the graves of Benj. Van Scyog, who died in 1872, aged 83 yrs. and Margaret, wife of Benj. Vanscyog, who died in 1870 aged 80 years. They are shown in Ambersons Valley, Fannett Twp., in 1800, selling land to John Harmoni. John Van Scyoc sells in 1803, and Wm. Vanscyoc in 1806, all in Fannett Twp. In 1796, Fannett Twp., Benjamin, John and Abel Scyhock are shown with land, horses, cattle &c.

Penna. Arch. 5th Ser. Vol. 4, p. 303, 304, 638.

JOHN SECRIST

Served under Capt. Samuel Royer, 1779-80-81 of the First Batt. Cumb. Co. Militia. He was probably a son of Bartholomew Seegrist, and in the will of John Secrist of Washington Twp., he names wife Mary; dau. Catherine, a minor; sons Solomon and John; Abraham; Dau. Elizabeth; Dau. Mary. The witnesses were: Solomon Secrist and Daniel Royer. The will dated Aug. 1797, was prob. March, 1798. In the will of the widow, Mary Secrist, she names dau. Elizabeth Frederick; Dau. Mary Small; Sons: Abraham; Solomon; John; Son-in-law John Small. Will dated June 1814; prob. Aug., 1823. Price's Graveyard, North of Waynesboro, Mary, wife of Soloman Segrist, b. Dec. 25, 1792, d. Feb. 24, 1860, aged 67 yrs. 3 mos.

Penna. Arch. 5th Ser. Vol. 6, p. 75, 90, 113, 542.

SOLOMON SECRIST

Served as private 1780-81, under Capt. Daniel Clapsaddle. Bartholomew Seegrist left a will at Carlisle, dated 1777, and prob., 1778, naming wife Susanna, and issue: Henry; Solomon; John, Michael; Peter; Catherine; Elizabeth of Antrim Twp. In the above will, Bartholomew willed to his sons, Henry and Solomon, a tract of land he had bought from Robert McCrea in 1773, which tract Henry and Solomon sold in 1792 to William Henderson. In 1817, Solomon Sechres, Sr,. conveys to Solomon Sechrest, Jr., Land called "Wisdom," 127 acres, also a tract "Wisdomsway" of 113 acres. Solomon Secrist, late of Quincy Twp., died Feb. 1838, leaving issue: 3 children, John; Mary mar. John Lehman and Martha mar. to Geo. Fry. In the Menser Graveyard, are old stones, showing, S-S 1838, C-S 1817.

Penna. Arch. 5th Ser. Vol. 6, p. 93, 116.

NICHOLAS SELHEIMER

Died in Franklin Co., 1823. He enlisted in Von Heer's; afterwards in Coultman's; served 3 years, 6 months; resided near Shippensburg in 1817. He was a private in Penna. Line and a pensioner.

Penna. Arch. 2nd Ser. Vol. 13, p. 202. 2nd Ser. Vol. 11, p. 230. Biographical Annals of Franklin Co., Penna.

THOMAS SELLERS (CELLARS)

Served as private under Capt. John Orbison, 1780-81. He mar. Sarah, dau. of John Flanagan, an early pew holder in the Welsh Run Church. Thomas Sellers & wife went to Delaware Co., Ohio.

Penna. Arch. 5th Ser. Vol. 6, p. 264, 274, 294.

LIEUTENANT EZEKIAL SEMPLE

Served in Capt. Samuel Patton's Ranging Company in the spring and summer of 1778-79, on the Frontiers of Bedford and Westmoreland Counties, in Col. Wm. Chambers Battalion. He served 1780-81-82 as Ensign with Capt. John Orbison.

Penna. Arch. 5th Ser. Vol. 6, p. 273, 293, 307, 601, 609.

ADAM SHAFFER

Rev. Soldier, died June 1, 1846, aged 91 years. Susannah, wife of Adam Shaffer, died 1847, aged 73 years. Enlisted in Capt. Abraham Smith's Company, Cumb. Co., Militia, Feb. 22, 1776. He also served in 1780-81-82 under Capt. Thos. Johnston, of Antrim Twp., Franklin Co., Penna. Shaffer home at King, Bedford Co., Penna.

Penna. Arch 5th Ser. Vol. 6, p. 85, 99, 115, 130. Pub. The Genealogical Society of Penna. Vol. XII, No. 3, March, 1935, p. 296.

PETER SHAVER

Served under Capt. Samuel Royer, 1777-78-79, and in 1780 under Capt. Wm. Long. He was an Ensign over that period. In 1796, Peter Shaver had 200 ac. land, horses and cattle in Montgomery Twp., and in 1827, he was one of three Executors to settle the estate of Jacob Angle of Welsh Run. The other Executors were: Frederick Smith and John Findlay, Esq. The 1790 Census shows Peter Shaver with two men, two boys and 4 females.

Penna. Arch. 5th Ser. Vol. 6, p. 273, 293, 511, 524, 532, 541, 557.

GEORGE SHANNON

Of Guilford Township served under Capt. James Young 1781. Court records show that Benj. Chambers and wife Jane sold a lot in Chambersburg to Charles Wright in 1778. In 1779 he conveyed it to George Shannon, who with Fanny his wife, sold in 1782 to Alexander Duncan, who with his wife Sarah sold to Henry Coyle. Mrs. Kate Bradfield Norris, born in Barnesville, Ohio, No. 52207, descendant of George Shannon, dau. of John Bradfield and Eliza Ann Shannon, grandau. of Thomas Shannon and Cassandra Anderson, great grandau. of George Shannon and Jane Milligan. George Shannon, 1759-1803, private in Capt. James Young's Co., 8th Batt. Cumb. Co. Penna. Militia, under Col. Abraham Smith, born in Ireland, died in Belmont Co. Ohio, also No. 50080.

Penna. Arch. 5th Ser. Vol. 6, p. 111, 630.

HUGH SHANNON

Served as a private under Capt. Thomas McDowell in 1780. He was a son of William. He was in Scott Co., Ky., in 1812.

Penna. Arch. 5th Ser. Vol. 6, p. 615.

JOHN SHANNON, SR.

Served as a private under Capt. William Huston, 1780-81. He lived in the "Corner" Montgomery Twp., and his will was probated 1792. He names wife Margaret; dau. Margaraet; son William McBroom; Five sons: William; Samuel; Joseph; Robert and Elijah. Letters on estate of Margaret Shannon were granted to Hugh Shannon in 1811. This family attended the Welsh Run Church, as Margaret and Joseph are shown as pew-holders.

Penna. Arch. 5th Ser. Vol. 6, p. 270, 276, 283.

JOHN SHANNON, JR.

Served under Capt. William Huston, 1780-81. He was a son of William and Mary Shannon and he mar. Susanna Alexander, July 8, 1772. They went south, being in Fayette Co., Ky., about 1812.

Penna. Arch. 5th Ser. Vol. 6, p. 269, 275, 282.

JOSEPH SHANNON

Served as private under Capt. William Huston, 1780-81, was probably a son of John Shannon, Sr. He mar. Mary, dau of James and Gwin Davis, and grandau. of pioneers Philip and John Davis of Welsh Run. They went to Kentucky.

Penna. Arch. 5th Ser. Vol. 6, p. 276, 284.

NATHANIEL SHANNON

Of William, served as a private in 1780, under Capt. Wm. Smith, (Huston's Company). He went to Scott. Co., Ky. His father had willed him his "right and title to a warrant for 400 acres in Cane Took Settlement."

Penna. Arch. Ser. Vol. 6, p. 276.

ROBERT SHANNON

A son of William and Mary Shannon, Montgomery Twp., Franklin Co., Penna., born Jan 23, 1753, mar. Feb. 24, 1780, Catherine, dau. of John Davidson, who moved to S. Carolina (York Co. later) mar. at her father's house (probably John Davidson from Antrim Twp.), moved to Lincoln Co. N. C., and in 1795, to Scott Co., Ky.; about 5 yrs. later to Fayette Co. then to Jessamine Co., and in 1812 to Henry Co., Ky. Robert Shannon died Jan. 22, 1827, in Henry Co., Ky. Widow applied for pension Jan. 8, 1840, claiming that Robert Shannon served from the commencement of war until about the close, as private and lieutenant, was in battles of Kings's Mountain, Cowpens, Eutaw Springs, served part of time under Capt. Henry and Col. Dickson. He took the Oath of Allegiance Aug. 29, 1778, and was discharged Oct. 20, 1781, from a 3 months tour as lieut. in Capt. James Little's Comp., in Col. Francis Lock's N. C., Regiment. The widow Catherine, born Dec. 2, 1762, died May 26, 1850. They had issue, 1781-1802; Nancy B; Mary; Catherine; Joseph W.; Pegy; Samuel, Lillie; John D. or B.; Elias. Pension Application R-9420.

THOMAS SHANNON

Served as private under Capt. James Young, 1777-78-79-81. His wife was Jane, and in 1781 and 1797, they sold lots in Chambersburg, bought by them from Benj. and Jane Chambers. They had a dau. Rachel who mar. Washington Porter

OF FRANKLIN COUNTY PENNSYLVANIA

in 1799; a dau. Jane and known sons were, Joseph; William; Samuel; buried in Moorifield Cemetery, near Mercer, Penna.

Penna. Arch. 5th Ser. Vol. 6, p. 76, 82, 111, 522, 526, 548.

WILLIAM SHANNON

Of Guilford Township, served as a private under Capt. James Young, 1779-80-81. In 1813, William Shannon and wife Margaret sold Lot 169 in Chambersburg to John Wickman (?)

Penna. Arch. 5th Ser. Vol. 6, p. 82, 547, 110.

JAMES SHARP

A Captain under Col. Hugh Mercer, 1758-59. Under Deeds, 1774, Capt. James Sharpe, of Letterkenny Twp., and wife Agnes, sell to Robert Sharp, farmer, for 600 pounds, 403 acres, land in said Township, warranted to James Sharpe, Apr. 16, 1765. Witness Will Sharp who was later in Harden County, Ky.

Penna. Arch. 5th Ser. Vol. 1, p. 130, 175, 184, 265.

JAMES SHARP

Appears as a private under Capt. Patrick Jack and Captain Noah Abraham. One James Sharp applied for land in Green Twp., 48 acres, 80 perches, Oct. 17, 1765; at a later date John S. Kerr applied for the above tract.

Penna. Arch. 5th Ser. Vol. 6, p. 139, 145, 147.

JOHN SHARP

Appears as a private 177-79-80-81 in service with Capt. Patrick Jack. He was probably one of the four sons of William Sharp of Letterkenny Township.

Penna. Arch. 5th Ser. Vol. 6, p. 20, 64, 145, 388, 401, 414.

MATTHEW SHARP

Served in the Light Dragoons, under James Culbertson, 1781, and under Capt. John Rea, 1777-79-80-81. He was a taxable in Letterkenny Twp., during the above years.

Penna. Arch. 5th Ser. Vol. 6, p. 72, 78, 523, 544, 585, 623, 640.

ROBERT SHARP

As Lieut. and Light Horseman appears under Capt. John McConnell, 1780-81-82. One Robert Sharp of Franklin County dying, Letters Admr. were issued to Hannah Sharp, Sept.,1785.

Penna. Arch. 5th Ser. Vol. 6, p. 267, 302, 309.

ROBERT SHARP

Is shown under Capt. Patrick Jack, at Newtown in 1779, and undated rolls.

Penna. Arch. 5th Ser. Vol. 6, p. 63, 144, 146.

ROBERT SHARP

One Robert Sharp appears under Capt. Chas. Maclay. A man of the name was a taxable in Lurgan Twp., in 1779. What appears as service for three men, named Robert Sharp, may all belong to one man.

Penna. Arch. 5th Ser. Vol. 6, p. 149, 150, 416.

WILLIAM SHARP

Served under Captains John Rea, and Samuel Patton, 1778-79-80-81. In 1778 William Sharp was taxed in Leterkenny Twp., with land, horses and cattle, and was a freeman. In 1779 "Major" William Sharp and William Sharp, Jr., were taxed as above. In 1781 "Major" William and William, Jr., again taxed with much land. In 1782, it is "William Sharp's heirs," and William, Jr., with a saw mill, 500 acres land, horses and cows. Patents were dated Feb. 1, 1775 to Wm. Sharp, land called "Angola" in Letterkenny Twp. William Sharp died, and in his will at Carlisle, he devised to eldest son William, and other three sons; John; David; George. Executors, Mary Sharp and James McConnell; the said Mary has since mar. John McDowell. The son David died intestate. In 1797-98 John Sharp of Shippensburg sells land to Captain William Rippey, of same place, Innkeeper, and to Peter Rudeback of Hamilton Twp., land in Greene and Letterkenny Twps. In Feb., 1800, Letters of Admr. on estate of John Sharp, were granted to Joseph McKinney, Esq., Capt. Matthew Henry and Robert Smith, as sureties. William Sharp occupied Pew No. 38 in the old Log Church at Rocky Spring, and Pew 22 in the new Brick Church, in 1794.

Penna. Arch. 5th Ser. Vol. 6, p. 78, 105, 536, 543, 584, 601, 610.

HENRY SHEARER

Served as private in Lancaster County Militia, 1779-1782, under Capt. Robert McKee. Henry, born about 1738 in Lancaster Co., Penna., mar. about 1758, Barbara Behme, dau. of Rudolph Behme of Lancaster Co., Penna. Henry Shearer died in Letterkenny Twp., Franklin Co., Penna., Jan. 4, 1812, his wife having died prior to him. Orphans Court held March 10, 1812, shows the following issue: Abraham; Henry; Peter; Dewalt; Christian; Mary; Joseph; Samuel; Hannah; Solomon, and the widow and issue of John Shearer, his son, who died about 4 days before the intestate; a widow Mary and 7 children: John; Sally; Simon; Mary; Henry; Peggy and Michael. Henry Shearer is also shown in Capt. Joseph Shippen's Company, March 10, 1756.

Penna. Arch. 5th Ser. Vol. 7 p. 207, 768.

HENRY SHEARER

Probably served from Berks Co., Penna., born

March 29, 1761, died 1839. His wife Christena, 1769-1828, was a dau. of Abraham Stump. They are buried at the White Church, Marion, Penna. The estate of Henry Shearer, late of Guilford Twp., was administered by Solomon Miller a son-in-law. A deed dated May 28, 1842 was from Solomon Miller, Esq., and Mary, his wife, of Franklin Co., Penna., and John Shearer and Margaret, his wife of Stark Co., Ohio, to Daniel Gelwix of Strasburg, conveyed to Henry Shearer, April 1, 1819, who left the above two children. Solomon Miller owned land in Guilford Twp., and died there. It is probable that the Shearers lived with them in their declining years.

Penna. Arch. 5th Ser. Vol. 4, p. 266.

PETER SHEARER

Appears serving in Lancaster Co., Penna., with Capt. John Gillchreest, in 1778-79, in the 4th Batt. of Militia. Deeds show Peter Shearer, Nov. 11, 1794, buying land in Peters Twp., from Edward Welch and Thomas McDowell, Exrs. of John Welsh, land joining Matthew Patton, Richard Cox, Benj. Chambers, "Barnell's Nobb;" also joining Hugh Carroll's land, Widow Donnalson, and John Welch's Dam. Peter left a will dated 1805, prob. 1806, naming wife Christina and son Jonathan to live with his mother. Young children were Rebecca; Benj.; Solomon; Daniel; Peter; and an expected child; land in Knoxville Co., Tenn. The Exrs., were Brother Fredk. Shearer, and son Jonathan. (The widow Christina probably mar. Conrad Stinger.) Under records of Trinity Reformed Church Mercersburg, Penna., as communicants, Dec. 23, 1804, were Peter, Fredk. and Jonathan Scherer. A deed of Oct. 1828, from Fredk. Shearer and wife Rebecca of Washington Twp., Fayette Co., Penna., to Adam Cromel (?), land in Peters Twp., conveyed to Fredk. Shearer Dec. 27, 1805, by Peter Shearer and Christina, his wife.

Penna. Arch. 5th Ser. Vol. 7, p. 386, 399, 410.

CAPTAIN EVAN SHELBY

Officers and Soldiers in the Provincial Service, Capt. Evan Shelby, Lieut. Reason Bell, Ensign Evan Shelby, Jr., May, 1759. Captain Evan Shelby, 1719-1794, was from what is now Washington Co., Md., a son of Evan and Catherine Shelby, the immigrants. Ensign Evan Shelby, Jr., was the son of Rees Shelby, who appears in the Little Cove. There were not enough Maryland troops in this French and Indian War, so they were sent up by Gov. Sharpe to General Forbes, who had them assigned to the Penna. Regt., and they served as part of the Provincial Troops. Capt. Evan Shelby, son of the immigrant, mar. 1st. in Maryland, 1744-45, Lititia Cox, dau. of David and Susanna Cox, and they had issue: John; Isaac; James; Evan.

He mar. 2nd Isabella Elliott, in N. E. Tenn., in 1787, a dau. of Thomas Elliott. Issue by Isabella Elliott: James; Letitia; Eleanor; He mar. 3rd Catherine Shelby, having issue: Moses and Catherina. They removed to what is now Sullivan Co., Tenn. In addition to service given, he is credited with a part in "Dunmores" war; a Captain in Fincastle Co., Va. troops under Lewis at battle of Point Pleasant, on the Ohio River, 1774. In the Rev. War as Major, Colonel, County Militia (Va) guarding the frontier, commanded the expedition against the Chickamauga tribe and Lookout Mountain South East Tenn., 1779. Post Revolution. His home, by running of the State line, was found to be in North Carolina instead of Virginia. Made brigadier general of the Washington (over Mountain) district by the N. C. legislature, 1787. Annals of Southwest Virginia 1769-1800, by Lewis Preston Summers, Wash. Co. p. 951, Jan. 29, 1770. Evan Shelby, Gentleman, produced his Excellency Patrick Henry the Governors commission appointing him Colonel of the Militia of the County of Washington, and took the Oath of office. Washington County Va., was one of the three new shires which were created out of the older and larger Fincastle Co., Dec. 6, 1776. Arthur Campbell was named County Lieutenant (or chief military officer), Evan Shelby as Colonal was in active command in the field. p. 1406. Rev. Soldiers: Col. Evan Shelby, Wash. County. James Shelby (son of Col. Evan) Capt. in Battle of L. I. Flats, Wash. Co. James, son of Col. Evan, was a private under his father at Point Pleasant, 1774. He was a Captain with George Rogers Clark. Isaac, 2nd son of Col. Evan Shelby, Col. Commandant, Sullivan Co., N. C. (Tenn) and one of the leaders at Kings Mt. later Governor of Kentucky. p. 1389. John and James Shelby, p. 1418. Capt. Evan Shelby, evidently Capt. Evan, lately, from Md., and now living in S. W. Virginia, 3000 acres land Jan. 7, 1774; John Shelby 2000 acres, same date. John was probably the brother of Capt. Evan, who removed from Franklin Co., Penna., to Wash. Co., Va., about same period as his brother Evan.

Penna. Arch. 2nd Ser. Vol. 2, p. 498.

LIEUTENANT JOHN SHELBY

1724-94, appears in 1758-59, under Col. Hugh Mercer, with Officers who serve in the Penna. Regt. Under lotts assigned to each man, Lieut. John Shelby is given two lotts. He was a son of pioneer Evan Shelby and wife Catherine and his issue by first wife is given as: John; Evan; Thomas; Isaac; Louisa who mar. Wm. McCrab, but not proven. The second wife of above John Shelby, was Sarah, dau of David Davis, one of the early Welsh settlers near Welsh Run. The will of David Davis, dated Apr. 1, 1764, prob. June

19, 1766 at Carlisle, Penna., names wife Catherine; only dau. Sarah Shelby; Grandau. Catherine Shelby; Grandson David Shelby; Brothers: James; Daniel and Samuel Davis; Wife's brother David Davis. An old Deed shows that in 1792, "David Shelby of Summer Co. and Territory of the United States of America, by John Shelby, Jr., of Sullivan County and Territory aforesaid, his Attorney &c." xxx Warrant dated the 15th day of March, 1744, there was surveyed to a certain David Davis a tract of land called "Dividend," on the Welsh Run, in Peters Twp., then in the County of Lancaster, part of a larger tract. David Davis in his will did devise this tract unto his "Grandson" the said "David Shelby and his heirs forever." This tract was in the Angle name for many years, the Deed having been written by James Maxwell. John Shelby was a witness in 1767, on a deed of John and Sarah Irwin of Hamilton Twp., to Samuel Smith of Peters Twp. Mr. Cass K. Shelby knows that "Grandson" David Shelby mar. Sarah, dau of Col. Anthony and Mary (Ramsey) Bledsoe, and that "Grandaughter" Catherine Shelby mar. her first cousin, Evan Shelby 3rd. We next hear of John Shelby, Sr., in Washington Co., Va., near his brother Evan, both prominent in Military affairs. Evan lived on the south side of the line now running between Virginia and Tenn., now Bristol, Tenn. John lived near Abingdon, Wash. Co., Va., about fifteen miles N. W. of Bristol. Mr. Cass K. Shelby adds the following: Since my early research, I have definitely discovered that the emigrants came from the town, or near the town, of Tregaron in Cardiganshire, mid-Wales. The entries of their names on the parish register at St. Caron's church (Anglican) there start with the year 1709, when there was an abrupt change in the spelling from Selby to Shelby, the first entry of the former being 1681. This and a tradition in Wales to that effect, would seem to confirm the opinion held here that the line came originally from England and that the pronunciation of the name became corrupted by the Welsh tongue into its present form. There is, as a matter of fact an English "family" by the name of Selby and neither that, nor Shelby is Welsh in form. We are indebted to Mr. C. K. Shelby, of Hollidaysburg for much of the Family data.

Penna. Arch. 5th Ser. Vol. 1, p. 266, 300.

JOHN SHENIFIELD (SHANEYFELT)

Served as a private under Capt. John Orbison, 1780-81-82. He was of vicinity of Welsh Run, left a wife Christina; sons, Peter; John; David; son-in-law Jacob Myers, to whom he left 50 acres land and a Mill Seat on Conococheague. His will was prob. Nov. 28, 1809.

Penna. Arch. 5th Ser. Vol. 6, p. 274, 294, 308.

DAVID SHIELDS

Served as Lieut. 1776 under Capt. George Matthews and 1777-78-80-81-82 under Capt. Samuel Patton. An unidentified Matthew Shields of Letterkenny Twp., "house carpenter," died Apr.—May 1816, naming a wife Rachael and 2 children: Jennet and David Shields, "if they die in minority," if all die to go to my half brother Robert Swan, and to my brother Joseph Shields. Moses Kirkpatrick again appears as a witness, with Robert Swan. The will of William Herron, 1828, names Matt. Shields, a son of decd., dau. Sarah. Exrs.: David Shields and William Herron.

Penna. Arch. 5th Ser. Vol. 6, p. 261, 277, 286, 310, 318, 368, 370, 377.

DAVID SHIELDS

The Chapter is indebted to Miss Isabel R. Sheilds for much of the following family data: David Shields served under Capt. Joseph Armstrong, Aug. 7, 1755. He, with his sons," heartily joined as a Company." His will dated May 27, 1766, names wife Mary and children Robert; Matthew; Isabel; Rebecca; Janet. Following the death of his wife, he added a Codicil "apriel ye 2nd 1773." The Warrant for land to David Shields was No. 17, May 1751. Warrant No. 87, was made to him in 1762. Quoting from the Shields Book, by Misses Jane E. and Isabel R. Shields, it is shown that a deed for land was given by David Shields, "Husbandman" to Samuel Culbertson, who "intermarried with Jennet, the daughter of said David."

Penna. Arch. 5th Ser. Vol. 1, p. 38.

GEORGE SHIELDS

Is shown serving in the Militia of Westmoreland Co., David McCraight of Franklin County, Penna., died leaving a tract of land; one dau. Mary, shown as the wife of George Shields, was living in Elizabeth Twp., Allegheny Co., Penna., in 1793. At the same time, the 2nd dau. Margaret, was the wife of Joseph Mitchell.

Penna. Arch. 5th Ser. Vol. 4, p. 455.

JOHN SHIELDS

Served with Capt. Thos. Askey, as Corporal, 1779-81, undated rolls.

Penna. Arch. 5th Ser. Vol. 6, p. 62, 132, 375, 408, 423, 424.

MATTHEW SHIELDS

(Son of David) Served 1777-80 under Captains John McConnell and Samuel Patton. Matthew Shields, Sr. and Jr., were among those who served Aug. 7, 1755, under Capt. Joseph Armstrong. Matthew Shields was an Elder in the Rocky Spring Church, and his name is on a pew in the present brick structure, built 1794. It is probable that

David Shields and family, Matthew Shields and Robert Shields and families, all lie in the old Rocky Spring Graveyard. Matthew Shields mar. Mary McKane (McKean) dau. of James and Martha McKean, in 1767. She had two sisters, Jane, wife of James Beard; Anne, wife of John Machan. Matthew and Mary (McKane) Shields had issue nine: (1) Mary b. Oct. 16, 1768, mar. Benj. Ramsey, 1795. Settled Washington Co., Penna. (2) Robert b. Jan. 26, 1770 mar. 1st Mary Shields; 2nd Mrs. Elizabeth Dickey, settled in Westmoreland Co., Penna. (James b. 4, 1772, d. July 2, 1841; mar. in 1799, Elizabeth Wilson, b. 1775, d. 1783, dau of John and Sarah (Strain) Wilson. The marriage by Dr. John King, Mercersburg, Penna. Both are buried in old "Congruity Cemetery," Westmoreland Co., Penna. A grandson, James Wilson Shields, returned to Franklin County and lives on one of the Wilson farms, "Locust Grove." (4) Martha, b. Apr. 4, 1774, d. May 4, 1856, buried Cross Creek, Washington Co., Penna. Mar. 1st John Ramsey in 1795; mar. 2nd John DeFrance. (5) Aggie Nancy b. Aug. 15, 1776, mar. Jan. 14, 1800, William Clark, of Beaver Co., Penna. (6) Rebecca b. March 15, 1779, mar. Moses Kirkpatrick, no issue: (7) David b. March 27, 1781, d. Dec. 11, 1851. He mar. May 11, 1829, Mrs. Elizabeth Todd Williamson. They are buried in Shippensburg. (7) George b. Aug. 8, 1785, mar. 1st Jane Craig; 2nd Elizabeth Smith. (9) Jean b. Aug. 29, 1786; probably died young. The will of Matthew Shields dated Oct. 18, 1809, prob. Nov. 1, 1809, gives to his wife all Household and kitchen furniture with the use of the fire room that is taken off the kitchen and the Little front Room in the house during her natural life.

Penna. Arch. 5th Ser. Vol. 1, p. 38. Vol. 6, p. 267, 373.

PETER SHIELDS

Was a private under Capt. Conrad Snider, 1780-81.

Penna. Arch. 5th Ser. Vol. 6, p. 87, 119.

ROBERT SHIELDS, SR. AND JR.

Served in the Company of Capt. Joseph Armstrong, Aug. 7, 1755. The above Robert Shields, Sr., was probably the son of pioneer David Shields. He died prior to his father, in 1766, leaving a widow Rebecca and issue: George; David; John; William; Matthew; Robert; James and Hannah. The widow and son George admr. on the estate. One Robert Shields was an Elder in Rocky Spring Church occupying Pew 54, wiht Joseph Swan, in the Brick Church built in 1794. Matthew Shields occupied Pew 43, in the Brick Church in 1800.

Penna. Arch. 5th Ser. Vol. 1, p. 38.

ROBERT SHIELDS

Served as private, 1780-81-82, under Capt. John McConnell. Under Oct. 9, 1804, the "Repository" gives the death of Mr. Robert Shields, on the 5th inst. Oct. 16, 1804, is recorded the death of Mrs. Nancy Shields, widow of the late Robert Shields, whose death we mentioned in our last. The will of Robert Shields of Letterkenny Twp., was "dated about 1st inst.," prob. Oct. 27, 1804. He names wife Ann; 2 daus. Ann and Isabella; youngest son Ralston; Sons John and Robert; Sons Abijah and Joseph now learning trades. Son Samuel; Grandau. Mary Duncan; Exr: wife; Son Robert; Moses Kirkpatrick. Wit: Matthew Sheilds and Matthew Shields.

Penna. Arch. 5th Ser. Vol. 6, p. 268, 303, 310.

DANIEL SHILLING

Was a private under Capt. Conrad Snider, 1780-81. In the will of Adam Stump (dated 1801) he names his dau. Elizabeth as the wife of Daniel Shilling. It is probable that Daniel Shilling left Franklin Co., early, as a Shilling descendànt writes from Ill., of a Barbara who mar. John Robinson. Barbara is said to have had two brothers carried off by Indians, also an Adam Shilling was born in Franklin Co., Penna., Feb. 11, 1792, the parents being John and Barbara Shilling. She further says that the one captive boy carried off by the Shawnese Indians later came back with the Indians to see his people at Falling Spring. Old Franklin Countians would add that they came to visit the graves of their ancestors, adjoining the Falling Spring Graveyard, Chambersburg.

Penna. Arch. 5th Ser. Vol. 6, p. 87, 119.

GEORGE SHILLITOE

Served as a pvt., in 1782, under Capt. Terrence Campbell. In 1781, Thomas Shannon and wife Jane sold Lots 298 and 299, in town of Chambersburg to George Shellito of Hamilton Twp. On Dec. 13, 1803, John House was mar. to Betsy Shellito, by Dr. David Denny.

Penna. Arch. 5th Ser. Vol. 6, p. 126, 296.

WILLIAM SHALOTOE

Served as private under Capt. Patrick Jack in 1781.

Penna. Arch. 5th Ser. Vol. 6, p. 292.

JACOB SHIRK

In Franklin County, 1826. Letters of Admr. March 15, 1826.

Penna. Arch. 2nd Ser. Vol. 13, p. 206.

JOSEPH SHIRK

Served as private under Capts. John Rea and John Reed, 1779-80-81. He was of Green Twp., but owned land in Letterkenny. He names 11 children: Casper; Fredk.; Joseph; Christly; Abraham; Jacob; Peter; Elizabeth mar. John Long; Barbara mar. Jacob Houser; Christina mar. John Leaman; Magdalena mar. Geo. Sellers; grandson Samuel of son John. This will was probated May 22, 1811.

Penna. Arch 5th Ser. Vol. 6, p. 78, 105, 544, 585.

ROBERT SHIRLEY

Born 1735, probably in Penna., mar. Susan Baker, b. 1742. He served in the Rev. War, and in 1792, came from the Conococheague Valley, and settled on Black-leg creek, near Sattsburg. He died 1834, aged 99 years, his wife Susan dying in 1843, at 101 years. They had issue John; Robert; Thomas; Jane; Joseph; Ann. Several of the sons lived to a great age. Under the 1790 Census for Franklin Co., Penna. the family of Robert Sherley shows 1 man, 4 boys, 3 females.

Caldwell's Hist. Indiana Co., Penna. p. 436.

THOMAS SHIRLEY

Served under Capt. Samuel Patton 1780-81-82. He is also shown as Sergt., in Penna. Militia, aged 84 years in 1834. John Irwin of Hamilton Twp., sold a tract of 63 acres to Thos. Shirley, and in 1775, he obtained a warrant for it, which he conveyed to John Deeds. In 1796 Thos. Shirley appears as a taxable in Peters Twp., a mason, and Robert Shirley is also shown. In 1803, a letter was addressed to Thos. Shirley at Chambersburg.

Penna. Arch. 3rd Ser. Vol. 13, p. 530. 5th Ser. Vol. 6, p. 278, 287, 312.

JACOB SHIVELY

Served as a private under Capts. Martin Huey and Alexdr. White in 1782. He was born Feb. 22, 1751, died Jan. 1, 1824. His wife Barbara born 1755, died Dec. 6, 1823. His wife Maria, 1787-1830. Deeds show he came from Arle (Earl) Twp. Lancaster Co., Penna. Buried in Shively graveyard on Brindle farm, Brookside, Franklin Co., Penna.

Penna. Arch. 5th Ser. Vol. 7, p. 68, 82, 84, 99.

JAMES SHOAFF

Served as a pvt., 1780-82, with Captains Alexdr. Peebles and William Strain. Mr. Orr states that James Shoaff was interested with Judge Hanna, of Ft. Wayne, in the Ft. Wayne and Chicago railroad, and that his family went to Ft. Wayne when it was a wilderness. Philip Shoaff of Fort Wayne, settled in Salt Lake, became the editor of the "Salt Lake Vidette," later removing to California. John Shoaff served in the House and the Senate of Indiana. The descendants of Peter Shoaff generally, removed to western Penna., Ohio and Indiana.

Penna. Arch. 5th Ser. Vol. 6, p. 142, 397, 428, 430.

PETER SHOAFF, SR.

Appears in service 1777-80-82, undated roll, with Captains Alex. Peebles and William Strain, Command of Col. James Dunlop. In Mr. John G. Orr's interesting article on Early Grist Mills of Lurgan Twp., he states that the mill on Row Run, and the first mill on this site, was erected in 1766, by Peter Shoaff, who bequeathed it to James Shoaff, Apr. 12, 1793, who conveyed it to John Herron, Oct. 13, 1799. By 1801, it had become the property of David Gish of Lancaster County, the price of 1200 pounds including the farms. In the will of Peter Shoaff, St., of Southampton Twp., dated and prob. 1795, he names oldest dau. Anne Kirbaugh, her oldest son Peter Shoemaker, and her dau. Anne Kirbaugh. Grandchild Margaret Stumback, dau. of my dau. Kartrout Stumback; dau. Elizabeth Stumback; dau. Katherine Painter; residue of estate between sons James and Peter, who were the Executors. John and James Brackenridge as witnesses.

Penna. Arch. 5th Ser. Vol. 6, p. 26, 143, 398, 430.

PETER SHOAF

Served as private under Capt. John Campbell and Lieut. William Strain.

Penna. Arch. 5th Ser. Vol. 6, p. 143.

JACOB SHOCKEY

Served as private 1780-81, under Capt. Daniel Clapsaddle. He was of Washington Twp., his will dated and prob. in 1803. He named Wife Anna, sons Isaac and Christian. He referred to land in Washington Co., Md., joining Balls Hill, Tise Young and John Funk's lines, also 20 acres called in Patent the land of Nob; Dau. Susanna, wife of Samuel Bigler; Son Jacob; Dau. Magdalena, wife of Balser Mowen; Dau. Barbara, wife of Peter Heck; Anna, wife of George Heck; Eve, wife of John Nicholas; The witnesses to the above will were Wm. Miner, Wm. Nichols, Jacob Weldy. In June of 1838, the will of Margaret Shockey was recorded. She appears to be a dau. of "Son Jacob," and a grandau. of Jacob Shockey, Sr. "To my mother Eve Shockey all my estate;" To Sarah Burns $25.00 to be paid to said Sarah, so soon as she finishes two Quilts of mine, that are now partly made. To my Aunt Mary Keefer $10.; Grave stones, viz: one pair or set of Marble stones to be placed at the head and foot of my grave; one pair of the same material to mark the grave of my brother John, decd.; and two pairs, similar, placed in like manner at the graves of my decd. sisters, Mary and Nancy, as soon as can, conveniently, be done. A similar pair to be placed at

the Grave of my Father, Jacob Shockey, decd. Exr.: John Bonebrake.
Penna. Arch. 5th Ser. Vol. 6, p. 94, 97.

BARNET (BARNEY) SHUTLER

Served as private in Lancaster Co., Penna., under Capt. Crage, Commanded by Col. Alexander Lowry. "The within class was called to randisvouse at the sign of the Barr this 12th of Apr., 1779 to march to Bedford town and it appears that only five Privates are willing to march as by the above road." In 1782 Barnet Shetler was serving in Cumb. Co. Militia under Capt. Noah Abraham. He mar. Barbara, dau. of John Keasy; she was the widow of William Stenger (of George) who died in 1795. They are buried in the Keasy graveyard, Fannett Twp. The will of Barnet Shetler was dated 1828, prob. Apr. 4, 1836. He names wife Barbara; son Jacob and other children: John; William; Mary; Elizabeth.
Penna. Arch. 5th Ser. Vol. 6, p. 127, 429. Vol. 7, p. 327.

ANDREW SIMMS

Served as private, 1781-82, with Capt. John McConnell.
Penna. Arch. 5th Ser. Vol. 6, p. 303, 310.

SAMUEL SIMMS

Is shown serving as a private, 1780-81, with Capt. William Huston.
Penna Arch. 5th Ser. Vol. 6, p. 276, 283.

HENRY SITES

Served as a private under Capt. John Woods, 1781-82. He was of Antrim Twp., and died intestate in 1814, leaving a widow Polly, and issue seven: John; Henry; Jacob; Catherine; Emanuel; Polly and David a minor, of whom Peter Kishner is guardian. He left 340 acres land. John and Maria Seitz appears in the record of Zion Reformed Church of Greencastle, having Henry baptized in 1818. The name continues, under Confirmation, thru the years until 1864.
Penna. Arch. 5th Ser. Vol. 6, p. 104, 138.

STOPHEL SIGHTS (SITES)

Appears in Service under Capts. Wm. Findley, James Poe and John Woods, 1778-80-81-82.
Penna. Arch. 5th Ser. Vol. 6, p. 76, 92, 104, 138, 530, 576, 583.

The will of Jacob Stotler of Antrim Twp., Feb.-March, 1790, names his wife Nancy and his father-in-law, Henry Sights.

JAMES SKILES

Appears in service, 1780, under Capt. James Young and again in March of 1781. In 1778, James "Schyles" was a taxable in Letterkenny Twp., with horses and cattle. An indenture made in 1841, James Skiles gives to his dau. Jane, wife of Robert King, in which he wills to her land along the Ohio river in a tract known as "Caledonia," of Alexander Co., Ill. A Patent having been granted to John Skiles (deceased) son of said James Skiles late of Caledonia, Ill. The other half of which section had by said John Skiles in his lifetime been conveyed to John Riddle. The said John Skiles having died intestate on or about June 28, 1828. By the laws of the State the said James Skiles became heir, &c., &c.
Penna. Arch. 5th Ser. Vol. 6, p. 83, 100.

JOHN SKILES

Was in service under Capt. Patrick Jack, with his company at Newtown and certified by Benj. Blythe, Sub-Lieut. on two undated rolls. Taxlists show a John Skiles, in Newton Twp., Cumb. Co. in 1778, with horses and cattle.
Penna. Arch. 5th Ser. Vol. 6, p. 145, 152.

Lancaster Co., Penna., Court House, Book F, Vol. 1, page 555. Will of James Clemson of Salisbury Twp.; wife Margaret; Henry Skiles five children; Son-in-law David Whitehill and Rachel, his wife; Herman Skiles and Elizabeth, his wife; John Watson and Margaret, his wife; John McCally and Sarah his wife; To Isaac Latty and Mary, his wife (Latta?); Sons James Clemson and John Clemson, who were executors. Will dated March, 1792. Wit: Joseph Dickinson and Gains Dickinson. Jane Skiles born June 4, 1798, mar. Robert King; John Skiles born Oct. 25, 1800; Elizabeth Skiles born Oct. 15, 1807; Clarissa Jane Latta, Jan. 18, 1826; Mary Scott Latta, Aug. 21 1828; Elizabeth McAdoo Latta, Dec. 2, 1830; Nancy Wallace Latta, June 24, 1833; Mary Riddle, born Dec. 17, 1767; Jane Riddle, born Apr. 27, 1769; Elizabeth Riddle, born Sept. 15, 1782. From: Mrs. James Johnston, Mercersburg, Penna.

GEORGE SKINNER

Private served in 1782, under Capt. Wm. Moorhead. He moved from Cumb. Co., to Horse Valley. He was born May 7, 1761, and twice married, names of wives unknown.
Penna. Arch. 5th Ser. Vol. 6, p. 439.

WILLIAM SKINNER

Private, served under Capt. Robert Quigley in 1781, Capt. Wm. Moorhead in 1782. He married Martha Duncan, born Dec. 4, 1759, died Dec. 1, 1845. They moved to Path Valley from Cumberland Co. Mr. Skinner is buried at Spring Run Graveyard, born March 7, 1757, died May 8, 1808.
Penna. Arch 5th Ser. Vol. 6, p. 416, 425, 439, 636.

ROBERT SLOAN

Served as private under Capt. Patrick Jack, 1778-81-82. Robert was the son of William Sloan and wife Ann Means, William dying in Peters Twp., prior to 1750. They had issue: John Sloan; William mar Francis Nesbit; Robert (above) mar. Mary McBrayer and Jane mar. William Oats. The widow, Ann Means Sloan, mar. 2nd John Wason, who was killed by Indians in 1756, and his wife taken captive. They had Thomas; James; Elizabeth. The above Robert Sloan moved to Westmoreland Co., Penna., and his will, dated 1812, prob., 1816, names dau. Susannah Sloan; son John Sloan; Ann; Elizabeth; Susannah; Mary; John; Dau. Ann Cowden's children; dau. Elizabeth McCleton; dau. Mary Cowden; son-in-law John Sloan of Bedford Co., Penna. and my son John Sloan of Westmoreland Co., Penna. Under Votes of Assembly, Nov. 10, 1760, is a bill for five pounds, "Ann Wasden (Wasson) to take her to Conococheague." In 1769, Ann was living with Jane and William Oats. Robert Sloan was a tax Collector in Hamilton Twp., in 1783, and some old papers are in possession of a descendant. One John Sloan was in Shippensburg in 1733.

Penna. Arch. 5th Ser. Vol. 6, p. 291, 295, 313, 380. 8th Ser. Vol. 7, p. 56, 58.

ADAM SMALL

Of Washington Twp., appears in service in 1779-80-81-82, an undated roll, under Capt. Samuel Royer. He was a taxable from 1778 for 48 acres land (Wash. Twp), to 217 ac. in 1782. In 1786 on 217 acres land 2 horses and 5 cows.

Penna. Arch. 5th Ser. Vol. 6, p. 89, 112, 123, 542, 585.

CAPTAIN ABRAHAM SMITH

6th Penna. Cont. Line, committioned Jan. 9, 1776, then living in Antrim Twp., Franklin Co., Penna. He had 3 tracts of land in Antrim, "Addition," "Mount Pleasant" and "Smith's Retirement." He was a brother of pioneer William Smith of Mercersburg, and after the Revolution, he removed to Mercersburg, where he bought the beautiful stone house on N. Main St., built by Col. Robert Parker. He was unmarried and died June 8, 1813, leaving a long will, naming nieces and nephews as legatees. He was Col. of the 8th Batt. Cumb. Co. Associators, 1777-80, member of Penna. Assembly 84-87, of the Supreme Executive Council of Penna. 1787-90, Senator 90-94. From the Ledger of Samuel Findlay, March, 1776, Abram Smith was charged wiht Sundry goods: To Broadcloth &c per Bills 53 pounds 5 shillings 6¼ pence. Five shillings for 1 pound Taylor's Thread; 132¼ yds. Linnen, 21 pounds 9 shillings 9¾ pence; To Ribbon given a Recruit, 1 shilling 3 pence.

Penna. Arch. 5th Ser. Vol. 2, p. 230.

ANDREW SMITH

Served as a private under Capts John Woods and James Poe in 1780-81-82. He is shown as a taxable from 1778 to 1782, is thought to have moved to Cleveland County, N. C. He was mar. 1st to a dau. of Andrew Colhoun; 2nd to Catherine Engelfinger; issue to 1st wife, Andrew; Eleanor; Sarah.

Penna. Arch. 5th Ser. Vol. 6, p. 91, 104, 138, 576, 583.

CONRAD SMITH

1st Penna. Cont. Line, also Pensioner, died in Franklin Co. 1833, aged 81. He is buried in the early Lutheran Graveyard at Greencastle, and his stone states he died July 16, 1839, aged 85 yrs. 11 mos. The late G. G. Rupley of Mercersburg, was born and raised in Greencastle; he names three Rev. Soldiers living in Greencastle when he was a boy: Conrad Smith, Conrad Coffroth, Jacob Van Pool.

Penna. Arch 2nd Ser. Vol. 10, p. 379. 3rd Ser. Vol. 23, p. 530.

GEORGE SMITH

Served as private under Capt. James Young and Capt. Terrence Campbell, 1777-79-80-81-82. Letters on the estate of George Smith of Guilford Twp., were issued Dec., 1802. Orphans' Court records show that George Smith died Dec. 14, 1802, leaving a widow Susana and issue: John; Jacob; Emanuel; Simon; Elizabeth; Catherine; Susannah and Lavina; also Sarah mar. to John Hicks, who died before her father, leaving one child, called Elizabeth, now mar. to John Clippinger. Said Catherine mar. to Fred. Heck, and said Susannah mar. to John Kern.

Penna. Arch. 5th Ser. Vol. 6, p. 110, 126, 524, 548, 557.

ENSIGN JAMES SMITH

Province of Penna., July 16, 1763, Lieut. James Chambers and Capt. Samuel Lindsay, under Lieut. Col. Asher Clayton. From Deed Book 6, p. 195, we have this: "Know all men by these presents that I, James Smith of Peters Twp. Cumb. Co., Penna., have sold and Made over my whole warrant, right and title of a tract of land, situate in said Twp., joining the land I now live on, unto James McClelan of said Twp., said warrant being granted for 50 acres, for consideration of 25 pounds. Dated Aug. 28, 1766." The heirs of James McClelland in 1811 sell the land to Jacob Stover, the warrant dated June 6, 1753, in the name of James Smith, 50 acres. From History

Westmoreland Co., Penna. 1882—G. D. A. p. 95. Col. James Smith taken Indian Captive in 1755. When free returned to Franklin Co.,—an Ensign in war of 1763, and in 1764, a Lieut. in State Militia. In 1766 he explored the Holstein River and the Kentucky Country and traveled thru the Carolinas. After opening of Land Office he bought land along the Youghiogheny and Jacobs Creek. In 1774, he was a Captain in the Penna Line, and with St. Clair and Proctor organized the rangers of that date. In 1776, he was a Major in the association, much to do with the resolutions of May 16, 1775. When independence was declared, elected a member from Westmoreland for the Convention and of the Assembly. In 1778, received a Colonel's commission, removed to Bourbon Co., Ky. In 1778 was a member of Assembly of that State nearly continuously to 1799.

Penna. Arch. 5th Ser. Vol. 1, p. 336.

JONATHAN SMITH

Died of Camp fever at Amboy, N. J., Oct. 13, 1776. He was a private under Capt. John McClelland of this Franklin Co. vicinity, and under Capt. Jeremiah Talbott, March 14, 1776. He left a wife Jean, but no issue. He was a brother of Col. James Smith, the famous Indian captive, of Blackboy fame. He left a will dated Sept. 17, 1776, prob. Nov. 15, 1776, naming his wife Jean, and his brothers and sisters. He was a Ruling Elder of the Presbyterian Church at Mercersburg. William Smith, who bought the land on which the town of Mercersubrg was laid out in 1786, came by way of Antrim Twp. A certain Samuel McFerran of Antrim Twp., left a will about 1753, in which he empowered his wife Jane (Jean) and William Smith, as Executors to dispose of his land, which they did to David Scott in 1764. He, McFerran, having obtained it from the Hon. proprietaries warrant, June 10, 1747. David Scott sold to Jonathan Smith. When Jonathan Smith appears in Church records at Mercersburg, as a Ruling Elder, 1769, his family consisted of a wife Jean, and a boy named Samuel McFerran. The other inmate was Eliza Brown. It is probable that Jonathan Smith mar. the widow McFerran. The marriage of Samuel McPherrin to Margaret McMullin took place May 22, 1781, by Rev. John King. After baptisms of several children, the family appear in or near Hancock, Md., where Samuel's estate was administered in 1791; his son Alexander's estate in 1824.

Penna. Arch. 5th Ser. Vol. 2, p. 241. Vol. 1, p. 427. Presbyterian Church records, Mercersburg, Penna.

SAMUEL SMITH

Of Antrim Twp., served as private, 1779-80-81, under Captains John Jack and Thomas Johnston. He was a son of Samuel Smith, who died 1763 and wife Mary. Samuel Smith mar. Mary, dau. of James McLene, Esq.; they lived in Cumberland, Md. Samuel Smith, Sr.'s children were: Rebecca mar. Jeremiah Talbot; Martha mar. 1st James Crawford; 2nd Dr. Wm. Magaw; Nancy mar. Walter Beatty; Ruth mar. John Heatherington.

Penna. Arch. 5th Ser. Vol. 6, p. 75, 84, 115, 130, 540.

SAMUEL SMITH

Of Welsh Run served as a private under Capt. John Orbisom, 1781-82. He was a son of Robert Smith and wife Catherine Wallace, early settlers on the Welsh Run. The will of Robert Smith was prob. June 22, 1787 and to the above Samuel he left 100 ac land; sons Oliver and Isaac to have the remainder of the land; Daus. Margaret, Ann and Elizabeth 150 pounds each. A deed to be made to the Trustees of the congregation for 3 acres. Oliver and Isaac Smith, Planters, of Montgomery Twp., sold their land to Samuel Smith, Blacksmith for 80 pounds. Samuel and wife Martha, also sold.

Penna. Arch. 5th Ser. Vol. 6, p. 294, 308.

CAPTAIN CONRAD SNIDER

Return of Officers on Parole, Aug., 1778. Col. Watt's regiment Flying Camp; Commissioned Sept. 7, 1776, taken at Fort Washington, Nov. 16, 1776. Again commissioned 1780, served in 1st Batt. Cumb. Co. Militia, 1780-81, and on the Western frontier. Captain Snider was appointed Coroner Oct. 25, 1787, by the Supreme Executive Council, for the County of Franklin. He died in 1802, leaving his widow Catherine (Stantz) and issue: John; Jacob; Samuel; Anthony; Catherine mar. George Hart; Mary mar. Michael Poorman; Elizabeth mar. Robert Philson.

Penna. Arch. 2nd Ser. Vol. 15, p. 649, 772. 5th Ser. Vol. 6, p. 70, 86, 118, 119.

HENRY SNIDER

Was a Sergt. under Capt. James Young, 1779-81. His wife was Anna Margaretta born Jan. 27, 1762, dau. of Jacob Harbaugh and wife Anna Margaretta Smith, dau. of George Smith. Henry Snider b. 1760, d. 1841. His will dated 1838, prob. Sept. 10, 1841, names Jacob Sumprood and wife Rebecca; heirs of Magdalena Brown; bro. Jacob Snider; bro. Nicholas Snider; sister Barbara Stands; Exrs.: friend John Snider (of Jacob), David Snider (of Nicholas) and Jacob Sumpro.

Penna. Arch. 5th Ser. Vol. 6, p. 111, 547.

CHRISTY SNIVELY

Served as private, 1780-81-82, under Capt. Thos.

Johnston. He mar. in 1762 Margaret Washabaugh, b. 1741, and they had issue: Elizabeth; John; Fanny; Henry; Susanna; Catherine; Maria; Joseph, b. 1781, went to Columbiana Co., Ohio. Further data in Histories of Franklin Co., Penna.
Penna. Arch. 5th Ser. Vol. 6, p. 84, 114, 130.

JAMES SNODGRESS

Is shown with Capt. Conrad Snider, 1780-81, under the Command of Col. James Johnston.
Penna. Arch. 5th Ser. Vol. 6, p. 87, 119.

ROBERT SNODGRASS

Served as Ensign during 1777-78-79-80-81, under Captains Conrad Snider, John Jack, and Wm. Long. Robert Snodgrass was a taxable in Guilford Twp., and a freeman in 1779-81-82.
Penna. Arch. 5th Ser. Vol. 6, p. 70, 86, 118, 169, 512, 514, 516, 580, 533, 535, 537, 545.

SAMUEL SNODGRASS

Was a private, 1777-78-79-81-82, under Captains William Long and James Poe. Samuel Snodgrass was a taxable in Guilford Twp., with land, horses and cattle and in 1781 he appears as a freeman. In the will of Elizabeth Devor, of Southampton Twp., dated 1800, she names a dau. Rebecca Snodgrass. In 1790 the family consisted of 1 man, 3 boys, 2 females.
Penna. Arch. 5th Ser. Vol. 6, p. 87, 119, 521, 523, 538, 546, 572.

WILLIAM SNODGRASS

Served as a Sergt., 1777-78-79-80-81, under Captains Conrad Snider, William Long and Samuel Royer. In 1790 Census shows his family as 1 man, 5 boys, 2 females.
Penna. Arch. 5th Ser. Vol. 6, p. 87, 118, 514, 538, 545, 580.

THOMAS SNODGRASS

Born 1748, of Lurgan Twp., served 1778-81-82 under Capts. Chas. Maclay, John McConnell and Isaac Miller. His will dated February, prob. March 11, 1808, gives to dau. Mary 133 lbs., and her spinning wheel; to dau. Elizabeth, wife of John Woods 30 lbs.; dau. Margaret 60 lbs., a case of drawers, all her clothes, coarse and fine, and her spinning wheel; Son James 133 lbs., clothes, his Harvesting tools; Son William 30 lbs.; Son Thomas 100 lbs., my family bible and his clothes, coarse and fine; Son Robert 100 lbs., and his clothes.
Penna. Arch. 5th Ser. Vol. 6, p. 36, 40, 149, 151, 303, 406, 435, 450.

ANDREW SNOWBERGER

Served as a private under Capt. Samuel Royer in 1779-80-81. He is buried in the Nunnery Graveyard,—"Here rests the devoted Strugler and brother Andreas Schneberger. He died the first day of August, and was 81 years and 14 days old." His will, dated Nov. 5, 1823, probated Aug. 16, 1825, names children: Anna; Barbara; Susanna; Andrew; Mary; John; Jacob; Elizabeth; each to get $81.75, a bond from the Society of seven day Baptists at Snowhill. This settlement north of Waynesboro, Penna., founded in 1795 at Snow Hill, by a religious sect known as Seventh Day Baptists, in 1775 gained enough followers to make practical the observance of Saturday as the Sabbath. About 1795, one Peter Lehman came as pastor. It was he who founded the Snow Hill branch of the order of the Solitary and convent life was soon after-wards begun in the large stone house erected by Andrew Snowberger in 1793. He was a prominent member of the Community, a cabinet maker by trade; a man of intense religious convictions, originally a member of the Amish branch of the Dunkard church, and had become a Seventh Day Baptist through his wife's influence. When the convent began, four or six young women, among them two of the daughters of Andrew Snowberger, became the first nuns. Several men joined the order and for some years its growth was rapid. Additions to the old house were built to furnish the saal, the refectory, the small sleeping rooms, the workshop &c. The men operated a mill where flour was made, hauled to Baltimore and found ready sale. They had a tin shop and farmed many acres of fertile land. In addition to the housework, the women spun flax and wool, wove tablecloths, woolen and linen fabrics. As part of the furnishings of this convent, Andrew Snowberger made a massive and unusual sideboard of curly maple, with feet, Capitals and Slabs of Mahogany. It was over seven feet long, with a mirror set in ebony, the original glass knobs were also set in ebony. It is now (1939) being cared for in a private home in Cove Gap, within a mile of the Birthplace of President James Buchanan. It is probable that the Barbara Snowberger, born July 11, 1743, died Jan. 14, 1810, was the wife of Andrew Snowberger. The Graveyard shows the following, presumably the children of Andrew Snowberger: Andrew, 1771-1830; John, 1776-1839; Jacob, 1779-1844; Barbara, 1768-1851; Elizabeth, 1779-1820. Obed, Veronica, Sarah, David and Benjamin Snowberger, also lie in this old graveyard. Catherine Snowberger, who died 1855 aged 78 years, probably the dau. of Joseph Mentzer, and wife of Andrew Snowberger, Jr., Joseph Mentzer names in his will dau. Catherine intermarried to Andrew Snowberger.
Penna. Arch. 5th Ser. Vol. 6, p. 89, 108, 112, 541.

HENRY SOCKMAN

Private in Penna. Militia, aged 86 in 1833. He was a pensioner and the Franklin Repository, under June 18, 1833, gives "Died at St. Thomas, on the 4th inst., in his 86th year, Mr. Henry Sockman, a soldier of the Revolution who lived beloved and esteemed." The Ledger of Matthias Nead, Esq., who had a Tannery in St. Thomas, shows accounts of Daniel, John and Henry Sockman 1821 to 1825, 1826 and 1827. John probably a potter, credited "By Crocks."

Penna. Arch. 3rd Ser. Vol. 13, p. 530.

JOHN SOOKE

Served as private 1781, under Capt. Daniel Clapsaddle.

Penna. Arch 5th Ser. Vol. 6, p. 117.

DANIEL SOURPIKE

Is shown in service in 1780, under Capt Samuel Patton, Command of Col. Samuel Culbertson. As Daniel Sowerpack he was a taxable in Hamilton Twp., 1778-79-80, and on Apr. 16, 1778, Daniel Sourbeek signed the Oath of Allegiance at Carlisle before Justice John Creigh.

Penna. Arch. 5th Ser. Vol. 6, p. 278.

EDWARD SPEAR

Second Lieut, Feb. 7, 1778, promoted to First Lieut. May 16, 1781, and transferred to the First Penna., Jan. 1, 1781. Lieut. Edward Speer killed at St. Clair's defeat, Nov. 4, 1791. "Genealogical Notes" by Seilhamer, state he was appointed a Lieut. in the U. S. Artillery Batt. Sept. 10, 1787 and Lieut. of Artillery, U. S. Army, Sept. 29, 1789. In 1769, Edward Spear was living near Mercersburg, Penna., with his mother, Jean Campbell, dau. of William and Frances Campbell, and widow of Andrew Spear. Lieut. Edward Spear was a member of the Society of the Cincinnati.

Penna. Arch 5th Ser. Vol. 3, p. 107, 159; 2nd Ser. Vol. 10, p. 335.

WILLIAM SPEAR

Was a Sergt., under Capt. Samuel Patton, June 22, 1779, at Legonere. He is also shown under Capt. William Huston in 1780, and as a Soldier of the Cont. Line, entitled to Dep. pay. He was a son of Andrew and Jean (Campbell) Spear, early members of "Upper West Conococheague" Church. His brother Edward was a Lieut. First Penna. and was killed Nov. 4, 1791, at St. Clair's defeat. William Spear mar. Barbara, dau. of Alex White, Dec. 23, 1788. They moved to Butler Co., Penna., and William Spear is buried in old Mt. Nebo Cemetery. He died 1840, aged 79 years, 9 mos. 16 days.

Penna. Arch. 5th Ser. Vol. 6, P. 275, 601, 609.

ALLEN SPEEDY

Served as private, 1780-81, under Capt. Wm. Huston. He may have mar. Margaret, dau. of James and Rebecca McCamish. Penna. Census, Franklin Co., 1790, shows Allen Speedy, with 1 man, 2 boys, 1 female.

Penna. Arch. 5th Ser. Vol. 6, p. 269, 275, 283.

ANDREW SPEEDY

Is shown under Capt. Walter McKinnie, 1781-82. Andrew Speedy was admitted to the Presby. Church of Mercersburg in 1784.

Penna. Arch. 5th Ser. Vol. 6, p. 298, 306.

ANDREW SPENCE

Is shown in service in 1780, with Capt. James Patton. His will, dated and prob. 1799, names: Wife Hannah; son Samuel's children; sons Isaac; Collen; William; Dau. Agnes; Dau. Hannah; and a son Thomas. They were living in Peters Twp., and members of the Presbyterian Church, Mercersburg, Penna. Samuel Spence mar. Miss McClelland, Sept. 15, 1785; Isaas Spence mar. Esther Walker, Dec. 10, 1793; Colin Spence to Elizabeth Walker, Jan. 7, 1800; Henry May to Agnes Spence March 25, 1802. The will of Samuel Walker of Peters Twp., shows his dau. Margaret (not Elizabeth) to have mar. Colin Spence, dated and prob. 1812. Letters of Admr. estate of John Spence granted to Cathreine Spence in 1815. Will Book c, p. 347, Chambresburg Court records. Catherine Spence of Guilford Twp., March 14, 1817; House and lot in Guilford Twp.; Dau. Sally and her heirs. A debt due me by John Friday (?) (Findley) to my dau. Polly; a some of money coming to me from the United States in right of my son John Spence, late a Soldier in the Army thereof I bequeath to my dau. Elizabeth mar. to Henry Ganter after deducting all just debts &c, funeral expenses, also to Elizabeth all my wearing apparel and one bed, allowing dau. Sally to say which one said Elizabeth shall have, and to dau. Elizabeth and her issue all my interest in and to any land that my son John, decd., was entitled to from the U. S. Ludwig Heck guardian of dau. Sally and John Durborow Executor. Wit: John Shillito and P. L. Dechert. Prob. Oct. 14, 1817.

Penna. Arch. 5th Ser. Vol. 6, p. 271.

GEORGE SPIELMAN, SERGEANT

Was in service 1780, undated roll, under Capt. Alexdr. Peebles.

Penna. Arch. 5th Ser. Vol. 6, p. 28, 395.

JACOB STAKE

And wife Barbara Ann (1765-1858) are buried in Upper Strasburg Union Cemetery, Franklin Co., Penna. In the will of Jacob Stake of Letterkenny Twp., dated 1820; prob. 1831, he names wife Barbara and two (2) nieces, now living with me: Mary and Elizabeth Boger, daughters of Elizabeth Freaker, decd., who mar. Joseph Boger; heirs of Eleanor Reed mar. to William Early, blacksmith, now living in Roxbury. Exrs.: wife Barbara and William Boggs. In the Methodist graveyard, Metal, Carrick Furnace, are buried Andrew W. Fraker, 1845-1917, wife Mary E. Stevens, 1851-1916. The will of Casper Reed of Letterkenny Twp., dated 1801, prob. 1840, names children of his dau. Margaret, decd., who was married to Andrew Fricher, also a son-in-law John Stake, mar. to dau. Eave. On Jan 4, 1798, Dr. David Denny married Catherine Fricker to Wm. McCammon.

HENRY STALL

Was in service 1777-78-80-81, under Captains James Young and William Berryhill. He appeared in Antrim Twp., for years as a taxable with horses, cattle and 475 acres of land. Letters of Admr. of estate of Henry Stahl were granted to Michael Stahl of Bedford Co., Penna. and Jacob Stahl, March 5, 1790. Sureties: William Berryhill and John Hill. A deed of March 30, 1797, gives the following: Whereas, Henry Stall, decd., of Antrim Twp., had certain lands and died intestate, leaving issue: John; Michael; Leonard; and Henry Stall; Susanna Stall; Barbara Hicks, wife of Jacob Hicks; and Henry Hawkersmith, son of Magdalen (Stall) Hawkersmith, decd.; Henry Hawkersmith of Frederick Co., Md., is the only surviving child of Magdalin Hawkersmith. Susanna Stall of Antrim Twp., (spinster) left a will dated 1797, prob. 1805, naming sister Barbara and brothers: Michael; Leonard; John; Jacob and Daniel. The above Henry Hawkersmith, as heir of Magdalin, petitions in 1792, for division of real estate. Henry Stahl died seized of 2 certain tracts; one of 340 acres in Antrim; one of 200 acres in Montgomery Twp., and stating that Henry Stahl died leaving eight children, besides the petitioner (a grandchild). On Dec. 17, 1772, Henry Stall was granted a tract of 219 acres in what is now Montgomery Twp., (vicinity of Welsh Run) called "Nonesuch," by Conococheague Creek, by the Meeting-house land, John Shelby, William McWhorter and John Mayse. On July 28, 1777, Henry Stall and Anne, his wife, sold the above land to Fredk. Darkiss, who with wife Margaret, sold in 1779 to William Scott.

Penna. Arch. 5th Ser. Vol. 6, p. 73, 80 102, 522, 526, 601.

JACOB STAHL

Was in service with Capt. William Berryhill, 1781. In 1797, Jacob Stall, of Antrim Twp., and Mary, his wife, sell to Daniel Stall certain land of Henry Stall, decd. In 1805, Jacob Stahl, of Montgomery Twp., and Mary, his wife, sell to John Angle of same place. A certain James Campbell obtained from the proprietaries 3 warrants—2 dated Feb. 20, 1754, and Aug 16, 1754, respectively; Campbell's right to this tract of land became vested in John Shelby and Robert Smith and was resurveyed to them Oct. 29, 1772. Said tract became vested in aforesaid Jacob Stahl by patent of Aug. 25, 1803, situate in Montgomery Twp. &c. In 1807 Jacob Stahl and Mary, his wife, of Montgomery Twp., sell to Peter Stinger, the Patent to Jacob Stahl in 1803, Montgomery Twp. Jan. 9, 1809, Jacob Stahl appointed Justice of the Peace under a deed of Apr., 1833, the heirs of Jacob and Mary Stahl appear to be: John Brosius and wife, Magdalena; Archibald Fleming and wife Eve; Jacob Wolff and wife Susannah; Martin Bear and wife Elizabeth; Catherine Stahl; Daniel Startzman and wife Anna; Sally Stahl; Christianna Stahl; Lydia Stahl; sell to John Stahl, part of the real estate of Jacob Stahl.

Penna. Arch. 5th Ser. Vol. 6, p. 102.

JAMES STALL

Was in service 1780-81-82, as a private under Capt. William Strain, command of Major Robert Culbertson. James Stall and John Stall were taxables in Southampton Twp., in 1788 to 1794; Andrew and Joseph continue to 1807, with John and Adam Stall ending the list.

Penna. Arch. 5th Ser. Vol. 6, p. 405, 430, 642.

JOHN STAHL

Was in service 1780-81, with Capt. William Berryhill, command of Col. James Johnston. In 1796, Tax lists show Daniel and Jacob Stall with Land, horses and cattle. One John Stall died in 1812. Letters of Admr. granted to Elizabeth Stall and Daniel Bittinger.

Penna. Arch. 5th Ser. Vol. 6, p. 81, 98, 102.

JOHN STAHL

Is shown in service in 1777, with Capt. Thos. Askey, and in 1780, under Capt. William Strain. It is probable that the following may connect with above John Stahl, but not proven: One John Stahl died in Hamilton Twp., in the Fall of 1821, leaving a widow Polly and issue ten children: Polly mar. Jacob Snider; Elizabeth mar. Peter Houser; Jacob. Barbara mar. Henry Houser; Ester mar. Henry Butz; Samuel; George; Eve Stahl; Michael and Nancy. By 1830 the widow had mar. Frederick Neville and there were 11 children. Peter Houser and wife Elizabeth were both dead leaving John, Mary, Sarah, Jacob and Elizabeth Houser. Eve mar. Henry Cromer; Nancy died unmarried.

Penna. Arch. 5th Ser. Vol. 6, p. 8, 10, 24, 142, 397.

LEONARD STALL

Served as a private 1777-78, under Capt. John Jack; in 1780-81, as an Ensign with Capt. Wm. Berryhill. He is shown as a freeman in Antrim Twp., 1778 to 1782. Leonard Stall, son of Henry, appears with Daniel, as Executors of the estate of their sister Susanna Stall, Feb., 1805. They filed the account Sept. 1806, and nothing further is shown on Leonard Stall.

Penna. Arch. 5th Ser. Vol. 6, p. 69, 79, 100, 169, 517, 519, 586, 599.

LOENARD STANS

Served as private under Capt. Pat. Jack, 1781-82. He was of Hamilton Twp., his will prob. Jan. 23, 1807. His wife was Catherine; Sons Henry; Leonard; Peter; Elizabeth; John; Jacob; Catherine.

Penna. Arch. 5th Ser. Vol. 6, p. 291, 295, 313.

ALEXANDER STANTON

Appears serving as private 1780-81, under Capt. Conrad Snyder. He is shown as a freeman, in 1780, in Guilford Twp. William Stanton appears in Peters Twp., in 1781-82, with 100 acres land, horses and cattle.

Penna. Arch. 5th Ser. Vol. 6, p. 88, 98.

ARTHUR STARR

Was in service 1778-82 with Capt. John Campbell; he also signed the Third Petition from the inhabitants of Fannett Township.

Penna. Arch. 5th Ser. Vol. 6, p. 31, 33, 443.

PHILIP STECK

Served as private in Lancaster Co., Penna., under Captains Alex. Scott, Jr., and Jacob Brandt, 1781-82. Deeds at Chambersburg, Penna., show that on April 19, 1808, Philip Steck of Manor Twp., Lancaster Co., Penna., bought from Jacob Snider and Christianna Elizabeth, his wife and Thos. G. McCulloh, of Chambersburg, a Plantation in Montgomery Twp. Franklin Co., Penna., for $3,420., 114 acres by Philip Davis, Mrs. McFerran and others. Orphans' Court Vol. E, p. 72, petition of John Cook son-in-law of Philip Stech, who died intestate in July 1839, leaving 11 children and one son decd.: Philip Stech; Susan Stech; Samuel Stech; Sophia mar. to John Hammond; John Stech; Eliza Stech; Jacob Stech; Catherine mar. Daniel Young; Mary Stech, all of Franklin County; also Nancy mar. John Cook in Washington Co., Md.; Elizabeth Stech mar. ―― Guise of Lancaster Co., Penna., and heirs of George Stech, decd., viz: Nancy; Susan; Martin and Mary Steck of Franklin Co., Penna., and Philip Stech and Elizabeth mar. to Jacob Zentmyer, both of Washington Co., Md. John Cook states his Father-in-law died owning land in Montgomery Twp., 116 acres, by David Wolff, John Kline &c, page 122; real estate taken by Samuel Stech; all heirs sign off. Susan, heir of George Stech was decd. Vol. D, p. 472, Aug. 13, 1839. Philip Stech and John Cook testified on July 29, last, at residence of Philip Stech, who was in his last sickness in his own house having resided in the said dwelling house for the last 20 or 30 years next preceding the said 29th day of July, 1839; he willed all property to wife Sophia during her life; son Samuel to work the farm; oldest dau. Polly to be particularly provided for during her life and family to remain together as they are as long as wife Sophia lives. Philip Steck died July 29, 1839. Before John Cook, his son-in-law and Dr. P. W. Little. Steck Graveyard on farm: Philip Steck, 1762-1839; Sophia Steck, 1770-1842. Will Book E, p. 332. Samuel Stech, Montgomery Twp., sisters Susana and Eliza, full brothers and sisters — brothers Philip and Jacob Stech. Dated March 19, 1850; prob. July 28, 1851.

Penna. Arch. 5th Ser. Vol. 7, p. 425, 426.

WILLIAM STEED

Corporal, Jan. 9, 1777, County of Bedford. William Stead was married Oct. 21, 1772, to Alice Woodworth, by the Rev. John King, pastor of the Presbyterian Church at Mercersburg. Penna. Arch. 5th Ser. Vol. 5, p. 67.

REV. JOHN STEEL

Captain, "at McDowell's Mill," 1755, and March 25, 1756 in 2nd Batt. Penna., Regt. of Foot, 1757, as Chaplain, and in same later under Staff Officers. "And among the first Companies organized in West Conococheague, on the bloody outbreak of the Delaware Indians in 1755, the Rev. John Steel, their pastor, was selected for its Captain. This command was accepted by Mr. Steel, and was executed with so much skill, bravery and Judgment as to commend him to the Provincial government, which appointed him a Captain of Provincial troops." In the war of Independence Mr. Steel took an active part; he was called the "Reverend Captain" as a title of honor. History of the Silver Spring Presbyterian Church (p. 13). The Rev. John Steel came to Carlisle in 1758 from West Conococheague, where he had been in the midst of perils of Indian depredation. He was pastor at Silver Spring, 1764-1776. He died Aug., 1779. His will "Rev. John Steel, Sr., Minister of Carlisle, Penna. Dau. Lydia's children by Robert Semple; Son John and children; Elizabeth McKindley and her children. Dau. Margaret and her children; To Mary and Sarah; To Robert and Andrew; To Steel McClean; To Dau. Jean 600 pounds and much else; To John my watch and chain; To Robert and Andrew each, one of my fowling pieces, &c. To Steel McClean and son Andrew each a pair of silver buckles. Dated May 24, 1779—2 Codicils, July 2, 1779.

Penna. Arch. 5th Ser. Vol. 1, p. 31, 46, 99, 109, 132.

CONRAD STENGER

Is it here stated that Conrad Stenger, a Revolutionary Soldier, became one of the leading business men of Franklin County. Under date of March 15, 1831, The "Franklin Repository" gives: "Died the 7th inst in St. Thomas Twp., Conrad Stinger in his 72nd year." The will fo Conrad Stinger of Peters Twp., dated Oct. 31, 1828, was prob. March 12, 1831. He named "wife Christina all the money that is or may become due to me at the time of my decease as her dowery out of her former Husband's Estate, in the hands of her son Jonathan Shearer." (The will of Peter Shearer shows a wife Christina). Conrad Stinger further names Son William Stinger; Dau. Maria and husband Joseph Hershey; Dau. Hannah and husband Daniel Shearer; Geo. Wime; 6 sons: Samuel; John; Conrad land in Stark Co., Ohio; Peter; Benj.; William; Rebecca Weirich; Amelia, dau. of Polly McMullin that now lives with me. His Exrs. were his sons, Samuel; John; Peter.

Biographical Annals, Franklin Co., Penna., by Geo. Seilhamer, p. 348.

WILLIAM STENGER

Served as private under Capt. John McConnell, 1780-81. Nancy Stinger, widow of William Stinger, desires that letters be granted to her father and father-in-law, Oct. 22, 1795. Letters were granted to John Kesey and George Stinger.

Penna. Arch. 5th Ser. Vol. 6, p. 268, 310.

JOHN STERN

Was in service 1781, with Capt. Wm. Huston, a freeman in Montgomery Twp., and in 1782, Jacob, John and Joseph Stern, all appear as freeman.

Penna. Arch. 5th Ser. Vol. 6, p. 283.

JOSEPH STERN

Was in service 1781, with Capt. Wm. Huston; Fredk. Stern was also in Montgomery Twp., in 1781.

Penna. Arch. 5th Ser. Vol. 6, p. 283, 643.

ALEXANDER STERRIT

Of Southampton Twp., is shown in service 1777-80, with Captains Alexander Peebles and William Strain. He left a will dated Jan., 1786, prob. March, 1786, naming a wife Mary to whom he gives 1/3 of all personal estate; 1/3 of the value of the rents of real estate yearly, best bed and furniture, a good horse and saddle, and one suite of black, that is Gown and Petticoat; Son Samuel; Sons Alexander; Benjamin; Robert; John and William land and houses to be valued and divided equally; dau. Sarah 100 pounds; dau. Margaret 100 pounds; dau. Bathshebah 100 pounds; dau. Mary Sharp 20 pounds; dau. Agnes Boyd 20 pounds. Exrs.: Wife and friend James Sharp. Mary widow of Alexander Sterrit of Southampton Twp., made a will dated June 1799, and which was prob. Oct., 1801. She names son Robert, all estate, he paying the following legacies: dau. Sarah Arbuckle 40 shillings; daus: Mary Sharpe; Margaret Breckenridge; Agnes Boyd; Bethsheba McCune, and Rosannah Sterrit each 40 shillings. I give unto my daughter-in-law for the purpose of buying them gowns; Sons Benjamin; John; William each 5 shillings. Exrs.: Son Robert and John Herron, Esq. Wit.: John Campbell and Andrew Thompson.

Penna. Arch 5th Ser. Vol. 6, p. 26, 143, 398.

JAMES STERRETT

Private served under Capt. Wm. Smith, Aug., 1780, in Cumb. Co. Militia. James Sterret was the son of Cairns and Mary (Mayes* Sterrett, early settlers in Montgomery Twp., from Lancaster Co., Donegal Twp. James Sterrett mar. Anne Dinwoodie (Dunwoody) Sept. 12, 1788. They removed to Williamsport, Md., where he was a tanner. His dau. Maria mar. Owen Edwards July 29, 1813. The distribution of his estate 1813, shows the widow of James Sterrett had become Mrs. Luckett, issue: Maria Edwards; Nancy; James and Joseph W. Sterrett.

Penna. Arch. 5th Ser. Vol. 6, p. 277.

JOHN STERRET

Served in Cumb. Co. Militia under Capt. Wm. Huston in years 1780-1781. He was the son of Cairns and Mary (Mayes) Sterrett (Lancaster Co.) early settlers in present Montgomery Twp. Franklin Co., Penna. John Sterret mar. Martille, dau. of Joseph and Violet (Porter) Irwin, April 5, 1785. John Sterret died March 16, 1811, aged 51; Myrtilla Sterrett died Jan. 19, 1824, aged 59. In the will of John Sterrett he requests that his body be deposited "in our family Burying Ground in the Church yard at Dr. King's old church," (Church Hill). He names Sons, John; Andrew and Joseph Irwin Sterrett; Dau. Ruhamah; sons Benjamin; James; Nathan; Daus. Maria (or Mary) Dau. Myrtilla; Son William; Brother-in-law Nathan McDowell. He bequeaths to his son Andrew "My sword, pistols and Light Horse Uniform, in order to deprive my estate from being injured as I have seen many others." Ruhama Sterret mar. Dr. Andrew Heatherington, June, 1811.

Penna. Arch. 5th Ser. Vol. 6, p. 265, 270, 283.

ROBERT STERRET

Appears as a private 1779-80-82, in service with Capt. William Moorhead. On Nov. 17, 1803, Letters of Admr. were granted on the estate of Robert Sterrett unto his widow Rosanna Sterritt, Benj. Sterrett, and John McCune. Robert was undoubtedly the son of Alexander and Mary Sterrett of Southampton Twp.; he had married Rosannah McCune, dau of Samuel McCune, Esq.

Penna. Arch. 5th Ser. Vol. 6, p. 66, 133, 400, 413, 439.

WILLIAM STERRIT

Killed at Crooked Billet, May 1, 1778. The will of John Sterrit of Antrim Twp., prob. 1762, names sons Alexander and William.

Presbyterian Church records, Mercersburg, Penna.

GEORGE STEVENSON

Served under Capt. John McConnell, as 2nd Lieut. and as private 1776-77-78, under the command of Col. Joseph Armstrong.

Penna. Arch. 5th Ser. Vol. 6, p. 317, 318, 370, 379.

JOHN STEVENSON

Served as private in the company of Capt. John McConnell, 1780-81-82. He also served in the Cont. Line from Washington Co., Penna. Deeds show that in May, 1790, John Stevenson and wife Jean, (a Dau. of John McComb) were of Cisel Twp., Washington Co., Penna., a yeoman. They sell to Robert Scott their interest in a tract of land surveyed to John McComb, in 1783 on warrant to John McComb, July 10, 1752, in Lurgan Twp.

Penna. Arch. 5th Ser. Vol. 6, p. 267, 268, 288, 302, 309. Vol. 4, p. 422.

JOSEPH STEVENSON

Served under Capt. John McConnell, as First Lieut. of the 8th Company, 6th Batt. Cumb. Co. Militia 1777-78. He continued under Capt. McConnell, 1780-81-82, as a private. Joseph Stevenson occupied Pew No. 33, with John Beard and John Beatty in the old Log Church at Rocky Spring and in 1800, when Rev. Francis Herron came, he occupied Pew No. 58, as "Lieut. Joseph Stevenson," and was clerk in Dr. Herron's ministry. The following man probably buried in Rocky Spring Graveyard. Joseph Stevenson, Sr., of Letterkenny Twp., dated 1787, prob. 1791; son John of Westmoreland Co.; grandson Joseph Stevenson, Jr.; Dau. Mary, wife of Stephen Caldwell; dau. Rebecca, wife of James Scott; grandau. Elizabeth, wife of Zachariah Sprigg and dau. of my son Robert Stevenson, decd.; grandau. Elizabeth; great-grand son George, son of my grandson

Joseph Stevenson, Jr.; Exrs.: Wm. Waddle; Samuel Culbertson.

Penna. Arch. 5th Ser. Vol. 6, p. 267, 302, 309, 370, 378.

ROBERT STEVENSON

Served as Lieut., also as Light Horseman, 1780-81-82, under Capt. John McConnell. He is said to have been born 1759, mar. Elizabeth Baird 1781; issue: Esther; Mary; Hannah; John; Elizabeth; William; Catherine; Robert; Joseph. He died July 23, 1835 near Decatur, Brown Co., Ohio, having gone there with his family about 1816.

Penna. Arch. 5th Ser. Vol. 6, p. 267, 303, 310.

NATHANIEL STEVENSON

Aug. 11, 1818, Butler Co., Penna, age 67, enlisted winter 1775-1776 under Capt. William Rippey in 6th, afterwards 7th Penna. Regt., Command Col. Irwin and April 20, 1777, received honorable discharge—in battles Three Rivers, etc. William Rippey, of Shippensburg, certifies July 5, 1819, that Nathaniel Stevenson was a soldier in his Company 1776—that he marched into Canada in Col. Irwin's Regt. Affidavit as to property—land—Jan. 3, 1820—wife Mary, age 67—one son married—James age 17—dau. Mary, age 22—living with him. Oct. 1, 1827, second application—under act May, 1820—(on account of property other pension dropped), no person except wife living with him, aged about 73. April 29, 1840. Petition Mary Stevenson, widow of Nathaniel Stevenson, late of Butler Co., Penna., (died Mar. 17, 1839), that they were married by Rev. Hughes on July 4, 1779, at Carlisle in Cumb. Co., Penna., her brother and Rev. Hughes only persons present at marriage and they are both dead. That she is now aged 86, and has had ten children, the eldest Jane was born 1780, that a record of their ages had been kept but that a little grandchild tore it out of the Bible and destroyed it. May 11, 1840. Hugh Stevenson presents application for his mother—he is 52 years of age last Aug. 27, and he is fourth child of Nathaniel and Mary Stevenson—sister Jane oldest, now 60.—May 11, 1840. Affidavit John St. Clair—known them since 1798 when they moved to his settlement—Jane then a young woman, George a young man—Jane now married with Thompson (late Commissioner, Butler Co)—Hugh Stevenson upward 50 years—Nathaniel Stevenson died Mar. 1839. July, 1849. Application Mary Stevenson, resident of North Butler Township, age 96—her maiden name was Mary Allen—that she had five children born to the said Nathaniel Stevenson prior to 1794—Jane; George; Elizabeth; Hugh; Mary, has not again married—shortly after marriage they resided in Westmoreland Co., Penna., for several years prior to 1797, moved to where now live. Nathaniel

Stevenson by trade a tailor. Sept. 1849. Affidavit —Jane Baer (Barr) age 76—knew Mary Stevenson when she was Mary Allen and resided in neighborhood of Carlisle—that she married at Carlisle when she (Jane Barr) came to reside with them soon after their marriage and was there for most of ten years—up to 1789 at which time they moved from Cumberland to where they now live—that four children were born in Cumberland Co.—the fifth born in this vicinity (Westmoreland Co.) that they subsequently moved to Butler Co. Hugh Stevenson mar. 1851—Pittsburgh, Justice Peace (?)
Pension Application W2266—Pennsylvania.

WILLIAM STEVENSON

Pensioner in Franklin Co., Penna., aged 88 years in 1830. Deed Book 4, p. 205, gives the following Nov. 5, 1787: William Stevenson and wife Ann of Chambersburg, Penna., sell to William Huston of same (House joyner). Lot 149 in Chambersburg for 30 lbs. Tax lists show Wm. Stevenson as a Taylor in Franklin Twp., 1796, with the usual Cow, a House and a half Lot. He was still living in 1835. Records at Harrisburg show that he died July, 1838.

ALEXANDER STEWART, SURGEON

Third Penna. Cont. Line, Oct. 6, 1779; he was surgeon's mate in the general hospital from 1776; died in Chambersburg, 1793. In his will he names a wife Margaret, to whom he wills 300 acres donation land in District No. 2; To his brother John 200 acres Congress lands; to his brother Robert 200 acres, Congress lands; to his brother William 300 acres district No. 7, "granted to me for services done in the last war." A legatee is Alexander Allison, son of Robret Allison. It is stated that Dr. Alex Stewart was a brother-in-law of Major Robert Allison. Dr. Stewart had in 1791, one house and lot; Tablespoons, 6; Teaspoons, 12; one horse and 2 cows.
Penna. Arch. 2nd Ser. Vol. 10, p. 459.

CHARLES STEWART, SR.

Is shown in 1780-81, under Capt. John McConnell. He spent the greater part of his life in Bedford County, Penna., serving from there in the State Legislature, and highly esteemed. The Repository, under Aug. 25, 1835 states that he died at his residence near Mercersburg, on the night of the 2nd in the 80th year of his age. His will, prob. Sept., 1835, names: Niece Mary McCreight; Niece Eleanor Harrison; Nephew S. Dearmond; Nephew John Rankin; Nephew Samuel Rankin; Nieces Elizabeth Miller; Matilda D. Raynolds; Charles S. Stoner and John Conner to have certain beds and bedding. Exrs.: David Hunter of Bedford County, and Andrew S. Dearmond. Eve Stuart, Consort of Charles Stuart is buried in the white Church Graveyard. It is probable that the above Charles Stewart is also buried there.
Penna. Arch. 5th Ser. Vol. 6, p. 267, 302.

GEORGE STEWART

Private 6th Penna. Cont. Line, died in Franklin County, June 18, 1823, aged 68. He was a pensioner.
Penna. Arch. 2nd Ser. Vol. 10, p. 605.

HUGH STEWART

April 1, 1777-81, Spencer's Regt. 4th Penna. Cont. Line, said to have died in Franklin Co., Penna., but died in Ohio. Deed Books at Chambersburg show that the Admr. of Legh Master sold land in Antrim Twp., to Hugh Stewart of Greencastle, for 120 pounds, Apr. 26, 1797; and that in 1802, he and wife Margaret sell land to Daniel Mowen. The following is from a descendant in Ohio: My Revolutionary ancestor, Hugh Stewart, (b. Dec. 19, 1757(?), Phila., Penna., d. May 1, 1824, Frankfort, Ohio). He married Margaret Roxburgh Smith on September 16, 1780. They lived about a year at Carlisle, Penna. Then, hearing that Hagerstown, Md., was a thriving place, they moved there and, as soon located, bought land at Ringgold Manor, Hagerstown, Md. From the dates of births, Hugh Stewart left Hagerstown between 1798 and 1802 and went to Greencastle, Penna., where the two younger children, Mary and Hugh, Jr., were born. He went to Ohio about 1809. On Mt. Pleasant, also called Prairie View, he built the mansion mentioned in the will which he often spoke of as Castle, saying it was modeled after the Castle of Bonkyl, in Scotland, a Stuart possession. This is near Frankfort, Ross County, Ohio. He is buried in the Family Cemetery on the hill above the mansion, a place he himself had selected. This Cemetery is still owned by the Stewart heirs. Part of his land was on the North Fork of Paint Creek and he came from Franklin County, Penna. He was a resident of Philadelphia, Penna., in 1776 where he was a private in Capt. Richard Barrett's Company of Major Nicolas' "City Guards." See Penna. Records, Penna. in the Revolution, 2nd Ser. Vol. X, page 576 for Hugh Stewart, Soldier.
Penna. Arch. 2nd Ser. Vol. 10, p. 534.

THOMAS STEWART

Under Applicants for State Annuities; Thomas Stewart, Franklin County, served under General Wayne in his campaign against the Indians. In 1796, in Antrim Twp., is shown under Taxables, Thomas Stewart, W. R. One House and Lot, One Cow. From State pension records at Harrisburg, Thos. Stewart appears Jan., 1828 and July 1831. The death of Mrs. Thos. Stuart is recorded at

Mercersburg, as March 15, 1833. Orphans' Court records (1842) show that Jane, widow of Thos. Stewart had died, leaving isuse 3: Absolom; Charles; Mary who mar. Robert T. Sterrett. Absolom and Charles died since; Charles unmar. but Absolom left widow Elizabeth and 2 minor children. Moss Spring Graveyard near Greencastle, Absolom Stewart died May, 1842, aged 53 yrs.

Penna. Arch. 2nd Ser. Vol. 15, p. 770.

WILLIAM STEWART

Served as private under Capt. Patrick Jack, 1780-81. Under Apr. 10, 1821, the Franklin Repository gives: "Died at his residence in Hamilton, Twp., on the 7th ult, at an advanced age, Mr. Wm. Stewart, he supported through life the character of an honest man and a sincere Christian." William Stewart names in his will his beloved wife Elizabeth, who probably was the dau. of Robert Elliott whose will was dated 1762 and prob. 1763. Elizabeth also left a will, prob. 1828. They name sons Robert; James; a dau. Jane Burns grandau. Jane Stewart Burns; sons John; William; Andrew and Alexander.

Penna. Arch. 5th Ser. Vol. 6, p. 292, 296, 313.

JAMES STITT

Served under the first Call of 1777-78-79-80-81, Captains James Young and Samuel Royer.

Penna. Arch. 5th Ser. Vol. 6, p. 74, 89, 112, 522, 526, 542.

JOHN STITT

Appears under Captains Noah Abraham, Thomas Askey and Samuel Royer, 1777-78-79, in "actual service" and as a Lieut. in 1780.

Penna. Arch. 5th Ser. Vol. 6, p. 20, 21, 24, 70, 139, 151, 541, 605.

THOMAS STITT

Served under Capt. Noah Abraham 1777, with Col. James Dunlap, stationed at Carlisle.

Penna. Arch. 5th Ser. Vol. 6, p. 20, 21, 140.

WILLIAM STITT

Appears serving in March, 1778, with Capt. John Rea. William Stitt mar. Dorothy English, dau. of Robert English of Guilford Twp. They had issue; Mary; Jane; Isabella; Margaret and an expected child. The will of William Stitt, dated Aug., 1776, was prob. Apr. 29, 1778. From Pension Records: William Stitt, Penn. 3 22544, Armstrong Co., Penna., Sept. 19, 1832, William Stitt, Sr., aged 77 years, Enlisted 1775. Capt. Abraham Smith, First Lieut. Andrew Irwin, 2nd Lieut. John Alexander. Our Colonel was Hartley from Little York, was attached to 6ht Regt. in (now) Franklin Co., went to Canada and in an engagement at Three Rivers we were defeated. Retreated to St. Johns, to Crown Point etc. To Mt. Independence and remained during winter. On 16 Feb., 1777 marched for Cannogogig, Penna., and arrived there Mar. 16. At the island of (?) or Ax Noase (Aux Noix) we were going to a house for the purpose of getting some beer when I saw Capt. Adams lying over the side of a Batteau. I went down into the water and found he was dead and raised him on my shoulder and carried him to another Batteau and took him to a camp and buried him. He had been struck with a tomahawk on the temple. I was born in Chester Co., Penna., 1755. At enlistment was living at Cannogogig a settlement 12 miles from Chambersburg. Since the war have lived in Westmoreland and Armstrong Counties. Served under Capt. Young 2 months and Capt. Jack 2 mos. in 1777 as I remember. Pensioned for proved service one year 4 months. (Robt. Robinson and Philip Mechling of Kittatinny Twp. and Gabriel A. Richard certified credence).

Penna. Arch. 5th Ser. Vol. 6, p. 528.

GEORGE STOCKTON

Served as private under Capt. James McConnell, 1776.

Penna. Arch. 5th Ser. Vol. 6, p. 317, 318.

ROBERT STOCKTON

Served as private under Capts James McConnell and Joseph Culbertson, 1776-1780. He mar. Mary Makemie. He was a son of Thomas Stockton of Peters Twp., will dated 1794. Thomas Stockton had sons Thomas; John; David; Robert; Daus.: Elizabeth Waddell; Isabella Neilson; Mary Bare; Margaret Johnston. Thomas Stockton, Sr., born 1709, died May 31, 1795. His wife was Margaret Fleming, pewholders in the Rocky Spring Church.

Penna. Arch. 5th Ser. Vol. 6, p. 317, 318, 279.

JACOB STOMBAUGH (STAMBAUGH)

Served as a private in 1780-82, under Capt. Wm. Strain. The will of Jacob Stambaugh was prob. Dec. 14, 1796, naming wife Elizabeth, son Jacob not yet 20, son John to maintain his mother; Jacob and John to learn any trade they may choose; to Dau. Margaret 100 pounds; mentions a legacy left him by his father Lawrence Stambaugh.

Penna. Arch. 5th Ser. Vol. 6, p. 143, 391, 398, 431.

JACOB STUMPAUCH (STUMBACK)

Served in 1780 with Capt. John Campbell, Lieut. Strain. Jacob Stumpauch appears as a taxable in Lurgan Twp., in 1782.

Penna. Arch. 5th Ser. Vol. 6, p. 143, 391.

PETER STAMBAUGH

Served as a private under Capts. Joseph Culbertson and William Strain in 1780-81. Under Census of Pensioners, Act of 1840, is shown Peter Stambaugh, aged 89 years. He was of Green Twp., Franklin Co., Penna.

Penna. Arch. 5th Ser. Vol. 6, p. 143, 290, 397.

PETER STUMPAUCH (STUMBACK)

Served with Capt. Joseph Culbertson, 1780-81. Lawrence Stumpauch is shown as a taxable in Lurgan Twp., 1778 to 1782, with land, saw mill, still, horses and cows.

Penna. Arch. 5th Ser. Vol. 6, p. 143, 290.

PHILIP STOMBAUGH

Served as private under Capt. Wm. Strain, 1780-81.

Penna. Arch. 5th Ser. Vol. 6, p. 389, 430.

ABRAHAM STONER

A son of John Stoner, served as private in 1780, under Capt. Daniel Clapsaddler and under Col. James Johnston. Abraham Stoner mar. Mary, dau. of Hans Michael Miller. They had issue: David, b. about 1765 mar. Mary Mack; Michael mar. Elizabeth Snively; John; Abraham b. 1791, d. 1860, mar. Susanna Benedict; Catherine b. 1769, mar. Daniel Royer; Elizabeth b. 1772 mar. Jacob Snively; Susannah b. 1787, d. 1845, unmar.; Rebecca b. 1784, d. 1855. Burials in the Stoner Graveyard near Welty's Mill southeast of Waynesboro, Penna. Small lime-stone markers.

Penna. Arch. 5th Ser. Vol. 6, p. 71, 94.

DAVID STONER

Served as private in 1780-81, under Capt. Daniel Clapsaddler. David Stoner was a son of John Stoner, and a brother of Abraham. His will is dated July 3, 1810. He names wife Margaret and daus.: Elizebeth Arnold; Susannah Funk; Margaret Coskery; Mary Funk; Sarah, wife of John Baker; Nancy wife of Martin Baer; Catherine wife of David Funk; David mar. Nancy Snively; John mar. Elizabeth Barr. John Stoner, Sr., sold land called "Egypt," on the north side of Antietam Creek, near Steiner Mill, March 18, 1750; John, Jr., son of John Stoner, Sr., sold to David and Abraham, a parcel of "Father's Good Will" also called "Content," 1350 acres. Records at Frederick, Md.

Penna. Arch. 5th Ser. Vol. 6, p. 93, 107, 116.

EMANUEL STOTLER

Was a private under Capt. John Woods and Capt. James Poe, 1777-78-81-82. He was a son of Jacob Stotler and wife Nancy. His estate administered March, 1831, shows a widow Catherine, since mar. to Henry Sellers and issue: Margaret, now decd., and having issue 4 minor children: Eliza; Catherine; Maria and Hannah; Samuel, since decd., without issue; Catherine mar. to Jacob Stoche, said Catherine being now decd., leaving issue, one son, since decd. They had land in Antrim Twp.

Penna. Arch. 5th Ser. Vol. 6, p. 76, 92, 138, 104, 522, 527, 576, 583, 623.

JACOB STATLER (STOTLER)

Was a Lieut. under Captains James Poe, John Woods, Samuel Royer in 1777-78-80-81-82. He was also a Ranger on Frontier.

Penna. Arch. 5th Ser. Vol. 6, p. 70, 90, 103, 137, 165, 512, 514, 516, 532, 574, 582. 3rd Ser. Vol. 23, p. 277.

JOHN STOTLER

Was a private under Captains James Poe and John Wods serving in 1780-81-82. He was a son of Jacob and Nancy Stotler.

Penna. Arch. 5th Ser. Vol. 6, p. 92, 99, 104, 576, 583.

LIEUT. COLONEL SAMUEL STATLER

The Franklin Repository, Chambersburg, Penna., March 7, 1804. "Died at Greencastle on the 27th ult., Lieut. Colonel Samuel Statler, in the 45th year of his age. The character of the deceased was that of a gentleman and a soldier, a Christian and a firm patriot and it may truly be said that he lived respected and died lamented. A number of officers belonging to his regiment who attended his funeral convened themselves after the interment of his remains, and resolved to ware scarf on the left arm until the first meeting of the militia in the Spring which is called the Drill day. 68th Regiment.

SAMUEL STOTLER

Served as Sergt. under Captains James Poe, John Jack and John Woods, in 1777-78-82. In the will of Jacob Stotler prob. 1790, he names Samuel as his brother.

Penna. Arch. 5th Ser. Vol. 6, p. 90, 103, 137, 517, 536, 575, 580, 582, 599.

DANIEL STOVER

Served 1779-80-81-82, under Capts. Samuel Royer and Thos. Johnston. His wife was Barbara, dau. of Peter Benedict, of Quincy Twp. Daniel Stover, 1757-1822, was a son of Rev. William Stover and wife Judiah (Shaeffer) Stover who erected Fort Stover as a defense against the Indians. They had issue: John Stover mar. Mary Deardorff; Catherine mar. Christian Royer; William mar. Nancy Gearheart; Elizabeth mar. Abraham Deardorff; Susan mar. Samuel Hess; Polly mar. Rev.

David Bock; Daniel mar. Nancy Holsinger; Jacob mar. Mary Royer.

Penna. Arch. 5th Ser. Vol. 6, p. 114, 124, 129, 542.

EMANUEL STOVER

Served as private under Capt. Thomas Johnston in 1780-81-82. His wife was Susanna, dau. of Rev. John Price (Johannes Preisz) of Montgomery Co., Penna., having settled at Germantown in 1719.

Penna. Arch 5th Ser. Vol. 6, p. 85, 99, 115, 130.

MICHAEL STOVER

Served as private, 1779-80-81-82 under Capt. Samuel Royer. Michael Stover, b. 1755, d. 1834, mar. 1776, Christina Hess, issue: Jacob Stover mar. Mary Ann Taylor; Susanna Stover mar. Rev. John Royer; Catherine Stover mar. Daniel Welty; Elizabeth Stover mar. Christian Good; Michael Stover; William Stover; Christina Stover mar. John Huber (Hoover); David Stover mar. Mary Hill; Mary Stover mar. David Stahl; Rebecca Stover mar. ———— Sheller; Sarah Stover mar. Jacob Good; Nancy Stover mar. Josiah Horn.

Penna. Arch. 5ht Ser. Vol. 6, p. 89, 112, 123, 542, 585.

JOHN STRAIN

Of Lurgan Twp., served as private and Sergt., under Captains Charles Maclay in 1778, and John Campbell in 1781. His will was probated Feb. 13, 1810. To dau. Mary and grandau. Isabella Caldwell annual rental from land; Son James; Dau. Margaret, wife of James Allsworth; Dau. Sarah wife of John Wilson; Dau. Mary and Grandau. Isabella Caldwell.

Penna. Arch. 5th Ser. Vol. 6, p. 36, 143, 406, 449, 434.

WILLIAM STRAIN

Served as Lieut. and Captain, 1777, 78, 80, 81, 82. The will of Martha Irwin of Southampton Twp., prob. Sept. 3, 1794, (and widow of Wm. Irwin, whose estate was administered Nov. 1792) shows that Jean Irwin was the wife of William Strain. She had sisters Mary wife of John Mitchell; Martha wife of David Simrall; Margaret Irwin; Ann, wife of John Ogilbe; Elizabeth Hunter, decd., and a brother William Irwin. Letters of Administration on the estate of William Strain were granted to Jannet Strain and James Strain, Nov. 28, 1794.

Penna. Arch. 5th Ser. Vol. 6, p. 13, 40, 45, 142, 386, 397, 399, 404, 405, 429, 431, 641.

MICHAEL STUFF

Served as private under Capts. John Jack and Wm. Berryhill, 1779-80-81.

Penna. Arch. 5th Ser. Vol. 6, p. 73, 80, 102, 540.

NICHOLAS STUFF

Served under Capts. John Jack and Wm. Berryhill, in 1779-80-81. He mar Catherine Mowen in 1781, and had issue: Elizabeth; George; John.

Penna. Arch. 5th Ser. Vol. 6, p. 80, 101, 540.

FELTY STULL

Is shown as a private serving under Capt. Samuel Royer, 1780-81.

Penna. Arch. 5th Ser. Vol. 6, p. 89, 113.

HERMAN STULT

A private 1781, under Capt. Daniel Clapsaddle. Penna. Arch. 5th Ser. Vol. 6, p. 117.

LUDWICK STULL

Served as private under Captain Samuel Royer, 1780-81. Deeds at Chambersburg show surveys to Ludwig Stull on 2 warrants, one to George Stover in 1755, the other to Ludwig Stull, April 30, 1765, who, in 1796, conveyed to Christian Miller. Lewis Stull of Washington Twp., left a Will dated and probated June, 1806. Sons Henry and Jacob my plantation xx division line near road from Fredk. Fisher's Mill; to Saml. Lean's Mill; other children, William; John; Mary.

Penna. Arch. 5th Ser. Vol. 6, p. 89, 112.

ADAM STUMP (STAMM-STUMM)

Served as a private under Capt. James Poe in 1777, under William Long in 1778-79, under Conrad Snider in 1780. His will dated 1801, was prob. Sept. 20, 1805, of Guilford Twp. He names a wife Isabella and a son John; Dau. Hannah, mar. John Mossholder; Dau. Margaret mar. Casper Coover; Dau. Elizabeth mar. Daniel Shilling; 2 Grandchildren, Catherine and Hannah Eley, daus. to my daughter mar. to Peter Eley; Dau. Susanna mar. Peter Smyth; Dau. Magdalena mar. Jacob Coover. Exr.: Henry Snider and my son John.

Penna. Arch. 5th Ser. Vol. 6, p. 87, 521, 523, 538, 546.

THOMAS SULLIVAN

Appears in service under Col. Samuel J. Atlee in the Musketry Battalion. He enlisted one year and nine months; wounded in the left leg at Fort Washington; re-inlisted at Mud Island, under Capt. Clark; resided near Shippensburg, Penna., in 1821.

Penna. Arch. 5th Ser. Vol. 2 p. 491.

JOHEPH SWAN

Served under Capt. Samuel Patton, 1781-82. Joseph Swan of Hamilton Twp., will probated June 25, 1806, names wife Katherine; sons Joseph; George; William; James; John; Ann, my dau., wife of Benjamin Jeffries; son William was of Huntingdon Co. Catherine Denny, wife of Joseph

Swan, died about May 4, 1818, shown in business transactions after her death. He was an Elder in the Rocky Spring Church occupying Pew 50 in the old Log church and Pew 54 in the Brick Church. Descendants state that Joseph Swan is buried in the Rocky Spring graveyard. A Deed refers to "Swansberry," a tract by Patent to Joseph Swan, who with wife Catherine, in 1804, sold to Samuel Liggett, Sr.

Penna. Arch. 5th Ser. Vol. 6, p. 287, 311.

JOSEPH SWAN, JR.

Served in 1782 under Capt. Samuel Patton.
Penna. Arch. 5th Ser. Vol. 6, p. 311.

WILLIAM SWAN

Served under Captains George Matthews, Patrick Jack and Samuel Patton, 1776, 77, 80, 81, 82. He was the son of Joseph and Catherine (Denny) Swan, and lived and died in Dublin Twp., Huntingdon Co., Penna. From Bibles owned by W. K. Swan, Oxford, Ohio, we have the following: William, Sr. born Feb. 28, 1753, died Aug., 1826. His wife Elinor (Chestnut) Swan, born Mar. 1, 1749, died July 4, 1829; they were mar. June 10, 1777. They had issue: Margaret b. 1779; Catherine b. 1780; Benjamin b. 1782; Joseph born 1784; John born 1786; Elinor born 1789; William born 1791; Ann born 1792; Martha born 1794.

Penna. Arch. 5th Ser. Vol. 6, p. 278, 287, 311, 318, 372.

JOHN TALLMAN

A private in the Cont. Line. Mrs. Helen Henderson of Vandergrift, Penna., states: John Tallman came from Wales shortly before the Rev. War, in which he served. He took up land near Shamokin, which he sold and came to Franklin County, where he bought property near Mercersburg. He operated a flour mill, selling the flour in Baltimore. In 1796, he was taxed with 3 horses and 2 cows, in Antrim Twp., a Cooper. He mar. Dorothy Ely and had issue one dau. and six sons: Isaac, b. 1775, went to Westmoreland Co., Penna.; George, born 1793, in Franklin Co., Penna. In the will of Jacob Detwiler of Montgomery Twp., dated 1824, he names his dau. Fanny's children, who was mar. to John Tallman; a grandson Jacob Tallman, a dau. Caty mar. to Abraham Barkman, and sons John and Jacob. One John Tallman owned a tract of land in Montgomery Twp. Franklin Co., Penna. The first tax list of Franklin Co., Penna., shows John Thallman, in Guilford Twp., 1786, 2 horses, 2 cows. One Henry Talman, private, is also shown in service in York Co., Militia.

Penna. Arch. 5th Ser. Vol. 4, p. 480.

JESSE TANYEAR (TANYARD)

Is shown in service 1781-82, with Captains John Woods nad Walter McKinnie.
Penna. Arch. 5th Ser. Vol. 6, p. 138, 298, 300.

JOHN TATE

Appears in service under Major Robert Culbertson, Captains Alexdr. Peebles and Wm. Strain, 1778-79-80-81. John and Robert Tate were freemen in Hopewell Twp.|, Cumb. Co., Penna.
Penna. Arch 5th Ser. Vol. 6, p. 58, 136, 389, 395, 404, 605, 641.

JOHN TATE

Is shown in service 1779-80-81-82, with Capt. Alexdr. Peebles.
Penna. Arch. 5th Ser. Vol. 6, p. 58, 136, 396, 422, 433.

JOHN TATE, JERSEY

Was in service 1781-82, under Capt. Alexdr. Peebles.
Penna. Arch. 5th Ser. Vol. 6, p. 421, 433.

JOHN TAIT

Was Serving in 1781, under Capt. Walter McKinnie, Cumb. Co. Militia.
Penna. Arch. 5th Ser. Vol. 6, p. 297, 300.

JOHN TATE

In 1780 one John Tate served with Capt. John Woods.
Penna. Arch. 5th Ser. Vol. 6, p. 76, 92.

ROBERT TATE, SR.

Served as Ensign with Capt. Alexdr. Peebles, 1779-80, also in 1778-82, as a private, command of Col. James Dunlop. He was a subscriber to the old Stone Church built 1781, at Middle Spring. From the Penna. Magazine of History, Jan., 1904. Under Francis Campbell of Shippensburg, it is stated that his dau. Nancy mar Robert Tate.
Penna. Arch. 5th Ser. Vol. 6, p. 30, 32, 57, 135, 385, 395, 444.

ROBERT TATE, JR.

Appears in service with Capt. Alexdr. Peebles, 1780-81-82. "Inlisted in ye Penna. Volunteers." Under baptisms in 1811 are Samuel Tate and Catherine, dau. of Samuel. In 1812, Samuel, son of Samuel. In 1814, Mary Jean, dau. of Samuel. In 1818 Sally Ann, dau. of Samuel.
Penna. Arch. 5th Ser. Vol. 6, p. 396, 421, 433, 389.

ANDREW TAYLOR

Served in 1781, as a private under Capt. Joseph Culbertson. He was probably the Andrew Taylor, who mar. Sarah, dau. of Wm. McBrayer (McBrier) of Hamilton Twp. One Andrew Taylor sold to John Jeffry, land in Hamilton Twp., granted in 1767 from the Penns. Under Aug. 30, 1813, he receipts for several payments, and states, "paid to us by David Brier himself on account, from estate of Wm. Brier, decd."

Penna. Arch. 5th Ser. Vol. 6, p. 290.

CHARLES TAYLOR

Was in service with Capt Samuel Patton, 1780, as were John and William Taylor.

Penna. Arch. 5th Ser. Vol. 6, p. 279.

EDWARD TAYLOR

Is shown in service 1777-79-80, under Captains Alexdr. Peebles and Noah Abraham, a taxable in Fannett Twp., in 1779.

Penna. Arch. 5th Ser. Vol. 6, p. 29, 32, 58, 85, 589.

GEORGE TAYLOR

From Harrisburg Republican, February 11, 1820. Died at his son's residence in Southampton Township, Franklin County, Friday morning the 4th inst. in the 79th year of his age, Mr. George Taylor an old and respectable citizen of that County. Mr. Taylor emigrated from Ireland in the year 1769 took an early and active part in the revolutionary war in which he sacrificed all his property for the furtherance of these principles which secured our independence and which he carried with him to his grave.

HUGH TAYLOR

Appears as a freeman in 1778 in Guilford Twp., and in 1781, he was in service under Captains James Young and John Woods. Cumberland County, Penna., records: Abstract of the will of Hugh Taylor; dated Dec. 17, 1781; proven Feb. 1, 1782. Sister's Daus., viz: Sarah and Elizabeth Vance, land in Westmoreland County, five miles south of Kitauning Town, one half mile east of the river Alleghany, and plantation Black Lick, in County aforesaid. Gives to Sister Jane Watson, wife of Josiah Watson, a beaver hat. William Nesbit a bible. Susannah McKee, wife of James McKee, a legacy. James McKee, Sr., also mentioned in will. A Box Iron, is given to Frances Sloan, wife of William Sloan. Jane Nesbit a legacy. Sarah Vance is bequeathed a silk gown formerly belonging "to my aunt." Elizabeth Vance is given a Scarlet cloth cloak, and each of the two just mentioned bequeathed linen smocks. Brother Andrew's dau. Elizabeth, a legacy. Exrs.: named in will are James McKee, Sr., and Andrew Reed. Brother Andrew is to receive everything remaining. George Dickson and George Dickey, a son-in-law of Hugh McKee. Carlisle Court records: Will Book 1, p. 156. Will of Alex. Finney, Cumb. Co. Well beloved sister Jean Nesbit; To my sister's dau. Jean Taylor ½ the plantation in Letterkenny Twp.; To nephew Andrew Taylor; To friend William Nesbit my boots; To John Coyl waistcoat &c; To Hance Hamilton a Fine Hat; Sister Sarah Taylor; Nephews, Andrew; Hugh; Sarah and James Taylor, the remainder. Exr.: Adam Hoops. Wit.: Geo. Brown and Robert Cummins. Dec. 6, 1765. No date of probate.

Penna. Arch. 5th Ser. Vol. 6, p. 104, 111.

JOHN TAYLOR

Served in the tenth Penna Regt. Cont. Line, residing in Franklin County in 1826. From records at Harrisburg, he appears to have received a "Gratuity" in 1827, — March 1829 — died May 1831. Through 1778-79-80, the Taylors were in Hamiltown Twp., as taxables. William; Robert; John; Andrew. John Taylor of Beech Creek, John only in 1782.

Penna. Arch. 3rd Ser. Vol. 10, p. 756. 5th Ser. Vol. 3, p. 582.

JOHN TAYLOR

Was serving 1779-80-81-82 under Capt Samuel Patton.

Penna. Arch 5th Ser. Vol. 6, p. 281, 288, 279, 312, 549.

ROBERT TAYLOR

Was in service 1780, under Capt. Wm. Huston. In 1769, his family consisted of wife Mary; Henry; Samuel; Sarah; Jean; William; Robert. William Huston was a member of the family and a descendant stated that William Huston had married either Sarah or Jean Taylor. Robert Taylor appears to have been on Licking Creek, where John Shannon joined him on a 1766 survey, also joining John Roberts. Robert Taylor sold land to James Scott, whose executors sold to Geo. Clark, Esq., of Greencastle, Penna. One Robert Taylor died Aug. 6, 1824, aged 84 yrs., and is lying in Long Run Presby Church Cemetery, Westmoreland Co., Penna.

Penna. Arch. 5th Ser. Vol. 6, p. 270.

SAMUEL TAYLOR

Was in service 1780,81, an undated roll, under Captains James Patton, Robert Dickey and Thomas McDowell. He was probably a son of Robert and Mary Taylor, and was mar. to Jean McGuire, Apr. 1, 1772. The baptism of a child is shown in April, 1781.

Penna. Arch. 5th Ser. Vol. 6, p. 271, 284, 289, 314.

SAMUEL TAYLOR

Appears in 1780-81, under Captains Robert Dickey, Thomas McDowell and James Patton.

OF FRANKLIN COUNTY PENNSYLVANIA

Penna. Arch. 5th Ser. Vol. 6, p. 271, 284, 289, 314.

WILLIAM TAYLOR

Was in service 1780-81-82, under Captains Alexander Peebles, Thomas Askey and Samuel Patton. He was of Fannett Twp., and appears 1779-81-82, with land, horses, cattle and a negro; under 1796 Taxables he had 400 acres of land, part unseated; horses, cows &c. John Taylor also had land, horses and cattle.

Penna. Arch. 5th Ser. Vol. 6, p. 278, 423, 441.

WILLIAM TAYLOR

Is shown in 1780-82, Captains Samuel Patton and Thomas Askey.

Penna. Arch. 5th Ser. Vol. 6, p. 278, 441.

ABRAHAM TEETER, JR.

Was in service 1781, under Capt. Walter McKinnie.

Penna. Arch. 5th Ser. Vol. 6, p. 297, 300.

JOHN TEETER

Served in 1782, under Capt. John Orbison. Abraham and John Teeter were Montgomery Twp. Taxables 1781, with horses and cattle.

Penna. Arch. 5th Ser. Vol. 6, p. 308.

GEORGE TEGARD

Was in service 1781 under Capt. Wm. Huston. Abram Tagarden a freeman in Montgomery Twp., tax list, 1781. Note: Abraham Tiegarden, Sr. and Jr. came over in ship Harle, Sept. 1, 1736, ages 48 and 18 years.

Penna. Arch. 5th Ser. Vol. 6, p. 283.

ALEXANDER TEMPLETON

Served under Captains Walter McKinnie and William Huston, 1780,81-82. He was a son of Samuel Templeton and wife Anne, members of the early Presbyterian Church near Mercersburg, Penna. Under a deed dated Feb. 25, 1803, Alexander Templeton of Conemaugh Twp. Westmoreland Co., Penna., is shown selling land in Peters Twp., Franklin Co., Penna., to James, John, Robert and Isabella McCoy, of Peters Twp.

Penna. Arch. 5th Ser. Vol. 6, p. 266, 298, 300, 306, 643.

JOHN TEMPLETON

Served from Fannett Twp., 1781-82, under Capt. Thos Askey. John Templeton, Jr. is also shown, "on a class Role duly made out according to law."

Penna. Arch. 5th Ser. Vol. 6, p. 409, 423, 441, 442, 424.

WILLIAM TEMPLETON

Served 1789-81 with Capt. Patrick Jack under the Command of Lieut. Col Samuel Culbertson, 1781-82. He was a son of Samuel Templeton and wife Anne. Samuel Templeton died May 24, 1777; Martha died about the same time; Anne, probably the widow of Samuel, died July, 1785. Samuel Urie mar. Anne Templeton June 22, 1779. John Smith mar. Mary Templeton, May 30, 1780, both daus. of Samuel Templeton and wife Anne.

Penna Arch. 5th Ser. Vol. 6, p. 292, 296, 313.

WILLIAM TEMPLETON

Served 1781-82, under Capt. Thos Askey. Both John and William Templeton are shown in 1779, signing a petition from Fannett Twp. Franklin Repository, Chambersburg, Penna., Aug. 18, 1829. St. Clairsville, Ohio, Aug. 8, married on Tuesday last by Rev. Joseph Anderson, William Templeton to Miss Sarah Wilson, all of this place.

Penna. Arch 5th Ser. Vol. 6, p. 409, 423, 441.

ARCHIBALD THOMPSON

Served as private under Capt. John Rea, 1779-1780. He was a miller in Green Twp., and left minor children, James; Jane; Agnes; Hannah. On June 28, 1770, John Robinson mar. Anne Campbell. In the will of Ann Robinson, widow and relict of John Robison of Chambersburg, Penna., she names her well beloved relation and friend Archibald Thompson and Ann, his wife,"my beloved niece,"—among legatees were nephew Wm. Campbell and nieces Polly, Jenny, and Madgey Campbell.

Penna. Arch. 5th Ser. Vol. 6, p. 73, 78, 106, 543, 584.

JOHN THOMPSON

Of Guilford Twp., served as private under Captains Terence Campbell and James Young. His will dated Sept., 1794, was prob. Jan., 1795, naming a dau. Martha McMurran; a dau. Jean "at her marriage"; 3 sons, William; John; Robert, when they arrive at 21 years; to be educated; Sons Henry and Samuel to each have one-half of my plantation in Guilford. Twp.

Penna. Arch. 5th Ser. Vol. 6, p. 82, 77, 111, 126.

WILLIAM THOMPSON

Son of Thos. and Martha Thompson, served with Capt. William Rippey's Company, of the 6th Penna. Batt., in the 2nd Canada expedition. He removed to Westmoreland Co., about 1780, where he was active against the Indians on the Western frontier. He later moved to Kentucky and died there. He mar. Mary, dau. of John Jack and grandau. of James and Elizabeth Jack, early settlers in the Conococheague Valley. John Jack of Westmoreland Co., Penna., names in his will (1808) a grandson Andrew Thompson.

Hist. of the Bard Family by George Seilhamer. Chambersburg, Penna., Orphans' Court Book A

p. 170-213, Sept. 16, 1806. On motion and proof of the existence of Catherine Thompson, widow of Genl. Wm. Thompson, decd., the Court makes an order for such allowance as she is entitled to by Law, on account of ½ pay &c, now due to her in pursuance of a widow's order made in her favor.

JAMES THORN

Was in service 1780-82, with Capt. Samuel Patton. One James Thorn mar. Agnes, dau of Thomas and Mary Dougherty.

Penna. Arch. 5th Ser. Vol. 6, p. 278, 303.

JOHN THORN

Appears in service with Capt. Conrad Snider, Lieut. Adam Harmony, 1778-80-82, a probable son of Joseph Thorn, Sr.

Penna. Arch. 5th Ser. Vol. 6, p. 87, 123, 538.

JOSEPH THORN, JR.

Son of Joseph Thorn, Sr., is shown in service 1781, with Capt. Patrick Jack. Joseph Thorn, Sr., of Hamilton Twp., left a will dated 1796, prob. May, 1799, in which the son Joseph is given the plantation of 154 acres of patented land; Dau. Esther 200 pounds, Lot No. 5, in Chambersburg, a deed of March, 1773, from Benj. Chambers and wife Jane. A dau. Martha Boyd, who is probably the Martha Thorn, who was taken with Ann, wife of John McCord, at McCord's Fort in Conococheague, and re-taken from the Indians at Kittanning. Martha was about seven years old at the time. Martha mar. Robert Boyd formerly of Chambersburg and they had sons Joseph Boyd and Steward Boyd, Martha to have the use of the Lot during her natural life. To sons John and Wm. Thorn, and dau. Mary Robeson, each the sum of 20 shillings. In the will of Robert Walker of Peters Twp., 1792, he mentions the heirs of dau. Jean Thorn, decd., and other daus.: Margaret Kerr, Sarah Kerr and Elizabeth Savage.

Penna. Arch 5th Ser. Vol. 6, p. 297.

WILLIAM THORN

Is shown serving with Capt. James Young, 1779-80-81, a probable son of Joseph Thorn, Sr.

Penna. Arch. 5th Ser. Vol. 6, p. 81, 110, 548.

HENRY TODD

Was a Sergt. 1778-79, under Capt. William Findley and under Capt. Samuel Patton 1780-81-82. The 1790 Census shows the family as 1 man, 1 boy, 6 females and the will of Henry Todd of Hamilton Twp., farmer, as Lettice Todd, my dearly beloved wife; Son John Daus. Dorcas; Martha; Mary; Lettice; Isabella; dated March 25, 1806. Ledger accounts of John and Polly Todd 1819-1822, and in 1828 John Todd and wife Gettys sell to Mary and Lettice Todd 300 acres land for $3000., part warranted and part located land.

Penna. Arch 5th Ser. Vol. 6, p. 277, 286, 289, 311, 529, 547, 596.

SAMUEL TODD

Was a private 1780, under Capt. John Orbison, vicinity of Welsh Run.

Penna. Arch. 5th Ser. Vol. 6, p. 274.

HENRY TOMS

Served as private, probably of the German Regiment, with Capt. Wm. Heyser, Col. Baron Arendt, Quibble Town, May 22, 1777. Henry Thomas mar. 1st Anna, dau. of Henry Detch (Ditch); He mar. 2nd Mary Detch (Ditch. See Carlisle Court records; will of Henry Detch of Antrim Twp.; dated Oct. 29, 1782; prob. Nov. 25, 1783; wife Eve; a dau. Anna, decd., wife of Henry Thomas and her children, 3 viz: John; Samuel and Molly Thomas. He also names daughter Mary Thomas, "as is now the 2nd wife of Henry Thomas to have her equal portion among the rest of my children." Henry Thomas mar. 3rd Rachel? who later married Henry Cauffman. Henry Thomas died in Bedford Co., Penna., Napier Twp., a farmer. His will dated Aug., 1816; prob. 1817, names wife Rachel; children: John; Samuel; Molly, wife of Conrad Bonebrake; David; Abraham; Henry; Daniel; Elizabeth; Jacob; Katherine; Michael; George; Nancy; William and the 5 youngest, viz: Frederick; Adam; Solomon; Eve and Joseph. Exrs.: John Rock and John Shell, and "I commend my young children to the care of my executors." McCauley's Hist. of Franklin Co., Penna., p. 288—Deed Book 5, p. 496 and Deed Book 7, p. 102, Zeamers Tax lists show in 1765, 150 acres for Henry Thomas (in 1781 as Henry Toms* xx in 1779 he had 200 acres. In 1796, listed as Henry Thomas, Sr. Under taxables in Warren Twp., 1799, are both Henry and Abraham Thomas, with land, horses and cows, presumably son of Henry of Washington Twp., Franklin Co., Penna. Certain land in Washington Twp., applications No. 4657 and 4954, in the name of George and Henry Thom, dated Dec., 1767 and Apr., 1768. Under a warrant to James McLanahan, June, 1762, who sold to Samuel Carrick in 1774, and sold by Carrick to Henry Thomas, Apr., 1789. In 1796, Henry Thomas was a witness on the will of Enoch Williams of Air Twp., Bedford Co., Penna., which strengthens the tradition that the Thomas' were Welsh and the records show that Wash. Co., Md., had many settlers named Thomas, of Welsh blood. Court records at Chambersburg show the admr. of Solomon Thomas, probably a grandson of Henry in 1811, leaving a widow Catherine.

Penna. Arch. 3rd Ser. Vol. 23, p. 389. 5th Ser. Vol. 3, p. 794, 805.

JOHN TOM (THOM)

Served as private 1779-80-81, under Captains William Long and Daniel Clapsaddler. Deeds show his heirs to have been John Toms; Jonas Toms; Susanna Wiles (late Toms); Catherine Peters late Toms); Michael Stoner in right of Elias Toms; Samuel Toms; who sold land to Abraham Ealy; also Thomas Barns and William Toms, of Moon Twp., Beaver Co., Penna., Attys. of Robert Long and Hannah his wife, Samuel Wilson and Susan, his wife, said Hannah and Susan being daus. of Abraham Toms, late of Moon Twp., decd., Abraham being a son of John Toms, of Washington Twp. Franklin Co., Penna. They now sell their shares.

Penna. Arch. 5th Ser. Vol. 6, p. 94, 116, 265, 546.

JOHN TOM

Served 1780-81 under Captains James Patton, Robert Dickey and Thos. McDowell. In Feb., 1785, he was granted a tract of 100 acres, including his improvement at the foot of Cove Mountain. In 1786, John Tom and wife Jane sold to James Buchanan 100 acres, for 200 pounds in Cove Gap, also all the dwelling houses, Store Houses, Stables and all other appurtenances, "where the said Tom now lives on." This is undoubtedly the tract on which Pennsylvania's only President was born.

Penna. Arch. 5th Ser. Vol. 6, p. 272, 285, 315.

GEORGE THOMAS

Appears with Capt. John Hodge, 1782.
Penna. Arch. 5th Ser. Vol. 6, p. 437.

JOHN THOMAS

Is shown serving in 1777, under Capt. Patrick Jack.
Penna. Arch. 5th Ser. Vol. 6, p. 372.

JACOB THOMAS

Appears in the Company of Capt. Noah Abraham, also in Capt. Thos. Askey's Company, 1780-81-82.
Penna. Arch. 5th Ser. Vol. 6, p. 121, 128, 407, 410, 477, 485.

SAMUEL THOMAS

Is shown in 1781 under Capt. Daniel Clapsaddle.
Penna. Arch. 5th Ser. Vol. 6, p. 117.

WILLIAM THOMAS

Gave service 1782.
Penna. Arch. 5th Ser. Vol. 6, p. 437.

ALBERT TORRENCE

Served as First Lieut. under Capt. John Rea and William Findley, 1778-80-81. He was of Green Twp., his will prob. 1804. He names a sister Jane, wife of Thos. McKean; brothers James and William; Sister Isabella, wife of John Ferguson; Sister Mary, wife of Hugh Wiley; also bequests to various nieces and nephews; mulatto girl Catey to be at the disposal of Elizabeth Ferguson, my sister's daughter. Albert Torrence occupied Pew No. 25, with Major Jas. McCalmont and Hugh Wiley, in the old log church at Rocky Spring. When Rev. Francis Herron came as pastor, in 1800, "Captain" Albert Torrence appears alone in Pew. No. 36.

Penna. Arch. 5th Ser. Vol. 6, p. 78, 106, 527, 534, 584.

DAVID TORRENCE

Was a private 1781-82, with Capt. Walter McKinnie, a taxable in Peters Twp. On June 19, 1787, Agnes Torrence was mar. to Andrew Long by Rev. John King of Mercersburg.
Penna. Arch. 5th Ser. Vol. 6, p. 298, 300, 305.

HUGH TORRENCE

Appears as a private 1777-79, undated rolls, with Capt. John Rea, Lieut. Albert Torrence, and privates James and Wm. Torrence. Hugh Torrence is also shown as Ensign in Cumb. Co. Associators in 1776. From 1778 to 1782, Tax lits show Albert, Wm. Hugh and James Torrence in Letterkenny Twp., with land, horses and cattle. Hugh Torrence occupied Pew No. 30, with John Ferguson and Joseph Clark in the old Log Church at Rocky Spring. He left a will, dated Aug. prob. Oct., 1795, of Green Twp., naming wife Gennet and a son Hugh, a minor, of whom Albert Torrence was appointed guardian.

Penna. Arch. 5th Ser. Vol. 6, p. 11, 448, 544, 585. 3rd Ser. Vol. 23, p. 465.

JAMES TORRANS

Was in service 1780-81, with Capt. John Rea, apparently afflicted with "Rumatism." It is probable that some of the family went to Westmoreland Co., Penna. One James Torrence was Captain of a Company of Rangers, from Westmoreland Co., Penna. In July, 1806, James Torrence was of Allegheny Co., Penna., certain lands in Franklin Co., Penna., bequeathed to James Torrence and his brother Albert Torrence, Jr. xx Hugh Ferguson acting Executor of Albert Torrence Jr. xxx.

Penna. Arch 5th Ser. Vol. 6, p. 78, 97, 106, 585, Vol. 4, p. 458, 758.

JOHN TORRANCE (TORRANS)

In 1777, serving under Capt. Thos. Askey, and in 1781-82 with Capt. Walter McKinnie. Aaron Torrance and others of the name were in Peters Twp., as taxables. On May 3, 1833, one John Torrence was aged 76 years, then living in Green Co., Ohio, and had been a private in the Militia of Penna.

Penna. Arch. 5th Ser. Vol. 6, p. 8, 10, 142, 297, 300, 305.

JOSEPH TORRENCE

As Lieut. with Capt. Jeremiah Talbot, Nov., 1777, 6th Penna. Batt., under Col. Wm. Irvine. They were in the Seventh Penna. Regt., later where Joseph Torrance was promoted to First Lieut., Feb. 2, 1778. He resigned Apr. 25, 1779.

McCauley's History of Franklin Co., Penna. p. 84.

SAMUEL TORRENS

Is shown in 1781 as a private under Capt. Walter McKinnie, a taxable in Peters Twp. On Dec. 31, 1778, Samuel Terrance was mar. to Jean McConnell, by Rev. John King.

Penna. Arch. 5th Ser. Vol. 6, p. 299.

WILLIAM TORRENCE

Is shown in service 1778-79-80-81, under Capts. John Rea and William Findley, undoubtedly a brother of Capt. Albert Torrence. Jean Torrence occupied a pew in the new Brick Church at Rocky Spring in 1794. A deed of Apr., 1790, shows Wm. Torrence and wife Martha of Wash. Co., Penna., selling to Albert Torrence of Green Twp., Franklin Co., Penna. A deed of Dec., 1805, further shows William Torrence of Hamilton Co., Ohio, one of the brothers and legatees of Albert Torrence. Hugh Ferguson appears in both deeds.

Penna. Arch. 5th Ser. Vol. 6, p. 585, 527, 530, 544, 106, 78, 73.

JOHN TOWNSLEY

Was in service March, 1776, in the Company of Captain Jeremiah Talbott, from Franklin County, 6th Penna. Batt. Official Roster, Rev. Soldiers of Ohio gives: John Townsley, b. May, 1753, Cumb. Co., Penna., mar. Hester Martin and died 1822, Cedarville, Greene Co., Ohio.

Penna. Arch 5th Ser. Vol. 2, p. 241.

PETER TRAUGH (TROUGH)

Is shown in the Cont. Line as entitled to Depreciation Pay. He served in Militia as a Ranger on Frontiers and under Captains Walter McKinnie and John Orbison. His son Peter also served. In his will, Peter Trough of Montgomery Twp., states he is advanced in years, weake in body. Son-in-law John Hicks. No sons nor daus. to receive anything except son Jonathan. His will was prob. Feb. 7, 1815.

Penna. Arch. 5th Ser. Vol. 6, p. 281, 299, 308. Vol. 4, p. 306. 3rd Ser. Vol. 23, p. 276.

WILLIAM GEORGE TRAYER

Was in service as a private, 1780-81, under Capt. John Rea.

Penna: Arch. 5th Ser. Vol. 6, p. 78, 105.

JONATHAN TREAKLE

Mattross, Germany, Aprr. 25, 1777. Jonathan Treakle served in the Penna. Artillery, Col. Thomas Proctor, 1779, also shown in the Cont. Line, entitled to Depreciation, pay. He was discharged Sept. 30, 1783, and living in Chambersburg in 1813.

Penna. Arch. 5th Ser. Vol. 3, p. 979, 1027. Vol. 4, p. 194.

DANIEL CALORY
(ULRICH, OLLERY, CALERY)

Served 1780-82 under Capt. John Orbison name probably Ulrick.

Penna. Arch. 5th Ser. Vol. 6, p. 274, 294.

JOHN ULRICH (OLLERY, CALERY)

Served as pvt., 1780-81-82 under Capt. John Orbison. He is shown in 1781, Montgomery Twp., with 2 Mills, Still, 380 ac. land, horses, cattle and was a freeman. He is the man who bought from the members of Welsh Run Church, the 93 acres given them by the Penns. The Indians had burned the "Meeting House" which was near the stone bridge, a mile from Welsh Run. It was thought advisable to build about where the present church now stands—on land from Robert Smith and later re-deeded by Jacob Angle and wife, Eleanor. The above John Ulrich moved to Huntingdon Co., Penna., and is buried there.

Penna. Arch. 5th Ser. Vol. 6, p. 273, 293, 307, 308.

JOHN ULRICH, JR.

Served as a private under Capt. John Orbison, 1780-81.

Penna. Arch. 5th Ser. Vol. 6, p. 274, 294.

FREDERICK UNSELL

W 22 472. Frederick Unsell was pensioned for his Rev. War service. Jane Unsell, widow of Frederick, was pensioned on Certificate No. 43, isued June 10, 1848; rate $80 per annum; act of Feb. 2, 1848; Springfield, Ill. Agency. He alleged that he enlisted about Aug.,1779; served in Capt. James "Hughs" Co., Col. Gibson's Penna. Regt., against the Indians; was in frequent skirmishes with them; was engaged as Spy and in guarding different forts; was discharged late in the fall of 1781. His alleged service in the Rev. War totaled 28 months. He alleged, also, that he served afterwards on Gen. St. Clair's Expedition in 1791 against the Indians, no other details of that service given. Frederick Unsell's parents names not shown, moved about 1770 to "Little Wheeling" where they lived a short time. His father died; and his mother moved to that part of Pennsylvania known as the "catfish country," which later became Washington County. During his service, and at different times after the war, he lived in Washington Co., Penna. In 1788 or 1789, he was a resident of Harrison Co., Va. He later moved to Miami Co., Ohio; thence to Muhlenburgh Co., Kentucky; he next lived on White River in Indiana. In 1822, he moved to Clark Co., Ill. His widow, Jane, was living in Clark Co. in 1840, and was still living there in 1848. Frederick Unsell, married Dec. 6, 1789, in Washington Co., Penna., Jane Masters, who was born March 17, 1772, place of her birth and names of parents not shown. She later mar. Peter Kitchel or Kitchello. Children: Margaret, the eldest, b. Sept. 26, 1790, 1791 or 1793. Mary, b. Feb. 18, 1795, in Virginia, and in 1841 the wife of ———— Oxendine. Henry, age not given. Jane, age not given; Ann or Anna, aged 40 years in 1841, when she was the wife of ———— Fuller. Susannah or Susan, who was aged about 38 years in 1841, when she was the wife of ———— Taylor. Jane, who in 1841 was aged 36 years and was then the wife of ———— Page. Frederick, Junior, born about June, 1807. Katherine, born about 1809, who in 1841 was the wife of ———— Gammon. Phebe, born about June, 1811. Peter, age not stated. Mahala or Mehala, b. in Sept., 1814, who in 1841 was the wife of ———— Wallen. James, born in May, 1817. The names of the daughters' husbands were not stated. The following places of residences for the veteran's children are shown for 1841: Mary Oxendine, Clark Co., Ill. Ann or Ann Fuller, Missouri, exact place not stated; Susannah or Susan Taylor, Clark, Co., Ill. Jane Page, Clark Co., Ill. Frederick, Clark Co., Ill.; Katherine Gammon, Clark Co., Ill. The veteran was born Aug. 25, 1765, in Frederick Co., Md., and died at his residence in Clark Co., Ill. Sept. 11, 1835. Frederick Unsell's dau. Margaret, died in Harrison Co., Va., prior to 1841. Three other children, Henry, Jane and Peter, died prior to 1841, exact dates and places not stated.

JOHN VANCE

Served as a private under Capt. Conrad Synder and William Long in 1779-80-81. He attended the Military Convention in Lancaster, July 4, 1776, as a private in the 5th Battalion, Cumb. Co., Militia. He also served as Ranger on the frontier. In 1782, John Vance appears with 510 acres of land, 5 horses, 10 cattle, 2 negroes. Presumably the son, John, had in 1804, a distillery, 457 acres of land, one slave, one powder mill, one grist mill, horses and cows. John Vance, Sr., died in 1784, leaving wife, Elizabeth, and the following children: John, Jr., b. 1770, d. April 17, 1834. He mar. Margaret, daughter of Robert McCulloch; children: George, Isabella, Mary. Rebecca Vance, b. 1769, mar. June 21, 1796 to John Watson of Greene Twp. Mary Vance, mar. prior to 1793 to George McCulloch. His widow, Elizabeth, later married David Adams (probably in 1789).

Penna. Arch. 5th Ser. Vol. 6, p. 87, 119, 546.

PATRICK VANCE

Brother of John Vance, served as a private under Capts. Conrad Snyder and William Long, in 1778-79-80-81. His wife's name was also Elizabeth. Patrick and John Vance, brothers, emigrated from Ireland and settled in Guliford Twp., Oct. 8, 1754. They bought a tract of land, jointly, from William Anderson and his wife Rebecca, for 242 pounds. This land had originally belonged to the Cavens, and on May 3, 1782, Alexander Caven, one of the heirs appeared and demanded of the Vances 250 pounds for his release to the property. This was paid him although the Vances had made payment in full under the original contract, by August 10, 1776. The first stone house in the vicinity of Stoufferstown was built by Patrick Vance in 1773. Patrick and John Vance helped to establish the Falling Spring Church. They were farmers and millers. Patrick became Justice of the Peace in 1777, and he took the Oath of Allegiance at Carlisle, Sept. 18, 1777.

Penna. Arch. 5th Ser. Vol. 6, p. 74, 88, 119, 538, 546. Deed Book Vol. 1, p. 232, 233. Deed Book Vol. 2, p. 421. Deed Book Vol. 5. p. 423.

JAMES VIRTUE

Served as pvt., 1780, under Capt. Saml. Patton. In the will of Samuel John of Letterkenny Twp., 1815, he names Ruthy Vertue and Rebecca Thomas. In 1790 the family of James Virtue consisted of 4 men, 2 boys, 4 females.

Penna. Arch. 5th Ser. Vol. 6, p. 278.

JAMES WADDELL

Took the Oath of Fidelity on Oct. 14, 1777, before Hugh Martin, Esq., in Westmoreland Co., Penna. He is also shown in the Cont. Line, serving from Westmoreland Co., Penna. When John Holliday, pioneer, of Peters Twp. made his will in 1770, the witnesses were William Thomas and Robert Waddell. John Holliday died March 27, 1770. One James Scott of Allegheny Co., Penna., in his will, dated 1822, names a dau. Sarah Waddle and grandson James Scott Waddle.

Penna. Arch 2nd Ser. Vol. 3, p. 31.

JOSEPH WADDLE

Appears in 1782, as a private with Capt. John McConnell. The Waddles are shown in Lancaster, Chester, Cumberland and elsewhere during the Rev. War. Samuel Waddle was a Lieut. under Col. Robert Magaw, 1777, in the Sixth Penna. Regt.

Penna. Arch. 5th Ser. Vol. 6, p. 309.

ROBERT WADDLE

Took the Oath of Fidelity, Oct. 13, 1777, before Hugh Martin, Esq., in Westmoreland Co., Penna. Deeds at Chambersburg, Penna., Book 1, p. 339, show the death of Thomas Waddle, whose tracts of land became the property of Robert Waddle by conveyance from the rest of Legatees. A tract was surveyed for the Reverend James Waddle, who in Aug., 1773, sold to Robert Waddle, who sold to Hugh Gibson, No. 5019. The will of Robert Waddel of Mercer Co., Penna., dated and prob. May-Dec., 1808, names wife Bathia (dau. of Thos. Orbison), 4 sons: Thomas; Robert; James; John. Division to be made by Wm. Agnew and Ephriam Harris. Daus.: Elizabeth Vandike; Jane; Mary; Sarah. Executors: Wife and sons, Thomas and James. The Rev. Z. M. Gibson states that Sarah, dau. of Robert Waddel, was born Aug., 1791, mar. Harvey Gibson. They lived in Armstrong Co., Penna., and he adds that Robert Waddell was a brother of Rev. James Waddell, of Virginia. Robert Waddle appears in the Cont. Line from Westmoreland Co., Penna.

Penna. Arch. 2nd Ser. Vol. 3, p. 31. 5th Ser. Vol. 4, p. 459. Deed Book Vol. 7, p. 229, 231.

WILLIAM WADDELL

Served as private in 1776-77-81-82, under Captains James McConnell, John McConnell and George Crawford. He mar. Elizabeth, dau. of Thos. Stockton. They had sons Thomas and Wiliam. Thomas mar. Catherine Long and Wiliam mar. Margaret McMullen. William Waddell, Sr., died 1830, aged 86 years. His wife Elizabeth born 1759, died 1808. They are buried in Fairview Cemetery, Mercersburg, Penna. (Removals). The Bard History, p. 383-384, Thomas Waddell, born in Peters Twp. Franklin Co., Penna., Dec., 1792, died June 23, 1852. He was a private in Capt. Thomas Bard's Co., that marched to the defence of Baltimore, in 1814. On the 4th of July of that year he was appointed brigadier general of the Franklin Co., Militia. Thomas Waddell mar. Catherine, dau. of Alexdr. and Mary (Poe) Long. She died Aug. 27, 1818. She was married in April 1796, to Thomas Waddell. They had issue: Alexdr. Waddell mar. Mary Erwin; John Waddell mar. Jane Allen; Thomas Waddell; William Waddell mar. Ruth Grubb; Archbd. Waddell born 1811, died 1849, mar. Maria Morrow; James Poe Waddell, born 1815, mar. Susan Flora; Eliza Waddell, mar Robert McKinnie.

Penna. Arch. 5th Ser. Vol. 6, p. 288, 301, 309, 317, 318, 371.

WILLIAM WADDLE

Pension Aplication of William Waddle of Penna., S-40645. Westmoreland Co., Penna., May 22, 1821, aged 73 years. Enlisted at Hannastown, April, 1776, Capt. Joseph Erwin's Company of Riflemen, Col. Brodhead's Regt., for 22 months, and was discharged at Valley Forge by Col. Walter Stewart. Participated in battles of Long Island, White Plains, Princeton, Brandywine, Trenton and Germantown. Was placed on the pension roll Oct. 22, 1818, Certif. No. 3847. Had not disposed of any property since that time, nor does he own any; resides with his son James and states further that his wife has been dead for 19 years and his children are all grown up and doing for themselves. On Apr. 15, 1818, Alexdr. McCurdy deposed service with Waddell in Capt. Joseph Irwin's Co. 2nd Regt. Penna. Riflemen from Apr., 1776 to spring of 1777, when Waddell was transferred to Capt. James Carnahan's Co., Col. Walter Stewart's Regt., where he served until Jan., 1778. At Chambersburg, Penna. Deed Book Vol. 1, p. 339, shows in 1777, William Waddle of Westmoreland Co., Penna., selling a tract of land in Peters Twp., to Alexdr and Andrew Biggers for 700 pounds. It further recited a certain Thomas Waddle, late of Peters Twp., died intestate, having sundry tracts in Peters Twp., which became the property of his son Robert Waddle by conveyance from the rest of the Legatees, the said Robert having conveyed a part of said land unto his brother William Waddle, one of the parties to these presents xx who now sells to A. &. A. Biggers, land by James Campbell, David Kisner, Hugh Gibson &c, 323 acres, 106 perches. On Aug. 19, 1778, William Waddle, signed the Oath of Fidelity before Hugh Martin, Esq., in Westmoreland Co., Penna. "On March 5, 1825, the pensioner certified that he was then residing in Westmoreland Co., Penna. The last payment was made March 14, 1825, at the Pension Agency in Phila., Penna., to John Horner, as attorney for the pensioner.

Penna. Arch. 2nd Ser. Vol. 3, p. 32.

JACOB WAGERMAN (WAGAMAN)

Is shown as private with Capt. Samuel Royer, 1779-80-81. He had 50 acres of land, horses and cattle in Washington Twp., and in 1790 Census, the family showed 1 man, 3 boys, 4 females.

Penna. Arch. 5th Ser. Vol. 6, p. 75, 90, 81-542.

OF FRANKLIN COUNTY PENNSYLVANIA 217

PHILIP WAGERMAN
Served in 1779, from Washington Twp., as a private under Capt. Samuel Royer.
Penna. Arch. 5th Ser. Vol. 6, p. 542.

CHRISTOPHER WAGNER
Served as a private 1777, as shown in the muster Roll of Capt. Wm. Heyser's Company of the German Regt., Commanded by Baron Arendt, Colonel; Quibble Town, May 22, 1777. Christopher Wagner of Washington Twp., left a will dated May, 1785, prob. Dec. 1789, in which he named Beloved Wife and children; Wife Elizabeth; 3 children; the witnesses being Geo. Hidler and Martain Jacob. Letters on the estate were granted to George Hidler, father of Elizabeth Wagner.
Penna. Arch. 5th Ser. Vol. 3, p. 794.

YOUST WAHL (JOOST WALB)
Of Chambersburg, Penna., yeoman; will dated Aug. 9, 1802; prob. Sept. 21, 1807; Beloved wife Catherine whole benefits of real and personal estate, residue amongst my three children, Jacob Josephine and Catherine, subject to the payment of the following sums: Son George 25 pounds; son-in-law Adam Burkholder, mar. to dau. Anna Mariah, 50 pounds; grandson John Burkholder, son to dau. Catherine, now intermarried to John Meesey, 30 pounds; son-in-law John Snell, intermarried with my dau. Margaret, hath already received his full share. Executors: wife Catherine and friend George Hetich; Wit: Thomas and George Hetich.
Penna. Arch. 5th Ser. Vol. 8. p. 94, 487, 457, 510.

JOHN WAID
Carlisle, Pa., Court records. The will of John Waid; a plantation in Conococheague near Rocky Spring (boundaries given) to son Ebenezer. Last wife's children each ½ crown. Dau. Fanny Boyd; Dau. Mary; Dau. Elizabeth; what money is due me for my service in the Provincial Troops, in years 1758 and 1759. When money is received, to pay for a deed for the above land. Dated and probated 1760. The executors were Samuel Boyd and Joseph Culbertson. Wit.: James Brice, George Small, Robert Hease.

JAMES WAKEFIELD
Served 1782, under Capt. Thos. Askey, from Fannett Twp. Andrew Campbell of Fannettt Twp., had a dau. Margaret, who married Andrew Wakefield.
Penna. Arch. 5th Ser. Vol. 6, p. 442.

JOHN WAKEFIELD
Served as private under Capt. Thos. Askey, 1781-82 from Fannett Twp., and was also in the Cont. Line. He signed a petition from Fannett Twp. in 1779.
Penna. Arch. 5th Ser. Vol. 6, p. 407, 410, 424, 442. Vol. 4, p. 306.

THOMAS WAKEFIELD
Of Fannett Twp., served in 1780-81 under Capt. Thos. Askey, as a private and he is also shown in the Cont. Line. He signed a petition from Fannett Twp., in 1779. It is stated that he married Elizabeth Morton, b. 1757, d. 1844. She was buried near New Florence, Penna. It is probable she was from Bedford, Penna.
Penna. Arch. 5th Ser. Vol. 6, p. 393, 409, 424, 620. Vol. 4, p. 306.

ALEXANDER WALKER
Pioneer, with his wife Mary, came from North Ireland, in 1737, settled at the Forks of the Brandywine. In 1761, they came to Path Valley settling in what is now Metal Twp., at a big spring, where he, Alexander, gave the land for the first church and graveyard. He died May 1, 1775, his wife Mary having died Oct. 16, 1774. They had five sons: (1) John mar. Miss McGuire and moved to Burnt Cabins. (2) James, an Indian Captive, died 1788. (3) Robert, unmar. died 1778. (4) David mar. Miss Elliott, moved to Burnt Cabins. (5) Samuel mar. Mary Noble. From: Walker Bible in possession of Mrs. Annie Walker.

ANDREW WALKER
Served as a private under Capt. Thos. Askey, in 1777. He is not identified as a son of either Alexander or of Robert Walker.
Penna. Arch 5th Ser. Vol. 6, p. 7, 10, 24.

BENJAMIN WALKER
Served as private under Capt. Noah Abraham, 1781-82. He was a son of Robert Walker and wife Mary of Path Valley. All evidence points to two (2) early and distinct Walker lines in Path Valley, as Deed Book 9, p. 186, shows Robert Walker granted 100 acres land in 1767, his heirs being a wife Mary who later mar. James Calhoun; children were Benjamin; Margaret; Alexander; Samuel; Mary mar. to David White; James; Robert; Abraham. Caldwell's His. Indiana Co., Penna., p. 428, "Benj. Walker and wife, Margaret Cunningham, of Path Valley, came to Armstrong Twp., in 1786. He died in 1843, over 80 years of age, his wife dying in 1818.
Penna. Arch 5th Ser. Vol. 6, p. 121, 128.

JAMES WALKER
Son of Alexdr. and Mary Walker of Metal Twp., was taken captive by the Indians when they burned the Walker barn. After great hardship, he finally escaped by stabbing an Indian who

guarded him, with a knife he had concealed in his boot. He reached home almost starved, travelling only at night, and in broken health. In June 1777, one James Walker signed the Oath of Allegiance before Robert Peebles. James Walker of Fannett Twp., left a will dated April and prob. Dec., 1788. To brother Samuel Walker of Fannett Twp., all my land, also my part of a Bond of 156 pounds, 16 shillings due from James Moor of the Forks of the Brandywine; to my brother Samuel and Robert's children; brother David, and John and sisters Susanna to be divided equally among them; sister Susanna Witherow thirty pounds; to brother Samuel out of the estate which I have bequeathed to him 3 pounds to be applied for repairing the Presby. Church in the Lower Congregation of Path Valley. Exrs.: brother Samuel and John Walker. Wit.: James Harve, Archbd. Elliott and James Moore.

JAMES WALKER

Son of Robert and brother of Samuel of Peters Twp., is shown in service under Captains James Patton and Thomas McDowell, 1778-80-81, undated rolls.

Penna. Arch 5th Ser. Vol. 6, p. 272, 286, 374, 382, 615.

JOHN WALKER

Brother of Samuel of Peters Twp., appears in service 1778-81, under Capt. James Patton.

Penna. Arch. 5th Ser. Vol. 6, p. 272, 286, 374.

ROBERT WALKER

Was a private under Capt. Noah Abraham, 1777-78, undated rolls. Deeds show Robert Walker of Fannett Twp., granted 100 acres of land in 1767. "We, Mary Calhoon, late Mary Walker, widow of Robert Walker, decd.,—James Colhoun her present husband;" also Benjamin; Margaret; Alexander; Samuel; David White and Mary, his wife; James; Robert; Abraham; all children of Robert Walker, decd., sell to John Elder, James Elder, Robert Elder, and Isabella Campbell, issue of Robert Elder of Metal Twp. The above sale was acknowledged by Robert Walker's heirs, Oct. and Nov., 1810, from Armstrong and Indiana Counties, Penna.

Penna. Arch. 5th Ser. Vol. 6, p. 18, 19, 21, 52, 53, 139, 141, 516.

ROBERT WALKER

Appears in service with Capt. Patrick Jack, undated rolls. One Robert Walker left a will, dated Jan. and prob. July, 1792. His sons were Andrew; Robert; John and Samuel; daus.: Margaret Kerr; Sarah Kerr, 10 pounds each; heirs of dau. Jean Thorn, decd., 24 pounds each; dau. Elizabeth Savage 2 Ews; dau. Mary Walker the one equal undivided half part of all my land in Peters Twp., with the Mansion house and barn, with half the Spring and the old meadow; about ½ the 600 acres for which I gave said Mary a deed of conveyance, March 3, 1789. James and William, sons of dau. Mary all my land in Virginia, which I have not already conveyed away; Grandson Robert, son of Samuel Walker, 20 pounds. The land, bonds &c to be divided between dau. Mary and son Samuel, except other personal property which goes to Mary. Exrs.: Thos. McDowell, James Chambers and John Morehead. Deeds of 1774 and 1784 show the following: Janet Barr; James Barr and wife Mary; Robert Barr and wife Mary of Cumb. Co., Peters Twp., Penna. to Robert and Samuel Walker of same, for 1,200 pounds xx by North Mountain, by Thos. McDowell, James Dickey, Robert Campbell, West Conococheague Creek, Enoch James xx Between Robert Walker and Samuel Walker, his son. Said tract contains "by computation 600 acres."

Penna. Arch. 5th Ser. Vol. 6, p. 145, 146.

SAMUEL WALKER

Son of Robert Walker, gave service under Captains Patton, Dickey and McDowell. His wife was Isabella, dau. of Samuel Brice of Cumb. Co., Penna. They are buried in the old Waddell Graveyard and have stones. When Samuel Walker made his will, March, 1812, he gives to his son James the farm "on which I now live," and to care for his beloved wife Margaret. Land bordered near the Mountain by Gen. James Chambers; land "I bought from Isaac Stark's estate," on the east by Conrad Stinger. He names: Son Robert; Dau. Esther, wife of Isaac Spence; Dau. Margaret, wife of Colin Spence; Dau. Sarah, wife of James Martin; James Martin and wife to get choice of 2 tracts of land in Ohio, about 300 acres and 2 or 3 miles east of the Miami; Dau. Jane Walker and heirs a tract of land in Ohio, after James and Sarah Martin choose; Jane is also to have bed and bedding, horse, saddle and bridle, 2 cows; 1st and 3rd choice of all my cows; my negroe girl Liddy to be freed; Negroes Dinah and Rosie to son James; sons Samuel and John. Exrs.: son James and trusty friends Archbd. Bard and Thomas Waddell. In the will of Samuel Brice of West Pennsboro Twp., Cumb. Co., Penna., he gives to wife Elizabeth, bed and bed clothes, her horse and a saddle, a good cow, two sheep and her spinning wheel xx so long as she is my widow. Five daus. and their children, viz.: To dau. Sarah, wife of John Murdock, and her children, the service of my mulatto boy, York, until the age of 21 years, when he shall be set free from them and all others whatsoever, also the 1/5 part of my estate; 1/5 part to my dau. Ann, wife of John Reed, and her children; 1/5 part to dau. Elizabteh, wife of Robert Walker, and her children; to Margaret wife of Peter Smith and her children 1/5 part; to dau. Isabel, wife of Samuel Walker and her children 1/5 part. Will dated May 27, 1783, prob. Oct. 3, 1786. The estate of Elizabeth, widow of Samuel Brice, was administered in 1786.

Penna. Arch. 5th Ser. Vol. 6, p. 271, 284, 314, 289.

SAMUEL WALKER

Appears as a Lieut., with Capt. Thos. Askey, July 31, 1777, First Batt. First Marching Company, First Call. In July, 1778, Battalions were called out by order of Council for ye first and second Classes ye second Tour for Three hundred Men to ye Standing Stone. Dated at Phila. July 14, 1778. Samuel Walker served through 1777-78-79 under either Capt. Askey or Noah Abraham. Lieut. Samuel Walker, born 1753, died ———; his wife Mary Noble died 1824. They had issue: (1) Mary, born 1779, mar. Robert Walker. (2) John, unmarried, born 1781. (3) Alexander, born 1783, mar. Mary McConnell. (4) Eleanor, born 1785, mar. Robert Ramsey. (5) Margaret, born 1788, mar. James McConnell. (6) Samuel, born 1794, mar. Martha McConnell. (7) James, born 1796, mar. Anna Skinner.

Penna. Arch. 5th Ser. Vol. 6, p. 7, 10, 12, 23, 43, 47, 49, 52, 383, 515.

SAMUEL WALKER

Seventh Penna. Cont. Line, private in Capt. Talbot's Company, May 12, 1778; afterwards fifer in Capt. John Alexander's Co.

Penna. Arch. 2nd Ser. Vol. 10, p. 631, 654.

DAVID WALLACE

Is shown in service 1780, under Capt. John Rea. Penna. Arch 5th Ser. Vol. 6, p. 72, 78.

GEORGE WALLACE

Was in service as a Lieut. in 1776, and also appears in 1781.

Penna. Arch. 5th Ser. Vol. 6, p. 6, 99.

JAMES WALLACE

Of Fannett Twp., was a private under Capt. Thos. Askey, 1779-1781, undated rolls. He was the oldest son of William and Margaret Wallace, the will of William being dated 1773, and probated Sept.,1816. William and Joseph Campbell identified signatures of witnesses, and William Campbell further deposeth and saith that xxx the will had been in possession of his father's family for safe keeping for more than 20 years. In 1791 James Wallace settles with part of the heirs, sisters as shown: Catherine Cowan (?); Joanna Elliott; James and Isabella Hill; Adam and Elizabeth Maxwell; William and Ann Carty (McCarty).

The will of above James Wallace, dated and prob. 1808, unmarried, and he first gives all real estate to Williaim B. Wallace, son of my brother William Wallace, of Newhaven, Conn., and named additional sisters: Catherine Carow; Mary Bary; Margaret Hamilton. The marriage of James Corran to Catherine Wallace, Dec. 17, 1770, is shown in records of Rev. John King.

Penna. Arch. 5th Ser. Vol. 5, p. 61, 131, 151, 409, 423.

JOHN WALLACE

Is shown 1778 under Capt. Chas. Maclay, Fannett Twp. men, under Capt. Thos. Askey, 1779-1781, and on guard at Frankstown 1781, under Col. James Dunlop.

Penna. Arch. 5th Ser. Vol. 6, p. 60, 42, 410, 631.

JOHN WALLACE

Served as private under Captains Daniel Clapsaddle and John Rea, in 1778-80-81. He laid out the town of Waynesboro in 1797, on land which his father, John Wallace, had on a warrantee title. John Wallace left neither wife nor direct issue.

Penna. Arch. 5th Ser. Vol. 6, p. 94, 97, 117, 537.

SAMUEL WALLACE

Is shown in service in 1779, under Capt. James Young. He was of Guilford Twp., and left a will dated 1792, prob. 1794, naming wife Mary, to whom he left all real and personal estate during her natural life. At her death "beloved son John shall have my dwelling house" and for acres of land bought first from John Coldwell; dau. Easter 3¼ acres of land which was bought last from John Coldwell; 10 pounds to dau. Elizabeth if she comes here from Ireland. In a Codicil, he bequeaths to dau. Agnes 6 pounds if she comes here from Ireland.

Penna. Arch. 5th Ser. Vol. 6, p. 548.

THOMAS WALLACE

Served as a Lieut. under Capt. Daniel Clapsaddler and others, Cumberland Co., Militia, in 1777-78-80-81. He was a son of John and Rachel Wallace, early settlers, John having made his will in 1777, and prob. March 24, 1778. Thomas Wallace was born Apr. 17, 1749, died May 21, 1804. (Family record). Under Orphans' Court Nov. 1815, is a petition from George and Mary (Wallace) Sheakley; the petitioner's father, Thomas Wallace had died about 11 years previously, leaving a widow Nancy and issue: Mary as above; Eleanor mar. Samuel Sloan; Esther mar. Wm. Sheakley; Sarah; John; Rebecca; Nancy; Joseph; Thomas and James; the last three minors. Land in Washington Twp.

Penna. Arch. 5th Ser. Vol. 6, p. 92, 115, 513, 528, 534, 536.

THOMAS WALLACE
As Sergt. 1780-81, with Capt. John McConnell.
Penna. Arch. 5th Ser. Vol. 6, p. 267, 301.

WILLIAM WALLACE
Second Co. 1st Batt., is shown in service April 19, 1778, under Capt. William Findley, probably of the family who laid out Waynesboro.
Penna. Arch. 5th Ser. Vol. 6, p. 597.

WILLIAM WALLACE
Appears in service 1780-82, under Capt. Wm. Strain.
Penna. Arch. 5th Ser. Vol. 6, p. 142, 397, 427, 430.

WILLIAM WALLACE
Is shown serving with Capt. Conrad Snyder, 1780-81.
Penna. Arch. 5th Ser. Vol. 6, p. 87, 118.

WILLIAM WALLACE
Was serving in 1780-81, with Capt. John McConnell.
Penna. Arch. 5th Ser. Vol. 6, p. 268, 303.

WILLIAM WALLACE
Served in 1781 under Capt. Robert Dickey, also under Capt. Joseph Culbertson.
Penna. Arch 5th Ser. Vol. 6, p. 284, 289, 314, 271, 290.

WILLIAM WALLACE, JR.
Son of William and Margaret Wallace of Fannett Twp., is shown in 1779, serving under Capt. Thos. Askey.
Penna. Arch. 5th Ser. Vol. 6, p. 61.

EDWARD WARD
Served as private 1781-82, under Capt. Thos. Askey of Fannett Township.
Penna. Arch. 5th Ser. Vol. 6, p. 407, 410, 424, 442.

JOHN WARD
Served 1781, under Capt. Patrick Jack.
Penna. Arch. 5th Ser. Vol. 6, p. 297.

JOHN WARD
Served 1781, under Lieut. John Stitt, Washington Twp., Franklin Co., Penna.
Penna. Arch. 5th Ser. Vol. 6, p. 113.

JOSEPH WARD, 1760-1826
Private appears in 1779-80-81-82, serving under Capt. Thos. Askey. The estate of Andrew Campbell of Fannett Twp., 1797, shows heirs to have been: Joseph Campbell; Andrew Campbell; Catherine wife of James Armstrong; Jean, wife of Joseph Ward; Elizabeth wife of Joseph McMackin; Margaret, wife of Andrew Wakefield; Esther, wife of Thomas Wilson. In the will of Andrew Campbell, dated 1788, he also names sons John; Mark; David; Alexander.
Penna. Arch. 5th Ser. Vol. 6, p. 62, 132, 394, 409, 424, 442.

WILLIAM WARD
Served under Capt. Thos. Askey, 1779-81.
Penna. Arch 5th Ser. Vol. 6, p. 61, 131, 408, 423.

JOSEPH WARNOCK
Is shown serving under Capt. Walter McKinnie in 1782. The name Warnock appears in both Chester and Lancaster Counties. Under Presbyterian Church records of Mercersburg is shown the death of Mary Warnock, on Oct. 21, 1776.
Penna. Arch 5th Ser. Vol. 6, p. 306.

GENERAL GEORGE WASHINGTON
"That great and good man, General Washington, president of the United States, set out from his house on Market Street, with Secretary Hamilton on his left and his private Secretary on his right, to head the troops called out to quell the insurrection to the westward." This was Tuesday, Sept. 30, 1794, and in the town on the way he found infantry and cavalry preparing to march to Carlisle. On leaving Harrisburg he forded the Susquehanna in his carriage which he, himself drove. He spent eight days in Carlisle, and on Sunday morning, at seven o'clock, October 12, he set out from Carlisle, after seeing the troops on their way. As Washington and his party came down Shippensburg's one long street the citizens were at their doors to see him. As they passed where William McConnell lived, Washington bowed to him as he stood at his door, and the regret of Mr. McConnell's life was he forgot, in his excitement, to return the salutation. He dined in Shippensburg, and coming up by the Harris Ferry road he arrived at Chambersburg that evening. He stopped at the stone tavern kept by Col Wm. Morrow, now the site of the Nicklas Store. Quoting from the Chambersbuhg Gazette Oct. 16, 1794, is this: "On Sunday evening last arrived in this town, His Excellency General Washington, and early on Monday morning he proceeded on his Journey to the Westward, by way of Williamsport and Fort Cumberland." "The next stop was at Greencastle, at the inn, kept by Robert McCulloh where they had breakfast. This tavern stood on the south-east corner of the Square, and has been enlarged at various times through the years and now presents a plastered front, but the back part is the original building in which President Washington was entertained.

As the story runs, Mr. McCulloh's son Thomas, was anxious to see and hear all he could of their distinguished guest and knowing he would not be allowed to remain in the room, he tried to hide under the table being laid for the meal, but his father spied him and spoiled the plan. This boy, Thomas G. McCulloh, was the first president of Cumb. Valley railroad. Leaving Greencastle by the Williamsport pike, General Washington and his company stopped at the handsome and hospitable home of Dr. Robert Johnston where he dined with the family. Dr. Johnston was present, as hospital surgeon, in the southern department, at the surrender of the British army under Lord Cornwallis at Yorktown, Va., in October, 1781. That night they lodged at Williamsport.

An account of this Philadelphia-Bedford journey:

"The President accompanied by Genl. Henry Knox, Secty. of War, Genl. Alexander Hamilton, Secty. of the Treasury and Judge Richard Peters of the U. S. District Court, set out for Western Pennsylvania on the first day of October. On Friday his Excellency reached Harrisburg and the day following, Carlisle where the main body of the army had preceded him.

"The President left Carlisle on the 11 of October, reaching Chambersburg the same day, Williamsport on the 13th and Fort Cumberland on the 14th, to review the left division of the army, consisting of the Virginia and Maryland Volunteers. On the 19th he reached Bedford, where he remained two or three days." Here the dates of setting out from Philadelphia and Carlisle differ from the ones given by Washington in his diary; that register showing he left Philadelphia a day earlier, on Tuesday, the 30th of September, and was on his way as far as Trappe on the morning of October 1st, also that he remained in Carlisle a day longer, not leaving until Sunday, the 12th of October. Quoting the diary, we have the itinerary of Washington's westbound journey as follows:—

"Tuesday, Sept. 30th, Having determined . . . to repair to the place appointed for the Rendezvous of the Militia of New Jersey, Pennsylvania, Maryland and Virginia, I left the city of Philadelphia about halfpast ten o'clock this forenoon accompanied by Colo. Hamilton and my private Secretary.

"Wednesday, Oct. 1st, Left Trappe early and breakfasted at Pottsgrove, 11 miles. We reached Reading for dinner, 19 miles further, where we found several detachments of Infantry and Cavalry preparing for their march to Carlisle.

"Thursday, Oct. 2nd, Reached Lebanon at night, 28 miles, etc.

"Friday, Oct. 3rd, Breakfasted at Hummelstown, 14 miles, and dined and lodged at Harrisburg on the banks of the Susquehanna, 23 miles from Lebanon. At Harrisburg we found the First Regiment of New Jersey, about 500 strong, commanded by Col. Turner, drawn up to receive us. Passed along the line to my quarters. Walked through and around the town.

"Oct. 4th, Forded the Susquehanna . . . On the Cumberland County side, I found a detachment of the Philadelphia Light Horse ready to receive and escort me to Carlisle, 17 miles, where I arrived about 11 o'clock. Two miles short of it I met the Governors of Pennsylvania and New Jersey with all the Calvary that had rendezvoused at that place, drawn up. Passed them and the Infantry of Pennsylvania I alighted at my quarters.

"Sunday, Oct. 5th, Went to the Presbyterian meeting and heard Dr. Davison preach a political sermon . . .

"Oct. 6th to 12th, Employed in organizing the several detachments, which had come in from different Counties of the State, in a very disjointed and loose manner, or rather I ought to have said, in urging and assisting Genl. Mifflin to do it; as I no otherwise took the command of the Troops than to press them forward, and to provide them with necessaries for their march.

"Sunday, Oct. 12th, Having settled these matters, having seen the troops off . . . given them their route and day's march . . . I set out from Carlisle about 7 o'clock this morning, dined at Shippensburg, 21 miles further, lodged at Chambersburg, 11 miles, where I was joined by Gen. Hand.

"From Carlisle along the left road which I pursued, to be out of the march of the army and avoid the inconvenience of passing the wagons belonging to it . . . . . .

"Along the road which the troops marched, both the road and the improvements were much better. The roads came together at the east end of town" (Shippensburg) . . . . . .

This army of Penna. and New Jersey troops, mobilized at Carlisle, numbered about five thousand, the greater part of which the infantry, artillery and wagon brigades, moved from Shippensburg westward over the Three Mountain Road to Strasburg, crossing North Mountain at that point, thence on to Bedford while the cavalry travelled the Old Loudon Road a longer route, by way of Thompson's Cove, now Cowan's Gap.

Genl. Washington and suite passed southward from Shippensburg over the Harris Ferry Road to Chambersburg, thence by way of Greencastle to Williamsport and Fort Cumberland, where the Maryland and Virginia troops rendezvoused and from there to Bedford which they reached a little after 4 o'clock in the afternoon of October 19th. Resuming the diary:

"October 20th, Called the Quartermaster General, etc . . . and others of the Staff department before me and the Commander in chief, at 9 o'clock this morning, in order to fix on the Routs of the two Columns and their stages.

"Upon comparing accounts, it was found that the army could be put in motion the 23rd, and it was so ordered . . . matters being thus arranged . . . I prepared for my return to Philadelphia in order to meet Congress, and to attend to the Civil duties of my office."

Returning from Bedford, General Washington traveled eastward over the same route the army followed in its westward march from Shippensburg to Bedford. This route was the Three Mountain Road, a State road, the latest and best. Its course was from Shippensburg to Strasburg, across the North Mountain to Skinners in Horse Valley, thence into Path Valley and on to Fort Littleton and Bedford. That this is the road Washington traveled is well established by the General himself in a letter to Alexander Hamilton. Quoting from it we have:

"Susquehanna, Wrights Ferry, 26 October, 1794. Dear Sir: "Thus far I have proceeded without accident to man, horse or carriage, altho the latter has had wherewith to try its goodness; especially in ascending North Mountain from Skinners by a wrong road, that is,—by the old road which never was good and is rendered next to impassable by neglect. "I heard a great complaint of Gurney's Corps, (and some of the Artillery) along the road to Strasburgh,—There I parted from their Rout. In some places, I was told they did not leave a plate, a spoon, a glass or a knife. I pray you to mention this to Gov. Mifflin with a request that the most pointed orders may be given and every precaution used to prevent the like on the return of the Army.

"I roade yesterday afternoon thro' the rain from York Town to this place." etc . . . (The Writings of George Washington. Edited by W. C. Ford, Vol. 12, p. 480. Original in New York City Library.)

That Washington left Bedford on Tuesday, the 21st of October is well attested; the Phila Gazette of Oct. 27, and the General Advertiser of Oct. 28, both having announced very cautiously that "We understand the President of the United States left Bedford on his return to Philadelphia on Tuesday last." Neither paper ventured into the wilderness to follow his course but as tradition hands it down, the President accompanied by his staff left Bedford in the morning of the 21st, by the Three Mountain Road; passing Sproats and Fort Littleton he arrived at Burnt Cabins that same day —having traveled a distance of 37 miles. Here Washington spent the night at the Red Tavern, a log inn since destroyed by fire and with it the old book in which he had written his name. Leaving Burnt Cabins the next morning, Oct. 22nd., he crossed the Tuscarora Mountains into Path Valley; passing through Fannettsburg and over a range of the Kittochtinny he entered Horse Valley and crossing it reached "Skinners," a tavern located near the foot of North Mountain. This Tavern-station marked "Skinner's" can be found on Howell's map of 1792. Not far from this tavern and close by the Ford in the Conodoguinet, the Three Mountain Road intersected the old Packer's Path. It was at this intersection that Washington, for once in his life, took the wrong way—"ascending the North Mountain from Skinner's by a wrong road;—"by the old road which never was good and is rendered impassable by neglect." Since the course of the old road and that of the new merged near the summit (original surveys) the General there regained the right way and continued his journey over the Three Mountain Road to Strasburg, thirteen miles distant from Burnt Cabins. From this point Washington's further course of travel through Franklin County remains an unsettled question. So far, with the exception of several miles on the "wrong road." The General has been travelling, in reverse, the same route the soldiers followed ten days earlier, but at Strasburg, as his letter states, he "parted from their Rout;" which can mean nothing else than at Strasburg he left the army-trodden Three Mountain Road, by this time badly wrecked in the passage of the artillery and "Waggon" brigades.

Yet, despite Washington's own statement, tradition continues his travels over that army route through Pleasant Hall, Orrstown, to the Black Horse, a log tavern kept by Daniel Nevin and thence to Shippensburg where he passed the night. Washington, himself, gives nothing concerning his journey between Strasburg and York but his expense account showing expenditures along the way includes Chambersburg in his route.

This account, along with the Washington letter to Hamilton, constitutes the only contemparary record of that Bedford-York journey.

Quoting from it, we have:—

19th,—Serv. between Bedford and Cumberland	3-9
21st,—Serv. at Bedford	7-8
Serv. between Bedford and Chambersburg	11-9
24th,—Cash to Mr. Dandridge for expenses 100D	37-10
25th,—Cash expended on Road from Chambersburg to York	7-6
27th,—Do at York and between that and Lancaster	11-3

(Division of Manuscripts—Library of Congress)

This record of Washington's route by way of Chambersburg leads to the assumption that at Strasburg, where he parted from the soldier's route, he turned his course toward Chambersburg—10 miles distant—traveling the road shown on Howell's map of 1792. Arrived at Chambersburg, Washington had the choice of two routes to York; the mountain way, a direct course through Black's Gap and over the South Mountains; the valley way, around about course skirting the range. Of proof of his choice, there is none for either way. But traditions, well founded and convincing, carry him over the valley route and offer nothing along the mountain road. General Washington's probable course from Chambersburg was over the Harris Ferry road to Shippensburg where tradition meets with him at the Black Horse, a stone tavern kept by William Rippey. Here, as tradition gives it, Washington spent the night, hospitably entertained by tavern and town, and continued his journey the following day over an undetermined course to Simpson's Ferry in York county where Gen. Michael Simpson "in 1794 had the distinguished honor of entertaining President Washington over night on his return from the Whiskey Insurrection. The next day President Washington journeyed to York. On Saturday, Oct. 25, he rode through the rain to Wright's Ferry, from which place he wrote to Hamilton on Sunday the 26th. Thence to Lancaster etc.—The next we hear of him through the Philadelphia papers is that the President of the United States arrived in town on the 28th and was in good health." Both papers assure us of this; the Gazette as before, beating the General Advertiser to it by one day.

Annie R. Rupley.

Washington's Diary
Washington's letter to Alexander Hamilton, from "The Writings of George Washington," by W. C. Ford. Original letter in New York Library, Fifth Ave. & 42nd St. General Washington in Franklin Co., Kittochtinny Soc. Hist. Pub. by John G. Orr, 1898, Vol. 1, p. 36. The Whiskey Insurrection, by C. P. Humrick, 1901, Vol. 111, p. 221. Early Highways—Three Mountain Road, by John G. Orr—Two papers, year 1905, Vol. V, p. 9 and 223. Early Travelled Highways about Upper Strasburg, by M. K. Burgner, Vol. X. 1886 History of York Co. p. 326. 1886 History of Cumb. County. Penna. Arch. 2nd Ser. Vol. IV, p. 16 & 17. McCauley's Hist. of Franklin Co. Notes by the late Chas. B. Carl, Judge Watson R. Davison and others.

DANIEL WASON

Was private under Captains Robert Dickey and Walter McKinnie, 1781-82. A probable son of Thomas Wason.

Penna. Arch. 5th Ser. Vol. 6, p. 285,306.

THOMAS WASON

Was a private under Captain McKinnie, 1781-82. He was of Peters Township, later "Rockdale," the Kieffer farm. His father was killed by Indians and his mother taken captive. The son James Wason went South, but Thomas lived and died here. His will was probated May 10, 1803, naming a wife Margaret; six sons, only John and James being named; a niece Mary Coleman. He was a member of the Welsh Run Presbyterian Church, and is probably buried there.

Penna. Arch. 5th Ser. Vol. 6, p. 289, 297, 299, 305.

WILLIAM WASON

Was a private under Captains William Smith and Thomas McDowell, probably a son of Thomas Wason. On Aug. 3, 1786, William Wason was married to Jean McDowell by Rev. John King, Mercersburg, Penna. They went to Butler Co., Penna., where Jane Wasson, widow and relict of William Wasson, decd., of Centre Twp., left a will, prob. Jan. 24, 1833, naming dau. Ann, now the wife of John Adams; son Thomas; John and William Thompson, sons of my said dau. Ann; son William's dau. mar. to William McCall; To Grandau. Anibel McCall; To Jane Thompson McCall and Jane Thompson McCall mar. to Joseph Adams. Grandaus: Jane McDowell Wasson and Mary Jane Wasson, daughters of son Thomas; To grandau. Anibel Thompson; To William Wasson, son of my son William; To Ann, wife of my son Thomas.

Penna. Arch. 5th Ser. Vol. 6, p. 276, 315.

COL. JAMES WATSON

In "Five Typical Scotch Irish Families of the Cumberland Valley," by Mary Craig Shoemaker, we have the following: Col. James Watson, 1743-1831, was the youngest son of John Watson and Ann Stephenson of Leacock Twp. Lancaster Co., Penna. His commission as Captain was dated July 8, 1776, and his commission as Colonel of the 2nd Batt. Lancaster Co. Militia was dated July 1, 1777. He was at Amboy, Long Island, then came with General Putman to Phila. Col. Watson mar. Jan. 25, 1766 Elizabeth Long, dau. of Hugh Long of Chestnut Level, Lancaster Co., Penna. After the close of the Revolution they moved to the vicinity of Greencastle. He was a tanner by trade, Justice of the Peace, and post master for more than thirty years. He died July 2, 1831, and was laid to rest beside his friends in Moss Spring Graveyard. Of his children: Mary mar. James Rankin; John mar. Rebecca Vance; Hugh mar. Susannah Crunkleton; Martha mar. Abram Prather; James mar. Charlotte Crawford. Three children died unmarried and four died in infancy.

JOSEPH WATSON

Presbyterian Church records, Mercersburg, Penna., show names of ten men of the congregation, who lost their lives in the Rev. War. Joseph Watson, killed in Battle, Dec., 1777. His will was dated Aug. 21, 1776, and prob. Apr. 23, 1778. Joseph Watson of Peters Twp., "To my mother, Thomas Dunwoody's wife and her four (4) children, the whole of my estate." Trusty friends, William and Thomas Dunwoody were Executors.

JAMES WATT

Served as private under Captains James Young and William Strain 1780-82.

Penna. Arch. 5th Ser. Vol. 6, p. 82, 431.

JOHN WATT

Is shown as a private 1780-82, with Captains James Young and Willaim Strain, command of Col. James Dunlop. On July 23, 1775, John Watt had a son Robert baptized and a dau. Mary Dec. 13, 1777, by Dr. John King of Mercersburg.

Penna. Arch 5th Ser. Vol. 6, p. 82, 431.

SAMUEL WATT

Is shown serving 1779, under Capt. James Young, Col. Abraham Smith, in command.

Penna. Arch. 5th Ser. Vol. 6, p. 548.

JACOB WEAVER

Seventh Penna. Cont. Line, Jacob Weaver, private in Capt. Talbot's Company; in wagon dept.; drove field officer's baggage wagon; discharged Oct. 15, 1782; resided in Adams Co. in 1825.

Penna. Arch. 2nd Ser. Vol. 10, p. 654.

GEORGE WEIR (WEAR)

Served under Captains Samuel McCune, Patrick Jack and Charles Maclay, 1776-79 and undated rolls.

Penna. Arch. 5th Ser. Vol. 6, p. 62, 63, 144, 146, 149, 587, 150.

CHRISTOPHER WEITER

Is shown in service, 1780, in Lancaster County with Capt. John Smuller, various spellings, Widnor-Widder and Weider. The tax list of 1796, shows him as Christopher Widnor of Antrim Twp., with a House, 2 lots and a Cow; one Isaac Widnor, a Potter, with a House and Cow. The will of Christopher Weiter of Greencastle, dated May, Prob. Sept. 1807, names Jacob as eldest son; son George; son Michael; son-in-law and dau. Frederick and Elizabeth Hauk. Executors: friends Michael Tice and George Beck. Quoting J. Edward Omwake in his excellent Historical Sketch of the Grace Reformed Congregation of Greencastle where he quotes Judge D. Watson Rowe's "Reminiscences of Greencastle," is the following: "On the 29th of November 1786, John Allison made a deed to Henry Sites, Jacob Zach- arias, Henry Stall and Christopher Widnor, to them and their successors in trust for the German Reformed Congregation of Greencastle." The consideration given was Five Shillings and the Lot conveyed was for the use of said congregation or for a burying ground. The Lot, as above conveyed, is the old German Reformed Graveyard on S. Carlisle Street, where a little log church was first used jointly by the reformed and Lutheran Congregations. In Deed Book 12, p. 186 at Chambersburg, Penna., the Weider records continue; We, Henry Frederic and wife Catherine (Weider) of Ross Co., Ohio; Charles Brotherlin (ton) and wife Elizabeth (Weider) of Huntingdon Co., Penna.; Henry Weider and wife Hannah of Ross County, Ohio; David Weider and wife Sarah of Ross County, Ohio; James Robinson and wife Mary (Weider), Harrison Co., Ind.; Daniel Musselman and wife Christina (Weider), Harrison County, Ind.; George Weider and wife Patience of Ross County, Ohio; Michael Weider and wife Nancy, of Ross County, Ohio; Julian Weider of Ross County, Ohio; Peter Thomas and wife, Sarah (Weider) Ross County, Ohio; ——— Sharp and wife Sarah (Weider) heir to George Weider of ——— County of Kentucky and 3 Weiders of Franklin Co., Penna., aforesaid, all of full age, legal heirs of Jacob Weider, Michael, George Weider; the only 3 sons and male heirs of Christopher Weider, decd., of the borough of Greencastle, appoint their trusty and beloved kinsman Henry Weider (above) of Ross County, Ohio, their attorney. Estate of Christopher Weider; all sign Oct. 31, 1818.

Penna. Arch 5th Ser. Vol. 7, p. 238.

DANIEL WELKER

Orphans' Court, Chambersburg, Pa., and Family records, Daniel Welker, 21, tailor, from Germany, enlisted in Col. John Patton's Regt. in 1777; wounded at Ash Swamp in New Jersey, discharged 1781, in consequence of said wound which has become so troublesome as to render him incapable of earning his subsistence by labour &c., entitled to Donation land &c. Commonwealth to Daniel Welker, soldier in Rev. War. Patent for 200 acres, tract No. 1934 in 2nd District Donation Land. (See Lawrence Co. Atlas) Daniel Welker, 1759-1824, mar. 1786, Susan Conrad. Issue: Daniel Welker mar. Anna M. Kesecker; Daniel, born York Co., Penna., Nov. 19, 1789, died Sept. 19, 1870. Christian, born 1796, died Lawrence Co., Penna., Aug. 13, 1868. Catherine mar. Samuel Clopper, died near Waynesboro, Aug. 18, 1868. Phoebe mar. Michael Sellers, died Peoria, Ill., July 9, 1864. Mary, died Mercersburg, Penna., July 13, 1864. Elizabeth mar. Robert Rule, died 1840, Greencastle, Penna., leaving issue three. Susanna mar. George McFerren, who since died in Ohio, leaving husband and nine children. Rachel lives in Bedford Co., Penna.

Penna. Arch. 5th Ser. Vol. 3, p. 650. 2nd Ser. Vol. 10, p. 811.

CASPER WELSH (GASPER-JASPER)

Served under Capt. Samuel Royer, 1780-81, also in 1779. From the application for pension it is inferred that there were ten children, the dau. Elizabeth, born May 22, 1777, mar. Adam Stonicker,, Oct. 11, 1791. They "moved west across the mountains to Fayette Co., Penna., where they settled."

Penna. Arch. 5th Ser. Vol. 6, p. 90, 99, 113, 543.

JAMES WELSH

Served as a private under Captains Thomas McDowell and Patrick Jack in 1782 &c. He was a son of John and Susanna Welsh, early settlers and members of "Upper West Conococheague" Presbyterian Church, near Mercersburg. He mar. Deborah Moore, Sept. 20, 1785, by Rev. John King. In 1809, Elizabeth Moore made him executor of her will. He probably left Franklin County.

Penna. Arch 5th Ser. Vol. 6, p. 313, 315.

JAMES WALSH (WELSH)

Served as private under Capt. James Young in 1779. He died October 22, 1806, aged 52 years. His son John, and John's wife Margaret are with him in Falling Spring graveyard, Chambersburg, Penna. He died leaving a widow Nancy and issue: Dau. Rebecca mar. Henry Thompson; dau. Mary mar. Samuel Peebles; sons Joseph and John; dau. Jinny; son James; dau. Nancy. Later marriages: Elizabeth mar. Jacob Grove; Jane mar. Samuel Thompson; Nancy mar. John Buchanan; James Welsh mar. Hannah Graham.

Penna. Arch. 5th Ser. Vol. 6, p. 547.

JOHN WELSH

Appears in 1777-78 as a Lieut., under Capt. James Patton. In 1779 he was at Ligonier, as a Ranger, with Capt. Samuel Patton, and in 1781, he is again in service with Capt. William Huston. In 1769, John Welsh and wife Susanna were living in the vicinity of Fort Loudon with a large family of children. There are baptisms and church admissions. John Welsh, Sr., died Dec. 29, 1784; his widow Susanna died Aug. 19, 1792. In his will, dated Dec. 19, 1784, he states he was of Peters Twp., "tho weak in body, yet of sound judgment and memory." To Susanna my beloved wife, 100 pounds, a horse and saddle, her bed and furniture, and all her other apparel, as also the whole service of a negro wench named Annack, during the life of her, my wife. xxxx I commit the care and education and support of my minor children to her my beloved wife, xxx they shall have a competency of English learning xx To dau. Margaret 10 pounds; son James 50 pounds, also the choice of any of the three tracts I have in that settlement called Kaintuck. Son Edward 100 pounds and a tract as aforesaid, which will remain after James and Andrew hath chosen theirs xx and if he shall stay such time with his mother xx for the support of the minor children, he is to have the further sum of 50 pounds. To Andrew, my son, 100 pounds, also the tract he shall choose after James hath made his choice. To dau. Mary 50 pounds, one mare, saddle, good bed and all its suitable furniture. To son John 100 pounds, horse and saddle, further tuition, clothing, support &c., during minority. To son Joseph 100 pounds, and as given to John during minority. To son William the same. To dau. Susannah 50 pounds and all as given above during minority. Any surplus after the above divides, to be equally parted between my minor children. Exrs.: my beloved wife Susannah, Edward, my son with my trusty friend Thomas McDowell. James Guthrey mar. Polly Welsh—March 3, 1785. William Guthrey mar. Mary Welsh—March 19, 1792

Penna. Arch. 5th Ser. Vol. 6, p. 368, 377, 602, 610, 643.

JOHN WHISNER (WHISTNOR)

Served during 1779-80-81-82 under Capt. Wm. Moorhead.

Penna. Arch. 5th Ser. Vol. 6, p. 66, 134, 388, 400, 401, 414, 440.

JOHN WHITE

The White family of Johnstown, Penna., contribute some notes on "Captain" John White, whose grave has been marked by descendants, members of the Quemahoning Chapter, D. A. R. Capt. John White was a son of pioneer Andrew and Jean White; the son of John was born near Antietam Creek, now Franklin County, in 1759. In 1776, he and a brother James went "west" to take charge of a tract of land granted their father, near Hannastown. John White served as a Scout during the Rev. War, and in the Whiskey rebellion. He mar. Margaret, dau. of Capt. James Patton, of Revolutionary fame, near Fort Loudon. Capt. White died at Ligonier, leaving many descendants. The Ledger of Samuel Findlay of Mercersburg, shows accounts of: Alexander White, Innkeeper, near Mercersburg; of Andrew White; of Robert White (neighbor) and of Robert White of Virginia.

Penna. Arch. 5th Ser. Vol. 4, p. 460, 759.

JOHN WHITE

Served as private under Capt. Chas. Maclay, 1778-81-82. He was of Lurgan Township, Farmer and Cordwinder. His will dated 1821, prob. 1823, names sons, James; John; Johnston; Charles M., and Isaac; Dau. Nancy Charlton; Son Edward's daus., Nancy and Eliza White. Son James' dau. Jane White. Codicil gives 3 grandsons: Samuel Eaton White; John Andrew White; James Morrison White; Sons of son Isaac White.

Penna. Arch. 5th Ser. Vol. 6, p. 36, 40, 149, 151, 406, 435.

JOSEPH WHITE

Served as private under Captains John Slaymaker and Alexander White. He was born in Lancaster Co., Penna., 1758, mar. Mary Fullerton, born 1767, married May or June, 1787. They had 3 sons born in Lancaster County; one son and 2 daus. born in Franklin Co., where two sons died in 1795. In 1798, the family moved to Westmoreland Co., Penna., settled near New Alexandria. Here two sons and four daus. were born, and even dozen. In the will of Jean Fullerton, of Antrim Twp., dated 1791, and prob. 1792, she appears as a sister of Humphrey Fullerton, Sr., of Lancaster Co., Penna., and as an Aunt to Humphrey Fullerton of Antrim Twp. She names first "my brother Humphrey Fullerton's dau. Susanna; his dau. Margaret's 2 children, John and Margaret McFadden; All the remaining estate into seven equal shares (excepting my stays) and that my brother's son Humphrey have one of said shares; his dau. Ann Wood one share; his dau. Elizabeth Miller one share; and likewise my stays; his son Thomas one share; his dau. Jean White one share; his son William to have one share; his dau. Mary White one share; The witnesses, Apr. 27, 1791, were William Burk, Anne Woods, William Woods, Jean Woods. When prob. Nov. 28, 1792, the witness was Jean Beard, late Jean Woods.

Penna. Arch. 5th Ser. Vol. 7, p. 97, 649.

Caldwell's History of Indiana Co., Penna.

WILLIAM WHITE

The data which follow were obtained from the papers on file in Rev. War pension claim, S.40671, based upon the military service of William White in that war. The data and place of birth and the names of the parents of William White are not shown. William Whtie enlisted in Cumb. Co., Penna., in February, 1776, served as a private in Capt. Jeremiah Talbot's Co., Col. William Irvine's Penna. Regt., went on the expedition to Canada, was in the battle of Three Rivers, and in Several skirmishes and was discharged Apr. 1, 1777 or 1778. He stated that he enlisted for one year but served "a greater length of time." He was allowed pension on his application executed May 21, 1818, while residing in Westmoreland Co., Penna., aged sixty-six years. It is not stated that soldier was ever married. In 1820, one James White made affidavit in Westmoreland Co., Penna., in support of soldier's claim for pension; no relationship was shown and there are no further family data. Probably enlisted in (now) Franklin Co., Penna.

PETER WHITSIDE

Served 1782, under Capt. John Orbison. He was a taxable in Montgomery Twp., 1781, and in 1796, a merchant and Inn Keeper. Under date of April 11, 1803, he offers for sale a two-story stone house, on the Square, in the town of Mercersburg, with a lot No. 9. The house is 43 ft. by 36 ft. a Store room, well shelved and a counting room &c. Also 123¾ acres of land within 6 miles of said town, with 100 bearing apple trees, a good spring, a large nursery of different kinds of fruit trees, a good dwelling house &c, also other tracts of land. The above stone house, lot 9, fits the early "Mansion House" of Mercersburg, but Peter Whitsides is lost in the past. Under the list of burials, Buelah Presby. Church in Pitt Township known still earlier as the preaching station at the Old Bullock Pens, is given, without dates, Captain Peter Whiteside. It is probable that Peter Whiteside had children who were mar. at Mercersburg. Kairns Sterrett to Elizabeth Whitesides, May 2, 1799; Robert Whitesides to Margaret Wilson, Feb. 14, 1805. The Franklin Repository, June 10, 1804, gives the following notice from Mercersburg; "Robert Whiteside states he has commenced the clock and watch-making business, in the house lately occupied by Major James Ramsey." The Census of 1790 shows James Whitesides in Allegheny Co., Penna., with one man, 4 boys and three females.

Penna. Arch. 5th Ser. Vol. 6, p. 307.

PETER WHITMER

Served as private 1780-81-82, under Captains John Woods and James Poe. In Dec. 1741, the Penns sold a tract of 200 acres to Hannis Gingery of Lancaster Co., Penna. He held it for twenty-five years, the place being sold to Peter Witmer, Jr., of Lancaster County Aug. 11, 1766. This tract known as the "Indian Spring Farm" came into possession of Henry Omwake in 1868. This bit of early lore is "Stolen" from a charmingly told tale of the Omwake Family showing the "Spring House" and much else of interest on the "Indian Spring farm." The will of Peter Whitmore of Antrim Twp., was dated Sept. and prob. Nov. 1801. He names wife Barbara; Son Jacob the plantation whereon he now lives in the Great Cove. Son Peter the plantation whereon I now live in Antrim Twp., and to look after his mother; Son Joseph the upper tract of land I bought from John Snively; balance of estate among my twelve children: Jacob; Elizabeth; Catherine; Barbara; Magdalena; Peter; Susanna; Mary; Ann; Esther;

Joseph; David. The witnesses were Andrew Snively and Jacob Lesher. On Dec. 5, 1804, Letters of Admr. were granted unto Peter Whitmore, on the estate of Barbara Whitmore.

Penna. Arch. 5th Ser. Vol. 6, p. 91, 103, 137, 576, 583.

CHRISTIAN WIEST

Under Hamilton Twp., Franklin Co., Penna., Christian Wiest of Paradise Twp. York Co. Penna., leaves Large Family Bible to son Jacob; to sell land in York Co., Penna., into 4 Shears. 1100 pounds to son Jacob; 1 shear to dau. Anna Mary, wife of Henry Appleman; 1 shear to grandson Henry Bentzel, son of dau. Barbara, decd., mar. to John Bentzel; 1 shear to dau. Eliabeth, widow of Samuel Hoke, decd. The will made in 1830, was prob. Dec. 5, 1842.

Census of Pensioners, 1840 Act.

MICHAEL WILAND

Served as private in 1782 in the 2nd Class of the First Batt. of Cumb. Co. Militia. Court records show that Michael Wiland died in Hamilton Twp., prior to April 19, 1794. He is probably buried on his farm in the Wiland graveyard, near Brake's saw-mill, now the C. J. Rumler farm. Dedes show that Michael Wiland bought land from Paul Barnet in 1787, and the land was patented in 1789. His widow, Christina bought land from Thomas Chestnut in 1812, which included a grist mill. On June 14, 1817, the heirs divide the land, John, eldest son taking the greater part of the land; John lived and died there and is buried in the grave yard. The other children of Michael and Christina Wiland were: Christian Wiland; Israel Jones and Elizabeth, his wife; John Mixhimer and wife Christina; John Coble and wife Susanna and Nancy Wiland.

Penna. Arch. 5th Ser. Vol. 6, p. 124.

HUGH WILEY

Of Franklin County, Ensign and Lieut. Will Book B, p. 274. Will of Hughey Wiley, Letterkenny Twp.; Son John Wiley; Son Hughey Wiley; Dau. Sally Wiley; Son James Wiley; Dau. Betsy, mar. to Joseph Culbertson. Her son Hughey Culbertson; Dau. Temperance, mar. to Wm. Means. Her Son John Means; Dau. Margaret mar. to Henry Davis. Her Son Hughey Davis. Dated Oct. 29, 1805; prob. Nov. 25, 1805.

Penna. Arch. 5th Ser. Vol. 6, p. 543, 614. Vol. 4. p. 643.

JAMES WILKENS

A commission by the Hon. George Thomas, Esq., to James Wilkens, Gentlemen,—"Reposing especial trust an confidence xx in your loyalty and courage xx I do constitute and appoint you, the said James Wilkens, to be Ensign of the Company of which Wm. Maxwell, Esq., is Captain in Rathmullin Twp., in Lancaster County. (Later Peters and Montgomery Twps., Franklin Co.) Given under my hand and seal Feb. 12, 1745-6. In 1769, James Wilkins and family were within the bounds of the "Upper West Conococheague" Church of Mercersburg. In his will, dated 1773, he states he was of Peters Twp., and names wife Jean; Daus.: Martha; Rachel; Jean; Rebekah; Mary; Minors. Sons, William and James, minors. Executors: Wife and brother-in-law James McFarland. Guardians, Johnston Elliott and Thos Dunwoody.

Penna. Arch. 5th Ser. Vol. 1, p. 5.

ROBERT WILKINS, JR.

First Lieut., 5th Penna. Batt. Col. Robert Magaw; West Nottingham, Chester Co., Commissioned Jan. 6, 1776; promoted Captain Nov. 4, 1776; taken Nov. 15, 1776. Lived and died in Franklin Co., was on the first Grand July, following the erection of Franklin County. Captain Robert Wilkins was a member of the society of the Cincinnati.

Penna. Arch. 2nd Ser. Vol. 10, p. 153.

GEORGE WILL

6th Penna. Cont. Line, First Lieut. Feb. 15, 1777; resigned Oct. 17, 1777; he had been eleven years in Prussian and English service. Franklin Repository, Chambersburg, Penna., 1829. Died at Adelphi in this county on the 13th of December, George Will, Senior, in his eighty-second year. He was a native of Prussia and came to New York in 1766. He was the head of the first company of Penna. Militia and later a Lieut. in the Continental Army, serving until 1779. In 1811, he moved to Adelphi and was appointed postmaster in 1813 and held that position until three months before his death. He was the father of nine children, the grandfather of forty-two children and great grandfather of eleven. He was an Elder in the German Lutheran Church and was buried on the 15th with military honors. Chillicothe paper.

Penna. Arch. 5th Ser. Vol. 3, p. 106, 108, 113, 114, 117, 128.

BENJAMIN WILLIAMS

Appears as a private in the Ranging Company of Capt. Thos. Paxton, also in the Cont. Line, from Bedford Co., Penna., and in the service with Capt. Thos. Davies. The Franklin Repository, June 14, 1825, states that "Benjamin Williams, Esq., died the 28th at Little Cove, aged 64 years and a few days." His will was dated 1820, prob. March 7, 1826, in which he names 3 children: Eli; Amos; Mary.

Penna. Arch. 5th Ser. Vol. 4, p. 254, 616. Vol. 5, p. 53, 56, 61, 62, 111.

ENOCH WILLIAMS

Served in the Company of Capt. Thos. Davies, Bedford Co. Militia, and is also shown in the Cont. Line from Bedford County, Penna. He left a will, dated 1796, prob. May, 1805. He was of Air Twp., and names first a dau. Mary Shelby (she mar. David Shelby, Jr., and died in Pickaway Co., Ohio in 1830); David, Jr., dying in 1845, their marriage having been in 1782. Enoch Williams further names a dau. Rachel Burns; a dau. Margaret Eaten; A dau. Hannah Eaten; Sons Benj. and Lewis as Executors; Son-in-law Augustus Bellew (Ballou); Son-in-law John Eavens and grandson Lewis Evans. Wit.: James Bala and Henry Thomas.

Penna. Arch. 5th Ser. Vol. 5, p. 111. Vol. 4, p. 254, 616.

HENRY WILLIAMS

Appears in the Company of Capt. Thomas Davies, also in Bedford Co. Militia, Cont. Line. An undated roll shows Henry Williams as Ensign in 1781, under Lieut Col. Charles Cessna.

Penna. Arch. 5th Ser. Vol. 4, p. 254, 616. Vol. 5, p. 111, 84.

LEWIS WILLIAMS

The record of Lewis Williams which follows was obtained from papers on file in claim for pension, S.40696, based upon his service in the War of the Revolution. The date and place of birth of Lewis Williams, and names of parents were not stated. Lewis Williams enlisted, place not given, March 15, 1778, served as private in Captain Samuel Brady's company, Col. Brodhead's Eighth Penna. Regt., and was discharged in the month of October, 1782, in Pittsburgh. The soldier, Lewis Williams, was allowed pension on his application executed May 4, 1818, at which time he was a resident of Muskingum County, Ohio, then in the seventy-seventh year of his age. He was still a resident of Muskingum County, in 1820, and then referred to his son-in-law, but did not give his name. The last payment of pension due Lewis Williams, a pensioner of the Rev. War, certificate No. 14,489, Ohio Agency, covering the period from Sept. 4, 1833 to March 1834, was made March 28, 1834, at the Pension Agency in Cincinnati, Ohio, to George Stratton, as attorney for the pensioner. On March 5, 1834, the pensioner certified to a Justice of the Peace in and for Morgan County, Ohio, that he had resided in the State of Ohio for the space of twenty-five years, and previous thereto he resided in the State of Pennsylvania. Lewis William and Thomas David applied for 800 acres land on Muddy Creek and Licking Run, Sept. 7, 1737. It was later surveyed for 1000 acres and adjoined (South of) Andrew Blair at a place called Clay Lick. Lewis Williams was allowed under a Blunston License. Under the Abington Presby. Church records is the following: Lewis Williams to Ann Watts, June 9, 1737. The estate of Lewis Williams, deceased, of Peters Twp., is shown at Carlisle, Aug., 1775. The son Enoch produced the account of his administration, the heirs being: To Lewis Williams in right of his grandfather, the deceased Lewis Williams, 3 pounds, 19 shillings, 6 pence; Grandaus.: Rachel; Mary; Sarah; Enoch in right of his father, and Mary, wife of John Lewis. Enoch Williams, son of Lewis Williams left a will dated 1796, prob. 1805. He was of Air Twp., and names first a dau. Mary Shelby (having mar. David Shelby, Jr. in 1782). and names other daus. and sons Benjamin and Lewis as Executors. One Lewis Williams was among the settlers evicted from the Little Cove and Connaloways in 1750, when Secretary Peters burned their cabins because the lands were not yet purchased from the Indians. The above notes are suggestions only to the Williams relationship.

THOMAS WILLIAMS

Second Penna. Regt. Cont. Line. He was of Franklin County, and died in Hamilton Co., Ohio, Jan. 25, 1826, aged 81 years.

Penna. Arch. 2nd Ser. Vol. 13, p. 242. 5th Ser. Vol. 2, p. 892.

HENRY WILLIAMSON

Is shown as a private with Captains Joseph Culbertson and Samuel Patton, during 1778-79-80-81. He was one of the Rangers with Captain Patton, at Ligonier during the spring of 1779, under Col. William Chambers.

Penna. Arch. 5th Ser. Vol. 6, p. 280, 290, 380, 602, 610.

ANDREW WILSON

Is shown serving in 1780 under Capt. John McConnell. A Patent was granted in 1788 to Andrew Wilson in Letterkenny Twp., called "Wilson's Choice," 181 acres; another Patent of 123 acres in 1788 in Letterkenny Twp., granted and called "St. Andrews;" a third tract to Andrew Wilson in Lurgan Twp., 24 acres, called "Blue Bonnet." Andrew Wilson died intestate, leaving a widow and issue 7: James; Charles; Stephen; and Andrew; Sarah, wife of John Skinner; Elizabeth, wife of Enoch Skinner; Jane, wife of Daniel Coyle. James Wilson, a son, sends Greetings from the State of North Carolina and sells his interest in estate to Stephen and Andrew Wilson.

Penna. Arch. 5th Ser. Vol. 6, p. 256, 267.

ISAAC WILSON

Served 1780 under Capt. William Smith. He was a son of William and Isabella Wilson. No Isaac Wilson until 1892 on estates. No Isaac Wilson until very late on deeds.

Penna. Arch. 5th Ser. Vol. 6, p. 267.

JAMES WILSON

In 1769, James Wilson and wife Isabella were living in the vicinity of Fort Loudon, and were members of the "Upper West Conococheague" Presby. Church. "Colonel (or Major) James Wilson was born 1741, in Cumb. Co. Penna., about three miles from where Mercersburg now stands. His wife was Isabella Barr, dau. of a neighbor," and probably the sister of James, Robert and Alexander Barr. Deeds at Chambersburg show that on Aug., 1779, James Wilson of Cumb. Co., Peters Twp., sells to Robert Wilson of same place, on Conococheague Creek, on south side of a branch which James Wilson holdeth by virtue of an article dated Apr. 27, 1770; also by his father's will, dated Aug. 7, 1776. Signed by James Wilson and Isabel Wilson. The parents of the above James Wilson, were James whose will was dated 1770, prob. 1786; the mother was Martha, who died Dec. 18, 1775. Mrs. Wilson and Mrs. Pomeroy are thought to have been the first white women to locate in Western Penna. On one occasion, the Indians being especially troublesome, Col. Wilson and James Barr hurried to the home of John Pomeroy, where they found Col. Pomeroy and wife Hannah upstairs, the children being stowed away unnder the puncheon floor, with orders to keep quiet. The Colonel had fought the savages over three hours. He had two good rifles, Hannah loading one while he was using the other, shooting through port holes, and hallooing to the Indians to come on, giving the impression there were many men in the house. Hannah was a great snuffer, and the Colonel said she deliberately took a pinch between the loadings. To Major Wilson is ascribed by tradition, the head to plan, and the hand to execute, for he was familiar with all manner of Indian strategy. After the wars, he devoted himself to the business of his farm, of about 800 acres of rich land, on which he resided till 1820, his family consisting of three sons and four daughters. His remains, with those of his wife, unmarried sons, and daughters, all repose on the farm, formerly Barr's Fort, where the bodies of the two brothers of Mrs. Wilson (Barrs) killed by the Indians, were buried in early days.
Frontier Forts of Western Penna., p. 344, 347, 348, 353, 355, 357, 371. Caldwell's Hist. of Indiana Co., Penna., p. 103, 104, 121, 122, 123.

JOHN WILSON

Son of William and Isabella Wilson, served under Captains William Huston and William Smith. He died April 2, 1788 and Letters of Administration were granted to Rachel Wilson and Matthew Wilson, June 3, 1788.

Penna. Arch. 5th Ser. Vol. 6, p. 275, 283.

MATTHEW WILSON

Served as private 1780-81 under Captains William Huston and William Smith. He was the son of William Wilson, who died Sept. 18, 1777, and his wife Isabella, died Oct. 3 1777. They were of Peters Twp., living in District 2 of the Presby. Church. They (Wm. and Isabella Wilson) had issue: Isaac; Sarah; Matthew; Elizabeth; John; William; Ann. Matthew Wilson, Peters Twp., died July, 1792. In his will he names Brother Isaac, son of William Wilson; sisters Sarah and Elizabeth; Brother John's son William; Brother William's land; Margaret McAfee to have the use of land. Elizabeth Smith 30 pounds; Sister Ann's children. The above will seems to prove this Ann Wilson to have been the wife of Col. James Smith, famous Indian Captive. Deed Book 5, p. 206, 207, shows James Irwin as the Executor of Matthew Wilson, who, with the aprobation and consent of Robert Newil, Esq., John Newil and others, heirs of said Matthew Wilson, decd. James Irwin sells to John Rowan, for 3 pounds, Lot No. 43 in town of Mercersburg, before Robert Newell, Justice of the Peace, Aug. 14, 1801.

Penna. Arch. 5th Ser. Vol. 6, p. 265, 270, 276, 283.

ROBERT WILSON

Served as a private 1780-81, under Captains James Patton and Robert Dickey. In 1781, he had 239 acres of land, Horses and Cattle. He left a will dated 1790, prob. 1793, naming wife Elizabeth; small children; sons Robert; James; William; Ralph; daus., not named and Nathaniel, born after 1790. The Patent to Robert Wilson was dated July 26, 1744. He was mar. to Elizabeth Hunt, by Rev. John King, Jan. 22, 1771. He died Jan. 10, 1793. In 1812, the heirs sold the land, Robert; James; William; Ralph; Nathaniel; Susan mar. Samuel Witherow, March 25, 1806. Sarah mar. Levi Woodward. Elizabeth mar. Enoch Bowen, May, 5, 1809. The land was sold to David Rankin, 297 acres for $12,181. The Witherows then in Butler Co., Penna. The Bowens then in Montgomery Co., Ohio. The Woodwards then in Warren Co., Ohio. The "Repository" under Feb., 1803, advertises a tract on West Conococheague, 2 miles from Mercersburg, adjoining "Sulphur Springs." Signed, Elizabeth Wilson, Admrx., Robert Wilson Admr. On May 14, 1803, Robert Wilson again requests persons indebted to Elizabeth and Robert Wilson, by note or account, to come and make payment. He stated several times that he intended to start for the Miami Country in a few weeks.

Penna. Arch. 5th Ser. Vol. 6, p. 271, 284, 289, 314.

CAPTAIN ROBERT WILSON

From Second Lieut. March 20, 1777; wounded at Paoli; living in Jefferson County, Ky., in 1834, aged 82 years. Pensioners in the state of Kentucky, Robert Wilson, Capt. Penna. Line, also Capt. Penna. Line, Nov. 2, 1832, aged 82 years. The date and place of birth and the names of the parents of Robert Wilson are not shown in the papers in the pension claim. While residing in Cumb. Co., Penna., Robert Wilson was appointed in Nov., 1775, Lieut. in Capt. James Wilson's (no relationship shown) Company. Col. Wm. Irvine's Penna. Regt. in the spring of 1777, was commissioned captain in same regiment; he was in the expedition to Canada, battles Three Rivers, Paoli, where wounded (nature of wound not shown) and Germantown and served until March, 1778. In November, 1778, or 1779, he was appointed Assistant Deputy Quartermaster under Col. John Davis, Quartermaster General of the Western Army nad served until April, 1781. He was allowed pension on his application executed May 9, 1818, while residing in Jefferson County, Ky. In 1820, he was aged sixty-six years. Robert Wilson died Sept. 10, 1835, in Jefferson Co., Ky. The soldier married in Hagerstown, Md., Jane, the daughter of John Elliott. The marriage license was dated Nov. 4, 1777. She was a resident of the state of Penna., about thirty-five or forty miles from Hagerstown, Md. Soldier's widow, Jane, was allowed pension on her application executed July 19, 1837, while residing in Jefferson Co., Ky., and aged seventy-four years. She died August 19, 1844. A daughter, Jane, is referred to in 1820, as aged 18 years. The following children survived their father: Emzy, living in Arkansas; Elliott; Patience, the wife of Joseph Blunk; David and Daniel Wilson. The widow left four children, Elliott having died in Louisiana. Elliott left four children, Jane and Julia only names of said Elliott's children shown. In 1849, Daniel Wilson was residing in Jefferson Co., Ky.; the places of residence of the other children are not shown.

Penna. Arch. 2nd Ser. Vol. 10, p. 618. 3rd Ser. Vol. 23, p. 560, 565.

ROBERT WILSON

Revolutionary War pension claim, S.39905, shows that Robert Wilson enlisted in Northumberland Co., Penna., in October, 1776, and served in Capt. Hawkins Boone's Co., Col. William Cooke's Penna. Regt.; he was in the battles of Brandywine, Germantown, Monmouth and several skirmishes, and was discharged in January, 1781, at Trenton (at the revolt of the Penna. Line), having served four years and four months. He was allowed pension on his application executed April 23, 1818, at which time he was living in Beaver Co., Penna., and was aged sixty-nine years. In 1820 he referred to his wife but did not give her name or age; to a son, Robert, aged twenty-one years, and to his daughter, Esther, aged thirteen years. Soldier died October 2, 1824. Thomas S. McClelland of Chicago adds to above, that Robert Wilson married Sarah Friend in the Path Valley, Penna., about 1784 or 85, and moved to Beaver Co., Penna. They had issue: James; Margaret; Hannah; Joseph; Nancy; Polly; Robert; Ann; Samuel; Elizabeth and Esther, the youngest, born 1807; all born at Darlington, Beaver Co., Penna. He further states that Sarah (Friend) Wilson became a pensioner at her husband's death in 1824, and drew a pension of $8.00 per month until her death in 1839.

WILLIAM WILSON

Son of William and Isabella Wilson, served 1780-81, under Capt. Wm. Huston.

Penna. Arch 5th Ser. Vol. 6, p. 270, 284.

MARTIN WINGERT

Of Green Twp., appears as a private with Capt. Joseph Culbertson, 1780-81. The will of Martin Wingert was written in 1812, and prob. Oct. 7, 1815. To son Abraham Wingert the Plantation whereon he and I now live, 222 acres, adjoining lands of Joseph Crawford, Henry Hoffman, and lands lately purchased of Wendle Shirk; also 178 acres of Pine land &c. To my son Michael Wingert the tract he now lives on 188 acres, also 11½ acres adjoining aforesaid tract, &c. To my dau. Barbara Eaby, and to her lawful Issue a certain tract lying in upper Canada on Grand River, Lot No. 3, for the sum of 200 pounds lawful money of Penna. xxx All my other children be first made equal, and I allow my other children to be paid in manner (to wit), the first gale to be divided amongst the two oldest of my children, and then to the next oldest and so on in rotation. Signed: Martin Wenger, In German. Witnesses: Abraham Wenger and George Hetich. The "Franklin Repository," Oct. 10, 1815. Departed this life, on Thursday the 23 ult, at his farm near this borough, Mr. Martin Wenger, in his 74th year. He was a man of unblemished character. He belonged to the respectable Society of Mennonites, in which he presided as elder. He came to America with his parents when he was but six years old, and resided on his lands, about two miles from town, nearly 50 years.

Penna. Arch. 5th Ser. Vol. 6, p. 280, 290.

JOHN WINN

Seventh Penna. Cont. Line, Sergeant John Winn, Capt. Alexdr. Parker's Co., resided Franklin Co., 1812. John Winn promoted ensign July 24, 1779. Orphans' Court Chambersburg, Penna. Book B, p. 102—1814 and p. 323—1819 and Book C, p. 22, all show the account of Archibald S. McCune, Esq., Guardian of John Winn (an old soldier) approved by Court. $181.29 in hands of accountant chargeable with interest, in June of 1824. Book B, p. 25, Aug. 16, 1813, Orphans' Court. On recommendation of the Board for the relief of disabled, aged and poor revolutionary officers and Soldiers, The Court appoints Archibald S. McCune, Esq., of Franklin County, Guardian of John Winn of said county, for the purpose of receiving and superintending the expenditure of a pension granted to the said John Winn by the Board aforesaid. Pension application of John Winn, April 20, 1818, from Fannetsburg, Franklin Co., Penna., in 1820, a day laborer, wife and 2 children at home, born 1752. Enlisted Feb. 3, 1776, in Shippensburg in Capt. Wm. Rippey's Company, 6th Penna. Regt., commanded by Col. Irwin for one year; again enlisted at Ticonderago under Capt. Parker in same Regt., Col. Hartley (then cammanding) for and during the war. Served until peace in 1783 when discharged at Phila.; in battles of Three Rivers; Springfield; White Horse; Brandywine; Paoli; Germantown; Monmouth; and at falling of Cornwallis. Sworn in Washington Co., Md. In 1821 in Franklin Co., Penna., no property, no family. Last pension certificate about Aug. 31, or early in Sept., 1820, "by having it washed up in his pocket," applied for new Certificate August 14, 1821, asks for change of place of payment from Penna. Agency to Maryyland.

Penna. Arch. 2nd Ser. Vol. 10, p. 653.

STEPHEN WINTER

Is shown in service 1776, in Capt. Paxton's Company, Bedford County Militia, with the Herods, Williams and others. Later he appears in the Cont. Line from Bedford Co., Penna. On Oct. 28, 1783, Stephen Winter was married to Mary Linn, by Dr. John King of Mercersburg, Penna. Under pensioners, Greene Co., Ohio, Stephen Winter appears July 27, 1833, aged 82 years.

Penna. Arch 5th Ser. Vol. 4, p. 225, 254, 616. Vol. 5, p. 62, 98.

CHRISTOPHER WISE

Served as a private March, 1778, under Capt. Wm. Findley. Christopher Wise mar. ———— McKinney, dau. of Wm. McKinnie, who was killed by Indians in 1757. Their son John Wise mar. Sarah Robinson; their dau. Mary Wise, 1786-1854, mar. Dec. 31, 1813, John Rowe born in Ireland 1776, died 1836. John Rowe, Jr., born Oct. 4, 1814, mar. Elizabeth Prather, Feb. 18, 1836.

Penna. Arch. 5th Ser. Vol. 6, p. 530.

EDWARD WISHARD

Served under Captains Daniel Clapsaddle and William Findlay, 1780-81-82. On June 2, 1777, Fergus Moorhead sold to Edward Wishard, both of Antrim Twp., for 1370 pounds, 5 shillings, 6 pence, land where Fergus now dwells, the one-half of his deceased Father's land made over to him by a conveyance or Instrument, under the hand seal of John Moorhead, decd., 248 acres 38 perches, also one other tract surveyed to Fergus 102 acres, 53 perches, in all 342 acres, 91 perches. Witnesses: James Moorhead and James Johnston. Edward Wishard died in 1804 leaving a widow and eight children; shown in Orphans' Court. Margaret mar. John Moorhead; Agnes mar. James McRoberts; Mary mar. Richard Scott; Ann mar. Samuel McCutcheon; Jacob the petitioner; Catherine mar. James Downey; John; Sarah mar. Robert Gibson. In 1793 the will of Agnes Wishart was prob., naming grandau. Jean, dau. of Joseph, decd.; Son Edward; Daus.: Mary and Nancy. A deed shows Ann to have been the wife of Edward Wishard, and further that John Moorhead and wife Margaret had gone to Red. Bank Twp., Armstrong Co., Penna.

Penna. Arch. 5th Ser. Vol. 6, p. 93, 116, 122, 586.

JAMES WISHARD

Served under Capt. Samuel Royer, 1779-80-81. From 1778 to 1782, the four Wisharts (Wishartt), Edward, John, James and Joseph, are shown as taxables in Washington Twp., with lands, Horses and Cattle.

Penna. Arch. 5th Ser. Vol. 6, p. 74, 90, 113, 542.

JOHN WISHARD

Served under Capt. Samuel Royer, 1779-80-81. John Gordon sold a tract of land to Edward and John Wishard in 1770, and in 1773, Margaret, widow of John Gordon, sold another tract to the same, John Gordon dying in 1772.

Penna. Arch. 5th Ser. Vol. 6, p. 89, 112, 542.

JOSEPH WISHARD

Served as private under Capt. Daniel Clapsaddle, 1780-81. In the will of Agnes Wishart, 1793, she names grandau. Jean, the dau. of son Joseph, decd.

Penna. Arch. 5th Ser. Vol. 6, p. 72, 94, 117.

JOHN WITHERSPOON, JR.

Princeton 1773, was son of the president of Princeton. He studied medicine and accompanied Washington to Boston in 1775. He was in the General Hospital at New York in 1776, and in the Trenton Hospital in 1777. In 1779, he was sent to France by Congress to purchase medical equipment. Later, he was surgeon on the American privateer De Graff, captured by the British in 1781. He was released through the efforts of Franklin. He returned to Princeton in 1782, but later broke with his father and his later life is uncertain . . . It is believed that he settled in South Carolina and was lost at sea in 1795.

Fithian's Journal, p. 60. Collins, Vol. 2, p. 49n.

WILLIAM WITHNEAL (WITHNEY)

Served as private under Capt. Patrick Jack in 1780. He was a farmer in Hamilton Twp., and in his will, prob. Dec. 20, 1805, he names wife Agnes and 5 children: Arthur; Jean; Elizabeth; Agnes and John; one of the Executors was son-in-law Thomas Kirby. The name William Withnal appears in 1757-58 in the Roll of Capt. John Potter's Company. Franklin Repository states William Withney was in his 78th year.

Penna. Arch. 5th Ser. Vol. 6, p. 291. 2nd Ser. Vol. 7, p. 269.

SAMUEL WITHROW

S22599 Pennsylvania, Samuel Withrow, pensioner, Franklin Co., Penna., April 10, 1833. Samuel Withrow of Metal Twp., will be 79 years in July next. He entered as a volunteer Sept., 1776, in the Township of Fannett, Franklin Co., Penna., under Command of Capt. Thos. Paxton and others. He was in service in Frankstown, Bedford Co., for protection against the Indians; drafted in same Company, Aug., 1777; discharged Oct. 15, 1777; was under Capt. Thos. Askey, Lieut., Adam Bratton; Brig. Genl. James Potter; Col. James Dunlap; at Wilmington and Newcastle, Del. In battle of Brandywine wounded in left leg. Under Capt. Askey 1778, along the Allegheny Mountain to guard the frontier. Born in Chester Co., Penna., July 4th, 1754.

HENRY WOLFKILL

Was serving from Bedford Co., Penna. in the Cont. Line and entitled to Depreciation pay. There are Wolfkill marriages by Rev. John Waldschmidt of Cocoalico and Lancaster Co.

Penna. Arch. 6th Ser. Vol. 6. 5th Ser. Vol. 4, p. 254.

PATRICK WOLFKILL

Was a private Aug., 1782, with Capt. Noah Abraham.

Penna. Arch. 5th Ser. Vol. 6, p. 128.

WILLIAM WOLFKILL

Is shown service Aug., 1781, with Capt. Snider. He was a son of Conrad Wolfkill of Guilford Twp., whose will was prob. Nov., 1813, naming wife Mary; Sons, Peter; John; William; Jacob; Grandson Elias Wolfkill; George Rouse mar. to dau. Dorothy; dau. Mary Whitmore; dau. Elizabeth mar. to Christian Cook. To son Jacob "my watch." Exrs.: Son Peter and John Ross. Jacob Wolfkill in War of 1812.

Penna. Arch. 5th Ser. Vol. 6, p. 119.

JAMES WOOD ESQ.

The Franklin Repository, Oct. 4, 1825, "Departed this life Wednesday last, in his 54th year, James Wood Esq., of Greencastle, Penna. He was with Wayne in 1794, and Major in the late war; was buried Thursday." Under Orphans' Court records June 12, 1827, is shown that James Wood died intestate leaving a widow Sarah and ten children: Mary; William; Elizabeth mar. to William Coffroth; Sarah; John; James; Agnes; Jane; Emmaline and Rebecca, the last five being minors.

LIEUTENANT COLONEL JOHN WORK

Battalions called out by order from Council, dated at Lancaster Jan., 1778, Lieut. Col. John Work, "back from Lan'r". He is also given under Col. Saml. Culbertson in 1777-78, and with Capt. Wm. Huston in 1780-81. Col. John Work and his brother Henry came here from Bart Twp. Lancaster Co., Penna. Their father, Capt. Andrew Work mar. in 1732, Isabell Koyle (Kyle?). He was a Captain in the Associated Companies of Lancaster Co., 1756. He was Sheriff 1749-50 and Justice of the Peace 1764. He died 1776-1779, owning a tract of land, 475 acres, patent in 1752, in what is now Montgomery Twp., which became the property of his two sons, John and Henry Work. John Davis who came from the Big Spring, Earl Twp. Lancaster Co., bought from Henry Work, the one half of his share of land. Col. John Work died Nov. 27, 1815. His wife Rachael Moore, died July 30, 1823. Descendants state they are buried in the grave yard at the Presby. Church at Welsh Run, with many other Welsh settlers. The son John and wife Lydia Huston are lying there and have stones. Col. John Work and wife Rachael, had issue: Sons, Andrew; John; dau. Rebeckah unmar. but who mar. John Davis, June 11, 1812, and shown in the will of her mother 1821.

Penna. Arch. 5th Ser. Vol. 6, p. 29, 265, 270, 276, 283, 367, 375, 608.

ROBERT WORK

Is shown serving in Franklin County Militia, in 1778, under Capt. John Rea, commanded by Col. A. Smith, and also in the Cont. Line from Cumb. Co. Penna. In the St. Clair Cemetery at Greensburg, Penna., is the grave of Robert Work, who died Apr. 27, 1832, aged 80 years. One Robert Work was married to Isabella McCullum, July 8, 1806, by Dr. David Denny of Chambersburg.

He may have been a relative of John D. Work of Greencastle.

Penna. Arch. 5th Ser. Vol. 6, p. 528, 529, 537. Vol. 4, p. 305, 642.

PATRICK WRIGHT

Served as private 1780-81, under Capt. John Rea. He was married to Ann, dau. of Samuel Rea of Green Twp.

Penna. Arch. 5th Ser. Vol. 6, p. 73, 78, 106.

CHRISTIAN YENEVINE

Served as pvt., under Capt. Jacob Brandt, Lancaster Co., Penna., in 1782. He died in Washington Twp., Franklin Co., Penna. His will, prob. Sept. 19, 1799, named Wife Mary; Two daus. Anna and Magdalena a legacy left them by their grandfather John Myers. Exrs.: Christian Myers of Washington Co., Md., and wife Mary. Wit.: Daniel Royer, Fredk. Nicodemus, Christian Grub.

Penna. Arch. 5th Ser. Vol. 7, p. 426.

ALEXANDER YOUNG

Served as pvt., under Capt. James Poe, First Call, Oct., 1777, and under Capt. Wm. Berryhill in 1780-81-82. His wife was Annas, daughter of Capt. John Potter, who died in 1757, and lies in an unmarked grave in Brown's Mill Graveyard. Alexander Young and wife Annas had a son James.

Penna. Arch. 5th Ser. Vol. 6, p. 80, 101, 521, 523, 572.

CAPTAIN JAMES YOUNG

Served 1777-78-79-80-81, from Guilford Twp. Franklin Co., Penna., under Col. Buchanan, Col. Abraham Smith, Col. James Johnston, of the First Batt. of Cumb. Co. Militia. The will of James Young of Guilford Twp., states: "Citizen of the United States, this instrument is written with my own hand." To my dearly and best beloved son William Young; To my darling son Robert Young; To my dearly beloved dau. Elizabeth Love, and her son James Love; To my dearly beloved dau. Mary Brisben. The will was prob July 18, 1822. Of the two sons we have the following: James, the eldest son of William, graduated from the University of Penna., in medicine, Apr. 4, 1823. ("I have his diploma"). He came south soon after and settled in Nashville Tenn., and was in partnership with Dr. Hogg, whose dau. Rebecca he married, later moving to Natchez, Miss. They had no issue and following the death of Rebecca, Dr. Young moved to Memphis, Tenn., where in 1850 he mar. Mary Brahan. They had James (my father), Rebecca and William. Dr. Young was born in 1800 and died in 1870; buried in Elmwood Cemetery, Memphis, Tenn. Deeds show James Young and wife Rebecca of Natchez, Miss., selling land to Philip Lemaster. Copy of letter and commission from Mary Young Barbee, Forest Ave., Memphis, Tenn. William Young mar. Polly Irwin, Jan. 2, 1800, the dau of Joseph Irwin (son of pioneer James and Jean Irwin) and his wife Violet Porter. From the Franklin Repository, Apr. 7, 1829, "Died at his residence in Guilford Twp., on the 30th ult. General William Young, a respectable farmer." Under Oct. 9, 1823, the above gives: "Died, at the house of her son-in-law, Qeneral Young, Mrs. Irwin, at an advanced age." The children of William Young and wife, Mary were: Robert; William; Violetta; Elizabeth; Martha, wife of Charles McFarland. In the Name and by the Authority of the Commonwealth of Pennsylvania,—Thomas McKean, Governor of said Commonwealth, To William Young of the County of Franklin, Greetings; Know that you, the said William Young (being duly elected and returned) are hereby commissioned Major of the Second Battalion in the Seventy third Regiment of the Militia of the Commonwealth of Pennsylvania, in the Second Brigade of the Seventh Division composed of the Militia of the counties of Cumberland and Franklin. To have and to hold this commission, exercising all powers and discharging all the duties thereto lawfully belonging and attached for the term of seven years from the day of the date hereof, of you shall so long behave yourself well. In testimony whereof I have set my hand and caused the Less (?) Seal of the State to be affixed to those presents, at Lancaster, the Second day of August in the year of our Lord one thousand eight hundred and of the Commonwealth the twenty-fifth. By the Govenor,

Jas. Trimble, Dy. Sec.

On the James Young farm, Guilford Township. Sale of the Last Slave North of Mason & Dixon Line was held under this old Tree. About two miles southwest of Chambersburg, in Franklin Co., stands an Oak Tree which deserves to be ranked as one of the historic trees of Pennsylvania, for under it slavery was publicly recognized as an institution for the last time by the people of the Keystone State. This venerable Oak stands on the edge of a public road leading through a farm which originally belonged to Colonel James Young, a scotch Irish soldier of the Revolutionary War. Slavery was abolished in Pennsylvania about the beginning of the last century, but the act of assembly provided that all children born into slavery before the act went into effect, were obliged to serve their respective masters for a period of twenty-eight years before they could be declared absolutely free. Hence it was that Colonel James Young continued to be the owner of two male slaves, and during the Spring of 1828 when a sale of his effects took place, these two slaves were sold along with his other property. A platform was erected under this Oak Tree and the auctioneer put the two slaves under the hammer and they were sold to the highest bidders. While the exact date and month of this memorable sale cannot now be definitely fixed, there is no doubt that it was the last time human flesh was legally and publicly exposed for sale in the Commonwealth of Pennsylvania. There is no record of the price for which these slaves were sold, but it is evident that they brought only a small sum, because they had only a few months more to serve. One of these slaves was knocked down to James Dunlap, a distinguished lawyer of Pennsylvania and author of "Dunlap's Digest." He put his purchase to work in an edge tool factory in Chambersburg and drew all the wages earned by the slave until the date of his freedom. The other slave was sold to Silas Henry, a contractor who was engaged in building King Street Bridge in Chambersburg. He was put to work on this bridge but became unmanagable and threatened his owner's life, when he too, was placed in the edge tool factory to serve out his time. The last witness to this remarkable sale died but two years ago at the age of ninety-one. Steps have been taken by the local Historical Society to place a marker under this old tree. Written for The Public Ledger, 1912, by J. H. Stoner, Waynesboro, Penna.

JACOB ZENT

Served as a pvt., in Lancaster Co. Penna., under Capt. Michael Moyer, 1778-79. His wife Susanna, born Apr. 30, 1765, died March 13, 1841, is buried in the White Church graveyard, in Guliford Twp., and it is probable he is beside her, but has no stone. The will of Jacob Zent is dated and prob., 1844-1845. He names Samuel Zent and Jacob Bowman of Stark Co., Ohio, the land on which dau. Susanna and husband Jacob Snider now live; in trust for said Susanna and her children; Samuel Cover, mar. to dau. Elizabeth $300., to purchase land in Crawford Co., Ohio; children of son John, decd., his son Jacob; children of dau. Catherine Myers, decd., her son Samuel Miller; son Samuel; dau. Sarah, mar. to Samuel Spoonhour; Polly Wingert mar. to John Wingert; dau. Mary mar. to Jacob Bowman; dau. Nancy, lately mar. to John M. Green and now decd.; Nancy's children; Son John, decd., has 4 children; The clothing belonging to me or my deceased wife are to be disposed of by my executors among my heirs at private sale, if that cannot be done, then to the poor. Executors: Grandson Samuel Miller, son of my dau. Catherine, decd. and Samuel Myers mar. to my grandau. Susanna, being a dau. of my son John Zent, decd. An additional executor was Jacob Eberly, mar. to my grandau. Polly, dau. of my son John Zent, decd.

Penna. Arch. 5th Ser. Vol. 7, p. 561.

JACOB ZIGLER

Served in the Cont. Line, 2nd Penna. Regt. The references do not clearly identify him. We offer for consideration Jacob Zigler of Antrim Twp., whos will dated June 7, 1787, was probated Aug. 7, 1787. The eldest son Jacob was given fifteen pounds specie and one large bible; dau. Christina Zigler seven pounds and ten shillings; dau. Mary Zigler five pounds; my brickyard to the above named legatees; real estate in Hagerstown, Md., to be sold; money divided as follows: Sons, Jacob; George and Joseph; daughters Elizabeth Heslick; Susanna Pruse; Cathrena Peated; Christeena; Mary and Mathalena Zigler. Exrs.: Son-in-law Nathaniel Peated and son Jacob Zigler. Wit.: Jacob Weider, George Sharrer, a German name.

Penna. Arch. 2nd Ser. Vol. 10, p. 407.

GRAVEYARDS

BROWNS MILL GRAVEYARD
Antrim Township, Franklin County, Pennsylvania

JAMES BORELAND

Antrim Twp., pvt., under Capt. John Jack in 1778, 79, and under Capt. Thos. Johnston, 1780-81-82. His will was dated and probated Oct. 1804. He named wife Mary; daus. Jean McDowell; Mary Horens; Isabella Clark and son John. Franklin Repository, Tuesday, Oct. 23, 1804. At his farm near Greencastle, on the 16th inst., "Mr. James Boreland, in the 71st year of his age. His remains were consigned to the silent tomb on the Wednesday following, in the burial ground near Mr. Lazarus Brown's Mill."

Penna. Arch. 5th Ser. Vol. 6, p. 84, 114, 124, 129, 169, 535, 540, 586.

THOMAS BROWN

One of the earliest settlers in the Brown's Mill district was Thomas Brown, founder of the family from which the graveyard derived its name. Records of land grants issued in Lancaster county show that in 1734 he received 300 acres and that he obtained an additional hundred acres in 1742. In 1738 he joined with Benjamin Chambers in an unsuccessful petition to the Donegal Presbytery for a pastor for East Conococheague. When Cumberland county was created in 1750 he was a member of the first grand jury, which convened on July 24th, probably at Carlisle. His will, dated December 20, 1768 contains interesting provisions. To his son-in-law, James McLene, he leaves his "still and vessels thereto belonging." Of my son Lazarus he declares that "his only part and portion shall be an English Crown." To his grand-daughter Finwell, or Fanuel, he bequeaths five pounds—"to be laid aside for her wedding suit if she lives to that time." For his "dear loving wife Marthew" he provided "three years living in my present dwelling house and a third of all crops raised by William Dean. At the expiration of three years she shall remove from the Mansion House to the house where John White now lives, taking household furniture which was hers before married; but if she change her estate by marriage she shall remove from the premises. He died in 1769. Six children survived this head of the house Brown:—George, who had come with his father to Brown's Mill prior to 1739 and had been in 1748 a captain in the Regiment of Col Benj.

Chambers; the unlucky Lazarus, whose portion was a crown, and four daughters—Rebecca, Ruth, Elizabeth, and Christina. The three latter daughters made notable matches. Ruth became the wife of John Rannells, Elizabeth the wife of Joseph Cooke, and Christina the wife of James McLene. George Brown married Agnes Maxwell. His children, also, were six in number. One son, William Maxwell Brown, married Hadassah Chambers, dau. of the pioneer Benjamin Chambers.

THOMAS BROWN

Second Lieut. served in the Company of Capt. Jeremiah Talbot, Col. Wm. Irvine's 6th Penna. Regt., Continental Line, 1776. He died Mch. 10, 1818, in his 56th yr. His wife was Margaret McLanahan. "Capt. Thomas Brown was a son of George and Ruth (Maxwell) Brown; Most notable of the sons of George Brown, and grandson of old Thomas Brown, was Capt. Thomas Brown. Born in 1762 he served in the Revolutionary War and apparently preserved his interest in military affairs. An advertisement in Franklin Repository, issue of Sept. 28, 1802, is headed "Attention Cavalry" and states that "Capt. Thomas Brown calls the members of the Franklin Guard to meet at the house of Mr. Henry Gordon, innkeeper, etc. Five members of the Brown family have markers in the Brown's Mill graveyard. Elizabeth wife of Joseph Cooke and dau. of the original Thomas Brown, lies buried beside her husband, a Rev. soldier. "Captain" Thomas Brown and his wife Margaret McLanhan had issue: James; George; Isabella Findly; Nancy; Susan; Rebecca; Sarah.

Penna. Arch. 5th Ser. Vol. 2, p. 201, 202.

JOHN CLUGSTON

Served in the Company of Capt. Thomas Johnston 1780-81-82, Cumberland Co. Militia. Agnes, wife of John Clugston, d. Apr. 15, 1830, aged 64 yrs. He d. Jan. 25, 1833, in his 73rd yr., leaving seven children: John; Jane mar. Abraham Hollinger; Thomas; Robert; Catherine, mar. John Hassler; Alexander; David.

Penna. Arch. 5th Ser. Vol. 6, p. 83, 108, 114, 129.

ROBERT CLUGSTON

Served as a private under Capts. Samuel Royer,

Thos. Johnston and John Jack, 1777-79-80-81. Robert Clugston died Sept. 3, 1834 in his 82nd yr. He left issue: Thomas; Jane mar. Daniel Huey; Nancy; Robert.

Penna. Arch. 5th Ser. Vol. 6, p. 83, 108, 114, 129, 514, 539.

JOSEPH COOK

Private in 1782, under Capt. John Woods. Joseph Cook of Antrim Twp., made his will Aug. 13, 1802; it was prob. Feb. 23, 1804. He named sons: David; Thomas; Joseph; dau. Sarah Scroges and her dau. Rachel; dau. Rebecca Mc Farlan; dau. Elizabeth Brown; bro. Alexander Cook; son Wm. to get the Plantation where the father lived. He died Feb. 5, 1804, aged 82 yrs. His wife Elizabeth, d. June 27, 1800. A dau. Phinwell had died June the 3rd, 1762, aged 19 months. Elizabeth was a dau. of pioneer Thomas Brown.

Ref. Penna. Arch. 5th Ser. Vol. 6, p. 138.

HUMPHREY FULLERTON

Served as a pvt. under Capt. Jas. Young, First Call Oct. 23, 1777, and in Jan. 1778; under Capt. John Woods in 1780; and in 1782, with Capt. James Poe. Miss Mary L. McFarland, a desc. stated that Humphrey Fullerton was buried at Brown's Mill Graveyard. His wife was Martha Mitchell of Lancaster Co., Penna. In his will he mentions his mother Ann, who died Mch. 14, 1804. On April 18, 1782, he was appointed a Justice of the Peace for Cumberland county and he continued to serve in the same capacity for Franklin county after its erection in 1784. That he was Greencastle's first justice of the peace and that by 1792 he maintained an office in the town is stated in the paper on "Early Days of Greencastle" prepared by the late Judge D. Watson Rowe. He died in January, 1792. His will, wated Dec. 15, 1791, provides that his widow shall have the sum of three hundred pounds, his negro wench Rachel, horse, saddle, 2 good cows, 6 sheep, her chest of drawers, a small table, five pounds with which to buy chairs and kitchen furniture and that she is to have the benefit of two rooms in the east of the house if she remains his widow. One of the witnesses to the will is Matthew Lind, Jr., evidently a son of the Rev. Matthew Lind and his wife who are buried in Borwn's Mill and the latter of whom is described as "among wives the most dutiful, among mothers the most affectionate, and among friends the kindest and most hospitable." To son David part of my tract adj. Muddy Run, including my mill, near John Woods bridge . . . to a meadow called Miller's Meadow; along the Great Road . . . my negroe servant Caesor. To son Humphrey the tract whereon I now live, 223 acres, also a long strip of my other tract along the Great road to Adam Hoop's line—my tract on Sugar Creek, Westmoreland Co.,—and my negro man Jack. To dau. Elizabeth the tract in my name on the waters of Sugar Creek adj. lands of Hugh, Henry and James Brown; also my negro wench Kate. To son Thomas a tract of land . . . . To dau. Anne a tract on Sugar Creek adj. lands of Elizabeth. Ta dau. Elinor a tract in Westmoreland County. To son Wm. remainder of the tract whereon my Mill now stands, &c. John Woods and son David guardians of Elizab. Anne, Elinor, Thomas and Wm. Humphrey Fullerton mar. Catherine Dixon. Went to Ohio. David Fullerton mar. Joanna Lind; Thomas Fullerton mar. Elizab. Stewart (of Hugh) Anne Fullerton mar. Robert Robinson (2nd wife) Eleanor (Nelly) Fullerton mar. John Blythe, 10-11-1799. Went to Westmoreland County, Penna. Elizabeth Fullerton mar. Mr. McCormick of Va. Wm. Fullerton mar. Barbara ?

Penna. Arch. 5th Ser. Vol. 6, p. 79, 92 138, 522, 526, 576, 583. Also 2nd Ser. Vol. 3, p. 661.

JOHN McCLEARY

Served in the Company of Capt. Thomas Johnston, 1780-81-82, Cumb. Co., Penna. His will was prob. Nov. 6, 1833, naming a son William.

Penna. Arch. 5th Ser. Vol. 6, p. 76, 84, 115, 130.

ROBERT McCLEARY

Served as a pvt. 1781, under Capt. Thos. Johnston. Letters of Admr. were granted to John Essick, Mch. 9, 1827, on est. of Robert McCleary. His widow, Jane McCleary, Sr., made a will July 28, 1847; prob. July 26, 1851. She named dau. Jane McLeary; son John; Catherine, wife of John Clugston; Alexander McLeary; Agnes McDowell; children of son John, the Exr. being Robert Clugston of Guilford Twp.

Penna. Arch. 5th Ser. Vol. 6, p. 115.

NATHAN McDOWELL

Served as private 1777-78-80, under Capts. James and Samuel Patton, a son of Wm. and Mary (Maxwell) McDowell. He died Feb. 1, 1830, aged 71 yrs. His wife Mary McLanahan, d. Oct. 22, 1818. They had issue: Wm. 1793-1825; Sarah, 1796-1856; Mary Maxwell, 1797-1843; Susanna Bella, 1799-1800; John Mclanahan, 1801-1882; Nathan, 1803-1860; Rebecca. Franklin Repository, Chambersburg, Penna. Feb. 9, 1830. Died of a lingering illness at his residence in Antrim Twp., on the 1st inst, Nathan McDowell, Esq., in the 72nd yr. of his age. In the 19th yr. of his age, Mr. McDowell was called to the army of his Country, then struggling for its independence. In 1788 he was attached to the army under Gen. Harmer and marched to the western frontiers to protect it from Indian outrages, &c.

Penna. Arch. 5th Ser. Vol. 6, p. 271, 314, 373, 380.

JAMES McLENE

Served in Congress 1779-80, was a member of the Provincial Conference of Penna., held at Carpenter's Hall, Phila., on the 25th of June 1776; was a member of the convention that formed the constitution of 1776, for the State of Penna.; a member of the Supreme Executive Council of Penna., from Cumb. Co. from Nov. 9, 1778 to Dec. 28, 1779; was elected to and served in the Council of Censors, from October, 1783 to October, 1784; was elected in October, 1784, a member of the Supreme Executive Council from this county and served for three years; and was also a representative from this county, in the convention of 1789, which formed the State Constitution of 1790; he was also a member of the House of Representatives of Penna., from this county in the sessions of 1787-88-89-90-91 and 1793-94. He died March 13th 1806, and was buried in the above graveyard. From the "Repository," Mch. 25, 1806, "On the 14th inst. James McLene, Esq., at his farm in Antietam —a Patriot of '76." In his will the tract of land on which he lived was called "Mount Pleasant." He names wife Christian, to whom he gives "all the gold in my possession as a free gift." Son Jas. a Plantation on which he lives in Indiana Co., Penna.; son Lazarus also in Indiana Co., Penna.; sons Danial and Thos. Brown McLene; son John (died without issue); son-in-law Samuel McPherrin; grandchildren McFarren; dau. Mary Smith; sister Margaret Thompson. Christian, widow of James McLene, Esq., left a will dated Nov. 1814, prob. Oct. 1818, in which she names sons; Thomas B. McLene; Lazarus; John; James; grandaus. Phinuel and Christian McLene, daus. of Thomas. Grandch., Samuel and Mary Ann McPherrin and a dau. Mary, wife of Samuel Smith.

Historical Sketch of Franklin County, by I. H. McCauley, p. 118.

HENRY POLAN (PAWLING)

Is shown as a First Lieut., 1777-78, also in 1780-81, serving under Capts. Elias Davison and Wm. Berryhill. The late Dr. Franklin A. Bushey, of Greencastle stated that Henry Pawling was a brother of one Thomas Paulding who assisted in the capture of Major Andre as the latter was returning from his meeting with Benedict Arnold. He died Feb. 15, 1794, aged 47 yrs. His estate was admr. by Benj. Price and wife Sarah in 1809. The ancestor of the Pawling family, according to information submitted through the courtesy of Dr. Mary A. Laughlin, was Capt. Henry Pawling, who came to the island of Manhattan in 1664 as a soldier in the expedition of the Duke of York against the Dutch. It is known that his sons, John and Henry Pawling, soon moved with their families from Kingston, N. Y., to what was then Philadelphia County, Penna. The Henry Pawling who is buried at Brown's Mill was a native of Montgomery County and was probably a grandson of the first Henry. Coming to the Conococheague settlement as an early settler, he married a daughter of Nicholas and Elizabeth Hicks, whose daughter, Elizabeth, married Henry Prather. He had two children, Henry, unmar., and Eleanor mar. Dr. Robert Johnston. Famous in the early history of Antrim Twp., was Pawling's or Pollen's tavern, which stood about two miles south of Greencastle near the present Williamsport pike and was conducted by Henry Pawling. This tavern was on the route from Philadelphia to Pittsburgh and was regarded as the western limit of safety for travelers. It is mentioned in Colonial documents as early as 1765 when, in spite of an order of the King forbidding the colonists to trade with the Indians, a number of Philadelphia merchants sent a caravan of goods to "Pollen's Tavern" and presumably disposed of them. His son Henry served in the militia during the Rev. War and his daughter Elinor mar. the distinguished Antrim surgeon, Dr. Robert Johnston. Henry Pawling was a delegate from 2nd. Batt. Cumb. Co. Militia to a meeting at Lancaster, July 4, 1776.

Penna. Arch . 5th Ser. Vol. 6, p. 513, 533, 581, 598. Penna. Arch. 5th Ser. Vol. 5, p. 21.

CAPTAIN JAMES POE

Was born in Antrim Twp., Franklin Co., Penna., Apr. 15, 1742. He mar. Elizabeth, eldest dau. of Maj. Gen. James Potter. At the beginning of the Rev. War, James Poe was a Lieut. in Col. John Allison's Batt. of Penna. Militia, which served under Gen. Hugh Mercer at Perth Amboy, N. J., in the autumn of 1776. He served as Captain under Col. Abraham Smith in 1777-79. The inscription on his tombstone is: "Sacred to the memory of James Poe, Esq., a patriot of the Revolution of 1776. A sincere friend and honest man, and a professor of the Christian religion, who departed this life June 22, 1822, aged 71 years." "Sacred to the memory of Elizabeth Poe, consort of James Poe, Esq. A worthy friend and a sincere christian, who departed this life, Sept. 11, 1819, aged 52 years." They had issue: Margaret Latimer, who mar. James Campbell of St. Thomas Twp.; Thomas was the eldest son of Capt. James and Elizabeth Poe; James Poe, Jr.; Mary Poe mar. Matthias Nead, Esq.; John Poe. "Sheriff John Potter, Thomas Poe, Sr., and their wives, and Gen. James Potter and his wife Elizabeth Cathcart, are all buried in Brown's burying ground, near Kauffman's Station. No stone marks any of their graves."

Penna. Arch. 5th Ser. Vol. 6, p. 91, 512, 520, 523, 532, 571, 575, 582. Kittichtinny Magazine, Vol. 7, p. 45.

MAJOR GENERAL JAMES POTTER

Col. Penna. Militia 1776-1777; wounded at Princeton 3rd Jan., 1777; Brig. Gen. Penna. Militia April 5, 1777; Maj. Gen. Penna. Militia May 23, 1782; served until the close of the war. James Potter was b. in Tyrone, Ireland, in 1729, and must have come to this country as a very young child. By 1755, at the age of 26, he had attained the rank of captain in the French and Indian war. In 1763-64 he was in active service as a major during the Pontiac war. When the Enoch Brown massacre occurred on July 26, 1764, it was Potter who led the expedition that attempted to overtake and punish the murders. In 1781 he was named a member of the Supreme Executive Council of Pennsylvania, on which James McLene had served a few years previously, and in the same year he was elected vice president of Pennsylvania. General Potter was twice married. His first wife was Elizabeth Cathcart, of Philadelphia, and his second was Mrs. Mary Patterson Chambers. His home during the latter part of his life was a fortified log house in Penn's Valley. He died in Antrim Township while visiting his daughter.

Letter to James H. Potter from General George Washington:

Headquarters Peter Wentz's, October 18, 1777. Sir:—I congratulate you upon the glorious success of our Armies in the North, an account of which is enclosed. This singular "fafour" of Providence is to be received with thankfulness and the happy moment which Heaven has pointed out for the firm establishment of American Liberty ought to be embraced with the coming spirit. It is encumbered upon every man of influence in his country to prevail upon the militia to take the field with that energy which the present crisis evidently demands. I have no doubt of your exarting yourself in this way. In the post which you now occupy, you may render the most important service by cutting off the enemy's convoys and communications with their fleet. For this purpose you should strain every nerve and there is another thing which I would suggest and leave you the judge of the practicibility of it. I think that you might harrass the parties who are located at Fort Mifflin . . . Let me again entreat you, and through you may every one of any influence among the militia, to exert it to the utmost in exciting them to the field where by renewed re-inforcements the glorious work we have in hand will be completed.

I am your most humble servant,
George Washington.

Heitman's Register of Officers of the Continental Army. p. 449.

WILLIAM REYNOLDS

Served as 1st Lieut. under Capt. Patrick Jack, 1777-78-80-81-82. Son of John and Ruth (Brown) Reynolds. His wife, Ruth Maxwell, is buried beside him. He was of Hamilton Twp. and names issue: dau. Mary Reynolds; sons Thomas; Wm.; John; James; daus. Susanna and Sarah; Susanna mar. Chas. Campbell; Wm. mar. Jane Holliday; Sarah mar. Thos. McLene; Thomas mar. Mary Speer. Members in 1769 of "Upper West Conococheague" Church, Mercersburg, Penna. Deeds show in 1794, that James Campbell and Wm. Reynolds, as Extris of the last Will of John Reynolds, Sell to Andrew LeMaster a tract of land granted in 1770 by the Prop. of Penna.; Said to be in Antrim Twp., but is actually in Guilf. Twp., now Franklin County. The tract called Rawnells Pasture, by Joseph Cook, Chas. McCormick and John Coyles land—100 acres, For £ 450 £ they sell to Andrew LeMaster.

Penna. Arch. 5th Ser. Vol. 6, p. 367, 376, 312, 291, 262.

ANDREW ROBISON

Shown serving under Capt. James Poe. His wife was Margaret Smith, dau. of James and Jennet Smith, early settlers in Antrim Twp. In the will of James Smith, May, 1764, he names Andrew Robinson as his son-in-law. It is probable he mar. twice; he names issue; Robert; Andrew; Joseph; James; Margaret; Mary; Esther; Rebeckah; Jennett. He appoints his sons Robert and Andrew as Executors, with Abhm. Smith and James Johnston as Guardians "to have Justice done to my young children." The will was dated Nov. 1794; prob. Jan. 1795. In Deed Book 10, 1832, is this: Mary Wason, sister of Andrew Robinson, of Antrim Twp., now all of Campbell Co., Ky., issue: Wm. Wason, wife Frances Jane; Henry Hawly, wife Elizabeth; John A. Goodson, wife Esther, legal representtaives.

Penna. Arch. 5th Ser. Vol. 6, p. 586.

RICHARD WRIGHT

Served under Capts. James Poe, John Jack and Thos. Johnston, under the First Call, 1777, in 1779-80-81-82. He died 1786, leaving a wife Jane who died Dec. 22, 1822, aged 78 yrs. Their dau. Rebecca mar. Charles Nill, she dying Mch. 1827, her husband dying June 1835, aged 72 yrs. Penna. Arch. 5th Ser. Vol. 6, p. 84, 114, 129, 521, 523.

CEDAR HILL CEMETERY
Greencastle, Penna.

JOHN ALLISON

On July 12, 1774, was a member of the Committee of Observation for Cumb. Co., Penna., with title of Colonel under "Officers in Service." He was appointed Justice of the Peace Oct. 17, 1764, May 23, 1770, April 6, 1771. His wife was Elizabeth Wilkin. He died June 14, 1795 in his 57th year. He lived esteemed and died regretted by the virtuous. His wife died May 15, 1815, aged 67 years, 8 days. They are buried in the above graveyard. To his wife he left 20 acres of land on which the town of Greencastle stands, and 200 pounds; brother Wm.; brother-in-law Wm. Henderson, Esq.; oldest son Wm.; 3 youngest sons Robert; Patrick; Wilkin; 7 daus: Mary, wife of Andrew Henderson; Catherine; Margaret; Agnes; Elizabeth; Lydia and Rebecca Allison. In 1791 John Allison is taxed with 608 acres and 80 acres land; 3 slaves; 8 cows; 6 horses; 1 house and lot; saw and grist mill; 1 lot; 1 chair; ground rent. In 1794 a similar tax, but 1 carriage is added to the above. John Allison was a Delegate to the Provincial Conference held at Carpenter's Hall, Phila., June 18, 1775, from the County of Cumberland.

Penna. Arch. 2nd Ser. Vol. 3, p. 594. Penna. Arch. 5th Ser. Vol. 6, p. 4, 5, 79, 586.

WILLIAM ALLISON

Was a pvt. under Captains Thomas Johnston and Wm. Berryhill. Under Taxables of Antrim in 1804, Wm. Allison is shown with 431 ac. land; 1 Distillery; 3 slaves; 6 horses; 12 horned cattle. His will was dated August and prob. Oct. 1825. He died Sept. 1825 in his 76th year, his wife being Mary McLanahan. They had issue: son James; dau. Mary; sons John and Robert; son Samuel; dau. Isabella Boggs. Some negro boys and a girl Priscilla were also named in the Will.

Penna. Arch. 5th Ser. Vol. 6, p. 81, 98, 102, 130.

LUDWIG EMRICK, SERGT.

Served under Capt. Wm. Laird in Lancaster Co. in 1781. He was b. July 1, 1754, d. Feb. 13, 1822. He signed the Test Oath in Hanover Twp. Lancaster Co. in 1778. His widow Susanah Eminger Emrick b. Jan. 3, 1757, d. May 18, 1848. She is lying in Quincy Graveyard near her dau. Elizabeth who mar. David Wertz. The will of Susanna Emrick was dated 1842; she named "8 of my children,"—son-in-law David Wertz; to Mary Bell, widow of Frederick Bell, decd.; Barbara mar. Jacob Bell; Margaret mar. Samuel Garver; Catherine mar. George Wertz; Peter Emerick; Magdalena mar. John Runkle; Elizabeth mar. David Wertz; Susanna mar. David Brumbaugh; sons John and George Emerick, decd.

Penna. Arch. 5th Ser. Vol. 7, p. 942.

JOHN GAFF

Served as pvt. 1778-80-81, under Capts. Wm. Findlay and Wm. Berryhill. The Ledger of Samuel Findlay, father of Governor Wm. Findlay, shows a charge against James Johnston, Aug. 11, 1775, for Broad-cloth and silk for John Gaff. His wife was Sarah, a dau. of John Rule. John Gaff d. Dec. 11, 1822, in his 87th year. He left issue: John; Mary Ann unmar. Jane mar. Alexdr. Latta; Elizabeth mar. John Scott; Sarah; Margaret.

Penna. Arch. 5th Ser. Vol. 6, p. 73, 80, 102, 527.

LIEUT. COL. JAMES JOHNSTON

The First Batt. in service March 1778. Under Commissary in 1778, is James Johnston. In 1780, John Jack was Major with Lieut. Col. Johnston. Page 103 lists the "Seventh Company of the first Battalion of Cumberland County, under Col. James Johnston" in 1781. The service of Col. James Johnston covered the years 1777-78-80-81-82, and the pages below attest that service. His wife was Jane Park of Bucks County, Penna.

Penna. Arch. 5th Ser. Vol. 6, p. 3, 38, 69, 77, 81, 83, 86, 90, 92, 100, 103, 105, 109, 113, 118, 137, 125, 129, 510, 531.

ROBERT JOHNSTON

Surgeon, appointed Jan. 16, 1776; in Service to 1781 when he was ordered by Gen. Greene to leave the regimental service and assist the wounded officers and soldiers of the American Army, prisoners in the British hospital in Charleston, S. C. Dr. Johnston d. Nov. 25, 1808, aged 58 yrs., near Waynesboro, Franklin Co., Penna. He was Major General of Seventh Division of Penna. Militia, appointed July 24, 1807. Chambersburg, Penna. Court records, Will Book B, p. 355. Will of Robert Johnston, Major General, of Antrim Twp.; wife Eleanor ½ personal est., her living in this my dwelling house, ½ the income of my plantation, and all my negroes; nephew John Boggs all my library . . . with a Bible, also my pistols and fire arms with my side arms, also the diploma I got of the Cincinata with the medal and appoint him to be my representative in the Society of the Cincinata; Eleanor Johnston Corman 100 lbs; Johnston Elliott, Jr. son to Eleanor Warden (formerly Elliott) 100 lbs; Aunt Brown's four daus. $200.; sons of Samuel Findlay decd., they being my nephews, and to Elizabeth Dunlop, dau. of Wm. Findlay, decd., and to the sons and daus. of my sister Mary Beatty, and the sons and daus. of my bro. John Johnston and the sons and daus. of my sister Elizabeth Boggs and the daus. of my sister Martha Campbell, all of said legatees being my nephews and nieces and to Rebecca Prather, a relation to my wife and to Elizabeth McLanahan (formerly Gordon) also related to my wife, the residue of my estate; trustees of Dickinson College at Carlisle 50 lbs; 50 lbs. to and for the use of the poor House near Chambersburg; brother James Johnston my canes; Adesa Dunlop, dau. to Andrew Dunlop, Esq., attorney in Chambersburg, 100 lbs. Exrs: Archibald Baird, Esq., John Findlay and Robert Johnston of John. Wit: Abm. Prather, Henry Prather, Wm. Shannon. Chambersburg, Penna., Court records show an Article of Agreement between Dr. Robert Johnston, James Dickey & James Buchanan of Franklin Co., Penna., having now purchased of Messrs Michael and Charles Campbell, of Nelson Co., Ky., 5900 acres land, Patents issued 1786, tenants in Common, under date of Mar. 11, 1796. In reply to a question concerning Eleanor Pawling, wife of Dr. Robert Johnston, Dr. Mary A. Laughlin sent the following some years ago: Her mother as you know was Mary Hicks, daughter of Nicholas Hicks, who was one of the earliest settlers in the Greencastle neighborhood; he died in 1749. The younger daughter was Elizabeth who married Henry Prather in 1754. My ancestor, Thomas Prather was their eldest son; Eleanor Pawling married Dr. Robert Johnston, the Revolutionary surgeon. They had no children, and her brother Henry died early, without issue. The wife of her cousin Thomas Prather died, leaving three boys and one little girl. She took the little girl and brought her up as a daughter; this child was Rebecca Prather, my great-grandmother, who married John M. Pawling, a relative of Mrs. Johnston on the Pawling side. Her father I believe was a man of means as was her husband. In her will probated 1818, she disposes of more than 1400 acres of land, some of the best in Franklin County. Most of her furniture she gave to John M. Pawling and it is still in the family. The stone mansions that belonged to her and husband are well preserved.

Penna. Arch. 2nd Ser. Vol. 10, p. 172.

THOMAS JOHNSTON

First Lieut. of the Flying Camp, appointed Jan. 21, 1777. In July, 1777, he was Adjutant under Col. Abhm. Smith in the Eighth Batt. with his brothers, Lieut. Col. James Johnston, Maj. John Johnston, with Terrance Campbell as Quarter Master. The arrangement the same in May, 1778, and in May, 1780, Thomas Johnston was Capt. of the 6th Co. First Batt. of Cumb. Co. Militia and Associators. Thomas Johnston, 1744-1819, mar. Martha Beatty, who died Aug. 1811; they had issue: James; Thomas; Nancy mar. James Moore; Elizabeth mar. John McLanahan; Martha mar. Stephen O. Brown. To his eldest son James Lieut. Johnston willed his sword and rifle.

Penna. Arch. 2nd Ser. Vol. 10, p. 281—also, 5th Ser. Vol. 2, p. 542, 544. 5th Ser. Vol. 6, p. 511, 530, 531, 70. McCauley's Hist. Franklin County, p. 87.

The Johnston brothers named in these records: James Johnston who died 1765, is named as one of the four early settlers in Antrim Twp., about 1735. His wife was Elizabeth Brown (Findlay) Johnston, and in addition to the four prominent Johnston sons, there were three daughters: Mary J. b. 1746 mar. Wm. Beatty; Martha J. b. 1749, mar. Dugal Campbell; Elizabeth J. b. 1751, mar. John Boggs.

JAMES MCCLENAHAN, SR.

Was a .pvt. under Capt. Wm. Berryhill, 1780-81-82. On pages 79, 101 James McClenahan is shown with James, Jr. presumably his son, years 1780-81. James McLanahan, Sr. mar. Isabella Craig. They are buried in above Cemetery.

Penna. Arch. 5th Ser. Vol. 6, p. 101, 123.

FREDERICK SHELE (SHEELY)

Served as a pvt. under Capt. Alexdr. Peebles, 1777, 78-79-80. He was b. Jan. 10, 1733, d. Mar. 31, 1800. Catherine, his wife, d. July 26,

aged 87 yrs. 10 mos. 20 days. Frederick Sheely b. Sept. 12, 1785, d. Sept. 6, 1858.
Penna. Arch. 5th Ser. Vol. 6, p. 51, 54, 57, 25, 395, 589.

JOSEPH SNIVELY

Served as pvt. under Capt. Wm. Berryhill, 1780-81-82. In 1810, Joseph Snively, Sr. of Antrim Twp., sold 2 tracts of land. One called "Hymen's Bower" in Antrim Twp., the other in Washington Twp., called "Wheatfield," both sold to Christian Shelly. Joseph Snively, 1748-1833, mar. 1771, Magdalena Stoner, who d. 1795. They had issue: Barbara, mar. Martin Baechtel; Jacob mar. Elizabeth Stoner; Anna mar. Isaac Garber; John mar. Catherine Poorman; Joseph mar. Nancy Baechtel.
Penna. Arch. 5th Ser. Vol. 6, p. 73, 80, 102.

ADAM VONDERAU

Born in Austria 1756, d. in Antrim Twp., Franklin County, 1819. He served in Lancaster County, Penna.; furnishing Forage and Service for the Revolutionary Magazines at Lancaster and Lebanon, 1778-79. He also signed the Oath of Allegiance. He mar. 1786, Margaret (Rupley) Snyder, widow, at Lancaster, Penna. Issue: Adam mar. Sarah Hines; Wm. mar. Mary Shaeffer; Jacob mar. Charlotte Kreps; Margaret mar. Matthias Walter; Kitty mar. Barnabas Walter.
Nat. Genealog. Society Quarterly, Vol. 16, No. 3, p. 41. June—1928.

JOHN ZOUSE

Served as a pvt. under Capt. Wm. Berryhill, 1780-81-82. His wife was Catherine Smith. John Joshua Yous, Oct. 6, 1740-Nov. 1, 1812. Catherine Yous, May, 6, 1757-Sept. 14, 1837. Orphans' Court Book C, p. 508. Petition of Solomon Eckert mar. to Catherine, dau. of John Youst, of Montgomery Twp., who d. intestate, in 1812, leaving a widow and 7 children: Mary; Margaret; Catherine mar. to Solomon Eckert; Elizabeth mar. to John Evert, or Ebbert; Jacob, since decd., unmar. no issue; John and Susanna.
Penna. Arch. 5th Ser. Vol. 6, p. 79, 101, 123, 586.

EARLY PRESBYTERIAN & LUTHERAN GRAVEYARD

St. Thomas, Penna.

BENJAMIN JEFFREY

Served under Capts. John McConnell and Patrick Jack, 1778-81-82. His wife was Ann Swan; his parents, John Jeffrey and Rachel (Chambers) Jeffrey, one of the three sisters of Col. Benj. Chambers. John Jeffrey was b. Nov. 5, 1788; Catherine Jeffrey was b. July 11, 1790. From his tombstone we have this: "A Soldier of our Independence, shot thru the right shoulder at the Battle of Brandywine by a British light-horseman; d. May, 1833, aged 81 years." Their son John, b. Oct., 1788, d. in defense of his country at Erie, Apr., 1814. John Jeffrey was born Nov. 5, 1788; Catheryn Jeffrey was born July 11, 1790; Rachel Jeffrey was born June 1, 1792; Rebekah Jeffrey was born July 28, 1794; Margaret Jeffrey was born Feb. 1, 1797; John Burtsfield and Rachel Jeffries, April 3, 1816; Thomas Eager and Catherine Jeffries, June 3, 1819; (Catherine Jeffries Eager mar. 2nd David Dixon); John Swan and Rebecca Jeffrey, Sept. 10, 1822; James Forbes and Margaret Jeffries, June 2, 1825; David Dixon and Catherine Eager, May 25, 1833; (Dr. J. H. Swan, St. Thomas, Penna., a descendant). Above marriages by Dr. David Denny "Translated Diligently Compared and Revised By His Majesty's Special Command Appointed to be read in Churches." Edenburg. MDCCLXXXIV (1784)
Benjamin Jeffrey Bible in the possession of Mrs. E. B. Diehl of St. Thomas, Penna.
Penna. Arch. 5th Ser. Vol. 6, p. 374, 281, 292, 313,—also Vol. 4, p. 629, as above—Cont. Line in Cumberland County, Penna.

FREDERICK KISSEL (KESSEL)

Served 1781-82, under Capt. Henry Custer (Kushter) Lancaster County, Militia. He came from Warwick Twp., to St. Thomas Twp., Franklin County. In his will, prob. May 24, 1841, he names his children: George; Frederick; John; Catherine; Rebecka; Elizabeth; Barbara; Mary; Susan. He outlived two wives; his consort Elizabeth d. Sept., 1827, in her 68th year; his consort Elizabeth d. June, 1832 in the 51st year of her age. A descendant states that Fredk. Kissell was buried between the two wives, and it is believed to be correct.

Penna. Arch. 5th Ser. Vol. 7, p. 265, 299, 301, 303, 616.

JOHN UNGER

Served as a pvt. in Lancaster County, Penna., under Capt. George Feather in 1778-79, and under Col. Geo. Feather and Capt. Michael Oberly in 1781-82. He was b. Mar. 23, 1755, and d. Mar. 19, 1825. His wife Christiana was b. Nov. 19, 1751, d. Oct. 20, 1821. He came from Warwick Twp., Lancaster County, Penna. He and his wife are buried in above graveyard. His will dated 1823, prob. Apr. 20, 1825, names his wife Christena; grandson John Coyner; dau. Elizabeth Swaggert and her heirs. He lived in Peters Twp.

Penna. Arch. 5th Ser. Vol. 7. p. 254, 308, 875, 897.

FAIRVIEW CEMETERY
Mercersburg, Penna.
(Removals)

HENRY SPANGLER

Born in York Town, Penna. Served as pvt. in York Town Guards in 1778. He was in the Upper District of same. He was born Feb. 2, 1761, died in Mercersburg, Penna., Aug. 17, 1837. His wife Susanna, b. Jan. 1, 1768, d. Sept. 5, 1855, aged 87 yrs. She was a dau. of Ignacius Lightner. They were buried in the old Reformed and Lutheran graveyard later removed to above cemetery. They had issue: George, b. 1789, mar. Mary Fields; Rebecca b. 1792, mar John Hart; Lenah, b. 1793, mar. Nathaniel Small; Henry, b. 1795, mar. Mary Aspey; Cassandra, b. 1797, mar. Henry Lightner; Margaret b. 1798, mar. John Gueyer; Catherine, b. 1800, mar. James Wilkins; Charlotte, b. 1801, mar. Henry Delebaugh; Nathaniel, b. 1802, mar. Sarah Scott; Susannah, b. 1805, mar. Samuel Palsgrove; John, b. 1807, mar. Eliza Keyser; Hannah, b. 1811, mar. John Black; Lydia, b. 1813, d. unmarried.

Penna. Arch. pth Ser. Vol. 2, p. 713—also Annals of the Spangler Family, p. 128.

WIILIAM WADDELL

Served as pvt in 1776-77-81-82 under Captains James McConnell, John McConnell & George Crawford. He mar. Elizabeth, dau. of Thos. Stockton. They had sons Thomas mar. Catherine Long & William mar. Margaret McMullen. William Waddell, Sr., d. 1830, aged 86 yrs. His wife Elizabeth b. 1759, d. 1808. William Waddell was a son of Thos. Waddell early settler in Peters Twp.; a Boulder with Tablet has been erected by Franklin County, Chapter, D. A. R., to mark the site of the Fort on Thos, Waddell's plantation.

Penna. Arch. 5th Ser. Vol. 6, p. 288, 301, 309, 317, 318, 371.

FALLING SPRING PRESBYTERIAN GRAVEYARD
Chambersburg, Penna.

The "Falling Spring" was the name given by pioneer Benjamin Chambers, to the place of his settlement, at the confluence of the large spring, with the Conococheague Creek. Col. Chambers, himself a Presbyterian, made an early appropriation of some suitable ground for a GRAVEYARD, SCHOOL HOUSE and PLACE of PUBLIC WORSHIP. This was the romantic Cedar Grove on the bank of the creek, on which the present church stands. In this grove, and near the spot which the present church occupies, there was erected a small log building, which was used for the double purpose of a school house and place of worship, and which Records of Presbytery show to have been in the year 1739. It was of logs, with doors on eastern and southern sides, and lighted by long narrow windows the width of two small panes of glass. When this building was not of sufficient capacity for all who wished to worship in it, the congregation abandoned it for the time in favour of the saw-mill of Col. Chambers, which stood on the bank of the creek, on what was known as "The Island" surrounded by a lovely green plot. On that grassy space the gathered crowd seated themselves and received with interest and eagerness the messages of God from his commissioned ambassador.

Ref. —Churches of the Valley.

JOSEPH ALLISON

Served from Little Britain Twp., Lancaster County, Penna., as a Captain 1777-79, 2nd Batt. Lancaster County Militia. In 1781-82 as a Clerk and pvt. under Capt. Robert Campbell. In the will of John Allison (1782) Lancaster, he bequeaths land to his son Joseph, who with wife Anne, of Chambers Town, Franklin County, Penna., sold to Robert McClelland of Lancaster County, Penna. One of the conveyances to Joseph Allison shows him buying Lot 217 in Chambersburg. He died Jan. 11, 1813, aged 61 yrs., and Anne died June 14, 1829, aged 70 yrs. Their dau. Mary d. Sept. 9, 1812, aged 15 yrs. They left issue: Hugh; Martha; Mary; Jane Ann; Eleanor Susannah. The Franklin Repository dated May 10, 1814, gives this: "Married in this boro on Tuesday evening, by Rev. Denny, James McCamey, of Washington, Penna., to Miss Martha, dau. of Joseph Allison, late of Chambersburg, decd."

Penna. Arch. 5th Ser. Vol. 7, p. 104, 108, 112, 114, 600, 622, 1130, 1131, 1132. Also Deed Books at Lancaster and Chambersburg, Penna.

ROBERT ALLISON

11th Penna. Regt., Mar. 16, 1780,—died in Franklin County, Apr. 24, 1836. Ensign, 1778, 11th Penna., Regt. Lieut. 1780. In 3rd Penna. Regt. in 1781. Lieut. Allison was a member of the Society of the Cincinnati. In his will he names wife Catherine and children—unmar. "The Whig," May 6, 1836, Died, Major Robert Allison, at his residence in this place (Chambersburg) on the 21" ult. The last officer of the Revolution whose lot was cast among us . . . A Military funeral . . . He entered the Army 1775 as pvt.,—1777 as Ensign; 1st and 2nd Lieut., Adjt., Col. Thos. Hartley's Regt. Penna. Line. In the pension application of Robert Allison, he stated he was 76 yrs. of age in 1818. Mary, dau. of Maj. Robert Allison was mar. to John Whetstone, May 22, 1827, by Rev. Rauhouser. Catherine, widow of Robert Allison applied for pension in 1837. In the will of Catherine Allison of Chambg., she names a dau. Eveline Catherine; also daus. Mary and Margaret, a son Wm. Allison and grandson Wm. Allison Whetstone, son of dau. Mary; son Alexander and his heirs. Will dated Sept. 23, 1840; prob. Mar. 9, 1846.

Penna. Arch. 5th Ser. Vol. 2, p. 976.
Penna. Arch. 2nd Ser. Vol. 11, p. 52, 55, 56, 59.
Penna. Arch. 2nd Ser. Vol. 10, p. 460, 462, 799.

OWEN ASTON (ASHTON)

Is shown as a Soldier in the Cont. Line, also as a Quarter Master and pvt. in Cumberland County Militia, 1779-80-81, under Capt. James Young. Isabella Barnet, in her Will (1800) names the three daus. of Capt. Owen Aston: The Misses Elizabeth, Williana and Sally Aston. The Franklin Repository, Sept. 30, 1806, gives: "On Thursday evening last, Mr. Elijah Mendenhall to Miss Betsy Aston, dau. of Capt. Owen Aston, all of this place." Quoting under Sept. 22, 1807, "Died on 14th inst., Mrs. Williana Magaw, wife of Samuel B. Magaw of Meadville, dau. of Mr. Owen Aston of this borough; she was on a visit to her friends in this place, left two small children, a tender husband, &c, &c." They were married by Dr. David Denny in 1802, who also married Sally Aston to Andrew Work (of Henry), Mar. 25, 1802. The Franklin Repository, Dec. 13, 1814: "Departed this life on Tuesday morning last in the 78th year of his age, Capt. Owen Aston of this Boro. He left an aged widow to bemoan the remnant of her days, the bereftment of a companion endeared by 50 years of connubial happiness." The Baltimore Chronicle, Feb. 8, 1830 gives: "Died in this Borough on Wednesday last in her 95th year, Mrs. Rachel Aston, relict of Capt. Owen Aston." Summers Annals of South West, Va., p. 583—Will Book A, p. 583, Botetourt County, shows the will of Joseph Phipps, prob. Feb. 11, 1772. He appears to have been from Chester County, Penna., and names a dau. Rachael Aston, wife of Owen Aston of Cumberland County, Penna., also a dau. Hannah Aston, wife of George Aston, of Bortetourt County, Va.

Penna. Arch. 5th Ser. Vol. 4, p. 619. Penna. Arch. 5th Ser. Vol. 6, p. 81, 109, 547.

MOSES BARNET

Served under Captains James Young and Terrence Campbell, 1780-81-82. He died Dec. 4, 1796, aged 61 yrs. His wife, Isabella, left a will prob. May 13, 1800, "To testify the esteem and regard for kindness during several indispositions, I will to the three daughters of Capt. Owen Aston, the whole of my estate—Miss Elizabeth, Miss Williana, Miss Sally Aston, a debt I owe them for their attention to me." Moses Barnet is shown as occupying Pew 48 in the old Log Church at Rocky Spring.

Penna Arch 5th Ser. Vol. 6, p. 83, 100, 111, 126.

JOHN CALHOUN (COLHOUN) (COLHOON)

Was on the Com. of Observation for the County of Cumberland, July 12, 1774. Dr. John Colhoon serving in 1777, with Capt. Alexdr. Peebles and as Dr. John Colhoon, 1779 with Capt. James Young. John Colhoon was a Delegate to the Conventions Meeting in Carpenter's Hall, Phila., June 18, 1775, and 1776, representing Cumberland County, Penna. Other men on that Committee from the present Franklin County, were in 1775 and 1776, James McLene; John Allison; John Maclay; Wm. Elliott. Dr. John Colhoon, b. 1740, d. 1782, "a gentleman of education," who had been regularly instructed in the science of medicine; as the settlement of Chambersburg increased in number a physician was needed and Dr. John Colhoon came to the place. We know little about his early life further than that he was a native of Cumberland County. He lived in the white weather-board house on the N. E. corner of Main & King Sts., for some years; in 1782 began the erection of a fine stone house now (1938) the Sellers Funeral Home. Dr. Colhoon died before this house was completed, but his widow Ruhamah Chambers lived there for some years, and it was here that her father Col. Benj. Chambers died in 1788 after an illness of a few hours. Dr. John Colhoon mar. Ruhamah Chambers, b. 1750, d. 1826. They had issue: Rebecca, b. 1775, d. 1839, mar. Edw. Crawford, Jr. b. 1757, d. 1833; Benjamin Colhoon mar. Lily Kennedy Risk; Jane; Elizabeth, unmar. buried in the Washington Plot, Pittsburgh, Penna. Ruhama, widow of Dr. John Colhoon, was taxed in Franklin Twp., 1791, with: House and Lot; 1 unimproved lot; 18 acres land; 1 negro; 2 cows; Teaspoons 10; Tablespoons & Ladle, 6.

Penna. Arch. 5th Ser. Vol. 6, p. 4, 549, 590. Penna. Arch. 2nd Ser. Vol. 3, p. 558, 577, 579, 594.

JOHN CALHOUN

Merchant, served as pvt. under Capt. James Young, 1780-81-82. He died 1822, aged 70 yrs. His first wife was Agnes, dau of Alexdr. Thompson of Green Twp., and wife Elizabeth. He left a widow Mary and minor children; Dorcas; Agnes; John; Samual; William and Mary; also Elizabeth, widow of John Cambell; Alexander; Eleanor, mar. to James Culbertson; Andrew; James.

Penna. Arch. 5th Ser. Vol. 6, p. 82, 110, 125.

COL. BENJAMIN CHAMBERS

On Mar. 30, 1734, Samuel Blunston granted to Benj. Chambers, 400 acres of Land at the Falling Spring's mouth and on both sides of the Conococheague Creek for the conveniency of a Grist Mill and plantation. It was a license, not a warrant, and he next built himself a house, which was burned, but he followed that with a better house, and then with a Mill for the benefit of the early settlers. In 1747-48, an Associated Regt. was formed, of which Benj. Chambers was made Colonel, with Robert Dunning as Lieut. Col., and Wm. Maxwell as Major. On the erection of Cumberland County, Col. Chambers was the first collector of the excise and one of the first Justices of the Peace. He was active in the defense of the frontier during the French and Indian War. Much has been written of his "great guns" and for eight years, 1756-64, Fort Chambers served as a place of retreat for the people of East Conococheague. In 1764 Colonel Chambers laid out a town "on both sides of the great Falling Spring where it falls into the said Creek." After the erection of Franklin County in 1784, with Chambersburg as the County Seat, the growth of the town was more rapid. On Jan. 1, 1768, Col. Chambers set apart grounds for the Falling Spring Church and graveyard, the consideration was the annual payment of one rose, if required. It has been said that the early meetings of the Falling Spring Church Members, were held in Benj. Chambers' saw mill. He mar. 1st in 1741, Sarah, dau. of Capt. Robert Patterson of Lancaster County; they had issue: James, 1743-1805. Col. Chambers mar. 2nd in 1748, Jane Williams, dau. of Rev. Wm. Williams, who was sent from Wales to America as a Presbyterian Missionary to the then Colony of Virginia. Under a Maryland Patent, Rev. Williams was granted a tract, Nov. 17, 1741, called "Green Bottom," known as the Rees Price farm. The will of Rev. Williams, 1759, names his three daus: Ahatama Chapline; Sarah Price; Jane Chambers. It was wife Jane who joined with Col. Chambers in selling Lots in the Town of Chambersburg. They had issue: Ruhamah; Williams; Benjamin; Joseph; George; Jane; Hadassah.

Penna. Arch. 5th Ser. Vol. 1, p. 24, 25, 31. Provincial Service.

FIRST LIEUT. BENJAMIN CHAMBERS

Served with Col. Wm. Thompson's Batt. of Rifflemen, and also in the Continental Line, First Penna., under Colonels Edward Hand and James Chambers. Lieut. Chambers was at Boston, Battle of Long Island, Brandywine and Germantown. He married Sarah Brown, dau. of George and Agnes (Maxwell) Brown in 1783. They had issue: George; Benjamin; William; Joseph; Thomas; Sarah; Susan. Their home "White Rock"was at Mont Alto. The Repository, under Jan. 4, 1814,—"Died on Wednesday last, Capt.

Benj. Chambers, in his 58th year. He left a wife and seven children. His widow, b. 1759, d. 1837.
Penna. Arch. 5th Ser. Vol. 2, p. 17, 629.

GEORGE CHAMBERS

Served as pvt. 1780-81-82, under Captains James Young and Terrence Campbell. He was b. 1760, d. unmar., in 1802. He joined with his brothers in establishing Mount Pleasant Iron Works, at the entrance of Path Valley in 1783. In 1791, George Chambers is taxed in Fannett Twp., with: 500 and 1200 acres of land; 1 mulato servant; 15 Horses; 9 Cows; 1 Furnace; 1 Grist Mill; 1 Saw Mill.
Penna. Arch. 5th Ser. Vol. 6, p. 82, 110, 126.

JOSEPH CHAMBERS

Served as pvt. 1779-80-81-82, under Captains James Young and Terrence Campbell and in 1781 he was in Capt. John Johnston's Light Dragoons for twenty-five days, under James Culbertson, Cornet. Mr. Chambers mar. Margaret Rippey (1769-1820), dau. of Capt. Wm. and Margaret Finley Rippey. They had a dau. Margaret, who mar. Rev. John McKnight (1789-1857), pastor of the Rocky Spring Church, 1816-1836. From the Repository, under date Dec. 27, 1814, "Died on his farm near Chambersburg, Mr. Joseph Chambers, the last of five sons of that deservedly respected gentleman, the late Col. Benj. Chambers. He was aged 55 yrs., lacking two days, departed at 6 A. M. 23rd inst He leaves a wife and one daughter. His confinement was only seven days.
Penna. Arch. 5th Ser. Vol. 6, p. 77, 82, 111, 126, 548, 640.

COL. JAMES CHAMBERS

Captain 1775 of a company raised in that part of Cumberland County, which is now Franklin County, company attached to Col Wm. Thompson's Batt. of Riflemen and was at Cambridge Aug. 13, 1775. Commissioned Lieut. Col. Mar. 7, 1776, promoted to Col. Sept. 28, 1776, and assigned to 10th Penna. Transferred Apr. 12, 1777, to 1st Penna. Continental Line, was wounded at Brandywine and retired from service Jan. 1, 1781, War of the Revolution. From letter of Col. James Chambers, to the Supreme Ex. Council, soliciting the appointment of Prothonotary for the proposed new County of Franklin, dated June 26, 1782: "I entered the Service June, 1775, first Captain in the first Regt., Ever Raised by Congress; about fifteen months after was promoted to the Command of the Regt., and continued in that capacity to the last Arrangement of troops, the first of January, 1781. The situation of my family at that time induced me to retire. I had served my County Six Campaigns —and I think I may say— with some propriety— almost for nothing and found myself." The will of Gen. James Chambers of Loudon Forge, Peters Twp., late Colonel commanding the first Regiment raised by Congress in the Revolutionary War of the United States; Dearly beloved wife Catherine the use and benefit of my real estate and personal property; the forge to be kept at rent; dau: Sarah Bella Dunlap 400 pounds; Two grandaus., Catherine and Charlotte Dunlop; dau. Charlotte Chambers Ludlow 400 pounds; grandson James Ludlow 300 acres, granted me by Congress for my services in the Rev. War; Grandau. Catherine Ludlow 200 acres granted me by Congress, the warrant for said lands I gave into the hands of Col. Israel Ludlow, their father; dau. Ruhamah Scott all that land I bot from Richard Harris, also 500 acres granted me by the State of Penna. for my services in the Rev. War; son Benjamin the residue of my real est. He died at Loudon Forge, Franklin County, Penna., Apr. 25, 1805, aged ——yrs. His son Lieut. Benj. Chambers, died in Saline County, Missouri, Aug., 1850. From the "Repository," Apr. 30, 1805: Major General James Chambers was farmly attached to the institution of Masonry . . . by his measures was this Lodge first established by him and by the unanimous voice of the Grand Lodge he was appointed our Master, in which capacity he continued until Dec. 1804, when with the greatest regret, we assented to his resignation. Gen. James Chambers was entitled to 1,000 acres of Donation Land. Andrew Dunlap was married to Sally Chambers, Nov. 18, 1790; Charlotte Chambers was married to Mr. Ludlow, Sept., 1796, and William B. Scott to Ruhamah Chambers July 9, 1795. The above three daughters of General James Chambers were married by Dr. John King of Mercersburg—as was, also, Benjamin, son of General Chambers, to his first wife Ruth McPherrin, on Dec. 27, 1796. Mrs. Catherine, relict of Gen. James Chambers, died at Cincinnati, Ohio, January 16, 1820.

Penna. Arch. 5th Ser. Vol. 2, p. 5, 15, 627. Heitman's Hist. Reg. of Officers of Cont. Army, p. 149. Nead's Hist. of Waynesboro, Penna. p. 371.

WILLIAM CHAMBERS

Served under his brother, Capt. James Chambers, in Col. Wm. Thompson's Batt. of Riflemen, and later under Captains James Young and Terrence Campbell. His estate was administered June 14, 1788.
Penna. Arch. 5th Ser. Vol. 6, p. 83, 100, 111, 126, 549. Penna. Arch. 5th Ser. Vol. 6, p. 17.

EDWARD CRAWFORD SR. PATRIOT

Born in County Donegal, Ireland, d. in Guilford Twp., Franklin County, Penna., in 1792. He mar. Elizabeth Sterritt (dau. of John Sterritt and wife Martha of Lancaster County, Penna.) They had issue: 1. Martha, b. 1743, d. 1837, mar. Edw. Cook and had issue James Cook, b. 1772, d. 1848. 2. John Crawford, b. 1745, d. 1827, mar. Anne Holmes, b. 1765, d. 1810, a native of Ireland. 3. James, b. 1748, d. Jan., 1798, mar. Martha the dau. of Samuel and Mary Smith, early settlers in Antrim Twp. (Said Samuel dying intestate in 1763), leaving no issue. His widow Martha mar. Dr. Wm. Magaw, as his 3rd wife; she died in or near Mercersburg Nov. 20, 1826, after which Dr. Magaw went with a son to Meadville. 4. Elizabeth, b. 1750, mar. John Fulton. 5. Sarah, b. 1752, d. 1833, mar. Henry Work, Esq.; they had issue: Andrew; James; Henry; Isabella; Martha; Sarah; Edward. 6. Ruth mar. Wm. Elliott, son of Robert Elliott, of Hamilton Twp. She was b. Nov. 11, 1754, and moved to Western Penna. 7. Edward, b. 1757, d. 1833, mar. 1st Elizabeth Holsinger; 2nd Rebecca Colhoun. 8. Joseph, b. 1759, killed by Indians. 9. Mary, b. 1761, mar. ——— Dunlevy. The above named and dated from notes by Edward Crawford, Jr., and information given by Miss Winifred Ross, Chambersburg, Penna. Edward Crawford, Patriot, took up a tract of 105 acres, 62 perchs' No. 444, which was called Guilford Manor.

The letter addressed to Mr. Hugh Crawford, Drumgavan, near Donegal, Ireland, is copied as follows:

Guilford Township Oct. 1, 1763.

Dr. Brother: these are to acquaint you that I and my wife is in good health at present but I have 3 children in the small Pox at the present and has four more to take them yet and I hope that these will find you and your family in the same good health you wrote to Brother James to know the . . . manner I lived or what my Circumstances are Brother Hugh I thought you might write to me I came to this Country . . . none that I received if you did I received none which you do not use me as a Brother ought to do we have another Indian War in these parts but I trust in the almighty that he will subdue them we had some trouble and with bad news they were a great many families gathered at my house but I thank the Almighty that we live at more peace than at first and all the Engagements that we had with the Indians Our Army kept the field which I trust they will ever do Dr. Brother you knew when I left Ireland my Riches was not great I thank God (here a brown stain and worn fold in paper makes it illegible) Patent which cost me 125 pounds and all my rent the year was half penny An Acre while I live and my Childrens Children after me Brother James had a Son named Edward died of the small Pox about the Tenth of September and the rest of the family is all recovered Brother Lindsay and family is in good health I heard lately from Brother Alexander that he and family is in good health and live very well Dr. Brother these is all but my wife and I joins with our love to you and Sister and all enquiring friends.

(Signed) Edward Crawford

P. S. I see Jack Kir . . . . . a brown stain again. "This letter was sent to Ireland but has come back" reads a statement on the outside faint and worn, also some other notations are illegible.

I do hereby certify, that Edward Crawford hath voluntarily taken and subscribed the oath of allegiance and fidelity, as directed by an act of General Assembly of Pennsylvania, Passed the 29th day of March, A. D. 1781.

Witness my hand and seal the 9th day of Oct. 1781 A. D.

Jno Scott

L. S.

CARLISLE: Printed by Kline & Reynolds

The original Oath of Allegiance is in possession of a descendant, Mrs. Janet W. Sharpe. Penna. Arch. 2nd Ser. Vol. 3, p. 42.

CAPTAIN AND PAYMASTER EDWARD CRAWFORD, JR.

Ensign in Capt. Grier's Co., 1st Penna.,		1776
3rd Lieut.	May 13,	1777
to rank as 2nd Lieut.	Sept. 11,	1777
1st Lieut.	March	1778
Captain		1781

First Penna. Cont. Line, War of the American Rev. He received a severe wound during one of the battles in New Jersey and came near to losing his life at the siege at Yorktowne, Va. A Member of the Society of the Cincinnati; In 1809 assisted in the organization of the Bank of Chambersburg, was its first President and to this office was re-elected for 23 yrs; elected Dec. 1814 a manager of the Franklin County Bible Society; served for some years as a Trustee of the Falling Spring Presbyterian Church; a veteran of the Rev. War, he was appointed to meet the soldiers on their return from the denfense of Baltimore, and addressed them; also a veteran of 24 years service as an official of the infant County of Franklin; he was appointed to the several offices of Prothonotary &c. To the capacity and fidelity with which the organization of these was made, the routine of business established and the various duties discharged throughout 24 years and upwards, the entire community could bear witness. The Franklin Repository,

Chambersburg, Penna., March 12, 1833: One of the oldest, one of the most useful and one of the most respected of the citizens of Chambersburg has fallen under the stroke that spares none. Edward Crawford, Esq., died on the morning of Wednesday the 6th March, inst. aged 75 years. So long a life necessarily carries with it more or less of the crosses and distresses of this world from which he was not entirely exempt—but in his cup was mingled an unusual portion of all that makes life valuable. The respect of the whole community, the sincere esteem of his fellow citizens to whom he was more intimately known and the ardent and devoted affections of those intimately connected with him conspired in and of a clear and excellent understanding and a warm and generous heart to encourage and invigorate the efforts of his life and to give enjoyment and happiness to his declining years. In the year 1776 and at the early age of 18 he entered the military service of his country as an officer of the Revolutionary army in which he continued until the war terminated and peace acknowledged us to be what we had declared we were an independent nation. Edward Crawford, Jr., b. Jan. 10, 1757, d. Mar. 6, 1833, mar. first Elizabeth Holsinger, of York County, Penna., b. 1762, d. 1792. They had issue: Thomas Hartley Crawford (Judge), b. Mar. 1786, d. 1863, buried Congressional Cemetery Washington, D. C.; Catherine b. July, 1789, d. 1818, mar. Robert Munro; no issue. Mar. 2nd, in 1793, Rebecca Colhoun, b. 1775, d. 1839. Issue; Ruhana Chambers Crawford, d. aged 13 yrs; Benjamin Chambers Crawford d. in infancy; Elizabeth Sterritt Crawford, b. 1802, d. 1877, mar. by Dr. David Denny Nov. 5, 1818, to Reade Macon Washington. In his will Edward Crawford mentions his property known as "Woodlawn" and later called "Hawthorne," near Stoufferstown. In 1791, he was taxed in Franklin Twp. with a House and Lot; 5 acres Land; a negro woman; 1 Horse; 1 Cow; Tablespoons 6; Teaspoons 12; a Profession.

Penna. Arch. 5th Ser. Vol. 2, p. 630. 645, 658, 665, 687. Men of Mark of the Cumberland Valley, p. 239.

EDWARD CRAWFORD

Served as pvt. under Captains Wm. Long and Conrad Snider, 1779-80-81. His wife Elizabeth died in 1838 aged 83 yrs., and was the dau. of Johnston Reynolds. Orphans' Court records show Edward Crawford as "farmer" with 500 acres land. He died April 1801, leaving a widow, Elizabeth and nine children: Hugh; Johnston R.; Edward; John; Frances, wife of John Lindsay; Nancy Crawford; Maria, wife of Wm. Ross; Elizabeth.

Penna. Arch. 5th Ser. Vol. 6, p. 74, 88, 119, 546.

JOHN CRAWFORD LIEUT.

Served in Watts Penna., Batt. of the Flying Camp, July, 1776; taken prisoner at Ft. Washington, Dec., 1776, exchanged in 1780. His wife Anne Holmes died in 1810 in the 45th yr. of her age. From the Franklin Repository, Feb. 20, 1827: "Died on the evening of Tuesday the 13th, at his residence in Guilford Twp., Mr. John Crawford, in his 82nd yr. The deceased had served his country faithfully in the great struggle by which she was happily freed from foreign domination. He was a Lieut. in the Rev. Army and one of the garrison that defended Ft. Washington in Nov., 1776; with the fall of that port he was captured and remained a prisoner for four years suffering all the privations and mortifications of his situation and which is believed more severe than those that ordinarily fall to a soldier's lot in civilized warfare." Lieut. John Crawford, b. Aug. 11, 1745, d. Feb. 13, 1827, mar. Anne Holmes, b. 1765,d. 1810. Issue: 1. Holmes, 1791-1874, mar. Martha ———; 2. James, 1800-1872, mar. Catherine Byers; 3. John mar. Margaret Black,—issue: Jane Anne, mar. Dr. H. K. Byers, and Martha mar. H. G. Greenawalt; 4. Joseph Cook; 5. Edward d. young; 6. Sarah, b. 1795, d. 1849, mar. J. S. Brown; 7. Martha, b. 1788, d.———, mar. Josiah Duffield; 8. Elizabeth, mar. in 1812 Hugh Crawford, issue: Anne Holmes, Elizabeth Reynolds, Catherine Munro, John Sterritt, Edward Crawford, James Crawford, Jane Duncan; 9. Rebecca mar. Matthew McKee in 1833; 10. Nancy died unmarried.

Heitman's Hist. Regular Officers of the Cont. Army, p. 177. Biographical Annals of Franklin County.

JOSIAH CRAWFORD

Served in 3rd Co., 4th Batt. Cumb. Co., Militia, 1780, Captains Joseph and Samuel Culbertson Commanding. From Boston Patriot and Chronicle, Jan. 23, 1819, "At Chambersburg, Penna., Col. Joseph (Josiah) Crawford, aged 83 yrs., of the Continental Army, a native of Ireland. He died Jan. 1, 1819, in 83rd year, buried in Falling Spring Graveyard." A letter from Secty. Dallas to Col. Josiah Crawford in 1794, suggests certain Committions, Col Crawford then being Brigade Inspector of Franklin County, Penna. The will of the above names: dau. Mary McDowell; dau. Elizabeth Greer; son John; son Josiah; dau. Margaret Crawford compensation for her good offices and time spent with me;

dau. Martha Crawford; dau. Anne Crawford; 2 sons, William and David; son-in-law, Michael Greer. He refers to that "invaluable book" Dr. Scott's family bible, each child to have a copy, or an equivalent. Dated Nov., 1818; prob. 1819. A deed shows the dau. Margaret, having mar. Robert Shields, of Union County, Ind. As Josiah Crawford named two grandaus. Margaret McDowell and Margaret Greer, it is probable that his wife was named Margaret. He also names a son James Mercer which may furnish another clue, with Lancaster County, Penna., as their first home in America. His dau. Martha, unmar., lies with him at Falling Spring.

Penna. Arch. 5th Ser. Vol. 6, p. 280. Penna. Arch. 2nd Ser. Vol. 3, p. 661. Josiah Crawford ap., Justice of the Peace, Cumberland County, May 17, 1780.

JOSEPH GRAHAM

Probable burial. From the Repository: "August 3rd, 1823, Died Sunday, Joseph Graham, of Hamilton Township, an Elder in Mr. Denny's Church."

MAJOR JOHN HOLLIDAY

Son of Lieut. James and Elizabeth (McDowell) Holliday, was First Lieut. in Col. Fredk. Watt's Batt., of the "Flying Camp," captured at Fort Washington, Nov. 6, 1776, prisoner for several years, reported on parole at Flatlands, L. I., in 1778; later Major, prominent in Chambersburg where he died Apr., 1818, in his 66th yr. He mar. Mary McDowell, dau. of Nathan and Catherine (Maxwell) McDowell. They had no issue. The Franklin Repository, in 1818 gave an obituary notice of the above Major Holliday, and the same paper, on Tuesday, Oct. 9, 1827, gave the following: "Died in Greencastle, on Saturday Morning last, in the 74th year of her age, Mrs. Mary Holliday, relict of Major John Holliday, late of this borough. The remains of this respectable and esteemed Lady were brought here on Sunday last agreeably to her own desire and deposited in the graveyard of Mr. Denny's church along-side of those of her husband." A Government Stone was placed by the Franklin County Chapter D. A. R.

Penna. Arch. 5th Ser. Vol. 4, p. 229.

CAPTAIN PATRICK JACK

In Camp at Fort Loudon, Aug. 16, 1764, 2nd Batt. Penna. Regt., under Lieut. Col. Clayton; order signed by Patrick Jack, Capt. Lieut; also shown July 21, 1763, as above. Served during 1777-78-79-80-81-82, Cumb. County, Militia. He was a Miller on Back Creek, and in 1773 there was a petition from settlers in Hamilton and Guilford Twps., stating "that they labor under great difficulty for want of a road from Patrick Jack's mill to the road leading through Black's Gap." Patrick Jack was married by the Rev. John C. Bucher, to Martha Findley, June the 27, 1765. The stone of Capt. Patrick Jack shows that he died 1821 aged 91 yrs. His wife Martha, dau. Jane Stewart, and dau. Mary who died in 1862. In the will of Miss Mary she bequeaths $100. to the Presby. Foreign Mission Board for a mission amongst the Cherokee Indians, "for their kindness, as a nation, to my father when a prisoner with them." In 1823, the son John F. Jack, Esq., was living in Granger County, Tenn.

Penna. Arch. 5th Ser. Vol. 6, p. 13, 28, 29, 31, 44, 62, 63, 95, 144, 146, 291, 295. Hain's History, Perry County, Penna. p. 97.

JOHN KERR

Of Guilford Twp., Prop. of Kerrstown, served as Second Lieut., in the 8th Batt. of Capt. James Young's Co., under Col. Abraham Smith, 1778-79. John Kerr mar. Mary Daugherty, Sept. 16, 1765. The will of John Dougherty and wife Lilly of Peters Twp., 1777, names dau. Mary, wife of John Kerr. John Kerr was b. in Ireland and d. in 1807; the will of his wife is dated 1815. They had issue: son Joseph; dau. Jean McKinley; son John; dau. Sarah Decamp; son James; dau. Mary Patterson and a son Samuel, b. 1778, d. 1823 in Ohio, who mar. 1799 Nancy Guin. A Government marker was placed at the grave of John Kerr by the Franklin County Chapter Daughters of the American Revolution,—the site having been marked by a descendant.

Penna. Arch. 5th Ser. Vol. 6, p. 530, 533, 547.

THOMAS KIRBY

Served as pvt. under Capt. Patrick Jack, 1781-82. He mar. Jean Witney. He came to Chambersburg as a preacher, poet and in 1806 a Justice of the Peace. He died July 25, 1815, in his 58th year. His wife Jane died Mar. 25, 1835 in her 68th yr. Thomas Kirby died owning lots in Chambersbrug, leaving a window and five children: Joanna, wife of Wm. A. Davis; Jemima, wife of John Cree; James Kirby, wife Rebecca; Martha, wife of Wm. Gilmore; Jane, wife of Silas Harry.

Penna. Arch. 5th Ser. Vol. 6, p. 292, 296, 313.

JAMES LINDSAY

Served as Wagon Master under Major Robert Culbertson, June 10, 1782. His stone states he d. Dec. 23, 1823, aged 87 yrs., 8 mos. 15 days. In his will he names various nieces and nephews, especially to the "children and grandchildren of my brother Fulton Lindsay, and to the children of my nephew, Fulton Lindsay, decd." In the will of Fulton Lindsay, (1788) he names as Exevutors James Lindsay, Batchelor, and James Lindsay, farmer, the will being prob. in 1789.

Penna. Arch. 5th Ser. Vol 6, p. 4, 598.

JAMES LINDSAY

Served in 1778 under Capt. Adam Harmony, also under Capt. Conrad Snider, 1780-81. His will was dated and prob. Sept.-Oct., 1804. His widow, Martha Breckenridge, d. in 1833, in her 87th yr. In his will he names children: John; James; Elizabeth; Martha; Jane; Agnes; Sarah; Mary. When the widow died in 1833, she names surviving children as: Elizabeth Thompson; Mary Davidson; Martha Thompson; James Lindsay.

Penna. Arch. 5th Ser. Vol. 6, p. 74, 88, 119, 538.

WILLIAM MOOREHEAD

Served as Ensign under Capt. Patrick Jack 1778-80-81. He was the son of Samuel Moorehead of Hamilton Twp., and wife Euphemia. John Lowery of Hamilton Twp., in his will (1795) named dau. Mary, wife of William Moorehead. William d. May 18, 1810; his wife Mary, April 29, 1838. Their children were: Euphemia, mar. Thomas Reed; Samuel; 3 minors, Martha, Jane (or Jeanie) and John. Martha later mar. Charles Punnion (?)

Penna. Arch. 5th Ser. Vol. 6, p. 29, 95, 292, 296.

ROBERT PEEBLES

Served as a pvt. under Capt. Samuel Patton, 1781. He mar. Peggy McClintic, June 10, 1802. He died 1824, aged 64 yrs. His widow d. in Cincinnati 1861, aged 80 yrs. They had issue: Eleanor; Mary mar. Robert Culbertson of Cincinatti; Robert; Jane d. 1893; Daniel McClintock; William Sharpe; Joseph; Nancy and perhaps Casandra. Robert Peebles lived in Chambersburg, —his property was sold to Silas Harry in 1826, —lot No. 29. "Eleanor, dau. of the late Robert Peebles, mar. May 23, 1826, Francis G. Patterson, by Dr. David Denny." "Robert Culbertson to Mary Peebles, Nov. 8, 1832, by Dr. Denny." The Chambersburg Times and Franklin Telegraph under Jan. 17, 1842 gives: "Married in Cincinnati the 27th ult, by Rev. Joshua Wilson, Thos. S. Stanfield of South Bend, Ind. to Miss Nancy Harper, dau. of Robert Peebles, decd. of Chambg., Penna." Also: "on the 26th ult, in Mercersburg, by Rev. Mr. Kennedy, Mr. Daniel M. Peebles of Cincinnati, to Miss Maria dau. of Jacob Wise, of Mercersburg."

Penna. Arch. 5th Ser. Vol. 6, p. 286.

SAMUEL PURVIANCE

Served as a pvt. under Capt. James Young, 1780-81-82. He d. Jan. 1829, in his 84th yr. His wife Nancy (Agnes) d. Oct. 1848, in her 84th yr. He names children: Elizabeth; Polly; Nancy; Jane; Samuel; John; James; Margaret. He is said to have been of French origin, and an early paper-manufacturer in Chambersburg. Peggy Purviance mar. Thos. G. McCulloh; Nancy Purviance mar. Dr. Samuel Culbertson; Jane Purviance mar. Samuel Blood.

Penna. Arch. 5th Ser. Vol. 6, p. 82, 110, 126.

ADAM ROSS

Served under Capt. Patrick Jack, 1779, and an undated roll. He was b. in Ireland 1754, mar. Jane, dau. of Col. Benj. and Jane (Williams) Chambers, in 1777. He d. nov. 30, 1827. Mrs. Ross, b. 1762, d. Mar. 19, 1825, the result of a fall from her horse. They are buried in the Chambers family enclosure. Adam Ross settled on a plantation in Guilford Twp., near Mont Alto, during or prior to the Revolution. It contained 700 acres, the deed for which was from John Penn, the Elder and John Penn, the younger, in 1789. The tract was called "Ross Common" on which Adam Ross lived and died. They had issue: 1. Benjamin, b. ——, d. Mar. 5, 1855, unmar. He was prominent in politics and member of City Council, Baltimore. II. William, b. Feb. 3, 1785, d. May 27, 1832, mar. Mary Crawford. They had issue: Edward Crawford; Adam; Wm.; Mary Ann; Benjamin Chambers. III. George, d. 1867; studied law in Chambersburg and was admitted to the Bar in 1810; he then removed to Somerset, Penna., where he practiced his profession. He is buried in Falling Spring graveyard. IV. James, b.——, d.——, unmar. V. Joseph, b.——, d. Jan. 16, 1838, unmar. VI. Adam, b.——, d. June 10, 1858, unmar. VII. John, b.——, d. Nov. 14, 1840, unmar. VIII. Mary, b. 1782, d. Oct. 22, 1862, mar. Wm. Drips, lawyer, Jan. 25, 1809. They had issue: Jane Chambers, mar. Horatio Dennison; George Ross Drips, lawyer, unmar. IX. Hadassah, mar. John Hanan, lawyer of Baltimore, issue: John, mar.;— a dau. Mary; Joseph, d. unmar. X. Jane mar. Henry George of Co. Derry, Ireland. She died May 8, 1876, issue: John, b.——, unmar.; Benj. Ross, mar. Lucy Chambers; Ruhamah, unmar.; Mary Jane, unmar. XI. Ruhamah, mar. Dr. Geo. Brown MacKenzie of Baltimore, June 6, 1832. They had issue: one son Benj. Chambers Ross, who d. in infancy. (Records given by Miss Winifred Ross).

Penna. Arch. 5th Ser. Vol. 6, p. 64, 147.

MAJOR JEREMIAH TALBOT

From Capt. of 7th Penna.; ranking from Sept. 22, 1777; retired Jan. 1, 1781; sheriff of Franklin County 1784; died at Chambersburg Jan. 19, 1791. He was one of the distinguished soldiers of the Revolution. He recruited largely in the West Conococheague; was commissioned Captain in the 6th Batt. Jan. 9, 1776. Court records show the following in 1787,—"The Supreme Executive Council, to Jeremiah Talbot, Esq.,—Reposing especial trust and Confidence in your Patriotism, Valor, Conduct, Constitute and appoint you to be Lieutenant of the County of Franklin." He mar. Rebecca, dau. of Samuel and Mary Smith, early settlers in Antrim Twp., —Samuel dying in 1763. After the death of Major Talbot, his widow and daughters moved to Mercersburg, or vicinity, where she was near her sister, Martha, wife of James Crawford. Deeds show that in 1801 Dr. James Martin and wife, Elizabeth, of Peters Twp., convey to Rebecca Talbot of same place, land sold to Dr. Martin in 1798 by Robert Smith, "on a line with the Main Street of Mercersburg." The will of Rebecca Talbot of Mercersburg, Pa., states that she is "Weke of body, but of sound mind and memory." To dau. Mary her choice of feather beds . . . one stand of curtains, looking glass,, copper tea kettle and what china ware may be in my cupboard, Dining Table, fire irons and brass candlesticks. To son Hillery the second choice in feather beds, silver table and teaspoons. Dau. Elizabeth Martin, grandson Jeremiah T. Martin; grandau., Matilda Crawford Talbot Martin. Rebecca Talbot d. Sept. 19, 1815. Her dau. Elizabeth Martin d. 1836, aged 60 yrs. Her dau. Mary Smith Talbot d. in 1836, aged 54 yrs. They are buried in the White Church Graveyard, where James Crawford is lying. A Government marker, to Major Jeremiah Talbot, was placed in Falling Spring Graveyard by the Franklin County Chapter, D. A. R.

Penna. Arch. 5th Ser. Vol. 3, p. 103, 121, 147. Also Penna. Arch. Vol. 2, p. 208. Hist. of the Bard Family, p. 465.

JAMES WALSH (WELSH)

Served as pvt. under Capt. James Young in 1779. He died Oct. 22, 1806, aged 52 yrs. His son John, and John's wife Margaret, are buried with him. He died leaving a widow Nancy and issue: Dau. Rebecca, mar. Henry Thompson; dau. Mary mar. Samuel Peebles; sons Joseph and John; dau. Jinny; son James; dau. Nancy. Later marriages: Elizabeth mar. Jacob Grove; Jane mar. Samuel Thompson; Nancy mar. John Buchanan; James Welsh mar. Hannah Graham.

Penna. Arch. 5th Ser. Vol. 6, p. 547.

* * * * *

Mrs. Sarah Denig, widow of Lewis Denig, died May 21, 1903, in her 97 year. "Among her recollections was the last visit of representatives of Indian tribes, who once inhabited our Valley, to see that the burying grounds, whe.e the remains of their ancestors reposed adjoining Falling Spring Presbyterian Church graveyard, were, in accordance with contract, kept sacred. The conditions were sacredly kept until 1834, when, for the last time they left the place, pitifully showing their distress as they marched up Main Street and started on the march back to their western reservations."

Hist. Zion Reformed Church, Chambersburg, Pa., p. 93.

FIRST LUTHERAN CHURCH GRAVEYARD

Chambersburg, Penna.

FREDERICK HOFFMAN

Served 1780-82 under Capt. James Beard; pages 422-1133, show Fredk. Hoffman serving as pvt. under Capt. Conrad Karver in Lancaster County, 1781-82, the latter man probably of Dauphin County. The gravestone of Fredk. Hoffman, gives his birth as Mar. 1761, and death Sept., 1830. His wife Catherine, b. Nov., 1760, d. June, 1838. In the will of Fredk. Hoffman of Chambersburg, he names wife Catherine; son Frederick; a dau. Catherine, wife of Stephen Keephart; grandchildren, the children of Geo. Overkersh, that has been mar. to my dau. Eve, decd; all my children. It may be of interest to add the following: Fredrich D. Hoffman, served as Serj. Major, under Col. James Burd on their march to Pittsburgh, Lancaster, May 11, 1761.

Penna. Arch. 5th Ser. Vol. 1, p. 316, 317. Penna. Arch. 5th Ser. Vol. 7, p. 412, 434.

JOHN IMMELL (EMBLE)

Was a pvt. 1779-81 under Capt. John Rea, undated rolls. The will of John Immell of Green Twp., was prob Mar. 1799. He names wife Anna Barbara; son John; land purchased of Wm. Sharp; sons Jacob and Michael; dau. Elizabeth and grandchild Elizabeth Diller; remaining legatees? son-in-law Martin Diller.

Penna. Arch. 5th Ser. Vol. 6, p. 78, 105, 543, 584.

PAUL IMMEL (EMBLE)

Served as a pvt. in 1779, and in 1781 under Capt. John Rea, some rolls undated. From the Franklin Repository we have the following,— dated May 16, 1804. "Died on Tuesday the 8th inst at his farm in Green Twp., in the 59th year of his age, Mr. Paul Immel, a very opulent farmer, and respectable citizen. On Wednesday last his remains, attended by a large and respectable concourse of citizens, were brought to town, and deposited in the silent grave." He was also a miller. He left a will dated May 1, 1804, prob. Jan 9, 1809; wife Dorothy; only daughter Magdalena, wife of Geo. Hetich; a grandson Paul Hetich.

Penna. Arch. 5th Ser. Vol. 6, p. 78, 105, 544, 585.

Notes by Geo. W. Immell of Chambersburg, Penna. JOHN AND PAUL IMMELL came to Franklin County, near Greenvillage, about 1760. The first and 2nd John Immell are buried in the Lutheran Graveyard, Chambersburg, Penna., no markers. "My grandfather, Jacob Immell told me his mother was a Miss Oberholtzer." The 2nd Johon mar. Elizabeth Barnett of Md. The 1st John had one dau. Elizabeth, who mar. Mr. Foreman of Baltimore and had 3 sons: Michael; Jacob; John. The first Michael Immell was a trapper in the Rocky Mountains and was killed by Indians.

PHILIP SCHOLL

Is shown giving service in 175, in Bucks County, Penna. Court records fail to show his arrival in Franklin County, but McCauley (p. 123) states that Philip Scholl, at a very early period, carried on at Chambersburg, the manufacture of cards for fulling mills, and for all other purposes. The "Repository" of July 26, 1814 gives the following: "Died on Thursday last in the 64th year of his age, Mr. Philip Scholl, a respectable citizen of this Boro. On Saturday his last remains were interred in the German Lutheran burial ground, the Rev. Mr. Moeller delivered an appropriate address." Under Jan. 12, 1830, is the marriage of George McFerron to Miss Elizabeth Scholl, on Thursday last, both of Guilford.

Penna. Arch. 5th Ser. Vol. 5, p. 401.

HOKES GRAVEYARD

(Near Greencastle, Penna.)

ANDREW UNANKE
(UNANX -- UNANGST -- ONAKKST)

Served as a pvt. in 1781, under Capt. Joseph Culbertson. Deeds show him early in Letterkenny and Green Twps. His will, Andrew Onakkst, of Peters Twp. names Widow; son-in-law Henry and Michael Hickman; dau. Elizabeth Felery of Faley; grandau. Elizabeth Faley to have a Kopper Kettle, &c. Andrew Lemaster and John Bryson were witnesses to the will, dated Oct. 4, 1810; prob. Apr. 18, 1812. Andreas Unangst b. Jan. 31, 1741, d. Apr. 4, 1812.

Penna. Arch. 5th Ser. Vol. 6, p. 290.

FREDERICK BYERS, SR. (BYER -- BOYER)

1732-1801, served as pvt. under Capt. John Jack in 179, and under Col. James Johnston 1780-81-82. He was of Antrim Twp., his will prob. Mar. 19, 1801, wife Margaret Hochlander; son Fredk.; dau. Catherine mar. Tobias Steaman; dau. Elizabeth mar. Gabriel Carpenter; sons Jacob and John; dau. Eve mar. Fredk. Fehl; dau. Margaret mar. Geo. Hochlander; dau. Feronica mar. Godlip Yeider; a grandson Andrew Fehl.

Penna. Arch. 5th Ser. Vol. 6, p. 75, 114, 130, 540.

GABRIEL CARPENTER

Served as pvt. under Captains John Jack, Thomas Johnston and James Poe, 1778-80-81-82. He and his wife Elizabeth Byer are buried in Hoke's graveyard near Greencastle. He was b. 1757, d. April 18, 1808; Elizabeth died Nov. 17, 1806, aged 44 yrs, 4 mos. They had issue: Elizabeth mar. Henry Wilhelm; Frederick mar. Margaret———; Margaret mar. Fredk. Wagner; John mar. Mary Eachus.

Penna. Arch. 5th Ser. Vol. 6, p. 76, 84, 115, 130, 169, 576, 583, 599.

JOHN GEARHART

Served as a Rev. Soldier. He died Oct. 12, 1817, in his 73rd yr., and is buried, with grave stone, in Hoke's Graveyard, east of Greencastle Reservoir. The line was approved by Nat. Soc. D. A. R. His land now, 1938, is owned by Daniel Grove, and is not far from the above graveyard. John Gearhart, Sr. and wife Margaret in 1804 deed to John Gearhart, Jr. and in 1816 they deed land to Jacob and Frederick Gearhart "provided they provide decently and comfortably for said Jacob and Margaret." Both tracts of land situate in Antrim Twp. The will of John Gearhart, Sr. of Antrim Twp., dated Sept. 14, 1816, prob. Oct. 24, 1817, names daus. Elizabeth mar. to John Besore; Catherine mar. to Abraham Crist; sons John, Jocab and Fredk.; daus. Peggy, Rosanna, Nancy and Susan; sons Samuel and George; sons Jacob and Fredk. to keep their mother comfortable and free of expense to my estate. Exrs: Jacob and John Gearhart.

Penna. Arch. 2nd Ser. Vol. 13, p. 80.

MOSS SPRING GRAVEYARD

Antrim Twp.

The Presbyterian Church at Moss Spring, adjacent to Greencastle, was evidently the oldest church building in this part of the County. It was built in 1737 or 1738, frame, 28 x 42, and called "Old Red Meeting House." The situation was a delightful one, and during the intermission of services the people, lunch in hand, would gather at the spring and drink of its cool, clear waters, or stroll at will among the rocks and woods of the surrounding groves."

JOSEPH DAVISON

"The Chambersburg Times," May 23, 1842. "On Friday the 13th inst., at his residence in Antrim Twp., Mr. Joseph Davison in the 89th year of his age. The deceased, during the War of the Revolution, endured the privations incident to that eventful period, by two terms of service in the Army; and through a long life of activity and usefulness, he enjoyed the esteem and confidence of his numerous friends and acquaintances." From the Moss Spring Graveyard, Antrim Twp., we have: Joseph Davison died May 13, 1842, aged 88 yrs. Margaret, formerly Margaret Brown, wife of Joseph Davison, died Feb. 25, 1779, aged 41 yrs. Margaret Robinson, wife of Joseph Davison, d. Nov. 10, 1836. The will of Joseph Davison of Antrim Twp., names: son Abraham S.; son James; son-in-law Jesse Craig; son Hugh, now decd.; son Wm. decd., widow and heirs; son John, decd., widow and heirs; dau. Jane Lindsay; dau. Elizabeth Craig; dau. Margaret Patton; son Andrew. The will was probated May 26, 1842.

DAVID KENNEDY

Served as pvt. under Capt. John Orbison in 1780-81-82. He died 1818, aged 55 yrs. In his will he states he is of Montgomery Twp.; names a wife, Mary; son Lazarus; dau. Harriet; dau. Sharlott. His wife was a dau. of Francis Robison.

Penna. Arch. 5th Ser. Vol. 6, p. 273, 293, 307.

JOHN KENNEDY

Served as pvt. under Capt. Wm. Berryhill, in 1780-81. He died in 1805, aged 70 yrs. In his will he names eldest dau. Mary Eaker; dau. Elly Lowrey; son David Kennedy; sister Mary Armstrong; son-in-law John Campble; grandson Allen Keiloh Campbell and other g-children.

Penna. Arch. 5th Ser. Vol. 6, p. 73, 80, 102.

JOHN MCCLELLAN, JR. (DR.)

Served as a pvt. under Capt. Walter McKinnie in 1781. His father served with him in 1781. John McClennan, 1762-1846, mar. May 1, 1804, Eleanor McCullough, dau. of Robert and Prudence (Grubb) McCulloh of Lancaster County, Penna. Issue: John McClellan, Brevet Lieut. Col. of the Corps of Topographical Engineers of the U. S. Army; Robert McCulloh McClellan, Secty. of the Interior in the Cabinet of Pres. Pierce and twice Governor of Michigan; George McClellan; Willm. McClennan of Chambersburg, Penna.; Prudence; Sidney (1812-1886) mar. John B. McLanahan of Chambersburg.

Penna. Arch. 5th Ser. Vol. 6, p. 299, 301.

JOHN MCCLENAHAN, SR.

Was a pvt. under Capt. Daniel Clapsaddle, 1780-81. He is also shown with John and James presumably his sons. John McLanahan mar. Rebecca Agnew.

Penna. Arch. 5th Ser. Vol. 6, p. 72, 93, 94, 117, 122.

ROBERT MCCULLOCH

Served as a pvt. under Capt. John Woods. He died 1824, b. 1750 in Lancaster County, Penna., son of George McCulloch. He mar. in 1778, Prudence Grubb, who d. 1809. The will of Robert McCulloch of Greencastle names sons: Thos. G. McCulloch; Robert Washington McCulloch; dau. Prudence McCulloch; dau. Eleanor, mar. to Dr. John McClelland; son Joseph; son George.

Penna. Arch. 5th Ser. Vol. 6, p. 138.

WILLIAM WALLACE

Served in 1778 under Capt. Wm. Findley, 2nd Comp., 1st Batt., and in 1780-82, under Capt. Conrad Snyder. In his will, dated 1805, prob. June, 1818, he names wife Martha, to whom he gives one half of his estate. The other half to three persons, named: Joseph Riddle, my sister Mary's son; to William Riddle, son of said Joseph; to John Towland, my sister Rachel's son. The executors were his wife and nephew John Towland. William Wallace d. Mar. 26, 1818, aged 80 yrs. Martha, his consort, d. Aug. 9, 1834, aged 86 yrs. Martha was a sister of Archibald Fleming. William Wallace Fleming, son of Archibald, was raised in the family of William Wallace.

Penna. Arch. 5th Ser. Vol. 6, p. 87, 123, 597.

OLD JOHNSTON GRAVEYARD

(Antrim Township)

JOHN BEATTY

Was a pvt., under Capt. Thos. Johnston 1780-81-82. He died 1839, aged 83 yrs. His consort Susannah Allen d. aged 85 yrs. From the Franklin Repository, July 30, 1839 we quote: "Died at his residence in Antrim Twp., on Wednesday last, Mr. John Beatty in his 83rd year. The deceased at an early period of his life entered the Rev. Army of the U. S. and was taken prisoner after the battle of Long Island at the capture of Fort Washington and with many more of his countrymen endured great privation when confined in a prison ship," etc, etc.

Penna. Arch. 5th Ser. Vol. 6, p. 84, 114, 129.

WILLIAM BEATTY

Served as a pvt., under Capt. James Young, 8th. Batt., 5th Co., First Call, Oct. 23, 1777-78. Under Capts. John Woods and James Poe in 1780-82. He married Mary, dau. of James Johnston, pioneer, of Antrim Twp. He died Feb. 15, 1802, in his 64th year. His wife Mary is buried near her dau. Elizabeth Bard in White Church graveyard 2½ miles from Mercersburg, Penna. Of the heirs, Johnston Beatty left a will in 1810. He wished his brother Henry to get his Gold buckles. The heirs in 1819 agree with the 1810 list: Robert Beatty and wife, Rebecca. John Beatty and wife, Elizabeth; Archibald Bard and wife, Elizabeth; Mary Beatty; William Beatty; Thomas Beatty; Samuel Beatty; Henry Beatty. In Aug. 1775, William Beatty bought a Regimental Hatt, value 2 pounds, from Samuel Findlay, Storekeeper, Mercersburg, Penna. In 1794, William Beatty is taxed with 200 and 100 acres of land, 5 Horses, 8 Cows, 2 Stills, 6 Teaspoons.

Penna. Arch. 5th Ser. Vol. 6, p. 76, 92, 522, 526, 576, 583.

"Memorial of Elizabeth Boggs, who d. July 11, 1815, aged 63 yrs. 11 mos. 25 days. Also her son Francis who died Jan. 18, 1792, aged 11 yrs." (Elizabeth, wife of John Boggs, was dau. of James Johnston, Sr. and wife Elizabeth Brown Findlay.) Graveyard above one-fourth mile N. E. of Shady Grove in Antrim Twp. About 60 graves, largely limestone markers.

OLD MCCLELLAN GRAVEYARD

(Near Upton)

CAPT. JOHN MCCELLAND

Minutes of a Convention of Associators of the Colony of Penna., at Lancaster, on the 4th day of July, 1776,—of the Officers and Privates of 53 Battalions: Cumberland (now Franklin) County. 2nd Batt. Officers—Capt. John McClelland, Capt. Elias Davidson. Pvts. Jonathan Smith, Henry Pauling. 5th Batt. Officers—Col. Joseph Armstrong. Maj. Jas. McCalmont. Pvts. James Findley, John Vance. Return for 1779—Roll of Capt. John McClelland's Company. Capt. John McCelland of Montgomery Twp., b. 1732, d. Dec. 12, 1817; mar. Sidney Smith Roddy, b. 1734, d. Aug. 20, 1818. "Mrs. Captain McClelland, widow," a dau. of James Roddy. They are buried on a farm which they owned, once a large graveyard. The farm today (1938) is owned by Leslie Hyssong, near Upton. It is probable that the Major Wm. Maxwell family was buried there. The issue of Capt. John and Sidney McCelland: (Dr.) John McCelland 1762-1846, mar. Eleanor McCulloh; Jane McClellan mar. 1788, Joseph Grubb; James McClellan mar. Mary Irwin; Alexander McClennan—unmar. Wm. McClelland mar. Agnes Dunwoody; Ruth McClelland mar. Robt. Galbreath.

Penna. Arch. 2nd Ser. Vol. 13, p. 264. Egle's Notes and Queries, Vol. 1896.

JOHN MCCULLOUGH

Served as pvt. under Capt. Walter McKinnie, 1781-1782. His brother Hance was a Lieut. in same Company. John McCullough lies buried in the old McClelland graveyard near Upton, Penna., (farm of Leslie Hyssong—1938). He was the famous Indian Captive, taken on July 26, 1756 and returned to his home, near Mercersburg, Penna., Dec. 1764. He left an interesting narrative of his life with the Indians. John McCullough mar. 1st Mary McKinnie, Nov. 8, 1774,—they had issue: Josiah; James; Mattie. He mar. 2nd Elizabeth Cunningham, Dec. 4, 1788, and had issue Susannah; John; Mary. He d. Jan. 4, 1823. The mother of Elizabeth Cunningham was Susanna King, wife of John Cunningham, early settlers near Mercersburg. She was killed by Indians in 1763, leaving issue: sons and the dau. Elizabeth, later wife of John McCullough. When Robert King, of Little Brittian, Lancaster County, and province of Penna., made his last will in 1763, he gives "to my dau., Susannah, wife of John Cunningham, the sum of seven shillings and six pence . . . in full for their share in my estate,"—but he also remembers their children, Robert and Elizabeth of John and Susannah Cunningham. John King (later Rev. John King), taught school in this vicinity until the death of his sister, Mrs. Cunningham.

Penna. Arch. 5th Ser. Vol. 6, p. 266, 298, 300, 305.

OLD REFORMED AND LUTHERAN GRAVEYARD

Mercersburg, Penna.

ANDREW LEYMEISTER

Gave service in Berks County, Penna., under Capt. Sebastian Emrick. His father Wilhelm Leymeister of Berks County, was naturalized Mar. 22, 1761. Andrew was baptized (records of Bern Reformed Church), Feb. 18, 1750. He died 1818 in Franklin County, and his wife Barbara Heck b. Dec. 28, 1755, d. Aug. 11, 1824. They both have stones. They had issue: Jacob, 1775-1861; John, 1778-1825; Catherine, 1780-1852; Philip, 1786, d. young; George, 1790-1863; Daniel 1796-1871; Philip, 1798-1883.

Penna. Arch. 3rd Ser. Vol. 6, p. 282, 306.

The following men are probably Rev. Soldiers: Jacob Geyer, b. 1759—d. 1824. Dorothy, relict of Jacob, b. 1766,—d. 1837. Jacob Geyer and wife Dorothy were members of St. John's Lutheran Ch. Hagerstown, Md. Baptisms of children shown, and came to Mercersburg from there.

John Long (From Lancaster County) b. 1758 —d.1826. Elizabeth, his consort, d. Sept. 6, 1845.

Frederick Smith d. 1829, in his 70th yr. Mary, consort of Frederick, d. 1832, in her 73rd yr. (from Lancaster County).

From the Church register of the Evangelical Reformed Zion's Church at Greencastle, Penna:

"God grant that the names of those persons which shall be written in this book, may also be written in the Book of Life-everlasting, and that they shall be sealed with the blood of the Lamb, Christ Jesus, for all eternity. Amen."

Frederick Augustus Scholl, Preacher of God's Word, October 13, 1818.—Translated from the original German by: Mr. and Mrs. Edward J. Omwake.

OLD REFORMED CHURCH GRAVEYARD

Greencastle, Penna.

JOHN HERR

Is shown in service under Capt. Thos. Robinson 1781-82, Lancaster County Militia. He was b. 1757, d. 1845; his wife Susan, b. 1762, d. 1841. They had a son Peter, b. 1799, d. 1848; a son Conrad, d. 1857, aged 59 yrs. The Baptismal Record of Zion's Reformed Church, Greencastle, Penna., shows the birth and baptisms in 1821, of George Isaiah Herr, for Daniel and Sarah Herr. They had a son John Herr, b. and baptized in 1823. A dau. Margaret Ann, baptized June, 1825. Conrad and Catherine Herr had Henrietta, b. July 3, 1821; Eleanor, b. Apr. 10, 1824; Elizabeth, b. May 11, 1826; Sara Jane, b. Feb. 1, 1828. The name continues on the Church Membership list. Hetty or Henrietta Herr (Harr) confirmed in 1841.

Penna. Arch. 5th Ser. Vol. 7, p. 688, 701, 725, 741, 758, 777, 785.

PHILIP ROEMER

Resident of Berks County, enlisted in spring of 1772, served as pvt., under Capts. Samuel Kearsley and Jackson and Lieut. Col. Aaron Burr and Col. Adam Hubley. He was in the battle of Brandywine and Monmouth and was with Gen. Sullivan during his Indian campaign and in the battle of Chemung. He was discharged Jan. 28, 1781. He was allowed pension on application executed June 8, 1824, then living in Antrim Twp., Franklin County, Penna., and stated he was aged "Sixty-one years and upwards." He d. May 26, 1831. He mar. in Dec. 1792, in Chambg., Penna., Elizabeth, maiden name not given. She was allowed pension on her application executed Nov. 9, 1838, then living in Antrim Twp., Franklin County, Penna. In 1842 she stated she was sixty-nine years of age and in 1848 she stated she was seventy-three years of age., and a resident of Antrim Twp., Franklin County, Pa. In 1824 the soldier stated that he had five daus. and 2 sons residing with him, and that the youngest child was six yrs. of age, and the others aged as follows: Eleven, fifteen, seventeen, twenty-two, twenty-five, and twenty-five years, their names not given.

War Pension Claim W. 3301.

The German Evangelical Reformed Zion's Church, Greencastle, Penna. Translated from German by Mrs. Edw. Omwake. Confirmations and communicants: Philip Roemer (Raymer), 1818; Elizabeth Roemer (Raymer), 1818; Peter Roemer, conf., 1819; Maria Roemer, conf., 1819; Magdalena Roemer, 1819; Martha Roemer, 1821; Elizabeth Roemer, 1824; Eleanor Roemer, conf., 1827; George Roemer, conf., 1832; Susan Roemer, conf., 1832; Charlotte Roemer, 1850. Penna. Pensioners: Philip Raymer, pr. P. L. May 21, 1819, aged 76; Philip Reymer d. 1831, aged 75 yrs. Elizabeth Raymer d. May 15, 1849, aged 71 yrs. 2 mos. 21 days. Philip Raymer and Michael Tice were County Commissioners in 1804.

Penna. Arch. 3rd Ser. Vol. 23, p. 580.

CONRAD SPEILMAN

Served as a pvt. under Capt. Caleb North, 4th Penna. Batt. Col. Anthony Wayne. He was b. Feb. 11, 1753, d. Dec. 4, 1829. His wife, Dorothea, b. May 6, 1784, d. —— Stone broken. The will of Conrad Speilman of Antrim Twp., dated Sept. 21, 1821; prob. Jan. 12, 1830, gives to son Conrad Speelman a quarter section land near Canton, Ohio, patented in the name of Charles Fout; son George quarter section land in Richland County, Ohio, patented 'in my own name'; as signee of Simon Eaker; dau. Elizabeth quarter section land near Canton, Ohio, patented 'in my own name', dated Oct. 10, 1815; son Valentine's son Conrad, who was named for me; residue to sons: Conrad; Jacob; George; and dau. Elizabeth; Executors: son George and friend Maj. Henry Snively. George Speilman, who died 1869, aged 85 years, is probably their son. Penna. Arch. 5th Ser. Vol. 2, p. 151.

MICHAEL TICE

Served as Ensign in Lancaster County, 1780-82, under Lieut. Col. Thos. Edwards and Capt. John Stone. He d. Feb. 20, 1821, aged 66 yrs. 11 mos. 13 days. His wife Barbara, d. Apr. 2, 1825, aged 59 yrs. 10 mos. 28 days. A dau. Eve Tice mar. John Wolgamott and had a dau. Nancy Jane, who mar. Wm. Gabriel, both families having come from Lancaster County Penna. Records of the Reformed Ch. Greencastle show the following: Confirmations and Communicants:—Michael Deisz, 1818; Magdalena Tice, conf., 1835; Henry Tice, conf., 1835; Martha Tice, conf., 1835; Eliza Tice, conf., 1835; Anna Maria, conf., 1841; Samuel and Anna Tice had baptized: David, b. Nov. 23, 1816; Henry, b. Aug. 21, 1818; Elizabeth Tice, b. May 8, 1820. The sponsors being, Michael Tice and wife Barbara and Elizabeth Corley. The will of Susannah Tice was prob. Nov. 29, 1824, in which she named five children: son David; dau. Barbara; who was mar. to Jacob Rutraugh; son Samuel; dau. Liddia Brentlinger and dau. Polly. They were of Antrim Township.

OLD SHANNON GRAVEYARD

(Now, The Academy Farm)

Mercersburg, Penna.

JAMES McFARLAND

The Franklin Repository, July 19, 1825. Died at his residence in Mercersburg on the 8th ult., Mr. James McFarland in his 79th year. He was removed very suddenly . . . It would be doing injustice to departed worth not to say that Mr. McFarland was a man of rare excellence. He possessed an equable and affectionate disposition which greatly endeared him to his friends. He was rigidly honest and as a member of society active and forward in promoting the public good. He had served his country faithfully during the Rev. War. His highest praise was that of a Christian. He was devoted to the interests of the Redeemer's cause and did much to promote it in the Society to which he belonged. He had long sustained the office of Ruling Elder in the Presbyterian Church the duties of which he discharged with rigid impartiality and very general acceptance. He is gone to his reward. The church mourns his loss. His friends will feel it. Let all however take comfort in the assurance that their loss is his unspeakable gain. The Census of 1790 shows the family of James Mc Farland to be,—4 men, 2 boys, 2 females. Under Aug. 7, 1835, "The Whig" of Chambersburg gives the following: "Died on the evening of the 18th ult., at the house of her son-in-law, Mr. Arthur Chambers, Mrs. Jane McFarland, in her 73rd year,"

WILLIAM SHANNON, CORPORAL

Served 1780-81, under Capt. Wm. Huston. The Ledger of Samuel Findlay shows him as Constable, Mar. 11, 1775. In 1769, he and wife Mary and their children were members of the "Upper West Conococheague" Presby., Church of Mercersburg. The above William and Hugh Shannon were 1751 taxables, Hugh buying land near Welsh Run which he sold to Robert Elliott of Peters Twp. He is said to have gone to Hampshire County, West Va. William Shannon had a Patent from Thomas and John Penn, Esqrs., dated 27th day of Nov., 1751, a certain tract of land called "Shannon's Industry," in Peters Twp., by lands of John Baird, James Black's land, John Huston and Joseph Bradner—300 acres and allowance. William Shannon died July 5, 1784, his wife was living in 1793 when their son David made his will. The children were, John, mar. Susanna Alexander, July 8, 1772, was in Fayette County, Ky., 1811-12. James was in Lincoln County, N. C., 1811-12. Wm. thought to have been killed by Indians. Robert Shannon in Carolina, 1793; in Fayette County, Ky., 1811-12. Joseph Shannon died 1805, in Franklin County, and a nephew Wm. of Fayette County, Ky., came north to settle the estate, a farm of 121 acres, which he sold to Chas. Gillespie in 1813. The dau. Jean, mar. Joseph Shannon of York County, Mar., 1778; of Woodford County, Ky., in 1811-12. Nathaniel Shannon of Scott County, Ky., in 1811-12. David Shannon mar. Eleanor Prather and left a son William. Samuel Shannon b. 1773, died 1811, mar. at Mercersburg, Mary, dau. of Johnston Elliott, Sept. 5, 1795. Joseph, David, Samuel lived and died in or near Mercersburg.

Penna. Arch. 5th Ser. Vol. 6, p. 269, 275, 282.

JOSIAH SMITH

Served as pvt. under Capt. Wm. Huston, 1780-81. Tax lists show name of Joseph, also, but the land and possessions are the same. In 1786, Josiah Smith acquired 100 acres of land bounded by Rev. John Black, Benj. Kirkpatrick, Patrick Campbell and other lands of Josiah Smith. Josiah Smith b. 1751, d. 1828. He mar. April 18, 1782, Esther, dau. of James Clarke and wife Nancy Reed. Esther b. 1757, d. 1821. They were members of the "Upper West Conococheague" Presbyterian Church, and they had baptized: Mary, Feb. 26, 1784; Samuel, Oct. 10, 1789. They had a dau. Nancy, b. 1793, d. 1876, who mar. John Johnston in 1812—(Lieut. in War 1812). He was b. Aug. 18, 1787, d. 1857. John and Nancy Johnston had a dau. Mary who mar. Samuel Bradley.

Penna. Arch. 5th Ser. Vol. 6, p. 269, 283.

SAMUEL SMITH

Was pvt. under Capt. Wm. Huston, 1780-81. He mar. Esther, dau. of James and Jean Rankin. Gravestones show: Samuel Smith d. Sept. 30, 1815, aged 72 yrs. and 6 mos. Esther Smith d. Mar. 21, 1826, aged 64 yrs.

Penna. Arch. 5th Ser. Vol. 6, p. 269, 275, 283.

PRESBYTERIAN GRAVEYARD

(Lower Path Valley)

List of Rev. Soldiers buried in above Graveyard,—list preserved by Capt. John Walker to the date of his death, (1900)—Joseph Noble being the only one who has a stone: Martin Miller; Samuel Walker; Robert Walker; Archibald Elliott; William Elliott; Francis Elliott; Joseph Noble (stone); Robert McConnell (Estate Admr. 1801).

ARCHIBALD ELLIOTT

Served as a Lieut. under Captains Noah Abraham and Alexander Peebles in 1777-78-79-81, —some undated rolls. His will was dated 1807— he left a wife Isabella and nephews and nieces. Capt. John Walker stated that Archibald Elliott was buried in Presbyterian Graveyard, Fannettsburg, Penna.

Penna. Arch. 5th ser. Vol. 6, p. 12, 22, 28, 43, 50, 54, 120, 383, 515, 596.

FRANCIS ELLIOTT

Served as a private under Capt. Noah Abraham in 1777-79-80-81-82. Some undated rolls. His will was dated 1797. His wife was Joanna Wallace. They had issue: sons John; William; Archibald; James; daus., Elizabeth; Isabella; Mary; James Wallace was executor. Capt. John Walker stated that Franics Elliott was buried in the Presbyterian Graveyard at Fannettsburg, Penna.

Penna. Arch. 5th Ser. Vol. 6, p. 18, 21, 85, 120, 127, 139, 140, 152, 515, 383.

The Valley Spirit, Chambersburg, Penna., May 11, 1850. Died at the residence of his son, near Fannettsburg, in this county on Monday the 15th ultimo, Mr. Martin Miller, aged 96 years. The deceased served as a soldier in the Revolutionary War and was present at the ever memorable surrender of Lord Cornwallis.

JOSEPH NOBLE

Of Path Valley served as Sergt., 1777-78-81-82 under Capt. Noah Abraham. His wife was Susanna, dau. of Wm. McClelland, Sr., of Fannett Twp., and named in his will. The will of Joseph Noble was dated 1822 and prob. 1823—in which he names wife Susanna; sons Johnston and John, "Ashbridges" land. Son Joseph "Conners Farm" and son William, land; a dau. Susanna, also daus. Ruthy and Polly. The Stills and vessels to John and William. Joseph Noble born 1753, died 1823; Susanna, his wife, born 1755, died 1830. The "Repository" states death of Susanna Noble: "She being one of three persons that only remained of the first inhabitants of the Valley."

Penna. Arch. 5th Ser. Vol. 6, p. 121, 128, 141, 515.

ROBERT WALKER

Served as pvt. under Capt. Noah Abraham 177-78. He died unmarried in 1778. He was a son of Alexdr. and Mary Walker, early settlers in Metal Twp.

Penna. Arch. 5th Ser. Vol. 6, p. 21, 53, 141, 139, 516.

SAMUEL WALKER

Served as 2nd Lieut. under Capts. Noah Abraham and Thos. Askey, 1777-78-79-81,—some undated rolls. Samuel Walker mar. Mary dau. of William Noble. They had issue: Mary b. Oct. 30, 1779, mar. Robert Walker, a cousin, son of John or David Walker. They moved to Indiana County, Penna; John, b. Mar. 30, 1781, unmar.; Alexander b. Mar. 3, 1783, mar. Mary McConnell; Eleanor b. Mar. 3, 1785, mar. Robert Ramsey; Margaret, b. Mar. 8, 1788, mar. James McConnell; Samuel, b. May 5, 1794, mar. Martha McConnell; James, b. June 30, 1796, mar. Ann Skinner.

Penna. Arch. 5th Ser. Vol. 6, p. 7, 10, 12, 23, 43, 47, 49, 52, 120, 140, 385, 417, 515.

QUINCY GRAVEYARD

Quincy, Penna.

FREDERICK FISHER

Served as a pvt., in 1779 under Capt. John Jack, and in 1780-81-82 under Capt. Thomas Johnston. He was born Dec. 27, 1749, died July 27, 1810, aged 63 yrs. His wife Susanna, b. Dec. 15, 1747, d. Nov. 9, 1817, aged 69 yrs.

Penna. Arch. 5th Ser. Vol. 6, p. 75, 84, 114, 130, 540.

GEORGE WERTS

Private in Penna. Line; died in Franklin County, Penna. The will of George Wertz of Washington Twp., dated July 16, 1798; prob. Jan. 3, 1799; names a wife Catherine; son George under 21; son David; other children; George Wertz had issue: George; David; Jacob; Elizabeth, mar. to Michael Emminger; Barbara, mar. to Henry Kyler; Catherine mar. to Ferdk. Fisher; Eve mar. to John Bushman; Mary mar. to Henry Cordel. Gravestone inscription:—George Wertz, Sr. d. Nov. 27, 1798, aged 53 yrs. Catherine Wertz, b. Sept. 27, 1758, d. Aug. 16, 1832.

Penna. Arch. 3rd Ser. Vol. 23, p. 817.

ROCKY SPRING GRAVEYARD

"Wherever the Scotch-Irishman went, one of his first efforts, after locating, was to secure the stated preaching of the gospel, and by the year 1740 Presbyterian Churches were found dotted over the broad bosom of this valley, almost invariably in a grove of shady trees, and near a spring of pure crystal water."

"Their pews of unpainted pine
straight-backed and tall;
Their gal'ries mounted high,
three sides around;
Their pulpits goblet-shaped,
half up the wall;
With sounding-board above,
with acorn crowned."

JOSEPH ARMSTRONG

Of Hamilton Twp., was Colonel of the 5th Batt., Cumb. Co., Militia in 1776. He left no issue and with his wife Elizabeth, lies buried in Rocky Spring graveyard. Joseph Armstrong 1739-1811. The legatees were nephew Joseph, son of John Armstrong of Orange County, N. C.; May Jack, dau. of Patrick Jack; May McConoughy, dau. of Robert, now mar. to Joseph Caset; Samuel Armstrong Finley (of John); Joseph Armstrong Blackburn, son of John of Ohio; George Armstrong, Esq., of Greensburg, Penna John Finley (of John).

Pena. Arch. 5th Ser. Vol. 6, p. 5, 316, 317, 318.

WILLIAM BARD (BEARD)

Served as pvt. under Capt. John McConnell 1776-81-82. He died in 1815, and his wife, Margaret Durborrow died 1825. William Beard, eldest son of William Beard, late of Letterkenny Twp., states that his father left a widow Margaret and 5 children: William; Martha, mar. to Balser Besore; Mary; Rebecca and James, last 3 are minors, guardians being John Durbarrow, Fredk. Shirk and John Poorman. Said intestate died owning 107 ac. land, with a dwelling house and barn theron erected.

Penna. Arch. 5th Ser. Vol. 6, p. 302, 312, 317, 318.

JAMES BRACKENRIDGE

Was a pvt. in Militia, also a Ranger on the Frontiers. b. 1742, d. 1809; his wife Elizabeth Culbertson b. 1760, d. 1835. Orphans' Court records show the issue as Martha, mar. to James Brown; Joseph; Molly; Elizabeth. Joseph and Martha Brackenridge attest that he, their father, died July 14, 1809. James, John and Robert Brackenridge occupied Pew No. 37 in the old Log Church at Rocky Spring.

Penna. Arch. 5th Ser. Vol 4, p. 392, 701.

REV. JOHN CRAIGHEAD

Served as a pvt. in 1776, under Lieut. John Culbertson in Armstrong's Batt. He had no issue, but left a widow Jane, and a sister Catherine, widow of William Gettys, of Cumberland County. He died Apr. 20, 1799, aged 57 yrs. He was installed Pastor of the Congregation of Rocky Spring on the 13th of April, A. D. 1768. In 1791, John and Jean Allison sold to Rev. John Craighead a tract called "Union" in Letterkenny Twp. The widow of Rev. Craighead died in Cumberland County, May 12, 1818. In 1796, he was taxed with 360 ac. land; 5 Horses; 5 Cows; 1 stone house; 1 cabin; 1 barn.

Penna. Arch. 5th Ser. Vol. 6, p. 316.

CAPT. JOSEPH CULBERTSON

Served 1777-78-80-81, under the Command of Lieut. Col. Samuel Culbertson. On pages 279-280, Aug., 1780, were the names of Samuel Culbertson, Jr., John Culbertson, Samuel Culbertson, Samuel Culbertson Clark and John Culbertson. The will of Joseph Culbertson, dated Oct. 9, 1817, prob. Nov. 17, 1818, names wife Margaret; sons Hugh and John, and to son Joseph land in Cumberland County, dau. Margaret, mar. to John Breakenridge; 4 daus: Mary; Martha; Elizabeth; Sarah.

Penna. Arch. 5th Ser. Vol. 6, p. 279, 280, 289, 369, 377, 290.

PIONEER JOSEPH CULBERTSON

He was of Letterkenny Twp., and his will was probated Jan. 1, 1785. He names wife Mary; sons Joseph; Samuel; Robert; daus: Martha; Elizabeth; Margaret; granddau. Mary Brackenridge. The will of the widow, prob. in Apr., 1791, names 3 sons as above; dau. Margaret Duncan; dau. Martha; dau. Elizabeth; garnddau. Mary Brechenridge. Exrs. were John Brackenridge and son-in-law Samuel Brackenridge. On death of Martha Culbertson, unmar., her estate was divided into 6 parts: bros: samuel; Joseph; Robert; legal heirs of Mary Brackenridge; a sister; Margaret Brackenridge, a sister; to James Brackenridge and Elizabeth, his wife, another sister.

COL. SAMUEL CULBERTSON

Took the Oath of Allegiance 1777-78, before John Creigh a Justice of the Peace for Cumberland County, Penna. His will, dated and prob. Oct., 1789, recites an agreement dated 1782, between himself and wife, Eleanor, "previous to our marriage." He names sons Samuel and John; son Robert, decd. Son-in-law Thos. McKean; grandson Samuel Culberson McKean, silver spurs; son Joseph negro boy Cuff; son Alexander a light blue fine coat; Samuel Culberson, son of Alexander; dau. Agnes Long 60 pounds; dau. Martha Culberson 50 pounds; Joannah Sharpe 50 pounds; dau. Mary Culberson 50 pounds; dau. Jennet Guthry 50 pounds; son James the whole of my plantation. Exrs: son Joseph; cozen Joseph Culberson and cozen or nephew Samuel Culberson.

Penna. Arch. 2nd Ser. Vol. 14, p. 472.

CHARLES CUMMINS

Served under Captains James Patton and John McConnell 1778-80-81. He died Sept., 1821, his wife Elizabeth having died in 1802. In his will he names wife Jane; eldest son John and his children, Charles and Rachel; son Allen, decd.; son Charles in education and bonds, in 1808; dau. Ann Gabby; son William; Agnes, mar. with Patrick Hayes; In 1796 Chas. Cummins was taxed in Letterkenny Twp., with 400 acres land; 50 acres Mt. Land; 3 horses; 4 cows; 1 Brick and 2 Log houses; 1 barn; 1 Grist Mill; 1 Saw mill. They occupied pew 27 in the old church and later in the Brick church.

Penna. Arch. 5th Ser. Vol. 6, p. 267, 302, 381.

WILLIAM DAVIS

As pvt. under Capt. Nicholas Patterson, 1780, Bucks County, Penna. He was b. May 15, 1730 in Ireland, was a son of James and Eliza

(Jennings) Davis, early settlers in Tinicum Twp. Bucks County, Penna. In 1747-48, he served as ensign under Col. Alex. Graydon. Wm. Davis also served in the Rev. War, and it is stated that he and his son James were in the battle of Princeton. He mar. Mary Means, in 1757. He removed to Franklin County, in 1784, where he bought land from Wm. Peebles, near Strasburg. They attended Rocky Spring Church for eleven years, then removed to near Meadville, Penna., where Wm. Davis d. Sept. 20, 1824.

Penna. Arch. 5th Ser. Vol. 5, p. 357, 395. Also History of the Davis Family, by Thos. Kirby Davis.

WILLIAM DAVIS

Son of William and Mary Means Davis, b. Apr. 22, 1762, in Bucks County, came with his parents to Franklin County. On Nov. 23, 1786, he was mar. to Sarah Stewart by the Rev. James Grier. They were attendants at Rocky Spring Church under three pastorates. Grave stones show Wm. Davis d. Oct. 6, 1823, his widow dying Apr. 12, 1825. They had seven children. On Nov. 3, 1823, Letters of Admr. were granted to Robert and William S. Davis.

HENRY DEYARMOND (DYARMAN)

Served as pvt. 1781 under Capt. James Irvin. He died in 1833, aged about 82 yrs. Jane Holmes, his wife b. 1757, d. Aug. 31, 1823. They are buried in one plot with the Gillans.

Penna. Arch. 5th Ser. Vol. 6, p. 195.

HUGH FERGUSON

Served under Capt. John Rea, 1779-80-81. The grave stone shows the birth of Hugh Ferguson as 1760, and his death in 1834. His wife Elizabeth dying in 1826. His will was dated Sept., and prob., Dec., 1834, in which he names Nephew John Ferguson; Niece Sally Ferguson, now living with me; Sister Isabella and Isabella McCoy.

Penna. Arch. 5th Ser. Vol. 6, p. 78, 106, 544.

JAMES FINLEY ESQ.

Of Greene Twp., served under Capt. Samuel Culbertson, in Armstrong's Batt. 1776, the Rev. John Craighead serving in the same company. In his will, dated May, 1809, prob. Oct. 21, 1812, James Finley names wife Jean; oldest son Samuel; son John; son James of Chambersburg. Lot No. 354, with the Brewhouse and Tan yard thereon erected, other buildings; younger son William where I now live; 4 daus: Elizabeth, mar. Stephen Duncan; Isabel, mar. James Gilbreth; Mary, mar. Joseph Culbertson; Jean mar. Samuel A. Rippey.

Penna. Arch. 5th Ser. Vol. 6, p. 290, 316.

ADAM HARBISON

Served as pvt. under Captains Joseph Sherer and George McMillan, 1776-81. He was b. July 15, 1754, d. Feb. 15, 1824. His wife Martha d. Apr. 6, 1840, in her 74th yr. They were of Greene Twp., Franklin Co., Penna., and in his will he gives to his wife Martha the "use and occupancy of the rooms on the first and second story in the west end of my Mansion house, also the privilege of the kitchen for cooking and other purposes," etc. He names son Samuel; dau. Maria, wife of Wm. McElhare; son Thomas and dau. Isabella. Mariah McElhare died Nov. 3, 1866, aged 70 yrs. 2 mos. 18 days.

Penna. Arch. 5th Ser. Vol. 7, p. 349, 1000, 1027.

CAPTAIN WILLIAM HUSTON

Probably the son of the Widow Huston, living in 1769 in Hamilton Twp.,—her children were: John and James; William; George; Mary; Margaret. The above later appears in Western Penna. Capt. Wm. Huston recruited largely in Peters Twp., and his service covers years 1776-78-80-81, probably more. He occupied Pew No. 47 in the old Log Church at Rocky Spring and he and his wife Margaret Nelson lie in the graveyard at the church, with tombstones. His will, dated Sept., 1823, was prob. Nov., 1823, in which he names "dear wife Margaret," sons Thomas; John; James; Wm.; Benj.; Joseph. Daus.: Isabella, Ann; Mary; Margaret; Mary and Margaret being minors. Deeds show that of the above issue Thos. Huston went to Adams Co., Ohio; John to Fayette Co., Ind.; Benjamin of Franklin Co., Penna. Isabella, wife of Wm. McKinstry of Franklin Co., Penna. N. Shields of Fayette Co., Ind. William moved to Fayette Co., Ind.; where he died leaving an only son James N. Huston. Ledger accounts of Samuel Findlay of Mercersburg, father of Gov. Wm. Findlay, show Aug. and Sept., 1775, Wm. Huston charged,—"To Broadcloth, Buttons, Hatt, Hose; Band and Feather" 2 lbs. 10S. 6d. In 1769, a Wm. Huston and wife and his brother Robert were living "on the Pike" near Mercersburg. On Jan. 14, 1775, the Findlay Ledger shows Robert Huston charged with "2 Indian Blankets and tobacco," 1 lb. 16S, 0d.

Penna. Arch. 5th Ser. Vol. p. 5, 262, 269, 282, 609, 642.

JOHN MAHAN

Served as pvt. under Captains Noah Abraham and Wm. Strain, 1777-78-80-82. Deeds in 1781 show the death James McKean, who left a dau.

Mary, wife of Matthew Sheilds; dau. Jane, wife of James Beard, and dau. Ann, wife of John Machan. The Hist. of Rocky Spring Church gives: John Machan, 1730-1805. Mary Machan 1728-1803. Elizabeth Machan 1750-1804.

Penna. Arch. 5th Ser. Vol. 6, p. 18, 21, 52, 142, 430, 397.

JAMES MCCAMANT, SR.

James McCamant, Jr., and Charles McCamant, "Heartily joined as a company Aug. 7, 1755, under Capt. Joseph Armstrong." The McCalmonts occupied a pew in the old Log Church at Rocky Spring and are buried there: "James McCalmont, departed this life July 2, 1780, aged 96 yrs. His wife Jane d. May 4, 1794, aged 100 yrs. Also their children,—Charles, Elizabeth and Isabella. From Carlisle, Penna., we have the following will of James McCalmont of Letterkenny Twp., Jan. 20, 1772. To wife Jean he gives 25 lbs., a horse crature, third best in value of all my Stock, one Cow chosen at her pleasure, 10 Bushels of Wheat, five Bushels of Rie, five Bushels of Indian Corn, Good Beef or Pork, Salt, Land sowed with flax seed, other Convenancys, Esteeming her bed and body cloaths her own; my dau. Margaret McCamount 15 lbs. exclusive of what I have already given her; to John McCamont my grandson, son of my son John decd. to Dau. Mary, wife of James Montgomery; to James Montgomery my Grandson; to Dau. Jean, now the wife of Patrick Hartford; to son James both real and personal property. Prob. Aug. 21, 1780.

Penna. Arch. 5th Ser. Vol. 1, p. 38.

MAJOR JAMES MCCALMONT

Served under Col. Samuel Culbertson, 1776-78-80, 6th Batt. Cumb. Co., Militia. He occupied Pew 25 in the old Log Church and his grave stone shows he died July 19, 1809, aged 70 yrs. He is said to have been famous as a runner and to have had many hairbreadth escapes from the Indians. The will of James McCalmont of Letterkenny Twp., Franklin Co., Penna., names first his wife Margaret; to Hannah Jameson, "my wife's Niece;" To Robert Hartford, James Hartford, John Hartford, Matthew and George Hartford, my 5 nephews, and Elizabeth Hartford, wife of Joshua Pierson, Jane Hartford, wife of Robert Wilson, Margaret Hartford, wife of James Smith; to Jane and Margaret McCalmont, daus. of Mary Hartford, who intermar. with James McCalmont of the town of Strasburg, Franklin Co., Penna. Will prob. Aug. 15, 1809, one witness being Isaac McCalmont.

Penna. Arch. 5th Ser. Vol. 6, p. 5, 39, 260, 310, 375, 608. Penna. Arch. 2nd Ser. Vol. 14, p. 434.

JOHN MCCONNELL

Served 1776 as a Lieut. and 1777-78-79-80-81, as a Captain in the 4th Batt. Cumb. Co. Militia under Lieut. Col. Samuel Culbertson. Capt. John McConnell occupied Pew No. 21, in the old Log Church at Rocky Spring and Pew 32 in the new brick church. In his will dated Oct., 1815, prob. Dec., 1815, he names wife Mary to whom he gives the largest looking-glass in the house; sons Robert; David; John; grandch: Mary; Wm.; and Margery Robinson, son and daus. of my dau. Margaret Robinson, decd., under 20 yrs.; dau. Rosanna Lawther; Dau. Elizabeth McConnell; excrs.: son Robert and Fredk. Foltz.

Penna. Arch. 5th Ser. Vol. 6, p. 34, 26, 266, 301, 308, 310, 318, 260, 317, 370, 374, 378, 614, 639.

JOHN REA

Served in Cumb. Co. Militia as Lieut. in 1777 and as Captain 1777-78-80-81. His wife was Elizabeth Culbertson; issue: 6 sons and 1 dau. Franklin Repository — Chambersburg, Penna.: Tuesday—Nov. 11, 1806. Married on Thursday last by the Rev. Mr. Herron, Gen'l. John Rea to Miss Elizabeth Culbertson, dau. of Col. Samuel Culbertson, all of this country. Franklin Repository—Feb. 10, 1829—No. 26, Vol. 33. Died on the morning of the 6th inst., General John Rea, after a very short illness aged 74 years . . . in less than a day and a half he breathed his last . . . In the career of his life he was early found among those who were engaged in the defence of Liberty and their country. He served several tours in the militia during the revolutionary contest and afterwards he was the uniform asserter of the rights of his country . . . highly esteemed—member of the State Legislature. (The mortal remains of General Rea were interred at Rocky Srring on Saturday last—they were escorted out of town by the "Franklin Blues," and the "Washington Grays" with solemn music and accompanied by the first named Company and an unusual concourse of relatives and neighbors—) Franklin Repository—June 21, 1836. Death of Mrs. John Rea, in her 52nd yr.—buried at Martinsburg, Bedford Co., Penna., at home of her son. She left six sons and one dau. A Government Stone has been erected in his memory, at Rocky Spring by the Franklin County Chapter, Daughters of the American Revolution.

Penna. Arch. 5th Ser. Vol. 6, p. 6, 69, 77, 78, 105, 514, 528, 534.

WILLIAM ROBERTSON

Served as pvt. under Captains Samuel Patton in 1777-78, and John McConnell in 1780-81-82. He was of Letterkenny Twp., his will prob. May

7, 1796. He names wife Margery; dau. Margaret, not yet 21; dau. Sarah; 4 sons: Wm. James; Thomas; David to be put to trades; son John; bro. Alexander Robertson.

Penna. Arch. 5th Ser. Vol. 6, p. 267, 302, 309, 373, 380.

ALEXANDER THOMPSON

An early settler in Greene Twp., came from Greenock, Scotland, in 1771, settling in Greene Twp., 1773. An active and prominent supporter of the Covenanter Church. His house a religious centre of a wide area of country. He served as a Lieut. with Capt. John Rea 1777-78 79-80, leaving a will dated and prob. in 1800. He named wife Elizabeth; son John; son William; dau. Agnes Colhoun; son Alexander; son Archibald; dau. Elizabeth Purviance; dau. Margaret Watson; dau. Barbara Watson; dau. Mary Cowan; dau. Jannet Shaw; son Andrew; dau. Ann Logan;

son James; dau. Jane Shields. In 1791, Alexander Thompson of Greene Twp., was taxed on 225 and 124 acres of Land; 5 horses; 16 Cows; 1 still; 1 Malt House; Teaspoons, 20.

Penna. Arch. 5th Ser. Vol. 6, p. 72, 78, 514, 534, 543, 584.

JOHN WILSON

Served as pvt. under Capt. Samuel Patton 1777-1780-1781-1782. The Franklin Repository, dated Feb. 7, 1826, states: "Died at his residence in St. Thomas Twp., Friday last, at an advanced age, John Wilson . . . He served one or more tours of duty during the Rev. War." His wife was Sarah, dau. of John Strain, of Lurgan Twp. He left issue: Elizabeth, mar. James Shields; Florence, mar. Matt. Patton; Moses; David; James; William; Robert; Sarah.

Penna. Arch. 5th Ser. Vol. 6, p. 279, 287, 312, 372.

THE ROYER GRAVEYARD

East of Waynesboro, Penna., near Shockey's Mill, Washington Twp.

CHRISTIAN KEAGY

Served from Lancaster Co., Penna., under Capt. Philip Baker, in 1782. Deed show that in 1787, Jacob Hollinger of Washington Twp., Franklin Co., Penna., sold to Christian Keagy, of Lancaster Co., Penna., 113 acres of land, for 700 pounds. The will of Christian Keagy was dated and prob. 1805, leaving a wife Mary and issue: Henry; Susanna; Nancy; Mary; Abraham; Christian; John; Elizabeth. Wife Mary was to have land and the use of the Spring called "Parkes." Christian Keagy was born Aug. 3, 1751, d. Aug. 31, 1805.

Penna. Arch. 5th Ser. Vol. 7, p. 1140.

DANIEL ROYER

Served as Ensign, 1780, under Capt. Samuel Royer, Lieut. John Stitt, being the 5th Co., of the First Batt., Cumb. Co., Militia under Lieut.

Col. Jas. Johnston. Daniel Royer b. Apr. 27, 1762, d. Mar. 26, 1838, aged 75 yrs. His wife Catherine b. Nov. 9, 1769, d. May 7, 1858, aged 88 yrs., 5 mos., 26 days. They had issue: David; Catherine; Nancy; Jacob; Samuel; Elizabeth, wife of David Good; Mary, wife of George Schmucker; John; Susannah, wife of Henry Reigart;; Rebecca, wife of George Smith.

Penna. Arch. 5th Ser. Vol. 6, p. 70, 88.

SAMUEL ROYER

Served as Capt. in Cumb. Co., Militia in 1777-78-80. His grave is marked by a plain limestone, and said to be the grave of Capt. Samuel Royer, 1738-1823. His wife was Catherine Lampshear, and they had issue: Daniel; Samuel mar. Susanna Mack; John; Jacob; Elizabeth; Catherine.

Penna. Arch. 5th Ser. Vol. 6, p. 88, 90, 511, 516, 531, 585, 609.

SLATE HILL GRAVEYARD

(Near Mercersburg, Penna.)

The Associate Reformed Church of West Conococheague, at Slate Hill, near Mercersburg, Franklin County, Penna. The pastors were: Rev. John Rodgers, 1772-1781; Rev. Matthew Lind, 1783-1798; Rev. John Young, 1799-1803; Rev. John Lind, 1808-1817. The Church building in which this Congregation worshipped was removed to Mercersburg, re-erected on LaFayette Street, and used as a dwelling house. Rev. Scouler stated that the dead of upwards of one hundred years lay buried in this graveyard.

Members of the West Conococheague Church. A list of the subscribers for the labours of the Rev. Matthew Lind of the West Conococheague Congregation. James Ramsey; David Humphrey; Samuel McCune; James Miller; Oliver Anderson; John Sterrit; James Stuart; Adam Rush; Robert Godgers (Rodgers?); Thomas McClelland; Ann Anderson; James and Andrew Read; Edward Mannon; John Bruce; Wm. Dickey; David Reed; Wm. Davidson; John Moore; Joseph Bogle; Daniel McCurdy; James Clark; John Martin; James Dodd; James McMaster; Thos. Rodgers; Samuel Reed; Thomas H. Sloan; Thomas Dunlop; Robert Miller; Thos. Shannon; James Bogle; Adam Lowry; James Clerk. In addition to above list, a receipt by James Ramsey Feb. 22, 1794, show names of Sarrah Davis and Walter Maxwell as paid "Steeppens for Mr. Lind."

Items from an unrecorded will of Oliver Anderson. 1st Bequeathment. To Beloved wife Jean 1/3 of my estate real and personal During life She continuing a widow, 1/2 during Life and at her death to return to the male part of the family, equally. 2nd Bequeathment, to my five daughters each 50 pounds out of my estate. My oldest dau. being married, Before her marriage I laid out for such things as she wanted 10 pounds. Likewise she got a Feather Bed and Bed Clothes. Likewise 2 cows, a mare worth 25 pounds, and a saddle. I likewise gave to dau. Elizabeth when she went to keep house for her brother Henry I laid out 10 pounds for her and gave her a mare at 25 pounds and saddle and a Feather bed and bed clothes but no cows as yet. The other 3 daus. to be provided for the same way and then each to get 50 pounds out of my estate. 3rd Bequeathment, The place or plantation to be sold after my decease the price to be equally divided among my 6 sons: Wm.; Henry; John; David; Samuel; Robert. My 2 oldest sons Wm.; and Henry Anderson got each of them a horse creature and those younger to get each of them a horse creature out of the estate and so making them equal to the 2 oldest . . . To my son John my watch which came to me, By my Brother John Anderson's Death, and so I allow him this upon account of the name. Some proven acc'ts., June 7, 1810,—

Hugh Cowan for coffin and shroud	$ 9.00
Jas. McCoy funeral expenses	28.70
Jas. Clark, Church Stipend Mar., 1811	14.00
Dr. P. W. Little	4.16
Robert Street, digging grave	2.00

To Jane and John Anderson Receipted bill from the Stores of T. & E. Lane & Jeremh. Evans of Mercersburg, Nov., 1814: To Mr. John Anderson and on which he added "Bills that I paid for Sister Anne when she was married." The items included: 1 Fancy fashionable Silk Bonnet and Box; 1 pair white kid slippers; 2 1/3 yards white Ribbond. 5 1/2 yards Silk; 1 shawl; muslin; dimity; cambrick; shirting; Lace. An Inventory of the Goods and Chattels, Rights and Credits of Oliver Anderson, Mar. 9, 1810, shows Puter plats and other dresser furniture; Breakfast and Dining Tables; Pepper Mille; Candle Sticks; Split bottomed Chairs; Books; Queensware; 7 Chaynay Cups and Saucers; 6 Silver Teaspoons &c, &c.

OLIVER ANDERSON

The War Department gives the following: He served in the Revolutionary War as a pvt. in a Company of the Second Batt. of Cumb. Co. Militia, commanded by Col. John Allison, now under the care of James Erwin, Captain. His name appears only on an undated Muster Roll from 6th of Dec. to the 24th . . . days inclusive, 1776. Oliver Anderson served as a pvt. Oct., 1777, with Capt. Samuel Patton, and in 1780-81 under Capt. Wm. Huston. Family tradition states that he kept the fires burning to deceive the British when Washington crossed the Delaware. Knowing the sterling worth and conscientious qualities of the Anderson family, the above statement is accepted as a fact by the neighborhood. Oliver Anderson mar. 1st Elizabeth Marshall, Mar. 14, 1770 and had issue: Wm. b. 1770; Henry b. 1772; Jeanette, b. 1774, who mar. John Burnsides. Oliver Anderson mar. 2nd Sarah Kyle, Feb. 22, 1780, and had issue Elizabeth, b. 1781; John b. 1783. Oliver Anderson mar. 3rd, Jean Humphrey, who d. Nov. 26, 1839 (?),—issue: Agnes, b. 1787; David b. 1788; Samuel b. 1790; Anne b. 1792; Robert b. 1795; Mary b. 1798. Of the above issue: Wm. b. 1770, mar. ———— Dewett, moved to Kentucky, had issue. Henry b. 1772, mar. Sallie McCune, moved to Mercer Co.—No issue. Jeanette Burnsides moved to Ohio, had issue, one Oliver. Elizabeth b. 1781, mar. Wm. Russell. Moved to Mercer Co., Penna. No issue. John b. 1783, d. 1850, unmarried. Anges b. 1787, mar. John Dodd, no issue. David b. 1788, unmarried. Samuel b. 1790 mar. Eleanor McCulloh; they had issue Ten. Anne b. 1792, mar. Matthew Newell. They moved to Tiffin, Ohio and had issue eight. Robert b. 1795, mar. Eve Ensminger d. Williamsport, Md. Mary b. 1798 mar. Wm. Dick, they moved to Tiffin, Ohio and had issue eight. Oliver Anderson, his three wives and son John are buried in the Slate Hill Graveyard. Their land was part of a tract taken up by James Galbreath in 1757.

Penna. Arch. 5th Ser. Vol. 6, p. 373, 269, 275, 282.

DAVID HUMPHREYS

Served as a pvt. under Capt. Wm. Huston, 1780-81-82. The will of David Humphreys, Sr., of Montgomery Twp., was dated 1790, prob. Dec. 1795. He names son David; son George; son Robert; son John; son Wm.; the lands he has located in Kaintucky; son-in-law Oliver Anderson and Jane, his wife . . . and to their three children, 29 pounds, 10 shillings; dau. Anne Humphreys ½ of the household furniture and 55 pounds in gold or silver. Of the above, David Humphreys, Jr., mar. Nancy dau. of James and Nancy (Reed) Clark. Anne mar. ———— McChesney.

Penna. Arch. 5th Ser. Vol. 6, p. 269, 275, 282, 304.

THOMAS JOHNSTON

Served from Lancaster Co., Penna., under Capt. Robert Buyers, Col. James Crawford, in Baergen Town Camp, Sept. 4, 1776 and 1777. The wife of Thomas Johnston was Anne Houston and they came from Lancaster to Franklin Co. about 1794, settling on a large tract of land two or three miles west of Mercersburg. It contained enough for a farm for each of his sons. His wife's brother James left a "day book" in which was written, "Thomas Johnston and Anne were married Dec. 31, 1778, aged 27 years and 11 months and 18 years and ten days." Anne died Aug. 18, 1823; Thomas died Feb. 5, 1829. They had issue: Mary Johnston b. Dec. 5, 1779 in Lancaster Co., Penna., mar. Apr. 1, 1800, John Hunter, b. Apr. 15, 1776; James Johnston mar. Nancy, dau. of Archibald Rankin; John b. 1787, mar. Nancy Smith, retained the homestead; he was a Captain in the War of 1812, in his later years he moved into Mercersburg, where he died Aug. 11, 1857. The early tract or home was called "Johnston Hall" and the Samuel Johnston home was known as "Poplar Hill;" Samuel Johnston b. 1792, mar. Maria Rankin. He, also, was in the war of 1812; Thomas Johnston b. 1795, d. 1827, in Wash. Co., Penna. He was attending Jefferson College, when taken ill with fever and is buried where the Daniel Houstons lie; Alexander b. Sept. 4, 1803, mar. Esther, dau. of Jeremh. and Mary Clark Rankin. He d. Apr. 25, 1870. Issue: Mary Clark and Thomas.

Penna. Arch. 5th Ser. Vol. 7, p. 458, 461, 463, 464.

ROBERT THOMPSON

Served with Capt. Wm. Huston, as Ensign, 1780-81. Robert Thompson left a will dated Sept. and prob. Oct. 5, 1824. He named sons: Wm.; James A.; Robert; also daus. Polly Templeton; Sally Reed;Nancy Thompson. Lands in the State of Ohio, in Stark County to 3 sons; "my road wagon and four of my horses." Grandch. Robert T. Templeton and Robert T. Reed.

Penna. Arch. 5th Ser. Vol. 6, p. 265, 270, 276, 642.

Probable burials: Samuel McCune; Joseph Bogle; James Clarke; James Dodd.

SNIVELY GRAVEYARD

Antrim Twp., Near Greencastle

ANDREW SNIVELY

Farmer of Antrim Twp., served 1779 under Capt. John Jack, and in 1780-81-82 with Capt. Thomas Johnston. He left a will dated 1812, prob. 1813, providing for wife Molly, among other things, the use of 6 apple trees, three her choice and three son Andrew's choice, also a piece of woolen cloth now in the house. He names sons John; Andrew; Henry; Jacob; daus. Catherine, wife of John Bowman; Susannah, wife of Jacob Newman; son Samuel; son Daniel land in Indiana Co., Penna.; Daus. Betsy Stoner, Nancy Stoner and Molly Snively; Samuel, Daniel and Molly minors. Andrew Snively died at the age of 62 years, his first wife Anna Funk dying in 1788; his second wife Mary Magdalena Shenk died in Oct., of 1830.

Penna. Arch. 5th Ser. Vol. 6, p. 75, 84, 115, 130, 540.

HENRY SNIVELY

Served under Captains James Poe and John Woods, 1780-81-82. His will dated 1801, prob. 1803, names wife Barbara, who was to be given 225 pounds and son Peter to maintain her; sons Jacob and Peter land; son Joseph land, also a house and Lot in Greencastle . . . and may take the water from the Meeting-house Spring; dau. Elizabeth Price; son Henry: the burying ground in my field shall be 'paled' around and remain as a burying place for the dead of my family and friends.

Penna. Arch. 5th Ser. Vol. 6, p. 91, 103, 109, 575, 582.

DEDICATION OF GRAVEYARD

at

SALEM REFORMED CHURCH

R. R. No. 3, Waynesboro, Penna.

June 21, 1931

The history of the "Graveyard" of Salem Church is closely linked with the erection of the log church, under the direction of Daniel Besore and Daniel Ledy. The founders and original members of this congregation who partook of the Lord's Supper at the first Communion service held in the log church on Easter Sunday, April 8, 1787, by the pastor Rev. Cyriacus Spangenberg von Reidemeister, were Elders, Henry Miller and Frederick Nicodemus; Deacons, Christopher Adam and Conrad Nicodemus, together with the following, Albert Heefner; John Heefner; Valentine Heefner; John Otto; Peter Schweitzer, Sr.; Elizabeth Miller; Catherine Heefner; Elizabeth Ruth; Veronica Otto; Catherine Adam; Margaret Nicodemus; Elizabeth Nicodemus; Anna Maria Steffen; Elizabeth Miller; Elizabeth Ledy; Magdalena Besore and Christina Besore. It is of interest to note that one hundred and forty-four years ago, twenty-two members communed at what was the first communion service in the log church that had been completed only a month earlier. Other early members were: Jacob and Catherine Omwake; John and Elizabeth Omwake; Henry and Christina Miller; David and Barbara Besore; George and Esther Carbaugh; Lewis Karbaugh; John and Sarah Scott; Jacob and Susan Wetzel; John and Margaret Nicodemus; George and Catherine Sheffler; Daniel and Susan Ledy; Daniel and Sarah Ledy; Samuel Miller; Samuel Omwake; Henry Omwake and others who were the forerunners of the Salem congregation, the Reformed constituency of Waynesboro and surrounding community.

DANIEL BESHORE

Served as a pvt., under Capt. Casper Steover and Capt. Wm. Skiles 1781-82, in Lancaster Co., Penna. Rev. John Waldschmidt records the marriage of "Daniel, son of the decd., Johann Bosshaar and Catherine, dau. of the decd., Rudolph Rudy, Mch. 30, 1756." Daniel Beshore of Washington Twp., b. July 30, 1733, d. Jan. 21, 1811. His wife Catherine b. Apr. 1, 1734, d. Apr. 30, 1814. They left issue: sons—David and John; daus.; Christina Tom; Elizabeth Rummell; Mary Stiffey; Margaret Sell; Catherine Adams; Maddeline, wife of Philip Sprahel. Daniel Beshore was one of the founders of Salem Reformed Church, near Waynesboro. He was a member of the building committee and for many years the church was called Besore's church, later changed to Salem.

Penna. Arch. 5th Ser. Vol. 7, p. 37, 171.

FREDERICK NICODEMUS

Was appointed by Council of Safety of Maryland, First Lieut. of Capt. Daniel Clapsaddle's Co. of Militia in Washington Co., Md. He died Oct. 26, 1816, aged 83 yrs, 8 mos. His wife Margaret d. Mar. 15, 1815, aged 67 yrs., 2 mos. Frederick Nicodemus mar. Margaret Ripple,—early German Settlers at Hoover's Mill, Washington Twp., Franklin Co., Penna., a founder of Salem Reformed Church. Fredk. Nicodemus and Henry Miller, Elders; Christopher Adam and Conrad Nicodemus, Deacons. Frederick Nicodemus and wife had issue: Conrad mar. Margaret Hartel; Susanna, b. 1781; John b. 1783 mar. Margaret Potter; Catherine b. 1787 mar. John Oellig; Elizabeth b. 1789; Madalene mar. Peter Adam.

Maryland Arch. Vol. 12, p. 301—Sept. 26, 1776.

THE ROBERT KENNEDY MEMORIAL PRESBYTERIAN CHURCH
Welsh Run, Penna.

The "Welsh Run Church" became known as "Lower West Conococheague" Presbyterian Church when separated from the "Upper West Conococheague" Church. It was organized A. D. 1741, and was supplied early by a Rev. Mr. Dunlap. The land was given by the Penns, but the early church was burned by the Indians in their Wars with the whites. The site was changed, one acre having been given by Robert Smith, of Welsh Run. As some trouble arose over a deed, Jacob Angle and wife Eleanor, later redeeded the land, on which the present building stands. A new edifice was erected about 1773, and a plan of seating still exists. Many pioneers and Rev. soldiers are known to be buried within the graveyard—Many of the early Welsh, altho they had a graveyard on a farm. The Works, Rheas, Duffields, Rankins, Davis' are known to be buried at this Church. Under probable burials, Col. Josiah Price, who was a pewholder, and whose plantation was just across the line in Maryland, and perhaps his parents who were among the very early Welsh. Thomas Wason, son of John Wason, the victim of Indian Cruelty. Hugh McKee; Fergus Moorhead, a pewholder, Andrew Mays, John Shannon, Sr. and Col. John Work—and many more. Probable burials Welsh Run Ch. Dr. Samuel Duffield; Wm. Duffield. Welsh Run—Patent in possession of John Martin; James Campbell pd. unto the Proprietaries at the granting of the Warrant—$449(now pd. by Jacob Stahl,) there is granted unto Jacob Stahl a tract called "Farmer's Hope"—Montgomery Twp., Franklin Co., by Wm. McWhirtir's land by Henry Stahl, Robert Mackey, David Davis—318 ac., 60 pchs., under 2 Warrants to James Campbell both in 1754 whose right became vested in John Shelby and Robert Smith, resurveyed in 1772.

GEORGE EAKER

d. Jan. 10, 1818. His grave stone has this inscription, "He fought for liberty and lived to enjoy it." He served 1780-81 under Lieut. Richard McLean and Capt. Thomas Johnston. He mar. Mary dau. of John Kennedy of Antrim Twp., and they had issue: Joseph; Elizabeth, wife of Wm. Scott; Catherine; Ruhanna mar. Nicholas Hooper; Polly; George Washington; Sarah. In the "Falling Spring" graveyard, Chambersburg, there is a stone to Sarah McDowell Eaker, who d. Oct. 16, 1856, aged 60 yrs. It is thought that her husband was the above George W. Eaker. They had one son who died young.

Penna. Arch. 5th Ser. Vol. 6, p. 83, 108, 114, 129.

FRANCIS ROBINSON

Served under Capts. James Patton, Robert Dickey, Thomas McDowell. The will of Francis Robinson of Montgomery Twp., prob. Dec. 3, 1829, names sons John; Charles; Joseph; Francis; Adam; dau. Margaret Gabrel's heirs; dau. Mary Kennedy; dau. Esther Campbell; dau. Jean Ritchey; dau. Martha Angle (wife of Samuel); dau. Ruth Fulk. The wife of Francis Robinson was Jean McMahon. Franklin Repository Tuesday, Feb. 10, 1829: "Departed this life on Wednesday the 28th ult. Mr. Francis Robinson of this county in the 85th year of his age after an illness of six days. He bore his afflictions with

Christian fortitude peacefully and calmly resigning his soul to God."

Penna. Arch. 5th Ser. Vol. 6, p. 271, 284. 314.

The will of Charles, son of Francis Robinson, requests that he be buried in the graveyard at the Presbyterian Church at Welsh Run, "Where my father and mother are buried."

JAMES WRAY

Pr. and pensioner, P. M. died Feb. 7, 1838, in his 83rd yr. His wife was probably Margaret Wray, who d. Sept. 7, 1804, in her 59th yr. They left issue: Sarah; Margaret, wife of John Anderson and Elizabeth, wife of Elisha Wilson.

Penna. Arch. 3rd Ser. Vol. 23, p. 530.

THE WHITE CHURCH GRAVEYARD

Churches of the Valley By the Rev. Alfred Nevin

Among the first objects which claimed the attention of the early settlers in their new home, was the organization of a Church according to the faith of their fathers. This took place, A. D. 1738, and was styled, "Upper West Conococheague," which covered about fourteen miles square. The two most prominent places selected were, the one, near what is now known by the name of Waddell's Graveyard, and which was then opened for interments in anticipation of the building being erected there, and the other the place where it now stands. In a spirit of compromise, and as being the most central and eligible, the latter place was chosen.

WHITE CHURCH GRAVEYARD

Early Presbyterian—2½ miles from Mercersburg, Penna.

ALLAN BROWN

Served as pvt. under Capt. Noah Abrahm from Metal Twp., in 1777-79-80-81-82. His will was probated Nov. 16, 1808, and he is buried at White Church graveyard. In his will he mentions his wife, his son John and John's nine children; dau. Mary Brown (now McCurdy); sons Joseph and Stephen Oliver Brown; granddau. Margaretta Johnston, dau. of Jane Brown, alias Johnston, decd. His sons and son-in-law James McCurdy were executors of the will.

Penna. Arch. 5th Ser. Vol. 6, p. 86, 121, 128, 141, 384, 393, 515.

RICHARD BARD

Served as a pvt. under Captains Walter McKinnie and Joseph Culbertson, 1778-81. He and his wife Catherine Poe were taken captive by the Indians in April, 1758. Mr. Bard escaping finally made many efforts to ransom his wife, going to Shamokin, thence to the Big Cherry Trees, where he started along an Indian path that he knew led to his wife's abode. He met a party of Indians who were bringing her in, and paid the forty pounds he had promised by letter; she had been a captive for two yrs. and 5 mos. Mr. Bard b. 1736, d. 1799; his wife b. 1737, d. 1811. They had issue: John; Isaac; Mary; Archibald; Olivia; Thomas; William; Elizabeth; Margaret; Catherine; Martha.

Penna. Arch. 5th Ser. Vol. 6, p. 266, 298, 300, 382.

JAMES CRAWFORD

Of Montgomery Twp., served 1780-81, under Capt. Wm. Huston. His will was probated Jan., 1798: "as soon as convenient a tombstone to be put over my grave, the dimensions of which I wish to be in length six feet and about two inches, and in breadth about four feet, and I rather desire it should come from Philadelphia." His wife Martha was a dau. of Samuel Smith of Antrim Twp.,—Jeremiah Talbot, Henry Work and Walter Beatty being his brothers-in-law. James Crawford was a son of Edward Crawford, Sr., of Fayetteville, and his legatees are largely nieces and nephews. Martha, widow of James Crawford, later mar. Dr. Wm. Magaw.

Penna. Arch. 5th Ser. Vol. 6, p. 265, 270, 275, 283.

JOHN DICKEY

Died 1842, aged 90 yrs. On Nov. 20, 1781, he was mar. to Betsy McCall, who also died in 1842, aged 87 yrs. This John Dickey was a brother of James Dickey whose grave is marked in the Waddell graveyard. John Dickey served under Capt. Robert Dickey in 1781, and under Capt. James Patton 1780. He lived for many years at McConnellsburg, Penna., and was an Associate Judge of Bedford County for nearly fifty yrs. He was a Penna., pensioner in Bedford Co., and his will proves his relationship to the Dickeys of Franklin Co., Penna.

Penna. Arch. 5th Ser. Vol. 6, p. 271, 284.

SAMUEL FINDLAY

Is shown in May, 1778, as Quarter Master in the Sixth Batt., under Col. Samuel Culbertson. He was in service, also, in 1781-82, under Capt. Walter McKinnie. His Ledger shows many interesting charges, over the period of the Rev. War. In his will, dated Oct., 1796, prob. Dec., 1804, he mentions two tracts of land not to be sold until son Nathan comes to age of twenty-one yrs. To Elizabeth Findlay, my niece, 25 pounds; residue to six sons: John; William; James; Jonathan; Thomas; Nathan. Deed book Vol. 1, p. 491,—Samuel Findlay of Peters Twp., tract in Antrim Twp., adjoining lands of John Mack and Catherine Thompson, 1762. In 1766 Samuel Findlay sells to James Thompson of Antrim Twp., 69 acres for 50 pounds, who sells to James McClenaghan in 1769. Under taxables, Peters Twp., in 1790, Samuel Findlay is shown with five tracts of land: 48, 264, 151, 153, 300 acres; 6 horses, 8 cows, 1 negro, 3 oz. Plate. In 1791 the Plate is increased to 8 oz. Samuel Findlay died 1804 in his 71st yr. His wife Jane Findlay died 1783 in her 35th year. She was a dau. of William Smith, Sr., of Mercersburg, Penna.

Penna. Arch. 5th Ser. Vol. 6, p. 298, 304, 375.

WILLIAM HAYES

Served as pvt. under Captains Wm. Huston and Wm. Smith, 1780-81. He died Aug. 25, 1804, aged 62 yrs.; his wife Jean Taylor, also died Aug. 26, 1804, aged 53 yrs. They were married by the Rev. John Roan. In his will, dated and prob. Aug., 1804, he names his wife Jean; sons Patrick; Samuel; David; daus. Nancy; Jean; Eleanor; Martha. They were members of the "Upper West Conococheague" Presby. Church, near Mercersburg. Their son Patrick Hays was a Captain in the War of 1812, from Franklin County.

Penna. Arch. 5th Ser. Vol. 6, p. 270, 276, 283.

REV. JOHN KING D. D.

b. Dec. 5, 1740, in Little Britain Twp., Lancaster Co., Penna., died July 15, 1813. He was Chaplain of Col. Samuel Culbertson's Batt., Cumb. Co. Militia. He was Pastor of the "Upper West Conococheague" Church from 1769 to 1811. Dr. King made a patriotic address to Capt. Wm. Huston's Co., when they were to start to the front. A marble tombstone was erected over his grave bearing this beautiful inscription: "As a tribute of respect to the memory of the Rev. John King, D. D. upwards of forty-two years the able, learned, and faithful pastor of the congregation of Upper West Conococheague, whose life exhibited the beauty of holiness; whose death declared the triumph of the cross, this monument is erected by the grateful children of his pastoral care." "They that be wise shall shine as the brightness of the firmament; and they that turn many to righteousness, as the stars forever and ever." In the will of Dr. John King, dated and prob. 1813, he provides for his wife,—furniture, real estate &c. To the Trustees of the Bible Society; nephews and nieces. To the Rev. Robert Kennedy my HEBREW BOOKS; to the Congregation of the Upper West Conococheague my hot press Bible. The will of his widow ELIZABETH KING, dated Jan., 1822, prob Dec., 1822,; "Mindful of the uncertainty of life." To nephew James King, my Tablespoons; to Mary Ray I give my set of black and white curtains and 600 dollars. I give Sister Brownson my black Bombasine frock; to Molly McDowell my cloath Cloak; to Elizabeth McDowell my black cloth shawl, and to my sister King the whole of the remainder of my wearing apparel; $40. to black Jean, now living with me, and $40. to Susy my small black girl. On April 2nd, 1771, Rev. John King was married by Mr. Lang to Elizabeth, dau. of John and Agnes (Craig) McDowell of Fort McDowell. In a Hymn Book which he gave to his bride, he inscribed the following poem:—

A Present to Mrs. Elizabeth King
Her heart may heavenly grace inspire
From Jesus her immortal King,
The Father's Love, the Spirits fire
Descend and teach her Soul to sing.

To sing, with sweetest Melody,
The Songs of Happy Saints above
To celebrate the eternal Three
And taste their everlasting Love.

In pleasing Concert let us join
Our Kindred Hearts his Name to praise

His glorious Name, who Deigns to hear
Nor will disdain our feeble lays.

Kindle our Fires, ye Glorious Hosts
In Heaven's high Courts, whose Flaming Tongues
Ne'er cease his glories to proclaim
Glories most worthy of your songs.

Be this our daily love and joy
Till this imperfect Life is gone,
And Jesus comes with mighty Grace
To raise us to his heavenly Throne.

(The Psalms of David in Metre, Printed by Alexander Adam, Glasgow. M.D.C.C.L.XXIII).

ALEXANDER MCCOY

Served in 1777-81, under Captains George Crawford and Patrick Jack. He died Jan. 30, 1823. His wife Jane died Nov. 18, 1802, aged 62 yrs; she was a dau. of John Watts. Alexander McCoy, 2nd., died Mar. 19, 1846, aged 60 yrs. 8 mos. His wife Jane Culbertson, d. Jan. 8, 1827, aged 38 yrs.
Penna. Arch. 5th Ser. Vol. 6, p. 295, 371.

ALEXANDER MCCUTCHEON

Served as pvt. under Capt. Patrick Jack, 1781-82. In 1769, Samuel McCutcheon and wife Catherine were living in District 9, of the Presbyterian Church of Mercersburg,—the children were: William; James; Alexander; Eleanor; Samuel. Alexander McCutcheon died Aug. 3, 1844, aged 88 yrs. Sarah, wife of Alexander, died Dec. 14, 1819, aged 59 yrs. (She was a dau. of Robert Crunkleton of Antrim Twp.
Penna. Arch. 5th Ser. Vol. 6, p. 313, 292, 296.

ROBERT MCFARLAND

Served as pvt. under Capt. William Huston, 1780-81. He was born in Bucks Co., Penna., Jan. 12, 1740, d. in Peters Twp., Jan. 22, 1823. His wife, Jean Faggs Cochran of Faggs Manor, was born Feb. 10, 1743, and died Apr. 2, 1827. He served under Capt. Nicholas Patterson in Tinicum Twp., Militia in 1775, and signed the Oath of Allegiance in Bucks Co., in 1777. He came to vicinity of Mercersburg in 1778 and served under Capt. Huston 1780-81. Issue: Joseph, b. 1771; Stephen; Prudence, b. 1774; Robert C. b. 1776; Ann, mar. Matthew Patton; John; Jane Cochran; Mary.
Penna. Arch. 5th Ser. Vol. 6, p. 269, 275, 282.

CAPTAIN ROBERT PARKER

(Son of Wm. and Elizabeth (Todd) Parker) b. 1754, died at Mercersburg, Penna., May 1, 1799. He entered the service from Phila., in 1777, 2nd. Lieut., in the 2nd Continental Artillery, under Col. John Lamb; 1st Lieut. in 1781; Capt. Lieut. 1782. At Brandywine and Germantown in 1777, Monmouth in 1778 with Gen'l. Clinton's brigade; in Gen'l. Sullivan's Expedition in 1779; Siege of Yorktown in 1781; Southern Army in 1782-83. His Journal of the Sullivan expedition was printed in the Penna. Magazine of History for Oct., 1902 and Jan., 1903. Captain Parker was a member of the Society of the Cincinnati. He built for himself in the town of Mercersburg a fine stone Mansion, still standing and in which he had his store. He mar. Mary, dau. of Wm. Smith, Sr., and wife Mary. Deeds show that on Nov. 17, 1787, the Supreme Executive Council of the Commonwealth appointed Robert Parker, Esq., of the County of Franklin, Collector of Excise.—under the hand of the Hon. Peter Muhlenberg, Esq., Vice President. Mary, wife of Robert Parker, died Dec. 4, 1843, aged 84 yrs. They had issue: Eliza Parker, who mar. John McFarland; and Mary Smith Parker who mar. Dr. Peter W. Little.
History of the Bard Family.

JAMES STUART

Served under Capt. Wm. Huston 1780-81. He died Apr. 27, 1813, in his 77th year. Eve Stuart, Consort of Charles Stuart, died Aug. 29, 1823, in her 39th (?) year. In the will of James Stuart, dated and prob. 1813, he names brothers Charles and Andrew Stuart; 3 nephews: John, William and James Rankin, sons of sister Mary Rankin, decd., $1000, to be divided among them. (Wm. Rankin to Mary Stewart, Feb. 28, 1774, by Dr. John King).
Penna. Arch. 5th Ser. Vol. 6, p. 265, 270, 276, 283, 643.

JOSEPH VAN LEAR

Served as a pvt under Capt. Pohn Orbison 1780-81-82. His will was prob. Aug. 17, 1819, in which he names wife Mary (who was a dau. of Rowland Chambers); son Joseph; dau. Ann Crawford; Jane wife of David Dunwoody; Mary, wife of Hugh Cowan; Elizabeth Crawford; Martha, wife of George Crawford; they were members of the Presbyterian Church. Joseph Van Lear is shown in Montgomery Twp., 1781, with land, horses and cows. Mrs. Van Lear b. 1746, d. 1836.
Penna. Arch. 5th Ser. Vol. 6, p. 274, 294, 307.

HENRY WORK

Served under Capt. William Huston, 1780-81.

He came from Lancaster Co., with his brother John about 1775. Their father, Andrew had bought a large tract of land in Franklin Co., in 1752. He mar. Sarah, dau. of Edward Crawford, Sr., of Fayetteville and he names in his will "Brother-in-law Edwd. Crawford, Esq." They had issue: Edward Work; son Andrew, decd., and his 7 children; (Owen; Henry; Elizabeth; Isabella; Wm.; Edward; Andrew;) son James Crawford; son Henry; dau. Martha; dau. Sally and granddau. Isabella Work Dickey. The son Andrew mar. Sally, dau. of Capt. Owen Aston of Chambersburg. Henry Work in his will said he was "old and infirm" and his stone in White Church Graveyard shows he died Mch. 6, 1819, aged 72 yrs. Sarah, consort of Henry Work, d. Sept. 10, 1833, aged 84 yrs.

Penna. Arch. 5th Ser. Vol. 6, p. 270, 276, 284.

HONOR LIST

From Records of "Upper West Conococheague"
Presbyterian Church, now Mercersburg, Penna.

Jonathan Smith, at Amboy, N. J., Oct. 13, 1776

John Campbell, Opression in Militia, Oct. 30, 1776

James McCoy, killed at Fort Washington, Nov. 16, 1776

Dugal Campbell, at Camden, N. J., Jan., 1777

Patt. McClelland, near Phila., by ill usage of enemy, 1777

Joseph Watson, killed in battle, Dec., 1777

Capt. Robert McCoy, killed at Crooked Billet, May 1, 1778

William Dean, killed at Crooked Billet, May 1, 1778

William Stewart (or Sterret), killed at Crooked Billet, May 1, 1778

William Dunwoody, killed at Crooked Billet, May 1, 1778

WADDELL'S GRAVEYARD
(Now Spring Grove)

"Joseph Howe did by early settlement obtain a Right and title to a certain tract of land in Peters Twp., bounding Thos. Waddle, Rev. John King and Conococheague Creek." Said Howe sold to Samuel Gettis, then of York Co., Penna., who later sold to his son James Gettis, who sold to Hamilton Ritchey, who, for 5 pounds, sells to SAMUEL WALKER, JAMES CAMPBELL and THOMAS MCDOWELL, JUNR., Trustees. All that land which contains the burying ground, lying on the eastern boundary of said land, joining Dobinses Spring, containing 80 pchs. The said Trustees to have and to hold said lands in trust for a public burying ground. (Joseph Howe and family went to Carolina 1771). The tract to Thos. Waddell was the land of Robert Newell, Sr., Patents of 231 acres in 1750, and 200 acres in 1766. Sold by Newell heirs in 1803.

JAMES DICKEY

Served as a pvt. under Capt. Robert Dickey in 1777-1781—undated rolls. He was a son of James and Isabel Dickey, early settlers. James mar. Rebecca Downey, and had sons, John and James, the line of Seth Dickey of Mercersburg, Penna. James d. in 1813, aged 59 yrs. His wife Rebecca lived until 1821.

Penna. Arch. 5th Ser. Vol. 6, p. 284, 289, 314, 371.

WILLIAM MCDOWELL

The Blensten License Book credits Wm. McDowell with 200 acres Dec. 13, 1736, "On the Northwest Branch of Conococheague, the Mountain and about 3 miles Northw. from Edward Parnells." The pioneer Wm. McDowell and wife Mary, fled during the Indian raids of 1755 to Wrights Ferry where Wm. died and is buried in the old Donegal Church yard. He was "late of Conococheague" and deceased here Sept. 12, 1759 aged 77 yrs. A list of the funeral expenses from family papers gives the following: To Expenses of Father's funeral. To cash for the Ferriage of the Company and some refreshments at Mr. Baylies. To cash for digging the grave. To cash for the Coffin. Mother's Funeral Expenses on Nov. 27, 1760. To Mourning Scarfs and gloves. To cash for making the Coffin. To Sundry other things.

WILLIAM MCDOWELL, PATRIOT
(From Tombstone)

"Who at the age of four-score and ten with the comfortable hope of a Christian, closed a long life here. Estimable for moral rectitude and venerable for sincere piety, Sept. 17, 1812. Filial Piety to a most deserving Mother has placed this marble over the remains of Mary McDowell, wife of Wm. McDowell and dau. of Wm. Wm. Maxwell, who d. Apr. 9, 1805, aged 78 yrs." WILLIAM MCDOWELL, son of pioneer Wm. and Mary McWowell, was appointed Justice of the Peace for Peters Twp., Nov. 3, 1778. In the will of Wm. McDowell, Sr., dated 1807, prob. Sept. 1812, he names sons: Wm.; John; Nathan; Alexander; Andrew; Patrick; Thomas; dau. Peggy; dau. Nancy; Susannah Martin; son Thomas the clock, desk, one feather bed and furniture, 2 melato boys, horses, cattle, Smith tools, Stills, farming utensils. Slave Dinna to be set free. In the will of Major Wm. Maxwell (1772) he gives to son-in-law, Wm. McDowell "my coat and silver buttons" and to Mary, wife of Wm. "the negro girl Dina." In 1769, Wm. McDowell was Presiding Elder over District 8, of the "Upper West Conococheague" Church, near Mercersburg.

JOHN MCDOWELL (FORT)

Son of pioneer Wm. McDowell and wife Mary, in 1769 was Ruling Elder over District 7 of the "Upper West Conococheague" Church. John McDowell mar. Agnes Craig, b. 1717, d. Aug. 8, 1766. John McDowell b. June 6, 1794, aged 78 yrs. They had a dau. (1) Mary, who mar. Dr. Richard Brownson, prior to 1769. (11) Agnes, mar. Elias Davidson, Mar. 19, 1771; (III) Elizabeth, mar. Rev. John King, Apr. 2, 1771; (IV) Catherine, mar. Hugh Davidson, Nov. 21, 1774; (V) Margaret, mar. George King, June 6, 1786; The above John McDowell, who was a Miller, built a fort, prior to 1755, and much can be gleaned from a study of the First Series Penna. Arch., to those interested in that period. In a letter from Adam Hoops to Governor Morris from Cannogogig, Nov. 3, 1755, he reports "that a certain Patrick Burns, a captive, had made his escape that morning, before the Tragedy in the Cove; John Potter, Esq., and self, sent Expresses through our Neighborhood, which induced many of them to meet with us as aforesaid, at John McDoole's Mill, where I, with many others had the unhappy prospect to see the smoke of two houses that was set on Fire by the Indians, vizt, Matthew Patton's and Meshech Jame's, where their cattle was shot down, and horses standing bleeding with Indian Arrows in them. The Rev. Mr. Steel, John Potter, Esq., and others to the number of an hundred, went in quest of the Indians, but no success."

FIRST LIEUT. WILLIAM MCDOWELL

1st Penna. Cont. Line., 2nd Infantry, Mar. 22, 1778; mustered out Nov. 3, 1783; died at St. Thomas, Franklin Co., June 19, 1835, aged 86. He was an original member of the Society of the Cincinnati. His membership in the Society was not continued. His tombstone states, "He was 7 years in Service of his Country in the Struggle for Independence under Washington." He left a Journal of his Southern Campaign, an interesting document. He left 3 daus.: Mary and Margaret unmar., and Jean Van Lear Davison; sons, Wm.; John; Thomas. He was entitled to 400 acres Donation land and in his will he divides his land between the sons and dau. Jean. Land in Dist. 1, Butler Co., on Muddy Creek; a tract in the 3rd Dist., Mercer Co., No. 446, also a tract in Ohio, as well as the Home place. To the daus. he gave shares in the Bank of Columbia, Farmers Bank of Md., and in the Bank of Alexandria, furniture, etc. A division between sons of "my wearing apparel, all my silver buttons, My Diploma, etc. The above Wm. McDowell was a son of Wm. McDowell and wife Mary Maxwell, and a grandson of pioneer Wm. McDowell. He was mar. by Dr. John King to Elizabeth Van Lear, Feb. 8, 1786.

Penna. Arch. 5th Ser. Vol. 2, p. 630.

JOHN MCDOWELL, L.L.D.

b. Feb. 11, 1751, d. Dec. 22, 1820. Under the call of July 28, 1777, he served as a pvt. in Capt. Samuel Patton's marching Co.

EPITAPH

Underneath this marble
Is deposited the body
of
John McDowell
Doctor of Laws
Once Principal of St. John's College
In the State of Maryland
And Late Provost
of the University of Pennsylvania
Distinguished for Learning,
Integrity and Piety,
Respected by the world,
Esteemed by his friends
And beloved by his relations,
He closed a life of useful labors
On the 22nd day of December
In the year of our Lord 1820
And of his age the 69th.

The "Repository" of Dec. 26, 1820, gives the following: "Departed this life on the evening of the 22nd inst., at the house of Mrs. Maris in this county in the 70th year of his age, John McDowell, L. L. D., late Provost of the University of Penna., and former Principal of St. Johns College, Annapolis, Md." The will of Dr. John McDowell is beautifully thoughtful of those near and dear to him. To the sisters and their children; to the orphan children of his brother Alexander in Venango County, "that distant county" where he hopes they will be visited by his brothers, ample compensation to such person for his expense and trouble; to Mrs. Maris who cared for him in her home in Mercersburg, and to his sister Nancy "for their tender care and assiduous attention to me in my weak and feeble condition." To the U. of Penna., Latin and Greek books and many others he hoped worthy of the acceptance of a learned institution. In addition to dividends, there was gold and silver coin; gold watch; gold sleeve buttons; horse; saddle and bridle, wearing apparel, stock in a Turnpike, and much else, all showing loving thought for his friends and relatives.

CAPT. SAMUEL PATTON

Served 1776-77-78-79-80-81-82; in 1779 the "Muster Roall of the third Cleas in the Servis of the State of Penna., under Col. Wm. Chambers." In 1782 under Col. Samuel Culbertson. From the "Repository," June 26, 1821. "Died recently in Hamilton Twp., Capt. S. Patton at a very advanced age. Any Eulogium on the character of Capt. Patton either as a most excellent moral citizen, would be superfluous as it is well known to the citizens of Franklin County." Capt. Patton died June 9, 1821, aged 80 yrs. He was a Capt. in Col. Joseph Armstrong's regt. of the Flying Camp in 1776, was Capt. of the 3rd Co., in Col. Samuel Culbertson's Batt., Cumb. Co. Associators 1777-80. He commanded a Marching Company under Col. Wm. Chambers in 1778, and on the Bedford frontier in 1779. Capt. Patton was married to Elizabeth McKinnie, dau. of Josiah and Isabel McKinnie. They had issue: Matthew; Betsy Gilmore; Isabel Marshal; Rebecca Patton; Catherine Cummins; Martha Patton.

Penna. Arch. 5th Ser. Vol. 6, p. 6, 261, 286, 310, 368, 372, 376, 609.

SAMUEL WALKER

Served as pvt., 1780, under Captain Patton, Dicky and McDowell. His wife was Isabella Brice. Samuel Walker d. Apr. 8, 1812. They had issue: son Robert; dau. Esther, wife of Isaac Spence; dau. Margaret, wife of Colin Spence; dau. Sarah wife of James Martin; dau. Jane

Walker; sons, Samuel; John; James. Will dated Mar. 26, 1812; prob. Apr. 13, 1812. Samuel Walker appears to have had a second wife, Margaret.

Penna. Arch. 5th Ser. Vol. 6, p. 271, 284, 314, 289.

JOHN HOLLIDAY

Pioneer, had a warrant for a tract of land Dec. 13, 1742, in Peters Twp., now St. Thomas Twp., Franklin Co., Penna. The tract contained 345 acres, 156 pchs., and adjoining it "other land of John Holliday." William Holliday and James Holliday were neighbors, as were Michael and Wm. Campbell, Samuel McCutcheon, Samuel Jack and Robert Hood. Campbell's Run crossed the tract. In 1769 when the Presbyterian Church of "Upper West Conococheague" was arranged into 10 Districts, John Holliday and family were in District 9,—the family including wife Jean and son Adam, undoubtedly living on the tract above mentioned. John Holliday, pioneer, d. Mch. 27, 1770, leaving a will in which he gave his land to his son Adam, with certain conditions. Jean, widow pioneer John Holliday, d. Aug. 18, 1776. In his will he gave her this privilege: "the Goods and Chattels to be disposed of at her Pleasure among my five sons, Wm.; Samuel; John; Adam and Joseph Hollidays."

WILLIAM HOLLIDAY

Earliest service seems to be in Bedford Co., Penna., Oct. 10, 1776, as one of Capt Thos. Paxton's Ranging Company. On Dec. 5, 1778, he was Paymaster of Militia for Bedford County, and Feb. 20, 1779, he and Adam Holliday are signers to a petition to the Assembly from Bedford Co. The Inhabitants on the Juniata part of the frontiers of Bedford Co. state their defenceless situation and appeal for help. In 1769, Wm. Holliday was head of a family in the "Upper West Conococheague" Church; in District 9, a neighbor to his father, John Holliday, pioneer. His wife was Mary, dau. of Pioneer John McClelland and wife Ruth, who lived near Upton. The family at this period consisted of Wm.; James; Samuel; Adam; Ruth; Patt; John, the eldest, presumably had left home, and the birth of Janet not on record here. McCauley's Hist., of Franklin Co., Penna., page 144, gives the following: "In 1768 a petition was presented for a public road from James Campbell's to the County line in Black's Gap; of the six Viewers appointed, Wm. Holliday was one, and they approved the project Jan. 1772. In Deed Book 1, p. 420, May 30, 1785, Samuel Smith of Peters., sold a tract of land to John Over of Lancaster Co., Penna., it being a warrant to ascertain Wm. Holliday, granted in 1770, in Peters Twp., and conveyed by Wm. Holliday to the above Saml. Smith, June 5, 1778, by land of Chas. Neely, James Jack, John Irwin, Robert Hood, Adam Holliday, and heirs of James Holliday, 272 acres, for 980 pounds. Samuel Smith sells to John Over. Deeds also show that on Oct. 20, 1790, Wm. Holliday of Frankstown Twp., Huntg. Co., and Mary his wife, sell to Benj. Chambers, 8 acres on Back Creek, Peters Twp., sold by Wm. Moore and wife Mary to Wm. Holliday, Sept. 5, 1761, from Back Creek to Giles Owen, a Mill seat. It has been stated that the Adam Holliday who was with Wm. in Bedford County was a cousin, which is quite probable, as Adam, son of pioneer John Holliday, lived on his land here for many years. From Quarter Sessions Docket, Carlisle, Penna., Vol. 3 X 3, Peters Twp., 1768, Wm. Holliday and Henry Anderson are given as Overseers of the Poor. In the will of Robert Elliott, of Hamilton Twp., dated Dec. 1762, prob. 1763, he names his friends (and neighbors) Wm. Campbell and Wm. Holliday, as Executors.

Penna. Arch. 5th Ser. Vol. 5, p. 49, 56, Sept. 12, 1776; also Penna. Arch. 2nd Ser. Vol. 3, p. 675, 242.

SAMUEL HOLLIDAY

Appears first as a pvt. in 1777, and as Capt. 1778-80-81-82 in Cumb. Co. He is said to have been born 1738, died 1792 in Mifflin Co., Penna. He was a son of pioneer John Holliday, and he mar. at Mercersburg, Dec. 12, 1769, Sarah Campbell, the first recorded marriage by Rev. John King. Sarah Campbell, b. 1744, d. after 1792, a dau. of Michael and Rebecca (Brown) Campbell. They had issue: John who mar. Margaret lived and died in 1812, in Fannett Twp.,; James; Adam; Michael; Samuel; Rebecca; Jane, mar. Thos. Provines.

Penna. Arch. 5th Ser. Vol. 6, 323, 334, 549, 563, 581, 635.

JOHN HOLLIDAY

Of Fannett Twp., is said to have served as a Soldier in Capt. Thos. Blair's company in 1778. He signed the Remonstrance against the alteration of the Constitution in 1779; he was elected an Elder of the "Upper Path Valley" Presby. Church in 1792. The will of John Blair of Fannett Twp., dated Feb., 1768, prob. in May 1769, names his son-in-law John Holliday. In the will of John Holliday, he mentions a brother James and his own children as: James; Adam; Elizabeth; John; Jean; Mary; the "Repository" gives the following: "Died at his farm in Fannett Twp., Franklin Co., on Monday, the 15th of

December, 1806, Mr. John Holliday, aged about 75 years, of a paralytic affliction with which he was attacked a few weeks since." Of the children of John Holliday, James and Adam died unmarried; Elizabeth Holliday was mar. at Mercersburg by Dr. John King, to Thomas Dunn, Feb., 1790. John Holliday, b. 1765, d. 1838, mar. June 15, 1791, Elizabeth Coulter, at Mercersburg. Jean Holliday is said to have mar. Alex. Wilson, of Butler Co., Penna. Mary Holliday, mar. in 1807, Charles Pomeroy. The baptisms of their four children are given in the records of Middle Spring church: Margaret in 1808; Thomas Blair in 1810; John Holliday in 1813; and Mary Elizabeth in 1815. Two quaint old letters from Mary Pomeroy, to her brother John are in existence. The Repository, Feb. 15, 1804. "Died a few weeks since of a lingering decay, Mr. Samuel Holliday, son of Mr. John Holliday, of this County in the 20th year of his age. To promising talents were added, in the deceased, those mild affections of the heart, which are calculated to render men estimable and society happy. His filial affection and dutiful demeanor toward his aged parents, will render the vacuum, occasioned by his death, severely felt by them. "This is the state of man; today he puts forth the tender leaves of hope; tomorrow blossoms, and bears his blushing honors thick about him; The third day comes a frost, a killing frost, and nips his roots."

ADAM HOLLIDAY

Served under Captains James Patton and Thos. McDowell, 1780, and an undated roll. Samuel Holliday, L. H., is shown with Adam, presumably his brother. Following the death of his mother in 1776, Adam Holliday mar. at Mercersburg, Penna., Sarah Campbell, Nov. 14, 1776. She was a dau. of Wm. and Jean (Coulter) Campbell and they had baptized: John, Apr. 19, 1778; Janet, Mch. 8, 1781; Jean, Dec. 15, 1782. In 1771, Adam Holliday is shown with 290 acres land,— 100 acres clear—Horses, Cows, Sheep, 1 negro. Samuel and Wm. Holliday shown in a similar way. Adam continued as a freeman 1772-73-74-75-76-78-79. and in 1780, he has 480 ac. land, 3 Horses, 10 Cows, 3 negroes. In 1782, Adam is shown with 486 acres, 8 Horses, 10 Cattle, 12 sheep and 3 negroes. John and Samuel appear with Adam through these years—having land horses and cows. On May 29, 1793, Joseph Armstrong 3rd, applied to Orphans' Court, Chambersburg, for partition of the land belonging to the Armstrong estate; the Sheriff chose 12 men, one being Adam Holliday and he appears several times as witness to a Will or Deed. In Deed Book 3, pages 152-153, May 15, 1793, Adam Holliday and Sarah his wife, of Peters Twp., Franklin Co., Penna., sell to John Brindle and Malchia Brindle, late of Cumberland Co., Penna., land under 2 warrants; one Dec. 14, 1742, the other, Sept. 6, 1744, there was surveyed to John Holliday land in Peters Twp., &c., land willed to Adam Holliday by his father John Holliday, 486 acres, 111 perches, for 2350 pounds. Under Deed Book 3, p. 456, May 16, 1794, the Brindles sold the above tract to Joseph Strock of Peters Twp. Adam Holliday and family probably removed to Huntingdon County about this period, where he died, his will dated 1799, Feb. 15. His son John is said to have married Mary Lowry, and his daughter Janet mar. Wm. Reynolds.

Penna. Arch. 5th Ser. Vol. 6, p. 272, 315.

JAMES HOLLIDAY

Lieut., Mch. 25, 1756, under Captain, the Rev. John Steel; Ensign, Archibald Irwin; also shown on Mch. 6, in the 2nd Batt., under Hugh Mercer. Rupp's Hist. of Dauphin, Cumb., &c. Counties, page 128, "June 9, 1757, James Holiday and fourteen men killed and taken." "At one o'clock this morning I received an express from Fort Loudon, with intelligence of Lieut. Holliday's having set out with seventy-five men, to reconnoiter the woods; and at the deserted house of one McClellan, in a place called the Great Cove, part of the men with the Lieut. went into the said house, whilst the residue were at some distance drinking water from the spring and were unhappily surprised and surrounded by a party of Indians, said to be one-hundred in number." This letter was from John Armstrong to Col. Stanwix. Under date of Aug. 18, 1756, Adam Hoops, in a letter to Hance Hamilton states,— "Lieut. Holliday sent to me last night for blankets, and says his men are all going to leave him for want of the same, as the inhabitants have all left the fort . . . If you have any blankets send them by the bearer," and further says, "the Courier has come to let me know that near John Lindsay's, five or six Indians were seen and that one was shot down near Grindstone Hill." Lieut. James Holliday mar. Elizabeth, dau. of Wm. and Mary McDowell, early settlers in Peters Twp. They had issue: John, known as Lieut. John Holliday, of the Flying Camp, Prisoner of War, 1778, who died in Chambersburg in 1818. His wife was Mary, dau. of Nathan McDowell; they had no issue and are buried in Falling Spring graveyard, Chambersburg, Penna. A son Wm. died young. A son Samuel, who mar. Jane or Jeanette Campbell, dau. of Wm. Campbell, who d. in 1803. They went to Presqu Ile, Erie Co., Penna.

Penna. Arch. Ser. Vol. 1, p. 46, 70, Province of Penna., 1744-1765.

JOHN HOLLIDAY

Pensioner,—S39706—Continental Pennsylvania, Huntingdon Co., Penna. He received the Commission of 2nd Lieut., signed by John Hancock, and dated June 25, 1775. He marched in July of same year to Boston, promoted to 1st Lieut., under Capt. Robert Cluggage, 1st Penna., Reg't. under Command of Col. Wm. Thompson. In 1776, before the battle of Long Island, was promoted to Captain, in the Reg't. of Col. Edward Hand, continued until 1778. His brother James a 1st Lieut. in his company was killed at the Battle of Brandywine, Sept. 1777. In 1778, a number of officers were reduced, and because of the exposed situation of his father and family in Bedford Co., now Huntingdon Co., he resigned his commission to assist his father and family. In 1778 there was a station at his father's house (moved furniture to out-house so men could have house) (attacked by Indians the out-house burned). In August 1779, his brothers Adam and Patrick and sister Jane were killed in Farnkston Twp., by Indians. In 1796 his father made his last will, bequesting him the Plantation in Frankston, Huntingdon Co., his father dying the same year. By erection of the land, by Edward and Joseph Nichols, Judgment was against him. Under date April 1, 1818, he states he will be 69 yrs. of age on Nov. 26. He was at the skirmish of——— near Boston; Battle of Long Island; Trenton; Princeton; Brandywine; Germantown; White Plains; White Marsh and Mill Square. He had a son and daughter; son about 40 yrs., the dau. about 30 yrs., the son does not contribute to support of family. He, John Holliday, is the sole support of the family. His wife about 70 yrs., of age; dated Aug. 17, 1820. The above John Holliday was the son of William Holliday and wife Mary McClennan of Peters Twp., Franklin Co., Penna. Capt. John Holliday was born Nov. 26, 1749 and died Aug. 19, 1823. His wife is said to have been Dorcas Roddy and two baptisms from Ch. records of Mercersburg lend color to the statement, John Holliday had bapt., Apr. 8, 1781, Alexander Roddy; John Holliday had baptz., July 25, 1784, Jean. It must be remembered that the "Conococheague Settlement" was home to the Hollidays—having taken up land as early as 1742, and James Roddy was one of the earliest settlers in Antrim Twp., nearby.

WILLIAM HOLLIDAY, JR.

Is shown in Bedford Co., Penna., in Militia, and in Mch. 21, 1777, as Sub-Lieut., of Bedford Co. Militia—probably a son of William and Mary Holliday. He is said to have served in Capt. Thos. Paxton's Company of Rangers, Oct., 1776, and called "Major." Records state that he died in Frankstown Twp., 1819.

Penna. Arch. 5th Ser. Vol. 4, p. 241. Vol. 5, p. 49.

SAMUEL HOLLIDAY

Son of Lieut. James Holliday and wife Elizabeth McDowell, served as pvt. under Capts., Patton, Dickey, McDowell, and in Capt. John Johnston's Pay Roll Light Dragoons under James Culbertson, Cornet, in 1781. Samuel Holliday mar. Jane or Jeanette Campbell, a dau. of Wm. Campbell, who died in 1803. They went to Presqu' Isle, Erie Co., Penna., where he died Nov. 26, 1841, his wife dying June 27, 1851, aged 81 yrs. They had issue: Elizabeth 1798-1834; Jane 1800-1871, mar. B. B. Whitley; John 1803-1872; Samuel 1805-1891; William 1808 mar. M. F. S. Post; Lucinda 1812-1875 mar.——— Rea.

Penna. Arch. 5th Ser. Vol. 6, p. 272, 285, 283, 615, 640.

INTERRED IN OLD UNION GRAVEYARD

Waynesboro, Penna.

REMOVED IN 1931 TO GREEN HILL CEMETERY

Waynesboro, Penna.

WILLIAM BOAL

Sergt. in Capt. Thos. Robinson's Co., Mt. Joy Twp., Lancaster Co., 1778-79. Chambersburg, Penna. Deed Book Vol 11, p. 15, shows William Boal of Lancaster Co., paying $16,000 for land in 1794-95. He died Dec. 17, 1831, in his 76th year. Agnes Boal d. 1829 in her 58th yr. Elizabeth Boal, d. Oct. 9, 1863, in her 81st yr. In 1817 Col. Wm. Boals was one of a Committee representing the Presbyterian Church of Waynesboro. Col. Wm. Boals appears to have left issue, three daus: Elizabeth, unmar. who died in

Quincy Twp., in 1863; Frances Boal, who mar. Thos. Mitchell, Oct. 17, 1815, by Dr. Robert Kennedy; they and their children were living in Butler Co., Ohio, in 1866; Mary Boal, who mar. James McKinley, they also are buried in Old Union Graveyard, Waynesboro, Penna.

Penna. Arch. 5th Ser. Vol. 7, p. 196, 203, 209, 452, &c.

JOHN BARNHEISEL

Pvt., July 22, 1776. In Barracks, Phila, Oct. 3, 1776, Capt. Benj. Weiser. Capt. John Robinson, Berks Co., Penna., pvt. John Barnhisel, 1781. John Barnheiser, old soldier of 1776, came to Hagerstown, Md., to draw his pension, d. in Quincy, Franklin Co., Penna. Gravestone inscription: In memory of John Barnhiser, d. June 2, 1848, in the 106th year of his age. In memory of Mary, wife of John Barnhiser, who died Jan. 6, 1813, aged 62 yrs. A dau. Mary mar. Fredk. Sheely, June 16, 1849. Barnheiser: "On Saturday last, John Barnheiser, a Revolutionary Soldier, departed this life in the 106th year of his age, in Quincy, Penna., and was buried with honors of war in the Union graveyard in this place on Wednesday the 4th inst. If we mistake not the deceased was the last survivor in this county, of those who fought to gain the liberties we enjoy." Records of St. John's Lutheran Church, Hagerstown, Md., show the following: Elias Lytle, Mary Barnhiser, July, 1821; John Barnhiser, Susan Brown, Aug., 1828. Fred Sheeley mar. Mary Barntizer, had a dau. Sarah who mar. William Brown.

Penna. Arch. 5th Ser. Vol. 2, p. 792. Vol. 5, p. 282. Hist. Washington County, Md. p. 259.

DAVID BASEOUR, (BASCHORE, BASORE)

Removed from Trinity Reformed, graveyard. David Baseour, (Baschore, Basore). Served under Capt. David Clapsaddler and Col. James Johnston, Cumberland Co. Militia, 1780-81. He was born in Lancaster Co., Penna., the son of Daniel and Catherina Rudy. He was married in Washington Twp., Franklin Co. to Barbara Schnaderlie by Rev. Weiner of Hagerstown, Md. He is shown in Washington Twp., Cumberland Co. tax list in 1779-80 with 285 acres of land, 2 houses, 3 cattle, left a will probated July 27, 1844 naming these children, Samuel b. 1790, Eva Elizabeth b. Dec. 24, 1792, Mar. George Uhler; Catharina b. Feb. 27, 1994, Mar. Christian Russel; John b. Oct. 5, 1795; Daniel b. Aug. 29, 1797, George b. Dec. 21, 1799, Mar. Eliza Snively; David b. Mar. 10, 1802, Jacob b. Feb. 12, 1804, d. Jan. 12, 1844, Henry b. Oct. 22, 1807, Mar. Mary Funk; Magdalena Barbara b. Oct. 25, 1809, Mar. Rev. George W. Glessner; Jeremiah b. Jan. 31, 1812 Mar Elizabeth Shank; Josiah b. Mar. 1, 1816, Mar. Sarah Vonderau.

Penna. Archives, 5th Series, Vol. 6, p. 72, 94, 117.

GEORGE FISHOOK (FISHOUCH-FISHOAK)

Served in Lancaster Co. Militia, as a private, under Capt. Abraham Forey and 1st Lieut. Noah Ceasey in 1777-1779, under Capt. Noah Ceasey in 1780-81-82. George Fishack (Fishauk &c) bought land in Washington Co., Md., 1792 to 1806. He d. Apr. 11, 1815, aged 75 yrs. 11 mos. 19 days. Mary Magdalen, wife of Andrew Oaks and dau. of George and Mary M. Fishack, d. Nov. 17, 1779, d. May 17, 1821, aged 41 yrs. 6 mos.

Penna. Arch. 5th Ser. Vol. 7. p. 193, 212, 697, 718, 729, 763, 790, 794.

ADAM HARTMAN

Pvt. in Penna., Militia, and a pensioner. He was of Washington Twp. His will, prob. Apr. 5, 1847 names children: George; Daniel; John David; Catherine, wife of Samuel Umstadt; Susannah, wife of Joseph Nail; Polly, wife of Robert Chestnut; Barbara, wife of Michael Gonder.

Penna. Arch. 3rd Ser. Vol. 13, p. 530.

JOHN POTTER, JR.

Served as pvt. under Capt. Daniel Clapsaddler 1780-81. In his will prob. July 23, 1821, he names wife Barbara; son Daniel; dau. Catherine Baker; dau. Polly Bashore; dau. Margaret, wife of John Nicodemus; dau. Barbara Leady; under July 3, 1821, the Franklin Repository states: "Died at his residence near Waynesboro, on Sunday the 24th ult., Capt. John Potter, and on Monday the 25th, his remains were interred at the Lutheran Graveyard in Waynesburg in the presence of perhaps the largest concourse of citizens that ever assembled there on a similar occasion." The Lutheran Graveyard was known as the "OLD UNION."

Penna. Arch. 5th Ser. Vol. 6, p. 94, 97, 117.

INTERRED IN OLD UNION GRAVEYARD

Waynesboro, Penna.

REMOVED IN 1931 TO BURNS HILL CEMETERY

Waynesboro, Penna.

FRANCIS SHOVER, PENSIONER

May 28, 1818, Frances Shover aged 63 yrs., resident of Washington Twp., Franklin Co., Penna., states he enlisted in Lancaster, Penna., in a Company Commanded by Capt. Jacob Weaver of the Tenth Reg't. of the Penna. Line under Col. Noggle (Nogel) and Hubley, in 1776-77; he continued in the same company until discharged 1781, in Trenton, N. J. Aug. 18, 1820, Francis Shover, aged 69 yrs., received pension certificate no. 4385 on Nov. 13, 1818. His family consists of wife, a grandchild; he is a weaver by trade but from disability unable to support them. Jan. 26, 1844. Franklin Co., Penna., Catherine Shover claims a pension, aged 69 on June 12, 1843, widow of Francis Shover, Rev. Soldier (his pension $96.00 year). She mar. 1792-1795 in York Co., (where they kept a house for public entertainment) now Adams Co., eldest child born nearly three years after marriage—bible with records burned, with property, July, 1820. Francis Shover died about Sept. 23, 1838. Affidavit of Mary Robinson, a dau. aged 48 yrs. on Dec. 29, 1843, bible record. Oct. 19, 1851, Catherine Shover again petitions for pension. John Renner, Sr., makes affidavit that in 1799, he stayed at Francis Shover's Tavern in York, now Adams Co., family then was: wife Catherine, dau. Mary, then 6 or 8 yrs. old—that Mary Shover mar., Andrew Robinson, that he knew them and lived near them at Hughes Forge in Franklin Co., that her oldest son Jacob Robinson is married and has 4 or 5 children. He heard of her living at Pinegrove Furnace in Cumb. Co., and of late they moved to Va.; John Renner further states that he lived within a few miles of the Shover family for 25 or 30 yrs. Affidavits of Wm. West and Elizabeth Bradley &c, &c. Cumb. Co., Penna., Mar. 19, 1855. Catherine Shover, aged about 80 yrs., was mar. to Francis Shover, 1793, by Rev. Davidson, Presby. Minister in (now) Adams Co., Penna. Her name before marriage was Catherine Todd, and asks to obtain bounty land she is entitled to. Gravestone inscription: "In Memory of Francis Shover, fought in the Revolution. Died Sept. 22, 1839, aged 88 yrs., 7 mos. 17days."

Pension No. W2009-B L W 5108 160 55.

GRINDSTONE HILL GRAVEYARD

(Guilford Twp.)

ADAM COOK

Served as pvt. under Capt. Samuel Royer 1779-80-81. He died in 1820, intestate, leaving issue: Adam; John; Matty mar. to Henry Small; Mary mar. to John Couchman; George; Catherine mar. to George Small; Peter; Christina Cook; Elizabeth Cook; Fanny Cook; all living in the commonwealth, except Mary Couchman. In 1838, Christina Cook had become the wife of William Sheetz; Elizabeth Cook had mar. Henry Fields. The will of John Harmon of Guilford Twp. (1801) states that his dau. Anna Mariah was the wife of Adam Cook. 1781,—"Here lies buried Anna Maria Kochin." Translation: "Rest well, you dead bones in the quiet lonliness; rest until that time shall appear when he shall call you out of your chains into the free Heaven's breezes."

Penna. Arch. 5th Ser. Vol. 6, p. 89, 112, 542.

GEORGE COOK

Served as pvt. under Capt. Samuel Royer, 1779-80-81. His brothers Adam, Michael and Jacob served with him, sons of George Adam Cook of Washington Twp., who died 1785. George Cook b. 1751, d. 1842. His wife Rebecca Ankeny died Jan. 21, 1832, aged 76 yrs.,—living a married life 57 yrs. and 9 mos.

Penna. Arch. 5th Ser. Vol. 6, p. 89, 112, 542.

ABRAHAM HASSLER

Pvt., gave service 1778-79-82 in Lancaster Co., Penna., under Capt. Joseph Gehr and others. Abraham Hassler, son of Abraham the emigrant and his wife Anna, baptized in Cocalico Congregation, Cocalico Twp., Lancaster Co., Penna., Jan. 29, 1759 by Rev. John Waldschmidt. In the year 1803 Abraham Hassler moved to Guilford Twp., Franklin Co., Penna. He bought 324 acres, 117, perches from Ezekiel Chambers in Guilford Twp., on June 20, 1803. He was born Jan. 29, 1759, died May 15, 1832 and is buried at Grindstone Hill Cemetery with his wife Catrina. At the time of his death, three children were living: Johannas, born 1787; Wilhelm, born 1800; Susan, born 1795, who married Samuel Frederick; 2 grandchildren, Henry and Susan Tritle. He married Catrina Waldschmidt, dau. of Rev. John Waldschmidt on Nov. 21, 1786. She was born Jan. 10, 1762, died ———.

Penna. Arch. 5th Ser. Vol. 7, p. 263, 270, 297, 877, 888.

LUDWIG HERMAN

Served from Berks County in the Cont. Line, 1780-81, under Capt. John Ludwig. He was b. 1720, d. 1790. His estate, Admr., 1793, also written Harmon. The widow Eberhart Ena (Dina); son Philip; dau. Fredrika, wife of Nicholas Coleman; dau. Catherine, wife of Henry Stouffer; dau. Elizabeth, wife of John Flack; son William. The gravestone gives issue as six, including Jeremiah.

Penna. Arch. 5th Ser. Vol. 4, p. 260; Vol. 5, p. 239. 285

PETER HERMAN HERMANY &c.

Served as pvt. under Capt. Conrad Snider 1780-81. He was of Guilford Twp., leaving a will dated and probated 1832. He left a son John; dau. Anna Maria Harmon; dau. Elizabeth; son Peter; dau. Rebecca; wife Elizabeth. His stone gives dates 1760-1832. His wife Magdalene d. Dec. 7, 1815.

Penna. Arch. 5th Ser. Vol. 6, p. 87, 108, 118.

JACOB KELLER

Capt. Conrad Snider, pvt. Jacob Keller, Aug. 16, 1780. Jacob Keller was born 1759, died 1830. Orphans' Court records show he died intestate in 1830, leaving a widow Margaret and 5 children: John; Frederick; David; Samuel; Henry. He lived in Guilford Twp.

Penna. Arch. 5th Ser. Vol. 6, p. 87.

DANIEL LEAP (LAPE)

Of Washington Twp., served in 1781 under Lieut. Stitt. His will, dated 1821, prob. 1824, names wife Mary and dau. Mary, wife of Samuel Lear; Christina, wife of Peter Heckman; Elizabeth; Susanna; Matty; Peggy; Nancy; Sally; grandchildren named Myer; son-in-law George Brandhefer. The dates on tombstones 1761-1823.

Penna. Arch. 5th Ser. Vol. 6, p. 108, 112.

GEORGE SMITH

Served 1780-81-82 under Capts. James Young and Terrence Campbell. George Smith of Guilford Twp., died Dec. 14, 1802, leaving a widow Susanna and issue: John; Jacob; Emanuel; Simon; Elizabeth; Catherine; Susannah and Lavina, also Sarah mar. to John Hick, who died before her father, leaving one child Elizabeth, now mar. to John Clippinger; said Catherine mar. to Fredk. Heck and said Susannah mar. to John Kern.

Penna. Arch. 5th Ser. Vol. 6, p. 82, 110, 126.

JACOB SNIDER

Served as pvt. under Capt. James Young 1779-80-81. He was born 1752, died 1819, as shown on gravestone. The will of Jacob Snider of Guilford Twp., was dated May 1819, prob. June 1819. Names sons Jacob; Samuel; John; grandson Leonard Seller, son of dau. Magdalene, decd.; wife Elizabeth; all my children; Exrs.: son John and friend Solomon Miller.

Penna. Arch. 5th Ser. Vol. 6, p. 82, 111, 546.

PETER SNIDER

Served as Corporal 1779-80-81 under Conrad Snider. Peter Snider of Guilford Twp., born 1729, died 1807, left a will dated 1805, prob. 1807, in which he names sons Henry and Jacob; dau. Mary wife of George Zigler; dau. Barbara wife of John Stans; dau. Elizabeth wife of Barnet Poorman; dau. Magdalene wife of Conrad Brown; sons Peter and Nicholas; heirs of son John: Catherine; Charlotte and Henry.

Penna. Arch. 5th Ser. Vol. 6, p. 87, 118. 548.

PETER WALBURN

Col. Arthur St. Clair, Peter Walburn, Pvt. b. 1759, d. 1832. His will dated Apr. 28, 1829; prob. May 24, 1832, says he was of Washington Twp. Names wife Catherine; 2 children of his son Leonard; son Peter; dau. Elizabeth mar. to George Kaufman; dau. Catherine mar. to Frederick Byer; dau. Anna mar. to Samuel Motter; son John.

Penna. Arch. 5th Ser. Vol. 2, p. 109. 2nd Penna. Batt.

ZION REFORMED CHURCH GRAVEYARD
Chambersburg, Penna.

There is record of the Rev. Jacob Weimer's visit to our people who 1778-1779 gathered at the home of Nicholas Snider on N. Main St. to organize a congregation which is still in existence. There is no actual record of the organization, but on the 1st May, 1780, Col. Benj. Chambers and wife Jane, conveyed the lot at the corner of Main and German (now Liberty) Sts., to Nicholas Snider, Leonard Stans, Peter Snider, John Harmon, Henry Coyle, George Smith and Capt. Conrad Snider, "for the love and affection they bear unto" these men and more especially for promoting religion in Chambersburg, as well as for and in consideration of the sum of 1 lb. 10 S . . . as trustees for building a Calvinist Church in Chambersburg . . . that they shall not put said lot of ground to any other use than the aforesaid house and a burying place or other seminaries of learning."

Consecration

On Saturday, the —— of June inst. the Corner-Stone of the New GERMAN REFORMED CALVANISTIC CHURCH intended to be built in this borough will be laid with appropriate Solemnity. Several Clerical Gentlemen from a distance are expected to assist in the ceremony, and the Citizens are respectfully invited to attend the same.

Franklin Repository, Chambersburg, June 11, 1811.

LUDWIG DENIG

Served as a private under Capt. Joseph Hubley, in 1781-82, Lancaster Co., Penna. He also signed the Test Oath in Lancaster. He was b. Sept. 17, 1755, d. July 1830 in Chambersburg. He mar. Barbara, dau. of Michael Guntaker, 1760-1801. They came from Lancaster Co. to Chambersburg, and are buried in Zion Reformed Church graveyard. They were mar. Oct. 28, 1779. He mar. second Catherine Roger (?) In his will dated 1826, prob. 1830, he names wife Catherine; Lewis; Louisa; Henrietta; Sarah; Ann; George; John; Margaret; Elizabeth; Grandch. Lewis and John Byerly.

Penna. Arch. 5th Ser. Vol. 7, p. 831, 851. Also 2nd Ser. Vol. 13, p. 439.

JACOB HOSSLER

Is shown in York Co., Penna., under Capt. Geo. Giselman, as pvt., Sergt. and Lieut., 1780-1782. Here rests the body in slumber and peace of Joseph Hassler, who was born 8 Sept., 1750. He honored his dear God, his wife Anna and his 9 children. Died 31 March, 1798 Joseph was born in Philadelphia County, Sept. 8, 1750. was the oldest son of Michael and Margretha Hassler. After 1761, his father moved with his family to Cordorus Twp., York Co. At his father's death in 1774 Joseph inherited 150 acres of land in Cordorus Twp. He lived there until the summer of 1793. He was a member of the York Co. Militia from the time of its organization at the beginning of the Rev. until he left the country. During the Rev. in the years 1780 and 1782 he is listed as Sergt. in the Company of Capt. Giselman, of the 7th Batt. of York Co. In 1783 he is listed as Lieut. of the Company of which Frantz Jacob Roemer was Col., in the 5th Batt. of York County. (See Penna. Arch. Ser. 6, Vol. 2) Joseph was a wagon-builder. In a deed dated May 12, 1792 in which he sells land to Andrew Heindorf, he is mentioned as "Joseph Hassler, wagon-maker." He mar. Anna Maria Roemer May 30, 1775, dau. of Fredrich and Anna Dorothea Miller Roemer. Fredrich Roemer was b. in Stadecken near Mainz, Germany in 1715, and Anna Dorothea Miller was b. in Beinen near Heidelberg in 1725. The nine children of Joseph and Anna Maria Hassler were baptized in the First Reformed Church of York and in St. Paul's Church of Codorus Twp. Joseph moved his family to Franklin Co. in 1793. He bought 318 acres of land south of St. Thomas from Melchor Brindle. Joseph died Mar. 31, 1798, and in accordance with a wish expressed in his will he is buried in the graveyard of the Zion Reformed Church of Chambersburg.

Penna. Arch. 6th Ser. Vol. 2, p. 570, 591, 647, 697, 675.

HENRY LOUTZENHEISER

Served as a pvt. under Capt. James Young, 1780-81. His estate was admr., Sept. 19, 1905. His wife was Elizabeth. A deed shows Col. Benj. Chambers and wife selling Lot No. 247 to Henry

Loutzenhiser Aug, 18, 1778, who with wife Elizabeth sold to Charles Wright in 1782.

Penna. Arch. 5th Ser. Vol. 6, p. 82, 110, 546.

JOHN RALPHSNIDER (RAFESNIDER)

Served as a pvt. under Capt. James Young, 1778-79-80-81. He was b. 1745, d. 1812. His will was prob. Oct. 19, 1812, of Letterkenny Twp.,—names wife Catherine; three older children: Henry, Catherine and Magdalene, each to get 100 lbs., in addition to equal division of estate; to "German Presbyterian" Congregation of Chambersburg $20. To son John his silver watch. Children equal shares. Son Henry and friend Henry Reges to be Execs.

Penna. Arch. 5th Ser. Vol. 6, p. 77, 111, 526, 548.

FREDERICK REAMER

Is shown as a Lieut. under Lieut. Col John King, 4th Batt., Militia of York Co., Penna. He came to Franklin County and settled in Chambersburg, Penna. The Corner Stone of Zion Ref. Church was laid June 29, 1811, "to erect this Church under God's blessing," the committee in charge being: Jacob Heyser; John Stump; Christian Wolff; FREDERICK ROEMER; Jacob Snider; Daniel Smith. The Repository, Aug. 27, 1822 gives: Died yesterday Frederick Roemer in his 68th year. He was mar. to Catherine Heitler Dec. 25, 1772, issue: Adam; Henry; Christian; Catherine; Robert; Frederick, b. 1784; Dolly; Jacob; Peggy mar. ———— Wertz; Elizabeth; Polly. Franklin Repository, Jan. 4, 1831,— "March 22, 1831. Died Tuesday, 8th in this borough, Mrs. Mary Roemer, aged 71 yrs."

Penna. Arch. 6th Ser. Vol. 2, p. 590.

HENRY GREENAWALT

Served in Capt. Henry Fry's Co., in 1775. They moved to Chambersburg, Penna. Johann Heinrich Greenawalt, b. 1732, d. Jan. 10, 1811. Wife Efa Michael, b. Aug. 30, 1745, d. Aug. 12, 1831. Issue: Henry 1772-1816, unmar. Godfrey b. Dec. 21, 1778, d. Dec. 1, 1847, mar. Anna Mary Rothbaust. Elizabeth, b. Nov. 14, 1787, d. July 3, 1818, mar. Heinrich Oberthier, no issue. Catherine b. Mar. 13, 1785, d. Dec. 8, 1831, mar. John H. Heffleman.

Prowell's Hist. of York Co., Penna. p. 265.

JOHN HENNEBERGER

In Penna Militia, was a pensioner. His wife was Margaret and in his will, prob. Oct. 23, 1845, he names children, Sophia; John; Elizabeth, wife of Daniel Shelby; Polly, wife of Frederick Best; Catherine, wife of John Henneberger; Susannah, wife of Jacob Beckley; Christian; Peter; grandson John Zettle.

Penna. Arch. 3rd Ser. Vol. 23, p. 530.

LIEUT. COLONEL FRANCIS JACOB REMER (REAMER)

Is shown in Service 1779-83, with the 5th Batt., Associators and Militia of York Co. He moved to Chambersburg, where his will was recorded in Dec., 1790. His wife was Catherine Wolf (brother-in-law Henry Wolf) and his five children named: Catherine; Frederick; Henry Francis; Jacob; John. The Roemers are known to have been buried in the front and to the extreme left of this graveyard, and attended Zion Ref. Ch., having been members of prominence in York, Penna.

Penna. Arch. 6th Ser. Vol. 2, p. 518, 590, 685, 678.

NICHOLAS SCHNEIDER

Served as a pvt. under Capt. James Young in 1780-81, and under Capt. Terrence Campbell in 1782. He was b. on the Rhine, Jan. 19, 1732, d. Mar. 20, 1786.

Here rests in God the body of the
departed Nicholaus Schneider,
born Jan. 19, 1732
died Mar. 20, 1786
aged 54 years 2 mos. 1 day
To the Great God alone shall
be all the glory.

He was an innkeeper in Chambersburg, and the present Zion Ref. Ch., was organized at his house 1778-79. His son Jeremiah was also an innkeeper, as the "Chambg. Weekly Advertiser" Mar. 16, 1797. JEREMIAH SNIDER informs his friends and the Public that he has taken the "HARP AND CROWN TAVERN" lately occupied by Capt. Abraham Chapman of Chambersburg. Orphans' Court records show that Nicholas Snider left a wife Catherine and issue: Jacob, age 16; Jeremiah, age 17; Catherine, age 15; John, age 11; Mary, age 6; Elizabeth, age 3; Nicholas b. after death of the father. On Nov. 12, 1756, Nicklas Schneyder was mar. to Cathrine Fischer, by Rev. J. C. Bucher. Quoting from McCauley in reference to early buildings in Chambg: "There were no brick buildings herein 1785, and only three stone ones: Chambers Fort, John Jack's tavern and Nicholas Snider's blacksmith shop. All the rest were of logs, small and inconvenient." Co. Chambers sold the lot Trostle's tavern now (1876) stands upon to Nicholas Snider for one pound, ten shillings, upon the condition that within two years, he should build a house upon it at least sixteen feet square, and forever pay an annual quit rent of fifteen shillings, to the said Chambers or his heirs.

Penna. Arch. 5th Ser. Vol. 6, p. 81, 110, 125. Also the History of Zion Ref. Church, Chambg. Penna.

JOHN STUMP

Served as a pvt. under Capt. Conrad Snyder 1780-81-82. In 1811 he was an Elder, and on the Building Committee of Zion Ref. Church, Chambersburg. His will was dated Oct. 31, 1823 and prob. Dec. 19, 1823. He states that he had a tan yard and house he occupied on the Falling Spring. He names wife Elizabeth; son David not yet 21; he and dau. Anna had gotten nothing; accounts charged against sons John and Jacob and daus. Elizabeth and Mary,—six children. Chambersburg, Penna. Deed Book Vol. 2, p. 447. On Nov. 8, 1828, the Exrs. of John Stamm show the house, lot and tanyard taken by David Stamm. Other heirs were: John Zent and wife Elizabeth; Christian Hostetter and wife Polly; John Shatter and wife Nancy. Franklin Repository: Dec. 16, 1823, died Tuesday last, John Stamm of the borough. March 9, 1824, Mrs. Stamm, widow of John Stamm. May 26, 1829, Married Thursday last by Rev. Moeller, David Stamm to Miss Nancy Reswick of this borough (Name also written Stamm).

Penna. Arch. 5th Ser. Vol. 6, p. 74, 88, 119, 572.

ABRAHAM SENSENICH

Served in Lancaster Co., Penna., as a pvt. under Capt. Wm. Skiles, 1781-82. He came to Chambersburg from New Holland, Lancaster Co., Penna. He and his wife Margaret are buried in Zion Reformed Graveyard. He names Magdalena Reges; son Jeremiah; son-in-law Henry Ruby; Polly Hershberger; son John; Eliza Strealy; son Jacob; Mrs. Heysinger; Mrs. Smith. He died Feb. 23, 1844, aged 82 yrs. 9 mos. 4 days.

"Farewell aged Father
Peace to thy ashes

Thy toils and troubles are ended;
Thy home is now where sickness,
Sorrow, pain and death are felt
and feared no more."

Penna. Arch. 5th Ser. Vol. 7, p. 37, 60, 84, 86, 282, 331, 654.

DANIEL SMITH

Served as 1st Lieut. under Capt. James Young, 1777-78-79-80-81, and in 1782 under Capt. Terrence Campbell. In deeds he is referred to as "Tobacconist," and Letters of Admr. were granted Aug. 2, 1815. Henry Smith, eldest son of Daniel, under date Mar. 10, 1818, states that Daniel died in July 1815, leaving a widow Mary and issue: 8 children: Henry; Elizabeth, mar. to Benj. Fanestock; Daniel; Mary; Catherine; John; Anna Barbara and Charlotte Matilda, last five minors. The Franklin Repository of Jan. 18, 1815, gives: "Married on Tuesday evening, the 10th inst., Mr. Benj. Fahnestock, Merchant, to Miss Elizabeth Smith, dau. of Mr. Daniel Smith, all of this place."

Penna. Arch. 5th Ser. Vol. 6, p 77, 82, 111, 126, 512, 522, 526, 547, 623.

CHRISTIAN WOLFF,

b. Dec. 6, 1762, d. Feb. 9, 1841. Mar. May 10, 1789 Anna Maria Krause. He was the son of Johann Barnhardt Wolff who came in 1739 with his parents from the Palatinate. At the age of 14 yrs. he helped to guard the Hession and other prisoners captured at Trenton and Princeton and went to Lancaster, where his parents then resided. He was a saddle and harness-maker. The Franklin Repository adds the following: Feb. 11, 1841. Died in this borough on the 5th inst. after a painful illness, Christian Wolf, Esq., in the 79th year of his age.

History of Zion Reformed Church, Chambersburg, Penna. p. 19. Biograph. Annals Franklin Co. Penna. p. 162.

Capt Michael Everly was probably buried in Zion Reformed Graveyard.

RANGERS ON THE FRONTIERS

Owen Aston
Capt. Thos. Askey
And. Alsworth

iWlliam Bleakney
Jas. Ballou
Jas. Breckenridge
Lawrence Barringer
Andrew Barringer
Jas. Brotherton
Peter Bonebrake
John Benefield
Sims Brown
John Blythe
John Beard, Ensign
William Beard
Hugh Barclay, Adjt.
Thos. Baldridge

Capt. Daniel Clapsaddle
John Clugston
Jas. Crooks
Jacob Cressy
Robert Cunningham
Jas. Canada
Charles Campbell
Edward Crawford
Josiah Crawford
Patrick Campbell
John Caisey
Jeremh. Calahan
Jas. Culbertson, Cornet

Samuel Dunwoody
James Dunwoody
Robert Dicky
Adam Dunwoody
Samuel Duffield
David Downy

George Elliott
Michael Everly
Arthur Eckles

Wm. Forsythe
Samuel Futhey
Christian Fordey
Charles Foster
Alex. French
Arthur French

Wm. Gabriel
John Guthrie
Capt. Wm. Guthrie

Saml. Holliday
Wm. Holliday, Paymaster
John Hogg
John Hood
Samuel Harden
Geo. Hufner
Felty Hufner
David Humphrey
John Hennesy
Levi Harod
Thos. Herod, Ensign
David Heron
Jas. Hindman

Jas. Irwine, Lieut.
Jas. Irwine, Jr.
Jas. Inness

John Jeffries
Evan Jenkins
Marmaduke Jamison
John Jamison
Lieut. Col Jas. Johnston
Major John Johnston
Capt. Pat. Jack
Thos. John
Lieut. Jas John
Benj. Jeffery

Samuel Kyle
Capt. John Kyle
Thos. Kennedy
Moses Kirkpatrick
John Kelly

Daniel Lavery
John Lindsay, Lieut.
Robert Leggett
Robert Lemon
John Laughlin
John Laycock
John Logan
Jas Leacock

Capt. Thos. McDowell
Robert McDowell
(Brother of our Thos)
Wm. McCasland
Alexander McDowell
James McDowell
Samuel McFerran
John Matthews
John Mitchell

Jas. McWilliams
Patrick Magee }
Patrick Magee } 2
Jas. McClenahan
Wm. McKee
Capt. Walter McKinnie
Patrick McCullough
John Martin
James Martin, 1st Lieut.
Capt. John McConnell
James Matthews
James McMichael
James McElhenny
Wm. McClellan
John Musholder
Fergus Moorehead
Thomas McCray
Robert McConnell
John Matthews
John Mitchell
Alex. Morehead
Wm. McNutt (Nitt)
Archibald McIlhatton
John Mardis
John McComb, Lieut.

John Newell
Daniel Nevans
Wm. Nichols
And. Nicodemus

James Patton
Thos. Patton
John Patton
Moses Porter
Col. John Pomeroy
Capt. Wm. Perry
Robert Parks
John Pollard
(d. near Mercersburg)

Jas. Roddy
Daniel Royer, Ensign
Jeremiah Rankin, Ensign
Wm. Reynolds, Ensign

John Simpson
Adam Scott
Lieut. Edward Spear
Lieut. Wm. Smith, Mercersburg
Robert Stoops
Lieut. Jacob Stotler
John Stall

Henry Smith
Geo. Shannon
Evan Shelby
Wm. Spear
Hugh Shannan (?)
Jacob Sailor

Peter Trugh
Jacob Trush (pens)

Henry Todd
Jesse Taylor

George Vance
John Vance

Stephen White
Wm. White
Stephen Winter
Wm. Wilson

Hugh Wylie
Enoch Williams
Benj. Williams
Wm. Waddle
Archd. Walker
Jas. Walker
Andrew Welsh
Robert Waddell
Andrew Wier
Robert Wier

This company is not shown in Penna. Arch., hence is included as representative of Capt. McClelland's vicinity.

Roll of Capt. John McClellan's Co.—7th Co. 6th Batt. of Cumb. Co. Militia.

Alex. White
Robert McClellan
James Dunlap
James Irwin, Sr.
James Irwin, Jr.
James McCoy
Thos. Watson (Wason)
Joseph Dunlap
Thos. Dunwoody
John Goulding
Robert Spicler

Richard Bard
James Maxwell
Thos. Laughlin
James Louery
Wm. Lamon
James Lamon
James Lamon
Joseph Lamon
Robert Lamon
Wm. McKnit, Jr.
Saml. Dinsmore

James Martin
James Robinson
Charles Stewart
John McCutcheon
Hugh McCutcheon
Peter Barncurt
Jacob Barncurt
George May
Daniel Lane (Lain)
Adam Dunwoody
James Dunwoody

Certified by me,
John McClellan, Capt.
Return for 1779 until 24th of May

Egles Notes and Queries, Vol. 1896, p. 204.

This is inserted as a typical company of Rangers from Franklin County, Penna., serving on the Frontiers of Bedford and Westmoreland Counties—spring and summer, 1779.

Col. Wm. Chambers' Batt.
Capt. Samuel Patton's Company

Lieut. Ezekiel Sample
Sergts. John Kincaid and Wm. Speare

Privates:
George Hunter
Wm. Lowery
Abraham Rosenberg
Samuel Howard
John Parker

John Lytle
Henry Marshall
John Hart
Wm. Patterson
Richard Cooper
Lorans McReady

Thomas Crottey
George Lamb
William Sharp
John Brand
John Mathis Wever
John Welsh
Henry Williamson

Legonere, June 22, 1779, Mustered then Capt. Samuel Patton's Company as specified in the above Roll.

Col. John Thomson
D. M. M. and R. P. M.

Penna. Arch. 2nd Ser. Vol. 14, p. 448, 449. Penna. Arch. 5th Ser. Vol. 6, p. 601-609.

COLONIAL RECORDS

Formation of Townships in Franklin County, Pa.
From the 1887 History, by Bates.

Antrim	1741	p.	555
Lurgan	1743	p.	564
Peters	1751	p.	567
Guilford	1751	p.	573
Hamilton	1752	p.	577
Fannett	1761	p.	579
Letterkenny	1762	p.	583
Washington	1779	p.	588
Montgomery	1781	p.	591
Southampton	1783	p.	593
Franklin	1784	p.	596
Greene	1788	p.	596
Metal	1795	p.	604
Warren	1798	p.	607
St. Thomas	1818	p.	609
Quincy	1838	p.	611

PROVINCIAL OFFICERS FOR CUMBERLAND COUNTY, PA.

Sheriff—John Potter	Oct. 6, 1750
	Oct. 4, 1753-55
Collectors—James Lindsay	1751-1756
Benj. Chambers	1758
John Lindsay	1761-1769
Assembly—Joseph Armstrong	1750-52-53-54-55
James Galbreath	1762
Coroner—Adam Hoops	Oct. 6, 1750-1764
James Jack	Oct. 5, 1765-1767

Justices of the Peace

William Maxwell	March 10, 1749-50
Benjamin Chambers	March 10, 1749
William Allison	March 10, 1749-1750
Benjamin Chambers	1750
James Galbreath	1750-1764
William Smith	July 13, 1757-1764
John Potter	July 13, 1757
Joseph Armstrong	July 13, 1757
Hugh Mercer	July 13, 1757
James Maxwell	Oct. 17, 1764-1770-1771
James Elliott	May 9, 1767
James Galbreath	May 23, 1770
John Allison	May 23, 1770-1771
William Maclay	May 23, 1770
Henry Prather	May 23, 1770-1771
John Maclay, Jr.	Apr. 6, 1771
William Elliott	Apr. 6, 1771
James Dunlap	Apr. 6, 1771

Penna. Arch 2nd, Ser. Vol. 9, p. 806, 807.

Roll of Capt. John Potter's Company 1757-58

Blackburn, John
Brown, George
Bulafui, Joshua
Burchill, Daniel
Burgess, Nathaniel

Carmichael, Daniel
Crof, (or Cross) Peter
Crow, Wm.
Curry, John

Davis, Elias

Eaker, Solomon
Evans, Wm.
Finley, Wm.
Fiste, Michael
Freeman, James
Fuchs, (Fox) Balzer

Gallagher, Wm.
Ganes, Edward
Gillespy, John
Gormanchon, Francis

Hayes, James
Harbridge, Edward
Hegney, Henry
Howe, Thomas

Jackson, James

Leith, Alexander
Lindsay, John
Lyon, Thomas

McCamey, Francis
McCombe, Wm.
McDowell, Allexander
McFaul, Michael
McGlaghlin, Henry
McKinney, Henry
McKinney, Wm.
Moak, Conrad
Money, John
Morrison, James

Nelson, Joseph

Patterson, Wm.
Peddan, Erastus R.
Purcil, Richard

Ramsey, John
Robinson, Wm.
Rorbrough, Adam

Smith, Alexander

Smith, John
Smith, John, Sr.
Thomson, James
Verner, Ludowick
Wache, Paul
Ward, John
Williams, John
Wilkins, James
Wilson, John
Withnall, Wm.
Wright, Joseph
Young, James
   Penna. Arch. 2nd Ser,. Vol. 7, p. 269, 270.

Petition of Defense from Cumberland County-1755
To Hon. Robert Hunter Morris, Esq., Governor of Penna.
A company under the care and Command of Joseph Armstrong, Esq., for Guns and Ammunition — Aug. 7, 1755.

Robert McConnel
Wm. McCord
James McCamond
Josh Mitchel
Jno. Irwin
Jno. Jones
Wm. Rankin
Josh. Patterson
James Barnet
Josh. Barnet
Jno. Hindman
Wm. Scott
Abram Irwin
James Norice
Jno. Norrice
Cristor Irwin
James Patterson
James Eatton
John McCord
James Guthrie
Thomas Barnet
John Barnet
Thomas Barnet
Wm. Dickson
Robert Dickson
George Gallery
Jon. McKeany
Charles McCamon
James Scott
Francis Scott
Pathk. Scott
Barnt Robertson
Jon. Wilson
Jon. Moor
James McCamon
James Mitchel
Bobt. Colwell
Alexander Colwell

Chas. Stuart
Jno. Stuart
Daniel Stuart
Samuel Brown
Josp. Swan
Jon. Swan
Robert Shields
David. Shields
Matw. Shields
Robert Shields
Matw. Shields
Wm. McCamish
Jas. McCamish
Jno. McCamish
Wm. Swan
Jon. Rippey
Jas. Dinney
Wm. Dinney
Jno. Eaton
Jno. Machan
James Elder
Josh. Eaton
Wm. Mitchel
Jon. Armstrong
Thomas Armstrong
John Boyd
Bobt. Groin
Devard Williams
Samuel Boun.
   Penna. Arch. First Series, Vol. 2, p. 385, 1748-1756.

Account of Ammunition sent to Frontiers (into the back Counties) for Defence—Sent to:
William Buchanan, Carlisle, Cumb. Co.
Justice Maxwell, Peters Township, Cumb, Co.
Capt. Alexd. Culbertson, Lourgan Twp., Cumb. Co.
Joseph Armstrong, Hamilton Typ., Cumb. Co.
   Penna. Arch. First Series, Vol. 2, p. 392.

p. 623—Letter from Reverend Capt. Steel to the Governor—April 21, 1756.
p. 611—McCord's Fort.
p. 602—Gov. Morris to John Potter, Esq.,—1756.
p. 601—Orders to John Steel, Esq.
p. 462—Letter from Adam Hoopes.
p. 239—Plan of Defence, Cumb, Co.
p. 173—Letter—Parnell's Knob—Wm. Maxwell.
p. 134—Distances—Mr. McDowell's Mill to Phil. Davids—8 mi. Davis' south of Welsh Run.
p. 14—Indian Traders—Aug. 1747-1748:
   Lazarus Lowry
   Alexander Moorhead
   George Croghan
   John Frazier
   John Galbreath
Thos. Magee
James Lowry

OF FRANKLIN COUNTY PENNSYLVANIA

Hugh Crawford
Peter Sheaver
Penna. Arch. First Series, Vol. 2.

OFFICERS AND SOLDIERS IN THE SERVICE OF THE PROVINCE OF PENNA., —1744-1765

Captain Wm. Maxwell
Ensign James Wilkins, Feb. 12, 1745-6
Raised in Rathmullen Twp., Lanc., Co., Pa.
 (Later Peters Twp., Franklin Co., Pa.)
"Over the River Susquehanna" 1747-8
Colonel Benjamin Chambers
Lieut. Colonel Robert Dunning
Major Wm. Maxwell
Captain Richard O'Kane
Lieut. Wm. Smith
Ensign John Mitchell

Captain Robert Chambers
Lieut. Andrew Finley
Ensign John Sesna

Captain James Carnahan
Lieut. James Jack
Ensign John Thompson

Captain George Brown
Lieut. John Potter
Ensign John Rannells (Reynolds)

Captain Benjamin Chambers
Lieut. Charles McGill
Ensign Robert Mull

Captain Wm. Maxwell
Lieut. John Winton
Ensign James Wilkey
 Penna. Arch. 5th Series, Vol. 1.

p. 36-37—Letters from Capt. Thos. Cambell—Hed Quarters Hanastown, Dec. 8, 1779.
p. 443-491-522—Letters to & from Col. Abraham Smith.
Penna. Arch. First Ser. Vol. 8.

p. 100 —Pet. of John Martin—Bedford—1762, wife and 5 children taken captive by Indians.
p. 222 —Deposition of John Shelby
p. 223 —Deposition of Jas. Wilkins
p. 224 —Wm. Smith gives a pass.
p. 228-29—Letters from James Smith
p. 230 —Dep. of John Smith
p. 237 —Dep. of Henry Prather
p. 244 —Fort Smith—Nov. 14, 1765, Wm. Smith to ——.
p. 245 —James Smith—McDowells
p. 246 —Obligation of Jonathan Smith—1765.

p. 409 —Magistrates 1771—Wm. Elliott, Path Valley.
p. 527 —Pet. of Inhab. of Pittsburgh—1774—John Shannon—Benj. & Robert Elliott.
Penna. Arch. First Ser., Vol. 4.

p. 27 Lancaster, Nov. 4, 1756.
Letter from Hugh Mercer to Mr. John Mifflin one of the Commissioners for the Province of Penna., Favor of Mr. Thomas Blair—stating that he and Coll. Armstrong recommend Mr. Blair for Surgeon of the Second Battalion.
p. 57 —Lancaster, Nev. 17, 1756, Hugh Mercer again urges that Dr. Blair be ap. Surgeon "of our Batt." "I intend to joyn, next week, my Company at Shippensburg (my Wound being in a fair way of being Cured) tho' it will be a considerable Time in healing up and rendering me fit for much Duty"—To Col. James Young, Esq.—Commissnr. Genl. of the Musters—In Philadelphia—By Favour of Dr. Blair.
p. 571—Captain Hugh Mercer to Gov. Denny—Camp at Loyal Hanning Dec. 3, 1758. Success of the Expedition against Fort Du Quesne

p. 624-25-26. Col. Mercer to ——— Pittsburgh—Apr. 25, 1759. In reference to Indians.
p. 674—Pittsburgh—July 17, 1759
p. 685—Pittsburgh—Sept. 15, 1759
p. 721—Col. Hugh Mercer to Gov. Hamilton, Fort Augusta, Apr. 23, 1760.
Penna. Arch. First Ser., Vol. 3.

President Reed appoints Thomas Campbell to a Captaincy of a Company of Rangers—owing to his claims or Standing in the Cont., Line—"I think you will serve yourself and your Country more effectually in this Corps" &c, &c,—Pr. 7, 1779.
Penna. Arch. First Ser., Vol. 7, p. 301.

10,000 Dollars by Major Boggs to Capt. Thos. Campbell—Mr. Carver of Carlisle to supply the men with Arms and as they are Cont. Troops the Commr. of Military stores will furnish the Accoutrements, &c, to be furnished by the Commissary under Gen. Sullivan, at Sunbury, when the Companies are to march with all Expedition as soon as completed.
Pres. Reed to Capt. Thos. Campbell—May 29, 1779.
Penna. Arch. First Ser., Vol. 7, p. 447.

p. 29 —Samuel Perry killed by Indians
p. 40 —Those killed at Canigojegg: John Archer & wife Elizabeth & 4 children
p. 58 —McDowell's Mill, &c.
p. 78-79—McDowell's Mill, &c.
p. 119 —Forts

p. 219 —Killed at John Cisney's Field, 1757
p. 220 —Killed at Joseph Steensons—1757
p. 239 —Security in Harvest
p. 308 —Pet. Margery Mitchell—Indian Scalp
p. 336 —Officers in Province—Hugh Mercer &c.
p. 396 —Richard Baird's Deposition, May 1758.
   Penna. Arch. First Ser., Vol. 3,—1756.

Men of Capt. Jameson's Company, Killed or Wounded near McCord's Fort, April 2, 1756.
   (A few miles N. W. of Loudon, Pa.)
Barnett, John
Blair, James, killed
Campbell, James
Chambers, William, killed
Gutton, Matthew
Hunter, William
James, Henry
McDonald, John
Mackey, Daniel, killed
Pierce, James, killed
Reynolds, John, killed
Reynalds, William
Robertson, James (tailor), killed
Robertson, James (weaver), killed
   Penna. Arch. 5th Ser., Vol. p. 41.

Roll of Capt. John Potter's Company
1757-1758

Blackburn, John
Brown, George
Bulafin, Joshua
Burchill, Daniel
Burgess, Nathaniel
Carmichael, Daniel
Crof, Peter
Crow, William
Curry, John
Davis, Elias
Eaker, Solomon
Evans, Williams
Finley, William
Fiste, Michael
McCombe, William
McDowell, Alexdr.
McFaul, Michael
McGlaughlin, Henry
McKinney, William
Moak, Conrad
Money, John
Morrison, James
Nelson, Joseph
Patterson, William
Peddan, Erastus R.
Purcil, Richard
Ramsey, John
Freeman, James
Fuchs, (Fox) Balzer
Gallagher, William
Ganes, Edward
Gillespy, John
Gormauchon, Francis
Hayes, James
Harbridge, Edward
Hegney, Henry
Howe, Thomas
Jackson, James
Leith, Alexdr.
Lindsay, John
Ligon, Thomas
McCamey, Francis
Robinson, William
Rorbrough, Adam
Smith, Alexdr.
Smith, John
Smith, John, Sr.
Thompson, James
Verner, Ludowick
Wache, Paul
Ward, John
Williams, John
Wilkins, James
Wilson, John
Withnal, William
Wright, Joseph
Young, James
   Penna. Arch, 2nd Ser., Vol. 7, p. 269.
   Penna. Arch. 2nd Ser., Vol. 4.

Eriction of Early Settlers Peters Township—1750
Sec'y Peters Report

William White
Geo. Calhoun
David Hiddleton
Geo. Galloway
Wm. Galloway
Andrew Lycon
Big Cove
Andrew Donaldson
John MacClelland
Charles Stuart
John McMeans
Robert Kendall
Samuel Brown
Wm. Shepherd
Roger Murphy
Robert Smith
Wm. Dickey
Wm. Millican
Wm. McConnell
Alex. McConnell
James Campbell
Wm. Carrell
John Martin
John Jamison
Hans Potter
John McClelland
Adam McConnell

James Wilson
John Wilson
Little Juniata
Thos. Parker
James Parker
Owen McKeeb
John McClure
Richard Kirkpatrick
James Hurray
John Scott
John Cowan
Simon Girtee
John Kilaugh
Burnt Cabins
Now Huntingdon Co.
then Cumberland
Path Valley
Abraham Slack
James Blair
Moses Moore
Arthur Dunlop
Alex McCarty
David Lewis
Adam McCarty
Felix Doyle
Andrew Dunlop
Robert Wilson

Jacob Pyatt
Jacob Pyatt, Jr.
William Ramage
Reynolds Alexander
Samuel Patterson
Robert Baker
John Armstrong
John Potts

Abstract of Letter from George Stevenson to R. Peters, 1758:

Must the men buy green Cloathing? I fear this will hurt us much. I think linnen Stockings, red below the Knee, Petticoat Trowusers, reaching to the thick of the Leg, made of strong Linnen, and a Sailor's Frock made of the same, would be best.

Young men that have Cloathing (especially Dutch) will not like to lay out their Money for more . . . . . etc., etc.

            I am, Dr. Sr.
                 Your most obedient
                        Hble Servt,
                            Geo. Stevenson

York, 8th May, 1758.
Mr. Peters.

    Penna. Arch. First Ser., Vol. 111, p. 392.

MCCONNELLSBURG

DAVID ANDREW

Was a Soldier of the Continental Line. He was a son of John and Hannah Andrew of Guilford Twp. He was married late in life by Dr. David Denny—"David Andrie to Sarah Ritchie, Nov. 3, 1818." They had two (2) daus. Misses Margaret and Sarah Andrew, who were school teachers in Mercersburg—both are buried in Fairview Cemetery. The parents lie Presbyterian Cemetery, McConnellsburg. David A. Andrews, b. Oct. 9, 1763, d. March 31, 1841, Sarah Andrews, d. Feb. 9, 1846, aged 56 yrs. 6 mos. 8 days.
Penna. Arch. 5th Ser. Vol. 4, p. 619.

ALEXANDER ALEXANDER

Appears in the Militia of Bedford Co. Pa., serving in Capt. Charles Taggart's Company of Militia. Robert and William Alexander were members of this company. Alexander Alexander was born in County Down, Ireland, in 1731, and mar. Agnes Kelly of Dromore in 1767. He came to America alone in 1770, settling first in the Conococheague Valley among those of his own descent, Scotch-Irish. From Wm. McConnell, Nov. 1772, he purchased a tract of land in Wells Valley, "Wm. McConnell, Esq. of Ayr Township, County of Bedford, do make over a Certain Tract . . . lying in Aughwick Valley . . . about three miles from the Great Road on the Top of Sideling Hill . . . about 280 acres, unto Alexander Alexander of Antrim Township, Co. of Cumberland, for the sum of 30 pounds. In the presence of Robert Scott and Hugh Alexander." The wife arriving, Alexander at once erected a cabin and was established as the first settler of Wells Valley. They next sought safety in the Conococheague in 1780, and returning in 1780, they again fled from the Indians in 1782, finally taking possession of the land. He was one of the first Elders in the Presbyterian Church of the Great Cove, a regular attendant until the time of his death. He died in Wells Valley, Nov. 8, 1815 and was buried on a lot reserved by him in his will. He left an interesting will, reserving from "any incumbrances forever, 40 ft. in length & 12 ft. in breadth, including my burying ground." His children were:
1. Joseph, 1768-1800, mar. Rebecca Osburn
2. John, 1770-1840, mar. Catherine Bradley
3. Elizabeth, 1774-1849, mar. Wm. Ready
4. Christiana, 1780-1827, mar. Wm. Grey
5. Agnes, 1783-1862, mar. John Gibson
6. Mary, 1785-1830, mar. 1st John Moore, Mar. 2nd, Abraham Copenhaver
7. Sarah, 1787-1855, mar. Benjamin Bradley
Penna. Arch. 5th Ser. Vol. 5, p. 114.

CAPTAIN JAMES GIBSON

Dec. 10, 1777. Of Bedford County, Pa. He was born 1745, died 1810; his wife was Margaret and they had issue: John mar. Sarah Dougherty; James, unmarried; Robert mar. Ruhamah Williams; Jane mar. Francis Kendall; Sarah mar. Robert McLean; Rebecca mar. Alex. Nesbitt; Isabel and Margaret, unmarried; Martha mar. John Gibbony; Ann mar. Robert Kendall. Descendants of Capt. James Gibson think he was buried in Big Spring Gr. yard, which at that period was a Community burial ground. There are many lime-stone markers, with no legible inscriptions.
Penna. Arch 2nd Ser. Vol. 14, p. 663.

From Mrs. Geo. F. Harper, Lenoir, N. C.; John Kerr, Adams Co. claim in 1741. Will at York, Penna., prob. 1759, 7 sons; George; Wm. M.; John; Samuel; James; Thomas; Andrew. Geo. Kerr's dau. Jean mar. Abram Scott—had son Wm. McClean Scott.

SAMUEL KERR

Moved to Bedford Co. Penna., near McConnellsburg, mar. probably, Margaret Rebecca McDowell. Samuel and Margaret Kerr had issue: Isabella mar. Charles Pettitt, May 7, 1818; Rebecca mar. James Irwin; Margaret mar. Nathaniel Pettitt, Apr. 18, 1815; George; Martha mar. Michael Downs; Jane mar. Wm. McClean Scott, a cousin; Elizabeth, unmar.; Mary mar. Thomas Douglass; Thomas mar. Maria Fleming; Samuel Jr., mar. Mary H. Blair.

ABRAHAM LESHER

Sergt. in Capt. Keefer's Company of Berks County Militia; he was born in Berks Co. Penna., May 15, 1757, died in Bedford Co. Penna., in 1839. He mar. Elizabeth Humbert about 1790. They are buried in the Lutheran Graveyard of McConnellsburg, Penna., and the stones show the following: "In memory of Abraham Lesher, Sr., who departed this life May 19th, 1839, In the 82nd year of his age. In memory of Elizabeth, wife of Abraham Lesher, who died Apr. 12, 1846, in the 74th year of her age." The will of Abraham Lesher dated March, 1836, was probated May, 1839. He was of Air Twp., and names wife Elizabeth; issue Margaret Reed; (Andrew) Elizabeth Smith; Catherine Pittman (Joseph); Susan Van Clief (Benjamin) Mary Miller; Barbara Logan (David); Sons: Wm.; John; Jacob; Isaac; Abraham and Grandson Abraham Van Clief; The will of the widow Elizabeth Lesher of Air Twp. dated Oct., 1845, was prob. at Hagerstown, Md., May, 1846. She names her six daus.: Peggy; Betsy; Catherine; Susy; Polly and Barbara; sons Isaac; Jacob; Abraham; Wm.; To son Isaac's wife the best bedstead and bedding, Standing in the White room upstairs, and the clock, and dining table and its Oilcloth. Bedford Co., Penna. Joseph B. Noble, Register. Additional from a Descendant—not in will. Isaac mar. Nancy Martin; Abraham mar. Elizabeth Keyser; Wm. mar. Hadassah Carroll; Jacob & John.

Penna. Arch., 3rd Ser. Vol. 18, p. 646, 774, also 5th Ser. Vol. 4, p. 263; 5th Ser. Vol. 5, p. 287.

JOHN MCKINLEY

The will of John McKinley of Air Twp., Bedford, Twp., Penna., Dated July 11, 1818; prob. Nov. 2, 1819. Exrs. my dau. Mary McKinley, my friend, David Hunter. To my dau. Elizabeth McKinley; To my 5 grandsons; James; Wm.; Alexander and David Hunter;; To my grandaus.: Nancy Culbertson; Grizzell; Mary and Martha Hunter; To my grandaus. by Elizabeth, Mary; Grizell; Sally; Betsy and Nancy; To Wm. McKinley and his son John McKinley; All the stock on the plantation at my decease, for my dau. Mary's use. Extra may be divided between the five Hunter grandsons, and the three Hunter grandaughters.

JAMES NELSON

Was in service with Capt. Chas. Taggart; born 1757, died 1828. His wife was Martha Sloan and they had issue: James Nelson, mar. Kezia Logan. Martha mar. John Murphy. Susan mar. John Forsythe; Fannie; Margaret and Sarah were unmarried; Wm. mar. Mary Peoples; Mary A. and John Nelson were unmarried. They are buried in Big Spring Graveyard.

Penna. Arch. 5th Ser. Vol. 5, p. 115.

JOHN RENKIN

Was an Ensign under Capt. Charles Taggart. John Renkin of Bedford in Cont. Line John Rankin d. Apr. 8, 1829, aged 75 yrs. His wife Mary d. Jan. 28, 1826, aged 68 yrs. Both are buried in Big Spring Graveyard, near McConnellsburg, Fulton Co., Pa.

Penna. Arch. 5th Ser. Vol. 4, p. 612; 5th Ser. Vol. 5, p. 114, 115, 84.

CAPTAIN CHARLES TAGGART

Of the First Batt. Bedford Co. Militia was in service 1782-83, undated rolls. There is an interesting list or "Just accompt" of the days spent in Public Service, in 1783. Charles Taggert and Mary Derby were married Nov. 17, 1778, by Rev. John King, Mercersburg, Pa. He was born 1753, died 1831, his wife born 1756, died 1835. They had issue: Andrew; John; Rebecca; Jane; Charles; Mary. They are buried in the Big Spring Graveyard, near McConnellsburg, Pa.

Penna. Arch. 5th Ser. Vol. 5, p. 83, 98, 102, 115, 114.

CHARLES TIPPER

A regular enlisted soldier in the Penna. Line. Served one year in a campaign to Canada. He was a Peters Twp. taxable, served under Capts. James Patton, Robert Dickey and Thos. McDowell 1780-81. U. S. Pension record: Charles Tipper, No. W 2883; applied for, Apr. 20, 1818; issue, Certif. No. 3002, Sept. 20, 1818 at $96 ann. Sent to John Dickey, McConnellsburg, Pa. Charles Tipper was born Feb. 14, 1753; died, McConnellsburg, Sept. 5, 1834. Served in Capt. Abram (Abraham) Smith's Co., 6th Penna. Regt., commanded by Col. Wm. Irwin; entered at Carlisle Mar., 1776; was in expedition to Canada; discharged in Apr., 1777. Also served tour in militia at time the British were in possession of Philadelphia; another tour when Washington marched against Cornwallis. Witness: Daniel Bloom, Sr., who knew him when in Canada and saw him in battle of Three Rivers, and at Ticonderoga during winter of 1777. Matthew Patton, b. 1776, Associate Judge, Franklin Co. states that Tipper lived with and worked for his father in Peters Twp. Mary Tipper, widow, nee Campbell, daughter of Robert Campbell of Franklin Co., born May 22, 1769, applied Nov. 12, 1839, from Franklin Co., having resided there since 1824; before that about 20 years in Bedford Co.; the rest of her life in Franklin Co. Certif. No. 5757 issued Sept. 11, 1840 for $40 ann. under Act July 7, 1838. Married Apr. 3, 1786 by James Maxwell, J. P. (died 1807) in Franklin Co., Bible Record (From original papers): Births: Andrew, b. May 23, 1787; Robert, b. June 25, 1788; Margaret, b. Sept. 20, 1791; John, b. Aug. 8, 1794; Charles, b. Apr. 4, 1797; Mary, b. Feb. 4, 1800; Susan, b. Apr. 6, 1805. Charles Tipper, Jr. received this family Bible ten years or so before his father's death. Mary, widow of pensioner, lived with son-in-law,

John Witherow, who married Susan Tipper in Aug., 1824, a Justice of the Peace.

Mary Tipper had a Son Andrew baptized in 1787, and A. Typer married Peggy Campbell, Path Valley, by Dr. McGinley in 1823. In 1786, Charles Tipper, Shoemaker and wife Polly sell to James Buchanan Lot No. 8 in the town of Mercersburg "likeways the logs fiting for a house, hewed and in good order to make a house of two Story high." Charles Tipper moved to Bedford Co., Penna., where as a private in the Penna Line he received a pension. He was 81 in 1818, and was buried in the Presbyterian graveyard at McConellsburg—a salute was fired over his grave, which had a nativestone. The will of Mary Typer of Fannettsburg, Penna., dated March 6, 1843, prob. Apr. 26, 1843, recorded Vol. E, page 30, Franklin County records, mentions sons Andrew and Charles; Daus. Margaret, Mary, Jane and Susan. Son-in-law John Witherow.

Penna. Arch. 5th Ser. Vol. 6, p. 265, 272, 285, 315, 643; Vol. 4, p. 504.

www.ingramcontent.com/pod-product-compliance
Lightning Source LLC
Chambersburg PA
CBHW020643300426
44112CB00007B/218